Newborn twin white-tailed deer fawns with doe.
Camera: Canon EOS-IN single-lens reflex
Lens: f 2.8 Canon EF 28-70mm Zoom
Exposure: f 5.6 @ 1/250 sec
Film: Fujichrome Provia 100 (ASA 100)
Fill flash: Canon 540 EZ Speedlite
Photographer: @Glenn D. Chambers

MISSOURI SHOW-ME BIG BUCKS CLUB

RECORDS OF WHITETAIL DEER

MISSOURI

SHOW-ME BIG BUCK CLUB

RECORDS OF WHITETAIL DEER

FIRST EDITION

Edited By

Dale H. Ream, Jr.

Records of Whitetail Deer Taken In Missouri

First Edition

Missouri Show-Me Big Bucks Club Records of Whitetail Deer

Library of Congress Catalog Card Number:
ISBN Number:
Published February 1998

Produced and published in the United States of America by:
The Missouri Show-Me Big Bucks Club
POB 9, Unionville, MO 63565-0009

ACKNOWLEDGMENTS

A SPECIAL THANKS TO ALL WHO CONTRIBUTED TO THIS BOOK.

CONTENTS

Missouri State Record Typical Whitetail Deer Score 205 0/8, Randolph County, 1971, Hunter: Larry W. Gibson, Owner: Missouri Show-Me Big Bucks Club

Missouri State Record and World Record Non-Typical Whitetail Deer, Score 333 7/8, St. Louis County, 1981, Found

HISTORY OF WHITE-TAILED DEER IN MISSOURI

by

WAYNE R. PORATH
WILDLIFE MANAGEMENT CHIEF
MISSOURI DEPARTMENT OF CONSERVATION

s the month when the deer rut (*Taxti Kithixi ike)* drew near, Wacabe began preparation for his hunt. Wacabe, r Black Bear, was a member of the Omaha Indian tribe. As he prepared his primitive but effective gear, Black ear prayed silently to the Talking God that his deer would lose its fear of being killed.

our days before the hunt, he and other young braves began their fast. At a time appointed by the old men, e young braves, either on foot or horseback, raced toward the war-post and took aim with knife, hatchet or bow. hose who missed retired from the hunt in disgrace and resumed eating--a small consolation. Black Bear's aim as deadly, and amid profound silence, he stole away from the village to hunt his deer.

hose at the village continued silent ceremony, praying that a deer would allow itself to be killed and that the ze of the herd would increase, easing the task of Black Bear and other braves. Wacabe whispered prayers s he stalked, being careful not to use the word *ta* (deer) so his animal wouldn't become frightened. He repeated,

> When hunting I want to see,
> The slender legged animals,

lack Bear had a dream the first night out. In the morning, he reflected on his overconfidence, evident in the ream.

> I, very eager,
> Grabbed a deer's forelegs,
> Thinking it my bow.
> I, over- brave,
> Grabbed the deer's tail,
> Thinking it my feathered arrow.

lack Bear was prepared. His equipment was well-hewn. His appeals that the deer would allow itself to be lled had been frequent. He spotted the quarry-- a large, fat buck. He hid in some bushes and positioned the ape and antler decoy over his head. With great skill, he thrashed the brush and lured the animal to him. Just efore releasing the arrow, Black Bear apologized to the animal for taking its life.

nother brave joined Black Bear, and together they packed the deer back to the village. There, the dead deer as treated like an honored guest--decorated with beads and sprinkled with pollen. Black Bear, having killed e deer, owned the skin and one side of meat. The remainder was processed by the women and divided nong those in the village. According to ancient ritual, the antlers were placed aloft on Black Bear's lodge.

Black Bear's hunt represents a chain of events that might have occurred within any of several midwestern india tribes any time during the past ten thousand years. His acts were directed in part by ceremony, but also by th need of his people for food and other staples. Throughout the hunt, he felt a genuine respect for the animal h hoped to kill. This respect was an important component of the ceremony--before, during and after the hunt.

As for the deer, Black Bear's intrusion on their lives had been relatively recent. The white-tailed deer is one of th mammals that became abundant during the Pleistocene Epoch, originating perhaps a million years ago. It cc evolved with several other North American ungulates, including the wapiti, or elk, mule deer, moose and caribou The whitetail's range was widespread, stretching across most of the eastern two-thirds of what is now Nort America, and from the boreal forests of Canada to the arid plains of northern Mexico. Whitetails had severa natural enemies, but the puma and gray wolf were most important. Densities no doubt ebbed and flowed, bu likely were held in check by those predators. Early naturalists in Missouri estimated historical populations be tween 10 and 20 deer per square mile, or more than 700,000 in the state prior to settlement by Europeans.

DEER USE BY NATIVE AMERICANS

Except possibly for the bison, the white-tailed deer is the most widely known and utilized native North Amer can hooved mammal. Archaeological evidence indicates that deer were an essential staple to the early hu man inhabitants, from the very early Mound Builders to the Senecas of New England, the Sioux Nation of th plains and the Aztecs of the arid southwest. They provided food, tools, utensils, clothing, ceremonial dress decoys and more. Leg bones, for example, were used to make awls (the marrow was removed for food needles, bodkins and forks. Shoulder blades were fitted to wooded handles for use as hoes. Antlers and skul caps were used in ceremonial dress and, when hides were added, the combination along with grunts, blea and fawn squeals decoyed deer for the kill. Tanned hides were used for dresses, tunics, leggings and mocca sins.

Depending on need, hides were stretched, dried, and scraped, sometimes multiple times, to make the thinner and lighter. If the hide was needed for a summer tent, the hairy side was scraped, then grease rubbe on the hide. Natives used the brains or liver and warm broth of the meat to treat the skin. After a few days sun-drying, they soaked the hide in water, then pulled it back and forth through a twisted sinew until it wa softened.

Many methods were used by North American Indians to capture deer. Some used fire-hunting, in which a fii was built in the bow of a canoe and the hunter sat in the back of the light (a forerunner of today's nigh lighting?). Deer driving was practiced by many tribes. Hundreds of people would participate. Drivers ar flankers would move deer toward narrow points, many times these would be into water, where they passed b hunters with bows posted on land or in canoes. A variation was a triangular enclosure made with woode stakes eight to ten feet tall with each leg of the triangle up to 1,500 feet long. Deer were driven into a narrov perhaps five foot wide opening in the triangle. Early in the drive, hunters would clash two sticks together i make noise. As the throat of the enclosure was neared, braves would shout and imitate the cry of wolve which terrified the deer so they would pass the throat into the kill pen.

Some tribes used deer snares. Typically, a loop snare was set in a runway to encircle the neck of a passir deer. Another type was laid in a small concealed pit to ensnare the leg.

Deer stalking as done by Wacabe was common among all Indian tribes. This normally involved the wearing antler and hide decoys. Some painted their arms and breasts like a deer's underside. Sticks were rubbe together to mimic the sound of a buck scraping his antlers. A variation used by some was the "sneak" metho in which bedded deer were stalked and shot.

final importance of deer in the lives of native Americans was in their lore. For example, within the Omaha [tri]be was a social clan called the Deer-Head Gens. Members could not touch the skin of any member of the [de]er family, nor could they use moccasins of deerskin or the fat for hair-oil, but they could eat the meat. This [cl]an used deer in their names, for example, He Who Wags his Tail, Deer Paws the Ground, Little Hoof of a [De]er, and Dark Chin of a Deer. On the fifth day following the birth of a child, the infant was placed within the [ci]rcle of adults. The face was painted red and red spots were placed down the back to imitate a fawn. Fawns [w]ere never killed by this clan, only adult deer.

[Be]cause of the prominent role deer played in the daily lives of native Americans, it is only natural that the [an]imal became associated with certain beliefs. For example, the barred owl was sometimes called the "deer [o]wl" because when deer heard it hoot, they began feeding. The "bezoar stone" was believed to come from the [e]sophagus of deer. When thrown up by a deer and found by a hunter, it was and worn on a necklace for its [pr]esumed curative power for rheumatism or heart trouble. Deer skins that were thin with short hair forecast a [mi]ld winter and, conversely, long, dense hair a severe winter.

[D]EER USE BY AMERICAN PIONEERS

[N]o doubt Christopher Columbus saw the white-tailed deer in his 1492 discovery of the new world. Captain [Ar]thur Barlowe, in landing on what was to be Roanoke Island, Virginia, reported to Sir Walter Raleigh "this [l]and had many goodly woods full of deer, conies, hares and fowl..." Colonists soon learned to value the deer, [wh]ich became the principle source of meat. Venison was more common than beef. Other interesting pioneer [us]es of deer were tallow for soap and candles, hides for breeches, jackets, waist-coats or entire suits and [m]occasins. Pioneers used deerskins for leather hats and gloves, as a substitute for glass in windows and as [ne]tting for snowshoes. Deer antlers were used for umbrella stands, chandeliers, jewelry, knife handles and [fo]rks. Interestingly, antlers were also used as a source of ammonia. Deer hair often was used as stuffing for [sa]ddles and furniture.

[Al]l of these uses created a tremendous demand for a continuous supply of deer as pioneers expanded west-[w]ard. Not only did they need deer to supply their own needs, but a huge market for deer products developed [to] meet the needs of "Easterners". Early frontiersmen, both hunters and trappers, included deer meat and [de]er hides in their fare. Deerskin often served as a medium of exchange for other goods or money, or in some [ca]ses, for liquor. One 1784 report states that, on the French Broad River, two deer skins would fetch one quart [of] an inferior grade of brandy. These tremendous impacts soon began to take their toll on deer populations.

[Co]ncurrent with high use of deer by pioneers, however, was an early expansion of both quality and quantity of [de]er habitat. Settlers inadvertently improved conditions for deer in the cutting or burning of thickets and for-[es]ts and the planting of farm crops, such as corn. However, these improvements were short-lived with subse-[qu]ent intensive grazing of plains and forests by cattle, sheep and hogs.

[IM]PACTS IN MISSOURI

[Mi]ssouri's deer were impacted along with those elsewhere as westward expansion progressed and human [po]pulations increased. As stated earlier, deer populations prior to European settlement likely ranged between [10]-20 per square mile, or more than 700,000 statewide. Settler activities reduced the herd in a remarkably short [ti]me. By 1890, deer were gone from most of the northern and western counties. By 1910, they remained in only [on]e or two counties north of the Missouri River, in the Mississippi Lowlands, the Ozarks and a few northern and [ea]stern Ozark border counties. The low point probably occurred around 1925 when the Missouri Game and Fish [D]epartment reported only 395 deer in 23 counties.

This decline was caused by year-round hunting for market, food or sport and from habitat depletion. Deer c all ages were killed with the gun as well as with traps, snares, nets and dogs. Earliest efforts at gam preservation consisted of local statues, the first of which applied only to St. Louis county. The first statewid game law was passed in 1874. It prohibited deer hunting and the sale of game from January 1 throug August 31. However, the law included no provision for enforcement and was largely ignored. Under th "Walmsley Law" of 1905 game wardens were hired and the deer season reduced to two months. Only on buck over one year old could be taken per day, with no season bag limit. This Law was unpopular with marke hunters and was repealed in 1907. However, sentiment continued in favor of deer and in 1909, concurrer with the creation of the office of State Game and Fish Commissioner, most provisions of the Walmsley Lav were restored.

But declines of deer continued. Deer supplied some families in the Ozarks with meat, but deer numbers wer dwindling. The result was a further reduction of the open season in 1921 to December. Finally, in 1925, th season was completely closed.

THE REBOUND OF DEER

The recovery of deer in Missouri was no accident. Missourians were alarmed at the scarcity of deer and othe wildlife. With reports of all-time low populations, such as 395 deer statewide in 1925, people were ready fc change. Some early restoration attempts were made. Between 1925 and 1930, 253 deer were live-trappe in Michigan and released on five ozark refuges (Meramec, Indian Trail, Deer Run, Sam A. Baker, and Bi Springs sites). Additionally, the Game and Fish Department purchased 91 deer from private individuals i Missouri and released them in the Ozarks. Limited recovery resulted from these efforts. In 1931 the stat legislature opened the deer season for antlered bucks during the last Thursday through Saturday in Octobe This season continued until 1938. In 1935, Bennitt and Nagel in their statewide game survey reported 2,24 deer distributed over 28 southeastern counties. However, at least half were located in and around the fiv Ozark refuges. They believed that the illegal kill equaled or exceeded the legal kill and was the chief limitin factor on growth of the deer herd. They considered stray dogs and competition from free ranging domest livestock for woodland forage as serious problems in the Ozarks. Gradual herd increases continued, and i 1937, when the current Conservation Commission was first established, the statewide population estimat was a meager 3,600 deer.

Bennitt and Nagel posed a number of research questions that they felt needed answers to assure soun deer management. They recommended studies on life history, food and cover requirements, and effects c various mortality factors and land use on deer populations. The newly established Department of Conserva tion took these questions seriously and immediately began a three-pronged deer management effort: re search to provide needed facts, restoration to enhance recovery and wildlife law enforcement to control an regulate human impacts.

Early research focused on life history studies, especially food habits, forage utilization and quality analys and techniques to survey deer numbers. These studies helped guide the restoration effort which began 1937. Over the next 20 years, 2,343 deer were trapped from refuge areas in southern and central Missou and were moved to 70 release sites in 54 counties. Strict wildlife law enforcement in every Missouri count backed by meaningful penalties, and a strong effort to educate Missourians on what was necessary to brir the deer back worked to turn things around.

Deer responded to these restoration, management and enforcement efforts. They rapidly expanded, both area and in density. Current deer numbers may exceed those of presettlement, around 800,000 statewid

Hunting of course has played a strong role in both the historical decline and in the recovery of deer populations in Missouri. Earlier, year-round unregulated market hunting took its toll. To facilitate other management programs that began in 1937 all deer hunting in Missouri was prohibited starting in 1938. Seasons remained closed until 1944 when the deer herd was estimated at 15,000 animals and limited bucks-only hunting was allowed in some counties. Seasons were liberalized as the herd grew and either-sex hunting was resumed by 1951 in 15 counties. By 1959, the entire state was opened to deer hunting. The deer population continued to grow rapidly in the 1960s, especially in northern Missouri. Hunter numbers and harvests also increased. By the 1970s, it became clear that more sophisticated regulations would be necessary to manage the annual harvest to keep populations in balance with food supplies and landowner tolerance. In 1970 a deer management unit system was adopted. This system provided for deer management by habitat type and capability, an improvement over the previous county-by-county method. Several unit boundary refinements have occurred since then, but the basic provision for regional management options has been retained. The deer management unit system, coupled with an any-deer quota system, first used in 1974, provide the management tools necessary to regulate Missouri's statewide deer herd. This requires a delicate balance between the needs of deer, and the wishes and concerns of Missouri citizens.

Deer are very important to Missouri hunters. More Missourians hunt deer than any other game animal. In 1996, over 400,000 hunters (modern firearms, muzzle loaders and archery included) harvested nearly 216,000 deer. Revenue from permit sales alone was about $8.4 million. Estimates of dollars spent by deer hunters annually in Missouri exceed $110 million with over $200 million in business activity generated.

In addition to hunting, deer add value to the quality of life for many citizens. People enjoy seeing deer and other wildlife and are willing to contribute financially through the 1/8 percent sales tax to their well-being. Deer also help attract tourists to the state.

Conversely, deer can cause significant damage to farm crops, orchards, vineyards, Christmas tree farms, nurseries and gardens, in both rural and urban settings. Deer-vehicle collisions are also a significant problem in many areas.

In the future, continued close population management will be required to maintain the delicate balance between too many and too few deer. This can by accomplished through the regulatory tools mentioned previously. Land uses resulting from expanding human populations will ultimately determine the fate of white-tailed deer in Missouri. It will be up to each of us to do our part to maintain the whitetail as an important component of Missouri's beautiful landscape.

A LOOK AHEAD

Black Bear might have said, *"Nikashiga no aba hoba ta ts'e tha bi ecka"* -- (How did the old men kill deer?). He and his fellow braves formed their traditions from ceremony and counsel provided by their ancestors. We too must use the traditions, knowledge and experience of those before us. To secure the success of whitetails in the future, we must learn from the mistakes and successes of the past. These are worth contemplating as we, "amid profound silence, steal away from our settlements to hunt deer."

REFERENCES

Baker, R. H. 1984. Origin, classification and distribution. Pages 1-18 in L. K. Halls, ed. whitetail deer ecology and management. Stackpole, Harrisburg, PA and Wildlife Management Institute, Washington , D.C. 870 pp.

LaFlesche, F. 1932. A dictionary of the Osage Language. Bureau of American Ethnology. Bulletin 109.

Murphy, D. A. 1970. White-tailed deer. Pages 129-138 in W.O. Nagel, ed. Conservation Contrasts. Missouri Conservation Commission. Jefferson City, MO 453 pp.

Porath, W. R. 1982. What makes a deer tick? Missouri Conservationist 43(4):16-19.

Robb, D. 1959. Missouri's deer herd. Missouri Conservation Commission. Jefferson City, MO. 44 pp.

Young, S. P. 1956. The deer, the Indians, and the American pioneers. Pages 1-27 in W. P. Taylor, ed. The deer of North America. Stackpole, Harrisburg, PA and Wildlife Management Institute, Washington, D.C. 668 pp.

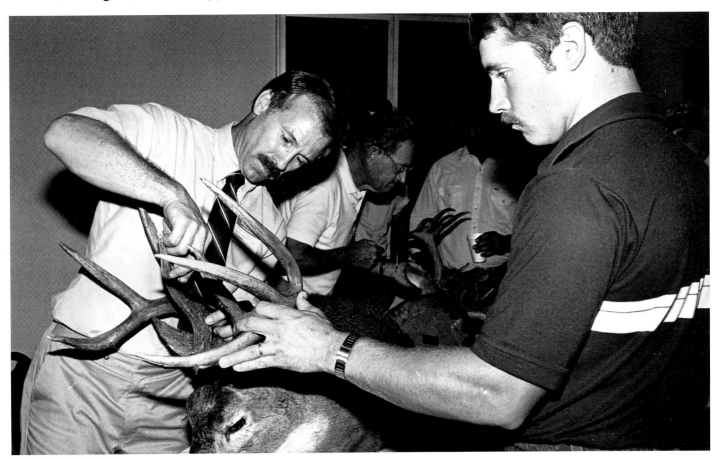

Wayne Porath measuring a trophy whitetail antler for an anxious hunter

Charles E. Hurst - 173 2/8 non-typical, Ste. Genevieve County

November Frost - Whitetail

A RECORDS KEEPING PROGRAM

"THE MISSOURI SHOW-ME BIG BUCKS CLUB"

by

R. SCOTT BRUNDAGE
Article compiled with information provided by the Missouri Department of Conservation.

While hunting, waiting on a deer stand sometimes for hours, one's mind tends to wonder, about a lot of things, but most often thoughts are of shooting a "trophy whitetail deer".

Suddenly, there was a slight rustling in the leaves, along the draw directly behind me. Was it another pesky squirrel or was it finally the real thing? Many previous false alarms that morning had not dulled the nerve-tingling anticipation, was it a deer? As I slowly turned and looked around the black oak I was leaning against, in my crudely constructed blind, the rustling stopped; no matter how hard I looked, I could see nothing.

Excitement slowly drained from me as I started to turn and continue my vigil, but a slight movement caught my eye, and all at once, there was a deer, where moments before there was nothing. My heart beat furiously, my hands trembled, my mouth went dry, as I slowly raised my rifle and looked through the scope. What I saw almost made me drop my gun, my knees went weak, there was the biggest buck I had ever seen. I tried not to breathe, for fear the movement might scare him, as he moved toward me through the woods. The buck stopped, looked back along its trail, my crosshairs centered quickly on the heart area, the rifle boomed, the buck dropped in his tracks. He thrashed the leaves, tried to rise, fell back, then all was silent.

I broke into a run, covered the 80 yards in record time, when I got to the buck I couldn't believe it. Thoughts flashed through my mind in the next few minutes: "talk about the hat-rack buck-this is it. I wonder if anyone has ever killed a bigger one in Missouri? Wait till Frank and the boys see this, they'll die! I wonder if it will qualify for the Boone and Crockett Club?, a trophy big game animals recognition program I read about once. Just think, a few years ago there were only a few deer in Missouri, now thousands".

With these thoughts still in mind, the idea for the big bucks club was born. Why not a state organization to recognize big trophy whitetail deer taken in Missouri and give the hunter credit for harvesting it? I knew that such an organization existed in Ohio, where I shot my first deer several years ago. The more I thought of it, the better the idea seemed. So, I wrote to Ohio and got some information on their club. With this information in hand, I contacted Dean Murphy and Dixie Robb, of the Game Division with the Missouri Department of Conservation.

After several sessions we decided to form a temporary Board of Directors and try to organize the "Show-Me Big Bucks Club". This was done and the Missouri Show-Me Big Bucks Club was now on its way.

The Big Bucks Club was officially formed in 1968 by interested hunters and some employees with the Missouri Department of Conservation. Our intended purpose in forming the club is: 1) To officially recognize Missouri Trophy deer heads and to honor the successful hunter: 2) To promote interest and appreciation in Missouri deer hunting: 3) To promote sportsmanship among deer hunters: 4) To establish and maintain a permanent records of trophy deer heads taken in Missouri: 5) To assist by whatever means possible the perpetuation of Missouri's deer population for the enjoyment of all: 6) To assist eligible members of the "Show-Me Big Bucks Club" to receive national recognition from the Boone and Crockett Club, the Pope and Young Club and the Longhunters Society.

How will a hunter become eligible for membership? By taking, through legal hunting methods, by high-powered rifle, muzzleloader, bow, pistol or found deer, a deer with antlers which will meet or exceed minimum standards set forth by the club. Measurements will be based on the system developed by the Boone and Crockett Club.

People hunt for sport and challenge, to get out-of-doors and with luck, get some delightful table fare. For most, the hunt itself is reward enough. They find satisfaction in recreating the role of their ancestor, the role of provider.

Others set a higher, and thus more elusive, standard. They are the trophy hunters, the ones who will probe deeper into the woods, scale higher bluffs, travel greater distances and endure greater hardships to attain their goal. They must seek and forebear and seek again until they find the one special trophy of a species. Their rewards are fewer in number but likely greater in satisfaction.

For whatever reason a person chooses to hunt, we are fortunate that our deer population can still provide the opportunity. And fortunate, too that the hunters are also good conservationists. If they were not, there would be no more rewards.

Pictured left to right: Wayne Porath, Ollie Torgison, Scott Brundage, Dean Murphy, Norb Giessman

1983 Banquet, in Columbia Missouri at the Ramada Inn.

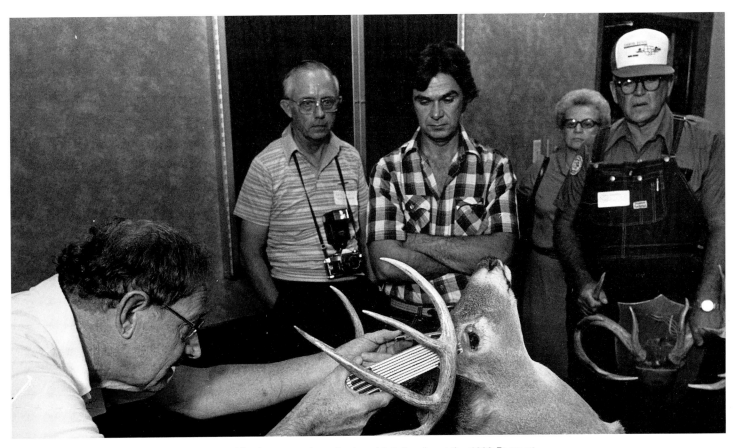
Dean Murphy measuring a trophy whitetail antler at the 1993 Banquet

21

Gibson, 205 0/8 typical and Jeff Brunk, 199 4/8 typical trophies

Paul Schwarz Official Boone and Crockett Measurer, Paul measured from 1960 - 1997 (now deceased)

Richard Stewart - 202 0/8 NT / Larry Penn -161 2/8 T / John Melton - 184 4/8 NT / Larry Ogle - 186 2/8 T

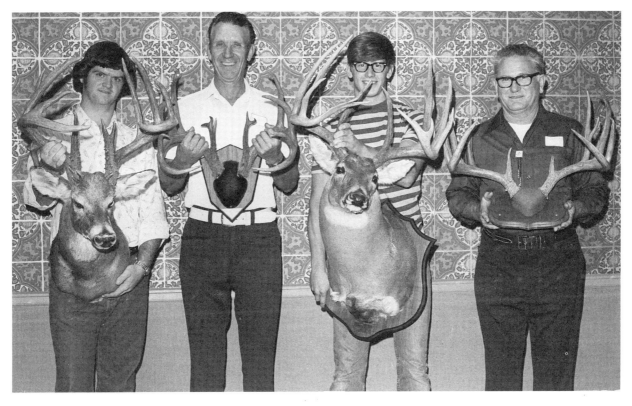

Steve Moreland - 193 1/8 NT / Donald Burnett - 194 6/8 NT / Joe Ditto - 187 1/8 T / James Wilson - 165 1/8 T

Gene Brown - 204 2/8 NT / Duane Linscott - 259 5/8 NT / David Smith - 171 7/8 T / David Allphin - 174 6/8 T

Charlie Montague and Larry Smedley
Charlie was Secretary-Treasurer of the Big Bucks Club for many years, Charlie passed away in 1992

Jerry Carter - 164 2/8 T / Stan McSparren - 218 5/8 NT / David Charlick - 186 5/8 NT / Carl Graham - 175 0/8 T

Gerald Drake - 217 7/8 NT / Burton Miller & Regan Nonneman - 215 5/8 NT / Roy Woodson -170 6/8 T / Danny Griffith - 174 5/8 T

Brian Branscomb - 168 3/8 T / Darren Dixon - 173 4/8 T / Jerry Cooper - 186 3/8 NT / George Johnson - 175 1/8 NT / Darrel Morgan - 168 3/8 T

Marvin Lentz - 183 4/8 Typical

Kenneth Lee - 208 7/8 NT

John Detjen - 187 4/8 NT

Virgil Ashley - 180 4/8 T / Karl Volz - 187 5/8 NT

Scott Brundage, David Mudd - 182 1/8 T

Jerry Calvert - 181 5/8 T

Gary Cokerham-193 0/8 NT/ Ray Banning-173 0/8 T / L.J. ByBee-164 4/8 T

17 NOV, 74
TO: MIKE
MILONSKI
19 PTS, 310 Rds
11TH LARGEST
FOR MISSOURI
Yours Truly,
David J. Roge

"GHOST FACE"

David Rogers, 153 2/8 typical, Daviess

James E. Williams - 223 7/8 non-typical, Warren County

Ken Umhoefer - 175 3/8 typical, Dent County

Gary Kinder - 197 1/8 non-typical, Worth County

Karl Volz - 187 5/8 non-typical, Ste. Genevieve County
If anyone knows the whereabouts of this trophy, please contact the Missouri Big Bucks Club

Jeff Brunk - 199 4/8 Typical, Clark County

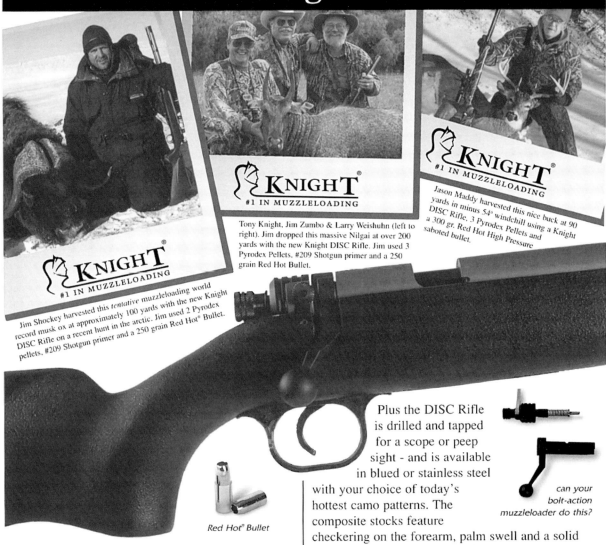

Old Rivals - Whitetail

THE PHILOSOPHY OF TROPHY HUNTING

by

KATHY ETLING

Trophy. A person who wins a trophy playing baseball, football, bowling or golf will be honored by friends and acquaintances alike. Yet mention the word in conjunction with hunting and you're bound to enrage at least a few people. What is it that makes this word so incendiary when used to describe the type of hunting for which most of us live and breathe?

Trophy. Here's Mr. Webster's definition of trophy as it pertains to the hunt: Any memorial of victory or conquest, as in trophies of the chase. We as hunters manage to keep ourselves in hot water with non-hunters because of this unfortunate definition of trophy as "memento of conquest."

Yet we conquer nature with an interstate highway system that gobbles up more wildlife habitat than any other public works project in history, and no one bats an eye. We can build mall after mall and subdivision on top of subdivision to shove nature even farther from our lives, and the response is basically "ho hum, so what else is new?" But woe to anyone who hunts a deer or an elk or a sheep simply because of the size of its antlers or horns. Trophy hunters find themselves tarred with the same broad brush of disapproval-- and, occasionally, downright hatred--that should be reserved for the true villains of our sport, the poachers.

As a trophy hunter myself I cannot understand why more outdoor writers and magazines and TV personalities don't attempt to explain the philosophy and ethics of trophy hunting. But then again, maybe I do. I recently queried an article on this very topic. MY idea was rejected as "too provocative." Rather than correct misconceptions, many editors go to extremes pretending that few trophy hunters exist, and the few who do exist are aberrations and nothing more. Rather than do what they can to instruct the approximately eighty percent of the public that perceive trophy hunting as always wrong, editors and producers ignore the subject entirely. But ignorance begets ignorance, and if we as trophy hunters don't start standing up for that in which we believe and, furthermore, explain exactly why we seek the biggest and the best, well, perhaps we deserve the scorn.

What do we believe? Funny, but few of us really know. Oh, we know we think it's okay to hunt trophy deer, but when it comes down to explaining why, many of us are at a loss for words. That doesn't mean we're stupid or foolish, it just means our everyday lives keep us so busy we rarely have a chance to formulate personal philosophies. That's what this chapter is all about: explaining my own trophy hunting philosophy and thereby providing readers of this book with enough thought-provoking information to start your own ruminations, if you haven't done so already.

I believe that when done properly trophy hunting is not only good, it's admirable. Trophy hunters who pursue wildlife both legally and ethically rank at the very top of hunting's hierarchy. Most of us have been hunters a long time. When we first started hunting, like everyone else we wanted to be outdoors, wanted to shoot our gun and hear it go 'bang' or to loose our bowstring and see an arrow bury itself in something, even if only a stump. Of course, we were hunters so we also wanted to kill an animal or two just to prove that we could. Over time we gained proficiency. As we did, we realized that not only was this sport called hunting mighty enjoyable, it kept us in fine physical shape, honed our skills as woodsmen and put food on the table, all good things. But after a while some of us found these goals, although still admirable, somewhat lacking. We began seeking greater challenges. Gradually, we became trophy hunters.

It begins innocuously enough. You might think, 'this season I will hold out for a buck.' And so you do. The next year you decide to wait for an eight-pointer. The following season your goals become even loftier, perhaps you're after a ten-point, or a buck with a 20-inch outside spread, or a 140-class Boone and Crockett, or something even more impressive. You, my friend, have morphed into a trophy hunter.

The author's trophy non-typical whitetail deer, 164 4/8 Boone and Crockett points. Taken November 21, 1991 in Ste. Genevieve County with a highpowered rifle.

Hunters of trophies practice voluntary restraint. Each of us passes up many deer in a quest for THE buck, and for that we're derided. "You're taking the biggest and the best; the survivor; the buck whose DNA should be kept in the gene pool, not eliminated so that its head may adorn some pompous hunter's wall." Such comments strike me with amazement. If a trophy buck has attained the age of 3 1/2, 4 1/2, 5 1/2, or 6 1/2 years, his genes have been liberally sprinkled throughout the gene pool ever since he was a basket-racked yearling, or maybe even a spike. These genes don't improve with age. The genes a buck possesses when he first sprouts velvet buttons are the ones he'll have when he dies. And if, as Dr. Larry Marchinton, a retired professor or wildlife biology, has often theorized, 98-percent of all whitetail bucks in the U.S. carry within their genetic makeup the capability of passing on to their progeny trophy-class antlers, then removing what to the laypersons' eye appears to be the 'best of the best' won't hurt the gene pool one whit. So what difference does it make if some lucky hunter harvests a bona fide trophy in its prime? Absolutely none.

Cathy's buck had 11 points right side, and 12 points left Inside, spread 14 6/8 inches, greatest spread 22 2/8

What's more, targeting animals in their prime or as they're going downhill removes them from the population before they can die cruelly from disease or starvation. I've read estimates that only about one percent of any wild population of deer dies peacefully in its sleep of natural causes. By concentrating on mature animals--and by practicing religiously with both bow and gun so we will always shoot straight and true--trophy hunters ensure not only will these deer live a reasonably long and full life but that they will also die quickly and humanely. Such a practice stands in stark contrast to the suffering endured by most older deer before dying.

Another important factor to consider is that during the rut even bucks in the peak of condition often run themselves ragged. Such individuals usually lose a significant amount of weight. They weaken and can become easy prey for predators. Once the rut has ended, bucks recover their vigor slowly. In some post-rut studies biologists have observed bucks refusing to eat even though food is available. Some Biologists speculate such behavior is a mechanism through which Mother Nature helps to ensure the survival of the upcoming generation. As for the buck, since he's already bred the doe, he's expendable. A cruel way of looking at it, but make no mistake: nature is cruel. One Texas A&I study estimated in some areas up to 25-percent of the bucks die annually from "post-rut mortality."

Another familiar objection to trophy hunting is simply that killing an animal for its antlers is always wrong. The scenario of a hunter shooting a buck and then whacking off its head while leaving the rest to rot must be vivid in most Americans' minds although ethical trophy hunters never kill animals solely for their antlers. Like any other hunter, a trophy hunter uses the meat from harvested animals. And when properly cared for, venison from a rank old buck can rival that of a yearling. In addition, trophy hunters often contribute part of their venison to programs that feed the needy. This notion that we harvest trophies solely for their horns is one that sorely needs clarification by the outdoor press. Word must be gotten out that even though trophy hunters are after deer with larger antlers, by no means is the meat from such animals ever wasted. To do so would be illegal, immoral and unethical.

Contrary to popular belief hunters don't hurt a population of whitetail deer, they help it. These hunters actually aid in the maintenance of herd vigor because by refusing to take smaller deer, more young bucks grow to maturity. The result is a better age-class distribution of bucks in areas favored by trophy hunters. When hunters opt not to shoot yearling bucks, the next season these are the bucks that will be doing most of the breeding. It doesn't take a rocket scientist to see how, after several years of passing up smaller bucks, the entire herd benefits. The herd's age structure becomes more diverse since it now includes bucks of many different ages instead of a preponderance of yearlings and the rare old survivor. And as everyone knows, knowledgeable whitetail managers strive diligently to maintain a diverse age structure in their own herds. They understand that a diversity of buck age-classes not only mitigates rut stress because breeding is performed by more and older animals, hunting usually improves because breeding competition increases. As competition increases, tactics such as calling, rattling and scrape watching become even more productive.

Now let's look at trophy hunting from an evolutionary perspective. Charles Darwin hypothesized--and the body of modern scientific knowledge seems to support--the idea that nature favors the "survival of the fittest." Yet killing the first foolish yearling to wander past your stand will do little to ensure that the 'fittest' will survive. In most cases a young buck has no idea of the danger in which he's placed himself. He may know all about coyotes and wild dogs and automobiles and even something about poachers, but hunters? We're out there only a few months each year. A buck is born in April, May or June. He'll often survive his fawn year with no or few bad human experiences. So why would such an animal be very wary the following season? It's only after a buck has lived through one or two truly dangerous encounters that he becomes savvy enough to evade most hunters. So having older or more experienced hunters--the trophy hunters--who almost certainly would be able to kill such a buck on the first try pass on the opportunity allows this buck to come into contact with less experienced hunters, folks who may not see animal coming, or who might experience buck fever, or who may simply miss. In any event, the trophy hunter has had the thrill of seeing the buck, the non-trophy hunter (s) have had the thrill of trying to shoot the buck and--if all goes well--the buck has learned a valuable lesson about the dangers of getting too close to hunters which may result in his attaining trophy status in years to come. And during all those years, the genes of this true survivor will continue to enhance the gene pool.

Trophy hunters pay for their tags like any other hunters. They fork over good money for the privilege of sitting in the outdoors waiting for a giant buck to happen by. That money--like the money collected from every other hunter--goes to state game and fish or conservation agencies. It goes to support wildlife conservation projects, pay agents' salaries and even buy or improve habitat. Yet more often than not, trophy hunters go home empty-handed. Think of it from this perspective: the more trophy hunters, the more money accumulating in state coffers to benefit wildlife. Yet trophy hunters place little added strain on the resource. In other words, the more trophy hunters there are, the more deer that will be available for the non-trophy hunter to harvest. This is an important point, one that almost no one ever contemplates. So if Hunter

A big body whitetail buck, had 8 points, shot in Ste. Genevieve County by the Author in '92

A is bound and determined to bag a twelve-point buck, he or she might allow ten smaller bucks to pass by unharmed. Now Hunter B might just be an 11-year old kid on his first deer hunt, Hunter C might be physically-challenged and Hunter D might be Hunter A's less particular buddy. Theoretically, if Hunters B, C and D all connect with bucks Hunter A's allowed to pass, you can readily see how trophy hunters help make hunting better for everyone. . . while satisfying all four hunters--A,B,C and D. Plus, it's unlikely all seven of those other bucks Hunter A passed up were killed. So in my opinion, the presence of ethical trophy hunters in the woods is a good deal for everyone. . . even the non-hunters who enjoy watching deer.

My next argument is elemental: hunting a trophy of almost any species provides an incredible challenge. A mature whitetail deer is probably as cunning an animal as can be found in nature. He has lived 3 1/2-years or more, so he's probably encountered hunters under a variety of circumstances. Such a buck comes equipped with great eyesight, wonderful hearing and a fantastic sense of smell. He possesses an incredible sixth sense that often allows him to intuit the presence of danger despite any concrete evidence--sight, sound or smell-- that it exists. Who among us hasn't seen a giant buck move almost within range, stop, appear to ponder something, then turn and go back the same way he came. . . even though everything was in your favor? Whitetail deer, when allowed to reach maturity, rank among the most intellectually worthy species humans can hunt. That's why so many giant bucks wind up on the walls of beginners who haven't got a clue. Since those hunters don't know anything about deer they do the last thing the deer expects them to do. Since giant bucks are phenomenal about patterning us, their hunters, when they do slip up it's often o a rookie.

The Reverend Theodore Vitali, a hunting priest who is also the chairman of St. Louis University's philosophy department, believes hunting--trophy hunting included--is a moral good when performed in a legal, ethical manner. "Hunting is a predatory pursuit," Father Vitali explained. "When you hunt, you place yourself at a primal level of experience. Hunting helps hunters recover what most urbanites lose; it reintroduces them to the experience of predation so as to regain their animality on a deep and reflective level. That is good. To be a trophy hunter requires so much more than luck; it takes a tremendous use of informed skill. To hunt the biggest, most mature buck in the woods requires instrumental intelligence and an advanced degree of outdoor skill and woodsmanship. Since a hunter must develop and hone these attributes to their highest levels to succeed, trophy hunting is both virtuous and a moral good."

Finally, sone people absolutely abhor the display of mounted trophies, which brings us full circle to the notion of a trophy as a "conquest." But I ask: who was conquered? The deer. . . or the hunter? Who's heart was really snagged for all eternity? Who has worked and slaved to accumulate the money and the vacation time to head into the whitetail woods for a mere chance at a trophy? I believe I speak for most of us when I say we don't mount deer as a symbol of their conquest, but to honor them for their beauty and intelligence and wild, untamed spirit.

I read about native Americans who performed rituals and ceremonies so that they might become more like the animal they hunted and I can't help but think of today's hunter: wearing silent clothes that approximate a deer's pelage; moving silently like whitetails through the woods; using scents taken from the deer's own body to confuse his wondrous nose; and saving antlers because, when all is said and done, they imbue the modern hunter--like the Native Americans--with "big medicine."

Big medicine. What is "big medicine' but that warm feeling within when you do what you set out to accomplish? If "big medicine" is both magical and inexplicable, then yes, hunting trophy deer and saving their hides or horns or mounting their heads or feet is big medicine indeed. The hunter looks at those antlers and feels a sense of pride, yet at the same time is humbled knowing he is just a cog in the greater mystery that is the universe. The hunter understands that he is as mortal as the deer he has just taken and thereby gains increasing acceptance of his own impending death. Rather than fearing death the way so many non-hunters do, hunters recognize it as a natural event simply because we are so intimately acquainted with it and because we have so much quiet time on land during which many of us contemplate its inevitability.

9 point whitetail buck taken in 1994, St. Genevieve County, by Author.

Last but not least, a whitetail in the wild lives eight or nine years, if he's lucky. A hunter may live to be 70, 80 or even 100 years old. A whitetail, with its great sensory perception and native intelligence, although a worthy adversary, possesses not our human capacities for love, for remembrance, for anticipating the future, or for creativity. Hunters such as William Faulkner and Ernest Hemingway have immortalized the creatures they hunted in brilliant works of literature. Hunter-artists from the Cro-Magnons down through the ages have immortalized them in sketches and paintings. We modern trophy hunters immortalize our beloved bucks through the photographs we take, the journal entries we make, the oral and written stories we tell, and glorious mounts we hang upon our walls. And for as long as the hunter lives, whenever his gaze falls upon his trophy buck that will immediately spring to life in the hunter's memory and imagination. Once more the animal will trot through a crisp dawn, sniff the cold north wind, chase a racing doe. For as long as the hunter draws breath, his buck will also live. And that is as close to bestowing immortality as we humans can come.

The Gibson Rack, 205 0/8 Typical, Randolph County

Double Trouble

MISSOURI DEER MANAGEMENT

by

LONNIE HANSEN
WILDLIFE REGIONAL BIOLOGIST
MISSOURI DEPARTMENT OF CONSERVATION

Deer management in Missouri has been a dynamic process. In 1939 the fledgling Conservation Commis-
n closed the deer season in hopes that faltering deer numbers would recover. Then, in 1944, modern
rvest management began when the deer season was reopened. Deer populations have changed dramati-
ly since then as have hunter interests, attitudes and harvest success. Early deer management goals were
provide hunting opportunity but ensure that deer numbers increased to fill all suitable range. Conservative
cks-only deer hunting seasons helped fulfill this goal. In more recent years, increasing deer populations
ve created new challenges and opportunities. Deer managers must now be concerned not only with
erharvest, but also, underharvest of deer populations. Increasing deer populations have allowed more
ral seasons and stimulated some hunters to seek something more than just shooting a deer. Some want
ger bucks and request trophy management. Some are looking for more challenging ways to hunt deer;
merous deer hunting user groups have resulted including among others, archers, muzzleloaders and
arms hunters. At the same time, increasing deer populations have resulted in more deer-human conflicts,
st importantly deer-vehicle accidents and agricultural crop damage. Deer management has become a
ancing act, part science, part art, that must consider both deer biology and human needs and desires.
lay the goal of deer management is to provide as much opportunity for hunting and viewing as possible
le minimizing deer-related conflicts. In the following sections I describe Missouri's current deer manage-
nt program, changing demands and problems associated with deer, and future challenges.

ulation Principles

he balance of reproduction and mortality determines if a deer population will grow, stay the same or
line. Deer reproductive rates in Missouri tend to be high with most does 2 years and older annually
ducing at least twins and between 10 and 15% producing triplets. Around 40% of fawn does produce a
le offspring their first year. Mortality due to factors other than hunting is low, only about 5% of deer 6
ths and older die each year. Fawn mortality is higher, averaging 40% during the first 6 months of life.
ler these conditions population growth rates without hunting are high (Figure 1, page 2).

unting is the most important deer mortality factor in Missouri and is the tool we use to manage deer
ulations. High buck harvests have little impact on the deer population because one male can breed with
erous females. Doe harvests are the key to managing deer numbers, therefore antlerless harvests have
ived most consideration in setting deer hunting regulations. Each year hunters take 40 to 70 percent of
antlered bucks and up to 25 percent of the does in Missouri. Buck harvests are high because we allow
e hunters to take bucks, hunters tend to select antlered over antlerless deer, and bucks are highly active
ng the hunting season because of rutting activities, thus exposing them more to hunters.

ncontrolled deer populations would eventually reach the land's carrying capacity (its ability to support
nals on a sustained basis). When this happens, reproductive rates decline and mortality rates increase
the population stabilizes. Accompanying this stabilization, however, are significant impacts on native

Figure 1. Deer Population Growth Potential

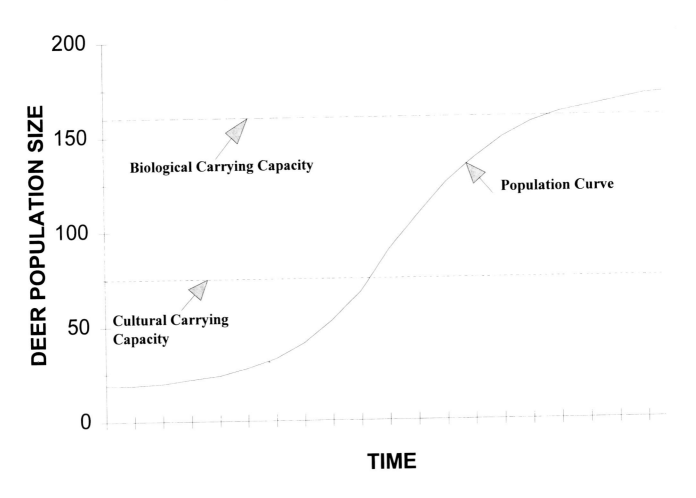

vegetation causing declines in other animal populations that depend on these plant communities. In Missouri deer populations are not near the biological carrying capacity because of the abundance of agricultural crops that deer use as a source of food. Much of northern Missouri could support several times the number of deer we have now. Deer numbers allowed to grow to the biological carrying capacit in Missouri, however, would lead to competition with man for his agricultural crops and create hazards such as deer collisions with vehicles. Therefore, the need to control deer numbers in most of Missouri is not related to the land's carrying capacity but to a typically lower cultural carrying capacity, the maximum number of deer that the public will tolerate. We determine this cultural carrying capacity by surveying landowners and hunters, the two groups that have the biggest stake in deer population management. Deer population goals are based on the cultural carrying capacity.

Historical management

The first modern-day deer season, held in 1944, was a modest affair in 20 Ozark and Ozark Border counties during which only bucks could be taken (Figure 2, page 3). Harvest regulations were intended provide some hunting opportunity but still allow for maximum growth of the deer herd. This "maximum growth" management continued until 1951. By this time deer had expanded throughout much of the southern Missouri deer range and densities in existing populations had increased. There were not serio problems with deer; only a few complaints about deer browsing on pines and some crop fields. Howeve early biologists recognized the need to take does to slow herd growth and provide additional harvest opportunity for hunters. The recommendation that some counties be opened to any-deer hunting receiv some public resistance but the 3-day any-deer hunt was opened in 15 counties; antlered-only deer hun ing continued in 17 counties. The season was successful.

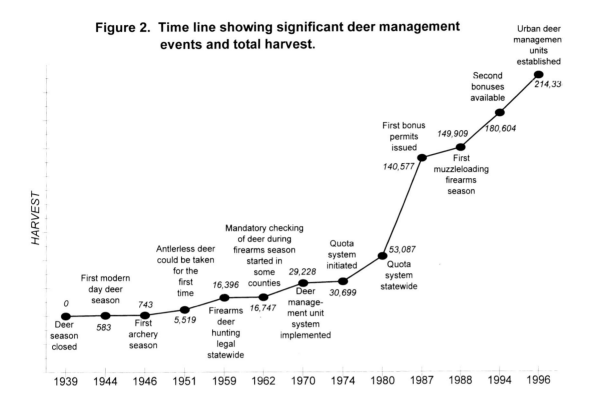

Figure 2. Time line showing significant deer management events and total harvest.

(Chart data points and labels:)

- Urban deer management units established — 214,33[3]
- Second bonuses available — 180,604
- First bonus permits issued — 140,577
- First muzzleloading firearms season — 149,909
- Quota system initiated
- Quota system statewide — 53,087
- Mandatory checking of deer during firearms season started in some counties — 29,228
- Quota system — 30,699
- Deer management unit system implemented — 16,747
- Firearms deer hunting legal statewide — 16,396
- Antlerless deer could be taken for the first time — 5,519
- First modern day deer season — 743
- First archery season — 583
- Deer season closed — 0

HARVEST

Years: 1939 1944 1946 1951 1959 1962 1970 1974 1980 1987 1988 1994 1996

he any-deer hunts allowed a person with a firearms deer hunting permit to take deer of any sex or age ng designated parts of the season. This system worked well but, as hunter numbers increased, any-r seasons in some counties resulted in overharvest. As a result, an any-deer season in a county often : followed by a bucks-only season to allow the deer population to recover. This "boon and bust" man-ment was confusing to the public and was an unsatisfactory way to manage deer. Also, short any-deer sons were a problem because weather could affect antlerless harvests. Finally, the public felt that many erless deer were killed illegally during seasons in which part was bucks only, and part any-deer. The souri Department of Conservation received many letters complaining about this waste of a resource. To ice these problems, in 1974 a quota system was implemented in one area. A few years earlier, in 1970, r management by unit instead of by county was introduced. Unit boundaries were based primarily on st cover, an important component of deer habitat. Under the quota system, there was a set number of -deer permits in a management unit that were distributed to applicants by random drawing. This system expanded until 1980 when any-deer permits in all management units were issued by random drawing er a quota system. As deer numbers increased, especially in northern Missouri, the public experienced easing problems with deer such as deer/vehicle accidents and crop damage. Hunter numbers were easing but doe harvests were not keeping pace with population expansion. In 1987, to increase erless harvest in selected units, bonus permits that allowed hunters to take an additional antlerless during the firearms season, were issued for the first time. Second bonuses were added in 1994 as we inued to liberalize harvest regulations, especially in northern Missouri.

anagement of deer in Missouri has emphasized monitoring and manipulating deer numbers. Generally, harvests have been relatively unrestricted compared to doe harvests which have been closely controlled. Our primary concern has been to maintain adequate deer numbers that provide hunters and viewers with a reasonable opportunity but low enough that problems associated with deer were tolerable. The result has generally been deer populations with more antlerless deer than antlered deer. Some state crop bucks at an extremely high rate, often greater than 80%. Few bucks get into older age classes as a result. In Missouri we take 40-70% of the antlered deer each year during the hunting seasons. Under the harvest rates, on average about 40% of the deer population is male and 20% is antlered bucks. Of the antlered bucks, around 60% are 1 1/2 years old.

Management Options

have been fortunate in Missouri to have public support for research on the biology and managem of white-tailed deer and good harvest information collected at mandatory check stations. We continue to be most concerned about deer densities, trying to keep numbers at optimal levels. Harvest opportunity been good, meeting the desires of much of the hunting public. However, increasing deer densities have made it relatively easy to harvest a deer. This has prompted some hunters to seek a more challenging deer hunting experience, either searching for that elusive trophy or using more "primitive" hunting equipment. This increasing interest in hunting for older bucks has been seen throughout the range of the whit tail. Trophy and quality deer management programs have resulted. Trophy management emphasizes th production of the largest racked buck possible. This requires intense management and control over larg blocks of land and is not practical in most situations in Missouri. Quality deer management is a less inter form of management where the primary concerns are to promote hunter ethics and responsible herd ma agement. Quality management requires minimal harvest of young bucks and doe harvest adequate to maintain populations at acceptable levels. In Missouri, because deer populations are already below the biological carrying capacity, the doe harvest is less critical, but still an important part of responsible dee management. One result of quality management is a herd with a more balanced sex and age ratio (Figu 3, page 5) so that hunters have a better opportunity to observe intense deer breeding activities and hav better chance to see and perhaps take an adult buck.

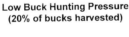

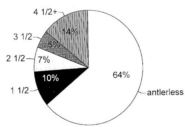

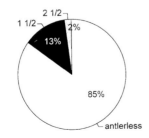

Quality management has been more popular in the South than in the Midwest because of land ownership
d harvest pressure differences. Much deer hunting in the southern states is done on leases. Historically,
ck populations were overexploited while too few does were taken. Deer populations highly skewed to-
rd antlerless deer and an antlered component that consisted mostly of yearlings led to increasing con-
rn from the public about the lack of adult bucks. Biologists have been mostly concerned about deer
pulations that surpassed the biological carrying capacity. Quality management was a logical solution to
s problem because emphasis was on increased harvests of does and reduced harvest of young bucks.
any leases in the south now practice quality management. The result in most areas practicing quality
anagement has been populations reduced to below the land's carrying capacity, a higher proportion of
cks in the population, and a higher proportion of bucks in older age classes.

Missouri offers a different management situation. Deer populations in most of the state are well below
rrying capacity. Although most land is in private ownership, the land holdings are small and leasing for
nting is not common. Missouri's firearms seasons are short compared to those in the south, resulting in
ver harvest rates of antlered bucks in most areas. In addition, Missouri hunters are not as resistant to
ing does. As a result, antlerless harvests generally exceed antlered harvests and the opportunity to take
ge-antlered bucks has been greater here than in the south. Because of this, public interest in quality deer
anagement programs has, thus far, not been great. However, in recent years we have noticed more
nters and landowners inquiring about this management practice.

Should we be doing more quality management in Missouri? Quality management has many good points
t promote responsible management. However, implementation on a large scale, such as a deer manage-
nt unit, would likely generate public concerns. The latest deer hunter survey in Missouri indicated that
% of the respondents would support management for adult bucks even if it meant they would not be
wed to take small-antlered bucks, 50% would not and 21% had no opinion. Of the respondents, 57%
t the first legal deer that offered a good shot. Apparently, most of our deer hunters still just want to shoot
eer and would not support management that restricted this opportunity. Surveys of the general public
icate that nonhunters do not approve of trophy management and may not accept the quality manage-
nt concept. Finally, quality management may promote large land leases and purchases, potentially
king deer hunting an elitist activity, preventing some persons from deer hunting.

It is clear that quality management is not without controversy and careful consideration must be given
fore attempting to manage this way on a large scale. Currently we advise landowners and managers on
w to do quality management on their own property; many are now trying it. Also, we are doing an evalua-
n of a quality management program on one of our public areas. Depending on the results, we may ex-
nd this program in the future. We will monitor public attitudes and adjust management strategies accord-
ly. If future public sentiment suggests we consider management alternatives, we will make appropriate
anges in the management program.

ture Challenges in Deer Management

he future of the white-tailed deer is bright in Missouri. Unfortunately, management is becoming increas-
y challenging because of changing property ownership and accessibility to land for hunting. Landowners
e the final say on how much hunting pressure their property receives. We can set deer hunting regula-
s that provide the opportunity to achieve desirable deer numbers through hunting. However, the success
ur management efforts depends on the persons who control access for hunting. Liberal seasons in-
ded to control deer numbers will not have the desired effect in places where hunters do not have access.

robably nowhere in Missouri will the deer management challenge be greater than in and around our
anding cities. Deer are highly adaptable and have survived, even taken advantage of, many man-

caused alterations in urban areas. Here we often lose hunting as a means of controlling deer populations because of safety concerns or public attitudes opposed to hunting. In some urban/suburban locations, carefully crafted and controlled hunting can be used to manage deer. Many of these hunts will produce some of our largest bucks because hunting pressure is generally light. In other urban areas it is inevitable that we will have to use non-traditional means of controlling deer, such as sharpshooting and trap and euthanasia. The human element will determine how we manage these populations.

The health and status of the deer population are primary concerns of our deer management program. However, human considerations will get equal consideration, especially in situations where deer become threat to human health and property. We will continue to monitor the hunting and nonhunting public's nee and desires concerning deer management and adjust our deer management strategies to serve Missouri citizens's best interest.

photo's by - Dale H. Ream, Jr.

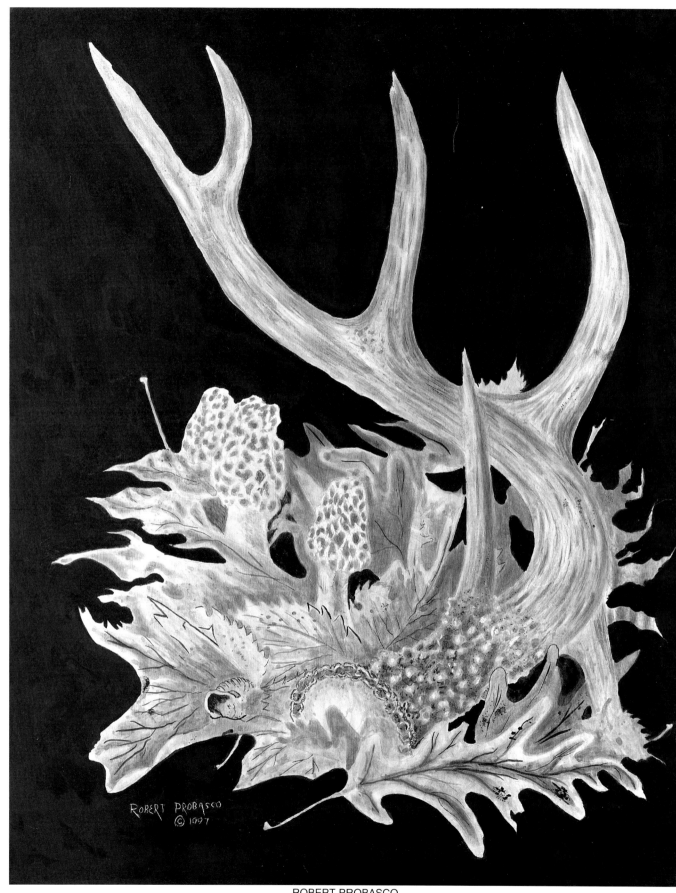

ROBERT PROBASCO
Specializes in Wildlife and Sporting Arts; Works mainly with: watercolor, acrylic and scratch board

Robert Probasco
Unionville, MO 63565
phone: 660/947-2738

SHED HUNTING

by

JOE REAM

The hunting of shed antlers has now become its own season. Avid hunters and whitetail enthusiasts have ⸱ many years spent time post-season scouting and looking for one of nature's most prestigious creations, ⸱ sheds of a majestic whitetail. The popularity of this sport has grown to the point where anyone who ⸱joys the outdoors can look forward to the mid to late season going with friends, family or by yourself. The ⸱ill of walking up on a unique shedded antler is an exciting experience all of its own. But to whitetail enthu-⸱sts like myself, it can also be very educational. The knowledge a hunter gains in the search can be ex-⸱mely helpful in the harvesting of a buck in the fall.

Let's start by looking at what causes antlers to shed. There are a number of reasons, but the majority of ⸱cks lose their antlers when the level of testosterone drops in their blood to a certain level. This is due ⸱rmally to the lack of estrus does in their breeding area. The length of daylight hours dictates a does ability ⸱breed, normally no later than mid December or early January. This is as late as mother nature will allow ⸱ this biological time clock. It is fairly well established that the strongest males generally cast earliest and ⸱unger subordinate bucks later. Bucks could cast their antlers for such reasons as: injuries, fever, disease ⸱overall health of a buck.

⸱Casting of antlers can occur from late December to April, but primarily in late January and February in ⸱ssouri. There are some main things to remember when you start looking for sheds. First, deer patterns ⸱ange during mid to late winter. A majority of deer will gather in groups called yarding. To conserve energy ⸱se groups will stay close to their feeding area during bad weather. Try driving roads, look for deer feeding ⸱d watch for heavily used trails, this is a good place to start. Topographical maps and aerial photos are ⸱dern visual aids that can increase your success. Using your map, mark it with different colors for trails, ⸱ding and bedding areas for future reference. Make sure you have acquired permission before entering ⸱vate property.

⸱Look in feeding areas especially along edges ⸱eeding areas. Corn, bean, winter wheat and ⸱y fields are all prime spots. Any other place ⸱ think bucks might be feeding in, check it out! ⸱en deer are feeding they are continuously ⸱sing and lowering their heads increasing the ⸱ds of their antlers falling off.

⸱When looking along travel corridors, remember ⸱celines and ditches are the best place to look. ⸱en bucks jump any obstacle the jar from land-⸱ can often cause an antler to fall off.

⸱dding areas will usually be in heavy cover, out ⸱he wind, allowing southern exposure. Most ⸱lly big bucks are solitary animals and chose

Joe Ream, with a shed found by a lucky hunter

53

Bob Mollick and his state record sheds, 187 0/8 found in the spring of 1996. Scoring 98 1/8 on its right side and 99 6/8 on its left side, with 2 abnormals totaling 3 4/8 inches, 7 3/8 difference Rt-Lt side, total deductions 10 4/8 inches. Add 2 inches of the G-5 point that was broken off (which the owner has), add a 19 inch inside spread. This antler in 1995 would have score 210 6/8 Boone and Crockett points.

54

bed away from the herd, usually not too far, but by themselves.

The best way to find sheds is by walking slowly and look for details. Many times you're only going to see art of the antler. Don't forget to take your binoculars. There is no exact explanation why sheds drop close each other or far apart. It makes sense to me that a buck with a big rack would like to drop both as quick s possible, due to the feeling of being off balance it would create. Your competitors for shed are, of ourse, other shed hunters. Antlers are a great source of minerals for many animals and can be consumed ery quickly, when found, or may last a long time if undetected.

A word of caution, winter can be very stressful on deer. Be careful not to disturb them to the point it ffects their physical condition, which could also hinder the antler development for the upcoming season.

Finding sheds is like hunting whitetails. All of a sudden there they are right in front of you. It takes pa- ence, persistence and dedication. Don't get discouraged. The one thing you have that no one can take is our attitude. So have fun. Take your family or friends and enjoy the world of the whitetail.

Mark Torrey and his dad Ed, with a set scoring 139 7/8 N-T

This big shed scores 91 7/8 typical

This shed scores 90 1/8 non-typical

Cornfield Buck

WHITETAIL,

THERE IS A DIFFERENCE

by

JAY GATES

They're all called whitetails. They all have that white flag on the underside of their tails. The males have ntlers. But somewhere back in the premortal stew, they were all the same animal. They were all deer of a nd.

But the simmering of that stew produced evolutionary changes that have better adapted these cloven-oofed, antler-headed beasts to habitat and breeding requirements. The current situation is that there are ore than 30 subspecies of whitetailed deer living on the North American and South American continents. nese can be placed in two major subspecies, the Northern and Eastern Whitetail (which we will refer to as e Northeastern Whitetail in the treatise) and the Coues Whitetail. These two groups are the only whitetail ecies recognized by the Boone and Crockett record keepers.

As different on cops and robbers, Republicans id Democrats, oil and water, night and day, ievies and Fords, these two deer have different iysical characteristics, live in totally different ibitat, and offer opposite challenges in hunting.

COMPARING SIZE, COLOR AND ANTLER CONFORMATION

The larger of the two deer is the Northeastern hitetail. They range from 140 to 350 pounds, Id dressed. Most western and central whitetails nge 140-190 pounds, while the Northeastern d Canadian deer often weigh over 250 unds.

The Northeastern animal is usually reddish-own in color with distinctive white eye circles d throat patch. The Coues is slate to gun metal ey with small amounts of white patching. Both e color matched to their habitat with the Coues owing the best camouflage features.

Antlers on both species are called "basket cks" with points protruding from the main ams. Both usually have long brow tines. The ference in the antler conformation is in the

Jay Gates, with a New Mexico Coues Deer, this buck scored 110 non-typical points

number of points. The mature Northeastern buck normally has five points on each side while the Coues normally sports four per side. Field judging for trophy purposes would have you looking for racks that extend past the ears, the farther the better. Look for long, heavy main beams and brow tines and for rack: that have good symmetry and proportion.

The Northeastern whitetail rack is much bigger; minimum Boone and Crockett typical score is 170 points compared to 110 points typical, for a Coues deer.

The doe-to-buck ratios for the two groups are also quite dissimilar, dictated by the hunting pressure, herd management, prolificacy, fawn survival ratios, and feed and water of the range. The ratio among the Northeastern animals runs from 1 : 1 all the way to a 50 : 1. and averages approximately 15 : 1. The Coues ratio, on the other hand, usually runs 1 : 1 and seldom more than 3 :1. This seems to be in direct response to drier, less vegetated habitat and less hunting pressure.

THE HABITAT FACTOR

The size and type of habitat of the two animals is perhaps the most major of the differences. The North eastern Whitetail ranges all over the U.S. (except Nevada, Arizona, Utah, and California), and Canada and northern Mexico. In the U.S. Coues deer range extends over less than 50,000 square miles compared to several million for the Northeastern deer.

The habitat type where you find the larger Northeastern Whitetail includes riparian areas such as river bottoms and shallow, broad canyons and breaks. They also frequent sage brush flats, woods, and some pine canyons, especially in Northwestern Montana.

Jay and 114 point typical buck taken in Old Mexico

The Deer Hunter, New Mexico 1981, 115 typical pts, 5x4

The Coues spends its life in some of the most rugged country in the western hemisphere, the volcanically spawned chaparral habitat of the southwest. Here sharp, hard rock ridges, brush choked draws, and boulder strewn, cactus infested hillsides are the most common features. In many cases, Coues hunters may think they will find desert big horned sheep before they find their deer. Water is scarce here.

HUNTING TECHNIQUES

All of the great whitetail hunters will tell you the best way to hunt whitetails is by stand hunting on scrapes, feeding or bedding areas, rattling, still hunting, foot drives, and by driving roads to find the animals before stalking them. Those methods work well, very well, for all except the coues. I have taken my share of the big whitetails using them, but they will not work for Coues Deer.

Because of their remote, rugged habitat, you have to go to the deer in Coues hunting. In most cases the roads end before you get there. For that reason, I prefer to backpack in and camp right in the hunting area. The other choice is to drive as far as you can and begin walking very early in order to arrive, before daylight, at a suitable ridge top from which you can glass the country. You may have to move several times during the day before you spot animals to stalk.

The best method for mid-day hunting is to "kick" brushy draws and the tops of canyons, attempting to jump the bucks who bed down in mid-day.

In Coues hunting, it is important to see the buck before he sees you. If you don't see him first, you will have almost no chance of catching up with him for a shot.

The single biggest factor that makes Coues hunting so different is probably the requirement that the hunter be in top physical condition. I have walked as many as 20 miles a day to find and harvest a good Coues buck. Once a kill is made, you have to get the meat back to the road. It is hard to imagine what a hunt would be like if the hunter was not in good physical condition.

THE GUNS AND GLASSES

I have a lot of money invested in good optics. I happen to think that my scopes and binoculars are as important to me as my rifle. This is especially true when you are hunting Coues in the vastness of the Southwest. Without high resolution optics, you could never pick out the well camouflaged little

Scoring 154, taken in New Mexico
Huge Velvet Coves buck

Taken in Arizona, 1988, scoring 101 Boone and Crockett points

Jay took this buck in Old Mexico, scoring 113 Boone and Crockett typical points. If you want to shoot a trophy buck like this one, you must pass 1 1/2, 2 1/2 year old bucks. Big bucks are like big bass, over harvesting of small bucks and trophy bucks will be in short supply.

This big 5x 5 Arizona Coues deer was taken by the Author in 1990, scoring 105 typical Boone and Crockett points.

deer, let alone field judge him.

I use Zeiss 10x40 and Docter 15x60 binoculars and a 13.5-37.5 power Docter spotting scope. My rifle scopes are Zeiss lenses. I easily have as much in optics as the rest of my gear. I use the same rifle for both types of whitetails----it's a good flat shooting Remington Model 700, 270 mounted on a Brown Precision fiberglass stock.

I also carry a walking stick which not only aids the walk, but serves as a steadying mount for binoculars when glassing.

THE THREE "P ' s"

Knowing more about the deer you hunt is one of the three "P's" by which I have taken whitetails every year since 1970. The first "P" stands for Preparation and includes knowing the animals and the habitat, preparing yourself physically, and having the right equipment.

The other two "P's" are for Patience and Persistence. You need both when hunting for trophy bucks. Whether you are sitting on a stand in zero weather or walking a ridge where the rocks are cutting away at your boots like machetes, you must commit yourself to the hunt and the fact that you may even have to pass up a lot of fine animals before you actually squeeze off a shot. If you have ten days to hunt, hunt all ten days, if you need to. Make the best use of daylight by being in the habitat when the dawn light appears.

Because Coues Whitetails are less plentiful and are often smaller than their whitetail cousins, they are often underrated as a game animal. But they have their own special place in the hearts of many serious hunters and students of deer habits. My personal favorite of the two whitetail subspecies is the Coues hunt, but whichever you choose, you'll find the crafty whitetails will lead you on as merry a chase as any deer will. When the chase is done, the meat is in the locker, and the rack is on the wall, the satisfaction is just as great for either animal.

Jay, with a 5x4, shot in Arizona 1983, 112 typical

This Arizona 4x4 shot in 1989 measured 100 typical

This Arizona 5x5 taken by Jay in 1986 scored 105 typical

This Texas Northeastern Whitetail taken by Jay in 1989, scored 140

Winter Sunrise - Whitetail

HUNTING ADVENTURES

AND PHOTOGRAPHS

by

MEMBERS OF THE MISSOURI SHOW-ME BIG BUCKS CLUB

Tom Philipps

t was the second day of Missouri's firearms deer season. My friend Kevin and I were heading back to the woods after
uneventful morning. We passed the turn off to Kevin's stand and proceeded to the end of the logging road where I
uld take my stand. He dropped me off, and not until he had gotten out of sight, did I realize that I had left my extra shells
hunting knife in the back storage box on his three wheeler. "I'll never get a deer anyway," I thought. As the sound of
three wheeler died in the distance, I settled in to watch a strip of
sh that was known as a good crossing. I sat there for about
ty minutes and started thinking about the day before. I had shot
nice six or eight point buck, emptying my gun and watching
walk away. I was kind of disgusted with deer hunting in
eral, and as I reviewed this spot, I was disgusted with it also.
cided to move a few hundred yards down a main ridge, nearer
where I had shot at the buck the morning before.

After a slow still hunt, I arrived at my desired location. I decided
nove a little deeper into the woods than I was yesterday and
ged down the ridge. This spot was good. I could stand vigil
r a brushy draw, but could also see well into the hollow below
As I cleared the leaves away from the base of the tree, I de-
:d to hunt here until dark. I sat down and decided to eat a snack
re getting down to business. I grabbed some food out of my
ket, and before I could open the lid, was startled by a deer
ating on the adjoining ridge. I put down the can and picked up
rifle. Again, I heard two more grunts; I was sure of it, this time.
onds later, I saw what I believed to be a nice buck meandering
ugh the brush hot on a scent trail. He slowly worked his way
n the ridge across from mine and upon reaching the base, he
ped. At this point, he could enter the brushy draw or go uphill

Tom Philipps & his trophy scoring 148 2/8 typical, Jackson County.

the open timber. My guess was the brush, and I quickly got ready to shoot. He stood facing me with his nose glued to
ground. I aimed right between the shoulder blades and fired. He acted as if nothing had happened. I slowly opened the
on my gun, capturing the spent shell in my gloved hand. I laid it on the ground then covered the breach with my other
l to muffle the sound, as I closed the action. Oblivious to my presence, he turned away from the thicket and started
king up the hill at a distance of a mere twenty-five to thirty yards. I was mad over missing the deer yesterday and had
done it again. This made me concentrate on shot placement. I aimed at the heart and when I squeezed the trigger, the

the deer kicked like a mule. He then swung into a full gallop up the hill in the direction he had come from. About th time he got out of sight, I heard a loud crash.

I waited about ten minutes and could stand it no longer. I walked to where I had last seen the deer and found a abundance of blood. I knew he had not gone far. I looked beyond the blood and there he lay. I was ecstatic. This was m first really good look at his antlers. They were magnificent. Eight long sweeping tines, dark in color, lots of mass. tagged my trophy.

After admiring the rack, I decided it was time to field dress my buck. This was going to be difficult since I had left m knife in the three wheeler. I fished in my pocket for my small knife and located it. I tried to make an incision, it was n use, to dull. I went to find Kevin. After a ten minute walk, or should I say run, I realized he was not on his stand. returned to my deer and started an exhausting pull some one to two hundred yards up the hill. This took me nearly a hour. I was wrung out by the time I heard the approaching three wheeler. I stood proudly over my trophy and lifted h head as Kevin approached. He nearly hit a tree when he saw the deer.

After a short celebration, I retrieved my knife and went about the task of field dressing the deer. Kevin added son much needed relief by helping me with the task. We loaded the buck on the back of the three wheeler and headed bac to camp. When we got on the logging road I told Kevin to hurry back to camp so I could show the deer to my dad. Kev said, "I want to take it slow, you don't kill a deer like this everyday." "You're right," I said, "slow down."

Jimmy O'Neal , 141 3/8 typical, Washington County, Bow

Norm Nothnagel, 174 2/8 non-typical, Greene County, Bow

Robin Lochridge, 151 5/8 typical, St. Clair County

Roy Everett Lewis III, 154 5/8 typical, Harrison County

Kevin Stroup, 203 5/8 non-typical, Chariton County

R.G. York, 162 7/8 non-typical, Barton County

Brian Anderson, 150 6/8 typical, Schuyler County

James Anderson, 168 7/8 non-typical, Adair County

Jeremy and Jeff Anderson, 163 0/8 typical, Caldwell County

Lester Wright, 144 2/8 typical, Morgan County

65

Jo Ann Robinson, 150 7/8 typical, Montgomery Co.

Jim Martin, 197 1/8 non-typical, Jackson County

Ed Nelson, 161 7/8 typical, Saline County

Evelyn Priebe, 223 4/8 non-typical, Clark County

Tom Philipps, 148 2/8 typical, Madison County

Eddie James, 189 4/8 non-typical, Morgan Co

Charles Sullivan, 176 6/8 typical, Laclede County

Curtis Powell, 144 1/8 typical, Benton County

Rita Legg, 151 0/8 typical, Benton County

MY BIG BUCK STORY

by

JANET WAYBILL

Janet Waybill, 170 1/8 non-typical, Adair Co.

Owning a sporting goods store, everyone knows how hard [i]s to find the time to hunt in your "favorite spot." So I [bid]ed my time, and took my second choice of spots to hunt, [wh]ere there was a good scrape line, and close enough to the [ho]use so I could hunt for about an hour and a half, before I [ha]d to go to work. I knew, in the back of my mind, that the ["B]ig Buck" was probably at my "favorite spot." I had seen a [gli]mpse of him a couple of weeks before gun season had [op]ened. After sitting and waiting, and not seeing a buck that [I w]ould have liked to harvest, I decided to head back to the [ho]use to get ready for work.

At the store I knew I would hear plenty of hunting stories [and] see some deer, but utmost on my mind was the thought [of] the afternoon hunt. My husband, Donnie, and I work [tog]ether, and since he was anxious to hunt also, we left the [sto]re around 2:30 p.m. because we knew we had to be in the [wo]ods and at our spot by 3:30 p.m., at the very latest. When we got home, we change into our hunting gear, and off to the [wo]ods for our hunt.

My favorite spot to hunt is where I've harvested the other 2 deer, the only 2 deer that I've ever harvested in my life. [W]e hunt on our 400 acre farm. Every year we set out food plots and practice wildlife management, working year around [to i]mprove our deer and turkey population.

[W]e have five hunters that hunt our land, including Donnie and myself. Traditionally, every weekend before season [op]ens, everyone sits around our kitchen table, and the conversation goes like this... "where are you going to hunt?" "I [don]'t know, where are you going to hunt?" This goes on for about an hour, and no one has a clue because no one wants [to t]ell where they really want to hunt.

[T]hree years ago, Donnie told me he had a place picked out for me to hunt. I had overheard him saying: "yeah, that [wo]uld be a good place for Janet to hunt," so I knew it was a spot no one else wanted. He did say there had been deer there [eve]ry evening, but I knew if anyone was interested in hunting a deer in that place, I sure wouldn't get that spot. I [har]vested my first deer there, an 8-point buck, whose antlers were so small, they would have fit in a grocery sack, so I [call]ed it my "sack-rack buck," but I was so proud that I had finally gotten my first deer, and it was a buck. I was sure [Don]nie figured I wouldn't get anything but a doe or a button buck, and my first deer had been a buck.

[N]ow that I have harvested deer two consecutive years in the same place, I'm loving this spot. So here I am, opening [day] of Firearms Season 1995. I'm heading to my "favorite spot" to hunt. Donnie's on his way to his "perfect place," [whi]ch he had chosen early that morning. I had carefully placed buck lure in various spots, the wind was in the right [dire]ction and I had my 6mm Remington. I like to hunt in a tree row and hunt from the ground, so I have to be very still. [I w]as in place and ready by 3:15 p.m. It was time for the longest wait.

[W]hat a beautiful day it was! One hour had gone by and no sight or sound of a deer, except me, using my grunt call. I [glan]ced up and... OH, MY! What a buck! He was walking straight towards me. I didn't want to shoot yet because he

67

hadn't turned at all, he was grazing and taking his sweet time. Finally, he turned about a third of a turn and I shot, missed! Shot, again... missed, again. I knew he was history, gone! Unbelievably, he turned to complete side profile, just as if he thought I couldn't kill him. I fired the third shot and down he came. He was MINE!

I ran to him as quickly as I could. I just stood there looking at him, not believing my eyes. I tagged my deer and sat down to wait for Donnie. I knew after shooting time he would be over to check on me. It was about 5:10 p.m., I turned around and saw Donnie coming over the ridge. I gave him thumbs-up sign, meaning I had my deer, not realizing at the time I had bagged a Missouri Big Bucks trophy deer that would score 170 1/8 non-typical points.

Donnie looked at me and said: "Janet, that's a really nice buck," and that was the last nice words I've ever heard from him about my deer.

Last year, I couldn't even get to my "favorite spot" for everyone else wanting to hunt there. It was like a super highway!!

Guy Richardson, 167 5/8 typical, Pike County

Shirley Hendrix, 179 0/8 non-typical, Randolph County

Jerry Stewart, 156 2/8 typical, Daviess County

George Schmutz, 177 4/8 non-typical, Pettis County

Bob Sutton, 151 0/8 typical, Morgan County

Fred Schrader, 151 2/8 typical, Gentry County

Brent Thorpe, 168 4/8 non-typical, Crawford County

Kent Nicholls, 152 1/8 typical, Harrison County

Lester Skouby, 174 0/8 non-typical, Dekalb County

John Buckner II, 153 7/8 typical, Carroll County

Don Copeland, 188 1/8 non-typical, Clay County

David Tillman, 141 7/8 typical, Jasper County

Dennis Schmidt, 194 2/8 typical, Mercer Co.

Rodney Carr, 183 2/8 non-typical, Shelby County

Dan Schmidt, 154 1/8 typical, Madison County

Brian Board, 159 7/8 typical, Bates County

James Ramsey, 151 6/8 typical, Jefferson County

David Jokerst, 141 4/8 typical, Ste. Genevieve Co.

Neal Breshears, 173 0/8 typical, Clay Coun

70

y DOUG G.PUITT

've been hunting whitetail for twelve years now, eight of them with an unsettling passion. I'm sure every hunter dreams taking a trophy and sometimes dreams do come true.

November 11, was opening day of the 1995 season. To say it was cold is putting it nicely. The snow covered ground ered the kind of conditions I love to take advantage of. That morning and early afternoon came and went with little ne moving. Action started at 3:15 p.m. when a 10 pointer made his way up a deep hollow to feed on top of an oak ridge. stayed at approximately 150 yards for the better part of 10 minutes. When he finally found enough acorns to stop his el and eat, he was broadside to me in the middle of a logging road. The first round clicked with no explosion. Soon r, I was able to send the next round aflight. By his reaction I knew it connected. I waited the standard time shaking, brating, and just hoping I would see him again. After the allotted time, the search was on. I knew where he was when

d shot him but, I found   no blood and no hair.
n doubt started to set in.   Darkness ended the
rch that night but, I knew   what the next day would
d in store for me.

nday morning came fast   and the search was on
in. I went back to the   place I had last seen him.
ok the one direction I   hadn't the night before.
fate would have it, 50   yards down the trail I
nd the first sign of blood.   After a short track, I
ted his body sticking out   from behind a big oak
. Once I was able to see   his head, I realized my
m had come true.

Doug Puitt, 164 2/8 typical, Ray County

BUCKS

by CAROLYN TAYLOR

re was a time
e Show-Me State
n the mighty buck
all you could take

k then, deer heritage
still in the molding
Conservation
slowly unfolding

Several deer seasons
The beast made us fail
  When hunters couldn't find
Those antlered whitetails

Measure this stag
  For Boone and Crockett
And if it's not even
  Please, don't dock it

"Next year", you say,
"I'll change my fate
  With a trophy buck
That will finally rate".

John Harris, 145 7/8, & 152 0/8 typicals, Laclede County

Ben Gibson, 154 4/8 typical, Chariton County

Carloss Kirkman, 151 1/8 typical, Texas County

Billy Schanks, 221 4/8 non-typical, Pike County

Donald Thompson, 152 0/8 typical, Lincoln County

Max Harden, 154 5/8 typical, bow, Nodaway County

THE NEW GROUND BUCK

by

FLOYD SIMMONS

The buck of my hunting life. Just riding around looking for deer one day. I saw a huge buck working a scrape line along the edge a small woods. Knowing that I could not hunt on that land, I thought I would never get a chance at this buck. After watching the ck from a distance with my binoculars, I could see that this was a nice eight or nine pointer.

This was in 1995 the day before gun season. I just knew someone was going to bag this buck before I could get a chance him. Finally the 1995 gun season was over. I was now hoping nobody would get him during the last part of the bow ason. I guess I sound a little selfish, but that buck was all "I could think about."

Bow season was all over, now if I could just see him again. About two weeks later I spotted him in the same area that ad before. Now knowing that he made it thought the hunting season, it gave me hope for the next deer season. Being a w and gun hunter, I would love to take this buck with my bow. But the land was posted no hunting, I contacted the land ner Mr. Herman Brands. I went to see Mr. Herman Brands about hunting on his land. After talking for awhile about er hunting with him, I asked him about hunting on his land. Mr. Brands told me that he had only forty to fifty acres of ods to hunt on. So, at this time he told me "no".

I thought there goes my chance for that big buck. Then out two weeks later Mr. Brands called and asked me to me and see him. At this time he gave me permission to nt his land.

At last I had a chance to pursue my big buck. The 1996 er season would not come fast enough for me. I was out king for deer signs just before bow season. Finding a v rubs and scrapes, I thought the buck was not in this a anymore. The rubs were small and not like any of the s he made the season before.

Later, during bow season, I started finding large rubs l more scrapes. I thought now I will get him, but all of first half of bow season not a single sighting of him. e day sitting around the cabin, that Mr. Brands has, we

Floyd Simmons, 153 3/8 typical New Madrid County

re talking about the big buck. About that time "Mr. Brands" showed me a shed from a large buck, that his nephew vid Brands had found. I just knew this was one of the sheds from the buck I had seen earlier the year before.

The 1996 gun season had arrived and I had only seen two bucks during the first part of bow season. I thought my nces of seeing him was very slim.

During the first week of gun season, Jimmy Swilly told me that he had spotted a large buck from his deerstand. Jimmy l "the huge buck was too far to get a clear shot at it, so I watched it walk out of site." With this news I had hope once in. Jimmy, Herman, and myself were about the only ones hunting this area. I thought one of us would get a chance to e this buck, I hunted every day during gun season. I had only one afternoon of hunting left, working until 3:00 p.m., I ught the big buck had made it through another deer season.

Just before leaving work I was talking to a friend, Larry Swilley, he asked me if I was going hunting this afternoon. told him "I didn't think so," Larry said, "you never know when that buck might show up." With that thought in mind when I left work, I went to my deer stand. With only two hours left in the 1996 season, I spotted three does coming fror the edge of the woods, then another doe came out, right behind her was THE BIG BUCK. I raised my thirty-thirty to m shoulder and fired a shot, missed! The doe turned and headed right at me with the buck still chasing her. I raised my gu again, this time looking through my iron sights, fired another shot, this time hitting him. He was still running toward m and I took another shot hitting him in the back. He dropped in his tracks!

I knew, I had my buck! Going crazy jumping up and down and yelling, "I got my big buck." Finally after calmin down a bit, I went and found Mr. Brands and thanked him for letting me hunt on his land. I call this buck "The Nev Grounds Buck" because the area where I killed this buck had just been cleared for farming. This buck was a huge eigh pointer, dressed out at two hundred pounds, and it scored 152 3/8 Boone and Crockett points. It is truly the trophy of m lifetime. I took my buck to Ken and Kay Bowman of 'Browman Taxidermy' to be mounted. What a way to end the 199 gun season.

Lloyd Schattauer, 143 5/8 typical, Cape Girardeau County, Glenn Brown

Norm Shaul, 170 4/8 non-typical, Atchison County

Bruce Jones, 185 0/8 non-typical, St Francois County

Melvin Reynolds, 150 3/8 typical, Clinton County

'MY SON'S FIRST BIG BUCK'

by

DON FEIGHERT
(Proud Dad)

was unable to take my 13-year-old son, Luke, to take his hunter safety course. He went with a friend of the family one ek before the opening day of deer season (1996).

)uring the week before deer season, I gave my son an old 30-30 I had bought years before. We were practicing shooting feed sack about 40 yards away. I told him to hit the middle of the feed sack, and he did. Then I told him to hit the D on feed sack, and he did that, too. Then I told him to hit the D again, which he also did. So I told him that was close enough ill a deer.

)n opening day, Luke and I went down by the creek and set up where I thought the wind would be blowing the deer's nt away from us. Luke had a hard time sitting still. After sitting for two or three hours, we went back to the house where found out a nephew of mine had killed a 4 pt. buck on the back side of our place. That afternoon, Luke and I went back to the same place we had gone that morning. I told Luke to take a book to read so he wouldn't move around so much. ld him to read a paragraph or two and then look around to see if he could see any deer. That seemed to help, but still no r. It started to rain and was about dark, so we went back to the house.

he next morning I could hear the wind blowing real hard. I went to wake Luke up and told him the wind was blowing hard, and it was going to be very cold outside. I asked him if he wanted to go and told him I was going anyway. He got ight away.

Ve went to the back side where my nephew had shot the 4 pt. k the day before. We went to the side of the pond where the d was blowing in our faces. We sat there for about 30 utes when a deer came from the north. Luke had his gun ed against a tree. When I saw it, I tried to get Luke's ntion so he could see it too, but it heard me. It had a pretty rack and when it turned away to take off, I shot it behind front leg. We sat there for about five minutes longer to let deer lay down. Then we heard some tree limbs breaking nd us.

uke was standing about 3 feet from me when he saw a deer. whispered, "Dad, there's a deer." I whispered, "Is it a buck?" he said "yeah." Then Luke said, "Can I shoot it?" and I led yes. I had told him to try and shoot in the middle of ody behind the front leg. Luke lifted up his gun and shot. r he shot, I saw antlers and a white tail running away. I d him, "Did you hit him?" Luke answered, "I think so." So vaited a few more minutes and went looking for the deer. ut that time, someone else shot from not very far away. We ed across the fence to see if there was blood from Luke's . We went about ten feet, and I saw the first buck that I had looking at us. I pulled and shot the deer in the neck. When

Luke Feighert, 154 6/8 typical, Clinton County

we got there, both deer were laying on the ground. One had a hole in his neck and four feet from it was the 11 pt. buck that Luke had shot in the side. When we got there, a doe was standing close by and wouldn't leave. We had to scare her off because someone else was hunting pretty close.

After we loaded the deer in the truck, I shook his hand and said, "Congratulations on your first deer!" I knew that the deer he shot was big, and I was very surprised it stood there long enough for Luke to shoot it, especially since the wind was blowing our scent the way of the deer. On our way back to the house, with a big smile on his face, Luke said, "Dad, my deer's bigger than yours!" But I told him, "It's not that you're such a good hunter, it's that I'm such a good guide."

When we got back to the house, Luke went to get his mom to show off his deer. Of course, she had to take pictures. We went to check it in, and everyone told him he had shot a nice deer. I thought since it was Luke's first deer, and it was so big, I would get it mounted for him. We took it to Jim Martin, a taxidermist near Cameron. When Mr. Martin saw the deer, he asked if we wanted him to score it. I asked him if he thought it was big enough. He told us he thought it might make Missouri's Big Bucks, so I told him to go ahead and score it. Six months later, we got the head mount back and found that is was big enough to make Missouri Big Bucks.

It gave me more pleasure to see my son kill his big buck than all the deer I've ever killed.

Dale Lawson, 150 7/8 typical, Sullivan County

Brent Buch, 152 4/8 typical, Bates County

Dale Brooks, 152 1/8, Madison County

Eldore Schwinke, 144 6/8 typical, Gasconade County

THE BACK DOOR BUCK

by MICHAEL ALBRIGHT

I took this buck behind my house in the Callao area. I started the morning hunt out of my stand. At about 9:30 a.m. I came restless, and began to walk to another location about 250 yards from the back door of my house. While crossing a fence, a buck and doe came running down the hill in front of me. When they were about 30 yards away from me, they pped and looked directly at me. I stood there with one leg on one side of the fence and the other leg on the other side of fence. Frozen!

Being awestruck by the size of this buck's rack, I remembered, I had a gun in my hand for a purpose. As I pulled up to ot, I realized my scope was cranked all the way up, I could only see a blur. I brought the gun down, adjusted the scope, n brought it back up, aimed, and fired. The buck and doe took off. At first I thought I had missed. I went and looked in area he was standing and I found a small amount of blood and began tracking. After tracking the buck about 200 yards, blood stopped. I couldn't find any sign of where he had gone.

I stopped to shed some of my cloths, and after reaching down to pick up my gun, I caught a glimpse of brown and ite off to my side. I looked up, and there he laid!

The buck had ran straight towards the house and had dropped about 50 yards from the back door! Unfortunately, it was he bottom of the steepest hill on the place. After dragging him for about 20 yards, I decided, I needed help. I recruited dad and a 4x4. We dragged it up the hill, I think I drove my dad nuts, making sure he did not harm the rack.

My buck weighed about 220 pounds, after being field dressed. It was the toughest deer I think I have ever eaten, but king back, I think it was the best tasting! I still can't understand why this buck and doe stood there as long as they did? ybe, we were all dumbfounded. Me, because of the size of the buck's rack, and the deer, looking at some idiot half-way oss a barbed-wire fence, drooling all over himself.

I think it was the strangest case of buck fever I'd ever had. I wasn't nervous until after I had shot. I guess I was just to nb struck to be nervous.

I shot this buck in 1984 and a year later my brother took it to Columbia and Nat Hussman measured it. When my ther walked in with the rack, Nat told him it wouldn't make it, but he would measure it anyway. After Nat measured it, tarted smiling and said "I think it made it." Nat measured it again and came up with the same score, 153 3/8 Boone and ckett points.

Courtney -1986 bow taken trophy -
ark County - scoring 146 5/8 typical

Scott Luthy, 225 5/8 non-typical, Laclede Co.

Christina Milburn, 185 3/8 non-typical, Putnam Co.

Richard Deuser, 160 6/8 typical, Phelps County

Gary Vails, 166 1/8 typical, St. Charles County

Kyle Rollins, 191 1/8 non-typical, Maries County

Walter Gregory, 157 0/8 typical, Linn County

Allen Courtney, 206 0/8 non-typical, Clark County

Allen Courtney, 178 0/8 typical, Clark County

Lonnie Courtney, 183 2/8 non-typical, Sullivan C

DEER HUNTING-MISSOURI STYLE

(Hopes, Frustrations, and Rewards)

by

E. E. GANN

After hunting the first 5 days of Missouri's 9-day, 1972 deer season without seeing a single deer, I had about decided that there must be something about successful deer hunting that I had not yet discovered.

Thursday's hunt started out as usual with me crawling out of bed at 4:45 a.m. for a quick breakfast before heading for the woods. I had decided to hunt an unfamiliar area east of Rolla which, according to my topographic map, contained several "points" or small ridges that looked promising. My previous nine years of hunting "white tails" had taught me that deer like such areas primarily because of the panoramic view and ready escape routes in case of danger.

I had killed deer before, but my best buck had been a 120-pounder with 6-inch spikes whose "rack" was proudly displayed in my family room. It was beginning to look like those 6-inch spikes would be my biggest trophy.

I parked my pickup in the woods at 5:30 a.m. and started the half-mile walk in the dark to my selected hunting stand. Unfortunately, the map did not indicate the density of small scrub brush and after stumbling through the dark for about 30 minutes, I arrived at the desired site only to find another hunter on "my" stand.

To an eager deer hunter there is nothing more frustrating than to have a well-planned hunt foiled by finding another hunter on his stand at the crack of dawn. I have often wondered if some of these guys don't actually spend the night in the woods just to be first on a choice stand. Anyway I started off in another direction to look for another site.

After walking most of the morning in the thick brush looking for a good stand and probably flushing every deer within a half mile, I finally walked down a long ridge in the opposite direction from my original stand to a point that had been planted in small pines about 5 years earlier. I immediately began to notice numerous deer tracks, skinned pines, and pawed areas indicating that this was a favorite hangout for an amorous buck. I hunted the area for about 45 minutes to no avail and remembering the Thanksgiving turkey in the oven at home, I headed for home.

During our Thanksgiving meal, I remarked to my wife that if I hunted the area that I had just found that morning long enough, I would eventually get a deer.

By 2:30 p.m., I was on the way back to the woods with visions of all those pines being skinned. I arrived at the point about 3:00 p.m. and selected a tall stump for my stand which afforded an excellent view over the top of the pines and from which I could also see the brushy ridge leading down to the point. I stood on that stump for an hour and a half, hardly moving a muscle, without so much as a glimpse of a deer.

Finally, about 4:30, tired of standing, I moved to another stump at the edge of the pine thicket and sat down facing the ridge to wait for dark and another disappointing trip home. About 5 o'clock my heart suddenly began to pound when I heard the unmistakable sounds of a deer trotting through the woods directly toward me, no doubt intending to spend the night in the pine thicket at my back. I raised my rifle in the direction of the sound and waited, still sitting on the stump. Suddenly, a large rack came into view and after about five steps, the buck stopped about 30 yards away and looked directly at me. With the telescope of my British 303 on his shoulder, I waited no longer. At the crack of the gun, the buck leaped into action. At full speed in the thick brush and waning light, he ran a 50-yard semicircle around me, heading for the pi[ne] thicket. I squeezed off two more shots, thinking that somehow my first shot had missed.

About 20 feet short of the pine thicket, the buck stopped but I was unable to locate him in my scope for another sh[ot.] Suddenly I heard him running again into the pine thicket. I moved cautiously in that direction, not wishing to encount[er] a wounded buck in the thick pines and poor light, with a growing sickening feeling that he had gotten away.

My heart fluttered when I heard a cough about 50 feet away as this was the first evidence that the deer had been hit. [I] moved on more cautiously and heard another cough and then silence. Working my way slowly into the dark pine[s,] expecting to be charged at any second, I suddenly saw the buck on the ground not 10 feet away drawing his final breat[h.] My heart really began to pound then, especially, when I counted the ten points on his huge rack.

After field dressing the buck in the dark, I tied a short rope to his rack and drug him headfirst around the pines and [off] the point to my parked pickup truck.

The buck weighed 163 pounds, field dressed. Unofficial Boone and Crockett measurements of the near-perfe[ct] typical rack indicated at least 150 typical points, sufficient for Missouri's Big Bucks Club.

Before skinning the deer, a lump was noticed under the skin of his right hip. When the skin was removed a spent bul[let] fell to the floor. Examination indicated that only the first of my three shots had scored. The bullet entered the left rib ca[ge] just behind the shoulder, traveled through the deer at an angle, and lodged just beneath the skin of the right hip, causi[ng] the previously noticed lump.

The buck's head was taken to a local taxidermist for mounting and the rack will be measured by an official Boone a[nd] Crockett scorer. Of course the mounted head will replace the 6-inch spike in my family room as a constant reminder [of] my once-in-a-lifetime experience. My buck officially scored 152 5/8 typical Boone and Crockett points, taken in Phe[lps] County, 1972.

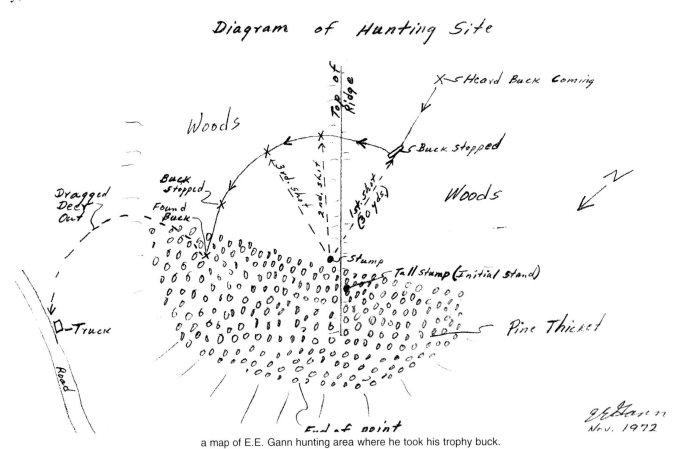

a map of E.E. Gann hunting area where he took his trophy buck.

Chuck Adkins, 170 1/8 typical, Pulaski County, 1986

Mike Cook, 156 1/8 typical, Cooper County

James Harlan, 160 1/8 non-typical, Howell County

Carl Gilfoy, 184 4/8 non-typical, Jackson County

Robert Reed, 140 6/8 typical, Cape Girardeau County, Bow

Patrick Blair, 167 7/8 non-typical, Johnson County

Larry Wooten, 145 4/8 typical, Atchison County

by GEORGE H. KOPPELMANN, JR.

Hunting in good old Missouri has been a pleasure to me since I was old enough to shoot a gun. I was 7 years old when [h]ad my first real gun. It was a single shot BB gun. I'll always remember it because I carry a copper BB in my jaw. My [c]usin accidentally pulled the trigger and there it went, right into my jaw. My nest gun was a single shot .22 that I received [fr]om my parents when I was 8 years old (Old Santa Clause brought it). With the .22 I was able to shoot squirrels. In those [da]ys we didn't see any wild turkeys or deer.

The first deer I remember seeing was in the early 40's, when I [ro]de one of our horses and lead one to the back end of our farm. I [w]as going to plow corn with a 5 shovel. When I got to the edge of a [sm]all corn field my horse, that I was riding, reared up and we were [al]l scared. There in this corn field was a huge buck, with a wide [sp]read rack, and his partner, a doe. They took off pretty fast.

George Koppelmann, 152 0/8 typical, Franklin County

I hunted deer, off and on, with borrowed guns, but in 1961 I bought [m]y first high powered rifle. It was a "Jap 7.7." I bagged my first [de]er that year. It was a beautiful 7 pointer. In 1963 I got my 12 point [tr]ophy buck that made the Missouri Show-Me Big Bucks Club, with [a]score of 152 0/8 typical points. I bagged it 5 miles north of Gerald, [in]Franklin County. I was one happy young man.

Since that time I have taken a 9 point, 3- 8 points and several [ot]hers that were does or small bucks. I think the Department of Con-[se]rvation has done a wonderful job in bring back our wild game that [w]as extinct in this area.

I turkey hunt and have gotten one or two in the fall, except for one [ye]ar. I have also bagged several in the spring. The largest gobbler I [ha]ve gotten had a double beard, one being 10 inches long and the [ot]her 7 inches long. It weighed in at about 28 pounds. I used a single [ba]rrel Winchester model 37 shotgun, with 4x6 shells to bag the tur-[ke]ys. I use the Jap 7.7 and a Teddy Roosevelt 30-30 lever action for [de]er. I had a 308 automatic with a flip-over scope, that I used some, [bu]t I recently sold it.

I consider all of us that hunt here in Missouri are really fortunate [to]have the diversity of game right here close. The unusual sights [yo]u see when you are out in the woods sure can vary. Such as what [I s]aw last fall during turkey season, a mature red fox chasing a small [bo]bcat across my wheat field. About 4 years ago I saw a black pan-[the]r, it came into the edge of my wheat field, it sat there quite a [wh]ile, then pounced on something, then ate it.

George shot this buck in 1963

I'm sure looking forward to November and deer season. Wow! A [ni]ce 8 point buck and doe just came into my wheat field!

Russell Wehmeyer, 150 6/8 typical, Gasconade Co.   Janie Wehmeyer, 148 0/8 typical, Gasconade Co.   Russell Wehmeyer, 140 4/8 typical, Gasconade C

Clayton Knepp, 140 0/8 typical, St. Clair County

Wayne Caldwell, 166 4/8 typical, Oregon County

Orlando Smith, 178 4/8 non-typical, St. Louis County

Steven Crain, 145 3/8 typical, Barry County

Jesse Perry, 190 3/8 typical, Pettis County

Donald Bell, 150 7/8 typical, Marion County

Robert Traub, 150 4/8 typical, Gasconade County

Rick Bray, 147 7/8 typical, St. Clair County

Anthony Bax, 151 5/8 typical, Miller County

Rogelio Bautista, M.D., 204 4/8 non-typical, Monroe County

85

Steve Angle, 154 1/8 typical, Gentry County

David Arnold, 151 4/8 typical, Scotland County

David Marti, 143 0/8 typical, Dent County

Danny Clifton, 159 6/8 typical, Bates County

Dwayne Corbett, 155 6/8 typical, Johnson County

Mike Cooley, 182 4/8 non-typical, Grundy Co

Chris Glaser, 171 5/8 typical, Crawford County

John Finley, 150 6/8 typical, Howard County

Curtis Fellhoelter, 141 6/8 typical, Henry Coun

1997 Iowa Habitat Stamp

WILDLIFE FRIEND OR FOE

by

DALE H. REAM, JR.

Managing private land for wildlife and profit. Is it possible? There are some entrepreneurs that think it is. Today in agriculture, making a "BUCK" is difficult. Are landowners tapping all of their available resources? The alternative to traditional agriculture could be, managing land for wildlife and profit.

What would it take to manage your land for wildlife. In the state of Missouri it would vary somewhat from the north to the southern part of the state. Regardless of location wildlife needs are basic for their survival. Habitat with, cover, food, water, protection, and management. Let's take a look at these ingredients.

Habitat, wildlife needs *cover*. It is not hard to create; leave brushy, grassy corners in your fields. Put a permanent or temporary fence around them to keep livestock out. You could fence off parts of standing timbers so livestock could not run in it. The thing is, if you want wildlife, wildlife needs areas of cover that is disturbed by livestock, cropping or man.

Good wildlife habitat needs alternative *food* sources close by. This could be done by planting food plots, leaving small parts of existing grain in the fields. Wildlife is very diverse in its eating habits and its needs. With a little help from us, survival for wildlife in harsh times of the year can be made a whole lot easier leaving portions of grain fields un-harvested or by planting food plots.

Water, doesn't sound like much of a problem for me, I just go into the kitchen and turn on the faucet. It doesn't matter if it is a 100 degrees above or 20 degrees below. But for wildlife this can be a problem. Availability of good clean water year round can be a problem for them. A pond with an all season water tank can be a determining factor; places like this is where wildlife spend a lot of their time. Some wildlife will travel great distances for food and water. If you're are a hunter, where do you want the game to be?

Protection, would you want a "thief" to break into your home and steal your guns, TV, your favorite lounge chair, etc. The poaching of wildlife is stealing from you and me. Let us say you have created a good wildlife habitat area, you have built a water structure, planted food plots. Now you need to let your neighbors know they can help with watchful eyes and ears. Have you ever been turkey hunting and tried to sneak a flock of wild turkeys? As hunters we need to become a flock of watchful eyes and ears. Hunting is a great sport it is quality time spent with family and friends. When we have permission to hunt a piece of property. We treat it with the respect as if it was ours. We also should have the same respect for property in which we do not have permission to hunt. Summed up in a nut shell, if you observe something going on, that shouldn't be, report it to the proper authorities. The balance between having plentiful amounts of wildlife or having none is a very fine line. POACHING IS EVERYONE'S PROBLEM!

Wildlife *management* is needed to have quality hunting. The Missouri Department of Conservation has done an outstanding job, and so has some of Missouri's private land owners. As trophy hunters of the Whitetail Buck Deer, we must also be a part of wildlife management, by taking our share of doe deer. Notice said Doe not fawn, when you shoot a fawn deer there is a 50-50 chance that you are shooting a button buck. If you want to shoot big bucks, big enough to make the Missouri Show-Me Big Bucks Club, then you have to let the button bucks, 1 1/2 year old bucks, and 2 1/2 year old bucks pass by. For a Whitetail Buck to make the minimum Big Bucks Club entry at 140 typical or 155 non-typical, this buck will have to be at least 3 1/2 years of age or older. If you are looking for meat, most adult does will out dress most 1 1/2 or 2 1/2 year old bucks. The oldest Doe recorded in Missouri is a road kill doe that was age by "Matson's Laboratory, LLC, in Montana" at 17 1/2 years of age.

With a 1000 acres of ground properly managed for wildlife. You could generate from $3000.00 to $25,000.00 dollars from hunting, possibly more. I'm not totally advocating this practice, I'm just stating fac In today's agriculture this could have a very positive effect on cash flows for private landowners.

What would happen if a very large percent of our private landowners would manage their land for wild-life and who would benefit from it? If thousands of acres of quality wildlife habitat were created state wide I would say wildlife. With thousands of acres of quality habitat, it spells good hunting, I would say hunters. If private landowners are seeing a profit from their land that was not there before, created by managing their land for wildlife, I would say private landowners. And if thousands of acres of good wildlife habitat created more hunters, I would say the Missouri Department of Conservation and thousands of businesse: Sounds as if it might be beneficial to all. The key trend of thought here is, owning land is not cheap. It takes lots of money to be a private landowner, taxes alone are astronomical. Wildlife management along with normal farming practices could be profitable for us all: private landowners, hunters, conservation department, businesses, and most importantly WILDLIFE.

Note: some private landowners and the Missouri Department of Conservation are and have been man-aging land for wildlife. But when I hear private landowners complaining about wildlife and hunters, I won-der "what if" they would take a look at managing land for wildlife and profit. This could be a way of turning a problem into "prosperity." You can lead a horse to water, but you can't make him drink. Taking that first sip could be very beneficial to all.

I mention these things because we are losing thousands of acres every year of natural wildlife habitat, for all kinds of reasons. A lot of it evolves from the economics of urban and rural America. Looking at alternative methods of farming, like managing private land for wildlife has a lot of potential.

This young trophy hunter learns at a young age the need to shoot does. Clint Ream with some mighty good table fare.

This young 1 1/2 year old whitetail buck needs a couple more years.

Autumn Encounter - Whitetail

TAXIDERMY READINESS

by

CARL SCHWARZ

There's nothing like a well mounted head to preserve the wealth of memories surrounding a successful White-tailed er hunt. There's nothing like a spoiled trophy to completely ruin the memories of the deer and the hunt! Delivering the r to your taxidermist in good condition should be as high a priority item on your checklist as sighting-in your rifle. re are some things for you to consider, taken from a taxidermist's point of view.

Be an optimist! There's nothing sadder than a hunter who's just taken a trophy-sized buck who then looks around and s, "what do I do now?" You've got to proceed, right from the beginning, with the thought that not only will you get a r, but that you'll get a trophy deer. Just as scouting is so important to hunting, scouting your taxidermist and meat cessor is equally important. The decision on which taxidermist and meat processor you will use should be made ore you go hunting, not after the deer is on the ground.

"SCOUTING"

Scouting for a taxidermist involves personally visiting the shops in your area, viewing the quality of the work, re-ching the costs involved, and possibly talking to someone who has had experience with the taxidermist (a reference). of your conversation with the taxidermist should be to ask "what should I do after I bag my deer?" Obviously, no ter what advice I may give you in this article or what you have heard from friends, the information you get from your icular taxidermist is the most important. Knowing in advance just what to do can take a tremendous load off your d and can assure that you will have a trophy to admire for the rest of your life.

couting your meat processor is just as important. Not only will the processor be handling the deer's meat, but he/she also be handling the head and skin. Again, actually talking to the processor is important. Find out what the business's rs are during deer season, what are the exact location or locations of the business, what are the options for processing meat, what are the prices, and what are the payment and pickup terms. Also you should find out whether the processor ws how to skin out a deer so that it will be suitable for a mount (discussed later) and whether he/she will keep it erly (frozen) until you can pick it up. Again, a reference from someone who has actually dealt with the processor is important.

Remember, that advance preparation for what to do after the hunt is just as important as scouting before the hunt. ember the Boy Scout motto, "Be Prepared."

"FIELD DRESSING"

ollowing are the basic steps for field dressing. Just like any other skill, field dressing is best learned by watching eone else. My father always said that "if a picture is worth a thousand words, then a demonstration is worth a

thousand pictures!" Seeing it actually done will teach you more than all the literature you can read and all the videos y
can watch.

A brief word about knives. The most dangerous knives are the dull ones. Sharp knives do what you want them to
and don't slip or catch. Have a good sharp knife with you and some means of honing the edge if it gets dull during t
field dressing or skinning process. If you watch someone who skins animals for a living (a taxidermist or meat proce
sor), you're very unlikely to see one of those over-sized survival knives. Professionals use relatively small bladed kniv
that are sharp and that can be easily re-sharpened.

Field dressing:
1. Be sure the deer is dead! The first cut of your knife might bring a stunned deer back to life. Immediately
   follow the current conservation department instructions and tag your deer.
2. Bleeding is not necessary. Prompt field dressing will do more good. Cutting the throat of a deer whose
   heart has stopped beating does not improve the quality of the meat and will ruin it as a trophy.
3. Make a deep close circle-cut around the anus.
4. Slit the belly skin from the anus to the brisket. Do not go any higher than the front legs. Make no cuts on
   the front of the neck!
5. Pull out the gut a little from around the rear vent and tie off with string at this point.
6. Remove sex organs.
7. Pull the rest of the intestines out of the body.
8. Cut the cartilage between the fore ribs over the chest cavity and reach up to cut the wind pipe loose.
9. Pull out remaining organs.
10. Drain blood out of the body cavity and wipe dry with clean rage or dry grass.
11. Prop open the body cavity with sticks and hang up to cool unless you plan to tote your deer out of the
    woods at once. Use loosely woven cloth as a cover to keep flies out while the meat is cooling.
12. If possible, get help to get the deer out of the woods. Do not tie a rope around the deer's neck to drag it.
    Many a head has been ruined by the rope. If you must drag the deer, pull it by the antlers to keep the head
    off the ground. This may still damage the skin, so getting help and keeping the deer from dragging is the
    best method. It goes without saying that you should never carry a deer on your shoulders!

Check your deer! Part of your pre-hunt scouting should also include locating the nearest deer check station. Know
rules about where and when you can check your deer. Do not give a biologist permission to cut the mouth (for determ
ing age) on any deer that you intend to mount.

"SKINNING"

Many hunters prefer to skin the deer themselves. Whether you skin it or the meat processor skins it, you should k
the correct method. When you scout your meat processor you should determine if he/she knows this method. No m
who does the work, it should be done AS SOON AS POSSIBLE! I'm going to say this now and I'll probably say it a
"Aging may be fine for the deer's meat, but it is not good for the skin!"

1. Either cut off the legs just below the knee joint (with a hack saw) or make a circular cut in the knee joint. I
   not try to cut out the scent glands on the rear legs or run your knife through them. The glands are r
   connected in any way to the meat, and removing them (by cutting away the legs) or ignoring them is the b
   policy. Trying to cut them out just taints the knife.
2. Slit the legs down to the belly. Take extra care to keep your knife toward the back edge of the front legs a
   go down from the armpits to the belly cut. Do not cut forward from the armpits to the belly cut.
3. Hang the deer by the rear legs. You can pass a rope or stick between the bone and tendon. You might want
   include a block and tackle in your equipment.
4. Starting at the rear, remove the skin from the legs. Use your knife or saw to disconnect the tail. After the le

have been skinned, much of the main portion of the skin can be removed by pulling down, and the knife will be needed only in the tight spots and for the front legs.

5. When you reach the brisket area, the skin should be peeled down the neck like pulling a sock off inside out. You'll need your knife in this area. Make no cuts anywhere in the neck. Skin all the way down to the base of the skull or as near to the head as possible.

6. Cut or saw the neck as close to the skull as possible.

7. You will now have the head and antlers with the entire skin attached to them. This needs to be kept cold in a cooler or refrigerator and taken to your taxidermist as soon as possible or the head, antlers and skin should be put into a trash bag and frozen. If your deer is skinned by a meat processor, make sure he/she freezes the head and skin. Remember, aging in the cooler may be good for the meat, but it is not good for the skin.

"MISC"

If you are only interested in the skin, separate it from the head, seal it in a plastic bag and freeze it as soon as possible.

If you are interested in a deer foot mount, seal them in a plastic bag and freeze them as soon as possible.

If you are interested in an antler mount it's best to let your taxidermist saw the antlers from the head. If you want to do yourself, cut along a line that goes through the eye socket and ear butt. Do not make a "V" cut or "butcher" cut. Your taxidermist will need a flat surface on the bottom of the antlers.

Removing the head skin or "cape" from the skull is a job that is best left to your taxidermist. However, many hunters want to know this process in case they are hunting out west or in Canada and find themselves in a position where there is no freezer facilities readily available. The Best person to teach you this process is your taxidermist. Most taxidermists will allow you to watch the caping of your deer or someone else's. Caping is not difficult to learn, but it is difficult to explain. Remember that "...a demonstration is worth a thousand pictures." After watching your taxidermist, you can practice on any small bucks or does that you don't intend to mount. Then when you go out west, you'll be ready.

"SUMMATION"

Remember, use common sense and be prepared. No question asked prior to the hunt is a dumb one. Try to gain as much information as you can before hunting, so that your trophy will keep the memory of the hunt alive and clear. Good luck!

Carl Schwarz is the president of :

> Schwarz Studio, Inc
> 1809 Lafayette Avenue
> St. Louis, MO 63104-2507

Schwarz Studio is the oldest commercial taxidermy studio in the United States. Carl is continuing the 115 year tradition the craftsmanship passed down by his:

Great-grandfather	-- Frank Schwarz
Grandfather	-- Paul Schwarz
Great-uncle	-- Max Schwarz
Father	-- Paul C. Schwarz

Editor note: I'm grateful to Carl for doing this article. His father, Paul, passed away this spring. Paul was an Official Measurer and supporter of the Missouri Show-Me Big Bucks Club for many years. He was an Official Measurer for the Boone and Crockett Club (prior to 1962-1997). His contributions to the hunting world will be remembered.

Broken Solitude - Whitetail

PHOTOGRAPHING the ELUSIVE WHITETAIL

by

GLENN D. CHAMBERS

The modern 35mm single-lens reflex camera with its wide range of accessories, new film emulsions/processing meth-, and the ability of people to reach wild animals in difficult locations have made all kinds of wildlife photography a iliar outdoor activity. Good wildlife photography has a very prominent place in today's emphasis on outdoor recre- on.

A recent survey conducted by the U.S. Fish and Wildlife Service reported that in 1996, there were about 16 million sons, 16 years or older, who photographed wildlife. They spent about $1.9 billion on cameras, special lenses, and other tographic equipment, and another $1.1 billion on film and processing. Needless to say, people enjoy photographing llife.

Photographing wildlife is demanding - but it has its' special rewards. It can be an educational experience as well as ing one gain an appreciation for the out-of-doors. But ultimately there is the freedom of expression in a blend of logical savvy and artistic skills. Photographs record the memory of a once-in-a-lifetime experience and become price-, endearing, treasures available for sharing in a tangible fashion.

Wildlife photography is a vital ingredient in today's public information and education programs. A conservation edu- on theme can often be "sold" by one sharp, well composed, eye-catching photograph. The scientific community com- ly uses the photographic "record" to document wildlife habitat as well as behaviors and numbers. Wildlife law en- ement personnel have found photography to be a great asset in difficult enforcement situations, especially as photo- hic evidence.

EQUIPMENT

Photographers today are not limited by the amount and kinds of photography equipment available but rather by the ense of that equipment. Camera bodies and lenses are primary expense items. Usually it is in the purchase of these ponents that people tend to "cut costs". But, in doing that, they very often sacrifice quality in favor of saving a dollar. 't do it!! Regardless of photographic expertise, inferior equipment results in inferior pictures.

erious wildlife photographers set goals and objectives concerning their desires. It makes a difference if one wants to tograph for a hobby versus profit, black and white versus color, or scientific versus popular publications. Once a sion is made, one can then evaluate how elaborate his/her photographic system needs to be.

ost is a major consideration, but I would advise you to stay in the top competitive lines for all photographic equip- t. Choosing among them is usually dictated by personal preference and budget! A good way to evaluate the quality of t cameras and lenses used by photographers today is to examine the cover photos on the leading conservation, envi- nental, and wildlife-orientated magazines. Then look inside the publication, usually on the title pages, and often it will the photographer's name, kind of equipment and film used to create the picture. Check out several sources and then can get an idea of the kind of equipment used by photographers whose work is publication quality.

CAMERA BODIES AND LENSES

The most basic piece of equipment is the camera body. They came in all sizes, shapes, orders of sophistication, price ranges. For whitetail photography, a 35mm single-lens reflex camera is the most popular. A wide variety of len and auxiliary equipment can be adapted to most 35mm cameras. I prefer to stay within the same manufacturer's syste For example, Nikon lenses with Nikon camera, etc. The top competitive brands of cameras are reliable and can prod quality photographs.

I am old-fashioned and like cameras that give the photographer the option of "manual" operation. Even most of top-of-the-line fully automatic cameras offer that option. But, if I am faced with a fully automatic camera versus a mar operation one - I'll go MANUAL. That's just my personal preference.

The fully automatic cameras now available (and I own two brands of them) are a boon in the hands of professio wildlife photographers. The "auto" systems are of great advantage when they are working, but all too often the user le of a malfunction after a once-in-a-lifetime photo opportunity is GONE!! So, the more conventional, manual models be more appropriate for the "casual" photographer and especially for beginners. Although point-and-shoot cameras popular, they are limited by the focal length of their lenses, and most serious photographers will want some telepl lenses in his/her gadget bag.

Good lenses are just as important as the camera body. As stated earlier, I always stay within the same "make" for car bodies and lenses. This is especially true if you are considering tele-extenders or "doublers" as they are often called.

The question of focal length depends on the objectives of the photographer. There are lots of good fixed focal-ler lenses and zoom lenses out there - go for quality! Let's talk fixed focal-length lenses versus zoomers. For years, the f focal-length lens was considered to be superior in quality, and was the case in the top-of-the-line lenses. But with advent of computer designing, the optical quality of zoom lenses dramatically improved.

Fixed focal-length lenses tend to be more compact, heavier, sharper at larger apertures, and very rugged. Those ar very important considerations for wildlife photographers. On the contrary, zoom lenses have a very important dimen of versatility - one lens can do the job of two or more fixed focal-length lenses. Other than reducing the number of f focal-length lenses in the gadget bag, perhaps the greatest advantage of the zoom lens, is its' ability to crop accurately quickly on the spot. This is very important for photographing a sequence when changing a lens could mean loss of a g photo opportunity.

Zoom lenses are even heavier than most fixed focal-length lenses; they are bulkier, more expensive, tend to be temperamental, and generally, produce poorer quality at larger apertures (especially true of economy-priced zoom len

A good selection of fixed focal-length lenses for photographing whitetail deer should include: (1) a wide-angle l 35mm (costing from $200 - $1,000), (2) a 50mm or "normal" lens ($75 - $500), (3) a 90 or 100mm lens ($200 - $1,1 (4) a 135mm ($100 - $12,00), (5) a 180 or 200mm ($200 - $1,700), (6) a 250 or 300mm ($450 - $2,500), (7) a 40C ($750 - $3,000), and (8) a 500 or 600mm lens. This array of lenses will give most whitetail photographers an opportu to get a good picture in about any situation.

Zoom lenses also come in several combinations. The most popular zoom lenses, according to price are: 80 - 20C ($300 - $3,000) or 70 - 210mm ($325 - $2,300). The 50 - 300mm (about $2,500) is probably the most ideal for photography. Longer zoom lenses often have smaller maximum apertures - definitely a serious disadvantage for ph graphing deer in limited, low-light conditions. Beyond the 300mm zoom range, I would carry long, fixed focal-le lenses to do the job.

Tele-extenders or "doublers" make long telephoto lenses out of shorter lenses. Their biggest drawback is that drastically reduce light intake. Depending on magnification, they can require twice as much light as is normally required e lens to which it is adapted without an extender. And remember, light in heavily wooded deer habitat is already at a emium.

FILM

As with cameras and lenses, the modern advances in film emulsion speeds has been dramatic and a wonderful boon to r photographers. Color film is the most popular with photographers for obvious reasons. But black-and-white prints popular with some publishers of books, journals, tabloids, and newspapers. Experienced professional wildlife photog- hers often carry two camera bodies (compatible with all the lenses) one loaded with black-and-white film and the other ded with color film.

Kodak is an "old line" of proven films. Kodachrome and Ektachrome are great basic color films. But they each have ir own strengths and weaknesses.

Kodachrome is extremely fine-grained and gives great natural color rendition for outdoors use - even with full flash. cessing Kodachrome film is best done by the professionals at processing laboratories across the country (see your rest photo center). Kodachrome, like all other film, "ages" if not kept in refrigeration. I usually keep it frozen until to day occurs. Be sure to take frozen film out of the freezer at least one hour prior to loading into your camera.

always buy true "professional" grade film, which means that it has been "aged" at the laboratory and is shipped to the ler under climate-controlled conditions where it is stored in refrigeration until the purchaser puts it to use. I sometimes large batches of professional film, all with the same emulsion number and freeze it for future use. I usually get sistent exposure results that way. My favorite Kodak film is Kodachrome 64 (ASA 64).

ktachrome film offers the widest ASA range of commercial Kodak film. Film speeds range from ASA 64 to ASA 400. not use much Ektachrome film as it is not the most "stable" film available on the market - it tends to discolor over a g period of time.

ecently, Fuji has come up with some good color transparency film. I use quite a lot of Fujichrome - both Velvia (ASA and Provia (ASA 100). I seldom use any kind of film rated over ASA 100, it's just too grainy. Fuji film can be cessed at most local film processing plants using conventional E6 processing methods.

What about "fast-emulsion" professional films? There are several available. Fuji provides Provia 400 (ASA) and via 1600 (ASA). Kodak has both Kodachrome and Ektachrome in "fast" films; i.e. Kodachrome 200 (ASA) and achrome 200 (ASA), Ektachrome 400 (ASA), and Ektachrome 1600 (ASA). These film emulsions are designed for use w-light conditions or extremely fast shutter-speed situations. But remember, the faster the film, the more "grainy" the lts will be.

rints versus transparency. It's a dilemma most photographers face sometime during their photographic journey. A lot hotographers will shoot transparencies rather than shoot with color negative film. Then they have the best of both lds. They can make prints from the transparency and still have the transparency to project. Most publishers want to lish from transparencies and will not work from a color negative or print - so if you are thinking about merchandising r work - think TRANSPARENCY.

PHOTO BLINDS

Another very important component of the whitetailed deer photographer's equipment is the photography blind. They be permanent or portable - I've used both kinds very successfully. The ploy is to place the blind or "hide" in the nity that deer frequent and hide inside and wait for deer to come nearby. It will require countless hours of patience and ting in order to get good pictures. However, the painstaking wait is worth it when that prize photo is taken or while erving some interesting deer behavior. And not every day will be a prize-winning photo day.

Photo blinds can be fabricated from native materials available in the woods or constructed of wood or canvas a[...] places in that special location. The deer adjust quickly to most blinds. Camouflage, using local vegetation, will help de[...] adjust quickly. Once they have accepted your make-shift, temporary home - they will consider it as part of the landsca[...] Then they will ignore it and behave quite normally as long as there are no alarming disturbances. I have found that t[...] longer a blind is left in place - the better it works. Therefore, I prefer to construct them out of wood and then just lea[...] them out there - all year-round. New camouflage must be added occasionally and certainly once every year. The be[...] camo is either oak or red cedar. Oak limbs retain their leaves real well and cedar just turns from green to brown. I oft[...] mix cedar and oak boughs - it gives a more natural look. Permanent wooden blinds are heavy enough to stand alone [...] the woods or along borders. But portable canvas blinds should be securely fastened to trees, rocks, or stakes driven in[...] the ground. Trees provide the best source for a secure place to fasten a blind in position. With a canvas blind be sure [...] tie down all lose, flapping ends - the flapping in the wind really frightens the deer. If livestock are running loose in t[...] woodlot, be sure to put a single or double stand wire fence around your blind - a few feet away. Livestock are curio[...] they are also destructive.

Deer have a very acute sense of smell. So, the wind direction cannot be ignored when attempting to photograph t[...] whitetail. No need to waste time in the blind when you are upwind from the place where deer approach or feed. Remem[...] ber that smoking, eating or drinking coffee can discourage deer from approaching your blind. Also stay at home wh[...] you have a severe cough - deer have good ears!!

I use bait to lure deer into photography range. I scatter it in close proximity to the blind. Sometimes I camouflage [...] when fresh bait is placed out, using leaves of the same species of trees from a nearby area. I bait with shelled corn, sli[...] apples, and sometimes commercial feed pellets.

One pleasant surprise that comes from attempting to photograph deer from a blind is the appearance of other ma[...] mals and birds that will come to feed on the bait that is put out for the deer. It is not uncommon to have photograph[...] opportunities for wild turkeys, quail, doves, crows, bluejays, squirrels, opossums, and even bobcats, coyotes, and fox[...] that visit the site.

To get some different deer poses and different behaviors, apply some commercially prepared deer scent to low[...] extremities of trees just at the periphery of the baited area. Deer are inquisitive and will investigate those scents - ha[...] your camera ready!! This is especially true during the rutting season. By strategically locating the blind, commerc[...] scent and bait, it is sometimes possible to lure a buck into a precise location for that very special picture.

Blinds should be situated in the photographic location well in advance of the first photo trip. Three weeks ahead [...] time is a good rule of thumb. Sometimes there is no way to put up a blind will in advance. In that situation, plan to arr[...] at mid-day when the animals are inactive, and make a temporary setup using netting on canvas and cover it with loca[...] available tree limbs as described above. Remember then to keep the wind and light in proper perspective. Don't get t[...] close - use longer telephoto lenses.

Amazingly enough, a vehicle makes a good blind. Deer pay little attention to parked vehicles because they encoun[...] all manor of parked farm machinery, pickups, and what have you in their territory. From a parked vehicle, use a wind[...] pod or sandbag cushion for a camera rest.

When I set up a blind, I often leave the lens opening pretty obvious to the animals. I will very often position a ma[...] believe lens in that opening and secure it there so the animals can get used to seeing it when I'm not there. I make m[...] lenses out of different sizes of tin cans with the sided painted flat black to resemble the lens on my camera.

CLOTHING

It's a good idea to wear camouflage clothing while photographing deer, but not during the hunting season. I d[...] photograph then anyway. Even when working from a blind camouflage clothing helps to conceal the photographer

100

side the blind. I even wear camouflage gloves because I use my hands to adjust lenses and focus and deer will notice the ghtest movement. Make your movements <u>very</u> <u>slow</u> and <u>very deliberate</u>. Keep the noise to a minimum.

TRIPOD

A tripod or some kind of a camera support is absolutely necessary. A telephoto lens protruding from the camera port in photo blind cannot usually be hand-held with enough stability to give a sharp image on the film. However, an image- bilized telephoto will help. So, set your tripod so that it will support your camera in ready-position to photograph mals in the vicinity. It may be hours of waiting and the tripod is the only way to be camera-ready when the subject bears. Tripods should also be camouflaged using flat, non-gloss paint.

STALKING

Stalking is a difficult, time consuming, method for photographing whitetailed deer. Stalking works best in refuges or serves where deer are used to seeing people and are not hunted. In stalking, the photographer is on the move and it gives reater chance to get pictures with different backgrounds. It's kind of like hunting too - and is less monotonous than ing in a blind.

Telephoto lenses are mandatory when you are in the stalking mode. With both you and your subject on the move, osures and focus distances are going to change continually - so be well-acquainted with your equipment. Some of the dern fabrics used by bow hunters should be worn when pulling off a successful stalk of a whitetail. Just as in the blind ove slowly and deliberately. Approach the animal at a passing angle - not directly. Approach from downwind and keep sun behind you. Let the deer set the pace. Do not "push" them. My photo files are full of deer with flags waiving and means <u>good bye</u>.

Remember a picture is worth a thousand words. And if you're a good deer photographer, you don't have to talk very ch. Good Luck.

GLENN D. CHAMBERS

Glenn D. Chambers, born in Butler Missouri in 1936, has achieved and received many awards in his long and prod[u]ctive career as: Educator, Photographer, Film Producer, and Conservationist.

In 1958 Glenn graduated from Central Missouri State University with a Bachelor of Science Degree in Biology [&] Chemistry. In 1960 he received his Master of Arts Degree in Wildlife Management from the University of Missouri.

His professional career started in 1960-1961 as, Wildlife Area Manager for August A. Busch Memorial Wildlife M[an]agement Area. 1961-1979 as, Research Biologist with the Missouri Department of Conservation. 1971-1979 as, Regio[nal] Biologist/Cinematographer with the Missouri Department of Conservation. 1979-1984 as, Regional Director Ducks [Un]limited, Inc.. 1984-1988 as, Corporate Photographer - Ducks Unlimited, Inc.. 1988-1995 as, Motion Picture Specia[list] with the Missouri Department of Conservation. Retired in 1995.

Some of Glenn's Publications (Photographic) work in the Audubon Magazine were: "Vultures" March 1988, "Yo[u]. Never See A Bobcat" 1979, "Swift Fox - Little Fox on the Prairie" July 1976, "Crows - Dance on Monkey Mountain [&] Other Crow Doings" January 1976, "Coyote - The Song Dog" September 1975 (includes front and back cover phot[os]. "Day of the Crane" March 1974, "Hudson Bay Album" May 1973.

Other publications include: National Geographic Books, Time-Life Books, McGraw Hill Books, The Hunting [&] Fishing Library, Science Magazine, National Wildlife, Ranger Rick and Hunting and Fishing Journal. Foreign publ[ica]tions featuring Glenn's work appear in five languages: German, French, Italian, Japanese and Spanish.

Glenn's Photographic Exhibits: U.S. Department of Interior, Washington, D.C., 1988; The Smithsonian, Washing[ton] D.C., 1988 (Traveling exhibit 1989-90); Ducks Unlimited, Inc., Sacramento, California, 1988; National Wildlife Show, Ducks Unlimited, Kansas City, Missouri, 1984.

Glenn has produced eleven award winning movies including: 1970 "Return of the Wild Turkey" (42 minutes); I[98?] "Wild Chorus" (Canada Goose story, 42 minutes); 1989 "Glenn & His Geese"; 1990 "It's Your Choice" (Hunter [eth]ics).

Glenn's awards have been many, but one of his most cherished honors was receiving the award:
Best Non-News Feature, Television Emmy Award.

End-Sheet photographs were provided by Glenn D. Chambers, for this first printing of the Missouri Show-Me [?] Bucks Club Records of Whitetail Deer.

BOONE AND CROCKETT CLUB

HISTORY AND

BIG GAME RECOGNITION PROGRAM

The Boone and Crockett Club was founded in 1887 by Theodore Roosevelt and a small group of his friends. It is one of r nations first conservation organizations. These men helped shape the course of conservation in America. The Boone d Crockett Club's earliest achievements were protection of Yellowstone and Glacier National Parks, establishment of leral forest reserves which became the National Forest System, support of national and state wildlife refuges, and the ming of wildlife protection laws, these are monuments to that legacy. The Club now promotes conservation and out- or ethics; supports wildlife research, education and management; and maintains records of North America's big game imals taken in fair chase.

The Records Program and Trophy Requirements

The first formal recognition of outstanding North American big game trophies by the Boone and Crockett Club was in

32 records book. It involved relatively few specimens that were listed by simple criteria of length and spread of horns, lers, or skulls. The 1932 book was followed by the 1939 records book that included informative chapters on a variety subjects related to big game hunting.

In 1947, the club held its first "competition" for outstanding trophies, ranking them by a series of measurements that re refined in 1950 into the current trophy scoring system. Since 1947 there have been 22 Awards Programs.

Trophy entry now occurs during a three year period, followed by public display of the finest trophies entered in each egory and an awards banquet. Presentation of Boone and Crockett Club big game medals and or certificates recognizes phy excellence. Only top trophies in each category are invited to the Final Awards Judging and only invited trophies neasured by the Judges' panel are eligible to receive awards. Place awards are reserved for Fair Chase trophies entered hunters. Other invited trophies, such as pickups and unknown origin invited trophies, are eligible for a Certificate of rit.

Entering A Trophy

The Boone and Crockett Club's copyrighted system of measurement is used for scoring entries. Make a preliminary asurement by use of a Boone and Crockett score chart and a 1/4-wide flexible steel measuring tape. Should such a asurement show your trophy to be above or very near the minimum score, contact an Official Measurer to have a asurement performed for trophy entry. A list of Boone and Crockett Club Official Measurers in your area will be sent on request. An official measurement cannot be made until the trophy has air dried for 60 days or more. Trophies taken hunters (archery, modern firearm, muzzleloader, etc.) in Fair Chase are eligible for listing in the records books and for eipt of awards. Pickups and trophies of unknown origin are not eligible for awards, but may be accepted for listing in ords books.

Trophies entered in an Awards Program that meet minimum requirements for the Awards Program, and minimu score for the All-Time Records Book, are automatically listed in the Awards Book and the All-Time Book. Trophi entered and accepted in one period cannot be entered in another entry period at a later date.

Deer, elk, caribou and moose trophies, for which the spread measurement is part of the score, are not eligible for ent if the skulls have been split, repaired or restored.

All Time Records Book

The All-Time Records Book, Records of North American Big Game, is published after two awards entry periods, when significant changes have occurred in trophy rankings, categories, or requirements. The 10th edition lists 12,7 trophies in 35 categories. The current minimum All-Time Records Book listing entry requirements for Typical Whitet Deer is 170 B&C points, for Non-Typical Whitetail Deer is 195 B&C points. The All-Time and Awards Books, Reco of North American Big Game, contain portraits, field photographs, and articles covering conservation and outdoor p grams. Plus the All-Time listings and ranking of North American Big Game.

The Awards Book

Awards books are both records books for single entry periods and supplements to the All-Time Record Book, Reco of North American Big Game. The Awards Book is a record for a three year entry period. Entry minimums for the th year awards period is less than that of the all-time listings. Minimum entry score for Typical Whitetail Deer is 160 B& points. The Non-Typical Whitetail Deer is 185 B&C points. The Awards Book contain portraits, field photographs, a hunting stories of top award recipients for that entry period and a listing of trophies accepted for that period.

Records of North American Whitetail Deer

Records of North American Whitetail Deer is now in its third edition. Containing tabulations of whitetail deer of No America as compiled from data in the Club's Big Game Records Archives. This book is a must for whitetail enthusia

B&C Associates Program and Lifetime Associates Program

The Boone and Crockett Club's Associates program was created in 1986 for people who support the Club's ideals a goals. To become an Associate or Lifetime Associate member contact the Boone and Crockett Club at:

Boone and Crockett Club
250 Station Drive
Missoula, MT 59801-2753
406/542-1888   phone
bcclub@montanna.com   email
www.boone-crockett.org website

Summary of Boone and Crockett minimum scores from 1950 to present for whitetail deer.

Category:	1950	1953	1963	1968>97
Whitetail Deer, Typical -	140	150	160	170
Whitetail Deer, Non-Typical -	140+20 -	---	160+20	195

The information is this article was taken from written material of the Boone and Crockett Club Record Books and b chures, with written permission granted to the Missouri Show-Me Big Bucks Club, for this 1st Edition Record Book. The listing of official score forms on the following pages was granted by: The Boone and Crockett Club, The Pope Young Club, and The Longhunters Society.

The Gun Library
at *Cabela's*

For more than 30 years, Cabela's World's Foremost Outfitter® has provided sportsmen worldwide with superior quality products and unequaled customer service.

The tradition continues with Cabela's Gun Library, designed to house the finest firearms from around the world. Located in the Sidney Retail facility, Cabela's Gun Library allows you to experience first-hand the World's Foremost Gunroom.

Cabela's experienced staff of **Wes Dillon** and **Dave Sanders** will assist you in meeting your requirements. Whether you are interested in classic antiques, collectibles or fine sporting firearms, the Gun Library staff will cater to your every need. Our inventory is constantly changing. Call today at **308-254-6560** or FAX your requirements to them at **308-254-6689.**

FLYING TO CABELA'S?

The Sidney Municipal Airport offers a 6,000-foot runway for your convenience. Radio the Sidney Unicom on 122.8 and have the airport call us. Cabela's will be happy to transport you to and from the airport when you visit the Gun Library.

The Gun Library
at
Cabela's

- *For more than 30 years, Cabela's has offered the discriminating sportsman the finest quality goods at the best prices*
- *Classic antique, collectible and fine sporting firearms*
- *Quality consignments welcomed*
- *Cash offers on single pieces or entire collections*
- *Appraisals and estate services*
- *Quarterly Fine Firearms Journal*

Cabela's, 115 Cabela Dr., Sidney, NE 69162
Phone (308) 254-6560 Contact Wes Dillon Or Dave Sanders FAX (308) 253-6689

1997, Cabela's, Inc.

OFFICIAL SCORING SYSTEM FOR NORTH AMERICAN BIG GAME TROPHIES

Records of North American
Big Game

BOONE AND CROCKETT CLUB®

250 Station Drive
Missoula, MT 59801
(406) 542-1888

TYPICAL
WHITETAIL AND COUES' DEER

Kind of Deer: _____

Minimum Score:	Awards	All-time
Whitetail	160	170
Coues'	100	110

Detail of Point Measurement

Abnormal Points	
Right Antler	Left Antler

Subtotals	
Total to E	

SEE OTHER SIDE FOR INSTRUCTIONS			Column 1	Column 2	Column 3	Column 4
			Spread Credit	Right Antler	Left Antler	Difference
A. No. Points on Right Antler		No. Points on Left Antler				
B. Tip to Tip Spread		C. Greatest Spread				
D. Inside Spread of Main Beams		(Credit May Equal But Not Exceed Longer Antler)				
E. Total of Lengths of Abnormal Points						
F. Length of Main Beam						
G-1. Length of First Point						
G-2. Length of Second Point						
G-3. Length of Third Point						
G-4. Length of Fourth Point, If Present						
G-5. Length of Fifth Point, If Present						
G-6. Length of Sixth Point, If Present						
G-7. Length of Seventh Point, If Present						
H-1. Circumference at Smallest Place Between Burr and First Point						
H-2. Circumference at Smallest Place Between First and Second Points						
H-3. Circumference at Smallest Place Between Second and Third Points						
H-4. Circumference at Smallest Place Between Third and Fourth Points						
TOTALS						

ADD	Column 1		Exact Locality Where Killed:
	Column 2		Date Killed: Hunter:
	Column 3		Owner: Telephone #:
	Subtotal		Owner's Address:
	SUBTRACT Column 4		Guide's Name and Address:
			Remarks: (Mention Any Abnormalities or Unique Qualities)
	FINAL SCORE		

Copyright © 1997 by Boone and Crockett Club®

I certify that I have measured this trophy on _____ 19 _____

at (address) _____ City _____ State _____
and that these measurements and data are, to the best of my knowledge and belief, made in
accordance with the instructions given.

Witness: _____ Signature: _____

B&C Official Measurer [ ][ ][ ][ ]

I.D. Number

INSTRUCTIONS FOR MEASURING TYPICAL WHITETAIL AND COUES' DEER

All measurements must be made with a 1/4-inch wide flexible steel tape to the nearest
one-eighth of an inch. (Note: A flexible steel cable can be used to measure points and main beams
only.) Enter fractional figures in eighths, without reduction. Official measurements cannot be
taken until the antlers have air dried for at least 60 days after the animal was killed.

A. Number of Points on Each Antler: To be counted a point, the projection must be at least one
inch long, with the length exceeding width at one inch or more of length. All points are measured
from tip of point to nearest edge of beam as illustrated. Beam tip is counted as a point but not
measured as a point.

B. Tip to Tip Spread is measured between tips of main beams.

C. Greatest Spread is measured between perpendiculars at a right angle to the center line of
the skull at widest part, whether across main beams or points.

D. Inside Spread of Main Beams is measured at a right angle to the center line of the skull at
widest point between main beams. Enter this measurement again as the Spread Credit **if** it is less
than or equal to the length of the longer antler; if greater, enter longer antler length for
Spread Credit.

E. Total of Lengths of all Abnormal Points: Abnormal Points are those non-typical in location
(such as points originating from a point or from bottom or sides of main beam) or extra points
beyond the normal pattern of points. Measure in usual manner and enter in appropriate blanks.

F. Length of Main Beam is measured from the center of the lowest outside edge of burr over
outer side to the most distant point of the main beam. The point of beginning is that point on
the burr where the center line along the outer side of the beam intersects the burr, then
following generally the line of the illustration.

G-1-2-3-4-5-6-7. Length of Normal Points: Normal points project from the top of the main
beam. They are measured from nearest edge of main beam over outer curve to tip. Lay the tape
along the outer curve of the beam so that the top edge of the tape coincides with the top edge of
the beam on both sides of the point to determine the baseline for point measurements. Record
point lengths in appropriate blanks.

H-1-2-3-4. Circumferences are taken as detailed for each measurement. If brow point is
missing, take H-1 and H-2 at smallest place between burr and G-2. If G-4 is missing, take H-4
halfway between G-3 and tip of main beam.

FAIR CHASE STATEMENT FOR ALL HUNTER-TAKEN TROPHIES

FAIR CHASE, as defined by the Boone and Crockett Club®, is the ethical, sportsmanlike and
lawful pursuit and taking of any free-ranging wild game animal in a manner that does not give
the hunter an improper or unfair advantage over such game animals.

Use of any of the following methods in the taking of game shall be deemed **UNFAIR CHASE**
and unsportsmanlike:

I. Spotting or herding game from the air, followed by landing in its vicinity for the
purpose of pursuit and shooting;

II. Herding, pursuing, or shooting game from any motorboat or motor vehicle;

III. Use of electronic devices for attracting, locating, or observing game, or for guiding
the hunter to such game;

IV. Hunting game confined by artificial barriers, including escape-proof fenced
enclosures, or hunting game transplanted for the purpose of commercial shooting;

V. Taking of game in a manner not in full compliance with the game laws or regulations
of the federal government or of any state, province, territory, or tribal council on
reservations or tribal lands;

VI. Or as may otherwise be deemed unfair or unsportsmanlike by the Executive Committee of
the Boone and Crockett Club.

I certify that the trophy scored on this chart was taken in **FAIR CHASE** as defined above by the
Boone and Crockett Club. In signing this statement, I understand that if the information
provided on this entry is found to be misrepresented or fraudulent in any respect, it will not
be accepted into the Awards Program and all of my prior entries are subject to deletion from
future editions of *Records of North American Big Game* and future entries may not be accepted.

Date: _____ Signature of Hunter: _____

(Signature must be witnessed by an Official Measurer or
a Notary Public.)

Date: _____ Signature of Notary or Official Measurer: _____

109

OFFICIAL SCORING SYSTEM FOR NORTH AMERICAN BIG GAME TROPHIES

Records of North American
Big Game

BOONE AND CROCKETT CLUB®

250 Station Drive
Missoula, MT 59801
(406) 542-1888

NON-TYPICAL
WHITETAIL AND COUES' DEER

Kind of Deer: _____

Minimum Score:	Awards	All-time
whitetail	185	195
Coues'	105	120

Detail of Point Measurement

Abnormal Points	
Right Antler	Left Antler
Subtotals	
E. Total	

SEE OTHER SIDE FOR INSTRUCTIONS				Column 1	Column 2	Column 3	Column 4
				Spread Credit	Right Antler	Left Antler	Difference
A. No. Points on Right Antler		No. Points on Left Antler					
B. Tip to Tip Spread		C. Greatest Spread					
D. Inside Spread of Main Beams		(Credit May Equal But Not Exceed Longer Antler)					
F. Length of Main Beam							
G-1. Length of First Point							
G-2. Length of Second Point							
G-3. Length of Third Point							
G-4. Length of Fourth Point, If Present							
G-5. Length of Fifth Point, If Present							
G-6. Length of Sixth Point, If Present							
G-7. Length of Seventh Point, If Present							
H-1. Circumference at Smallest Place Between Burr and First Point							
H-2. Circumference at Smallest Place Between First and Second Points							
H-3. Circumference at Smallest Place Between Second and Third Point							
H-4. Circumference at Smallest Place Between Third and Fourth Point							
			TOTALS				

ADD	Column 1	
	Column 2	
	Column 3	
	Subtotal	
SUBTRACT Column 4		
	Subtotal	
ADD Line E Total		
	FINAL SCORE	

Exact Locality Where Killed:

Date Killed: Hunter:

Owner: Telephone #:

Owner's Address:

Guide's Name and Address:

Remarks: (Mention Any Abnormalities or Unique Qualities)

Copyright © 1997 by Boone and Crockett Club®

110

I certify that I have measured this trophy on _____ 19 _____

at (address) _____ City _____ State _____
and that these measurements and data are, to the best of my knowledge and belief, made in
accordance with the instructions given.

Witness: _____ Signature: _____

B&C Official Measurer | | | |
                                                                      I.D. Number

INSTRUCTIONS FOR MEASURING NON-TYPICAL WHITETAIL AND COUES' DEER

All measurements must be made with a 1/4-inch wide flexible steel tape to the nearest
one-eighth of an inch. (Note: A flexible steel cable can be used to measure points and main beams
only.) Enter fractional figures in eighths, without reduction. Official measurements cannot be
taken until the antlers have air dried for at least 60 days after the animal was killed.

A. Number of Points on Each Antler: To be counted a point, the projection must be at least one
inch long, with the length exceeding width at one inch or more of length. All points are measured
from tip of point to nearest edge of beam as illustrated. Beam tip is counted as a point but not
measured as a point.

B. Tip to Tip Spread is measured between tips of main beams.

C. Greatest Spread is measured between perpendiculars at a right angle to the center line of the
skull at widest part, whether across main beams or points.

D. Inside Spread of Main Beams is measured at a right angle to the center line of the skull at
widest point between main beams. Enter this measurement again as the Spread Credit **if** it is less
than or equal to the length of the longer antler; if greater, enter longer antler length for
Spread Credit.

E. Total of Lengths of all Abnormal Points: Abnormal Points are those non-typical in location
(such as points originating from a point or from bottom or sides of main beam) or extra points
beyond the normal pattern of points. Measure in usual manner and enter in appropriate blanks.

F. Length of Main Beam is measured from the center of the lowest outside edge of burr over the
outer side to the most distant point of the main beam. The point of beginning is that point on
the burr where the center line along the outer side of the beam intersects the burr, then
following generally the line of the illustration.

G-1-2-3-4-5-6-7. Length of Normal Points: Normal points project from the top of the main beam.
They are measured from nearest edge of main beam over outer curve to tip. Lay the tape along the
outer curve of the beam so that the top edge of the tape coincides with the top edge of the beam
on both sides of the point to determine the baseline for point measurement. Record point lengths
in appropriate blanks.

H-1-2-3-4. Circumferences are taken as detailed for each measurement. If brow point is missing,
take H-1 and H-2 at smallest place between burr and G-2. If G-4 is missing, take H-4 halfway
between G-3 and tip of main beam.

FAIR CHASE STATEMENT FOR ALL HUNTER-TAKEN TROPHIES

FAIR CHASE, as defined by the Boone and Crockett Club®, is the ethical, sportsmanlike and
lawful pursuit and taking of any free-ranging wild game animal in a manner that does not give
the hunter an improper or unfair advantage over such game animals.

Use of any of the following methods in the taking of game shall be deemed **UNFAIR CHASE**
and unsportsmanlike:

I. Spotting or herding game from the air, followed by landing in its vicinity for the
purpose of pursuit and shooting;

II. Herding, pursuing, or shooting game from any motorboat or motor vehicle;

III. Use of electronic devices for attracting, locating, or observing game, or for guiding
the hunter to such game;

IV. Hunting game confined by artificial barriers, including escape-proof fenced
enclosures, or hunting game transplanted for the purpose of commercial shooting;

V. Taking of game in a manner not in full compliance with the game laws or regulations
of the federal government or of any state, province, territory, or tribal council on
reservations or tribal lands;

VI. Or as may otherwise be deemed unfair or unsportsmanlike by the Executive Committee of
the Boone and Crockett Club.

I certify that the trophy scored on this chart was taken in **FAIR CHASE** as defined above by the
Boone and Crockett Club. In signing this statement, I understand that if the information
provided on this entry is found to be misrepresented or fraudulent in any respect, it will not
be accepted into the Awards Program and all of my prior entries are subject to deletion from
future editions of *Records of North American Big Game* and future entries may not be accepted.

Date: _____ Signature of Hunter:_____
                              (Signature must be witnessed by an Official Measurer or
                              a Notary Public.)

Date: _____ Signature of Notary or Official Measurer:_____

I certify that I have measured the above trophy on _____19_____

at (address)_____ ___ _____ _____ City_____

State_____ Zip Code_____ and that these measurements and data are, to the best

of my knowledge and belief, made in accordance with the instructions given.

Witness:_____Signature_____
　　　　　　(To Measurer's Signature)　　　Pope & Young Club Official Measurer

　　　　　　　　　　　　　　　　　　　　_____
　　　　　　　　　　　　　　　　　　　　MEASURER (Print)

　　　　　　　　　　　　　　　　　　　　_____
　　　　　　　　　　　　　　　　　　　　ADDRESS

　　　　　　　　　　　　　　　　　　　　_____
　　　　　　　　　　　　　　　　　　　　CITY　　　　　　　　STATE　　　　　　ZIP

INSTRUCTIONS

Measurements must be made with a flexible steel tape or steel cable to the nearest one-eighth of an inch. To simplify addition, please enter fractional figures in **eighths.** Official measurements cannot be taken for at least sixty days after the day the animal was killed. **Please submit photographs (see below).**

A. Number of Points on each antler. To be counted a point, a projection must be at least one inch long AND at some location at least one inch from the tip, the length of the projection must exceed its width. **Beam tip is counted as a point but not measured as a point.**

B. Tip to Tip Spread is measured between tips of main beams.

C. Greatest Spread is measured between perpendiculars at right angles to the center line of the skull at widest part whether across main beams or points.

D. Inside Spread on Main Beam is measured at right angles to the center line of the skull at widest point between main beams. Enter this measurement again in "Spread Credit" column if it is less than or equal to the length of longer antler; if longer, enter longer antler length for spread credit.

E. Total of Length of all Abnormal Points. Abnormal points are generally considered to be those non-typical in location. Sketch all abnormal points on antler illustration (front of form) showing location and approximate size. Measure in usual manner and enter in appropriate blanks.

F. Length of Main Beam is measured from lowest outside edge of burr over outer curve to the most distant point of the main beam. The point of beginning is that point on the burr where the center line along the outer curve of the beam intersects the burr.

G-1-2-3-4-5-6-7. Length of Normal Points. Normal points project from the top of the main beam as shown in illustration. They are measured from nearest edge of beam over outer curve to tip. To determine nearest edge (top edge) of beam, lay the tape along the outer curve of the beam so that the top edge of the tape coincides with the top edge of the beam on both sides of the point. Draw line along top of tape. This line will be base line from which point is measured.

H-1-2-3-4. Circumferences. If first point is missing, take H-1 and H-2 at smallest place between burr and second point. If G-4 is missing, take H-4 halfway between G-3 and tip of main beam. Circumference measurements must be taken with a steel tape (a cable cannot be used for these measurements).

Photographs: All entries must include photographs of the trophy. A right side, left side and front view photograph is required for all antlers. A photograph of the entire animal, preferably at the site of kill, is requested if at all possible.

Drying Period: To be eligible for entry in the Pope & Young Records, a trophy must first have been stored under normal room temperature and humidity for at least 60 days after date of kill. No trophy will be considered which has in any way been altered from its natural state.

THIS SCORING FORM MUST BE ACCOMPANIED BY A SIGNED POPE & YOUNG FAIR CHASE AFFIDAVIT, 3 PHOTOS OF ANTLERS, AND A RECORDING FEE OF $25.00.

I certify that I have measured the above trophy on _____ 19_____

at (address) _____ City _____

State _____ Zip Code _____ and that these measurements and data are, to the best

of my knowledge and belief, made in accordance with the instructions given.

Witness: _____ Signature_____

(To Measurer's Signature)

Pope & Young Club Official Measurer

_____

MEASURER (Print)

_____

ADDRESS

_____

CITY   STATE   ZIP

INSTRUCTIONS

Measurements must be made with a flexible steel tape or steel cable to the nearest one-eighth of an inch. To simplify addition, please enter fractional figures in **eighths**. Official measurements cannot be taken for at least sixty days after the day the animal was killed. **Please submit photographs [see below].**

A. Number of Points on each antler. To be counted a point, a projection must be at least one inch long AND at some location, at least one inch from the tip, the length of the projection must exceed its width. **Beam tip is counted as a point but not measured as a point.**

B. Tip to Tip Spread is measured between tips of main beams.

C. Greatest Spread is measured between perpendiculars at right angles to the center line of the skull at widest part whether across main beams or points.

D. Inside Spread on Main Beam is measured at right angles to the center line of the skull at widest point between main beams. Enter this measurement again in "Spread Credit" column if it is less than or equal to the length of longer antler; if longer, enter longer antler length for spread credit.

E. Total of Length of all Abnormal Points. Abnormal points are generally considered to be those non-typical in location. Measure in usual manner and enter in appropriate blanks.

F. Length of Main Beam is measured from lowest outside edge of burr over outer curve to the distant point of the main beam. The point of beginning is that point on the burr where the center line along the outer curve of the beam intersects the burr.

G-1-2-3-4-5-6-7. Length of Normal Points. Normal points project from the top of the main beam as shown in illustration. They are measured from nearest edge of beam over outer curve to tip. To determine nearest edge (top edge) of beam, lay the tape along the outer curve of the beam so that the top edge of the tape coincides with the top edge of the beam on both sides of the point. Draw line along top of tape. This line will be base line from which point is measured.

H-1-2-3-4. Circumferences. If first point is missing, take H-1 and H-2 at smallest place between burr and second point. If G-4 is missing, take H-4 halfway between G-3 and tip of main beam. Circumference measurements must be taken with a steel tape (a cable cannot be used for these measurements).

Photographs: All entries must include photographs of the trophy. A right side, left side and front view photograph is required for all antlers. A photograph of the entire animal, preferably at the site of kill, is requested if at all possible.

Drying Period: To be eligible for entry in the Pope & Young Records, a trophy must first have been stored under normal room temperature and humidity for at least 60 days after date of kill. No trophy will be considered which has in any way been altered from its natural state.

THIS SCORING FORM MUST BE ACCOMPANIED BY A SIGNED POPE & YOUNG FAIR CHASE AFFIDAVIT, 3 PHOTOS OF ANTLERS, AND A RECORDING FEE OF $25.00.

BIG GAME   RECORDS

KIND OF DEER _____

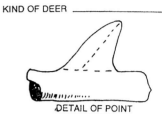

DETAIL OF POINT
MEASUREMENT

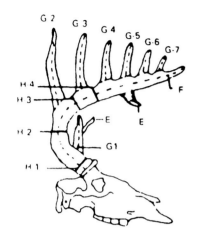

TYPICAL
WHITETAIL AND COUES DEER

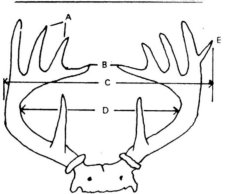

Abnormal Points	
Right	Left

Total To E

SEE OTHER SIDE FOR INSTRUCTIONS		Supplementary Data		Column 1	Column 2	Column 3	Column 4
		R	L	Spread Credit	Right Antler	Left Antler	Difference
A.	Number of Points on Each Antler						
B.	Tip to Tip Spread						
C.	Greatest Spread						
D.	Inside Spread of MAIN BEAMS	Spread credit may equal but not exceed length of longer antler					
E.	Total of Lengths of all Abnormal Points						
F.	Length of Main Beam						
G-1	Length of First Point, if present						
G-2	Length of Second Point						
G-3	Length of Third Point						
G-4	Length of Fourth Point, if present						
G-5	Length of Fifth Point, if present						
G-6	Length of Sixth Point, if present						
G-7	Length of Seventh Point, if present						
H-1	Circumference at Smallest Place Between Burr and First Point						
H-2	Circumference at Smallest Place Between First and Second Points						
H-3	Circumference at Smallest Place Between Second and Third Points						
H-4	Circumference at Smallest Place between Third and Fourth Points Or half way between Third point and Beam Tip if Fourth Point is missing						
TOTALS							

ADD	Column 1		Exact locality where killed	(County)	(State)
	Column 2		Date killed	By whom killed	
	Column 3		Present owner	•Phone ( )	
	Total		Address		
	SUBTRACT Column 4		Guide's name and Complete Address		
	FINAL SCORE		Remarks: (Mention any abnormalities)		

I certify that I have measured the above trophy on _____ 19_____

at (address) _____ City _____

State _____ Zip Code _____ and that these measurements and data are, to the best

of my knowledge and belief, made in accordance with the instructions given.

Witness: _____ Signature _____

(To Measurer's Signature)

Pope & Young Club Official Measurer

_____

MEASURER (Print)

_____

ADDRESS

_____

CITY   STATE   ZIP

INSTRUCTIONS

Measurements must be made with a flexible steel tape or steel cable to the nearest one-eighth of an inch. To simplify addition, please enter fractional figures in **eighths.** Official measurements cannot be taken for at least sixty days after the day the animal was killed. **Please submit photographs [see below].**

A. Number of Points on each antler. To be counted a point, a projection must be at least one inch long AND at some location, at least one inch from the tip, the length of the projection must exceed its width. **Beam tip is counted as a point but not measured as a point.**

B. Tip to Tip Spread is measured between tips of main beams.

C. Greatest Spread is measured between perpendiculars at right angles to the center line of the skull at widest part whether across main beams or points.

D. Inside Spread on Main Beam is measured at right angles to the center line of the skull at widest point between main beams. Enter this measurement again in "Spread Credit" column if it is less than or equal to the length of longer antler; if longer, enter longer antler length for spread credit.

E. Total of Length of all Abnormal Points. Abnormal points are generally considered to be those non-typical in location. Measure in usual manner and enter in appropriate blanks.

F. Length of Main Beam is measured from lowest outside edge of burr over outer curve to the distant point of the main beam. The point of beginning is that point on the burr where the center line along the outer curve of the beam intersects the burr.

G-1-2-3-4-5-6-7. Length of Normal Points. Normal points project from the top of the main beam as shown in illustration. They are measured from nearest edge of beam over outer curve to tip. To determine nearest edge (top edge) of beam, lay the tape along the outer curve of the beam so that the top edge of the tape coincides with the top edge of the beam on both sides of the point. Draw line along top of tape. This line will be base line from which point is measured.

H-1-2-3-4. Circumferences. If first point is missing, take H-1 and H-2 at smallest place between burr and second point. If G-4 is missing, take H-4 halfway between G-3 and tip of main beam. Circumference measurements must be taken with a steel tape (a cable cannot be used for these measurements).

Photographs: All entries must include photographs of the trophy. A right side, left side and front view photograph is required for all antlers. A photograph of the entire animal, preferably at the site of kill, is requested if at all possible.

Drying Period: To be eligible for entry in the Pope & Young Records, a trophy must first have been stored under normal room temperature and humidity for at least 60 days after date of kill. No trophy will be considered which has in any way been altered from its natural state.

THIS SCORING FORM MUST BE ACCOMPANIED BY A SIGNED
POPE & YOUNG FAIR CHASE AFFIDAVIT, 3 PHOTOS OF ANTLERS, AND A
RECORDING FEE OF $25.00.

Records of North American
Big Game

BOONE AND CROCKETT CLUB

National Muzzle Loading
Rifle Association
P.O. Box 67.
Friendship, Indiana 47021

250 Station Driv
Missoula, MT 598
(406) 542-18

B&C LHS
130
70

Minimum Score: Awards All-time
whitetail   160   170
Coues'   100   110

TYPICAL
WHITETAIL AND COUES' DEER

Kind of Deer: _____

Abnormal Points	
Right Antler	Left Antler
Subtotals	
Total to E	

Detail of Point Measurement

					Column 1	Column 2	Column 3	Column 4
A. No. Points on Right Antler		No. Points on Left Antler			Spread Credit	Right Antler	Left Antler	Difference
B. Tip to Tip Spread		C. Greatest Spread						
D. Inside Spread of Main Beams		(Credit May Equal But Not Exceed Longer Antler)						
E. Total of Lengths of Abnormal Points								
F. Length of Main Beam								
G-1. Length of First Point								
G-2. Length of Second Point								
G-3. Length of Third Point								
G-4. Length of Fourth Point, If Present								
G-5. Length of Fifth Point, If Present								
G-6. Length of Sixth Point, If Present								
G-7. Length of Seventh Point, If Present								
H-1. Circumference at Smallest Place Between Burr and First Point								
H-2. Circumference at Smallest Place Between First and Second Points								
H-3. Circumference at Smallest Place Between Second and Third Points								
H-4. Circumference at Smallest Place Between Third and Fourth Points								
				TOTALS				

SEE OTHER SIDE FOR INSTRUCTIONS

ADD	Column 1		Exact Locality Where Killed:
	Column 2		Date Killed: Hunter:
	Column 3		Owner: Telephone #:
	Subtotal		Owner's Address:
SUBTRACT Column 4			Guide's Name and Address:
			Remarks: (Mention Any Abnormalities or Unique Qualities)
FINAL SCORE			

I certify that I have measured this trophy on. _____ 19 _____

at (address) _____ City _____ State _____

and that these measurements and data are, to the best of my knowledge and belief, made in accordance with the instructions given.

Witness: _____   Signature: _____

                                                 B&C Official Measurer   ☐☐☐☐

                                                              I.D. Number

INSTRUCTIONS FOR MEASURING TYPICAL WHITETAIL AND COUES' DEER

All measurements must be made with a 1/4-inch wide flexible steel tape to the nearest one-eighth of an inch. (Note: A flexible steel cable can be used to measure points and main beams only.) Enter fractional figures in eighths, without reduction. Official measurements cannot be taken until the antlers have air dried for at least 60 days after the animal was killed.

A. Number of Points on Each Antler: To be counted a point, the projection must be at least one inch long, with the length exceeding width at one inch or more of length. All points are measured from tip of point to nearest edge of beam as illustrated. Beam tip is counted as a point but not measured as a point.

B. Tip to Tip Spread is measured between tips of main beams.

C. Greatest Spread is measured between perpendiculars at a right angle to the center line of the skull at widest part whether across main beams or points.

D. Inside Spread of Main Beams is measured at a right angle to the center line of the skull at widest point between main beams. Enter this measurement again as the Spread Credit **if** it is less than or equal to the length of the longer antler; if greater, enter longer antler length for Spread Credit.

E. Total of Lengths of all Abnormal Points: Abnormal Points are those non-typical in location (such as points originating from a point or from bottom or sides of main beam) or extra points beyond the normal pattern of points. Measure in usual manner and enter in appropriate blanks.

F. Length of Main Beam is measured from the center of the lowest outside edge of burr over outer side to the most distant point of the main beam. The point of beginning is that point on the burr where the center line along the outer side of the beam intersects the burr, then following generally the line of the illustration.

G-1-2-3-4-5-6-7. Length of Normal Points: Normal points project from the top of the main beam. They are measured from nearest edge of main beam over outer curve to tip. Lay the tape along the outer curve of the beam so that the top edge of the tape coincides with the top edge of the beam on both sides of the point to determine the baseline for point measurements. Record point lengths in appropriate blanks.

H-1-2-3-4. Circumferences are taken as detailed for each measurement. If brow point is missing, take H-1 and H-2 at smallest place between burr and G-2. If G-4 is missing, take H-4 halfway between G-3 and tip of main beam.

FAIR CHASE STATEMENT FOR ALL HUNTER-TAKEN TROPHIES

FAIR CHASE, as defined by the Boone and Crockett Club®, is the ethical, sportsmanlike and lawful pursuit and taking of any free-ranging wild game animal in a manner that does not give the hunter an improper or unfair advantage over such game animals.

Use of any of the following methods in the taking of game shall be deemed **UNFAIR CHASE** and unsportsmanlike:

I. Spotting or herding game from the air, followed by landing in its vicinity for the purpose of pursuit and shooting;

II. Herding, pursuing, or shooting game from any motorboat or motor vehicle;

III. Use of electronic devices for attracting, locating, or observing game, or for guiding the hunter to such game;

IV. Hunting game confined by artificial barriers, including escape-proof fenced enclosures, or hunting game transplanted for the purpose of commercial shooting;

V. Taking of game in a manner not in full compliance with the game laws or regulations of the federal government or of any state, province, territory, or tribal council on reservations or tribal lands;

VI. Or as may otherwise be deemed unfair or unsportsmanlike by the Executive Committee of the Boone and Crockett Club.

I certify that the trophy scored on this chart was taken in **FAIR CHASE** as defined above by the Boone and Crockett Club. In signing this statement, I understand that if the information provided on this entry is found to be misrepresented or fraudulent in any respect, it will not be accepted into the Awards Program and all of my prior entries are subject to deletion from future editions of *Records of North American Big Game* and future entries may not be accepted.

Date: _____ Signature of Hunter:_____
                    (Signature must be witnessed by an Official Measurer or a Notary Public.)

Date: _____ Signature of Notary or Official Measurer:_____

OFFICIAL SCORING SYSTEM FOR NORTH AMERICAN BIG GAME TROPHIES

Records of North American
Big Game

BOONE AND CROCKETT CLUB®

National Muzzle Loading
Rifle Association
P.O. Box 67.
Friendship, Indiana 47021

250 Station Dri~
Missoula, MT 598~
(406) 542-18~

B&C   LHS

Minimum Score:	Awards	All-time	**160**
Whitetail	185	195	
Coues'	105	120	**75**

NON-TYPICAL
WHITETAIL AND COUES' DEER

Kind of Deer: _____

Detail of Point Measurement

	Abnormal Points	
	Right Antler	Left Antle~
Subtotals		
E. Total		

SEE OTHER SIDE FOR INSTRUCTIONS				Column 1	Column 2	Column 3	Column 4
A. No. Points on Right Antler		No. Points on Left Antler		Spread Credit	Right Antler	Left Antler	Difference
B. Tip to Tip Spread		C. Greatest Spread					
D. Inside Spread of Main Beams		(Credit May Equal But Not Exceed Longer Antler)					
F. Length of Main Beam							
G-1. Length of First Point							
G-2. Length of Second Point							
G-3. Length of Third Point							
G-4. Length of Fourth Point, If Present							
G-5. Length of Fifth Point, If Present							
G-6. Length of Sixth Point, If Present							
G-7. Length of Seventh Point, If Present							
H-1. Circumference at Smallest Place Between Burr and First Point							
H-2. Circumference at Smallest Place Between First and Second Points							
H-3. Circumference at Smallest Place Between Second and Third Point							
H-4. Circumference at Smallest Place Between Third and Fourth Point							
			TOTALS				

ADD	Column 1		Exact Locality Where Killed:
	Column 2		Date Killed: Hunter:
	Column 3		Owner: Telephone #:
	Subtotal		Owner's Address:
SUBTRACT Column 4			Guide's Name and Address:
	Subtotal		Remarks: (Mention Any Abnormalities or Unique Qualities)
ADD Line E Total			
FINAL SCORE			

118

Copyright © 1997 by Boone and Crockett Club®

I certify that I have measured this trophy on _____ 19 _____

at (address) _____ City _____ State _____

and that these measurements and data are, to the best of my knowledge and belief, made in
accordance with the instructions given.

Witness: _____ Signature: _____

B&C Official Measurer ☐☐☐☐

I.D. Number

INSTRUCTIONS FOR MEASURING NON-TYPICAL WHITETAIL AND COUES' DEER

All measurements must be made with a 1/4-inch wide flexible steel tape to the nearest
one-eighth of an inch. (Note: A flexible steel cable can be used to measure points and main beams
only.) Enter fractional figures in eighths, without reduction. Official measurements cannot be
taken until the antlers have air dried for at least 60 days after the animal was killed.

A. Number of Points on Each Antler: To be counted a point, the projection must be at least one
inch long, with the length exceeding width at one inch or more of length. All points are measured
from tip of point to nearest edge of beam as illustrated. Beam tip is counted as a point but not
measured as a point.

B. Tip to Tip Spread is measured between tips of main beams.

C. Greatest Spread is measured between perpendiculars at a right angle to the center line of the
skull at widest part, whether across main beams or points.

D. Inside Spread of Main Beams is measured at a right angle to the center line of the skull at
widest point between main beams. Enter this measurement again as the Spread Credit **if** it is less
than or equal to the length of the longer antler; if greater, enter longer antler length for
Spread Credit.

E. Total of Lengths of all Abnormal Points: Abnormal Points are those non-typical in location
(such as points originating from a point or from bottom or sides of main beam) or extra points
beyond the normal pattern of points. Measure in usual manner and enter in appropriate blanks.

F. Length of Main Beam is measured from the center of the lowest outside edge of burr over the
outer side to the most distant point of the main beam. The point of beginning is that point on
the burr where the center line along the outer side of the beam intersects the burr, then
following generally the line of the illustration.

G-1-2-3-4-5-6-7. Length Of Normal Points: Normal Points project from the top of the main beam.
They are measured from nearest edge of main beam over outer curve to tip. Lay the tape along the
outer curve of the beam so that the top edge of the tape coincides with the top edge of the beam
on both sides of the point to determine the baseline for point measurement. Record point lengths
in appropriate blanks.

H-1-2-3-4. Circumferences are taken as detailed for each measurement. If brow point is missing,
take H-1 and H-2 at smallest place between burr and G-2. If G-4 is missing, take H-4 halfway
between G-3 and tip of main beam.

FAIR CHASE STATEMENT FOR ALL HUNTER-TAKEN TROPHIES

FAIR CHASE, as defined by the Boone and Crockett Club, is the ethical, sportsmanlike and
lawful pursuit and taking of any free-ranging wild game animal in a manner that does not give
the hunter an improper or unfair advantage over such game animals.

Use of any of the following methods in the taking of game shall be deemed **UNFAIR CHASE**
and unsportsmanlike:

I. Spotting or herding game from the air, followed by landing in its vicinity for the
purpose of pursuit and shooting;

II. Herding, pursuing, or shooting game from any motorboat or motor vehicle;

III. Use of electronic devices for attracting, locating, or observing game, or for guiding
the hunter to such game;

IV. Hunting game confined by artificial barriers, including escape-proof fenced
enclosures, or hunting game transplanted for the purpose of commercial shooting;

V. Taking of game in a manner not in full compliance with the game laws or regulations
of the federal government or of any state, province, territory, or tribal council on
reservations or tribal lands;

VI. Or as may otherwise be deemed unfair or unsportsmanlike by the Executive Committee of
the Boone and Crockett Club.

I certify that the trophy scored on this chart was taken in **FAIR CHASE** as defined above by the
Boone and Crockett Club. In signing this statement, I understand that if the information
provided on this entry is found to be misrepresented or fraudulent in any respect, it will not
be accepted into the Awards Program and all of my prior entries are subject to deletion from
future editions of *Records of North American Big Game* and future entries may not be accepted.

Date: _____ Signature of Hunter: _____

(Signature must be witnessed by an Official Measurer or
a Notary Public.)

Date: _____ Signature of Notary or Official Measurer: _____

MISSOURI

SHOW-ME

BIG BUCKS CLUB

RECORDS OF WHITETAIL DEER

RECORDS BY COUNTY

TYPICAL & NON-TYPICAL

by

DALE H. REAM, JR.

COUNTY	COUNTY RANK	SCORE	YEAR TAKEN	WEAPON	HUNTER	FIRST NAME	STATE RANK
ADAIR	1	182 1/8	96	HP/RIFLE	LUSHER	SELBY	27
	2	181 5/8	92	HP/RIFLE	SIMONSON	L.D.	30
	3	181 0/8	92	HP/RIFLE	HILL	MIKE	35
	4	173 2/8	86	HP/RIFLE	HATFIELD	ERIC	95
	5	173 0/8	82	HP/RIFLE	PINKERTON	DENNIS E.	100
	6	170 7/8	85	HP/RIFLE	HATFIELD	ERIC	134
	7	170 0/8	89	HP/RIFLE	YANTIS	DONNIE	151
	8	168 3/8	78	HP/RIFLE	CONLEY	ROGER	184
	9	167 5/8	72	HP/RIFLE	ASHER	JERRY	205
	10	167 4/8	80	HP/RIFLE	SCHEMPP	JIMMY K.	213
	11	166 5/8	87	HP/RIFLE	ELFRINK	DAN	238
	12	166 0/8	74	HP/RIFLE	DANIELS	NELSON	262
	13	164 1/8	93	HP/RIFLE	BAUMGARTNER	RODNEY	345
	14	163 3/8	74	HP/RIFLE	CAMERON	MIKE	378
	15	162 4/8	79	HP/RIFLE	LEDFORD	STEVE	431
	16	162 0/8	81	HP/RIFLE	MAGNESS	MIKE	462
	17	161 4/8	90	HP/RIFLE	ZEIGLER	LEON	493
	18	161 3/8	89	HP/RIFLE	MOYER	ANN	503
	19	161 2/8	90	HP/RIFLE	HUGHES	BRIAN W.	512
	20	161 1/8	94	HP/RIFLE	FIXX	VIVAN	520
	21	160 7/8	70	HP/RIFLE	HUTCHESON	RUSSEL	535
	22	159 3/8	66	HP/RIFLE	BRAGG	PAUL	665
	23	159 0/8	59	HP/RIFLE	DOUGLAS	LEON	695
	24	158 4/8	87	BOW	CLAY	TERRY	739
	25	157 6/8	73	HP/RIFLE	FLEAK	DAVID	812
	26	157 2/8	96	HP/RIFLE	ROHDE	WILLIAM A.	853
	27	157 0/8	95	HP/RIFLE	HOFFLAND	SCOTT A.	875
	28	155 4/8	93	HP/RIFLE	ERWIN	MIKE	1040
	28	155 4/8	93	HP/RIFLE	HOMAN, JR.	KENNETH	1040
	30	155 3/8	72	BOW	EASLEY	GARY L.	1059
	30	155 3/8	87	HP/RIFLE	FLOYD	TRAVIS	1059
	32	155 2/8	88	HP/RIFLE	YOUNG	BURT	1068
	32	155 2/8	95	HP/RIFLE	MORROW	MARTY	1068
	34	153 7/8	92	HP/RIFLE	JOHNSON	JERRY	1238
	35	153 6/8	94	HP/RIFLE	NOVINGER	GLEN	1256
	36	153 2/8	72	HP/RIFLE	WADDILL	ELLIS	1327
	36	153 2/8	87	HP/RIFLE	MOOTS	FERREL A.	1327
	38	153 1/8	79	HP/RIFLE	COY	ELDON	1344
	39	152 7/8	95	HP/RIFLE	KLUG	KEVIN L.	1370
	40	152 5/8	92	HP/RIFLE	IVIE	MICHAEL	1399
	41	152 4/8	89	HP/RIFLE	BEATTY	LEONARD	1423
	42	152 2/8	84	HP/RIFLE	FARLEY	BILL	1469
	43	152 1/8	82	HP/RIFLE	LEDFORD	OWEN	1493
	43	152 1/8	92	HP/RIFLE	SPARKS	ROBERT	1493
	43	152 1/8	96	HP/RIFLE	STEWART	RYAN	1493
	46	151 6/8	90	HP/RIFLE	RUBLE	ROBERT	1566
	47	151 5/8	90	HP/RIFLE	WILSON	CHRIS	1586
	47	151 5/8	95	HP/RIFLE	PARTIN	GAROLD	1586
	49	151 3/8	78	HP/RIFLE	ELLIS	WAYNE	1637
	50	151 2/8	83	HP/RIFLE	STEWART	RON	1656
	51	151 1/8	71	BOW	TRANSANO	EDDY	1690
	51	151 1/8	88	HP/RIFLE	TUGGLE	TOMMY	1690
	53	150 4/8	91	HP/RIFLE	PHILLIPS	RICHARD	1811
	53	150 4/8	91	HP/RIFLE	RECKNER	CUB	1811
	55	150 2/8	74	HP/RIFLE	FLOWERS	JIM	1853
	55	150 2/8	85	HP/RIFLE	WOMACK	WILLIAM	1853
	57	150 1/8	91	HP/RIFLE	BAUMGARTNER	RODNEY	1879
ANDREW	1	186 7/8	89	HP/RIFLE	TILL	KENNETH	13
	2	180 4/8	67	HP/RIFLE	ASHLEY	VIRGIL M.	38

MISSOURI SHOW-ME BIG BUCKS CLUB RECORDS OF WHITETAIL DEER BY COUNTY, TYPICAL

COUNTY	COUNTY RANK	SCORE	YEAR TAKEN	WEAPON	HUNTER	FIRST NAME	STATE RANK
ANDREW	3	176 7/8	95	HP/RIFLE	MADDOX	BRIAN	57
	4	166 0/8	86	HP/RIFLE	SHIFFLETT	RANDY	262
	5	160 2/8	90	HP/RIFLE	SHEETS	NINA	584
	6	160 0/8	79	HP/RIFLE	HORN	BILL	605
	7	159 6/8	88	HP/RIFLE	MANN	ROGER	628
	8	158 5/8	93	HP/RIFLE	FLORA	PATTY	735
	9	156 1/8	92	HP/RIFLE	LANCE	RONNIE	967
	10	154 2/8	90	HP/RIFLE	FISHER	JERRY	1186
	10	154 2/8	94	HP/RIFLE	KENDALL	BEN	1186
	12	154 1/8	69	HP/RIFLE	SMITH	JERRY	1207
	13	152 2/8	92	HP/RIFLE	BARNETT	TIM	1469
	14	152 1/8	81	HP/RIFLE	HOSKINS	ROBERT	1493
	14	152 1/8	95	HP/RIFLE	JONES	RICHARD	1493
	16	151 4/8	72	HP/RIFLE	DEGENHARDT	JOHN	1613
	17	150 4/8	76	HP/RIFLE	MORAN, SR.	ROBERT L.	1811
	18	150 1/8	95	HP/RIFLE	COX	TONY	1879
	19	148 2/8	94	HP/RIFLE	PFLUGRADT	LARRY	2071
	20	143 4/8	90	BOW	WOLF, JR.	BILL	2577
	20	143 4/8	96	HP/RIFLE	DEERING	SHANE	2577
ATCHISON	1	186 7/8	68	HP/RIFLE	MOODY	MIKE	13
	2	170 5/8	80	HP/RIFLE	MUNSEY	ROY	137
	3	165 4/8	88	HP/RIFLE	HOWELL	MIKE	283
	4	165 0/8	89	HP/RIFLE	RHOADES	VERNIE	299
	5	161 1/8	95	HP/RIFLE	GROFF	GREG	520
	6	159 2/8	74	HP/RIFLE	SCHOMBURG	WARREN	675
	7	156 0/8	91	HP/RIFLE	SLENKER	TIM	981
	8	155 2/8	70	HP/RIFLE	GRIMES	HAROLD	1068
	8	155 2/8	92	HP/RIFLE	KUHNS	JEFF	1068
	10	155 1/8	72	HP/RIFLE	HULETT	DAVID	1091
	11	154 6/8	60	HP/RIFLE	COOK	JIM	1130
	12	154 1/8	83	HP/RIFLE	HARMON	BRITT	1207
	13	153 4/8	94	HP/RIFLE	AVRETT	MIKE	1287
	14	153 3/8	94	HP/RIFLE	WENNIHAN	JOHN	1310
	15	153 2/8	78	HP/RIFLE	JENSEN	JANET	1327
	16	153 1/8	81	HP/RIFLE	LONG	RALPH	1344
	17	152 6/8	93	HP/RIFLE	HOWELL	BILL	1385
	18	152 0/8	90	HP/RIFLE	GEBHARDS	RAYMOND	1519
	19	151 4/8	94	HP/RIFLE	WATKINS	TRAVIS	1613
	20	145 4/8	94	HP/RIFLE	WOOTEN	LARRY D.	2331
AUDRAIN	1	167 2/8	90	HP/RIFLE	WHALEN	LARRY	221
	2	164 3/8	95	HP/RIFLE	QUALLS	DAVE	328
	3	161 4/8	89	BOW	HENDRIX	WILLIAM	493
	4	161 2/8	88	HP/RIFLE	DAY	JOHN	512
	5	158 7/8	80	HP/RIFLE	SMITH	LARRY D.	712
	6	158 2/8	87	HP/RIFLE	DUNGAN	TERRY	763
	7	156 4/8	93	HP/RIFLE	LYNN	ROY E.	925
	8	155 0/8	95	HP/RIFLE	HEADINGS	SANFORD O.	1102
	9	153 7/8	71	HP/RIFLE	ROBERTS	BOB	1238
	9	153 7/8	88	HP/RIFLE	SIMS	SCOTT W.	1238
	11	153 1/8	89	HP/RIFLE	LYBARGER	DWAYNE	1344
	12	153 0/8	84	HP/RIFLE	BEABOUT	RANDY	1355
	12	153 0/8	93	HP/RIFLE	CAMPBELL	RICK	1355
	14	152 6/8	93	HP/RIFLE	BURNS	GLEN E.	1385
	15	152 0/8	80	HP/RIFLE	TERRY	JEFF	1519
	15	152 0/8	92	HP/RIFLE	PEAK	PAUL	1519
	17	151 3/8	78	HP/RIFLE	BRANSTETTER	BOB	1637
	18	151 1/8	93	BOW	GRAWE	MIKE	1690
BARRY	1	158 6/8	75	HP/RIFLE	FAIRCHILD	PAUL	719
	1	158 6/8	85	HP/RIFLE	THOMAS	CLYDE L.	719

MISSOURI SHOW-ME BIG BUCKS CLUB RECORDS OF WHITETAIL DEER BY COUNTY, TYPICAL

COUNTY	COUNTY RANK	SCORE	YEAR TAKEN	WEAPON	HUNTER	FIRST NAME	STATE RANK
BARRY	3	158 5/8	87	HP/RIFLE	THURMAN	RICHARD	735
	4	156 0/8	71	HP/RIFLE	TOWE	TED	981
	5	155 0/8	95	HP/RIFLE	DODSON	JOHN	1102
	6	154 7/8	67	HP/RIFLE	PRIER	WINFRED	1118
	7	154 1/8	71	HP/RIFLE	RENFRO	CLEO	1207
	8	152 5/8	84	HP/RIFLE	UTTER	CARMEN W.	1399
	9	150 4/8	90	HP/RIFLE	SHOCKLEY	MICHAEL	1811
	10	145 3/8	95	BOW	CRAIN	R. STEVEN	2350
	11	145 1/8	71	HP/RIFLE	DAVIS	DOYLE	2379
	12	143 5/8	91	HP/RIFLE	ONEY	CHARLES E.	2564
	13	143 4/8	95	HP/RIFLE	RENKOSKI	DENNIS	2577
BARTON	1	155 5/8	80	HP/RIFLE	TEFERTILLER	RICHARD	1023
	2	154 6/8	80	HP/RIFLE	BRUMMETT	DAVE M.	1130
	3	154 0/8	92	HP/RIFLE	EHLERS	KIM C.	1219
	4	152 1/8	83	HP/RIFLE	BICKFORD	JERRY	1493
	5	150 4/8	93	HP/RIFLE	RAY	RICHARD	1811
	6	144 2/8	90	HP/RIFLE	RANDALL	RODNEY	2483
	7	144 1/8	88	HP/RIFLE	HAGENSICKER	JAMES M.	2498
	8	143 6/8	75	HP/RIFLE	VANGILDER	RANDY	2550
	9	142 4/8	96	HP/RIFLE	GORDON, IV	DAVID P.	2678
	10	142 0/8	95	HP/RIFLE	FRIEDEN	KURT	2725
	11	141 2/8	87	HP/RIFLE	LAFON	WAYNE	2828
	12	140 6/8	88	HP/RIFLE	FRIEDEN	KURT	2895
BATES	1	177 7/8	95	HP/RIFLE	WHITE	DAN	51
	2	170 0/8	69	HP/RIFLE	ROSIER	GARY	151
	3	166 5/8	90	HP/RIFLE	MORELAND	DALLAS	238
	4	161 4/8	81	HP/RIFLE	NULL	MARVIN	493
	5	160 2/8	88	HP/RIFLE	LEEMASTERS	MIKE	584
	6	159 7/8	93	HP/RIFLE	BOARD	BRIAN E.	620
	7	159 6/8	89	HP/RIFLE	CLIFTON	DANNY	628
	8	154 7/8	92	HP/RIFLE	VANGORDON	JOHN L.	1118
	9	153 7/8	92	HP/RIFLE	TILLERY	HOWARD	1238
	10	152 4/8	82	HP/RIFLE	BURCH	BRETT	1423
	11	151 2/8	88	HP/RIFLE	ANDULA	RAY	1656
	12	151 1/8	82	HP/RIFLE	WILSON	WILLIAM J.	1690
	13	150 6/8	89	HP/RIFLE	CLINTON	MARK E.	1756
	14	150 4/8	89	HP/RIFLE	WILEY	CHAD	1811
	15	149 7/8	73	BOW	BETHEL	RONNIE A.	1915
	16	149 3/8	82	HP/RIFLE	DURST	MIKE	1959
	17	148 7/8	65	HP/RIFLE	HATTON	CHARLIE	2012
	18	148 6/8	95	HP/RIFLE	TIFFEY	GARY	2024
	19	146 3/8	76	HP/RIFLE	LEFEVRE	RANDY	2252
	20	144 6/8	95	HP/RIFLE	SIMMS	DOUG	2425
	21	140 5/8	85	HP/RIFLE	GOLLADAY	JOHN D.	2908
BENTON	1	169 4/8	68	HP/RIFLE	BYBEE	L.J.	160
	2	163 0/8	85	HP/RIFLE	THOMAS	ROBERT	393
	3	162 3/8	95	HP/RIFLE	KESTNER	MARK	439
	4	161 4/8	72	HP/RIFLE	ROGERS	DUANE	493
	5	159 6/8	83	HP/RIFLE	KREISLER	DILLARD	628
	6	158 1/8	71	HP/RIFLE	PERRY	E.R.	777
	7	157 6/8	92	BOW	OWEN	RODNEY	812
	8	157 5/8	77	HP/RIFLE	VAN NATTA, SR.	JAMES E.	821
	9	155 4/8	75	HP/RIFLE	BEYER	DAN	1040
	10	154 7/8	95	HP/RIFLE	MEYER	DENNIS	1118
	11	154 6/8	68	HP/RIFLE	O'CONNOR	PAT	1130
	12	152 5/8	78	HP/RIFLE	HOSTERMAN	LARRY	1399
	13	152 0/8	86	HP/RIFLE	BACON	DALLAS	1519
	14	151 5/8	86	HP/RIFLE	MEDLOCK	JOHNNY	1586
	15	151 4/8	95	BOW	PENNINGTON, JR.	JIM	1613

MISSOURI SHOW-ME BIG BUCKS CLUB RECORDS OF WHITETAIL DEER BY COUNTY, TYPICAL

COUNTY	COUNTY RANK	SCORE	YEAR TAKEN	WEAPON	HUNTER	FIRST NAME	STATE RANK
BENTON	16	151 0/8	88	HP/RIFLE	LEGG	RITA F.	1715
	17	150 3/8	84	BOW	PRITCHETT	MERLIN L.	1834
	18	149 6/8	68	HP/RIFLE	FISHER	BOB	1926
	19	149 0/8	74	HP/RIFLE	NEWKIRK	SCOTTY	1998
	20	148 5/8	90	HP/RIFLE	LEGG	RITA	2035
	21	148 4/8	75	HP/RIFLE	FISHER	BOB	2048
	22	147 5/8	85	HP/RIFLE	SWEENEY	GREG	2138
	23	147 1/8	71	BOW	CHANCE	BILL	2183
	23	147 1/8	82	BOW	KNOX	ARNOLD	2183
	25	146 4/8	89	HP/RIFLE	BAIN	RICK	2242
	26	146 3/8	69	HP/RIFLE	COOPER	LOUIS A.	2252
	27	146 2/8	91	HP/RIFLE	KEPHART	ARMOND R.	2266
	28	146 1/8	94	HP/RIFLE	COX	DAVID	2281
	29	145 7/8	78	HP/RIFLE	CHURCH	WAYNE	2302
	30	145 5/8	86	HP/RIFLE	ANDREWS	RICHARD	2324
	31	144 5/8	88	BOW	TAGTMEYER	VIRGIL	2442
	32	144 3/8	84	HP/RIFLE	FINDLEY	STEVE	2466
	33	144 1/8	88	BOW	POWELL	CURTIS A.	2498
	34	143 6/8	88	HP/RIFLE	SEDGWICK	BILLY T.	2550
	35	141 7/8	90	HP/RIFLE	WYATT	MICHAEL W.	2747
	36	141 4/8	94	HP/RIFLE	GERLT	LONNIE J.	2787
	37	141 2/8	82	HP/RIFLE	JEFFRIES	CLINTON	2828
	38	141 2/8	95	HP/RIFLE	HADDOCK	SAM	2828
	39	140 7/8	82	HP/RIFLE	VAUGHAN	ROBERT	2877
	40	140 3/8	96	HP/RIFLE	GILES	BRIAN	2935
	41	140 2/8	87	HP/RIFLE	GRAVES, JR.	STEVE	2952
	42	140 0/8	83	HP/RIFLE	KOLL	RICK	2990
BOLLINGER	1	172 2/8	66	HP/RIFLE	FORNKAHL	HADLEY E.	109
	2	162 5/8	72	BOW	GOCKEL, JR.	JOE	417
	3	156 3/8	79	HP/RIFLE	ASLINGER	HARLOD G.	940
	4	155 6/8	95	HP/RIFLE	WELKER	DALE	1004
	5	151 7/8	80	HP/RIFLE	CLEMENTS	RALPH	1550
	6	150 5/8	92	HP/RIFLE	GLAUS	STACEY	1789
	7	149 1/8	90	HP/RIFLE	GREER	BRUCE	1988
	8	148 6/8	88	HP/RIFLE	ANTHONY	W. SCOTT	2024
	9	147 7/8	92	BOW	WESBECHER	RONNIE	2114
	10	146 2/8	86	HP/RIFLE	MYRACLE	JERRY	2266
	11	146 1/8	90	HP/RIFLE	PRUETT	BILLY	2281
	12	145 3/8	87	HP/RIFLE	ENDERLE	RON	2350
	13	144 0/8	94	HP/RIFLE	BROSHUIS	RICK	2514
	14	143 4/8	85	HP/RIFLE	MORGAN	SCOTT	2577
	15	143 0/8	64	HP/RIFLE	ROPER	RONNIE D.	2626
	16	141 6/8	93	HP/RIFLE	CLINGINGSMITH	DONALD L.	2756
	17	140 4/8	65	HP/RIFLE	VANDEVAN	KEN	2925
	18	140 2/8	85	HP/RIFLE	PROVAZNIK	MICHAEL JOHN	2952
BOONE	1	182 1/8	94	HP/RIFLE	MILLER	JEFF L.	27
	2	177 7/8	94	HP/RIFLE	FRITCHEY	TRACY	51
	3	174 5/8	95	PICK-UP	LOVEKAMP	TERRY L.	73
	4	170 0/8	91	HP/RIFLE	BARROWS	NORMAN	151
	5	167 4/8	86	HP/RIFLE	CALDWELL	SCOTT	213
	6	166 1/8	93	HP/RIFLE	HARMON	SCOTT	259
	7	164 1/8	80	HP/RIFLE	WYATT	CHRISTOPHER	345
	8	163 3/8	73	HP/RIFLE	THOMPSON	CHESTER	378
	9	163 2/8	73	HP/RIFLE	WELLS	JAMES K.	383
	10	161 1/8	96	HP/RIFLE	SCHULTE	LARRY	520
	11	160 0/8	66	HP/RIFLE	PENBERTHY	LARRY	605
	11	160 0/8	91	HP/RIFLE	RAY	LARRY	605
	13	159 6/8	88	HP/RIFLE	MUELLER	GARY	628
	14	159 0/8	86	HP/RIFLE	SHAWVER	CHARLES	695

MISSOURI SHOW-ME BIG BUCKS CLUB RECORDS OF WHITETAIL DEER BY COUNTY, TYPICAL

COUNTY	COUNTY RANK	SCORE	YEAR TAKEN	WEAPON	HUNTER	FIRST NAME	STATE RANK
BOONE	15	158 0/8	92	HP/RIFLE	WISE	MIKE	788
	16	157 7/8	86	HP/RIFLE	HAGANS	ROBERT	806
	17	157 6/8	90	PICK-UP	THORNHILL	CURTIS	812
	18	156 7/8	80	HP/RIFLE	McCLINTOCH	WAYNE	893
	18	156 7/8	85	HP/RIFLE	MITCHELL	GARY	893
	20	156 5/8	79	HP/RIFLE	COOK	LARRY	911
	20	156 5/8	87	HP/RIFLE	NICHOLS	HAROLD	911
	22	154 7/8	90	HP/RIFLE	LOVELESS	JIM	1118
	23	154 5/8	72	HP/RIFLE	STORM	DEAN	1146
	23	154 5/8	92	HP/RIFLE	McKEE	DANNY	1146
	25	154 2/8	85	BOW	SMALLWOOD	DON	1186
	26	153 7/8	76	HP/RIFLE	THORNHILL	STEVE	1238
	27	153 5/8	84	BOW	GARRETT	JACK	1273
	28	153 4/8	91	HP/RIFLE	DOMETRORCH	BRENT	1287
	29	153 0/8	89	BOW	BEAN	WILLIAM	1355
	30	152 2/8	89	HP/RIFLE	BERGSIEKER	VERNON	1469
	31	151 7/8	85	HP/RIFLE	ALLEN	JOHN	1550
	32	151 4/8	82	PICK-UP	CRANE	MURIEL	1613
	33	151 2/8	74	HP/RIFLE	HUFFMAN	FRANK	1656
	34	151 1/8	87	HP/RIFLE	SHELTON	SAM	1690
	35	150 6/8	84	HP/RIFLE	DOUGLAS	JOE	1756
	36	150 5/8	76	HP/RIFLE	PHILLIPS	BOB	1789
	37	150 4/8	82	HP/RIFLE	HINES	ROGER	1811
	38	150 3/8	96	HP/RIFLE	THORNHILL	CURTIS	1834
	39	150 0/8	82	HP/RIFLE	DAWSON	DAVID	1897
	39	150 0/8	88	HP/RIFLE	SCHINDLER	DON	1897
	41	149 4/8	95	HP/RIFLE	McMANAMA	SCOTT	1936
	42	148 7/8	96	HP/RIFLE	KUSTER	JOSEPH W.	2012
	43	140 0/8	93	HP/RIFLE	THORNHILL	CURTIS	2990
BUCHANAN	1	167 7/8	62	HP/RIFLE	COOK	DWAYNE	197
	2	166 4/8	82	HP/RIFLE	FIMPLE	MIKE	244
	3	165 2/8	85	HP/RIFLE	FARRELL	JAY	293
	4	163 2/8	91	HP/RIFLE	DONALDSON	JEFF	383
	5	162 2/8	75	HP/RIFLE	DONALDSON	FRED	451
	6	152 0/8	60	HP/RIFLE	MARRIOTT	RODGER	1519
CALDWELL	1	169 3/8	91	HP/RIFLE	ROBESON	MIKE	162
	2	168 6/8	89	HP/RIFLE	KELLETT	DANIEL T.	174
	3	166 4/8	92	HP/RIFLE	HUNTER	RON	244
	4	163 0/8	96	HP/RIFLE	ANDERSON	JEFFREY B.	393
	5	161 1/8	88	BOW	MYERS	GARY	520
	6	160 2/8	88	HP/RIFLE	CAMPBELL	SCOTT	584
	7	160 0/8	80	HP/RIFLE	SWEENEY	GREG	605
	8	159 7/8	88	HP/RIFLE	FIELDS	RICHARD	620
	9	159 4/8	74	HP/RIFLE	SHELTON	J.T.	654
	10	159 2/8	84	HP/RIFLE	MYERS	GARY	675
	11	158 6/8	73	HP/RIFLE	TITTLE	GARY	719
	12	156 5/8	93	HP/RIFLE	McCALLISTER	TOM	911
	13	156 1/8	91	HP/RIFLE	STANLEY	BOB D.	967
	14	155 4/8	88	HP/RIFLE	KAVANAUGH	MATT	1040
	15	155 2/8	91	HP/RIFLE	SWINDLER	DARREN	1068
	16	153 4/8	66	HP/RIFLE	DEWEESE	CECIL	1287
	17	152 1/8	92	HP/RIFLE	CREWS	BILL	1493
	18	151 4/8	83	HP/RIFLE	SPARKS	RAYMOND W.	1613
	19	150 0/8	96	HP/RIFLE	RUPERT	SCOTT	1897
	20	141 5/8	96	HP/RIFLE	JONES	GAYLEN D.	2772
CALLAWAY	1	190 0/8	95	HP/RIFLE	BARKS	BEN	5
	2	174 1/8	68	HP/RIFLE	LAFON	JAC	83
	3	172 0/8	90	PICK-UP	QUICK	LARRY	112
	4	168 2/8	63	HP/RIFLE	BENSON	RUSSELL	190

MISSOURI SHOW-ME BIG BUCKS CLUB RECORDS OF WHITETAIL DEER BY COUNTY, TYPICAL

COUNTY	COUNTY RANK	SCORE	YEAR TAKEN	WEAPON	HUNTER	FIRST NAME	STATE RANK
CALLAWAY	5	166 0/8	88	HP/RIFLE	WURM	TIM	262
	6	164 7/8	86	HP/RIFLE	QUICK	BOB	303
	7	164 6/8	93	HP/RIFLE	JUNGERMANN	GARY	307
	8	164 2/8	83	HP/RIFLE	UNDERWOOD	LARRY	332
	9	164 1/8	92	HP/RIFLE	RAILTON, JR.	EDGAR J.	345
	10	163 7/8	88	HP/RIFLE	PRETTYMAN	MARK	356
	11	162 2/8	82	HP/RIFLE	THOMAS	RANDY	451
	12	161 2/8	74	HP/RIFLE	UNDERWOOD	LARRY	512
	13	160 7/8	91	HP/RIFLE	ATTERBERRY	TIM	535
	14	160 1/8	85	HP/RIFLE	BACKER, SR.	FORREST	599
	15	159 5/8	72	HP/RIFLE	WEKENBORG	THOMAS L.	641
	16	159 4/8	88	HP/RIFLE	MEINHARDT	SHAWN	654
	17	158 7/8	81	BOW	NEAL	LARRY	712
	18	158 3/8	81	HP/RIFLE	BURRE	KELLY	753
	19	158 2/8	89	HP/RIFLE	SUTTON	DOYLE	763
	19	158 2/8	93	HP/RIFLE	BROWNE	CHRIS	763
	21	158 0/8	70	HP/RIFLE	WYMAN	DANNY	788
	22	157 5/8	94	HP/RIFLE	WALLACE	JAMES O.	821
	23	157 2/8	78	HP/RIFLE	BODE	GERALD	853
	24	157 0/8	89	HP/RIFLE	REVELLE	JOEL	875
	25	156 3/8	83	HP/RIFLE	BURRE	KELLY	940
	25	156 3/8	86	HP/RIFLE	McGRATH	MARK	940
	27	156 2/8	58	HP/RIFLE	WINDSOR	O.V.	953
	27	156 2/8	87	HP/RIFLE	BECKERMAN	SCOTT	953
	29	156 1/8	76	HP/RIFLE	FERGUSON	JAMES F.	967
	30	155 7/8	85	HP/RIFLE	SCHINDLER	DON	994
	31	155 6/8	89	HP/RIFLE	GIBONEY	JEFF	1004
	31	155 6/8	91	HP/RIFLE	NEELY	STANLEY B.	1004
	33	155 5/8	78	HP/RIFLE	BUSKEN	LEONARD	1023
	34	155 4/8	95	HP/RIFLE	HARTSOCK	ALAN L.	1040
	34	155 4/8	96	HP/RIFLE	WEBB	JAMES	1040
	36	155 0/8	92	HP/RIFLE	CLARK	LARRY J.	1102
	37	154 6/8	87	HP/RIFLE	CONNER	ALLEN	1130
	38	154 5/8	91	HP/RIFLE	TRACY	JIM	1146
	39	154 1/8	91	HP/RIFLE	MORRIS	ROBBY	1207
	40	154 0/8	72	HP/RIFLE	WILDEISEN	ORVILLE	1219
	41	153 6/8	73	HP/RIFLE	BUSKEN	LEONARD	1256
	42	153 4/8	80	BOW	GIBONEY	MARVIN	1287
	43	152 7/8	77	HP/RIFLE	DOERHOFF	GREGORY	1370
	43	152 7/8	85	HP/RIFLE	DANUSER	JERRY	1370
	45	152 5/8	57	HP/RIFLE	WINDSOR	O.V.	1399
	46	152 4/8	84	HP/RIFLE	ORSO	TOM	1423
	46	152 4/8	84	HP/RIFLE	SEBASTIAN	BRIAN	1423
	48	152 1/8	92	HP/RIFLE	WEKENBORG	TOM	1493
	49	151 7/8	80	PICK-UP	CRANE	DENNIS	1550
	50	151 6/8	78	HP/RIFLE	SPATAFORA	JOE	1566
	51	151 5/8	76	HP/RIFLE	CUNO	LARRY	1586
	51	151 5/8	77	HP/RIFLE	LONG	STEVEN	1586
	53	151 2/8	92	BOW	VARNADORE	TRACY	1656
	54	151 0/8	93	HP/RIFLE	WILSON	MONICA	1715
	55	150 7/8	94	HP/RIFLE	HAAS	MARK	1734
	56	150 5/8	65	HP/RIFLE	WHANGER	ROY	1789
	56	150 5/8	84	HP/RIFLE	BARTON	OVA	1789
	56	150 5/8	90	HP/RIFLE	McVEIGH	DAVID	1789
	59	150 3/8	94	BOW	COGORNO	GENE	1834
	59	150 3/8	96	HP/RIFLE	ROESNER	GREG	1834
	61	150 0/8	88	HP/RIFLE	DAWSON	DRAKE Q.	1897
	62	148 2/8	88	HP/RIFLE	MASCHGER	JERRY	2071
	62	148 2/8	96	HP/RIFLE	JORDAN	SCOTT	2071

MISSOURI SHOW-ME BIG BUCKS CLUB RECORDS OF WHITETAIL DEER BY COUNTY, TYPICAL

COUNTY	COUNTY RANK	SCORE	YEAR TAKEN	WEAPON	HUNTER	FIRST NAME	STATE RANK
CALLAWAY	64	147 5/8	83	PICK-UP	BEVL	DALE	2138
	65	147 1/8	90	HP/RIFLE	UNDERWOOD	LARRY	2183
	66	147 0/8	91	BOW	BARKS	BEN	2195
	67	146 6/8	90	PICK-UP	SPURGEON	DAVID D.	2225
	68	145 0/8	92	PICK-UP	UNDERWOOD	LARRY	2391
	69	144 2/8	93	HP/RIFLE	NARZINSKI	MATTHEW L.	2483
	70	141 7/8	91	HP/RIFLE	UNDERWOOD	LARRY	2747
CAMDEN	1	170 3/8	80	HP/RIFLE	GREEN III	TREY	144
	2	166 2/8	79	HP/RIFLE	WOLFE	NELLIE JANE	255
	3	164 5/8	89	PICK-UP	CAPPS	LESTER	313
	4	162 6/8	91	HP/RIFLE	SCHMITT	BOB	411
	5	161 4/8	86	HP/RIFLE	GOLDSBERRY	DAVID	493
	6	160 5/8	88	HP/RIFLE	STENSON	LEROY	553
	7	160 4/8	81	HP/RIFLE	DORF	MICHAEL P.	560
	8	160 2/8	86	HP/RIFLE	BEASLEY	WADE	584
	9	160 0/8	80	HP/RIFLE	FREDERICK	GARY	605
	9	160 0/8	82	HP/RIFLE	WILLIAMS	JACK	605
	11	157 4/8	89	HP/RIFLE	HEISLEN	DALE	833
	12	156 1/8	88	HP/RIFLE	BRAILE	ED	967
	13	156 0/8	87	HP/RIFLE	YAEGER	WILLIAM	981
	14	154 1/8	93	HP/RIFLE	MURPHY	JACK	1207
	15	152 6/8	82	HP/RIFLE	WORLEY	JOHN	1385
	16	152 3/8	67	HP/RIFLE	RAMSEY	JAMES E.	1453
	17	151 3/8	84	HP/RIFLE	SHRAUGER, JR.	RUSSELL	1637
	18	150 7/8	71	HP/RIFLE	ESTHER	W.S.	1734
	19	150 3/8	73	HP/RIFLE	THOMAS	LARRY D.	1834
	19	150 3/8	91	HP/RIFLE	McDANIEL	BRUCE	1834
	21	150 0/8	58	HP/RIFLE	SMENTKOWSKI	A.J.	1897
	22	149 7/8	86	HP/RIFLE	KAISER	JOHN	1915
	23	149 6/8	82	HP/RIFLE	SHARP	CLIFFORD	1926
	24	149 0/8	62	HP/RIFLE	WOODALL	LESLIE LEE	1998
	24	149 0/8	74	HP/RIFLE	CAMPBELL, JR.	KEN L.	1998
	26	148 6/8	54	HP/RIFLE	GREEN	ARNOLD	2024
	27	148 2/8	79	HP/RIFLE	PRYOR	TERRY	2071
	28	147 6/8	86	HP/RIFLE	WHITMORE	BILLY	2126
	28	147 6/8	88	HP/RIFLE	JENNINGS	LENN	2126
	30	147 5/8	72	HP/RIFLE	WESTFALL	DAN	2138
	31	147 0/8	88	HP/RIFLE	ARNONE	GUY	2195
	32	146 4/8	92	HP/RIFLE	ABBOTT	CEANN	2242
	33	146 2/8	95	HP/RIFLE	ACKERSON	ART	2266
	33	146 2/8	95	HP/RIFLE	STEWARD	ROBERT L.	2266
	35	145 6/8	71	HP/RIFLE	FRANKS	CHARLES	2311
	35	145 6/8	91	HP/RIFLE	SCHAFFNER	BRYAN C.	2311
	37	145 3/8	93	HP/RIFLE	FRY	EDDIE	2350
	38	145 2/8	82	HP/RIFLE	HANKS	GLEN	2361
	39	144 5/8	89	HP/RIFLE	CARROLL	KENNY	2442
	39	144 5/8	90	HP/RIFLE	MOORE	DENNIS	2442
	41	144 4/8	88	HP/RIFLE	PROPST	KEVIN	2459
	42	143 7/8	89	BOW	CARTWRIGHT	JOHN	2533
	43	142 6/8	79	HP/RIFLE	EDWARDS	JOE DAVID	2647
	44	142 5/8	76	HP/RIFLE	BLANKENSHIP	LILBURN F.	2660
	45	142 4/8	88	HP/RIFLE	STEELE	ROBERT C.	2678
	46	142 3/8	69	HP/RIFLE	JOHNSON	RON	2691
	47	141 7/8	85	BOW	WEST	STEVE	2747
	48	141 1/8	66	HP/RIFLE	GROVES	DAVID	2844
	48	141 1/8	87	HP/RIFLE	PATTON	TOMMY	2844
	50	140 0/8	90	HP/RIFLE	BROWN	PAUL	2990
	50	140 0/8	96	HP/RIFLE	HEISLEN	CORY	2990
CAPE GIRARDEAU	1	165 3/8	87	HP/RIFLE	BURGFELD	LAWSON	288

MISSOURI SHOW-ME BIG BUCKS CLUB RECORDS OF WHITETAIL DEER BY COUNTY, TYPICAL

COUNTY	COUNTY RANK	SCORE	YEAR TAKEN	WEAPON	HUNTER	FIRST NAME	STATE RANK
CAPE GIRARDEAU	2	161 2/8	84	HP/RIFLE	BEUSSICK	PHILIP J.	512
	3	159 3/8	88	HP/RIFLE	HINDMAN	KIM	665
	4	158 4/8	66	HP/RIFLE	JONES	EUGENE	739
	5	157 7/8	59	HP/RIFLE	BOREN	ROLAND	806
	6	155 7/8	91	HP/RIFLE	LIVINGSTON	GARRETT	994
	7	155 5/8	94	HP/RIFLE	FARROW	MIKE	1023
	8	155 1/8	91	HP/RIFLE	AINSWORTH	JOE	1091
	9	154 6/8	83	HP/RIFLE	SEIBEL	HARRY H.	1130
	9	154 6/8	89	HP/RIFLE	FEE	BRUCE A.	1130
	11	153 1/8	85	HP/RIFLE	LOWES	PAUL	1344
	12	152 7/8	91	HP/RIFLE	VINES	BOB	1370
	13	152 6/8	89	HP/RIFLE	ABERNATHY	GERELD	1385
	14	152 4/8	92	PICK-UP	ALLEN	JEREL	1423
	15	152 3/8	91	HP/RIFLE	RUCH	LARRY F.	1453
	16	152 0/8	92	HP/RIFLE	BROWN	CHARLES	1519
	17	148 6/8	85	HP/RIFLE	LANDS	DALLAS K.	2024
	18	148 1/8	81	HP/RIFLE	BROWN	ALBERT	2088
	19	147 2/8	87	HP/RIFLE	SMITH	TIM B.	2167
	20	147 0/8	91	HP/RIFLE	WALLIS	WILLIAM E.	2195
	21	146 1/8	65	HP/RIFLE	RIDINGS	CHARLES	2281
	22	146 0/8	89	HP/RIFLE	WILKENS	JANET	2290
	23	145 5/8	95	BOW	HOBBS	DARRELL W.	2324
	24	145 3/8	93	HP/RIFLE	KLINGEMAN	PHIL	2350
	25	144 5/8	67	HP/RIFLE	DRAKE	PAUL	2442
	25	144 5/8	96	HP/RIFLE	FORD	MICHAEL	2442
	27	144 2/8	89	HP/RIFLE	SAWYER	DEAN	2483
	28	143 7/8	76	HP/RIFLE	ZIEGLER	JEROME	2533
	29	143 5/8	68	HP/RIFLE	SCHATTAUER	LLOYD	2564
	30	142 5/8	87	PICK-UP	WIBBENMEYER	LES	2660
	31	141 4/8	87	HP/RIFLE	SLINKARD	THOMAS E.	2787
	32	141 1/8	78	HP/RIFLE	ZIEGLER	JEROME	2844
	33	141 0/8	87	HP/RIFLE	SLINKARD	RICHARD	2863
	34	140 6/8	95	BOW	REED	ROBERT	2895
	35	140 5/8	90	HP/RIFLE	NOLAN	LAURA J.	2908
	36	140 0/8	89	HP/RIFLE	GRASS	NORMAN	2990
CARROLL	1	166 5/8	73	HP/RIFLE	HUNDLEY	RONNIE	238
	2	164 5/8	84	HP/RIFLE	GOEDEKE	RANDY	313
	3	163 7/8	72	HP/RIFLE	MANSFIELD	HAROLD G.	356
	4	163 0/8	88	HP/RIFLE	WEBB	JARED E.	393
	5	161 7/8	88	HP/RIFLE	MOORE	RAYMOND	467
	6	161 2/8	90	HP/RIFLE	DAVIES	DANNY	512
	7	160 3/8	93	HP/RIFLE	DREW	GARY C.	574
	8	159 2/8	93	BOW	PARKER	JAMES	675
	9	158 6/8	90	HP/RIFLE	AVERSMAN	DONALD	719
	10	155 7/8	95	HP/RIFLE	GREGG	RUSSELL	994
	11	155 4/8	82	HP/RIFLE	RODENBURG	CHARLES	1040
	12	154 5/8	91	HP/RIFLE	PATTERSON	AVA	1146
	13	154 0/8	83	HP/RIFLE	ADKISON	DALE	1219
	14	153 7/8	88	HP/RIFLE	BUCKNER II	JOHN	1238
	15	153 3/8	95	HP/RIFLE	GUGLIELEMENCCI	CRAIG	1310
	16	152 4/8	90	HP/RIFLE	OWEN	HEATH THOMAS	1423
	17	152 3/8	84	HP/RIFLE	KIRKHOLM	MARK	1453
	18	151 7/8	82	HP/RIFLE	SHERWOOD	WILLIAM G.	1550
	19	151 4/8	84	HP/RIFLE	MORITZ	LEE	1613
	20	150 7/8	77	HP/RIFLE	MOORE	DEARL	1734
	21	150 6/8	87	HP/RIFLE	BARTLETT, JR.	ROY E.	1756
	22	149 1/8	83	PICK-UP	FLOYD	CHARLIE	1988
	23	145 4/8	96	HP/RIFLE	WILCOX	MARK	2331
CARTER	1	186 0/8	63	HP/RIFLE	GOGGIN	RICHARD N.	17

MISSOURI SHOW-ME BIG BUCKS CLUB RECORDS OF WHITETAIL DEER BY COUNTY, TYPICAL

COUNTY	COUNTY RANK	SCORE	YEAR TAKEN	WEAPON	HUNTER	FIRST NAME	STATE RANK
CARTER	2	168 5/8	79	HP/RIFLE	LEACH	LEWIN	179
	3	164 2/8	82	HP/RIFLE	GOLDSCHMIDT	A.L.	332
	4	158 3/8	91	PICK-UP	LINDSEY	SCOTT	753
	5	157 3/8	77	HP/RIFLE	REDMAN	JOHN	848
	6	151 5/8	68	HP/RIFLE	SEYMOUR	MICHAEL J.	1586
	7	151 0/8	82	HP/RIFLE	BUTLER	HAROLD	1715
	8	149 7/8	96	HP/RIFLE	SCHAFER	KELLY	1915
	9	149 5/8	94	BOW	WALKER	PHILLIP DON	1936
	10	148 7/8	66	HP/RIFLE	JUERGENS	ROY E.	2012
	11	146 2/8	37	HP/RIFLE	LEBARON	FRANK	2266
	12	145 0/8	94	HP/RIFLE	PAYNE	BERT	2391
	12	145 0/8	95	HP/RIFLE	BARNETT	SAM	2391
	14	143 7/8	92	HP/RIFLE	POGUE	RANDY	2533
	15	142 7/8	92	HP/RIFLE	WILKINS	BILL	2641
	16	142 5/8	71	HP/RIFLE	BARDWELL	VINCE	2660
	17	141 2/8	82	HP/RIFLE	SONTHEIMER	MICHAEL C.	2828
	17	141 2/8	83	HP/RIFLE	LAYTON	JEFF	2828
	17	141 2/8	92	BOW	BENEDICK	BOB	2828
	20	140 4/8	91	HP/RIFLE	YANCEY	JAMES	2925
	21	140 2/8	92	HP/RIFLE	BOTKIN	DALE	2952
CASS	1	181 5/8	91	HP/RIFLE	WATSON	WILLIAM MARTI	30
	2	162 7/8	93	HP/RIFLE	GOOSEY	RICK W.	406
	3	160 3/8	96	HP/RIFLE	ATKINSON	MARVIN	574
	4	160 2/8	94	HP/RIFLE	GARRETT	DONNY	584
	5	159 6/8	87	HP/RIFLE	RUPARD	ROGER E.	628
	6	157 5/8	93	HP/RIFLE	McCALL	WILLIAM E.	821
	7	154 5/8	89	HP/RIFLE	RAYMOND	DAVID	1146
	8	152 3/8	86	HP/RIFLE	HOCKER	GORDON	1453
	9	152 2/8	84	HP/RIFLE	HOOK	GEORGE E.	1469
	10	150 6/8	90	HP/RIFLE	HEAPER	C.W.	1756
	11	150 2/8	88	HP/RIFLE	VIAR	FRED W.	1853
	12	150 0/8	95	HP/RIFLE	AYLER	JERRY	1897
	13	149 4/8	93	HP/RIFLE	THOMAS	DAVID	1936
	14	149 2/8	88	HP/RIFLE	HELPHREY	ROGER	1973
	15	149 0/8	89	HP/RIFLE	BROOKS	WILLIAM O.	1998
	16	147 1/8	88	HP/RIFLE	HAMBLIN	RICHARD	2183
	17	146 5/8	94	BOW	GARDNER	JOHN S.	2235
	18	143 0/8	86	HP/RIFLE	WHITLOCK	HARRY	2626
	19	141 6/8	88	HP/RIFLE	BEARD	ED	2756
	19	141 6/8	96	HP/RIFLE	DEMPSEY	STEVE	2756
	21	141 4/8	90	HP/RIFLE	MOORE	SHERRI	2787
CEDAR	1	157 0/8	71	HP/RIFLE	HARVEY	GENE	875
	2	155 1/8	70	HP/RIFLE	UNDERWOOD	WESLEY	1091
	3	151 0/8	74	HP/RIFLE	MONTGOMERY	FARREL	1715
	4	149 0/8	94	HP/RIFLE	LANE	MIKE	1998
	5	147 6/8	85	HP/RIFLE	RUTLEDGE	TOM	2126
	6	147 0/8	75	HP/RIFLE	BURNS	ROBBIN	2195
	6	147 0/8	86	BOW	BARNARD	DAVID.	2195
	8	146 4/8	80	HP/RIFLE	EASON	ROGER	2242
	9	145 0/8	92	HP/RIFLE	LUCIUS	KENNETH	2391
	10	144 7/8	59	HP/RIFLE	MOON	ORAN B.	2412
	11	144 6/8	93	HP/RIFLE	BRAKE	RALPH	2425
	12	142 2/8	80	HP/RIFLE	RUMMEL	JOHN	2701
	13	141 1/8	67	HP/RIFLE	ROY	ROBERT L.	2844
CHARITON	1	183 4/8	68	HP/RIFLE	LENTZ	MARVIN	23
	2	181 5/8	91	BOW	CALVERT	JERRY	30
	3	180 1/8	82	HP/RIFLE	PEARMAN	RICKY	41
	4	168 4/8	67	HP/RIFLE	MONTAGUE	CHARLES	181
	5	167 3/8	88	HP/RIFLE	SHARP	RONALD	217

COUNTY	COUNTY RANK	SCORE	YEAR TAKEN	WEAPON	HUNTER	FIRST NAME	STATE RANK
CHARITON	6	166 6/8	90	HP/RIFLE	BERTSCH	DAVID C.	235
	7	166 5/8	67	HP/RIFLE	KLINE	LARRY	238
	8	166 2/8	95	HP/RIFLE	MILONSKI	MIKE C.	255
	9	165 6/8	92	M/L	HAGANS	ROBERT	273
	10	165 4/8	79	HP/RIFLE	BURRIS	OWEN	283
	10	165 4/8	94	HP/RIFLE	GIOVANINI	MICHAEL D.	283
	12	164 4/8	70	HP/RIFLE	JOHNSON	WILLIAM	319
	12	164 4/8	88	HP/RIFLE	DUNIVENT	SEAN	319
	14	163 5/8	93	HP/RIFLE	PATTERSON	FRED	368
	15	163 4/8	74	HP/RIFLE	ROBERTS, SR.	VIC	373
	16	163 0/8	89	HP/RIFLE	STILL	EDDIE	393
	17	162 3/8	76	HP/RIFLE	JOHNSON	SAM	439
	18	161 5/8	89	HP/RIFLE	FULLINGTON	DON	486
	19	161 3/8	60	HP/RIFLE	PENNINGTON	MARION	503
	19	161 3/8	80	HP/RIFLE	POPE	GARY	503
	21	160 6/8	93	HP/RIFLE	POPE	ROGER	543
	22	160 3/8	94	HP/RIFLE	GROSVENOR	CHARLES H.	574
	23	159 7/8	86	BOW	ARGETSINGER	BRIAN D.	620
	24	159 2/8	90	HP/RIFLE	WRIGHT	GARY	675
	25	159 1/8	84	HP/RIFLE	WARD	ROBERT	687
	26	158 6/8	96	HP/RIFLE	GOOCH	JERRY	719
	27	158 3/8	96	HP/RIFLE	HALL	REV. RICKY L.	753
	28	158 2/8	59	HP/RIFLE	WOHLGEMUTH	VERNON	763
	29	157 7/8	94	HP/RIFLE	LAUHOFF	GREG	806
	30	157 2/8	95	HP/RIFLE	IGO	SAMUEL DAVID	853
	31	156 6/8	80	HP/RIFLE	MITCHELL	LARRY	900
	32	156 5/8	91	BOW	LEONARD	NATHAN	911
	33	155 6/8	76	HP/RIFLE	MILLER	MARK	1004
	34	155 2/8	84	HP/RIFLE	BATTAGLIA	ANTHONY	1068
	34	155 2/8	89	HP/RIFLE	MONNIG	CHARLIE	1068
	34	155 2/8	92	BOW	GORDON	CHARLES	1068
	37	154 4/8	91	HP/RIFLE	GIBSON	BEN	1164
	38	153 6/8	84	HP/RIFLE	RODGERS	BILL	1256
	38	153 6/8	95	HP/RIFLE	SMITH	PHILLIP	1256
	40	153 5/8	93	BOW	HOWARD	BOB	1273
	41	153 4/8	80	HP/RIFLE	LENTZ	LINDY	1287
	41	153 4/8	86	HP/RIFLE	SMITH	TOM	1287
	43	152 7/8	96	HP/RIFLE	BLACKWELL	ROD	1370
	44	152 5/8	69	HP/RIFLE	BLOSS	GARY	1399
	45	152 4/8	74	HP/RIFLE	BELT	BOB H.	1423
	45	152 4/8	87	HP/RIFLE	SCHMITT	CLARENCE	1423
	45	152 4/8	89	HP/RIFLE	HURT	RANDY	1423
	48	152 2/8	79	HP/RIFLE	LINEBAUGH	DEBORAH	1469
	49	151 3/8	92	PICK-UP	BERTSCH	DAVID C.	1637
	50	151 1/8	90	HP/RIFLE	WOMACK	ROBERT	1690
	51	151 0/8	93	HP/RIFLE	SUNDERLAND	HARDIN	1715
	52	150 6/8	88	HP/RIFLE	ERICKSON	TEDDY	1756
	53	150 4/8	95	HP/RIFLE	ATKINSON	STEVEN S.	1811
	54	150 2/8	71	HP/RIFLE	GORDON	WILLIAM	1853
	54	150 2/8	81	HP/RIFLE	PARKER	RONNIE	1853
	54	150 2/8	91	HP/RIFLE	BLALOCK	BRUCE	1853
	57	150 1/8	90	HP/RIFLE	LINSCOTT	DUANE R.	1879
	57	150 1/8	96	HP/RIFLE	MOREHEAD	DANNY H.	1879
	59	150 0/8	76	HP/RIFLE	RUKAVINA	JOE	1897
	60	148 5/8	95	HP/RIFLE	WOMACK	MIKE	2035
	61	145 0/8	94	HP/RIFLE	PALMER	TERRY	2391
	62	144 5/8	96	HP/RIFLE	ODOWD	BRADLEY	2442
	63	144 2/8	96	HP/RIFLE	BROKKS	SCOTT	2483
	64	140 0/8	89	HP/RIFLE	RODGERS	BILL	2990

COUNTY	COUNTY RANK	SCORE	YEAR TAKEN	WEAPON	HUNTER	FIRST NAME	STATE RANK
CHRISTIAN	1	171 0/8	83	HP/RIFLE	HERNDON	MELBA	129
	2	160 6/8	69	HP/RIFLE	SHIPMAN	FARRIS	543
	3	151 6/8	70	HP/RIFLE	HILTON	GARY	1566
	4	148 1/8	68	HP/RIFLE	STAFFORD	DALE	2088
	5	146 6/8	79	HP/RIFLE	LINDSEY	DAVID L.	2225
	6	145 6/8	78	HP/RIFLE	ROUSSELL	PHILLIP	2311
	7	141 1/8	87	HP/RIFLE	KUENZ	STEVE	2844
CLARK	1	199 4/8	69	HP/RIFLE	BRUNK	JEFFREY	2
	2	178 0/8	66	HP/RIFLE	COURTNEY	ALLEN L.	50
	3	177 6/8	85	HP/RIFLE	NOBLE	BILLIE	53
	4	177 1/8	93	HP/RIFLE	BANASZEK	JOHN	55
	5	174 3/8	65	HP/RIFLE	PRUETT	DICK	78
	6	169 2/8	89	HP/RIFLE	BUTLER	KENNY	163
	7	167 5/8	80	HP/RIFLE	BINGHAM	ED	205
	8	167 1/8	87	PICK-UP	MOHR	CHAD	225
	9	166 7/8	95	HP/RIFLE	THOMSON	MARY F.	230
	10	164 4/8	86	HP/RIFLE	REDDING	JERRY	319
	11	164 3/8	89	HP/RIFLE	BERHORST	ALAN	328
	12	160 1/8	65	HP/RIFLE	ACKLIE	NEAL	599
	13	159 5/8	91	HP/RIFLE	WILKINSON, JR.	PHIL E.	641
	14	159 3/8	95	HP/RIFLE	STURM	ROCKY	665
	15	158 7/8	80	HP/RIFLE	COCHENOUR	GERALD	712
	16	158 0/8	76	HP/RIFLE	SMITH	ALBERT	788
	16	158 0/8	95	HP/RIFLE	MORSE	BILL	788
	18	156 7/8	82	HP/RIFLE	MORTON	DON	893
	19	156 4/8	85	HP/RIFLE	BROOKS	BRIAN	925
	20	156 3/8	73	HP/RIFLE	BRUNK	ARNOLD	940
	21	155 2/8	88	HP/RIFLE	YATES	STEVEN	1068
	22	155 0/8	86	HP/RIFLE	CAMPBELL	JOHN	1102
	23	153 3/8	92	HP/RIFLE	ALDERTON	RRIAN	1310
	24	152 3/8	76	HP/RIFLE	STEWART	BILL F.	1453
	25	152 2/8	85	HP/RIFLE	DUNNING	MIKE	1469
	26	152 1/8	70	HP/RIFLE	COURTNEY	ALLEN L.	1493
	27	151 2/8	87	HP/RIFLE	FIFE	FRED R.	1656
	28	149 3/8	95	HP/RIFLE	ELFRINK	DAVID E.	1959
	29	146 5/8	86	BOW	COURTNEY	ALLEN L.	2235
CLAY	1	173 0/8	96	BOW	BRESHEARS	NEAL B.	100
	2	157 2/8	87	HP/RIFLE	RUKAVINA	BILLY J.	853
	3	156 3/8	75	HP/RIFLE	CLEVENGER	KEN	940
	4	152 3/8	88	HP/RIFLE	BALDWIN	TRACY	1453
	5	148 5/8	91	BOW	DUTTON	DONALD	2035
CLINTON	1	187 6/8	94	HP/RIFLE	LOONEY	SCOTT E.	7
	2	163 6/8	85	HP/RIFLE	MICK	DENNIS	363
	3	162 6/8	88	HP/RIFLE	NORTON	DAVID	411
	4	159 6/8	89	HP/RIFLE	CAIN	MICHAEL	628
	5	157 1/8	80	HP/RIFLE	NORTON	DAVID	864
	6	156 6/8	88	HP/RIFLE	GRIFFIN	BEN	900
	7	156 5/8	70	HP/RIFLE	KISKY	DON	911
	8	154 6/8	96	HP/RIFLE	FEIGHERT	LUKE	1130
	9	154 0/8	82	HP/RIFLE	BURNETT	SHAWN	1219
	10	153 4/8	74	HP/RIFLE	MILLER	RONNIE	1287
	11	152 1/8	87	HP/RIFLE	WATERS	CHARLES	1493
	12	150 3/8	91	HP/RIFLE	REYNOLDS	MELVIN	1834
	13	150 2/8	91	HP/RIFLE	BOSLEY	DAVID	1853
	14	150 2/8	93	HP/RIFLE	VOGT	DOUG	1853
COLE	1	175 1/8	95	HP/RIFLE	BRUEMMER	BRIAN	67
	2	164 3/8	87	HP/RIFLE	LEPPER	CURTIS A.	328
	3	163 7/8	84	HP/RIFLE	LISTER	RICK	356
	4	162 1/8	96	BOW	RACKERS	CARL	455

COUNTY	COUNTY RANK	SCORE	YEAR TAKEN	WEAPON	HUNTER	FIRST NAME	STATE RANK
COLE	5	158 4/8	87	HP/RIFLE	SCHEPERLE	RAY	739
	6	158 2/8	87	HP/RIFLE	CROCKER	DENNY	763
	7	156 7/8	86	HP/RIFLE	SWANIGAN	GENE	893
	8	153 4/8	77	HP/RIFLE	KLIETHENMES	LEON	1287
	9	152 6/8	87	HP/RIFLE	OUSLEY	HAROLD	1385
	10	149 2/8	87	HP/RIFLE	ADRIAN	JAMES	1973
	11	147 6/8	87	HP/RIFLE	HUFF	ROBERT	2126
	12	147 4/8	94	BOW	BOESSEN	ANTHONY N.	2148
	13	147 3/8	93	HP/RIFLE	WHEELER	STEVE	2155
	14	146 5/8	84	BOW	STUCKEY	NORMAN	2235
	15	146 3/8	89	HP/RIFLE	STROESSNER	BILL	2252
	16	145 0/8	77	HP/RIFLE	JEAGER	JOHN	2391
	17	144 6/8	79	HP/RIFLE	MELLER	KEITH	2425
	18	142 6/8	84	HP/RIFLE	SCHNEIDER	GARY	2647
	19	141 3/8	88	HP/RIFLE	DISTLER	DON	2812
	20	141 2/8	87	HP/RIFLE	BINKLEY	BILL	2828
	21	140 7/8	78	HP/RIFLE	HEMMEL	CHARLES	2877
	22	140 2/8	88	HP/RIFLE	OTT	PAUL G.	2952
	23	140 0/8	77	HP/RIFLE	WIEBERG	HENRY	2990
	23	140 0/8	91	HP/RIFLE	PLANK	JIM	2990
COOPER	1	187 1/8	74	HP/RIFLE	DITTO	JOE	10
	2	174 0/8	88	HP/RIFLE	SCHLUP	MIKE	84
	3	172 4/8	60	HP/RIFLE	KUHN	DALE	105
	4	170 3/8	90	HP/RIFLE	BINNIE	JIM	144
	5	168 6/8	78	HP/RIFLE	BURNETT	GUY	174
	6	167 2/8	83	HP/RIFLE	ROBERTSON	DAN	221
	7	164 4/8	92	HP/RIFLE	PAINTER	BOB	319
	8	162 4/8	85	HP/RIFLE	THURMAN	DENNIS	431
	9	161 3/8	80	HP/RIFLE	BRENGARTH	FRANCIS	503
	10	160 4/8	90	HP/RIFLE	WOOD	TOM	560
	11	160 0/8	84	BOW	SMITH	NANCY	605
	12	159 5/8	62	HP/RIFLE	JEWETT	GILL	641
	13	159 4/8	82	HP/RIFLE	JOBE	CARL	654
	14	159 3/8	96	HP/RIFLE	VOSS	ALLEN A.	665
	15	158 0/8	90	HP/RIFLE	KOLLER	SCOTT	788
	16	157 0/8	84	HP/RIFLE	PENNINGTON	LEROY	875
	17	156 6/8	85	PICK-UP	PRICE	JEFF	900
	18	156 5/8	88	HP/RIFLE	STRECK	CHRIS	911
	19	156 1/8	90	HP/RIFLE	COOK	MIKE	967
	20	154 5/8	95	HP/RIFLE	SPENCE	TERRY	1146
	21	154 2/8	93	HP/RIFLE	WOOD	TOM	1186
	22	153 6/8	83	HP/RIFLE	MADDOX	RAYMOND	1256
	23	153 2/8	94	HP/RIFLE	KNEDGEN	DARRELL J.	1327
	24	152 1/8	88	HP/RIFLE	ROOT	RODGER	1493
	25	151 3/8	78	HP/RIFLE	RENTSCHLER	DAVID	1637
	25	151 3/8	88	HP/RIFLE	JEWETT	JEFF	1637
	25	151 3/8	91	HP/RIFLE	MEYER	RICK E.	1637
	28	151 2/8	90	HP/RIFLE	HOFSTETTER	ROSS	1656
	29	151 1/8	93	HP/RIFLE	MARTIN	STEVE W.	1690
	30	151 0/8	83	HP/RIFLE	HECKMAN	HAROLD	1715
	31	150 3/8	82	HP/RIFLE	POTTER	RANDY	1834
	32	150 1/8	91	HP/RIFLE	GREER	JACK	1879
	33	149 1/8	89	HP/RIFLE	PEASE	TOM	1988
	33	149 1/8	93	HP/RIFLE	MILLER	STEVEN	1988
	35	148 5/8	92	HP/RIFLE	FERGUSON	ALAN	2035
	36	148 4/8	95	HP/RIFLE	DUVALL	TWILLA D.	2048
	37	148 0/8	73	HP/RIFLE	SCHUPP	BILL	2101
	38	146 5/8	73	HP/RIFLE	WALTHER	ERNIE	2235
	39	146 4/8	89	HP/RIFLE	FRIEDRICH	JERRY	2242

COUNTY	COUNTY RANK	SCORE	YEAR TAKEN	WEAPON	HUNTER	FIRST NAME	STATE RANK
COOPER	39	146 4/8	93	HP/RIFLE	AGGELER	LYLE	2242
	41	146 2/8	80	HP/RIFLE	MEYER	ALVIN J.	2266
	42	146 0/8	95	HP/RIFLE	GRAPES	MIKE	2290
	43	145 4/8	77	HP/RIFLE	SIECKMANN	TERRY	2331
	44	145 2/8	82	HP/RIFLE	REAGAN	DARRIN	2361
	44	145 2/8	90	HP/RIFLE	THIESSEN	RONDA	2361
	46	144 5/8	83	HP/RIFLE	QUINT	JOHN	2442
	47	144 4/8	82	HP/RIFLE	RILEY	CHRIS WAYNE	2459
	48	144 1/8	93	PICK-UP	WESSING	JEFF	2498
	49	143 7/8	76	HP/RIFLE	FRIEDRICH	ALFRED	2533
	50	143 5/8	82	HP/RIFLE	FARRIS	DAN	2564
	51	143 1/8	87	HP/RIFLE	GREER	JACK	2615
	52	142 5/8	82	HP/RIFLE	PFEIFFER	LOGAN	2660
	53	142 3/8	68	HP/RIFLE	RINACKE	ERV	2691
	54	142 1/8	85	PICK-UP	PRICE	JEFF	2709
	55	142 0/8	77	HP/RIFLE	HURST	ROBBIE	2725
	55	142 0/8	93	PICK-UP	CLEVENGER	MICHAEL	2725
	55	142 0/8	95	PICK-UP	WESSING	JEFF	2725
	58	141 5/8	82	HP/RIFLE	REAMS	LARRY	2772
	59	141 2/8	78	HP/RIFLE	JOHNSTON	RAY	2828
	60	141 1/8	72	HP/RIFLE	FISHER	CLAUDE	2844
	60	141 1/8	89	BOW	THURMAN	TROY	2844
	62	141 0/8	95	HP/RIFLE	LOESING	MARK	2863
	63	140 7/8	83	HP/RIFLE	JOBE	BRIAN	2877
	64	140 3/8	75	HP/RIFLE	STEGNER	JOHN	2935
	64	140 3/8	83	HP/RIFLE	IMHOFF	MIKE	2935
	64	140 3/8	87	HP/RIFLE	HUMFELD	BILL	2935
	67	140 2/8	92	HP/RIFLE	VOSS	ALLEN A.	2952
	68	140 1/8	90	HP/RIFLE	YOUNG	KENNY	2978
CRAWFORD	1	171 5/8	82	HP/RIFLE	GLASER	CHRIS	118
	2	168 3/8	93	PICK-UP	TURNBOUGH	GLENWOOD	184
	3	164 2/8	87	HP/RIFLE	LARUE	PHIL	332
	4	162 4/8	71	HP/RIFLE	MOUTRAY	TERRY	431
	5	160 6/8	82	HP/RIFLE	VALLEY	GEORGE	543
	6	160 0/8	77	HP/RIFLE	HUBLER	JOE	605
	7	159 0/8	86	HP/RIFLE	WILMESHERR	STANLEY	695
	8	157 1/8	92	HP/RIFLE	MARNATI	FATHER (LOUIS)	864
	9	156 7/8	92	HP/RIFLE	GILLESPIE	RANDY	893
	10	155 3/8	82	HP/RIFLE	HEMSATH	DON	1059
	11	154 5/8	87	HP/RIFLE	PAYNE	NORMAN	1146
	12	154 2/8	87	PICK-UP	OGLE	STEVE	1186
	13	153 2/8	55	HP/RIFLE	HELLE	FRANK E.	1327
	14	152 4/8	53	HP/RIFLE	LEA	WILLIAM L.	1423
	15	152 4/8	64	HP/RIFLE	MABE, JR.	RICHARD	1423
	16	151 4/8	63	HP/RIFLE	SHOEMAKE	BOB	1613
	16	151 4/8	86	HP/RIFLE	KELLER	RANDY	1613
	16	151 4/8	87	HP/RIFLE	ROBERTSON	VERNON	1613
	19	151 2/8	91	HP/RIFLE	LEM	TOM	1656
	20	150 7/8	95	HP/RIFLE	COLE	BRITT L.	1734
	21	150 6/8	89	HP/RIFLE	LOGAN	CLAY	1756
	22	150 3/8	81	HP/RIFLE	VAUGHN	LAURA	1834
	23	148 6/8	95	HP/RIFLE	ORTON	JAMES	2024
	24	148 5/8	95	HP/RIFLE	PAYNE	MARK	2035
	25	148 3/8	70	HP/RIFLE	McMILLEN	ROBERT	2060
	26	148 0/8	49	HP/RIFLE	FARRIS	HAROLD	2101
	26	148 0/8	60	HP/RIFLE	PETERSON	PAUL F.	2101
	28	147 5/8	82	HP/RIFLE	LOGAN	ROBERT R.	2138
	29	147 4/8	89	HP/RIFLE	FARRIS	RICK	2148
	30	147 2/8	86	HP/RIFLE	HARTLEY	DR. DENNIS	2167

COUNTY	COUNTY RANK	SCORE	YEAR TAKEN	WEAPON	HUNTER	FIRST NAME	STATE RANK
CRAWFORD	30	147 2/8	86	HP/RIFLE	DOTSON	DANIEL	2167
	30	147 2/8	88	HP/RIFLE	PIAZZA	LARRY	2167
	33	147 0/8	69	HP/RIFLE	LAFFERTY	JOHN	2195
	34	146 7/8	55	HP/RIFLE	McCOY	JOHN RILEY	2214
	35	146 2/8	93	HP/RIFLE	BASS	STEPHEN	2266
	36	145 3/8	95	BOW	ISOM	BRIAN	2350
	37	145 2/8	80	PICK-UP	WEBER	MIKE	2361
	38	145 0/8	83	HP/RIFLE	HEDRICK	DAVID	2391
	39	145 0/8	92	HP/RIFLE	MARTIN	A.B.	2391
	40	144 7/8	50	HP/RIFLE	CROSS	GEORGE	2412
	41	144 3/8	84	HP/RIFLE	SCOTT	LONNIE	2466
	42	144 0/8	80	PICK-UP	SAPPINGTON	COLIN	2514
	43	143 7/8	86	HP/RIFLE	SMITH	FRANCIS L.	2533
	44	142 6/8	87	HP/RIFLE	MOUTRAY	TERRY	2647
	45	142 1/8	82	HP/RIFLE	IVES	DAVE	2709
	46	141 4/8	45	HP/RIFLE	LEA	WILLIAM L.	2787
	47	141 2/8	90	HP/RIFLE	SAMMELMAN	MIKE	2828
	48	141 1/8	82	HP/RIFLE	JEPSEN	PAUL	2844
	49	140 5/8	96	PICK-UP	HOPWOOD, JR.	EUGENE F.	2908
	50	140 4/8	82	HP/RIFLE	SAPPINGTON	COLIN	2925
	51	140 3/8	57	HP/RIFLE	BRUCE	EDMON S.	2935
	51	140 3/8	81	HP/RIFLE	SLONE	MIKE	2935
DADE	1	159 5/8	87	PICK-UP	BARTHOLOMEW	EDWARD	641
	2	158 0/8	85	HP/RIFLE	MYERS	CHARLES A.	788
	3	154 7/8	85	HP/RIFLE	KING	BILL	1118
	4	153 6/8	86	HP/RIFLE	TEFERTILLER	LARRY	1256
	5	149 5/8	87	HP/RIFLE	JOHNSTON	JERRY	1936
	6	148 0/8	82	HP/RIFLE	HEDRICK	RON	2101
	7	144 4/8	73	HP/RIFLE	HEMBREE	JOHN	2459
DALLAS	1	185 5/8	86	HP/RIFLE	HEADINGS	JAMES	18
	2	184 5/8	92	HP/RIFLE	GARNER	LYNN	21
	3	160 6/8	69	HP/RIFLE	EVANS	JERRY	543
	4	153 2/8	82	HP/RIFLE	REED	DAVE	1327
	5	149 5/8	69	HP/RIFLE	ALLEN	JAMES E.	1936
	6	149 5/8	91	HP/RIFLE	LUTTRELL	BOB	1936
	6	149 5/8	91	HP/RIFLE	WILSON	BART	1936
	8	149 4/8	91	HP/RIFLE	WALKER	WADE	1936
	9	146 2/8	87	HP/RIFLE	RAMBO	LYNETTE	2266
	10	145 2/8	95	HP/RIFLE	HOSTETLER	MARION	2361
	11	144 7/8	82	HP/RIFLE	MORGANS	GREG	2412
	12	144 0/8	73	BOW	GILLHAM	MIKE	2514
	13	143 0/8	96	BOW	SWEANEY	JAMES A.	2626
	14	142 2/8	63	HP/RIFLE	REED	DALE	2701
DAVIESS	1	181 0/8	75	HP/RIFLE	OLIPHANT	F.D.	35
	2	174 7/8	86	PICK-UP	HOOVER	BRANDON	70
	3	171 5/8	92	HP/RIFLE	DEWEESE	DAVE	118
	4	166 3/8	88	HP/RIFLE	KLINE	HOMER	249
	5	166 0/8	95	HP/RIFLE	LEWALLEN	GARY	262
	6	165 6/8	73	HP/RIFLE	HELDENBRAND	GERALD	273
	7	164 2/8	89	PICK-UP	MORT	KENNETH	332
	8	160 4/8	87	BOW	BOYD	SAM	560
	8	160 4/8	92	HP/RIFLE	BROWN	JOHN T.	560
	10	160 3/8	88	HP/RIFLE	BOWMAN	BRENT	574
	11	160 2/8	71	HP/RIFLE	STOUT	CLAUDE	584
	12	159 3/8	91	HP/RIFLE	FULLER	NORMA C.	665
	13	159 0/8	76	HP/RIFLE	SALMON	RALPH	695
	14	158 6/8	71	HP/RIFLE	IDDINGS	ED	719
	15	158 0/8	96	HP/RIFLE	LEE	MELVIN	788
	16	157 0/8	92	HP/RIFLE	HOLCOMB	STEVE	875

135

COUNTY	COUNTY RANK	SCORE	YEAR TAKEN	WEAPON	HUNTER	FIRST NAME	STATE RANK
DAVIESS	17	156 2/8	93	HP/RIFLE	STEWART	JERRY	953
	18	154 7/8	94	HP/RIFLE	STIGALL	GENE	1118
	19	154 4/8	68	HP/RIFLE	MORT	K.H.	1164
	20	153 6/8	85	HP/RIFLE	COLLINS	DENNIS	1256
	21	153 5/8	88	HP/RIFLE	WIDEMAN	JOEL	1273
	22	153 2/8	74	HP/RIFLE	ROGERS	DAVID	1327
	23	153 0/8	89	HP/RIFLE	RENFRO	DAVID	1355
	24	152 7/8	78	HP/RIFLE	MOORE	MIKE	1370
	25	151 7/8	94	HP/RIFLE	MYERS	JOHN	1550
	26	151 6/8	88	HP/RIFLE	REYNOLDS	RUSSELL	1566
	27	151 2/8	78	HP/RIFLE	GARDNER	ALBERT	1656
	27	151 2/8	93	HP/RIFLE	HIGHTREE	JOHN	1656
	27	151 2/8	95	HP/RIFLE	CARTER	SCOTT	1656
	30	151 1/8	79	HP/RIFLE	LEE	MICHAEL	1690
	31	151 0/8	84	HP/RIFLE	STRAIN	SCOTT	1715
	32	150 7/8	85	HP/RIFLE	POLEYN	SHANE	1734
	32	150 7/8	88	HP/RIFLE	TEEL	BRIAN	1734
	34	150 6/8	95	HP/RIFLE	COULSON	STAN	1756
	35	150 5/8	76	HP/RIFLE	BASSETT	JERRY	1789
	35	150 5/8	91	HP/RIFLE	THOMPSON	HOWARD K.	1789
	37	150 2/8	94	HP/RIFLE	COX	RALPH	1853
	38	141 5/8	96	HP/RIFLE	HULLINGER, JR.	LAWSON H.	2772
DEKALB	1	174 5/8	88	HP/RIFLE	HOOVER	MONTE	73
	2	172 0/8	91	HP/RIFLE	DAVIS	DEAN	112
	3	167 7/8	94	HP/RIFLE	STAHL	HANK	197
	4	167 1/8	92	HP/RIFLE	WEIGAND	KENDALL	225
	5	166 5/8	94	HP/RIFLE	NIECE	PAUL	238
	6	164 0/8	89	HP/RIFLE	FURGESON	ARLEY	349
	7	162 0/8	92	PICK-UP	CROWLEY	DOYLE	462
	8	161 7/8	89	HP/RIFLE	OWEN III	SAM	467
	8	161 7/8	91	HP/RIFLE	COURTNEY	CHAD	467
	10	161 5/8	88	HP/RIFLE	MARTIN	JIM W.	486
	11	157 7/8	89	HP/RIFLE	YOUNG	LARRY	806
	12	157 6/8	92	HP/RIFLE	ELLIS	JEREMY	812
	13	157 2/8	88	HP/RIFLE	LAWSON	MIKE	853
	14	155 6/8	90	HP/RIFLE	LESLIE	LLOYD A.	1004
	15	154 2/8	90	HP/RIFLE	MARTIN	JIM W.	1186
	15	154 2/8	91	BOW	MARTIN	JIM W.	1186
	17	154 0/8	95	HP/RIFLE	MARTIN	JIM W.	1219
	18	152 7/8	87	HP/RIFLE	MARTIN	JIM W.	1370
	19	152 2/8	91	HP/RIFLE	MALLEN	SCOTT	1469
	20	151 3/8	81	HP/RIFLE	SIMMONS	JACKIE	1637
	21	151 2/8	83	HP/RIFLE	HILL	DON	1656
	22	151 1/8	86	HP/RIFLE	LEIVAN	NEAL	1690
	23	150 5/8	85	HP/RIFLE	ALLAN	DAVE	1789
	24	150 1/8	85	HP/RIFLE	GAISER	ROGER E.	1879
DENT	1	175 3/8	82	HP/RIFLE	UMHOEFER	KEN	66
	2	174 5/8	90	HP/RIFLE	WYLIE	THOMAS P.	73
	3	164 4/8	89	HP/RIFLE	BOOKER	LYNDELL	319
	4	160 3/8	83	HP/RIFLE	CONLEY	CHRIS	574
	5	159 0/8	86	HP/RIFLE	KEENEY	ED	695
	6	158 6/8	87	HP/RIFLE	HINKLE	CARL	719
	7	158 3/8	94	HP/RIFLE	LIGHT	HERSHEL	753
	8	155 6/8	87	PICK-UP	WARDEN	DARREL	1004
	9	153 7/8	78	HP/RIFLE	GULLET	RANDY	1238
	9	153 7/8	92	HP/RIFLE	DANZ	DARA	1238
	11	153 6/8	92	HP/RIFLE	PORDORSKI	JEROME L.	1256
	12	152 2/8	95	HP/RIFLE	TODD	ANDY	1469
	13	152 1/8	92	HP/RIFLE	RUTLEDGE	LAWRENCE J.	1493

MISSOURI SHOW-ME BIG BUCKS CLUB RECORDS OF WHITETAIL DEER BY COUNTY, TYPICAL

COUNTY	COUNTY RANK	SCORE	YEAR TAKEN	WEAPON	HUNTER	FIRST NAME	STATE RANK
DENT	14	151 6/8	93	HP/RIFLE	JONES	MARK B.	1566
	15	151 3/8	96	HP/RIFLE	LAPLANT	MARK	1637
	16	150 7/8	94	HP/RIFLE	WHITAKER	RUSSELL	1734
	17	150 4/8	92	HP/RIFLE	GREEN	MICHAEL	1811
	18	150 2/8	94	HP/RIFLE	DILLON	TOM M.	1853
	18	150 2/8	95	HP/RIFLE	SCHNARR	LARRY	1853
	20	149 7/8	61	HP/RIFLE	ADAMS, JR.	CLIFFORD	1915
	21	149 3/8	68	HP/RIFLE	KING	COLLEEN	1959
	22	148 5/8	90	HP/RIFLE	CAMPBELL	TONY	2035
	23	148 2/8	89	HP/RIFLE	ENKE	GILBERT	2071
	24	148 1/8	87	HP/RIFLE	DIEM	FRED	2088
	25	147 5/8	68	HP/RIFLE	WILDT	AL	2138
	26	147 1/8	47	HP/RIFLE	KAHRS	JAMES W.	2183
	27	145 2/8	89	HP/RIFLE	ADAMS	MARVIN	2361
	27	145 2/8	89	HP/RIFLE	SCHAFER	JOHN L.	2361
	29	144 3/8	90	HP/RIFLE	FISHER	ANDREW C.	2466
	30	144 1/8	86	HP/RIFLE	CARTY	LARRY	2498
	31	143 3/8	86	HP/RIFLE	BATSCHELET	DON	2591
	32	143 0/8	86	HP/RIFLE	MARTI	DAVID	2626
	33	142 1/8	96	HP/RIFLE	MORTON, SR.	RONALD D.	2709
	34	141 4/8	86	HP/RIFLE	FISHER	ANDREW C.	2787
	35	140 7/8	73	HP/RIFLE	JONES	BUFORD	2877
	36	140 6/8	88	HP/RIFLE	CAMDEN	RANDY	2895
	37	140 4/8	85	HP/RIFLE	CARTY	LARRY	2925
DOUGLAS	1	154 0/8	95	HP/RIFLE	McPHERSON	JEFF	1219
	2	153 1/8	92	HP/RIFLE	SCHINDLER	WILLIAM C.	1344
	3	151 5/8	82	HP/RIFLE	DUCKWORTH	RANDY	1586
	4	149 0/8	84	HP/RIFLE	JOHNSON	GENE	1998
	5	148 4/8	81	HP/RIFLE	DODSON	DAVID	2048
	6	144 6/8	90	HP/RIFLE	MOORE	HAROLD E.	2425
	7	144 0/8	57	HP/RIFLE	CAIN	HAROLD L.	2514
	8	143 6/8	76	HP/RIFLE	RHOADS	JOHNNY	2550
	9	140 2/8	91	BOW	JOHNSTON	CHARLIE	2952
FRANKLIN	1	165 7/8	80	HP/RIFLE	REITZ	CARL J.	269
	2	165 5/8	90	HP/RIFLE	FELLER	KEVIN	269
	3	165 1/8	46	HP/RIFLE	WILSON	JAMES F.	296
	4	162 6/8	84	HP/RIFLE	KRIEFALL	DAN	411
	5	162 5/8	79	HP/RIFLE	VAN LEER	DAN	417
	6	161 7/8	54	PICK-UP	KOPPELMANN	TERRY	467
	7	159 7/8	63	HP/RIFLE	SCHUTTENBERG	THEODORE T.	620
	8	159 3/8	40	HP/RIFLE	BRUEGGEMANN	ADOLPH	665
	9	159 2/8	74	HP/RIFLE	HAID	DANNY	675
	10	158 7/8	87	HP/RIFLE	LAWRENCE	TINA M.	712
	11	157 5/8	87	HP/RIFLE	NOVOTNEY	WILLIAM R.	821
	12	156 6/8	79	HP/RIFLE	FRANKENBERG	DONALD	900
	12	156 6/8	88	HP/RIFLE	ROTHWEIL	GERALD A.	900
	14	155 0/8	81	HP/RIFLE	OVERSCHMIDT	VERNON	1102
	15	154 4/8	74	HP/RIFLE	BRUEGGEMANN	KENNETH R.	1164
	16	154 3/8	84	HP/RIFLE	PILGRAM	PHIL	1174
	17	152 1/8	51	HP/RIFLE	SCHROEDER	DON	1493
	18	152 0/8	63	HP/RIFLE	KOPPELMANN, JR.	GEORGE H.	1519
	19	151 6/8	70	HP/RIFLE	MYRICK	AVERY	1566
	20	150 7/8	68	HP/RIFLE	WEBB	BENTON	1734
	21	150 0/8	71	HP/RIFLE	BOLTE	GARY	1897
	22	149 6/8	80	HP/RIFLE	LANDERS	LARRY	1926
	22	149 6/8	86	HP/RIFLE	BOWEN	GLORIA	1926
	24	149 3/8	60	HP/RIFLE	UNGER	EDWARD	1959
	25	149 1/8	63	HP/RIFLE	BRUEGGEMANN	PAUL	1988
	26	148 3/8	92	HP/RIFLE	KOPP	GERALD E.	2060

MISSOURI SHOW-ME BIG BUCKS CLUB RECORDS OF WHITETAIL DEER BY COUNTY, TYPICAL

COUNTY	COUNTY RANK	SCORE	YEAR TAKEN	WEAPON	HUNTER	FIRST NAME	STATE RANK
FRANKLIN	27	148 0/8	81	HP/RIFLE	DIMMETT	RONALD	2101
	28	148 0/8	86	HP/RIFLE	HELLING	ROLLIN	2101
	28	148 0/8	86	HP/RIFLE	VAN WINKLE	RICHARD	2101
	30	147 6/8	66	HP/RIFLE	DOOR	NEIL	2126
	31	147 6/8	75	HP/RIFLE	WILSON	JOHN	2126
	32	147 1/8	85	HP/RIFLE	WARGIN, SR.	RICHARD W.	2183
	33	146 7/8	69	HP/RIFLE	ANDERSON	DENNIS	2214
	34	146 4/8	62	PICK-UP	FRIZZELL	CHRISTOPHER	2242
	35	146 0/8	81	HP/RIFLE	PALMER	KEVIN	2290
	36	145 3/8	92	HP/RIFLE	BAKER	DAN	2350
	37	145 2/8	88	HP/RIFLE	HUSSEY	KEN	2361
	38	145 0/8	56	HP/RIFLE	WEBB	BENTON	2391
	39	144 7/8	84	HP/RIFLE	JOHNSON	GERALD	2412
	40	144 6/8	49	HP/RIFLE	MEYER	R.A.	2425
	40	144 6/8	89	HP/RIFLE	SCHMELZ	JOHN J.	2425
	42	144 5/8	74	HP/RIFLE	MOLL	RON	2442
	43	144 1/8	79	HP/RIFLE	TIMLIN	WILLIAM J.	2498
	44	143 7/8	87	HP/RIFLE	SMITH	ROBERT D.	2533
	45	143 6/8	72	HP/RIFLE	VOSS	RUDOLPH	2550
	46	143 5/8	81	HP/RIFLE	COOK, JR.	JOSEPH M.	2564
	47	143 2/8	74	HP/RIFLE	KLOEPPEL	RAYMOND J.	2598
	47	143 2/8	92	HP/RIFLE	SCHOWE	BLAKE	2598
	49	142 6/8	84	HP/RIFLE	TERSCHLUSE	MARVIN	2647
	50	142 3/8	91	HP/RIFLE	DIMMETT	RONALD	2691
	51	142 1/8	59	HP/RIFLE	VOSS	ROBERT	2709
	52	142 0/8	85	HP/RIFLE	FIGGEMEIER	KENNETH M.	2725
	53	141 7/8	93	HP/RIFLE	BORGMEYER	GREG	2747
	54	141 6/8	66	HP/RIFLE	ROWDEN	WALTER M.	2756
	54	141 6/8	72	HP/RIFLE	YOUNG	HARLAN	2756
	56	141 4/8	77	HP/RIFLE	RICHESON	JOHN O.	2787
	57	141 0/8	74	HP/RIFLE	STACK	DOYLE	2863
	57	141 0/8	85	HP/RIFLE	NULL	KURT A.	2863
	59	140 7/8	79	HP/RIFLE	STRAATMAN	AL J.	2877
	60	140 6/8	83	HP/RIFLE	LAWRENCE	MIKE	2895
	61	140 5/8	64	HP/RIFLE	DIAZ	DENNIS	2908
	61	140 5/8	83	HP/RIFLE	CUNNINGHAM	ROBERT W.	2908
	63	140 1/8	88	HP/RIFLE	LASCHKE	JOSEPH E.	2978
GASCONADE	1	174 5/8	74	HP/RIFLE	GRIFFITH	DANNY	73
	2	166 6/8	90	HP/RIFLE	APPRILL	CURT	235
	3	161 4/8	78	HP/RIFLE	HAVENER	DELBERT	493
	4	160 2/8	95	HP/RIFLE	GOODMAN	RICK	584
	5	160 0/8	75	HP/RIFLE	FRICKE	VIRGIL	605
	6	159 6/8	85	HP/RIFLE	RUWWE	CLYDE	628
	7	159 6/8	87	HP/RIFLE	THEISSEN	DANNY	628
	8	159 2/8	89	HP/RIFLE	AHONEN	JOHN	675
	8	159 2/8	89	HP/RIFLE	OLDFATHER	RAY	675
	8	159 2/8	UNK	PICK-UP	WEST	RON	675
	11	158 2/8	95	HP/RIFLE	TUSCHHOFF	RAYMOND	763
	12	156 3/8	79	HP/RIFLE	GOODMAN	JERRY L.	940
	12	156 3/8	86	HP/RIFLE	BRANDT	EUGENE E.	940
	14	155 2/8	82	HP/RIFLE	PETERS	RAYMOND A.	1068
	15	154 5/8	96	HP/RIFLE	BOLAND	JEFFREY J.	1146
	16	154 4/8	58	HP/RIFLE	MOTTER	MARION	1164
	17	154 2/8	69	HP/RIFLE	ENKE	ARTHUR	1186
	18	154 0/8	83	HP/RIFLE	OLIVER	DELTON	1219
	18	154 0/8	93	HP/RIFLE	MASTERS	GARY	1219
	20	153 6/8	96	HP/RIFLE	BUSCHMANN	ALFRED	1256
	21	153 0/8	93	HP/RIFLE	ROST	ED	1355
	22	152 3/8	85	BOW	HAWKINS	JOHN	1453

MISSOURI SHOW-ME BIG BUCKS CLUB RECORDS OF WHITETAIL DEER BY COUNTY, TYPICAL

COUNTY	COUNTY RANK	SCORE	YEAR TAKEN	WEAPON	HUNTER	FIRST NAME	STATE RANK
GASCONADE	23	152 0/8	69	HP/RIFLE	APPRILL	MELVIN	1519
	23	152 0/8	72	HP/RIFLE	POSEY	STEVEN A.	1519
	25	151 5/8	86	HP/RIFLE	WILLIAMS	ED	1586
	26	151 2/8	81	HP/RIFLE	SEAMON	TIM	1656
	27	151 0/8	95	HP/RIFLE	MEHRHOFF	KEN	1715
	28	150 6/8	87	HP/RIFLE	WEHMEYER	RUSSELL	1756
	29	150 4/8	90	HP/RIFLE	TRAUB	ROBERT	1811
	30	150 2/8	88	HP/RIFLE	FREDRICK	MAYNARD	1853
	31	150 1/8	82	HP/RIFLE	SPURGEON	JERRY L.	1879
	32	149 4/8	67	HP/RIFLE	DUNCAN	LARRY	1936
	33	148 5/8	71	HP/RIFLE	SWOBODA	M.F.	2035
	34	148 0/8	95	HP/RIFLE	WEHMEYER	JANIE	2101
	35	147 2/8	95	HP/RIFLE	HABERBERGER	DAVID	2167
	36	147 1/8	91	PICK-UP	GIEDINGHAGEN	KURT	2183
	37	147 0/8	88	HP/RIFLE	WHITTALL	STEVE	2195
	38	146 3/8	89	HP/RIFLE	APPRILL	KENNETH	2252
	39	146 2/8	94	HP/RIFLE	ISAAK	STEVE	2266
	40	146 0/8	84	HP/RIFLE	WEHRLE	HOWARD	2290
	40	146 0/8	95	HP/RIFLE	McGEE	TRAVIS H.	2290
	42	145 7/8	72	HP/RIFLE	SPURGEON	DOYLE	2302
	43	145 4/8	86	HP/RIFLE	SCHNEIDER	JAMES	2331
	44	145 3/8	90	HP/RIFLE	SCHULTE	JUDY	2350
	45	145 2/8	50	HP/RIFLE	LANGENDOERFER	AUGUST	2361
	46	145 0/8	88	HP/RIFLE	PEARSON	DOUG	2391
	47	144 6/8	63	HP/RIFLE	LANDOLT	BOB	2425
	47	144 6/8	92	HP/RIFLE	SCHWINKE	ELDORE W.	2425
	49	144 2/8	92	HP/RIFLE	BARCH	RON	2483
	50	144 1/8	74	HP/RIFLE	SPURGEON	DON	2498
	51	144 0/8	85	HP/RIFLE	FRICKE	DENNIS	2514
	52	143 7/8	63	HP/RIFLE	AHLBON	B.G.	2533
	52	143 7/8	76	HP/RIFLE	GERSCHEFSKE	MILDA	2533
	54	143 4/8	79	HP/RIFLE	SCHNEIDER	JIM	2577
	55	143 2/8	85	PICK-UP	SCHNEIDER	JIM AND BOB	2598
	56	142 5/8	72	HP/RIFLE	HEIDEL	DALE	2660
	57	142 3/8	52	HP/RIFLE	BAUR	FRANK E.	2691
	57	142 3/8	68	HP/RIFLE	FRANKENBERG	ALAN	2691
	57	142 3/8	81	HP/RIFLE	MUELLER	TIM	2691
	60	141 4/8	86	HP/RIFLE	APPRILL	KENNETH	2787
	60	141 4/8	91	HP/RIFLE	EPPLE	GLENNON	2787
	62	141 2/8	73	HP/RIFLE	BINKHOLDER	MICHAEL	2828
	63	141 0/8	82	HP/RIFLE	GORMAN	BRAD	2863
	64	140 4/8	90	HP/RIFLE	WEHMEYER	RUSSELL	2925
	65	140 3/8	45	HP/RIFLE	QUICK	OREL R.	2935
	66	140 3/8	92	HP/RIFLE	NAGLE	DOUGLAS	2935
	67	140 2/8	78	HP/RIFLE	SCHNEIDER	DONNA	2952
	68	140 0/8	73	HP/RIFLE	WACKER	JAMES	2990
	68	140 0/8	79	HP/RIFLE	WITTE	LESLIE	2990
	68	140 0/8	79	HP/RIFLE	WATSON	STEVE	2990
GENTRY	1	173 5/8	69	HP/RIFLE	OBERBECK	WILLIAN F. (BILL)	89
	2	166 7/8	89	HP/RIFLE	DIERENFELDT	CLARENCE	230
	3	165 5/8	86	HP/RIFLE	BYRANT	JIM	269
	4	164 2/8	91	HP/RIFLE	WILLIAMS	LLOYD	332
	5	162 4/8	87	HP/RIFLE	BUERKY	GARY	431
	6	162 1/8	90	HP/RIFLE	PARMAN	MARK	455
	7	160 7/8	79	HP/RIFLE	JENSEN	JOE	535
	8	160 0/8	94	HP/RIFLE	LEDBETTER	CURTIS	605
	9	158 6/8	88	HP/RIFLE	SUTTON	ROBERT	719
	10	158 4/8	82	HP/RIFLE	YOUNG	RANDALL	739
	11	158 1/8	75	PICK-UP	DARNELL	KEVIN	777

COUNTY	COUNTY RANK	SCORE	YEAR TAKEN	WEAPON	HUNTER	FIRST NAME	STATE RANK
GENTRY	12	157 2/8	88	PICK-UP	HENRY	MARK	853
	13	156 1/8	89	HP/RIFLE	LAU	ROGER	967
	14	155 1/8	81	HP/RIFLE	WALLACE	RICHARD	1091
	15	154 5/8	77	HP/RIFLE	GILLESPIE	CRAIG	1146
	16	154 1/8	90	HP/RIFLE	ANGLE	STEVE	1207
	17	153 6/8	76	HP/RIFLE	RENO	RAYMOND	1256
	18	152 5/8	74	HP/RIFLE	DARNELL	KEVIN	1399
	19	152 4/8	80	HP/RIFLE	DOOLITTLE	BILL	1423
	20	151 2/8	95	HP/RIFLE	SCHRADER	FRED	1656
	21	151 0/8	89	HP/RIFLE	McFADDEN	MIKE	1715
	22	150 6/8	83	HP/RIFLE	HENSLEY	JOHN	1756
	22	150 6/8	85	HP/RIFLE	LIPPARD	MIKE	1756
	24	143 7/8	95	HP/RIFLE	CRAWFORD	BRYON	2533
	25	140 7/8	87	HP/RIFLE	RODERIQUE	CAROL	2877
GREENE	1	168 4/8	91	HP/RIFLE	ANDREWS	DON	181
	2	160 6/8	95	HP/RIFLE	KROPF	STEPHEN	543
	3	160 0/8	72	HP/RIFLE	ROBERTS	MIKE	605
	4	159 5/8	86	HP/RIFLE	BENNETT	MARK	641
	5	157 6/8	88	BOW	ANDREWS	DON M.	812
	6	155 0/8	70	HP/RIFLE	JOHNSON	RICHARD	1102
	7	154 4/8	86	HP/RIFLE	LAMBERT	BRENT	1164
	8	148 4/8	87	HP/RIFLE	SCHREINER	CLIFF	2048
	9	143 6/8	79	HP/RIFLE	LASSLEY	DELBERT	2550
	10	143 4/8	93	HP/RIFLE	BARNHOUSE	JEFFERY L.	2577
	11	143 2/8	87	HP/RIFLE	FLETCHER	RICK	2598
	12	141 4/8	86	HP/RIFLE	PULLEY	TOM	2787
	13	140 6/8	83	HP/RIFLE	BRAY	BRETT	2895
GRUNDY	1	170 5/8	88	HP/RIFLE	WEATHERS	MICHAEL C.	137
	2	165 3/8	89	HP/RIFLE	HARRIS	CLAUDE	288
	3	164 6/8	89	HP/RIFLE	TODD	RANDALL	307
	4	163 5/8	83	BOW	COPELAND	KENNETH A.	368
	5	163 3/8	94	HP/RIFLE	NICHOLS	RONALD S.	378
	6	162 6/8	90	HP/RIFLE	NOE	J.R.	411
	7	161 3/8	81	HP/RIFLE	STAMPER	JUNIOR	503
	8	160 4/8	94	HP/RIFLE	KASEY	JAMES	560
	9	159 6/8	94	HP/RIFLE	RICKETTS	BOB	628
	10	158 2/8	90	HP/RIFLE	REED	ALLAN D.	763
	11	156 2/8	91	HP/RIFLE	HALL	TIM	953
	12	154 6/8	95	HP/RIFLE	STILES	W.J.	1130
	13	154 0/8	73	HP/RIFLE	THOGMARTIN	LEROY	1219
	14	153 3/8	87	HP/RIFLE	SCHMIDT	GERALD	1310
	15	151 3/8	70	HP/RIFLE	GIBSON	WESLEY	1637
	16	151 2/8	90	HP/RIFLE	HUGHS	TIM	1656
	17	150 3/8	92	HP/RIFLE	KOENIG	EDDIE	1834
	18	150 1/8	87	HP/RIFLE	McDANIEL	RONALD	1879
	19	150 0/8	87	HP/RIFLE	HILL	BILL	1897
	20	144 0/8	95	HP/RIFLE	CREASON	RICHARD	2514
HARRISON	1	185 3/8	95	HP/RIFLE	RHEA II	JOHN W.	20
	2	175 0/8	74	HP/RIFLE	GRAHAM	CARL	68
	3	170 3/8	91	HP/RIFLE	GENTRY	GLEN	144
	4	168 1/8	93	HP/RIFLE	GARRETT	MICHAEL C.	193
	5	165 6/8	94	HP/RIFLE	FERREE	CLARK	273
	6	165 3/8	95	HP/RIFLE	SCHNEIDER	ROBERT S.	288
	7	165 1/8	74	HP/RIFLE	MAXWELL	ROGER L.	296
	8	164 7/8	85	HP/RIFLE	ROBERTSON	JUNIOR	303
	9	163 0/8	84	HP/RIFLE	GIBSON	DONALD	393
	10	162 5/8	69	HP/RIFLE	HILLYARD	LARRY	417
	11	161 6/8	92	HP/RIFLE	MEEKS	BOB	476
	12	161 4/8	78	HP/RIFLE	BOOTHE	WAYNE	493

MISSOURI SHOW-ME BIG BUCKS CLUB RECORDS OF WHITETAIL DEER BY COUNTY, TYPICAL

COUNTY	COUNTY RANK	SCORE	YEAR TAKEN	WEAPON	HUNTER	FIRST NAME	STATE RANK
HARRISON	13	159 6/8	89	HP/RIFLE	RICHARDSON	JERRY	628
	14	159 5/8	92	HP/RIFLE	VANDEVENDER	KEITH	641
	15	159 2/8	79	HP/RIFLE	McBROOM	JAMES K.	675
	16	158 3/8	70	HP/RIFLE	LEWIS	ERNIE	753
	17	158 2/8	77	HP/RIFLE	BENNETT	CARL	763
	18	158 1/8	82	HP/RIFLE	BENNETT	FRED	777
	18	158 1/8	89	HP/RIFLE	HILL	JARALD R.	777
	20	158 0/8	63	HP/RIFLE	BROWN	CLARENCE R.	788
	21	157 4/8	71	HP/RIFLE	WHITE	JIM	833
	22	157 0/8	67	HP/RIFLE	DAVIS	MARCO	875
	23	156 4/8	88	HP/RIFLE	McBROOM	CHRIS	925
	24	156 3/8	67	HP/RIFLE	HENDERSON	JERRY	940
	25	155 6/8	92	M/L	JAMES	JERRY	1004
	26	155 5/8	79	HP/RIFLE	BENNETT	DAVID O.	1023
	26	155 5/8	83	HP/RIFLE	JEANES	CHARLES	1023
	26	155 5/8	85	HP/RIFLE	ALLEN	WAYNE	1023
	29	155 4/8	71	HP/RIFLE	HALE	ROBERT E.	1040
	30	154 5/8	94	HP/RIFLE	LEWIS, III	ROY EVERETT	1146
	31	154 3/8	89	HP/RIFLE	WRIGHT	TOBY	1174
	32	154 2/8	67	HP/RIFLE	FORDYCE	MAX	1186
	33	153 6/8	70	HP/RIFLE	HARDING	MARVIN	1256
	34	153 5/8	86	HP/RIFLE	BURNS	MITCHELL	1273
	35	153 4/8	88	HP/RIFLE	CLARK	ROBERT W.	1287
	35	153 4/8	96	HP/RIFLE	HILLYARD	TODD	1287
	37	153 3/8	91	M/L	CHANDLER	ROBERT L.	1310
	38	152 5/8	83	HP/RIFLE	FRAME	DAVID	1399
	39	152 2/8	71	HP/RIFLE	COMER	GORDON	1469
	40	152 1/8	96	HP/RIFLE	NICHOLLS	KENT	1493
	41	151 6/8	90	HP/RIFLE	ALLEN	WAYNE	1566
	42	151 1/8	77	HP/RIFLE	DEVER	GUS	1690
	43	151 0/8	76	HP/RIFLE	BAYLESS	ROGER	1715
	43	151 0/8	88	HP/RIFLE	McGINNES	DEAN	1715
	45	150 7/8	91	HP/RIFLE	MITCHELL	JUSTIN	1734
	46	150 6/8	70	HP/RIFLE	HARDING	SAMMIE	1756
	46	150 6/8	88	HP/RIFLE	KELLEY	BRIAN	1756
	48	150 3/8	79	HP/RIFLE	HUSKEY	LARRY	1834
	48	150 3/8	86	HP/RIFLE	PARKHURST	DOYLE	1834
	50	150 2/8	67	HP/RIFLE	PRESTON	RAYMOND	1853
	51	150 1/8	67	HP/RIFLE	GIBSON	NORMAN L.	1879
	52	147 2/8	96	HP/RIFLE	GARRETT	MARVIN	2167
	53	146 3/8	93	HP/RIFLE	CRAIG	VERNON L.	2252
	54	145 4/8	95	HP/RIFLE	HAGEN	MICHAEL J.	2331
	54	145 4/8	96	HP/RIFLE	EASTON	STEVE	2331
HENRY	1	169 1/8	95	HP/RIFLE	WHEELER	KENT	166
	2	168 6/8	86	HP/RIFLE	NORMAN	LYMAN	174
	3	168 3/8	76	HP/RIFLE	MORAN	DARRELL	184
	4	164 2/8	96	HP/RIFLE	WILLIAMS	RONALD	332
	5	164 2/8	96	HP/RIFLE	MILLER, JR.	LARRY G.	332
	6	163 0/8	86	HP/RIFLE	SOELDNER	JAMES	393
	7	161 2/8	91	HP/RIFLE	POWELL	JIM	512
	8	158 7/8	88	BOW	RUCKER	LAVERNE	712
	9	157 4/8	93	HP/RIFLE	McCALMON	KEVIN	833
	10	157 1/8	96	HP/RIFLE	BUTLER	JAMES	864
	11	154 7/8	94	HP/RIFLE	DENISON	BARRY	1118
	12	154 0/8	91	BOW	HULL	MATTHEW L.	1219
	13	152 3/8	89	HP/RIFLE	CLAUNCH	DAVID	1453
	13	152 3/8	93	BOW	COOK	PHIL G.	1453
	15	151 7/8	86	HP/RIFLE	KEDIGH	BILL	1550
	16	151 2/8	86	HP/RIFLE	SMITKA	BILL	1656

MISSOURI SHOW-ME BIG BUCKS CLUB RECORDS OF WHITETAIL DEER BY COUNTY, TYPICAL

COUNTY	COUNTY RANK	SCORE	YEAR TAKEN	WEAPON	HUNTER	FIRST NAME	STATE RANK
HENRY	17	151 0/8	79	HP/RIFLE	PARKS	BOB	1715
	18	150 6/8	88	HP/RIFLE	BAILEY	JOE	1756
	19	149 4/8	56	HP/RIFLE	HAMILTON	MAX C.	1936
	20	149 2/8	93	HP/RIFLE	NIDA	CALVIN	1973
	21	149 0/8	96	HP/RIFLE	BAUER	BRETT	1998
	22	147 4/8	87	HP/RIFLE	DENNIS	CARY	2148
	22	147 4/8	90	HP/RIFLE	SWATERS	BILL	2148
	24	147 3/8	93	HP/RIFLE	CANNON	JEREMY	2155
	25	146 7/8	87	HP/RIFLE	BAILEY	DANNY	2214
	26	146 5/8	94	HP/RIFLE	GOTH	BRETT	2235
	27	145 0/8	87	HP/RIFLE	HEANY	RANDY	2391
	28	144 5/8	94	HP/RIFLE	SIMMERMON	RENEE	2442
	29	144 4/8	85	HP/RIFLE	NORTHINGTON	MIKE	2459
	30	144 2/8	93	HP/RIFLE	KENNEY	DOUG	2483
	31	143 7/8	95	HP/RIFLE	KIELY	JAMES	2533
	32	142 5/8	82	HP/RIFLE	CARNEY	KENT	2660
	33	142 3/8	86	HP/RIFLE	HILLS	RUSSELL	2691
	34	142 2/8	70	HP/RIFLE	BAILEY	W.E. (BILL)	2701
	35	142 1/8	75	HP/RIFLE	KIDWELL	DON	2709
	36	142 0/8	90	HP/RIFLE	HOLMGREN	CHRISTOPHER	2725
	37	141 6/8	95	HP/RIFLE	FELLHOELTER	CURTIS	2756
	38	141 4/8	81	HP/RIFLE	SMART	BRAD	2787
	39	140 6/8	65	HP/RIFLE	TIRMAN	JERRY	2895
	40	140 3/8	87	HP/RIFLE	KEDIGH	BILL	2935
	41	140 1/8	96	HP/RIFLE	SANDERS	JACKSON D.	2978
HICKORY	1	166 7/8	83	HP/RIFLE	DRISKILL	JEFF	227
	2	163 0/8	86	BOW	PEARSON	GARY	393
	3	161 5/8	66	HP/RIFLE	HEARE	CHARLES E.	486
	4	161 1/8	87	HP/RIFLE	DORMAN	MARVIN L.	520
	5	157 3/8	82	HP/RIFLE	FLESHMAN	WILLIAM	848
	6	155 4/8	85	HP/RIFLE	WEYER	TOM	1040
	7	153 0/8	71	HP/RIFLE	HOCKMAN	ARNOLD	1355
	8	151 2/8	60	HP/RIFLE	O'CONNOR	PAT	1656
	9	148 1/8	81	HP/RIFLE	MATTHEWS	KIRBY	2088
	9	148 1/8	87	HP/RIFLE	LANGTON	DAVID	2088
	11	147 5/8	91	HP/RIFLE	PALMER	FORREST A.	2138
	12	147 0/8	72	HP/RIFLE	MERTGEN	JULIA	2195
	13	146 2/8	95	HP/RIFLE	JOHNSON	PAM	2266
	14	144 6/8	92	HP/RIFLE	ROARK	KATHLEEN	2425
	15	143 6/8	88	HP/RIFLE	PUMMILL	LAURA	2550
	16	141 0/8	66	HP/RIFLE	MOORE	LAWSON P.	2863
	17	140 5/8	85	HP/RIFLE	THOMPSON	FLOYD	2908
	18	140 3/8	88	HP/RIFLE	TAYLOR	GENE R.	2935
	19	140 0/8	87	HP/RIFLE	GILLOTTE	MICHAEL	2990
HOLT	1	175 4/8	62	HP/RIFLE	SCHAEFFER	ORRIE L.	65
	2	164 0/8	92	HP/RIFLE	MONTGOMERY	EDWARD	349
	3	161 1/8	74	HP/RIFLE	TURNER	BRUCE	520
	4	159 5/8	81	HP/RIFLE	ARNDT	RANDY	641
	5	159 1/8	91	HP/RIFLE	DEGENHARDT	JOHN	687
	6	159 0/8	82	HP/RIFLE	MUNYAN	LARRY	695
	7	157 4/8	84	HP/RIFLE	RAMSAY	TERRY	833
	8	157 2/8	88	M/L	BERENDZEN	JAY	853
	9	157 1/8	84	PICK-UP	SQUAW CREEK	NWR	864
	10	157 0/8	70	HP/RIFLE	CURRAN	DENNIS	875
	10	157 0/8	88	HP/RIFLE	BLANKENSHIP	GLEN	875
	12	156 4/8	73	HP/RIFLE	DYE	ROBERT L.	925
	13	155 6/8	92	HP/RIFLE	BARKER	CARROL	1004
	14	152 3/8	70	HP/RIFLE	COTTON	GEORGE	1453
	15	151 5/8	84	PICK-UP	REYNOLDS	JERRY	1586

COUNTY	COUNTY RANK	SCORE	YEAR TAKEN	WEAPON	HUNTER	FIRST NAME	STATE RANK
HOLT	16	151 4/8	88	HP/RIFLE	RASMIC	MIKE	1613
	17	151 3/8	76	HP/RIFLE	SCARBROUGH	FRANK	1637
	18	150 5/8	75	HP/RIFLE	McGUIRE	BILL	1789
	19	145 7/8	96	HP/RIFLE	CUNNINGHAM	MIKE	2302
	20	144 1/8	82	HP/RIFLE	BULLOCK	LEONARD	2498
HOWARD	1	174 6/8	85	HP/RIFLE	ALLPHIN	DAVID	71
	2	173 0/8	78	HP/RIFLE	BANNING	RAY	100
	3	171 3/8	92	HP/RIFLE	POWELL	DERRICK	121
	4	167 7/8	87	HP/RIFLE	TAYLOR	R.W.	197
	5	167 5/8	84	HP/RIFLE	PROCTOR	MIKE	205
	6	163 7/8	87	HP/RIFLE	HUGGANS	MIKE	356
	7	163 4/8	90	HP/RIFLE	BREWSTER	JIM	373
	8	163 0/8	91	HP/RIFLE	NICHOLS	KEITH	393
	9	162 7/8	93	HP/RIFLE	KAYLOR	JAY	406
	10	162 5/8	91	HP/RIFLE	POWELL	DERRICK	417
	11	162 3/8	94	HP/RIFLE	DOBSON	KEVIN	439
	12	161 4/8	94	HP/RIFLE	PRENTZLER	LARRY RAY	493
	13	160 6/8	87	HP/RIFLE	WOOD	ROB	543
	14	159 2/8	81	HP/RIFLE	BUCK	DEAN	675
	15	156 0/8	59	HP/RIFLE	AHOLT	ROY	981
	16	155 4/8	90	HP/RIFLE	REAGAN	DEAN	1040
	16	155 4/8	93	HP/RIFLE	SIMS	NORMAN L.	1040
	18	154 2/8	89	HP/RIFLE	CAIN	RICKY	1186
	19	153 5/8	87	HP/RIFLE	KOLKS	BOB	1273
	20	153 3/8	72	HP/RIFLE	HILGEDICK	GLENN	1310
	21	152 6/8	87	HP/RIFLE	LEISURE, JR.	BAXTER	1385
	22	152 2/8	74	HP/RIFLE	SUNDERLAND	WOODROW	1469
	23	151 5/8	92	HP/RIFLE	CARTON	JOHN	1586
	24	151 2/8	91	HP/RIFLE	SENTER	DANIEL LEE	1656
	25	150 7/8	87	HP/RIFLE	BRAITHWAIT	JIM	1734
	26	150 6/8	90	HP/RIFLE	FINLEY	JOHN	1756
	27	150 4/8	94	HP/RIFLE	BOSTON	KEVIN	1811
	28	150 2/8	90	HP/RIFLE	CUNDIFF	RICKY	1853
	29	147 7/8	95	HP/RIFLE	WESTHUES	GEORGIA	2114
	30	147 2/8	93	HP/RIFLE	MAXFIELD	DAVID	2167
	31	145 4/8	95	HP/RIFLE	HILGEDICK	GLENN	2331
	32	140 2/8	95	HP/RIFLE	SUNDERLAND	HARDIN	2952
HOWELL	1	170 6/8	74	HP/RIFLE	WOODSON	ROY	136
	2	168 4/8	68	HP/RIFLE	HOFF	GERRY	181
	3	157 3/8	68	HP/RIFLE	SMITH	DR. H.D.	848
	4	154 6/8	90	HP/RIFLE	SPENCER	SCOTT	1130
	5	154 3/8	74	HP/RIFLE	HIGHLEY	DANNY	1174
	6	153 7/8	79	HP/RIFLE	COLLINS	JIM	1238
	7	153 6/8	76	HP/RIFLE	HOWELL	EARL	1256
	8	152 7/8	87	HP/RIFLE	HOWARD	GLENN	1370
	9	152 6/8	75	HP/RIFLE	WOMACK	JERRY	1385
	10	149 5/8	92	BOW	FRENCH	THOMAS E.	1936
	11	149 1/8	67	HP/RIFLE	ANSTINE	GERALD	1988
	12	148 5/8	68	HP/RIFLE	HENDRIX, Jr.	JOHN	2035
	13	145 6/8	80	HP/RIFLE	DOCK	FRED W.	2311
	14	145 4/8	72	HP/RIFLE	BERZINA	JIM	2331
	15	144 1/8	92	BOW	GROSZE	GARY	2498
	16	143 6/8	72	HP/RIFLE	BRADDISH	RICK	2550
	17	143 2/8	72	HP/RIFLE	JOHNSON	BILL	2598
	18	140 3/8	73	HP/RIFLE	EMERICK	W.R.	2935
IRON	1	168 6/8	82	HP/RIFLE	WIGGER	MARK	174
	2	168 0/8	89	HP/RIFLE	BUTERY	SCOTT	194
	3	166 3/8	83	HP/RIFLE	CLIBURN	JAMES	249
	4	160 3/8	73	HP/RIFLE	STEWART	JAMES	574

COUNTY	COUNTY RANK	SCORE	YEAR TAKEN	WEAPON	HUNTER	FIRST NAME	STATE RANK
IRON	5	155 4/8	68	HP/RIFLE	RONEY	CHARLES G.	1040
	6	151 7/8	64	HP/RIFLE	RONALD	ARTHUR L.	1550
	7	151 1/8	91	HP/RIFLE	HARTWICK	CHARISSE	1690
	8	149 6/8	92	BOW	CAMPBELL	TERESA L.	1926
	9	147 4/8	88	PICK-UP	JENKINS, JR.	MARVIN	2148
	10	147 0/8	89	HP/RIFLE	INMAN	BYRON B.	2195
	11	144 6/8	91	HP/RIFLE	AUBUCHON	BARRY	2425
	12	144 3/8	67	HP/RIFLE	POINSETT	CHARLES	2466
	13	142 1/8	69	HP/RIFLE	MERKEL	LARRY	2709
	14	141 4/8	88	HP/RIFLE	TIEFENAUER	LARRY L.	2787
	15	140 5/8	73	HP/RIFLE	WEADON, JR.	JOE	2908
JACKSON	1	176 6/8	96	HP/RIFLE	WILLIAMS	CHARLES	58
	2	176 0/8	95	BOW	HIESBERGE	MICHAEL A.	63
	3	173 5/8	95	BOW	SYTKOWSKI	MIKE	89
	4	169 6/8	86	HP/RIFLE	TROTTER	BRYAN	158
	5	168 0/8	84	HP/RIFLE	ALLEN	RON	194
	6	163 5/8	85	BOW	SHOTTON, JR.	CHARLES C.	368
	7	162 3/8	86	HP/RIFLE	COOKSTON	STEVE	439
	8	158 3/8	93	HP/RIFLE	GARRETSON	SHAYNE	753
	9	156 5/8	89	HP/RIFLE	COLLINS	JAMES E.	911
	10	155 4/8	87	BOW	SHOTTON, JR.	CHARLES C.	1040
	11	155 1/8	95	HP/RIFLE	STEPHENS	JAMES	1091
	12	155 0/8	88	HP/RIFLE	HARRIS	LYNN	1102
	13	154 7/8	92	BOW	SCHLEIF	JOHN T.	1118
	14	151 5/8	76	HP/RIFLE	GIESEKE	MIKE DAVID	1586
	14	151 5/8	85	HP/RIFLE	OSBORN	ROY A.	1586
	16	150 3/8	83	BOW	THOMEY	MARVIN	1834
	17	149 7/8	74	HP/RIFLE	SHINNEMAN	HOMER	1915
	17	149 7/8	88	BOW	EASLEY	TYRON	1915
	17	149 7/8	93	HP/RIFLE	THOMPSON	JOHN	1915
	17	149 7/8	94	HP/RIFLE	BISACCA	MARK	1915
	21	149 2/8	84	BOW	THOMEY	MARVIN	1973
	21	149 2/8	85	BOW	THOMEY	MARVIN	1973
	23	148 0/8	93	HP/RIFLE	SCHUBERT	CHESTER	2101
	24	147 3/8	84	BOW	THOMEY	MARVIN	2155
	25	147 0/8	83	HP/RIFLE	McCURRY	L.O.	2195
	26	145 6/8	94	BOW	STAHL	JEFF	2311
	27	144 2/8	88	BOW	VAN RADEN	DAVID	2483
	27	144 2/8	92	HP/RIFLE	GARRETSON	SHAYNE	2483
	29	142 7/8	72	HP/RIFLE	COX	GARY	2641
	30	141 3/8	91	BOW	HOOD	WENDELL E.	2812
	31	140 2/8	83	HP/RIFLE	LANGENSAND	WAYNE C.	2952
	31	140 2/8	89	BOW	TERRY	BOB	2952
	33	140 0/8	80	BOW	THOMEY	MARVIN	2990
JASPER	1	157 1/8	76	HP/RIFLE	MORT	RICHARD B.	864
	2	156 2/8	84	HP/RIFLE	WREN	JEFF	953
	3	154 3/8	80	HP/RIFLE	CROUCH	LARRY	1174
	4	153 1/8	87	HP/RIFLE	WEBB	JIM	1344
	5	152 2/8	94	HP/RIFLE	BYNUM	THERON D.	1469
	6	151 2/8	92	HP/RIFLE	SMITH	GREG	1656
	7	150 7/8	85	HP/RIFLE	McWILLIAMS	ELMER	1734
	8	147 7/8	84	HP/RIFLE	CLINE	GAYLE	2114
	9	145 4/8	91	HP/RIFLE	PIERCE	EDDY G.	2331
	10	143 7/8	93	HP/RIFLE	PIERCE	ED	2533
	11	141 7/8	95	HP/RIFLE	TILLMAN	DAVID L.	2747
JEFFERSON	1	155 7/8	94	HP/RIFLE	ASELMAN	JAMES	994
	2	151 6/8	95	HP/RIFLE	RAMSEY	JAMES H.	1566
	3	151 1/8	88	BOW	NORTH	STEVE	1690
	4	150 7/8	67	HP/RIFLE	COOPER	AUSTIN	1734

MISSOURI SHOW-ME BIG BUCKS CLUB RECORDS OF WHITETAIL DEER BY COUNTY, TYPICAL

COUNTY	COUNTY RANK	SCORE	YEAR TAKEN	WEAPON	HUNTER	FIRST NAME	STATE RANK
JEFFERSON	5	148 5/8	62	HP/RIFLE	BRINLEY	CLYDE H.	2035
	6	148 4/8	85	HP/RIFLE	MONTGOMERY	KENNETH A.	2048
	7	145 4/8	87	BOW	NORTH	STEVE	2331
	8	142 1/8	60	HP/RIFLE	HARPER	WILLIAM W.	2709
	9	141 6/8	84	HP/RIFLE	SULLIVAN	ALONZO	2756
	10	141 3/8	54	HP/RIFLE	HAYES	DONNELL E.	2812
JOHNSON	1	176 1/8	90	BOW	STEPHENS	JAMES	61
	2	161 3/8	95	HP/RIFLE	SHEETS	JIM	503
	3	157 5/8	87	HP/RIFLE	STEPHENS	JAMES	821
	4	157 4/8	89	HP/RIFLE	STEPHENS	JAMES	833
	5	156 1/8	90	HP/RIFLE	JACKSON	JOHN	967
	6	155 6/8	79	HP/RIFLE	CORBETT	DWAYNE	1004
	7	154 3/8	83	BOW	ADAMS	DALE	1174
	8	151 7/8	86	HP/RIFLE	BALDWIN	IRA	1550
	9	150 1/8	86	HP/RIFLE	SLAUGHTER	STEVEN	1879
	10	149 3/8	86	HP/RIFLE	BURKE	GARY	1959
	11	147 0/8	86	HP/RIFLE	MEADS	WAYNE	2195
	11	147 0/8	91	HP/RIFLE	SMITH	WILLIAM E.	2195
	13	146 6/8	76	HP/RIFLE	BRACKEN	CHARLES E.	2225
	14	145 4/8	87	HP/RIFLE	PETTY	HOMER	2331
	15	145 3/8	91	HP/RIFLE	LENZ	EDWARD	2350
	16	144 3/8	83	HP/RIFLE	BYERS	JOHN	2466
	17	142 5/8	87	HP/RIFLE	MORRIS	HUGH	2660
	18	140 0/8	95	BOW	WRIGHT	MELFORD L.	2990
KNOX	1	174 3/8	72	HP/RIFLE	SIMMONS	JON	78
	2	169 0/8	71	HP/RIFLE	MEEK	EDWARD M.	170
	3	168 7/8	82	HP/RIFLE	KLINE	CLAYTON	173
	4	166 4/8	87	HP/RIFLE	MAUZY	TOM	244
	5	165 4/8	82	HP/RIFLE	BOES	BRUCE	283
	6	163 2/8	67	HP/RIFLE	PARTON	BOBBY DEAN	383
	7	162 5/8	96	HP/RIFLE	PERRIGO	DOUG	417
	8	162 0/8	96	HP/RIFLE	LINDEMANN	STEVE	462
	9	161 3/8	86	HP/RIFLE	DIXSON	DALE	503
	9	161 3/8	95	HP/RIFLE	McARTHUR	BRAD	503
	11	160 3/8	87	HP/RIFLE	HOOD	LARRY	574
	12	160 0/8	93	HP/RIFLE	HARSELL	MICHAEL	605
	13	159 5/8	87	HP/RIFLE	KLOCKE	MARK RALPH	641
	14	158 4/8	96	HP/RIFLE	HETTINGER	RUSSELL	739
	15	158 1/8	86	HP/RIFLE	MASTERS	GARY	777
	16	156 4/8	76	HP/RIFLE	HITCHCOCK	ROBERT	925
	17	156 2/8	76	HP/RIFLE	HAMILTON	MELVIN	953
	18	155 2/8	73	HP/RIFLE	MORROW	ELVIN RAY	1068
	19	154 7/8	64	HP/RIFLE	COLE	WILLARD C.	1118
	20	154 4/8	87	HP/RIFLE	SCHRAGE	JERRY L.	1164
	21	153 2/8	94	HP/RIFLE	BERGMAN	DAVID	1327
	22	153 0/8	90	HP/RIFLE	TAYLOR	KEVIN	1355
	23	152 4/8	78	HP/RIFLE	SCHUSTER	IRVIN E.	1423
	23	152 4/8	86	HP/RIFLE	BRUMBAUGH	DAVID A.	1423
	25	151 7/8	94	HP/RIFLE	COULTER	TERRY	1550
	26	151 5/8	80	HP/RIFLE	EASLEY	LEROY	1586
	27	151 2/8	71	HP/RIFLE	HUSE	RICKY	1656
	28	150 4/8	74	HP/RIFLE	LAY	KEITH	1811
	29	150 3/8	86	HP/RIFLE	BOECKMAN	TERRY	1834
	30	147 3/8	95	HP/RIFLE	SCHULTZ	RANDALL	2155
	31	146 4/8	95	HP/RIFLE	DENT	DALE	2242
	32	145 4/8	85	HP/RIFLE	HOUSE	BOYD	2331
	33	145 1/8	96	BOW	HOUSE	BOYD	2379
	34	144 1/8	93	HP/RIFLE	DAVIS	DONNIE L.	2498
	35	141 3/8	96	HP/RIFLE	DAVIS	DONNIE L.	2812

COUNTY	COUNTY RANK	SCORE	YEAR TAKEN	WEAPON	HUNTER	FIRST NAME	STATE RANK
KNOX	36	140 6/8	95	HP/RIFLE	STRANGE	KEVIN	2895
LACLEDE	1	186 2/8	72	HP/RIFLE	OGLE	LARRY	16
	2	176 6/8	76	HP/RIFLE	SULLIVAN	CHARLES	58
	3	170 4/8	86	HP/RIFLE	SHERRER	KEITH D.	140
	4	167 2/8	89	HP/RIFLE	KRUEGER	ELDAR R.	221
	5	166 3/8	88	HP/RIFLE	MOYERS	GERALD D.	249
	6	157 2/8	78	HP/RIFLE	TAGGART	KEITH	853
	7	155 6/8	92	BOW	McCANN	ROY	1004
	8	154 0/8	80	HP/RIFLE	WILSON	WALLACE	1219
	9	153 5/8	92	HP/RIFLE	TAGGART	KEITH	1273
	10	152 5/8	81	HP/RIFLE	DICKINSON	KENNETH LEE	1399
	11	152 0/8	93	HP/RIFLE	HARRIS	JOHN M.	1519
	12	150 2/8	78	HP/RIFLE	FREDERICK	BILL	1853
	13	149 6/8	73	HP/RIFLE	ESTHER	W.S.	1926
	14	149 2/8	72	HP/RIFLE	SMITH	DEE	1973
	14	149 2/8	91	HP/RIFLE	YOUNG	ROBERT A.	1973
	16	147 1/8	88	HP/RIFLE	FULKERSON	BRUCE	2183
	17	145 7/8	95	HP/RIFLE	HARRIS	JOHN M.	2302
	18	145 0/8	64	HP/RIFLE	MANION	ED	2391
	19	144 5/8	81	BOW	PETERSON	RICHARD	2442
	20	144 0/8	72	HP/RIFLE	McMURDO	MIKE	2514
	21	143 7/8	89	HP/RIFLE	YOUNG	ROBERT A.	2533
	22	143 6/8	93	HP/RIFLE	TREMBLER	JOEL	2550
	23	143 5/8	75	HP/RIFLE	SULLIVAN	CHARLES	2564
	24	143 3/8	85	HP/RIFLE	RAINES	MIKE	2591
	25	142 5/8	87	HP/RIFLE	UDER	KENNY	2660
	26	142 4/8	82	HP/RIFLE	WALLANDER	JACK	2678
	26	142 4/8	84	HP/RIFLE	BAKER	BOBBY	2678
	28	142 1/8	94	BOW	LEMERY	GARY	2709
	29	142 0/8	81	HP/RIFLE	HILTON	DELMAR	2725
	29	142 0/8	95	HP/RIFLE	VANDERHOEF	WILLIAM C.	2725
	31	141 7/8	82	HP/RIFLE	FUGITT	BOB	2747
	32	141 3/8	89	HP/RIFLE	SULLIVAN	BRANDON	2812
	32	141 3/8	93	HP/RIFLE	PATTON	MARY	2812
	34	141 1/8	88	HP/RIFLE	MASSEY	DENNIS	2844
	35	140 3/8	82	HP/RIFLE	HILTON	MATT	2935
	36	140 2/8	88	HP/RIFLE	McCORMICK	BRANDON	2952
	37	140 0/8	95	HP/RIFLE	MIZER	TIM W.	2990
LAFAYETTE	1	156 2/8	71	HP/RIFLE	BUESING	MERLE	953
	2	148 7/8	70	HP/RIFLE	LARKIN	THOMAS	2012
	3	147 0/8	91	HP/RIFLE	KRAUS	KEN	2195
	4	146 7/8	91	HP/RIFLE	RUNNELS	TRACY	2214
	5	145 6/8	91	HP/RIFLE	WODRICH	DARRELL	2311
	6	144 0/8	94	HP/RIFLE	BEUMER	DEAN	2514
	7	141 4/8	85	HP/RIFLE	KEY	MIKE	2787
	7	141 4/8	91	HP/RIFLE	LIMBACK	WILLIAM	2787
	9	140 7/8	95	HP/RIFLE	WILLIAMS	CHARLES	2877
LAWRENCE	1	159 4/8	94	HP/RIFLE	BAX	DEREK A.	654
	2	151 6/8	85	HP/RIFLE	JOHNSON	LARRY	1566
	3	147 2/8	94	BOW	GRAFF	JASON	2167
	4	145 4/8	84	HP/RIFLE	HAMM	MELVIN	2331
	5	144 4/8	84	HP/RIFLE	CLAYTON	JERRY	2459
LEWIS	1	167 7/8	89	HP/RIFLE	MULLEN	SCOTT	197
	2	166 7/8	93	HP/RIFLE	ELLISON	JOHN	230
	3	165 3/8	67	HP/RIFLE	HUDNUT	GILVIA B.	288
	4	164 1/8	83	HP/RIFLE	EWING	L. DALE	345
	5	162 5/8	70	HP/RIFLE	SIMMONS	ART	417
	6	161 5/8	86	HP/RIFLE	MASON	GENE	486
	7	161 2/8	89	HP/RIFLE	FOUST	LONNIE	512

COUNTY	COUNTY RANK	SCORE	YEAR TAKEN	WEAPON	HUNTER	FIRST NAME	STATE RANK
LEWIS	8	161 1/8	72	HP/RIFLE	PENN	LARRY	520
	9	158 6/8	90	HP/RIFLE	SEAY	JAMES H.	719
	10	157 5/8	94	HP/RIFLE	HITTLER	TRACY	821
	11	156 2/8	86	HP/RIFLE	MILLER	RICHARD D.	953
	12	155 5/8	70	HP/RIFLE	SPARKS	RILEY P.	1023
	12	155 5/8	86	HP/RIFLE	McDONALD	JAMES	1023
	14	154 0/8	81	HP/RIFLE	BARICKMAN	TOM	1219
	15	153 5/8	79	HP/RIFLE	McCUTCHAN	DENNIS	1273
	16	153 2/8	75	HP/RIFLE	PINSON	KENNETH R.	1327
	17	152 4/8	83	HP/RIFLE	SCHULTZ	JEFF	1423
	18	151 5/8	94	HP/RIFLE	SHUMAN	MARK	1586
	19	151 4/8	90	BOW	EMRICK	BLAINE	1613
	20	151 2/8	73	HP/RIFLE	STEWART	EDWARD L.	1656
	20	151 2/8	85	HP/RIFLE	ST. CLAIR	STEVE	1656
	22	150 4/8	84	HP/RIFLE	TODD	CRAIG	1811
	22	150 4/8	93	HP/RIFLE	ASKEW	LARRY	1811
LINCOLN	1	182 1/8	88	HP/RIFLE	MUDD	DAVID	27
	2	173 1/8	92	HP/RIFLE	NARUP, DDS	DANIEL A.	97
	3	171 2/8	92	HP/RIFLE	NORTON	NEIL	123
	4	162 0/8	60	HP/RIFLE	STARKEY	ROBERT	462
	5	161 6/8	86	PICK-UP	NEUSUS	JACK	476
	5	161 6/8	88	HP/RIFLE	SITZE	RICHARD	476
	7	161 5/8	83	HP/RIFLE	BRAUNGARDT	JASON	486
	8	161 0/8	84	HP/RIFLE	WELLS	RON	530
	9	160 3/8	95	BOW	CREECH	SCOTT	574
	10	159 7/8	88	HP/RIFLE	OWENS	BILL	620
	11	159 2/8	96	HP/RIFLE	CHARTRAND	LONNIE	675
	12	158 2/8	83	HP/RIFLE	PORTER	RAY	763
	13	158 0/8	93	BOW	GNADE	MARK	788
	14	157 7/8	87	HP/RIFLE	McCARTNEY	GARY	806
	15	156 6/8	81	PICK-UP	HEITMAN	GERALD	900
	15	156 6/8	83	HP/RIFLE	EICHLER	KEN	900
	17	156 5/8	58	HP/RIFLE	NIEHOFF	JOE	911
	18	156 3/8	89	HP/RIFLE	BRAUNGARDT	GARY	940
	19	156 2/8	95	PICK-UP	HURD	J.D.	953
	20	156 0/8	85	HP/RIFLE	BOWERS	BRUCE	981
	21	155 4/8	94	HP/RIFLE	STEPHENS	CARLIS	1040
	22	154 4/8	84	HP/RIFLE	HUPP	JERRY	1164
	23	154 2/8	77	HP/RIFLE	BRIGGS	GARY E.	1186
	23	154 2/8	90	HP/RIFLE	SHOCKLEE	DERON A.	1186
	25	154 0/8	79	HP/RIFLE	WOMMACK	DAVE	1219
	26	153 7/8	86	HP/RIFLE	KENNEDY, JR.	RICHARD J.	1238
	27	152 2/8	77	HP/RIFLE	SOMMER	RICHARD	1469
	28	152 1/8	95	BOW	DIETIKER	STEVE	1493
	29	152 0/8	88	HP/RIFLE	CONNETT	SQUIRE	1519
	29	152 0/8	89	BOW	THOMPSON, JR.	DONALD E.	1519
	31	151 4/8	84	HP/RIFLE	DETJEN	BRYON	1613
	32	150 4/8	87	HP/RIFLE	HERMANN	STEVE	1811
	33	150 1/8	74	HP/RIFLE	CREECH	MIKE	1879
	34	150 0/8	89	HP/RIFLE	EISENBATH	DAVID C.	1897
	34	150 0/8	93	HP/RIFLE	MENNEMEYER	ED	1897
	36	142 5/8	95	HP/RIFLE	MUDD	BILLY	2660
	37	142 3/8	80	HP/RIFLE	TWELLMAN	RON	2691
LINN	1	193 4/8	96	HP/RIFLE	KEARNS	TIM J.	3
	2	180 2/8	70	HP/RIFLE	BURCH	E.L.	40
	3	173 7/8	91	HP/RIFLE	SIMPSON	DANNY	86
	4	171 2/8	92	HP/RIFLE	MUELLER	BRYAN	123
	5	170 4/8	76	BOW	SPAINHOUR	DONALD	140
	6	168 2/8	94	HP/RIFLE	VANRADEN	DAVID	190

COUNTY	COUNTY RANK	SCORE	YEAR TAKEN	WEAPON	HUNTER	FIRST NAME	STATE RANK
LINN	7	167 4/8	91	HP/RIFLE	FITZGERALD	JIM	213
	8	164 0/8	89	HP/RIFLE	YARDLEY	BRADY	349
	9	162 7/8	94	HP/RIFLE	MORRIS	BILL	406
	10	160 7/8	91	HP/RIFLE	BURNS	KEVIN	535
	11	160 4/8	96	HP/RIFLE	ATKINSON	CAMDEN	560
	12	157 2/8	91	HP/RIFLE	ROSANBALM	LARRY	853
	13	157 0/8	95	HP/RIFLE	GREGORY	WALTER D.	875
	14	153 1/8	84	HP/RIFLE	SCHUENEMAN	LESTER	1344
	15	152 5/8	73	BOW	SCHUENEMAN	LESTER	1399
	15	152 5/8	76	HP/RIFLE	GANN	ROBERT	1399
	17	152 2/8	68	HP/RIFLE	MARTENS	C.E.	1469
	18	151 4/8	86	HP/RIFLE	CLAIBORNE	JAMES	1613
	18	151 4/8	96	HP/RIFLE	PAULUS	JOHN	1613
	20	151 1/8	87	HP/RIFLE	CAMPBELL	KEITH	1690
	21	150 5/8	86	HP/RIFLE	ATKINSON	PAUL H.	1789
	22	150 4/8	90	HP/RIFLE	FITZGERALD	JIM	1811
	23	140 5/8	94	HP/RIFLE	KOENIGSFELD	RAY	2908
LIVINGSTON	1	171 1/8	86	HP/RIFLE	WEST	RICHARD	127
	2	164 2/8	87	HP/RIFLE	THOMPSON	MARK E.	332
	3	162 5/8	90	HP/RIFLE	THOMPSON	CLARENCE	417
	4	157 0/8	84	HP/RIFLE	MOORE	RICKY	875
	5	155 3/8	95	HP/RIFLE	SHILT	JOE D.	1059
	6	155 1/8	84	HP/RIFLE	BUSWELL	DENNIS	1091
	7	154 2/8	87	HP/RIFLE	MILLER	FOREST D.	1186
	8	153 5/8	80	BOW	COLEMAN	FRED	1273
	9	152 4/8	67	HP/RIFLE	YOS	RAYBURN	1423
	10	152 0/8	88	HP/RIFLE	SMITH	ROGER	1519
	11	151 6/8	86	HP/RIFLE	CARLSON	DOROTHY	1566
	12	151 3/8	91	HP/RIFLE	BUCKNER	E.W.	1637
	13	151 1/8	86	HP/RIFLE	MENEELY	HOWARD	1690
	14	150 6/8	94	HP/RIFLE	ROMESBURG	ROY	1756
	15	150 0/8	90	HP/RIFLE	LOLLAR	MIKE	1897
MACON	1	179 6/8	88	HP/RIFLE	YOUNG	JOHN W.	43
	2	179 4/8	95	HP/RIFLE	RICKWA	MARK	46
	3	177 0/8	91	HP/RIFLE	FREEMAN	W.R.	56
	4	174 2/8	59	HP/RIFLE	RUNNELS	ALVIN	82
	5	173 3/8	69	HP/RIFLE	WHITE	RICHARD	94
	6	170 2/8	92	HP/RIFLE	DEWEESE	RENEE	148
	7	165 7/8	95	HP/RIFLE	PHILLIPS	JOHN A.	269
	8	165 4/8	93	HP/RIFLE	STEVENS	TONY	283
	9	164 4/8	94	HP/RIFLE	WISDOM	GEORGE W.	319
	10	164 2/8	77	BOW	DEMORY	LLOYD	332
	11	163 4/8	91	HP/RIFLE	ALLEN	CALVIN	373
	12	163 2/8	77	HP/RIFLE	KOGER	RICHARD	383
	13	162 7/8	76	HP/RIFLE	PIKE	FRANK	406
	13	162 7/8	88	HP/RIFLE	WOOD	JERRY	406
	15	162 3/8	70	HP/RIFLE	WILLIAMS	DWIGHT	439
	16	161 1/8	83	HP/RIFLE	CARNAHAN	MAURIEDA	520
	17	160 5/8	90	HP/RIFLE	LENZINI, JR.	JOHN	553
	18	159 1/8	80	HP/RIFLE	HOUPT	CARL	687
	19	158 7/8	73	HP/RIFLE	BURKHART	VERN	712
	20	157 5/8	96	HP/RIFLE	BOND	DWAYNE	821
	21	157 1/8	59	HP/RIFLE	EASLEY	RAY	864
	22	156 6/8	96	HP/RIFLE	BASLER	ERIC J.	900
	23	156 4/8	84	HP/RIFLE	HOBBY	CHARLES	925
	23	156 4/8	86	HP/RIFLE	MEYER	DALE	925
	25	155 7/8	75	HP/RIFLE	AMEDEI	JOHN	994
	26	155 2/8	73	HP/RIFLE	BRADLEY	HAROLD	1068
	27	155 2/8	90	HP/RIFLE	SIMMONS	STEVEN	1068

MISSOURI SHOW-ME BIG BUCKS CLUB RECORDS OF WHITETAIL DEER BY COUNTY, TYPICAL

COUNTY	COUNTY RANK	SCORE	YEAR TAKEN	WEAPON	HUNTER	FIRST NAME	STATE RANK
MACON	28	154 7/8	69	HP/RIFLE	LARSON	ALBERT	1118
	29	154 3/8	88	HP/RIFLE	SMITH	KEN	1174
	30	153 7/8	84	HP/RIFLE	HEPWORTH	BERNARD	1238
	31	153 5/8	74	HP/RIFLE	POWELL	GARY R.	1273
	32	153 3/8	83	HP/RIFLE	ALBRIGHT	MICHAEL KEITH	1310
	33	153 2/8	76	HP/RIFLE	BANE	ARTHUR	1327
	33	153 2/8	94	HP/RIFLE	SLOAN	KENT	1327
	35	153 0/8	87	HP/RIFLE	RICHARDSON	BOBBY	1355
	36	152 7/8	85	HP/RIFLE	SMEDLEY	LARRY	1370
	37	152 5/8	87	BOW	HULL	MARTIN	1399
	38	152 4/8	69	HP/RIFLE	MILLER	CHARLES K.	1423
	39	151 5/8	92	HP/RIFLE	BARRON	GREGG	1586
	40	151 4/8	78	HP/RIFLE	WILSON	JIM	1613
	41	150 6/8	84	HP/RIFLE	CLEMENS	JOE	1756
	41	150 6/8	92	HP/RIFLE	BRISCOE	JOHN	1756
	43	150 5/8	89	HP/RIFLE	AKINS	ROBERT P.	1789
	44	150 4/8	95	HP/RIFLE	TAYLOR	JAMES	1811
	45	150 3/8	92	HP/RIFLE	McELROY	KEVIN D.	1834
	46	148 3/8	96	HP/RIFLE	HERRMANN	STEVE	2060
	47	145 6/8	95	HP/RIFLE	REPLOGLE	EVAN W.	2311
	48	145 2/8	95	HP/RIFLE	BALDWIN	PORTER	2361
	48	145 2/8	96	HP/RIFLE	SIZEMORE	DONNIE	2361
	50	144 6/8	76	HP/RIFLE	KEUNE	RONALD	2425
	51	142 6/8	96	HP/RIFLE	MILLIRON	STEVE	2647
	52	142 0/8	96	HP/RIFLE	BOGEART, JR.	ROBERT L.	2725
MADISON	1	165 7/8	94	BOW	HELM	TONY JOE	269
	2	162 1/8	83	HP/RIFLE	MORICE	VIRGIL C.	455
	3	156 5/8	96	HP/RIFLE	SCHMIDT	DANIEL D.	911
	4	155 1/8	64	HP/RIFLE	GANN	KENNETH	1091
	5	154 4/8	90	HP/RIFLE	TRIPP	GABRIEL W.	1164
	6	152 1/8	95	HP/RIFLE	BROOKS	DALE B.	1493
	7	149 1/8	86	HP/RIFLE	HARDING, JR.	JOHN A.	1988
	8	148 3/8	86	HP/RIFLE	THOMAS	DONALD M.	2060
	9	148 2/8	86	HP/RIFLE	PHILIPPS	THOMAS E.	2071
	10	144 3/8	89	HP/RIFLE	MOWRY	CHRIS	2466
	11	143 4/8	74	HP/RIFLE	PALUBIAK	GARY	2577
	12	143 3/8	71	HP/RIFLE	SCHULTZ	BILL	2591
	13	142 7/8	94	BOW	SHY	JUNIOR	2641
	14	141 1/8	67	HP/RIFLE	HENSON	IRA	2844
	15	140 6/8	68	HP/RIFLE	REICHERT	GEORGE	2895
	16	140 2/8	64	HP/RIFLE	WHITE	FRED	2952
	17	140 1/8	79	HP/RIFLE	BOYD	JIM	2978
	18	140 0/8	92	HP/RIFLE	LOWERY	GREG	2990
MARIES	1	180 7/8	94	HP/RIFLE	BILYEU	JESSE MATT	37
	2	169 2/8	80	HP/RIFLE	MITCHELL	JAMES	163
	3	166 7/8	82	HP/RIFLE	VERHOFF	PAUL	227
	4	165 0/8	84	HP/RIFLE	GRUBER	ROBERT W.	299
	5	164 0/8	83	HP/RIFLE	POGUE	JOHN	349
	6	163 0/8	86	HP/RIFLE	HEMPE	JOHN E.	393
	7	162 4/8	73	HP/RIFLE	THOMAS	GREG	431
	8	162 3/8	93	HP/RIFLE	MESSERSMITH	RICHARD	439
	9	160 6/8	77	HP/RIFLE	BENNEKE	ANTHONY	543
	10	160 2/8	87	HP/RIFLE	YORK	DARREL J.	584
	10	160 2/8	92	HP/RIFLE	SEYMORE	MURL	584
	12	158 4/8	95	HP/RIFLE	BOYD	PATRICK J.	739
	13	158 1/8	67	HP/RIFLE	HONSE	HENRY	777
	14	157 6/8	79	HP/RIFLE	MARSHALL	TOM	812
	15	156 4/8	86	HP/RIFLE	BUCKOWITZ	ART	925
	15	156 4/8	89	HP/RIFLE	WILES	GARY	925

MISSOURI SHOW-ME BIG BUCKS CLUB RECORDS OF WHITETAIL DEER BY COUNTY, TYPICAL

COUNTY	COUNTY RANK	SCORE	YEAR TAKEN	WEAPON	HUNTER	FIRST NAME	STATE RANK
MARIES	17	155 2/8	67	HP/RIFLE	HONSE	WESLEY	1068
	18	153 2/8	74	HP/RIFLE	KERR	ROBERT	1327
	19	152 7/8	85	HP/RIFLE	GADDY	LYNN	1370
	20	151 5/8	69	HP/RIFLE	HELTON	ROGER	1586
	21	151 1/8	75	HP/RIFLE	SCHEULEN	DANIEL	1690
	22	151 0/8	76	HP/RIFLE	WELLER	JERRY	1715
	22	151 0/8	93	HP/RIFLE	STEVENS, SR.	ROBERT L.	1715
	22	150 1/8	82	HP/RIFLE	HEMMINGHAUS	JOHN	1879
	25	149 4/8	92	HP/RIFLE	BRUNNERT, JR.	DON	1936
	26	149 3/8	95	HP/RIFLE	KLEFFNER	DON	1959
	27	149 2/8	79	HP/RIFLE	MOLKENBUR	DAVE	1973
	28	149 0/8	81	HP/RIFLE	MAHANEY	BOB	1998
	29	148 2/8	73	HP/RIFLE	JONES	RALPH	2071
	30	148 1/8	71	HP/RIFLE	SAPPINGTON	BILLY	2088
	31	147 5/8	86	HP/RIFLE	BARNHART	JOHN	2138
	32	146 3/8	75	HP/RIFLE	WEST	JOSEPH	2252
	33	146 2/8	92	HP/RIFLE	SINDEN, JR.	WILLIAM R.	2266
	34	146 0/8	90	HP/RIFLE	SKOUBY	JUDY	2290
	35	145 7/8	72	HP/RIFLE	RAMSEY	GABE	2302
	36	145 2/8	89	HP/RIFLE	KLEFNER	DON	2361
	37	145 2/8	95	PICK-UP	SCHWEER	JEFF	2361
	38	145 0/8	87	HP/RIFLE	NOBLETT	DENNIS	2391
	39	144 7/8	92	HP/RIFLE	STUEKEN	ROGER	2412
	40	144 3/8	89	HP/RIFLE	TOEBBEN	MIKE	2466
	41	144 2/8	89	HP/RIFLE	BELL	FRANZ	2483
	42	144 0/8	92	HP/RIFLE	RAGAN	DONALD G.	2514
	43	143 7/8	82	HP/RIFLE	RAGAN	ROGER	2533
	44	143 6/8	86	HP/RIFLE	FRITCHEY	JUSTIN D.	2550
	45	143 2/8	85	HP/RIFLE	WEBER	PAUL A.	2598
	46	143 2/8	87	BOW	RIDENHOUR	DANNEY	2598
	47	143 1/8	84	HP/RIFLE	FRITCHEY	CARL	2615
	48	143 0/8	78	HP/RIFLE	BUTLER	DOUG	2626
	49	142 6/8	82	HP/RIFLE	KLEFNER	MIKE	2647
	50	142 0/8	72	HP/RIFLE	PERKINS	ROBERT	2725
	50	142 0/8	72	HP/RIFLE	REDEL	LAWRENCE	2725
	50	142 0/8	92	BOW	ALEXANDER	MICHAEL	2725
	53	141 6/8	82	HP/RIFLE	KOEHLER	FRANK	2756
	54	141 4/8	95	HP/RIFLE	BUSCHMANN	RICK	2787
	55	141 0/8	79	HP/RIFLE	WILSON	BOB J.	2863
	56	140 7/8	72	HP/RIFLE	CORDSMEYER, JR.	ELMER	2877
	56	140 7/8	87	HP/RIFLE	GEMMING	DON	2877
	58	140 5/8	95	HP/RIFLE	YOUNG	JOHNNIE	2908
	59	140 2/8	75	HP/RIFLE	ROWE	DALE	2952
MARION	1	161 7/8	87	BOW	SCHAEFER	JAMES	467
	2	158 2/8	61	HP/RIFLE	McELWEE	BURYL	763
	3	152 2/8	93	HP/RIFLE	MILLER	PHILLIP	1469
	4	151 4/8	95	HP/RIFLE	BOHRER	RYAN	1613
	5	151 2/8	84	HP/RIFLE	BLOMBERG	CHRIS	1656
	6	150 7/8	94	HP/RIFLE	BELL, JR.	DONALD E.	1734
	7	142 5/8	90	BOW	CARSON	BOB	2660
	8	140 2/8	95	HP/RIFLE	DAVID	LARRY	2952
McDONALD	1	160 2/8	89	HP/RIFLE	BRIXEY	WILLARD	584
	2	157 0/8	71	HP/RIFLE	MITCHELL	NEAL	875
	3	154 2/8	76	HP/RIFLE	LYSTER	CLINT	1186
	4	152 4/8	67	HP/RIFLE	HARPER	ROYCE	1423
	5	152 0/8	70	HP/RIFLE	MURRAY	JAMES B.	1519
	6	150 7/8	58	HP/RIFLE	JOHNSON	JACK	1734
	7	149 2/8	91	HP/RIFLE	WARDEN	SUSAN RAE	1973
	8	145 2/8	74	HP/RIFLE	WASMAN	BOBBY	2361

MISSOURI SHOW-ME BIG BUCKS CLUB RECORDS OF WHITETAIL DEER BY COUNTY, TYPICAL

COUNTY	COUNTY RANK	SCORE	YEAR TAKEN	WEAPON	HUNTER	FIRST NAME	STATE RANK
McDONALD	9	144 7/8	92	HP/RIFLE	ANDERSON	RANDY	2412
	10	144 5/8	88	HP/RIFLE	STARCHMAN	RON	2442
	11	143 1/8	67	HP/RIFLE	WELLESLEY	ALLAN	2615
	12	141 6/8	71	HP/RIFLE	MICHAEL	RICHARD	2756
	13	141 1/8	73	HP/RIFLE	RING	GERALD	2844
	14	140 0/8	73	HP/RIFLE	BUSH	DR. S.S.	2990
MERCER	1	187 1/8	86	PICK-UP	SUMMERS	BOB	10
	2	173 0/8	65	HP/RIFLE	CLAPHAM	CODA	100
	3	172 3/8	88	HP/RIFLE	SIMPSON	JARIN	107
	4	172 2/8	93	HP/RIFLE	HOLT	BRAD	109
	5	167 6/8	67	HP/RIFLE	BARNETT	ALLEN R.	204
	6	166 5/8	88	HP/RIFLE	GOODIN	JERRY	238
	7	163 2/8	90	HP/RIFLE	TRAVIS	DAMON K.	383
	8	163 0/8	83	HP/RIFLE	NELSON	TRACY	393
	9	162 3/8	71	HP/RIFLE	THOMPSON	E.J.	439
	10	159 6/8	75	HP/RIFLE	SHAFFER	REVA L.	628
	11	159 1/8	89	HP/RIFLE	RALSTON	MIKE	687
	12	158 0/8	89	HP/RIFLE	EAKES	JASON	788
	13	156 1/8	78	HP/RIFLE	EASTIN	CURTIS	967
	14	154 7/8	89	HP/RIFLE	DeMOSS	KENNETH	1118
	15	154 3/8	90	HP/RIFLE	KEEN	MICHAEL J.	1174
	16	154 1/8	73	HP/RIFLE	HERIFORD	ART	1207
	17	154 0/8	84	HP/RIFLE	BIERLE	JEFF	1219
	18	153 4/8	71	HP/RIFLE	HODGES	FRANK D.	1287
	19	152 7/8	72	HP/RIFLE	CLEM	VELDON T.	1370
	20	152 0/8	75	HP/RIFLE	MOORE	RICHARD	1519
	20	152 0/8	75	HP/RIFLE	GEORGE	JERRY	1519
	20	152 0/8	94	HP/RIFLE	SLAUGHTER	DAVID	1519
	23	151 6/8	90	HP/RIFLE	CRAIG	DARRYL D.	1566
	23	151 6/8	93	HP/RIFLE	BAKER	ROBERT	1566
	25	151 2/8	77	HP/RIFLE	NOE	JUDITH M.	1656
	26	150 7/8	91	HP/RIFLE	SHARP	CHRIS	1734
	27	148 4/8	96	HP/RIFLE	FINNEY	GRAG	2048
	28	142 1/8	82	HP/RIFLE	MARTIN	JAMES W.	2709
MILLER	1	173 4/8	96	HP/RIFLE	BERRY	STEVE	92
	2	172 1/8	92	HP/RIFLE	BELL	JIM	111
	3	170 3/8	71	HP/RIFLE	JOHNSON	RAY	144
	4	166 0/8	92	HP/RIFLE	CASTEN	BRUCE	262
	5	165 0/8	92	HP/RIFLE	MOSELEY	RANDY B.	299
	6	164 6/8	54	HP/RIFLE	ROBINETT	OSBY L.	307
	7	163 2/8	81	HP/RIFLE	KINDER	JIM	383
	8	159 5/8	94	HP/RIFLE	SCHULTE	WAYNE	641
	9	158 6/8	83	HP/RIFLE	GRAVES	TOM	719
	10	158 0/8	96	HP/RIFLE	HOWSER	EDWARD A.	788
	11	157 4/8	88	HP/RIFLE	DUNCAN	TIM	833
	12	157 1/8	60	HP/RIFLE	PEMORTON	OSCAR D.	864
	13	156 6/8	85	HP/RIFLE	MYERS	BILL	900
	14	154 6/8	95	HP/RIFLE	WILDER	KERRY	1130
	15	152 4/8	94	HP/RIFLE	MYERS	JIM J.	1423
	16	152 1/8	83	HP/RIFLE	GROOSE	CHRIS	1493
	17	151 7/8	86	HP/RIFLE	BOWMAN	CHUCK	1550
	18	151 5/8	88	HP/RIFLE	BAX	ANTHONY	1586
	19	150 4/8	89	HP/RIFLE	FRITCHEY, JR.	LARRY	1811
	20	149 2/8	89	HP/RIFLE	BLOMBERG	ALAN	1973
	21	149 0/8	83	HP/RIFLE	PLEMMONS	JIMMIE	1998
	21	149 0/8	91	HP/RIFLE	MINNICK	TROY	1998
	23	148 6/8	94	HP/RIFLE	TIPTON	EDGER	2024
	24	148 4/8	87	HP/RIFLE	WALL	CLARK	2048
	25	148 3/8	87	HP/RIFLE	GOLDEN	EARL	2060

151

COUNTY	COUNTY RANK	SCORE	YEAR TAKEN	WEAPON	HUNTER	FIRST NAME	STATE RANK
MILLER	26	148 1/8	87	HP/RIFLE	MORGAN	ANTHONY	2088
	27	147 3/8	91	HP/RIFLE	PEMBERTON	DAVID	2155
	28	145 4/8	92	HP/RIFLE	PHILLIPS	PATSY J.	2331
	29	145 1/8	91	HP/RIFLE	VESTAL	TIM	2379
	30	144 2/8	93	HP/RIFLE	LUTTRELL	TONY RAY	2483
	31	143 6/8	92	BOW	STONER	MIKE	2550
	32	143 5/8	74	HP/RIFLE	RACKERS	STANLEY	2564
	33	143 2/8	94	HP/RIFLE	HERIGON	NATHAN	2598
	34	143 0/8	86	HP/RIFLE	WILSON	JERRY	2626
	35	142 2/8	73	HP/RIFLE	STRANGE	JACK	2701
	36	141 1/8	82	HP/RIFLE	SCHINSA	MICHAEL	2844
MISSISSIPPI	1	146 3/8	83	HP/RIFLE	DUENNE, JR.	HENRY	2252
	2	145 0/8	91	HP/RIFLE	DILL	DEE	2391
MONITEAU	1	164 4/8	76	HP/RIFLE	HICKAM	J.R.	319
	2	164 0/8	74	HP/RIFLE	McPHERSON	JOHN	349
	3	163 7/8	86	HP/RIFLE	WILSON	RANDY	356
	4	163 4/8	81	HP/RIFLE	WHITE	CHRIS	373
	5	156 2/8	83	HP/RIFLE	FARRIS	NICK	953
	6	155 7/8	84	HP/RIFLE	HOBACK	DENNIS H.	994
	7	152 0/8	76	HP/RIFLE	NIVENS	NORMAN	1519
	8	150 5/8	88	HP/RIFLE	HOWARD	KENNETH R.	1789
	8	150 5/8	95	HP/RIFLE	BIERI	JASON	1789
	10	149 6/8	82	HP/RIFLE	WYCOFF	LARRY	1926
	10	149 6/8	88	HP/RIFLE	KUNZE	WAYNE	1926
	12	148 3/8	90	HP/RIFLE	BURLINGAME	PHILLIP	2060
	13	148 2/8	88	HP/RIFLE	WOLFRUM	GAIL E.	2071
	13	148 2/8	91	HP/RIFLE	REDDEN	CHARLES	2071
	15	148 1/8	92	HP/RIFLE	BARNETT	TERRY	2088
	16	147 7/8	83	HP/RIFLE	PORTER	LANNY	2114
	17	147 0/8	91	HP/RIFLE	FLEISCHMANN	GARY	2195
	18	145 7/8	89	HP/RIFLE	JENKINS	DANIEL R.	2302
	19	144 5/8	87	HP/RIFLE	HEES	DAVID	2442
	20	144 3/8	92	HP/RIFLE	PAYNE	COLE	2466
	21	144 1/8	96	HP/RIFLE	KUNZE	WAYNE	2498
	22	143 5/8	81	HP/RIFLE	LITTLE	HEATH	2564
	23	143 3/8	80	HP/RIFLE	DIETZEL	JOHN	2591
	24	142 5/8	90	HP/RIFLE	LIGHT	KEVIN	2660
	25	142 2/8	82	HP/RIFLE	GOLLADAY	AL	2701
	26	142 2/8	93	HP/RIFLE	ZIEHMER	ROBERT L.	2701
	27	142 0/8	86	HP/RIFLE	ENOWSKI	BOB	2725
	27	142 0/8	92	HP/RIFLE	DOWELL, JR.	HARLAN	2725
	29	141 1/8	86	HP/RIFLE	YORK	WAYNE	2844
	29	141 1/8	92	HP/RIFLE	HEES	DAVID	2844
	31	140 5/8	84	HP/RIFLE	JONES	GARY	2908
	32	140 0/8	93	HP/RIFLE	WOLFE	DANNY	2990
MONROE	1	179 0/8	88	HP/RIFLE	GARNETT	TOMMY	49
	2	172 3/8	67	HP/RIFLE	BRAY	CLARK E.	107
	3	167 5/8	82	HP/RIFLE	BIRD	JERRY	205
	4	167 3/8	92	HP/RIFLE	McMURDO	WES	217
	5	165 3/8	93	BOW	MEIER	LARRY	288
	6	163 7/8	83	HP/RIFLE	BALL	DARREN	356
	7	162 6/8	96	HP/RIFLE	BOWMAN	RALPH	411
	8	160 5/8	69	HP/RIFLE	YUSKO	ANDREW	553
	9	159 2/8	94	HP/RIFLE	LEHENBAUER	BOB	675
	10	159 0/8	73	HP/RIFLE	BOZOIAN	DR. HARRY	695
	11	158 6/8	87	HP/RIFLE	WHEELER	MIKE	719
	12	158 4/8	86	HP/RIFLE	McMORRIS	JAMES R.	739
	12	158 4/8	89	HP/RIFLE	RENCH	STEVE L.	739
	14	157 7/8	88	HP/RIFLE	MAYES	BILL	806

COUNTY	COUNTY RANK	SCORE	YEAR TAKEN	WEAPON	HUNTER	FIRST NAME	STATE RANK
MONROE	15	157 5/8	90	BOW	WILLINGHAM	RAY	821
	16	155 2/8	88	BOW	HAYS	DON LEO	1068
	17	154 5/8	90	HP/RIFLE	STROPPEL	CALVIN	1146
	18	153 4/8	70	HP/RIFLE	GILLIAM	ROBERT J.	1287
	19	153 2/8	74	HP/RIFLE	DIXSON	MICHAEL R.	1327
	20	153 0/8	93	HP/RIFLE	PEIRICK	TOM	1355
	21	152 6/8	73	HP/RIFLE	MINOR	FRED	1385
	22	152 3/8	73	HP/RIFLE	ABBOT	JOE	1453
	23	151 7/8	71	HP/RIFLE	BOZOIAN	STEVE	1550
	24	151 5/8	82	HP/RIFLE	MAGRUDER	MIKE	1586
	25	149 4/8	93	HP/RIFLE	ASHER	VERNON	1936
	26	149 2/8	96	HP/RIFLE	WEST	JUSTIN	1973
MONTGOMERY	1	176 0/8	96	HP/RIFLE	KNOEPFLEIN	DAVE	63
	2	175 0/8	76	HP/RIFLE	WOODRUFF, JR.	RICHARD	68
	3	174 3/8	77	HP/RIFLE	DIXON	DARREN D.	78
	4	170 0/8	88	HP/RIFLE	MASKEY	KENNETH	151
	5	169 0/8	77	HP/RIFLE	SPENO	SAM J.	170
	6	168 6/8	94	HP/RIFLE	VANBOOVEN	DAVE	174
	7	166 3/8	90	HP/RIFLE	HAM	THOMAS	249
	8	164 2/8	94	HP/RIFLE	GROSSE	BEN	332
	9	161 7/8	94	HP/RIFLE	ROSNER	MARK	467
	10	160 7/8	87	HP/RIFLE	ALVAREZ	DENNIS	535
	11	160 5/8	87	HP/RIFLE	WAELDER	KEVIN	553
	12	160 0/8	71	HP/RIFLE	SCHULTE	GERALD	605
	13	159 3/8	78	HP/RIFLE	DEVLIN	GENE	665
	14	159 1/8	86	HP/RIFLE	SCHLANKER	FRANK	687
	15	159 0/8	93	HP/RIFLE	GRIMES	STEVE	695
	16	156 4/8	87	HP/RIFLE	KICKER	ROBERT	925
	16	156 4/8	89	HP/RIFLE	DEBENPORT	ROGER G.	925
	18	156 0/8	91	HP/RIFLE	HAYES	GARY	981
	19	155 5/8	95	HP/RIFLE	SULLIVAN	KEVIN P.	1023
	20	155 0/8	93	HP/RIFLE	HAM	RICHARD	1102
	21	154 3/8	94	HP/RIFLE	UTHLAUT	RONALD	1174
	22	153 7/8	73	HP/RILFE	SCHULTE	GERALD	1238
	23	153 6/8	93	HP/RIFLE	CARTEE	GREG	1256
	24	153 3/8	90	HP/RIFLE	CULLOM	DAVID	1310
	25	152 3/8	85	HP/RIFLE	RUPPEL	RUSSELL	1453
	26	152 2/8	79	HP/RIFLE	HIATTE	KENNETH	1469
	27	151 5/8	79	HP/RIFLE	LANG	MIKE	1586
	27	151 5/8	93	HP/RIFLE	WALTON	SCOTT	1586
	29	151 3/8	95	HP/RIFLE	SHELTON	DOUG	1637
	30	151 2/8	88	HP/RIFLE	RETHERFORD	JUDY	1656
	31	150 7/8	95	HP/RIFLE	ROBINSON	JoANN	1734
	32	148 2/8	95	HP/RIFLE	KNOEPFLEIN	JACK	2071
	33	147 0/8	95	HP/RIFLE	GRAVE	DOUG	2195
MORGAN	1	162 5/8	85	HP/RIFLE	AVEY	JEFFREY	417
	2	162 1/8	91	HP/RIFLE	DOUGLAS	ERNIE	455
	3	160 2/8	92	HP/RIFLE	BRUNJES	MARK	584
	4	159 5/8	94	HP/RIFLE	WALSH	JEFF	641
	5	158 6/8	96	HP/RIFLE	NOLTING	JEFF	719
	6	157 6/8	96	HP/RIFLE	SHULTZ	GENE	812
	7	157 4/8	82	HP/RIFLE	SANDERS	GRACE	833
	8	156 3/8	96	HP/RIFLE	HOLSTEN	YRONNE	940
	9	154 2/8	95	HP/RIFLE	WOHLT	GEORGE H.	1186
	10	154 0/8	94	HP/RIFLE	ROSS	MICHAEL E.	1219
	11	152 1/8	58	HP/RIFLE	PARRISH	ROBERT	1493
	12	152 0/8	55	HP/RIFLE	GILL	CLYDE	1519
	13	151 2/8	86	HP/RIFLE	KNUTH	KENNY	1656
	14	151 0/8	89	HP/RIFLE	McCURRY	L.O.	1715

COUNTY	COUNTY RANK	SCORE	YEAR TAKEN	WEAPON	HUNTER	FIRST NAME	STATE RANK
MORGAN	14	151 0/8	96	BOW	SUTTON	BOB	1715
	16	150 6/8	86	HP/RIFLE	MITCHELL	CHARLEY	1756
	16	150 6/8	94	HP/RIFLE	BONDURANT	STEVE	1756
	18	149 6/8	78	HP/RIFLE	MEYER	HAROLD	1926
	19	149 5/8	82	HP/RIFLE	HIBBON	JOHN	1936
	19	149 5/8	91	HP/RIFLE	MILLER	DAVID	1936
	19	149 5/8	95	HP/RIFLE	ROSS	MATT	1936
	22	148 4/8	68	HP/RIFLE	EARNEST, JR.	L.M.	2048
	23	148 3/8	66	HP/RIFLE	JONES	JOHN E.	2060
	23	148 3/0	82	HP/RIFLE	VOGT	STEVE	2060
	25	148 0/8	91	HP/RIFLE	SIMMONS	DAVID	2101
	25	148 0/8	92	HP/RIFLE	MARRIOTT	PHILLIP C.	2101
	27	147 3/8	83	HP/RIFLE	HALL	GARY	2155
	27	147 3/8	88	HP/RIFLE	DITTO	JOE	2155
	29	147 0/8	80	HP/RIFLE	HEIMSOTH	MARK D.	2195
	30	146 7/8	72	HP/RIFLE	ZIMMERMAN	ELWOOD	2214
	31	146 3/8	91	HP/RIFLE	HOLEM	LURLEEN	2252
	32	145 5/8	88	HP/RIFLE	BORTS	JOANN	2324
	33	145 0/8	96	HP/RIFLE	MILLER	BRIAN S.	2391
	34	144 6/8	94	HP/RIFLE	MAHNKEN	KEVIN	2425
	35	144 3/8	80	HP/RIFLE	RIGHT	MAXRY L.	2466
	35	144 3/8	80	HP/RIFLE	YOUNG	GARY L.	2466
	37	144 2/8	66	HP/RIFLE	VIEBROCK	BOB	2483
	37	144 2/8	94	HP/RIFLE	WRIGHT	LESTER	2483
	39	144 0/8	78	HP/RIFLE	WHITE	LORAN	2514
	40	143 2/8	91	HP/RIFLE	McPHERSON	MARTIN	2598
	41	143 1/8	91	HP/RIFLE	WILLIS	WISLEY DALE	2615
	42	142 4/8	94	HP/RIFLE	WOOLERY	WALTER	2678
	43	141 7/8	68	HP/RIFLE	LANGEWISCH	HARRY	2747
	44	141 4/8	94	HP/RIFLE	WENIG	ROBERT D.	2787
	45	141 1/8	83	HP/RIFLE	SCHRECK	LARRY	2844
	46	141 0/8	93	HP/RIFLE	NOLTING	RONNIE	2863
	47	140 4/8	82	HP/RIFLE	THEISEN	DAVID	2925
	48	140 2/8	69	HP/RIFLE	HICKSON	JACK	2952
NEW MADRID	1	153 3/8	96	HP/RIFLE	SIMMONS	FLOYD	1310
	2	144 0/8	85	HP/RIFLE	DANIELS	AVERA	2514
	3	143 6/8	83	HP/RIFLE	JAMES	RILEY	2550
	4	140 5/8	95	BOW	GLAUS	BILL R.	2908
NEWTON	1	174 3/8	94	HP/RIFLE	WOLFE	SCOTT	78
	2	160 2/8	82	HP/RIFLE	REYNOLDS	HARLAN	584
	3	159 4/8	84	HP/RIFLE	VERMILLION	BOB	654
	4	158 0/8	78	HP/RIFLE	LUMMIS	PERRY	788
	5	154 3/8	87	HP/RIFLE	MAYBERRY	TOM	1174
	6	152 4/8	54	HP/RIFLE	GRANE	JOHN R.	1423
	7	151 6/8	82	HP/RIFLE	SHOBE	BOB	1566
	8	150 6/8	76	HP/RIFLE	ELBRADER	DENNIS R.	1756
	9	150 5/8	86	HP/RIFLE	KING	TONY	1789
	10	148 5/8	77	HP/RIFLE	BINGHAM	DALE	2035
	11	147 2/8	67	HP/RIFLE	WELSH	TOM	2167
	12	145 6/8	85	HP/RIFLE	HORNOR	CURTIS	2311
	13	145 5/8	65	HP/RIFLE	COOPER	DAVID F.	2324
	13	145 5/8	85	HP/RIFLE	SWARTZ	GARY	2324
	15	140 7/8	83	HP/RIFLE	GARCIA	JEFF	2877
	16	140 5/8	68	HP/RIFLE	LOPRESTI	ANTHONY F.	2908
NODAWAY	1	173 4/8	87	HP/RIFLE	HART	GARY	92
	2	172 4/8	85	BOW	DAVISON	LARRY	105
	3	167 5/8	78	HP/RIFLE	BALDWIN	LARRY	205
	4	166 7/8	95	HP/RIFLE	HOLTMAN	STEVE	230
	5	164 7/8	72	HP/RIFLE	McKEE	ROBERT	303

MISSOURI SHOW-ME BIG BUCKS CLUB RECORDS OF WHITETAIL DEER BY COUNTY, TYPICAL

COUNTY	COUNTY RANK	SCORE	YEAR TAKEN	WEAPON	HUNTER	FIRST NAME	STATE RANK
NODAWAY	6	163 3/8	89	HP/RIFLE	DAVISON	JEFF	378
	7	162 3/8	59	HP/RIFLE	ADKINS	FRANKLIN T.	439
	8	161 5/8	74	HP/RIFLE	HILSABECK	ED	486
	9	160 4/8	83	HP/RIFLE	WALLACE	DICK	560
	10	160 1/8	82	PICK-UP	AUFFERT	CHARLES	599
	11	157 4/8	72	HP/RIFLE	McGINNESS	J.D.	833
	12	156 0/8	88	HP/RIFLE	PEVE	BOB	981
	13	155 1/8	72	HP/RIFLE	DAVISON	LARRY	1091
	14	154 5/8	96	BOW	HARDEN	MAX	1146
	15	154 0/8	86	HP/RIFLE	FARRELL	STEVEN	1219
	15	154 0/8	88	HP/RIFLE	OWENS	RICHARD	1219
	17	153 5/8	85	HP/RIFLE	ANDREWS	RONALD	1273
	18	153 1/8	81	HP/RIFLE	McINTYRE	BASIL	1344
	19	152 7/8	96	HP/RIFLE	WILHELM	JIM	1370
	20	152 4/8	84	HP/RIFLE	GRAHAM	GALEN	1423
	20	152 4/8	86	HP/RIFLE	DURBIN	FRANCIS	1423
	22	150 6/8	85	BOW	DAVISON	JEFF	1756
	23	150 5/8	80	HP/RIFLE	LINDSTRON	C.B.	1789
	24	149 3/8	95	HP/RIFLE	FOSTER	WILLIAM L.	1959
OREGON	1	156 6/8	83	HP/RIFLE	VESTAL	JACK	900
	2	153 2/8	90	HP/RIFLE	SUTTON	DONALD	1327
	3	152 0/8	81	HP/RIFLE	BARTON	GARY	1519
	4	150 2/8	77	HP/RIFLE	SIMMONS	ROSCOE	1853
	5	149 3/8	76	HP/RIFLE	BARTON	GARY	1959
	5	149 3/8	87	HP/RIFLE	WALKER	GARY	1959
	7	148 4/8	83	HP/RIFLE	ALSUP	BRENT	2048
	8	147 7/8	89	HP/RIFLE	EMERY	MIKE	2114
	9	147 2/8	68	HP/RIFLE	BRUMLEY	DONALD	2167
	10	146 1/8	93	HP/RIFLE	PARROTT	WOODROW	2281
	11	144 7/8	95	HP/RIFLE	HOLLIS	RICK	2412
	12	142 2/8	57	HP/RIFLE	CLINE	GLEN	2701
	13	141 4/8	71	HP/RIFLE	PARROTT	WOODROW	2787
	14	141 0/8	70	HP/RIFLE	MILLER	WILLIAM M.	2863
	15	140 5/8	96	HP/RIFLE	McFANN	JERRY S.	2908
	16	140 3/8	89	HP/RIFLE	COLLICOTT	BILL	2935
OSAGE	1	177 6/8	95	HP/RIFLE	LANGFORD	CHUCK	53
	2	168 2/8	86	HP/RIFLE	GRANNEMANN	MARK	190
	3	167 3/8	95	HP/RIFLE	MORFELD	SCOTT	217
	4	164 6/8	89	HP/RIFLE	KAISER	MARK A.	307
	5	164 4/8	94	HP/RIFLE	ROESLEIN	DERRICK	319
	6	161 4/8	95	HP/RIFLE	TITUS	RUSSELL	493
	7	161 3/8	80	HP/RIFLE	WEBER	ROGER	503
	8	160 4/8	92	BOW	LUECKE	LEON	560
	9	158 7/8	90	HP/RIFLE	COX	MIKE	712
	10	158 2/8	82	HP/RIFLE	BOLTEN	DELBERT	763
	11	157 1/8	80	HP/RIFLE	PFAHL	RICHARD	864
	12	157 0/8	88	HP/RIFLE	REYNOLDS	DENNIS	875
	13	156 7/8	90	HP/RIFLE	HURST	DANNY	893
	14	155 7/8	80	HP/RIFLE	MONROE	JERRY	994
	15	155 5/8	94	HP/RIFLE	VOSS	ADRIAN	1023
	16	154 2/8	71	HP/RIFLE	GAULT	HAROLD E.	1186
	17	154 2/8	91	HP/RIFLE	STUCKEY	MARK	1186
	18	153 4/8	72	HP/RIFLE	WATERS	JAMES	1287
	19	152 0/8	70	HP/RIFLE	ADKINS	GENE	1519
	20	151 7/8	96	HP/RIFLE	HENDRIX	GENEVIEVE	1550
	21	151 6/8	96	HP/RIFLE	FICK	PATRICK J.	1566
	22	151 4/8	63	HP/RIFLE	BODE	FRED F.	1613
	22	151 4/8	84	HP/RIFLE	FITZPATRICK	WAYNE	1613
	24	151 2/8	81	HP/RIFLE	BRANDT	URBAN	1656

COUNTY	COUNTY RANK	SCORE	YEAR TAKEN	WEAPON	HUNTER	FIRST NAME	STATE RANK
OSAGE	25	151 1/8	93	HP/RIFLE	BERHORST	JACOB	1690
	26	150 7/8	87	HP/RIFLE	RUSH	ALBERT	1734
	27	148 2/8	95	HP/RIFLE	ROESLEIN	RUDI	2071
	28	148 1/8	78	HP/RIFLE	WEBER	ROGER	2088
	29	147 7/8	88	HP/RIFLE	VOSS	DEREK A.	2114
	30	147 6/8	92	HP/RIFLE	HAFLEY	SAM	2126
	31	147 3/8	75	HP/RIFLE	KOELHER	WILLIAM	2155
	32	147 1/8	83	HP/RIFLE	BACON	AARON	2183
	33	146 6/8	77	HP/RIFLE	TOWNLEY	STEVEN	2225
	34	146 2/8	95	HP/RIFLE	WULFF	JEROME H.	2266
	35	146 1/8	73	HP/RIFLE	OTTO	DAVE	2281
	36	145 0/8	86	HP/RIFLE	BUDNIK	STEVEN	2391
	37	144 7/8	90	HP/RIFLE	FINOCCHIARO, SR.	ROBERT	2412
	38	144 5/8	58	HP/RIFLE	BACKES	HUBERT	2442
	38	144 5/8	68	HP/RIFLE	TEMMEN	J.R.	2442
	40	144 3/8	77	HP/RIFLE	SCHELL	GARY	2466
	40	144 3/8	87	HP/RIFLE	BAX	CHRIS C.	2466
	42	144 0/8	71	PICK-UP	NILGES	LAWRENCE G.	2514
	43	143 4/8	95	HP/RIFLE	OLIGSCHLAEGER	TIM	2577
	44	143 1/8	86	HP/RIFLE	SCHAEFER	RON	2615
	45	142 7/8	82	HP/RIFLE	LUECKE	DEAN	2641
	46	142 6/8	78	HP/RIFLE	VOSS	HERBERT H.	2647
	47	142 6/8	81	HP/RIFLE	MATTHEWS	JAMES	2647
	48	142 5/8	89	HP/RIFLE	PFAHL	EDWARD	2660
	49	142 4/8	70	HP/RIFLE	LUECKE	KENNY	2678
	50	142 1/8	71	HP/RIFLE	HOFFMAN	CHARLES	2709
	51	141 7/8	91	HP/RIFLE	BOEN, III	JAMES M.	2747
	51	141 7/8	95	HP/RIFLE	REHAGEN	RON	2747
	53	141 5/8	67	HP/RIFLE	RADEMANN	ELMER	2772
	53	141 5/8	90	HP/RIFLE	SMITH	STEPHEN C.	2772
	55	141 2/8	72	HP/RIFLE	KOENIGSFELD	ANDREW	2828
	55	141 2/8	83	HP/RIFLE	McFADDEN	RALPH	2828
	57	141 0/8	68	HP/RIFLE	SANDBOTHE	EDWARD	2863
	58	140 7/8	67	HP/RIFLE	DICKNEITE	DENNIS	2877
	58	140 7/8	94	HP/RIFLE	DIAL	KEITH	2877
	60	140 5/8	91	HP/RIFLE	STROPE	MICHAEL R.	2908
OZARK	1	167 7/8	82	HP/RIFLE	JENKINS	REX E.	197
	2	158 4/8	84	HP/RIFLE	HIXON	RAY	739
	3	155 7/8	82	HP/RIFLE	BLACKBURN	JIMMY JOE	994
	4	155 5/8	82	HP/RIFLE	JAMES	IVAN	1023
	5	153 6/8	66	HP/RIFLE	PIPIN	DON A.	1256
	6	153 5/8	79	HP/RIFLE	ROBERTSON	HENRY	1273
	7	147 3/8	67	HP/RIFLE	McNEIL	BERT	2155
	8	146 3/8	88	HP/RIFLE	ROGERS	RON	2252
	9	145 4/8	82	HP/RIFLE	HORINE	BRUCE	2331
	9	145 4/8	90	HP/RIFLE	POORE	DAVID	2331
	11	145 1/8	90	HP/RIFLE	BEACH	JERRY	2379
	12	145 0/8	78	HP/RIFLE	McDANIEL	MICHAEL	2391
	13	144 3/8	72	HP/RIFLE	LOSCHKY	DAVID	2466
	13	144 3/8	73	HP/RIFLE	ROBERTS	JIM	2466
	15	144 0/8	82	HP/RIFLE	FREEMAN	DAVID	2514
	16	142 5/8	93	HP/RIFLE	COLEMAN	R. DENNIS	2660
	17	142 4/8	82	HP/RIFLE	HARTGRAVES	JIMMIE	2678
	17	142 4/8	88	HP/RIFLE	LLOYD, JR.	JOHN A.	2678
	19	140 1/8	86	HP/RIFLE	COLE	GARY L.	2978
	20	140 0/8	70	HP/RIFLE	SKAGGS	DON	2990
PERRY	1	161 1/8	88	HP/RIFLE	RENAUD	DARYL	520
	2	158 1/8	77	HP/RIFLE	WELKER	ROBERT	777
	3	157 1/8	93	HP/RIFLE	DENNINGER	STANLEY	864

MISSOURI SHOW-ME BIG BUCKS CLUB RECORDS OF WHITETAIL DEER BY COUNTY, TYPICAL

COUNTY	COUNTY RANK	SCORE	YEAR TAKEN	WEAPON	HUNTER	FIRST NAME	STATE RANK
PERRY	4	155 5/8	94	HP/RIFLE	PETZOLDT	TROY	1023
	5	154 5/8	84	HP/RIFLE	WEBER	JAMESON	1146
	6	152 6/8	79	HP/RIFLE	AUSTIN	PAUL	1385
	7	151 2/8	87	HP/RIFLE	STENGEL	TOM	1656
	8	150 4/8	92	HP/RIFLE	WEITH	STANLEY	1811
	9	150 2/8	87	HP/RIFLE	GUTH	ED	1853
	10	149 0/8	83	HP/RIFLE	LEUCKEL	PAUL A.	1998
	11	148 2/8	60	HP/RIFLE	VINSON	HAROLD D.	2071
	11	148 2/8	84	HP/RIFLE	KOENIG	ALAN	2071
	11	148 2/8	91	HP/RIFLE	BALL	PAM	2071
	14	148 0/8	86	HP/RIFLE	TUCKER	JIM	2101
	15	146 4/8	79	HP/RIFLE	THOMPSON	QUINTIN	2242
	16	146 2/8	80	HP/RIFLE	HAERTLING	CLINTON	2266
	17	146 1/8	77	HP/RIFLE	COFFELT	CHARLES E.	2281
	18	146 0/8	85	HP/RIFLE	SCHROETER	JERRY	2290
	19	145 3/8	72	HP/RIFLE	MEYER	JOE	2350
	20	145 1/8	85	HP/RIFLE	STUEVE	DAVID	2379
	21	145 0/8	78	HP/RIFLE	HUBER	LARRY M.	2391
	22	144 6/8	94	HP/RIFLE	HAGAN	ROBERT H.	2425
	23	144 3/8	87	HP/RIFLE	KIRN	BRENT	2466
	24	144 1/8	80	HP/RIFLE	SCHMIDT	BRAD	2498
	24	144 1/8	85	HP/RIFLE	HECHT	MIKE	2498
	26	144 0/8	87	HP/RIFLE	PETZOLDT	MARVIN P.	2514
	27	143 4/8	96	HP/RIFLE	RELLERGERT	DAVID L.	2577
	28	143 1/8	73	HP/RIFLE	BURROUGHS	LARRY	2615
	29	143 0/8	68	HP/RIFLE	MARTIN	ROBERT L.	2626
	29	143 0/8	78	HP/RIFLE	LIX, JR.	LOUIS	2626
	29	142 0/8	75	HP/RIFLE	HOOD	JAMES L.	2725
	32	141 4/8	90	HP/RIFLE	KIRN	NELSON E.	2787
	33	141 3/8	92	HP/RIFLE	ROLLET	DAVID F.	2812
	34	140 6/8	85	HP/RIFLE	STEFFENS	RANDALL R.	2895
	35	140 2/8	96	HP/RIFLE	PETZOLDT	TOMMY	2952
PETTIS	1	190 3/8	86	HP/RIFLE	PERRY	JESSE A.	4
	2	169 1/8	84	HP/RIFLE	MEYER	ALVIN J.	166
	3	164 4/8	87	HP/RIFLE	TEMPLETON	LARRY	319
	4	160 2/8	82	HP/RIFLE	LAWTON	ARTHUR	584
	5	159 6/8	92	HP/RIFLE	CORNINE	GARY	628
	6	159 4/8	86	HP/RIFLE	SIMON	BOB	654
	7	155 3/8	91	HP/RIFLE	MORRISON	JOHN D.	1059
	8	155 2/8	91	HP/RIFLE	ANNERSON	SAM	1068
	9	154 1/8	89	HP/RIFLE	ELLISON	RONNIE	1207
	10	154 0/8	95	HP/RIFLE	RAY	GEORGE W.	1219
	11	153 7/8	86	HP/RIFLE	HOLTGERWE	RICHARD	1238
	12	152 6/8	91	HP/RIFLE	BALKE	JERRY M.	1385
	13	152 1/8	86	HP/RIFLE	RHODUS, JR.	LEWIS M.	1493
	13	152 1/8	96	BOW	RHODUS III	LEWIS M.	1493
	13	151 1/8	77	HP/RIFLE	TAYLOR	CHESTER	1690
	16	150 6/8	84	HP/RIFLE	LEFTWICH	JEFF	1756
	17	150 3/8	94	HP/RIFLE	AKER	STEVEN	1834
	18	148 6/8	90	HP/RIFLE	KIZER	KEITH	2024
	19	148 3/8	76	HP/RIFLE	SHACKLES	ROBERT L.	2060
	20	145 6/8	72	HP/RIFLE	CATON	MARVIN E.	2311
	21	145 4/8	80	HP/RIFLE	NEVILS	EDDIE R.	2331
	22	144 7/8	80	HP/RIFLE	CHARLES	LYONEL	2412
	23	144 5/8	90	HP/RIFLE	ARNETT	RICHARD	2442
	24	143 7/8	90	HP/RIFLE	PARKHURST	ROBERT RICHARD	2533
	24	143 7/8	91	HP/RIFLE	ELLISON	RUSTY	2533
	26	143 5/8	95	HP/RIFLE	JEFFERIS	DAVID	2564
	27	143 4/8	88	HP/RIFLE	DOVE	JAMES J.	2577

COUNTY	COUNTY RANK	SCORE	YEAR TAKEN	WEAPON	HUNTER	FIRST NAME	STATE RANK
PETTIS	28	142 6/8	79	HP/RIFLE	MONTGOMERY	JAMES	2647
	29	142 5/8	95	HP/RIFLE	ELLISON	RANDY	2660
	30	141 5/8	96	HP/RIFLE	TYLAR	RICK	2772
	31	141 3/8	89	HP/RIFLE	WILLIAMS	RONNIE	2812
	31	141 3/8	92	BOW	LORENZ	TRAVIS G.	2812
	33	141 1/8	96	HP/RIFLE	WHITLOW	JOSEPH E.	2844
	34	140 2/8	89	HP/RIFLE	GATSCHET	MIKE	2952
	34	140 2/8	91	HP/RIFLE	VAUGHAN	HAROLD	2952
	36	140 1/8	95	HP/RIFLE	FISHER	ERIC	2978
PHELPS	1	186 7/8	76	HP/RIFLE	LANCASTER		13
	2	184 5/8	88	PICK-UP	DAVIDSON	DON	21
	3	182 4/8	89	PICK-UP	DAVIDSON	DON	24
	4	182 2/8	96	HP/RIFLE	GABEL	DAVE	26
	5	180 1/8	73	HP/RIFLE	HAGENHOFF	BILLY	41
	6	165 5/8	79	HP/RIFLE	BLACK	STEVE	269
	7	164 5/8	81	HP/RIFLE	MAXWELL	WAYNE	313
	8	160 6/8	90	HP/RIFLE	DEUSER	RICHARD	543
	9	159 6/8	82	HP/RIFLE	SPENCER	ALLEN C.	628
	10	155 6/8	67	HP/RIFLE	GOLLAHON	JOHN P.	1004
	11	155 5/8	79	HP/RIFLE	PONZER	BRUCE	1023
	12	155 2/8	73	HP/RIFLE	MONTGOMERY	CLYDE	1068
	13	153 7/8	94	HP/RIFLE	MACORMIC	JIM	1238
	14	152 5/8	72	HP/RIFLE	GANN	E.E.	1399
	14	152 5/8	95	HP/RIFLE	YELTON	RICHARD	1399
	16	152 1/8	73	HP/RIFLE	RHODES	ROCKY	1493
	17	152 0/8	96	HP/RIFLE	WASSILAK	JIM	1519
	18	151 4/8	96	HP/RIFLE	KINSLOW	ARNOLD W.	1613
	19	151 1/8	86	HP/RIFLE	DAVIS	DOUG	1690
	19	151 1/8	95	HP/RIFLE	FABICK, III	JOHN	1690
	21	150 1/8	81	HP/RIFLE	JOHNSON	LEONARD	1879
	22	149 5/8	79	HP/RIFLE	KLIPFEL	E. ALAN	1936
	22	149 5/8	92	HP/RIFLE	POUND	DAVID	1936
	24	148 7/8	66	HP/RIFLE	WOOLMAN	BILL	2012
	26	147 7/8	57	HP/RIFLE	DESHURLEY	REX	2114
	27	147 0/8	89	HP/RIFLE	CARROLL	DEREK	2195
	28	146 7/8	72	HP/RIFLE	WATSON	DONALD LEROY	2214
	29	146 6/8	82	HP/RIFLE	LANE	RONNIE	2225
	30	146 3/8	94	HP/RIFLE	FEELER	GARY	2252
	31	146 1/8	95	HP/RIFLE	PLANK	ROBERT	2281
	31	146 0/8	71	HP/RIFLE	FRUEH	BOB	2290
	31	146 0/8	85	HP/RIFLE	BLACK	LOGAN	2290
	33	145 3/8	65	HP/RIFLE	WATSON	RAY	2350
	34	145 1/8	88	HP/RIFLE	FITZGERALD	SEAN	2379
	35	144 4/8	51	HP/RIFLE	FEELER	GALE	2459
	36	143 6/8	92	HP/RIFLE	BURNS	EARL	2550
	37	143 2/8	84	HP/RIFLE	DARLINGTON	ROBERT	2598
	39	142 7/8	69	HP/RIFLE	COX	ROBERT	2641
	39	142 6/8	79	HP/RIFLE	BURNS	WILSON	2647
	40	142 3/8	82	HP/RIFLE	CLIFTON, SR.	DAVID N.	2691
	41	142 1/8	80	HP/RIFLE	PIAZZA	GEORGE	2709
	42	141 2/8	71	HP/RIFLE	MYERS	NICK D.	2828
	43	140 2/8	85	HP/RIFLE	BARKS	TIM	2952
	44	140 1/8	83	HP/RIFLE	SPURGEON	JOHN	2978
PIKE	1	181 4/8	87	PICK-UP	PENROD	RALPH	33
	2	172 0/8	88	PICK-UP	HIPES	MARK R.	112
	3	171 0/8	82	BOW	HOLDENRIED	JIM	129
	4	168 5/8	74	HP/RIFLE	STROOT	EDWARD	179
	5	167 7/8	73	HP/RIFLE	DEWEY	LESTER	197
	6	167 5/8	95	HP/RIFLE	RICHARDSON	GUY H.	205

COUNTY	COUNTY RANK	SCORE	YEAR TAKEN	WEAPON	HUNTER	FIRST NAME	STATE RANK
PIKE	7	166 2/8	75	HP/RIFLE	NICOSIA	RAYMOND	255
	8	165 2/8	89	HP/RIFLE	HENDERSON	JAMES	293
	9	164 7/8	95	HP/RIFLE	KIMBRO	BILL	303
	10	163 6/8	73	HP/RIFLE	MILAN	PHILLIP	363
	11	162 0/8	86	HP/RIFLE	DROSTE	LOUIS N.	462
	12	161 5/8	80	HP/RIFLE	PRESTON	ROGER	486
	13	160 1/8	94	HP/RIFLE	BURNER	MATT	599
	14	158 6/8	73	HP/RIFLE	NOBLE	JOHN R.	719
	15	158 3/8	67	HP/RIFLE	SHOTTEN	CHARLES	753
	16	158 0/8	92	HP/RIFLE	BROWN	KENNETH	788
	17	157 3/8	86	HP/RIFLE	LAWRENCE	GREG	848
	18	156 4/8	93	HP/RIFLE	GROTE	BOBBY	925
	19	156 2/8	63	HP/RIFLE	MORRIS	GEORGE	953
	20	155 6/8	90	HP/RIFLE	MORRIS	SEAN	1004
	21	155 5/8	71	HP/RIFLE	SPARKS	CHARLES F.	1023
	22	155 2/8	91	HP/RIFLE	McINTURFF	JOHN P.	1068
	23	153 6/8	79	HP/RIFLE	STUMBAUGH	KEVIN	1256
	24	152 2/8	90	HP/RIFLE	SCHUMAN	FRED A.	1469
	25	151 6/8	84	BOW	BOULWARE	DEAN	1566
	26	151 3/8	80	PICK-UP	MUFF	EDWARD	1637
	27	150 7/8	92	HP/RIFLE	HOLTSMAN	LLOYD	1734
	28	150 6/8	85	HP/RIFLE	ROBINSON	STEVEN	1756
	29	150 5/8	75	HP/RIFLE	HUCKSTEP, JR.	RICHARD	1789
	29	150 5/8	85	HP/RIFLE	WHEELER	CHRIS	1789
	31	150 4/8	72	HP/RIFLE	SCHULZ	CLIFF	1811
	32	150 2/8	86	HP/RIFLE	HENDERSON	CURTIS	1853
	33	150 0/8	93	HP/RIFLE	DAVIS, III	JAMES M.	1897
	34	145 1/8	67	HP/RIFLE	MARTIN	EDDIE E.	2379
PLATTE	1	180 4/8	87	BOW	MARTIN	JIM	38
	2	165 1/8	91	HP/RIFLE	STEWART	MICHAEL	296
	3	164 5/8	95	HP/RIFLE	HIATT	CHRIS	313
	4	163 6/8	95	HP/RIFLE	BASH	JEFF	363
	5	157 4/8	85	HP/RIFLE	CALLEHAN	MELVIN	833
	5	157 4/8	91	HP/RIFLE	ASHPAUGH	JAMES W.	833
	7	156 5/8	81	HP/RIFLE	FREEMYER	BILL	911
	7	156 5/8	82	HP/RIFLE	WHEELER	STEVE	911
	9	156 4/8	85	HP/RIFLE	STACKHOUSE	GUY	925
	10	156 2/8	93	HP/RIFLE	HEYDINGER	JEFF	953
	11	155 1/8	89	HP/RIFLE	SHAFER	SCOTT	1091
	12	154 5/8	86	HP/RIFLE	PERKINS	ANDREW	1146
	13	152 4/8	86	HP/RIFLE	WHITE	STEPHEN C.	1423
	14	150 1/8	81	BOW	COONS	RICHARD	1879
	15	150 0/8	71	HP/RIFLE	CHAPIN	LOREN L.	1897
	16	148 7/8	94	HP/RIFLE	JAMISON	FRANK	2012
POLK	1	164 5/8	95	HP/RIFLE	BUCKNER	LLOYD	313
	2	163 0/8	90	HP/RIFLE	WELLS	STACY	393
	3	152 2/8	90	HP/RIFLE	CAMPBELL	TOM	1469
	4	148 1/8	89	HP/RIFLE	ELLIS	KENNETH N.	2088
	5	144 0/8	91	HP/RIFLE	PAXSON	BRUCE	2514
	6	143 2/8	93	HP/RIFLE	DURYEE	JIM	2598
	7	141 6/8	80	HP/RIFLE	ROBERTS	DWIGHT	2756
	9	140 2/8	95	HP/RIFLE	EIGSTI	WILLIS	2952
PULASKI	1	170 1/8	86	HP/RIFLE	ADKINS	CHUCK	150
	2	161 7/8	53	HP/RIFLE	SHOCKLEY	JOSEPH C.	467
	3	160 5/8	54	HP/RIFLE	CHAMBERS	HERBERT	553
	4	160 5/8	94	HP/RIFLE	KOECHLING	RICHARD	553
	5	157 2/8	76	HP/RIFLE	LOGAN	ROBERT	853
	6	155 5/8	86	HP/RIFLE	AGEE	BRUCE	1023
	7	155 2/8	77	HP/RIFLE	SHELDEN	WILLIAM J.	1068

MISSOURI SHOW-ME BIG BUCKS CLUB RECORDS OF WHITETAIL DEER BY COUNTY, TYPICAL

COUNTY	COUNTY RANK	SCORE	YEAR TAKEN	WEAPON	HUNTER	FIRST NAME	STATE RANK
PULASKI	8	153 3/8	81	BOW	SCOTT	ROBERT W.	1310
	9	152 5/8	84	HP/RIFLE	HAGE	RICHARD	1399
	10	151 3/8	90	HP/RIFLE	SHELDEN	MARK	1637
	11	149 0/8	87	HP/RIFLE	DOYLE	TOMMY	1998
	12	148 1/8	89	HP/RIFLE	DOYLE	ROY LEE	2088
	13	146 5/8	87	HP/RIFLE	ENTWISTLE	KENNETH P.	2235
	14	146 4/8	75	HP/RIFLE	HELFRICH	DR. LORING R.	2242
	14	146 4/8	84	HP/RIFLE	BELL	IRVIN G.	2242
	16	145 6/8	94	HP/RIFLE	CLARK	GARY	2311
	17	145 4/8	69	HP/RIFLE	MYERS	J.D.	2331
	18	143 5/8	67	HP/RIFLE	BARCLAY	JAMES B.	2564
	19	142 0/8	74	HP/RIFLE	CLARK	WILLIT B.	2725
	20	141 5/8	84	HP/RIFLE	DICKENS	TERRY	2772
	21	141 4/8	82	HP/RIFLE	CHAPMAN	MATT	2787
	22	141 2/8	76	HP/RIFLE	HUTTON	RANDALL	2828
	23	140 4/8	92	BOW	WIGLEY	MARVIN T.	2925
	24	140 2/8	80	HP/RIFLE	CORE	ANDY O.	2952
	25	140 1/8	94	HP/RIFLE	THILTGEN	EUGENE	2978
	26	140 0/8	68	HP/RIFLE	HEISSERER	FRANK L.	2990
PUTNAM	1	179 5/8	92	HP/RIFLE	SEATON	WES	44
	2	169 4/8	60	HP/RIFLE	TRENT	GLEN	160
	3	168 3/8	76	HP/RIFLE	BRANSCOMB	BRIAN	184
	4	167 7/8	80	HP/RIFLE	RILEY	CURTIS	197
	5	167 3/8	81	HP/RIFLE	SMITH	EARL	217
	6	167 2/8	77	HP/RIFLE	MICHAEL	MONTE	221
	7	162 5/8	84	HP/RIFLE	PICKETT	DAVID	417
	7	162 5/8	94	HP/RIFLE	YOUNG	BRANDON	417
	9	162 4/8	78	HP/RIFLE	LARUE	LLOYD	431
	10	162 3/8	96	HP/RIFLE	HABERBERGER	MARK E.	439
	11	160 4/8	90	HP/RIFLE	TORREY	MARK	560
	12	159 5/8	79	HP/RIFLE	FISHER	MARK	641
	13	159 3/8	83	HP/RIFLE	LARUE	LLOYD	665
	14	159 0/8	91	HP/RIFLE	RYERSON	RICK L.	695
	15	158 3/8	95	HP/RIFLE	COWIE	KAREN	753
	16	157 5/8	91	HP/RIFLE	BUSHNELL	TONY	821
	17	157 4/8	96	HP/RIFLE	HALLEY	HEATH	833
	18	157 1/8	90	HP/RIFLE	TUCKER	MATT	864
	19	156 6/8	81	HP/RIFLE	SMITH	PAUL W.	900
	20	156 0/8	86	HP/RIFLE	GADBERRY	RONNIE	981
	21	155 6/8	92	HP/RIFLE	BRYAN	MIKE	1004
	22	155 3/8	88	HP/RIFLE	WILLIAMS	LAWRENCE	1059
	23	155 2/8	90	HP/RIFLE	REAM	JOE	1068
	24	154 6/8	91	HP/RIFLE	O'BRIEN	MATTHEW DAVID	1130
	24	154 6/8	92	PICK-UP	LARUE	LLOYD	1130
	26	153 4/8	95	HP/RIFLE	BURNS	KRIS	1287
	27	153 2/8	92	HP/RIFLE	KOTTWITZ	ANDREW	1327
	28	153 0/8	88	HP/RIFLE	HURLEY	LARRY	1355
	28	153 0/8	91	HP/RIFLE	LARUE	JOYCE	1355
	30	152 5/8	90	HP/RIFLE	VIGGERS	LEE	1399
	31	152 4/8	77	BOW	SUMMERS	JIM	1423
	32	152 0/8	95	HP/RIFLE	PARKER	MICHAEL	1519
	33	151 6/8	92	PICK-UP	LARUE	LLOYD	1566
	34	150 5/8	88	HP/RIFLE	MITCHELL	DANNIE	1789
	35	150 2/8	88	HP/RIFLE	LARUE	LLOYD	1853
	35	150 2/8	90	HP/RIFLE	LARUE	LOYD	1853
	35	150 2/8	91	HP/RIFLE	DEFREITAS	JACK	1853
	38	148 7/8	60	HP/RIFLE	CLEM	VELDON T.	2012
	39	145 2/8	96	HP/RIFLE	REAM, JR.	DALE H.	2361
	40	143 5/8	92	HP/RIFLE	PERKINS	BRIAN LEE	2564

MISSOURI SHOW-ME BIG BUCKS CLUB RECORDS OF WHITETAIL DEER BY COUNTY, TYPICAL

COUNTY	COUNTY RANK	SCORE	YEAR TAKEN	WEAPON	HUNTER	FIRST NAME	STATE RANK
PUTNAM	41	142 1/8	95	BOW	PEARSON	BOBBY	2709
	42	140 7/8	96	HP/RIFLE	MARVIN	WADE	2877
	43	140 6/8	84	HP/RIFLE	REAM	JOE	2895
	43	140 6/8	86	HP/RIFLE	TORREY	MELODY	2895
	45	140 2/8	95	HP/RIFLE	GADBERRY	RONNIE	2952
RALLS	1	179 1/8	92	HP/RIFLE	FAHLE	STEVE	47
	2	173 1/8	88	PICK-UP	JAMES	LES	97
	3	163 2/8	82	HP/RIFLE	FORD	FRANKIE	383
	4	159 3/8	80	HP/RIFLE	RILEY	HARRY L.	665
	5	157 6/8	86	HP/RIFLE	FIEDLER	DAVE	812
	6	154 5/8	91	HP/RIFLE	SMITH	TROY M.	1146
	7	154 1/8	80	HP/RIFLE	COUCH	BILL	1207
	8	153 7/8	88	HP/RIFLE	UNDERWOOD	BOB	1238
	9	153 3/8	82	HP/RIFLE	LONG	RONALD L.	1310
	10	152 5/8	59	BOW	CURLESS	DONALD	1399
	11	152 4/8	88	HP/RIFLE	MURPHY	DONALD W.	1423
	12	151 5/8	87	HP/RIFLE	WEST	ALLEN	1586
	13	151 1/8	64	HP/RIFLE	PEERY	TOMMY	1690
	14	150 2/8	72	HP/RIFLE	FENDRICK	DICK	1853
	15	150 1/8	93	HP/RIFLE	RIEDINGER	REGGIE	1879
	16	150 0/8	85	HP/RIFLE	CERNEA	MIKE	1897
	17	141 6/8	96	HP/RIFLE	BURNETT	BOB	2756
RANDOLPH	1	205 0/8	71	HP/RIFLE	GIBSON	LARRY	1
	2	174 0/8	95	HP/RIFLE	SEINER	ROGER	84
	3	172 0/8	68	PICK-UP	SIMMERMAN	GENE	112
	4	166 7/8	75	HP/RIFLE	SCOTT	STEVE	227
	4	166 7/8	96	HP/RIFLE	CRUTCHFIELD	ART	230
	6	165 5/8	66	HP/RIFLE	MESSER	DAVID	276
	7	165 5/8	77	HP/RIFLE	RICKERTSEN	CHRIS M.	269
	8	164 2/8	79	HP/RIFLE	CATER	JERRY	332
	9	164 0/8	75	HP/RIFLE	THOMAS	JAMES	349
	10	163 0/8	77	HP/RIFLE	JOHNSON	GEORGE	393
	11	162 5/8	75	HP/RIFLE	RICHARDS	MR.	417
	12	161 6/8	74	HP/RIFLE	BROWNING	EDDIE	476
	12	161 6/8	92	HP/RIFLE	BLOCK	NEIL	476
	12	161 6/8	96	HP/RIFLE	CONGER	KERRY	476
	15	160 5/8	88	HP/RIFLE	POLLARD	MARK W.	553
	16	160 4/8	85	HP/RIFLE	HAYES	ROY	560
	17	159 7/8	89	HP/RIFLE	RICKERTSEN	CHRIS M.	620
	17	159 7/8	90	HP/RIFLE	STOEBE	DONNIE	620
	19	159 3/8	93	HP/RIFLE	WILSON	DARRELL	665
	20	158 4/8	59	HP/RIFLE	CHISM	ROBERT	739
	20	158 4/8	69	HP/RIFLE	BOWDEN	DANNY	739
	22	155 7/8	93	HP/RIFLE	RICE	JAMES	994
	23	154 4/8	89	HP/RIFLE	HUDSON	RANDY	1164
	24	154 2/8	80	HP/RIFLE	THOMAS	FRANK	1186
	25	154 1/8	66	HP/RIFLE	WAGNER	DAVID	1207
	26	154 0/8	82	HP/RIFLE	WATKINS	FLOYD	1219
	27	153 5/8	83	HP/RIFLE	WOODY	CLAYTON	1273
	28	153 4/8	91	BOW	MONTGOMERY	HAROLD	1287
	29	153 3/8	96	HP/RIFLE	COLLEY	TERRY	1310
	30	152 7/8	87	HP/RIFLE	WHITE	STEPHEN C.	1370
	31	152 0/8	72	HP/RIFLE	O'BRYAN	DAN	1519
	32	151 6/8	96	HP/RIFLE	DALE	ROY	1566
	33	151 2/8	92	HP/RIFLE	BATES	JOHN F.	1656
	34	150 6/8	84	HP/RIFLE	MAUPIN	ALLEN	1756
	35	150 4/8	72	HP/RIFLE	WOGOMON	GERALD	1811
	36	149 7/8	84	HP/RIFLE	VITT	JOE	1915
RAY	1	174 5/8	90	HP/RIFLE	BALES	DENNIS B.	73

MISSOURI SHOW-ME BIG BUCKS CLUB RECORDS OF WHITETAIL DEER BY COUNTY, TYPICAL

COUNTY	COUNTY RANK	SCORE	YEAR TAKEN	WEAPON	HUNTER	FIRST NAME	STATE RANK
RAY	2	172 0/8	78	HP/RIFLE	LINDLEY	DWIGHT	112
	3	171 2/8	82	HP/RIFLE	HIGHTOWER	RON	123
	4	171 0/8	66	HP/RIFLE	SIEGEL	DALE	129
	5	170 0/8	87	HP/RIFLE	KING	LARRY	151
	6	169 0/8	96	HP/RIFLE	JAMES	MICHAEL	170
	7	165 7/8	82	PICK-UP	JOY	RICHARD P.	269
	8	164 2/8	95	HP/RIFLE	PRUITT	DOUG	332
	9	163 3/8	94	HP/RIFLE	HAYES	KERRY	378
	10	162 5/8	59	HP/RIFLE	WRIGHT	PAUL	417
	11	162 4/8	70	HP/RIFLE	OFFUTT	SAM	431
	12	160 4/8	85	HP/RIFLE	KIRK	DOUGLAS	560
	13	160 0/8	67	HP/RIFLE	WRIGHT	DALE	605
	14	159 4/8	95	HP/RIFLE	TEMPLETON	EDDIE	654
	15	159 0/8	94	BOW	HOLDER	KELLY D.	695
	16	158 2/8	87	HP/RIFLE	WHITE	BRAD	763
	17	158 0/8	89	HP/RIFLE	BELLIS	RAYMOND L.	788
	18	157 4/8	71	HP/RIFLE	BEARD	ELBERT	833
	19	156 2/8	90	HP/RIFLE	HEWITT	WESLEY	953
	20	153 7/8	88	HP/RIFLE	KIRK	CHRISTOPHER	1238
	21	153 4/8	76	HP/RIFLE	MYNATT	LARRY	1287
	22	153 0/8	70	HP/RIFLE	CLEMMONS	ED	1355
	22	153 0/8	86	HP/RIFLE	LAMAR	DON	1355
	24	152 7/8	89	HP/RIFLE	DICKEY	LLOYD A.	1370
	25	151 4/8	83	HP/RIFLE	ALBRECHT	DONALD	1613
	25	151 4/8	88	HP/RIFLE	KIRK	DOUGLAS	1613
	27	151 3/8	95	HP/RIFLE	HIATT	PHILLIP R.	1637
	28	151 2/8	87	HP/RIFLE	ESTES	NOAH	1656
	28	151 2/8	87	HP/RIFLE	HICKS	LARRY	1656
	28	151 2/8	91	HP/RIFLE	BROCK	WADE	1656
	28	151 2/8	92	HP/RIFLE	HOLTZCLAW	TONY	1656
	32	150 7/8	85	HP/RIFLE	BARNETT	J.E.	1734
	33	150 3/8	92	BOW	KING	JOHNNIE	1834
	34	150 2/8	87	HP/RIFLE	BRANHAM	KENDALL	1853
	35	150 0/8	70	HP/RIFLE	IMGARTEN	FRED	1897
	36	148 6/8	96	HP/RIFLE	KIRK	DOUG	2024
	37	146 0/8	94	HP/RIFLE	KIRK	DOUGLAS	2290
REYNOLDS	1	168 3/8	90	HP/RIFLE	SUTTON	RANDY	184
	2	159 4/8	90	HP/RIFLE	COWIN	RANDY L.	654
	3	158 1/8	93	HP/RIFLE	VOLNER	CLINTON S.	777
	4	152 6/8	93	HP/RIFLE	HALL	ELVIS	1385
	5	152 5/8	89	HP/RIFLE	TURNER	TERRY G.	1399
	6	152 1/8	83	HP/RIFLE	SMITH	RICHARD	1493
	6	152 1/8	90	HP/RIFLE	RANEY	CARL	1493
	8	150 2/8	93	HP/RIFLE	HEDGER	JOHN	1853
	9	147 6/8	92	HP/RIFLE	MARTIN	ROCKY	2126
	10	146 6/8	60	HP/RIFLE	CARR	DICK	2225
	11	145 7/8	95	HP/RIFLE	SMITH	DARREL	2302
	12	144 3/8	90	HP/RIFLE	CROCKER	APRIL	2466
RIPLEY	1	166 4/8	91	HP/RIFLE	McGOWAN	JACK	244
	2	153 4/8	91	HP/RIFLE	YORK	LYLE D.	1287
	3	152 2/8	92	HP/RIFLE	KEEL	BRUCE	1469
	4	150 5/8	82	HP/RIFLE	FREEMAN	ELDIE T.	1789
	5	149 4/8	69	HP/RIFLE	SMITH	LUTHER	1936
	6	148 7/8	94	BOW	EDDINGTON	BRAD	2012
	7	147 6/8	94	HP/RIFLE	MUSE	STEVEN E.	2126
	8	144 6/8	96	HP/RIFLE	WHISNAT	PETE	2425
	9	143 7/8	89	M/L	BYERS	TED R.	2533
	10	143 0/8	92	HP/RIFLE	TROTTER	JESSE	2626
	11	140 1/8	73	HP/RIFLE	CLAYTON	GILLIE	2978

162

MISSOURI SHOW-ME BIG BUCKS CLUB RECORDS OF WHITETAIL DEER BY COUNTY, TYPICAL

COUNTY	COUNTY RANK	SCORE	YEAR TAKEN	WEAPON	HUNTER	FIRST NAME	STATE RANK
SALINE	1	173 7/8	71	HP/RIFLE	DICKEY	WILLIAM	86
	2	171 2/8	95	HP/RIFLE	EDWARDS	JEFFREY E.	123
	3	170 4/8	94	HP/RIFLE	PICK-UP		140
	4	169 5/8	94	HP/RIFLE	RAMEY	BILL	159
	5	164 3/8	92	HP/RIFLE	RICHARDSON	WILLIAM L.	328
	6	163 0/8	73	HP/RIFLE	OWENS	STEVEN	393
	7	162 3/8	78	HP/RIFLE	CRAMER	DAVID L.	439
	8	161 7/8	90	HP/RIFLE	ALFREY	ROBERT	467
	8	161 7/8	94	HP/RIFLE	NELSON	ED	467
	10	161 6/8	81	HP/RIFLE	LAND	VIRGIL A.	476
	10	161 6/8	90	HP/RIFLE	EDMONDS	PAUL	476
	12	161 1/8	83	HP/RIFLE	LEATHERS	MARK	520
	13	160 4/8	92	HP/RIFLE	CRIST	WILLIAM E.	560
	13	160 4/8	95	HP/RIFLE	EVANS	BRAD	560
	15	159 0/8	89	HP/RIFLE	GARR	MARK	695
	16	158 0/8	91	HP/RIFLE	WISE	K. WAYNE	788
	17	157 4/8	74	HP/RIFLE	VAUGHAN	GREGORY L.	833
	18	157 0/8	88	HP/RIFLE	HUNTER	DAVID	875
	19	156 7/8	95	HP/RIFLE	VOGL	KENNETH	893
	20	156 5/8	96	HP/RIFLE	DAVIS	GERRY D.	911
	21	156 4/8	85	HP/RIFLE	BOSSALLER	ELDON	925
	22	156 1/8	95	HP/RIFLE	ZINN	TOMMY D.	967
	23	155 5/8	89	HP/RIFLE	ENGLAND	LARRY	1023
	24	154 5/8	66	PICK-UP	NORMAN	VINCE	1146
	24	154 5/8	91	HP/RIFLE	PLUMMER	CHARLES L.	1146
	26	154 3/8	88	HP/RIFLE	NORMAN	NOEL	1174
	27	153 5/8	90	HP/RIFLE	MURDOCK	JIM	1273
	28	153 3/8	92	HP/RIFLE	KNOX	ROBERT	1310
	28	153 3/8	93	HP/RIFLE	DOHERTY	TOM	1310
	30	153 1/8	92	HP/RIFLE	GREEN	KEITH	1344
	31	152 5/8	95	HP/RIFLE	CRAWFORD	CHARLES	1399
	32	152 4/8	94	HP/RIFLE	KLASING	JAMES	1423
	32	152 4/8	94	HP/RIFLE	LOESING	THOMAS	1423
	34	152 0/8	88	PICK-UP	KELLEY	JOHN	1519
	35	151 6/8	92	HP/RIFLE	O'BRYAN	ROBBIE	1566
	36	151 3/8	95	HP/RIFLE	PARRISH	ROBERT	1637
	36	151 3/8	95	HP/RIFLE	EDDY	JOE	1637
	38	151 0/8	95	HP/RIFLE	MURPHY	STEVE	1715
	39	150 7/8	87	HP/RIFLE	COPELAND	DAVID	1734
	40	150 6/8	85	HP/RIFLE	RHODES	CHESTER	1756
	40	150 6/8	87	HP/RIFLE	SCOTT	WILLIAM W.	1756
	40	150 6/8	91	HP/RIFLE	EVANS	JEFF	1756
	43	149 4/8	95	HP/RIFLE	MOBILE	MICHAEL R.	1936
	44	149 1/8	86	HP/RIFLE	MARSH	TOM	1988
	45	148 7/8	95	HP/RIFLE	WISEMAN	JAMES	2012
	46	148 6/8	94	HP/RIFLE	TUCKER	BRIAN P.	2024
	47	148 4/8	75	HP/RIFLE	HIGHBARGER	RONALD	2048
	48	147 7/8	74	HP/RIFLE	LAND	BOB	2114
	49	147 4/8	96	HP/RIFLE	ROGERS	TIM	2148
	50	147 2/8	89	HP/RIFLE	KLASING	JERRY	2167
	50	147 2/8	92	PICK-UP	DRISKELL	JOHN E.	2167
	52	146 7/8	84	HP/RIFLE	VOGL	KENNETH	2214
	53	146 5/8	87	PICK-UP	SYLVESTER	LEON	2235
	54	146 0/8	95	HP/RIFLE	RAMEY	BILL	2290
	55	145 6/8	76	HP/RIFLE	JOHNSON	KENNETH E.	2311
	56	145 4/8	95	HP/RIFLE	WISEMAN	SAM	2331
	57	145 2/8	95	HP/RIFLE	HURSMAN	TONY	2361
	58	145 1/8	79	HP/RIFLE	RAYL	ALAN	2379
	58	145 1/8	79	HP/RIFLE	TENNILL	RONNIE	2379

163

MISSOURI SHOW-ME BIG BUCKS CLUB RECORDS OF WHITETAIL DEER BY COUNTY, TYPICAL

COUNTY	COUNTY RANK	SCORE	YEAR TAKEN	WEAPON	HUNTER	FIRST NAME	STATE RANK
SALINE	58	145 1/8	89	HP/RIFLE	BRADSHAW	DON	2379
	61	145 0/8	86	HP/RIFLE	MORTON	LARRY	2391
	61	145 0/8	93	HP/RIFLE	HARRIS	DARREN	2391
	63	144 1/8	86	HP/RIFLE	BLEDSOE	RICK	2498
	63	144 1/8	92	HP/RIFLE	MALTER	JUSTIN	2498
	65	144 0/8	79	HP/RIFLE	BRUNS	LESLIE	2514
	65	144 0/8	89	HP/RIFLE	ADAMS	BILL	2514
	67	143 5/8	91	HP/RIFLE	McDANIEL	CRAIG	2564
	68	143 1/8	88	HP/RIFLE	EDDY	ALAN	2615
	69	143 0/8	91	HP/RIFLE	ALDREDGE	LARRY	2626
	70	142 5/8	85	HP/RIFLE	SLEEPER	RANDY	2660
	71	142 4/8	89	HP/RIFLE	ZIMMERSCHIED	BRIAN	2678
	72	142 1/8	89	BOW	UNDERWOOD	JERRY	2709
	73	142 0/8	74	HP/RIFLE	HOLLINGSWORTH	KENNY K.	2725
	73	142 0/8	88	HP/RIFLE	STEDING	ED	2725
	73	142 0/8	90	HP/RIFLE	LARUE	DALE	2725
	76	141 6/8	86	HP/RIFLE	KRUGER	DARRYL	2756
	77	141 5/8	82	HP/RIFLE	MASTERS	NORMAN	2772
	77	141 5/8	88	HP/RIFLE	THIEL	DON	2772
	77	141 5/8	91	HP/RIFLE	KNOX	MIKE	2772
	80	141 4/8	88	HP/RIFLE	MALTER	TOM	2787
	80	141 4/8	89	HP/RIFLE	DRAFFEN	WILLIAM	2787
	80	141 4/8	91	HP/RIFLE	McMASTERS, JR.	JOHNNY	2787
	80	141 4/8	92	HP/RIFLE	KRUGER	DARRYL	2787
	84	141 3/8	87	HP/RIFLE	WISKUR	DOYLE	2812
	85	141 1/8	85	HP/RIFLE	ADCOCK	WAYNE	2844
	85	141 1/8	89	HP/RIFLE	HARE	PHIL	2844
	87	141 0/8	93	HP/RIFLE	McGUIRE	RICK	2863
	88	140 7/8	88	HP/RIFLE	MASTERS	NORMAN	2877
	89	140 5/8	79	HP/RIFLE	TYRE	JIMMIE D.	2908
	90	140 4/8	92	HP/RIFLE	SMITH	LUCAS	2925
	91	140 2/8	93	HP/RIFLE	JOHNSON	LEON	2952
	91	140 2/8	93	HP/RIFLE	CROKA	ALVIN	2952
	93	140 1/8	86	HP/RIFLE	DAVIS	JERRY	2978
SCHUYLER	1	167 4/8	95	HP/RIFLE	CHANCE	LARRY	213
	2	161 0/8	83	HP/RIFLE	GIBSON	DEAN	530
	3	160 6/8	92	HP/RIFLE	SUMMERS	JOE	543
	4	160 0/8	95	HP/RIFLE	LEWIS	WILLIAM R.	605
	5	159 5/8	77	HP/RIFLE	WHEELER	TERRY	641
	6	159 1/8	74	HP/RIFLE	FREMON	W.G.	687
	7	158 1/8	96	HP/RIFLE	BAILEY	MIKE C.	777
	8	157 4/8	86	HP/RIFLE	WEBSTER III	THOMAS M.	833
	9	157 0/8	94	HP/RIFLE	McCORMICK	DONALD L.	875
	10	156 0/8	91	HP/RIFLE	BAILEY	WAYNE	981
	11	155 3/8	76	HP/RIFLE	FREMON	BOB	1059
	12	152 2/8	90	BOW	PIERCEALL	JIM	1469
	13	152 0/8	87	HP/RIFLE	BYRN	BRIAN	1519
	14	151 7/8	93	HP/RIFLE	PARSONS	CHARLIE	1550
	15	150 6/8	96	HP/RIFLE	ANDERSON	BRIAN N.	1756
SCOTLAND	1	187 2/8	71	HP/RIFLE	BERHORST	ROBIN	9
	2	181 2/8	89	HP/RIFLE	KENNEDY	JERRY	34
	3	179 1/8	85	HP/RIFLE	SMITH	DAVID ROY	47
	4	176 0/8	72	HP/RIFLE	MORTON	JIMMY	62
	5	171 7/8	84	BOW	SMITH	DAVID	117
	6	171 4/8	89	HP/RIFLE	ROBESON	HARRY	120
	7	171 0/8	94	HP/RIFLE	ANDERSON	RICK	129
	8	170 0/8	74	HP/RIFLE	YOUNG	CHESTER JAMES	151
	9	169 2/8	67	HP/RIFLE	PARRIS	ADREN	163
	10	166 0/8	81	HP/RIFLE	HYDE	ROY C.	262

MISSOURI SHOW-ME BIG BUCKS CLUB RECORDS OF WHITETAIL DEER BY COUNTY, TYPICAL

COUNTY	COUNTY RANK	SCORE	YEAR TAKEN	WEAPON	HUNTER	FIRST NAME	STATE RANK
SCOTLAND	11	163 5/8	94	HP/RIFLE	WATKINS	DALE E.	368
	12	163 4/8	84	HP/RIFLE	BRANDRIFF	RAYMOND E.	373
	13	162 2/8	85	HP/RIFLE	McBEE	JIM L.	451
	14	162 1/8	90	M/L	POHLERS	MIKE	455
	15	161 6/8	66	HP/RIFLE	CHANCE	KEITH	476
	16	161 2/8	88	HP/RIFLE	HARLAN	ROGER	512
	17	161 0/8	71	HP/RIFLE	WAGNER	MICHAEL E.	530
	18	160 3/8	70	HP/RIFLE	SHELLEY	LARRY	574
	19	159 5/8	84	HP/RIFLE	ADAMS	JOHN W.	641
	20	159 4/8	76	HP/RIFLE	YORK	DARRELL	654
	21	159 1/8	76	HP/RIFLE	BARICKMAN	TOM	687
	22	159 0/8	88	HP/RIFLE	HURST	TONY	695
	23	158 6/8	65	HP/RIFLE	HOLTON	ROBERT E.	719
	23	158 6/8	88	HP/RIFLE	YOUNG	DAVID	719
	25	158 4/8	67	HP/RIFLE	HOSKINSON	BILL	739
	26	158 3/8	78	HP/RIFLE	FRANKLIN	PAUL R.	753
	26	158 3/8	88	HP/RIFLE	BAIR	DOUG	753
	28	158 1/8	92	HP/RIFLE	LEWIS	ROGER W.	777
	29	157 6/8	88	HP/RIFLE	HOLT	MARK	812
	30	157 5/8	83	PICK-UP	SMITH	DAVID	821
	30	157 5/8	86	HP/RIFLE	VASSHOLZ	FRITZ	821
	32	156 5/8	95	HP/RIFLE	STOTT	TRAVIS	911
	33	156 3/8	84	HP/RIFLE	SMITH	DAVID	940
	34	155 2/8	79	HP/RIFLE	HATFIELD	RODNEY	1068
	35	155 0/8	73	HP/RIFLE	BUNCH	JOHN	1102
	35	155 0/8	74	HP/RIFLE	ARNOLD	JUDY	1102
	37	154 6/8	79	HP/RIFLE	GUNDY	MICHELE	1130
	38	153 4/8	94	HP/RIFLE	CREEK	ALLEN W.	1287
	39	153 3/8	91	HP/RIFLE	DAVIS	JOHN	1310
	40	153 2/8	84	HP/RIFLE	YOUNG	DAVID	1327
	41	153 1/8	96	HP/RIFLE	DeNOON	BILL	1344
	42	153 0/8	88	HP/RIFLE	BRADLEY	BOBBY R.	1355
	43	152 6/8	85	HP/RIFLE	ROBINSON	RON	1385
	44	152 5/8	88	HP/RIFLE	GUNDY	KEVIN	1399
	45	152 3/8	70	HP/RIFLE	SLAYTON	TIM	1453
	45	152 3/8	88	HP/RIFLE	TAGUE	DIANE	1453
	47	152 0/8	78	HP/RIFLE	TRIPLETT	BOB	1519
	47	152 0/8	82	HP/RIFLE	KICE	JAMIE	1519
	49	151 7/8	90	HP/RIFLE	McVEIGH	KEN	1550
	49	151 7/8	93	HP/RIFLE	SCHUMACHER	DAN	1550
	51	151 6/8	88	HP/RIFLE	MEINHARDT	MIKE	1566
	51	151 5/8	82	HP/RIFLE	HOSKINSON	BILL	1586
	51	151 5/8	83	HP/RIFLE	AUSTIN	JOHN	1586
	54	151 4/8	88	HP/RIFLE	ARNOLD	DAVID L.	1613
	55	151 2/8	71	HP/RIFLE	HILPERT	GARY	1656
	56	151 0/8	88	HP/RIFLE	ANDERSON	STEVE	1715
	57	150 2/8	79	HP/RIFLE	SPARKS	JOHN R.	1853
	58	149 1/8	96	HP/RIFLE	GARNETT	JAMES MICHAEL	1988
	59	145 5/8	96	HP/RIFLE	HOLT	BRANDON	2324
	60	144 0/8	95	HP/RIFLE	SMALL	MICHAEL	2514
	61	143 0/8	71	HP/RIFLE	CHILDRESS	SCOTT	2626
	62	140 5/8	73	HP/RIFLE	DAVIS	DARL	2908
SCOTT	1	156 3/8	95	HP/RIFLE	DANIELS	TIMOTHY L.	940
	2	148 1/8	81	HP/RIFLE	MILLER	JOHN	2088
	3	140 4/8	96	HP/RIFLE	SMITH	KEVIN	2925
SHANNON	1	179 5/8	89	HP/RIFLE	FRY	ROBERT K.	44
	2	174 6/8	92	PICK-UP	LINDSEY	SCOTT	71
	3	170 5/8	71	HP/RIFLE	BLAND	GARRY	137
	4	166 6/8	94	HP/RIFLE	ELLIOT	LARRY	235

COUNTY	COUNTY RANK	SCORE	YEAR TAKEN	WEAPON	HUNTER	FIRST NAME	STATE RANK
SHANNON	5	166 4/8	83	HP/RIFLE	GEORGE	DENVER D.	244
	6	163 5/8	86	HP/RIFLE	REYNOLDS	PAUL	368
	7	157 0/8	88	HP/RIFLE	LINDSEY	ROGER	875
	8	156 3/8	93	PICK-UP	LINDSEY	SCOTT	940
	9	156 2/8	95	HP/RIFLE	LINDSEY	SCOTT	953
	10	155 4/8	92	HP/RIFLE	STROTHER	LARRY M.	1040
	11	155 0/8	87	HP/RIFLE	VERMILLION	RAY	1102
	12	151 6/8	62	HP/RIFLE	HOWELL	GORDON	1566
	13	147 6/8	79	HP/RIFLE	SEARCY	DONALD D.	2126
	14	147 1/8	61	HP/RIFLE	HEDRICK	RON	2183
	15	146 6/8	84	HP/RIFLE	YOUNG	CHUCK	2225
	16	145 1/8	93	HP/RIFLE	LANHAM	BUD	2379
	16	145 1/8	94	HP/RIFLE	FOSTER	TERRY	2379
	18	144 6/8	82	HP/RIFLE	COOLEY	SHAWN	2425
	19	144 2/8	84	M/L	DEBLOIS	DOUG	2483
	20	143 6/8	72	HP/RIFLE	REIMINGER	DAVE	2550
	21	143 2/8	87	HP/RIFLE	BLAND	GARY	2598
	22	143 0/8	72	HP/RIFLE	ARTHUR	TED	2626
	23	142 6/8	87	HP/RIFLE	STUCKEY	F. DAVID	2647
	24	142 4/8	90	HP/RIFLE	BLAND	BOBBY W.	2678
	25	140 3/8	89	HP/RIFLE	LINDSEY	ROGER	2935
SHELBY	1	187 6/8	84	HP/RIFLE	WILLEY	RODNEY	7
	2	185 4/8	88	PICK-UP	PARSONS	RONALD L.	19
	3	173 1/8	81	HP/RIFLE	LIGHT	WILLIAM	97
	4	170 0/8	73	HP/RIFLE	GANDER	RUSTY D.	151
	5	166 0/8	70	HP/RIFLE	HAMMOND	JACK	262
	6	165 2/8	66	HP/RIFLE	CALDWELL	JAMES R.	293
	7	165 0/8	78	HP/RIFLE	ELLIOTT	JACKSON D.	299
	8	164 6/8	71	HP/RIFLE	PETERS	DONALD H.	307
	9	161 0/8	77	HP/RIFLE	LONG	DAVID	530
	10	159 0/8	80	HP/RIFLE	COLLINS	JIM	695
	11	158 2/8	88	BOW	McEWEN	RANDY	763
	12	158 1/8	67	HP/RIFLE	BOUDREAU	WILLIAM L.	777
	13	157 3/8	83	HP/RIFLE	GORDON	DWAYNE	848
	14	157 1/8	60	HP/RIFLE	WILLEY	MERRILL	864
	15	155 0/8	83	HP/RIFLE	BLAINE	REESE	1102
	16	154 5/8	89	HP/RIFLE	LARRICK	JOHN L.	1146
	17	153 5/8	69	BOW	SMOOT	RONALD C.	1273
	18	152 6/8	87	HP/RIFLE	MAYES	BILL	1385
	19	152 3/8	70	HP/RIFLE	RESA	ED	1453
	20	151 1/8	73	HP/RIFLE	BROWN	NOBLE	1690
	21	151 0/8	95	HP/RIFLE	HAWKINS	KENNY	1715
	22	150 5/8	72	HP/RIFLE	CLINE	VICTOR R.	1789
	23	150 3/8	84	HP/RIFLE	BICHSEL	DAVID	1834
	24	150 1/8	91	HP/RIFLE	BUCKMAN	MIKE	1879
	24	150 1/8	95	HP/RIFLE	SMOOT	DOUG	1879
	26	141 2/8	81	BOW	McWILLIAMS	JAMIE	2828
ST. CHARLES	1	172 7/8	80	HP/RIFLE	SATTLER	NOBERT J.	104
	2	170 2/8	94	HP/RIFLE	VEHIGE	LEROY	148
	3	169 1/8	90	HP/RIFLE	HOPEN	PAUL	166
	4	166 1/8	89	HP/RIFLE	VAILS	GARY	259
	5	164 6/8	74	HP/RIFLE	HEALEY, JR.	COL. CR	307
	6	162 5/8	85	BOW	HEILIGER	ROLAND	417
	7	160 7/8	76	BOW	SCHULTE	DANIEL D.	535
	8	160 1/8	87	HP/RIFLE	FITZPATRICK	MAURICE	599
	9	159 0/8	82	HP/RIFLE	BOLLMANN	JEFF	695
	10	158 6/8	88	HP/RIFLE	COLYER	JOHN D.	719
	11	158 4/8	86	HP/RIFLE	BUEKER	HARLAN	739
	12	156 1/8	94	HP/RIFLE	KOEHLER	KEITH	967

MISSOURI SHOW-ME BIG BUCKS CLUB RECORDS OF WHITETAIL DEER BY COUNTY, TYPICAL

COUNTY	COUNTY RANK	SCORE	YEAR TAKEN	WEAPON	HUNTER	FIRST NAME	STATE RANK
ST. CHARLES	13	156 0/8	72	PICK-UP	HERGERG	RANDALL O.	981
	14	155 6/8	88	HP/RIFLE	BURBES	JERRY	1004
	15	155 2/8	95	HP/RIFLE	KORTZEDORY	MICHAEL	1068
	16	155 0/8	81	HP/RIFLE	DYER	GARY J.	1102
	16	155 0/8	87	HP/RIFLE	RAGSDALE	ROGER	1102
	18	154 1/8	89	BOW	STEPHENS	CARLIS	1207
	19	152 5/8	84	HP/RIFLE	COLYER	JOE	1399
	20	151 1/8	90	HP/RIFLE	HALE	GREG	1690
	21	150 6/8	95	HP/RIFLE	OSTMANN	WILLIAM G. (BILL)	1756
	22	149 5/8	86	HP/RIFLE	THOMPSON	DON	1936
	23	148 6/8	96	BOW	HOLDMEYER	CLARENCE L.	2024
	24	148 5/8	80	BOW	DAVIDSON	EDWARD J.	2035
	25	146 7/8	85	HP/RIFLE	DUNKMANN	DWAIN	2214
	26	146 1/8	92	BOW	HAMRICK	BENJAMIN F.	2281
ST. CLAIR	1	159 4/8	90	HP/RIFLE	MOORE	CHARLES L.	654
	2	155 0/8	82	HP/RIFLE	HULSEY	HEATH	1102
	3	154 4/8	76	HP/RIFLE	BROWN	LARRY	1164
	4	153 4/8	82	HP/RIFLE	HARRIS	JACK T.	1287
	5	152 2/8	88	HP/RIFLE	BURCHETT	TRAVIS L.	1469
	6	151 7/8	69	HP/RIFLE	FLETCHER	DONALD W.	1550
	7	151 5/8	90	HP/RIFLE	LOCHRIDGE	ROBIN	1586
	8	150 4/8	59	HP/RIFLE	BOUGH	JOHN	1811
	8	150 4/8	90	HP/RIFLE	HAMILTON	JEFF	1811
	10	150 0/8	88	HP/RIFLE	HOSTETTER	NELSON L.	1897
	11	149 2/8	72	HP/RIFLE	STODDARD	NELSON	1973
	12	148 2/8	83	HP/RIFLE	QUICK	LARRY GENE	2071
	12	148 2/8	87	HP/RIFLE	WILLIAMS	ROBERT D.	2071
	14	147 7/8	90	HP/RIFLE	BRAY	RICK	2114
	15	146 6/8	95	HP/RIFLE	GENGLER	MIKE	2225
	16	146 2/8	95	HP/RIFLE	MARSHALL	DEONNE	2266
	17	144 7/8	92	HP/RIFLE	BOURLAND	SHEILA M.	2412
	18	144 4/8	88	HP/RIFLE	FARRIS	JAY	2459
	19	144 2/8	87	HP/RIFLE	COLLINS	DONALD	2483
	20	144 1/8	89	HP/RIFLE	HUTTON	OLIVER	2498
	21	143 1/8	80	HP/RIFLE	BARNES	KIRBY W.	2615
	21	143 1/8	89	BOW	SHOUSE	MARK	2615
	23	142 6/8	89	PICK-UP	ABBOTT	ELMER	2647
	24	142 3/8	85	HP/RIFLE	HARRIS	JACK T.	2691
	25	142 0/8	83	HP/RIFLE	KNEPP	CLAYTON M.	2725
	26	141 5/8	90	HP/RIFLE	DEITCH	BOBBY	2772
	27	141 4/8	83	HP/RIFLE	HENDRICKS	STEVE	2787
	27	141 4/8	90	HP/RIFLE	WILLIAMSON	JIM	2787
	29	140 5/8	95	HP/RIFLE	SMITH	RANDY	2908
	30	140 0/8	92	HP/RIFLE	HARPER	WILFORD N.	2990
ST. FRANCOIS	1	164 0/8	89	HP/RIFLE	HENSON	SHARON	349
	2	160 1/8	67	HP/RIFLE	SMITH	JAMES	599
	3	155 7/8	88	HP/RIFLE	MAY	MATTHEW	994
	4	155 3/8	95	HP/RIFLE	CALLAHAN	LARRY	1059
	5	144 7/8	95	HP/RIFLE	TEDDER	JESSE MICHAEL	2412
	6	144 6/8	71	HP/RIFLE	STROUP	JUNIOR C.	2425
	7	144 0/8	85	HP/RIFLE	BYERS	TED R.	2514
	8	143 5/8	92	PICK-UP	FREEMAN	DENNIS P.	2564
	9	143 2/8	93	HP/RIFLE	STOTLER	HOMER	2598
	10	142 5/8	86	HP/RIFLE	COLLINS	ROGER	2660
	11	142 4/8	88	HP/RIFLE	DAVIS	GARY	2678
	12	141 5/8	83	PICK-UP	WALKER	DARREN R.	2772
ST. LOUIS	1	187 1/8	72	HP/RIFLE	TUCKER	MACK	10
	2	167 5/8	87	HP/RIFLE	MEYER	MERVIN J.	205
	3	163 6/8	71	HP/RIFLE	KNIGHT	VEARL	363

COUNTY	COUNTY RANK	SCORE	YEAR TAKEN	WEAPON	HUNTER	FIRST NAME	STATE RANK
ST. LOUIS	4	162 4/8	92	HP/RIFLE	LEUTHAUSER	SCOTT	431
	5	160 2/8	68	HP/RIFLE	WATTS	THEODORE C.	584
	5	160 2/8	92	HP/RIFLE	SHELTON	ERIC	584
	7	159 0/8	94	HP/RIFLE	KREIENKAMP	STEVE	695
	8	156 1/8	72	HP/RIFLE	DELANEY	DAVE	967
	9	155 6/8	84	HP/RIFLE	ECKSTEIN	MARTIN H.	1004
	9	155 6/8	93	HP/RIFLE	WHITTENBERG	ALAN E.	1004
	11	154 2/8	96	BOW	WIGGINS	JESSIE	1186
	12	151 5/8	71	HP/RIFLE	SIDWELL	WILLIAM E.	1586
	13	151 3/8	85	HP/RIFLE	LEUTHAUSER	RONALD	1637
	14	151 2/8	90	HP/RIFLE	RUFFINO	PHIL	1656
	15	151 1/8	93	HP/RIFLE	HILL	WILLAIM H.	1690
	16	149 7/8	86	HP/RIFLE	HOFFMAN	EARL R.	1915
	17	149 3/8	79	HP/RIFLE	ZERWIG	ALAN	1959
	18	148 5/8	92	HP/RIFLE	WISNIEWSKI	JAY	2035
	18	148 4/8	95	HP/RIFLE	BAUER	DONALD J.	2048
	20	147 7/8	83	BOW	BERGMANN	DAVID	2114
	21	146 3/8	84	PICK-UP	CHRISTIE	DAN	2252
	21	146 3/8	96	HP/RIFLE	GILL	BUTCH	2252
	23	146 1/8	86	HP/RIFLE	GUEMMER	GERALD	2281
	24	145 3/8	96	BOW	McCONNELL	DAVID	2350
	25	143 4/8	82	HP/RIFLE	BERGMANN	DAVID	2577
	26	143 1/8	82	HP/RIFLE	SARTORS	DANNY	2615
	27	142 1/8	95	BOW	WERGES	ROBERT O.	2709
	28	141 3/8	92	HP/RIFLE	LEUTHAUSER	RONALD	2812
	29	141 0/8	82	HP/RIFLE	WILES	JACK	2863
	30	140 7/8	82	BOW	REPP	JACK	2877
	31	140 6/8	61	HP/RIFLE	ZERWIG	RAYMOND	2895
STE. GENEIEVE	1	158 0/8	80	HP/RIFLE	DRURY	KEITH	788
	2	156 0/8	71	HP/RIFLE	MANION	JAMES C.	981
	3	155 6/8	62	HP/RIFLE	STEARNS	KEN	1004
	4	155 2/8	87	HP/RIFLE	DAVITZ	KERMITH C.	1068
	5	150 5/8	90	HP/RIFLE	GEGG	NORMAN	1789
	6	148 7/8	79	HP/RIFLE	VOGEL	EDWIN	2012
	7	148 5/8	82	HP/RIFLE	GEARY	GEORGE	2035
	8	147 3/8	91	HP/RIFLE	HICKMAN	DALE	2155
	9	147 2/8	85	HP/RIFLE	HILL	CHRIS L.	2167
	10	147 0/8	77	HP/RIFLE	BOYER	VIRGIL	2195
	11	146 7/8	73	HP/RIFLE	HUCK	JEFFREY PAUL	2214
	12	146 3/8	89	HP/RIFLE	FOLKERTS	WIL A.	2252
	13	144 7/8	86	HP/RIFLE	VOLMAR	LINDA	2412
	14	144 5/8	52	HP/RIFLE	GYURICA	PHILLIP	2442
	14	144 5/8	67	HP/RIFLE	HOLLIS	DORRIS C.	2442
	16	143 1/8	95	HP/RIFLE	VOGT	RICHARD	2615
	17	142 5/8	79	HP/RIFLE	JOKERST	GENE	2660
	18	142 4/8	82	HP/RIFLE	BREWSTER	JOE	2678
	19	142 0/8	90	HP/RIFLE	McCLANAHAN	ROBERT	2725
	20	141 6/8	61	HP/RIFLE	KINKEAD	TERRY	2756
	21	141 5/8	94	HP/RIFLE	CLUKIES	PAUL A.	2772
	22	141 4/8	95	HP/RIFLE	JOKERST	DAVID L.	2787
	23	141 3/8	88	HP/RIFLE	VINCENT	DAVID A.	2812
	24	140 3/8	79	HP/RIFLE	MENGE	DAVID	2935
STODDARD	1	161 0/8	95	BOW	LANDEWEE	PAUL F.	530
	2	155 6/8	90	HP/RIFLE	HEDSPETH	LINUEL	1004
	3	153 6/8	80	HP/RIFLE	BARTON	GARY	1256
	4	148 3/8	90	BOW	BARNFIELD	CLINT	2060
	5	146 6/8	96	BOW	REYNOLDS	DON	2225
	6	141 1/8	86	HP/RIFLE	HARDIN	RICK	2844
	7	141 0/8	87	HP/RIFLE	PAGE	GAVIN	2863

MISSOURI SHOW-ME BIG BUCKS CLUB RECORDS OF WHITETAIL DEER BY COUNTY, TYPICAL

COUNTY	COUNTY RANK	SCORE	YEAR TAKEN	WEAPON	HUNTER	FIRST NAME	STATE RANK
STODDARD	8	140 1/8	90	BOW	WRIGHT	JOHN M.	2978
STONE	1	151 5/8	75	HP/RIFLE	BLADES	WAYNE	1586
	2	150 6/8	81	HP/RIFLE	SCHULZ	EARL	1756
	3	149 0/8	86	HP/RIFLE	CREEL	TODD	1998
	4	147 5/8	73	HP/RIFLE	RICE	JOE	2138
SULLIVAN	1	171 0/8	72	HP/RIFLE	HARVEY, JR.	FORNEY	129
	2	170 4/8	81	HP/RIFLE	TUCKER	RANDY	140
	3	168 0/8	90	HP/RIFLE	HINES	JAMES E.	194
	4	167 5/8	69	HP/RIFLE	MICHAEL	KENNETH L.	205
	5	166 1/8	82	HP/RIFLE	GLIDEWELL	GREG	259
	6	165 5/8	90	HP/RIFLE	MAGGART	DENNIS	269
	7	164 5/8	81	HP/RIFLE	MURPHY	MARK D.	313
	8	162 5/8	71	HP/RIFLE	BOWE	LLOYD	417
	9	162 3/8	67	HP/RIFLE	JEFFRIES	EDWIN	439
	10	162 2/8	73	HP/RIFLE	CREASON	JOHN	451
	11	160 3/8	94	HP/RIFLE	GLIDEWELL	BRANDON	574
	12	159 4/8	90	HP/RIFLE	HOCKER	ROGER	654
	13	158 0/8	86	HP/RIFLE	MARTIN	CHARLES	788
	14	157 0/8	74	HP/RIFLE	WHEELER	TERRY	875
	14	157 0/8	95	HP/RIFLE	GROFF	RODNEY S.	875
	16	156 1/8	86	HP/RIFLE	GANN	KENNY	967
	17	156 0/8	96	HP/RIFLE	ANDERS, SR.	GARY	981
	18	155 4/8	91	HP/RIFLE	HIGH	DUANE	1040
	19	155 1/8	92	HP/RIFLE	GUION	LONNIE	1091
	20	154 6/8	86	HP/RIFLE	GILVIN	JOE	1130
	21	154 3/8	89	HP/RIFLE	SCHROCK	JERRY L.	1174
	21	154 3/8	95	M/L	CUNNINGHAM	WESLEY	1174
	23	153 7/8	89	HP/RIFLE	WHITLOCK	MARCUS	1238
	24	153 3/8	89	HP/RIFLE	MILDWARD	RICHARD L.	1310
	25	153 2/8	90	HP/RIFLE	FOSTER	RUSSELL A.	1327
	26	153 1/8	91	HP/RIFLE	WILCOX	WILLIAM B.	1344
	27	152 4/8	89	HP/RIFLE	OTTO	ART	1423
	28	152 2/8	88	HP/RIFLE	SMITH	BRUCE	1469
	29	152 1/8	89	HP/RIFLE	PARKS	DOUG	1493
	30	151 4/8	85	HP/RIFLE	GANN	KENNY	1613
	31	151 1/8	67	HP/RIFLE	SAYRE	PHILLIP	1690
	32	150 7/8	94	HP/RIFLE	LAWSON	DALE	1734
	33	143 4/8	95	HP/RIFLE	McDONALD	AARON	2577
	34	143 0/8	94	HP/RIFLE	HALTERMAN	KEN	2626
	35	140 7/8	93	PICK-UP	SCHOONOVER	TOM	2877
	36	140 0/8	96	HP/RIFLE	SHOOP	MARCUS	2990
TANEY	1	162 3/8	74	HP/RIFLE	NEWBERRY	DAVID	439
	2	150 6/8	85	HP/RIFLE	HOLIDAY	LARRY	1756
	3	147 5/8	73	HP/RIFLE	ROSSNER	HERMAN	2138
	4	147 4/8	81	HP/RIFLE	OUSLEY	CHUCK	2148
	5	147 2/8	89	HP/RIFLE	COFFELT	JIM	2167
	6	145 7/8	82	HP/RIFLE	McINTURFF	RON	2302
	7	143 3/8	91	BOW	HAMMONS	GEORGE	2591
	8	141 3/8	76	HP/RIFLE	HANNAH	RICK	2812
	9	140 2/8	80	HP/RIFLE	McMAHON	JUNIOR	2952
TEXAS	1	173 7/8	81	BOW	BELEW	DON	86
	2	169 1/8	90	HP/RIFLE	CHIPPS	DALLAS	166
	3	166 3/8	90	HP/RIFLE	PAMPERIEN	GREG	249
	4	163 7/8	89	BOW	NEUGEBAUER	LONNIE	356
	5	159 0/8	76	HP/RIFLE	FUNK	DAVID	695
	6	158 5/8	93	BOW	SCANTLIN	DAVID	735
	7	156 5/8	65	HP/RIFLE	SULLINS	HAROLD	911
	8	155 5/8	77	HP/RIFLE	HANCOCK	JERRY	1023
	9	155 1/8	81	HP/RIFLE	SULLINS	NARVEL	1091

169

COUNTY	COUNTY RANK	SCORE	YEAR TAKEN	WEAPON	HUNTER	FIRST NAME	STATE RANK
TEXAS	10	154 1/8	81	HP/RIFLE	MENDENHALL	MIKE	1207
	11	153 4/8	89	HP/RIFLE	TUNE	ROGER	1287
	12	153 3/8	75	HP/RIFLE	OGDON	CARL	1310
	13	152 5/8	67	HP/RIFLE	JORDAN	BUD	1399
	14	151 5/8	91	HP/RIFLE	WELLS	DON	1586
	15	151 1/8	94	HP/RIFLE	KIRKMAN	CARLOSS	1690
	16	150 3/8	94	HP/RIFLE	SMITH	RODNEY T.	1834
	17	150 2/8	88	HP/RIFLE	UMKNOWN		1853
	18	150 0/8	65	HP/RIFLE	LEADFORD	GLEN	1897
	19	149 6/8	93	HP/RIFLE	QUESENBERRY	BASIL	1926
	20	149 3/8	89	HP/RIFLE	BUCHHEIT	DENNIS	1959
	20	149 3/8	96	BOW	GASTON	DON	1959
	22	149 2/8	85	HP/RIFLE	LIPSCOMB	ROY	1973
	24	149 2/8	87	HP/RIFLE	CARR	RUSSELL	1973
	25	149 1/8	73	HP/RIFLE	KEITH	KENNETH J.	1988
	26	148 7/8	58	HP/RIFLE	ICE	ELMER	2012
	27	147 6/8	89	PICK-UP	GIVENS	GARY	2126
	28	147 1/8	81	HP/RIFLE	CAMPBELL	HERBERT	2183
	29	147 0/8	55	HP/RIFLE	STILLEY	VAUGHN	2195
	30	146 7/8	87	HP/RIFLE	GOINS	RICK	2214
	31	146 3/8	76	HP/RIFLE	BARTON	ELMER	2252
	31	145 6/8	77	HP/RIFLE	ICE	RONALD	2311
	32	145 2/8	74	HP/RIFLE	BATES	KENNETH	2361
	33	144 3/8	96	HP/RIFLE	LINDSEY	ROGER S.	2466
	34	144 1/8	96	HP/RIFLE	STONE	DONALD	2498
	35	143 7/8	90	HP/RIFLE	YOAKUM	DELMAR	2533
	36	143 4/8	73	HP/RIFLE	OGDON	CARL	2577
	36	143 4/8	86	HP/RIFLE	FRAMPTON	LLOYD	2577
	38	143 2/8	91	HP/RIFLE	LUTZ	THOMAS	2598
	39	143 0/8	91	HP/RIFLE	JUNG	STANLEY V.	2626
	40	142 7/8	93	HP/RIFLE	TAYLOR	ARLAN	2641
	41	142 5/8	87	HP/RIFLE	JAUDES	KIRK A.	2660
	42	142 4/8	88	HP/RIFLE	McCARTER	W. GENE	2678
	43	142 2/8	91	HP/RIFLE	STAFFORD	KEN	2701
	44	142 1/8	59	HP/RIFLE	AUSTIN	LARRY B.	2709
	44	142 1/8	88	HP/RIFLE	RHODES	JONATHAN	2709
	46	142 0/8	83	HP/RIFLE	SHEPPARD	EDWARD F.	2725
	47	141 6/8	80	HP/RIFLE	BONNER	JOE	2756
	48	140 6/8	90	HP/RIFLE	VOGELIE	MICHAEL A.	2895
	49	140 3/8	69	HP/RIFLE	DOUGLAS	DAVID	2935
VERNON	1	189 5/8	96	HP/RIFLE	GUINN	BRAD	6
	2	166 2/8	90	HP/RIFLE	BRANNAN	ERWIN	255
	3	153 7/8	89	HP/RIFLE	ROBINSON	BILL	1238
	4	150 6/8	91	HP/RIFLE	FOX	SCOTT R.	1756
	5	150 5/8	72	HP/RIFLE	GASTEL	K.J.	1789
	6	148 0/8	89	HP/RIFLE	MOONEY II	TOM R.	2101
	7	147 7/8	86	HP/RIFLE	PARRISH	KEVIN	2114
	8	147 3/8	91	HP/RIFLE	McGRATH	FRANK	2155
	9	147 2/8	79	HP/RIFLE	COUCH	PHIL	2167
	10	147 1/8	93	BOW	BOGART	LARRY D.	2183
	11	146 6/8	86	BOW	BURRELL	JEFF	2225
	12	145 2/8	82	HP/RIFLE	ARTHUR	LAWANNA	2361
	13	143 2/8	90	HP/RIFLE	ANDERS	ED	2598
	14	143 0/8	93	HP/RIFLE	NEWTON	BILL W.	2626
	15	141 6/8	66	HP/RIFLE	JENKINS	MIKE	2756
	15	141 6/8	95	HP/RIFLE	MASON	CLEM V.	2756
	17	141 3/8	95	HP/RIFLE	GRUENHAGEN	ARON	2812
	18	141 0/8	84	HP/RIFLE	MORLAN	ED	2863
	19	140 4/8	82	HP/RIFLE	NELANDER	ED	2925

MISSOURI SHOW-ME BIG BUCKS CLUB RECORDS OF WHITETAIL DEER BY COUNTY, TYPICAL

COUNTY	COUNTY RANK	SCORE	YEAR TAKEN	WEAPON	HUNTER	FIRST NAME	STATE RANK
WARREN	1	182 4/8	68	HP/RIFLE	TANNER	DONALD L.	24
	2	173 5/8	95	HP/RIFLE	SKELTON	GLENN	89
	3	173 2/8	80	HP/RIFLE	LEY	JEROME	95
	4	171 1/8	90	HP/RIFLE	CASPER	JIM	127
	5	165 5/8	85	HP/RIFLE	GILDEHAUS	JAMES H.	269
	6	164 2/8	85	HP/RIFLE	HANDLANG	MELVIN	332
	7	163 2/8	59	HP/RIFLE	AVERY	ALTON	383
	8	162 1/8	88	HP/RIFLE	KLEWEIS	ED	455
	9	159 1/8	94	HP/RIFLE	KLEIMAN	KENNETH M.	687
	10	159 0/8	92	M/L	KREPS	STEVE	695
	11	158 4/8	84	HP/RIFLE	GERARD	TRAVIS	739
	12	158 0/8	73	HP/RIFLE	BIERBAUM	EMMET W.	788
	13	157 0/8	73	HP/RIFLE	EDWARDS	NORMAN J.	875
	14	156 1/8	94	HP/RIFLE	COX	PAUL R.	967
	15	155 6/8	84	HP/RIFLE	NICKS	DEAN	1004
	16	155 4/8	67	HP/RIFLE	ELLIS	D.C.	1040
	16	155 4/8	96	HP/RIFLE	MOORE	CECIL M.	1040
	18	154 2/8	87	HP/RIFLE	BALLMANN	MARK A.	1186
	19	153 4/8	69	HP/RIFLE	SZACHNIESKI	BARRY	1287
	19	153 4/8	69	HP/RIFLE	TANNER	DONALD L.	1287
	19	153 4/8	88	HP/RIFLE	ENGEMANN	DAVID	1287
	22	153 0/8	95	HP/RIFLE	JOERLING	GENE	1355
	23	152 5/8	67	HP/RIFLE	JOERLING	LAWRENCE	1399
	24	152 4/8	91	HP/RIFLE	JONES	MICHAEL R.	1423
	25	152 3/8	82	HP/RIFLE	DUFRENNE	KENNY	1453
	26	152 2/8	59	HP/RIFLE	PLACKEMEIER	ROY	1469
	26	152 2/8	94	HP/RIFLE	FENSOM	JOHN	1469
	28	152 0/8	57	HP/RIFLE	WEST	IRVIN G.	1519
	28	152 0/8	93	HP/RIFLE	FEHLINGS	SCOTT	1519
	30	150 1/8	85	HP/RIFLE	SMITH	DWAIN	1879
	31	148 3/8	94	HP/RIFLE	CASPER	JIM	2060
	32	147 5/8	68	HP/RIFLE	CASPER	TIMOTHY W.	2138
	33	146 7/8	86	HP/RIFLE	KESSELHEIM	JEFF	2214
	34	143 6/8	86	HP/RIFLE	CASPER	JIM	2550
	35	143 2/8	79	HP/RIFLE	MASCHGER	JERRY	2598
WASHINGTON	1	171 3/8	87	HP/RIFLE	BOUSE	JERRY	121
	2	166 3/8	49	HP/RIFLE	ROUSAN	BERN	249
	3	160 7/8	66	HP/RIFLE	PENNOCK	NORBERT	535
	3	160 7/8	69	PICK-UP	CLANTON	BYRON	535
	5	160 6/8	62	HP/RIFLE	SUMPTER	MONROE	543
	6	159 7/8	57	HP/RIFLE	MASON	GEORGE	620
	7	158 5/8	95	HP/RIFLE	JOHNSON	JEFFREY	735
	8	156 4/8	69	HP/RIFLE	PHIPPS	LEE	925
	9	156 1/8	86	HP/RIFLE	HARNESS	WAYNE	967
	10	154 7/8	73	HP/RIFLE	BISHOP	DEAN R.	1118
	11	154 6/8	85	HP/RIFLE	LANDS	PAUL	1130
	12	154 2/8	95	HP/RIFLE	SITZES	JAMIE E.	1186
	13	152 6/8	86	HP/RIFLE	RIGEL	BILL	1385
	14	152 5/8	72	HP/RIFLE	GROSS	ARTHUR B.	1399
	15	149 7/8	77	HP/RIFLE	RUFKAHR	MIKE	1915
	16	149 5/8	72	HP/RIFLE	SIMPSON	WILLIS HENRY	1936
	17	149 4/9	77	HP/RIFLE	MERCER	MERLIN	1936
	18	149 2/8	85	HP/RIFLE	POLITTE	TERRY	1973
	19	148 6/8	94	HP/RIFLE	HUBBLE	DAVE	2024
	20	148 4/8	85	HP/RIFLE	CHRISTOPHER	ROBERT	2048
	21	148 2/8	87	HP/RIFLE	JACOX	RANDY	2071
	22	147 7/8	89	HP/RIFLE	MEDLIN	GREGORY D.	2114
	23	147 6/8	96	HP/RIFLE	GOODSON	KELLY E.	2126
	24	147 3/8	85	HP/RIFLE	BUST	JOE	2155

COUNTY	COUNTY RANK	SCORE	YEAR TAKEN	WEAPON	HUNTER	FIRST NAME	STATE RANK
WASHINGTON	25	147 2/8	92	HP/RIFLE	MEDLIN	GREGORY D.	2167
	26	145 6/8	69	HP/RIFLE	MERCER	CURTIS D.	2311
	27	145 5/8	58	HP/RIFLE	RUSSELL	RICHARD	2324
	28	144 7/8	77	HP/RIFLE	WORLEY	LARRY	2412
	29	144 2/8	77	HP/RIFLE	PHILLIPS	G.D.	2483
	30	143 5/8	89	HP/RIFLE	FRANKLIN	ALAN D.	2564
	31	143 3/8	71	HP/RIFLE	SULLENTROP	HOWARD	2591
	31	143 3/8	82	HP/RIFLE	STACK	DEAN R.	2591
	33	143 2/8	96	HP/RIFLE	CLICK	BRYAN	2598
	34	141 5/8	75	HP/RIFLE	KLOPPE	ROWAN R.	2772
	35	141 3/8	95	BOW	O'NEAL, JR.	JIMMY J.	2812
	36	140 7/8	84	HP/RIFLE	WILLIAMS	JOHN	2877
WAYNE	1	170 7/8	89	HP/RIFLE	BOSTIC	DARRELL	134
	2	163 1/8	67	HP/RIFLE	FOX	JAMES	392
	3	162 6/8	89	PICK-UP	STANFILL	RICK	411
	4	160 4/8	88	HP/RIFLE	ROACH	CARL	560
	5	158 2/8	95	HP/RIFLE	ROSE	LARRY E.	763
	6	157 5/8	89	BOW	BOWLING	ROD	821
	7	157 2/8	63	HP/RIFLE	WILDERMAN	WILLIAM	853
	8	153 6/8	82	HP/RIFLE	RUNNELS	LINDELL	1256
	9	152 5/8	89	HP/RIFLE	CRUTCHFIELD	WINFRED	1399
	10	152 2/8	95	BOW	WATKINS	CARL L.	1469
	11	152 1/8	87	HP/RIFLE	VANNOY	MARVIN	1493
	12	152 0/8	96	HP/RIFLE	GOLDBECK	MIKE	1519
	13	150 7/8	87	HP/RIFLE	GREEN	DALE	1734
	14	149 3/8	84	HP/RIFLE	WILFONG	RAY	1959
	14	149 3/8	89	HP/RIFLE	KEPPIER	JOHN	1959
	16	149 0/8	87	HP/RIFLE	COX	JEFF	1998
	17	148 7/8	84	HP/RIFLE	WELLS	ANDY	2012
	18	146 2/8	88	BOW	GROOM	VIRGIL E.	2266
	19	146 0/8	75	HP/RIFLE	ROPER	DONALD P.	2290
	20	145 7/8	95	HP/RIFLE	FRYMIRE	JACKIE	2302
	21	142 6/8	87	HP/RIFLE	TONEY	MIKE	2647
	22	141 3/8	96	HP/RIFLE	LOAFMAN	BYRON	2812
	23	141 2/8	89	HP/RIFLE	DENKINS	BILL	2828
	24	140 7/8	78	HP/RIFLE	NEAL	JERRY	2877
	25	140 0/8	89	HP/RIFLE	LEMMON	JODY	2990
WEBSTER	1	161 4/8	67	HP/RIFLE	ALCORN	BILLY J.	493
	2	140 2/8	95	HP/RIFLE	BIGLEY	JIMMIE L.	2952
WORTH	1	168 3/8	81	HP/RIFLE	NIGH, JR.	WESLEY	184
	2	163 2/8	85	HP/RIFLE	SPICER	GARY	383
	3	162 1/8	88	HP/RIFLE	LYNCH	MIKE	455
	4	161 6/8	90	HP/RIFLE	JAMES	DUANE	476
	5	157 4/8	96	HP/RIFLE	MERCER	MARVIN	833
	6	156 0/8	85	HP/RIFLE	SASSANI	KOUROS	981
	7	155 4/8	89	HP/RIFLE	VON GEYSO	FRANK	1040
	8	155 3/8	72	HP/RIFLE	THURMAN	DAVID	1059
	9	155 0/8	96	HP/RIFLE	DeFREECE	SHAWN E.	1102
	10	154 6/8	89	HP/RIFLE	LYNCH	LESLIE	1130
	11	152 7/8	79	HP/RIFLE	STEVENS	PREN	1370
	12	152 4/8	93	HP/RIFLE	ALLEN	RICHARD	1423
WRIGHT	1	176 3/8	86	HP/RIFLE	NAPIER	MIKE	60
	2	163 6/8	80	HP/RIFLE	WHITE	TONY	363
	3	152 1/8	90	HP/RIFLE	FLAKE	DAVID	1493
	4	151 4/8	81	HP/RIFLE	DUDLEY	JAMES L.	1613
	5	150 6/8	90	HP/RIFLE	DODSON	EDWIN	1756
	6	148 1/8	79	HP/RIFLE	TURNER	LARRY	2088
	7	145 0/8	78	HP/RIFLE	WILLIAMS	GARRY	2391
	8	144 6/8	79	HP/RIFLE	HYLTON	LLOYD	2425

COUNTY	COUNTY RANK	SCORE	YEAR TAKEN	WEAPON	HUNTER	FIRST NAME	STATE RANK
WRIGHT	9	141 5/8	95	HP/RIFLE	THRONE	CURTIS	2772
	10	140 3/8	79	HP/RIFLE	WERKMEISTER	GENE	2935
	11	140 1/8	76	HP/RIFLE	MARTIN	DON	2978

COUNTY	COUNTY RANK	SCORE	YEAR TAKEN	WEAPON	HUNTER	FIRST NAME	STATE RANK
ADAIR	1	207 7/8	94	HP/RIFLE	HIGGINS	LARRY	30
	2	207 2/8	88	HP/RIFLE	ELSEA	KEVIN	32
	3	201 7/8	90	HP/RIFLE	CAIN	RONALD	54
	4	188 6/8	91	BOW	REID	DAVID C.	148
	5	187 2/8	87	HP/RIFLE	GIBBS	JOHN R.	163
	6	183 5/8	95	HP/RIFLE	GROSSNICKLE	JOHN B.	209
	7	183 4/8	61	PICK-UP	SEVITS	WENDELL	211
	8	178 4/8	86	HP/RIFLE	FARLEY	BILL	276
	9	172 3/8	91	HP/RIFLE	STRIBLING	SONNY	373
	10	170 4/8	76	HP/RIFLE	GIBSON	JOHN	410
	11	170 1/8	94	HP/RIFLE	WAYBILL	JANET	417
	12	168 7/8	88	HP/RIFLE	ANDERSON	JAMES M.	422
ANDREW	1	207 2/8	81	HP/RIFLE	KELSO	FRANK	32
	2	203 6/8	89	HP/RIFLE	HOWARD	MARTY	43
	3	203 2/8	95	HP/RIFLE	SCHWEIZER	CRAIG	46
	4	193 3/8	76	HP/RIFLE	HERBERT	RICHARD	106
	5	188 6/8	59	HP/RIFLE	CORDONNIER	DAVID	148
	6	184 4/8	72	HP/RIFLE	MARTIN	LOREN	199
	7	183 1/8	96	HP/RIFLE	WAEGELE	RANDY	218
	8	180 2/8	85	HP/RIFLE	KAPP	BRENT	251
	9	177 0/8	94	HP/RIFLE	COLE	MIKE	301
	10	176 7/8	73	HP/RIFLE	SMITH	LUCIAN	302
	11	173 4/8	93	HP/RIFLE	SCHOTTEL	ROD	350
	12	171 4/8	81	HP/RIFLE	TAYLOR	CAROLYN	387
	13	170 1/8	72	HP/RIFLE	PELLERSELS	DAVID	418
ATCHISON	1	223 2/8	83	HP/RIFLE	SUTTER	JERRY	10
	2	208 7/8	64	HP/RIFLE	LEE	KENNETH W.	25
	3	205 7/8	90	HP/RIFLE	POPPA	LARRY	36
	4	201 3/8	88	HP/RIFLE	THOMPSON	STEVE	59
	5	170 4/8	86	HP/RIFLE	SHAUL	NORM	410
	6	157 3/8	94	HP/RIFLE	HEANY	RONNIE	540
AUDRAIN	1	183 1/8	86	HP/RIFLE	McCUBBIN	DENNIS	218
	2	174 2/8	96	HP/RIFLE	DAY	JUSTIN	337
BARTON	1	212 5/8	91	HP/RIFLE	CRYSTAL	DAVID	21
	2	177 3/8	85	HP/RIFLE	RANDALL	RODNEY	297
	3	168 0/8	91	HP/RIFLE	CARDER	GEORGE E.	451
	4	162 7/8	91	HP/RIFLE	YORK	ROBERT GLENN	501
	5	160 7/8	90	HP/RIFLE	TODD	DONALD	522
BATES	1	208 7/8	95	HP/RIFLE	FERGUSON	BRAD	25
	2	169 0/8	84	HP/RIFLE	DURST	MIKE	438
	3	167 7/8	91	HP/RIFLE	PIPES	MARK	454
BENTON	1	181 5/8	66	HP/RIFLE	WISE	CHARLES	232
	2	177 4/8	79	HP/RIFLE	DRENNON	CHIP	294
	3	175 0/8	95	HP/RIFLE	KOLL	BOB	327
	4	173 7/8	70	HP/RIFLE	COCKERELL	EDWARD	344
	5	170 0/8	89	HP/RIFLE	McKINNEY	TROY	423
	6	169 4/8	94	HP/RIFLE	MACKAY	ALAN D.	431
	7	168 1/8	85	HP/RIFLE	HILTY	JOHN	449
	8	163 0/8	84	HP/RIFLE	DURRILL	RANDOLPH	496
	9	160 5/8	96	HP/RIFLE	IRWIN	JACOB	526
BOLLINGER	1	191 3/8	94	HP/RIFLE	DEROUSSE	DAVE	123
BOONE	1	204 2/8	85	HP/RIFLE	BROWN	GENE	41
	2	199 5/8	91	HP/RIFLE	KRUEGER	STEVEN LEE	71
	3	193 7/8	92	HP/RIFLE	QUEVREAUX	AL	104
	4	191 7/8	83	HP/RIFLE	WIESCHAUS	PAUL	118
	5	186 6/8	86	HP/RIFLE	PALMER	DALE	170
	6	180 4/8	94	HP/RIFLE	CALVERT, JR.	HOWARD	249
	7	178 4/8	83	BOW	LADDON	PHIL	276
BUCHANAN	1	189 2/8	84	PICK-UP	DELK	DEAN M.	143

MISSOURI SHOW-ME BIG BUCKS CLUB RECORDS OF WHITETAIL DEER BY COUNTY, NON-TYP

COUNTY	COUNTY RANK	SCORE	YEAR TAKEN	WEAPON	HUNTER	FIRST NAME	STATE RANK
BUCHANAN	2	173 2/8	89	HP/RIFLE	BILLINGTON	PAUL	357
	3	170 5/8	80	HP/RIFLE	MUSSER	ROBERT	408
CALDWELL	1	206 1/8	96	HP/RIFLE	MIDDLETON	PAUL	34
	2	197 1/8	90	HP/RIFLE	NICKLES	JAMES	77
CALLAWAY	1	202 0/8	95	HP/RIFLE	MENG	MARC	51
	2	187 2/8	86	BOW	COX	BRUCE	163
	3	182 2/8	84	HP/RIFLE	BROWN	ROGER	227
	4	181 6/8	95	HP/RIFLE	FOWLER	DONALD	230
	5	179 5/8	89	HP/RIFLE	BUCKHOLZ	KENNY	259
	6	173 6/8	88	HP/RIFLE	SCHAEFER	RONALD ERIC	346
	7	173 3/8	95	HP/RIFLE	REANY	BILL	354
	8	172 3/8	75	HP/RIFLE	SHANNON	MIKE	373
	9	170 3/8	90	HP/RIFLE	EDMUNDS	JAMES THOMAS	413
	10	170 2/8	88	BOW	MURPHY	LARRY	417
	11	161 6/8	96	HP/RIFLE	HOOK	BRIAN K.	514
CAMDEN	1	208 5/8	91	HP/RIFLE	DUNCAN	DAVID	27
	2	195 3/8	82	HP/RIFLE	STEPHENS	CARLIS	89
	3	189 3/8	74	HP/RIFLE	SULGROVE	A.D.	141
	4	182 3/8	55	HP/RIFLE	COURTNEY	BERT	224
CAPE GIRARDEAU	1	190 6/8	89	HP/RIFLE	SNELL	GARY	129
	2	167 3/8	90	HP/RIFLE	TALLEY	KENNY	459
	3	162 1/8	88	HP/RIFLE	FARROW	BRYAN	509
CARROLL	1	197 1/8	90	HP/RIFLE	OSER	DALE	77
	2	178 2/8	96	HP/RIFLE	GERMANN	MARK	286
	3	172 5/8	76	HP/RIFLE	BROOKE	WALTER	369
	4	171 7/8	89	HP/RIFLE	STARK	LEE	381
	5	170 7/8	93	HP/RIFLE	HUTCHINSON	DENNIS	397
	6	170 1/8	92	HP/RIFLE	BAGGS	TODD	417
CARTER	1	191 7/8	92	HP/RIFLE	DENNIS	MICHAEL	118
	2	180 6/8	87	HP/RIFLE	BOSTIC	IVAN	243
	3	169 0/8	59	HP/RIFLE	DAWSON	GEORGE	438
CASS	1	174 0/8	95	HP/RIFLE	THOMAS	DAVID	341
	2	173 2/8	84	HP/RIFLE	STARK	ED	357
	3	172 2/8	92	BOW	WALTON	JERROL	375
	4	167 6/8	93	HP/RIFLE	GRAVES	ED	456
	5	160 4/8	84	HP/RIFLE	JOHNSON	STEVE	527
CEDAR	1	165 1/8	74	HP/RIFLE	ESSEX	NORMA	480
	2	162 5/8	71	HP/RIFLE	DURHAM	LARRY	504
CHARITON	1	259 5/8	85	HP/RIFLE	LINSCOTT	DUANE R.	2
	2	218 5/8	79	HP/RIFLE	McSPARREN	STAN	14
	3	203 5/8	53	HP/RIFLE	SOWERS	VERNON	44
	3	203 5/8	95	HP/RIFLE	STROUP	KEVIN RAYMOND	44
	5	193 0/8	71	HP/RIFLE	COKERHAM	GARY	108
	6	191 5/8	96	HP/RIFLE	GLADBACH	TIM	121
	7	190 2/8	83	HP/RIFLE	WALTON	ANN	133
	8	186 4/8	59	HP/RIFLE	CHILDERS	HARLEY	174
	9	183 5/8	92	PICK-UP	CUNNINGHAM	PATRICK	209
	10	175 5/8	96	HP/RIFLE	WEIMER	MICHAEL	317
	11	164 5/8	90	HP/RIFLE	BILLUPS	RANDY	483
CHRISTIAN	1	160 3/8	92	HP/RIFLE	PLANK	TERRY	530
CLARK	1	223 4/8	67	HP/RIFLE	PRIEBE	EVELYN	9
	2	206 0/8	83	HP/RIFLE	COURTNEY	ALLEN L.	35
	3	199 3/8	73	HP/RIFLE	ARNOLD	BOB	73
	4	198 2/8	95	HP/RIFLE	WARD	STEWART W.	75
	5	194 4/8	88	HP/RIFLE	WHEATON	RALPH	97
	6	185 0/8	81	HP/RIFLE	HARMON	TOM	192
	7	184 5/8	91	HP/RIFLE	HOWARD	J. DAVID	197
	8	184 4/8	85	HP/RIFLE	YATES	KEVIN	199
	9	178 5/8	67	HP/RIFLE	O'DAY	ROSS L.	275

COUNTY	COUNTY RANK	SCORE	YEAR TAKEN	WEAPON	HUNTER	FIRST NAME	STATE RANK
CLARK	10	172 4/8	94	M/L	COPPLER	BRUCE H.	371
	11	172 2/8	87	HP/RIFLE	YOUNG	RONALD L.	375
	12	170 3/8	90	HP/RIFLE	COOK	JIM	413
CLAY	1	216 6/8	91	BOW	THOMEY	MARVIN	17
	2	214 3/8	96	HP/RIFLE	MYNATT II	JERRY W.	19
	3	199 0/8	90	HP/RIFLE	CALLAHAN	PATRICK M.	74
	4	188 1/8	92	HP/RIFLE	COPELAND	DON	155
	5	171 0/8	83	HP/RIFLE	NAPPI	VICTOR A.	393
CLINTON	1	201 5/8	89	HP/RIFLE	EADS	DAVID	55
	2	200 4/8	91	HP/RIFLE	NORTON	REA	64
	3	189 5/8	84	HP/RIFLE	AITKENS	RONNIE	138
	4	188 7/8	94	HP/RIFLE	JONES	MARTIN	146
	5	172 6/8	95	HP/RIFLE	KECK	JIM	366
	6	166 0/8	96	BOW	THOMAS	CHRIS	471
COLE	1	171 4/8	86	HP/RIFLE	VARNADORE	ROBERT	387
COOPER	1	194 6/8	70	HP/RIFLE	BURNETT	DONALD	95
	2	190 0/8	71	HP/RIFLE	NIXON	H.A.	134
	3	188 5/8	94	HP/RIFLE	DEUSCHLE	STEVE	154
	4	183 7/8	86	HP/RIFLE	THURMAN	TROY	207
	5	177 4/8	73	HP/RIFLE	WALJE	WILLARD	294
	6	176 5/8	82	HP/RIFLE	TEMPLETON	JESSIE	305
	7	173 6/8	71	HP/RIFLE	FRIEDRICH	RON	346
	8	167 6/8	95	HP/RIFLE	ZUMSTEG	PAUL	456
	9	167 0/8	91	HP/RIFLE	HUTH	STEVE	462
	10	164 1/8	74	HP/RIFLE	FRIEDRICH	TOMMY	490
	11	163 0/8	87	HP/RIFLE	REX	MIKE	496
CRAWFORD	1	189 0/8	68	PICK-UP	TAYLOR	HAROLD	144
	2	185 1/8	95	HP/RIFLE	YOUNG	EUGENE P.	190
	3	184 2/8	65	HP/RIFLE	ROBINSON	JAMES R.	203
	4	183 4/8	67	HP/RIFLE	HARTKE	WARREN	211
	5	177 5/8	62	HP/RIFLE	WEBB	RAYMOND	292
	6	168 6/8	89	HP/RIFLE	LEACH	JAMES C.	444
	7	168 4/8	94	HP/RIFLE	THORPE	BRENT C.	447
	8	163 5/8	92	HP/RIFLE	MATHEWS	BRIAN	491
DADE	1	175 0/8	83	HP/RIFLE	SLATTEN	DANNY	327
DALLAS	1	183 3/8	62	HP/RIFLE	HAMLET	D.W.	215
	2	177 7/8	94	HP/RIFLE	LEWIS	BOBBY A.	290
DAVIESS	1	202 6/8	83	HP/RIFLE	HELDENBRAND	DENNIS	48
	2	180 5/8	96	PICK-UP	SHAUL	NORM	247
	3	177 2/8	91	HP/RIFLE	EADS	JOHN	299
	4	172 2/8	74	HP/RIFLE	YOST	KENNETH	375
	5	169 6/8	96	HP/RIFLE	COLE	CHARLES R.	429
DEKALB	1	174 0/8	89	HP/RIFLE	SKOUBY	LESTER	341
	2	170 6/8	86	HP/RIFLE	PENCE	BARB	403
DENT	1	179 2/8	83	HP/RIFLE	SIMPHER	MICHAEL	263
DOUGLAS	1	200 2/8	79	HP/RIFLE	STITES	JOE	65
	2	169 4/8	71	HP/RIFLE	ROY	RONNIE R.	431
	3	162 3/8	74	HP/RIFLE	CLAYTON	JOHN	506
FRANKLIN	1	187 6/8	94	PICK-UP	NUNN	BOBBY	159
	2	175 7/8	67	HP/RIFLE	GLATZ	HILMAR	312
	3	175 2/8	56	HP/RIFLE	WAGNER	J.L.	321
	4	168 6/8	79	HP/RIFLE	KOSSMANN	MIKE	444
	5	167 4/8	75	HP/RIFLE	KERBY	JESSE	458
	6	166 1/8	91	HP/RIFLE	CAREY	MIKE	469
	7	162 1/8	92	HP/RIFLE	FUNKHOUSER	GERRY	509
	8	160 3/8	91	HP/RIFLE	MINKS	DAN	530
GASCONADE	1	179 3/8	70	HP/RIFLE	FARRIS	JOHN W.	261
	2	173 4/8	73	HP/RIFLE	SCHNEIDER	ROBERT	350
	3	168 5/8	78	HP/RIFLE	FILECCIA	JOE	446

MISSOURI SHOW-ME BIG BUCKS CLUB RECORDS OF WHITETAIL DEER BY COUNTY, NON-TYP

COUNTY	COUNTY RANK	SCORE	YEAR TAKEN	WEAPON	HUNTER	FIRST NAME	STATE RANK
GASCONADE	4	164 4/8	67	HP/RIFLE	MEYER	LOUIS H.	485
	5	160 4/8	52	HP/RIFLE	BRANDT	WESLEY E.	527
GENTRY	1	208 2/8	90	HP/RIFLE	SYBERT	ERIC	29
	2	173 0/8	89	HP/RIFLE	PIERICK	FRANK	361
	3	171 3/8	93	HP/RIFLE	ROBERTS	KEATON	389
	4	170 7/8	87	HP/RIFLE	LUPFER	JOEY	397
	5	163 2/8	73	HP/RIFLE	HEATH	JOE	495
GREENE	1	174 2/8	93	BOW	NOTHNAGEL	NORM	337
	2	166 4/8	72	HP/RIFLE	TRACY	CLAUDE	464
	3	165 3/8	90	HP/RIFLE	HAYNES	JAMES L.	477
GRUNDY	1	190 0/8	88	HP/RIFLE	WHITAKER	JACY F.	134
	2	182 4/8	87	HP/RIFLE	COOLEY	MIKE	222
	3	178 7/8	94	HP/RIFLE	SHERLEY	STANLEY	273
	4	174 6/8	83	HP/RIFLE	TUTTLE	LARRY	331
	5	170 6/8	90	HP/RIFLE	JONES	JEFF	403
HARRISON	1	193 1/8	75	HP/RIFLE	MORELAND	STEVE	107
	2	192 4/8	85	HP/RIFLE	SHAIN	ROD	114
	3	180 1/8	81	PICK-UP	IRVIN	MICHAEL	252
	4	178 0/8	81	HP/RIFLE	PERKINS	DENNIS	288
	5	176 4/8	83	HP/RIFLE	HYRE	LARRY	307
	6	174 5/8	79	HP/RIFLE	O'NEIL	TOM	332
	7	171 7/8	74	HP/RIFLE	WILCOXSON	DANA	381
	8	169 1/8	89	HP/RIFLE	HARROLD	GLEN	437
	9	162 0/8	95	HP/RIFLE	BOWEN	BOBBY	512
	10	156 6/8	96	HP/RIFLE	HARTSCHEN	TRACY	541
HENRY	1	171 3/8	88	BOW	ALBIN	WOODY	389
	2	170 7/8	70	HP/RIFLE	EASTER	ROBERT LEE	397
	3	165 5/8	77	HP/RIFLE	CHRONISTER	DAVID	474
	4	161 5/8	70	HP/RIFLE	KERNS	BOBBIE	515
	5	160 0/8	74	HP/RIFLE	WISKUR	HENRY	536
HICKORY	1	199 7/8	71	HP/RIFLE	STOGSDILL	DARWIN	68
	2	181 3/8	68	HP/RIFLE	PLUMMER	CHARLES L.	237
	3	174 3/8	69	HP/RIFLE	CHAMBERS	DOUGLAS	335
	4	165 3/8	91	HP/RIFLE	ANDERSON	MARK	477
HOLT	1	200 1/8	94	HP/RIFLE	COPSEY	BRUCE	66
	2	197 6/8	86	HP/RIFLE	WILSON	RON	76
	3	189 5/8	82	HP/RIFLE	LONG	MIKE	138
	4	189 3/8	88	HP/RIFLE	REHN	JOHN A.	141
	5	185 1/8	83	HP/RIFLE	HALEY	BECKY BREWER	190
	6	179 1/8	81	HP/RIFLE	ARCHER	DAVE	267
	7	178 4/8	90	HP/RIFLE	NANCE	LARRY R.	276
	8	177 3/8	86	HP/RIFLE	VOLTMER	DALE	297
	9	175 5/8	91	HP/RIFLE	GILLELAND	MAX	317
	10	170 7/8	61	HP/RIFLE	NASH	JAMES H.	397
	11	170 3/8	81	HP/RIFLE	WRIGHT	ROBERT	413
	12	170 1/8	72	HP/RIFLE	HOOD	JOHN	417
HOWARD	1	201 5/8	83	HP/RIFLE	O'BRIAN	GREG	55
	2	201 0/8	72	HP/RIFLE	WYATT	ROBERT LEE	60
	3	194 2/8	87	HP/RIFLE	RAYMORE	DAVID	98
	4	193 0/8	82	HP/RIFLE	FUEMMELER	MYRL	108
	5	174 4/8	83	HP/RIFLE	KIRRANE	GARY	334
	6	172 4/8	90	HP/RIFLE	COLVIN	ERIC	371
	7	159 2/8	95	BOW	BELSTLE	GARY	537
HOWELL	1	162 6/8	91	HP/RIFLE	MYRICK	JOHN R.	503
	2	160 1/8	89	HP/RIFLE	HARLAN	JAMES	534
IRON	1	176 2/8	93	HP/RIFLE	WILSON, JR.	WILLIAM T.	308
	2	169 0/8	83	HP/RIFLE	SUTTON	NORMAN	438
JACKSON	1	259 1/8	96	PICK-UP	LOVEKAMP	TERRY L.	3
	2	199 6/8	89	BOW	HOLLINGSWORTH	JACK	69

COUNTY	COUNTY RANK	SCORE	YEAR TAKEN	WEAPON	HUNTER	FIRST NAME	STATE RANK
JACKSON	3	197 1/8	84	BOW	MARTIN	JIM	77
	4	190 7/8	88	PICK-UP	POTTS	DAVID	128
	5	188 1/8	90	HP/RIFLE	BUCHANAN	CHAD E.	155
	6	183 4/8	94	HP/RIFLE	GILFOY	CARLTON	211
	7	181 4/8	88	PICK-UP	BARNES	BOB	236
	8	171 5/8	87	PICK-UP	DICKEY, SR.	GLEN S.	385
	9	160 3/8	91	BOW	HOOD	WENDELL E.	530
JASPER	1	201 0/8	91	PICK-UP	MORRIS	RICHARD	60
	2	179 2/8	86	HP/RIFLE	THORNTON	JACK	263
	3	173 1/8	91	HP/RIFLE	GETTINGS	DOYLE	359
JEFFERSON	1	180 3/8	92	HP/RIFLE	RICHARDSON	DALE C.	250
	2	167 0/8	87	HP/RIFLE	JOHNSON	BARNEY	462
JOHNSON	1	188 6/8	83	HP/RIFLE	MILLER	CHARLES E.	148
	2	185 0/8	95	M/L	COEN	ROCKY	192
	3	173 4/8	72	HP/RIFLE	WALTERS	VAUGHN	350
	4	167 7/8	79	HP/RIFLE	BLAIR	PATRICK	454
KNOX	1	185 4/8	67	HP/RIFLE	RHOADES	RAYMOND G.	186
	2	183 2/8	74	HP/RIFLE	DAVIS	HASKEL	216
	3	178 7/8	71	HP/RIFLE	SCHRAGE	DAVID	273
	4	176 6/8	75	PICK-UP	DENT	DALE	303
	5	174 0/8	88	HP/RIFLE	PETERS	STEVE	341
	6	173 4/8	72	HP/RIFLE	SIMMONS	LARRY	350
	7	173 0/8	92	HP/RIFLE	DOSS	RANDY	361
	8	166 0/8	86	HP/RIFLE	WHITMIRE	KEVIN	471
LACLEDE	1	225 5/8	90	PICK-UP	LUTHY	SCOTT	7
	2	196 1/8	72	HP/RIFLE	WEST	JOHN	85
	3	171 5/8	83	HP/RIFLE	HUNT	RON	385
	4	170 3/8	96	HP/RIFLE	ALKIRE	RAYMOND	413
	5	164 2/8	96	BOW	GOANS	JERRY	488
LAFAYETTE	1	164 2/8	92	HP/RIFLE	WRIGHT	MITCH	488
LEWIS	1	210 7/8	95	HP/RIFLE	MEAD	RON	24
	2	177 6/8	94	HP/RIFLE	MILLER	CLIFTON A.	291
	3	172 1/8	95	HP/RIFLE	MYERS	EARL J.	378
	4	170 4/8	93	HP/RIFLE	GUERDAN	LARRY	410
LINCOLN	1	218 6/8	62	HP/RIFLE	GUTERMUTH	SYLVESTER	13
	2	217 0/8	91	HP/RIFLE	MITTS	PAT D.	16
	3	207 3/8	55	HP/RIFLE	ZUMWALT	MELVIN	31
	4	200 0/8	83	HP/RIFLE	RODRIGUEZ	RALPH	67
	5	194 2/8	96	HP/RIFLE	THIEMET	DAVE	98
	6	194 1/8	88	HP/RIFLE	VAUGHAN	DOUG	103
	7	184 1/8	76	HP/RIFLE	KEETEMAN	HAROLD	204
	8	180 6/8	89	PICK-UP	HATCHER	DON	243
	9	179 1/8	86	HP/RIFLE	KERKER	EUGENE	267
	10	171 0/8	74	HP/RIFLE	SCHLESINGER	RONALD	393
	11	168 1/8	96	HP/RIFLE	REED	DENIS	449
	12	165 5/8	91	HP/RIFLE	COAN	JASON	474
LINN	1	200 6/8	91	HP/RIFLE	YOUNG	JASON	63
	2	192 2/8	69	HP/RIFLE	NICKERSON	MARK	115
	3	186 6/8	72	HP/RILFE	SCHUENEMAN	LESTER	170
	4	186 3/8	77	HP/RIFLE	COOPER	JERRY	176
	5	185 6/8	89	HP/RIFLE	QUIGLEY	DAVE	184
	6	181 2/8	70	HP/RIFLE	BELZER	BILL	240
	7	178 4/8	84	BOW	SCHUENEMAN	LESTER	276
	8	176 2/8	65	HP/RIFLE	WALTZ	FLOYD	308
	9	173 0/8	92	HP/RIFLE	BERRY	DON	361
LIVINGSTON	1	212 0/8	61	HP/RIFLE	HUGHES	MARSHALL	22
	2	203 1/8	54	HP/RIFLE	DAVIS	CLIFFORD	47
	3	183 7/8	78	HP/RIFLE	LAMP	DONALD	207
	4	180 1/8	68	HP/RIFLE	WOOD	FRANCIS P.	252

COUNTY	COUNTY RANK	SCORE	YEAR TAKEN	WEAPON	HUNTER	FIRST NAME	STATE RANK
LIVINGSTON	5	175 2/8	89	HP/RIFLE	HUSSEY	JAMES	321
MACON	1	205 7/8	94	HP/RIFLE	EASLEY	CLINT	36
	2	202 0/8	94	HP/RIFLE	ALLEN	LARRY	51
	3	185 3/8	60	HP/RIFLE	BRAGG	RONALD	187
	4	184 4/8	95	HP/RIFLE	LATCHFORD	BRUCE	199
	5	179 0/8	74	HP/RIFLE	DILLINGHAM	THEODORE	270
	6	175 6/8	70	HP/RIFLE	MORRIS	LARRY W.	315
	7	173 3/8	85	HP/RIFLE	PAGLIAI	DANIEL R.	354
MADISON	1	161 4/8	86	HP/RIFLE	STEPHENS	ERNEST J.	516
MARIES	1	217 7/8	74	HP/RIFLE	DAKE	GERALD	15
	2	191 1/8	83	PICK-UP	ROLLINS	GARY KYLE	125
	3	175 7/8	75	HP/RIFLE	REDEL	LAWRENCE	312
MARION	1	185 7/8	74	HP/RIFLE	STOUT	LARRY	181
	2	182 5/8	96	HP/RIFLE	HILLS	TIM	220
MERCER	1	211 0/8	95	HP/RIFLE	GRAY	TREVE	23
	2	202 6/8	90	HP/RIFLE	MOORE	MIKE	48
	3	194 5/8	83	PICK-UP	GALETTI	DAN & JIM	96
	4	194 2/8	89	HP/RIFLE	SCHMIDT	DENNIS	98
	5	192 1/8	71	HP/RIFLE	STOTTS	MELVIN E.	117
	6	188 7/8	85	HP/RIFLE	NOLAND, JR.	JIM L.	146
	7	174 7/8	85	HP/RIFLE	HASHMAN	FRED	329
	8	174 5/8	96	HP/RIFLE	HENLEY	TRACY	332
	9	173 0/8	67	HP/RIFLE	CLAPHAM	CODA	361
	10	170 0/8	85	HP/RIFLE	CLEM	VELDON	423
	11	169 2/8	89	HP/RIFLE	RIDENHOUR	KEITH	434
MILLER	1	196 3/8	82	HP/RIFLE	HEDDEN	RICK	84
	2	176 0/8	89	HP/RIFLE	HAWK	TIM	310
	3	160 7/8	96	HP/RIFLE	WHITNEY	JON	522
MONITEAU	1	219 7/8	83	PICK-UP	STOKES	BARNEY	12
	2	187 1/8	84	HP/RIFLE	KUEFFER	GARY	165
MONROE	1	204 4/8	96	HP/RIFLE	BAUTISTA, M.D.	ROGELIO L.	39
	2	190 5/8	89	HP/RIFLE	STRUNK	MIKE	131
	3	188 1/8	74	HP/RIFLE	HOLLINGSWORTH	PAUL	155
	4	186 5/8	76	HP/RIFLE	CHARLICK	DAVID	172
	5	182 4/8	96	HP/RIFLE	SAUNDERS	GEORGE L.	222
	6	160 6/8	96	HP/RIFLE	MUDD	JAMIE	524
MONTGOMERY	1	191 3/8	74	HP/RIFLE	CARPENTER	PHILIP	123
	2	170 6/8	94	HP/RIFLE	BOKERMANN	JIM	403
	3	166 4/8	87	HP/RIFLE	STRUBE	KENNY	464
MORGAN	1	226 0/8	62	HP/RIFLE	SOUSLEY	ART	6
	2	190 3/8	86	HP/RIFLE	DOYLE	MARCUS D.	132
	3	189 4/8	96	HP/RIFLE	JAMES	EDDIE	140
	4	185 7/8	92	HP/RIFLE	GANT	BRIAN	183
	5	174 7/8	93	HP/RIFLE	UPTEGROVE	MICAH	329
	6	171 0/8	81	HP/RIFLE	BLAKE	THOMAS A.	393
	7	161 7/8	94	HP/RIFLE	HILDDON	JAMES	513
NEWTON	1	196 5/8	93	HP/RIFLE	PRITCHARD	WALTER P.	83
NODAWAY	1	233 1/8	92	HP/RIFLE	BARCUS	KEN	4
	2	212 7/8	81	HP/RIFLE	BARCUS	KENNETH	20
	3	202 0/8	72	HP/RIFLE	STEWART	RICHARD	50
	4	188 6/8	85	PICK-UP	AUFFERT	CHARLES	148
	5	186 5/8	93	HP/RIFLE	BOWLIN	DENNIS	172
	6	186 4/8	85	HP/RIFLE	RAUCH	VALERIE	174
	7	179 0/8	66	HP/RIFLE	PEVE	BOB	270
	8	170 6/8	79	HP/RIFLE	McBRIDE	DARRELL W.	403
	9	170 0/8	70	HP/RIFLE	BRUSHWOOD	HENRY	423
OREGON	1	166 4/8	94	HP/RIFLE	CALDWELL	WAYNE	464
OSAGE	1	190 6/8	92	HP/RIFLE	POINTER	GREG	129
	2	182 5/8	95	BOW	TYREE	RONNIE LEE	220

179

COUNTY	COUNTY RANK	SCORE	YEAR TAKEN	WEAPON	HUNTER	FIRST NAME	STATE RANK
OSAGE	3	181 3/8	69	HP/RIFLE	SESTAK	PAUL	237
	4	179 7/8	78	HP/RIFLE	BRANDT	DAVE	256
	5	171 7/8	71	HP/RIFLE	WEBSTER	MURRAY	381
	6	170 1/8	73	HP/RIFLE	KAUFFMAN	BOB	417
	7	167 2/8	84	HP/RIFLE	GENTGES	PHILIP	460
	8	166 6/8	81	HP/RIFLE	LAUX	JOHN	464
	9	163 0/8	66	HP/RIFLE	BACON	SCOTT	496
	10	161 3/8	73	HP/RIFLE	WILSON	BILL	518
OZARK	1	181 3/8	96	HP/RIFLE	WARREN	MARK	237
	2	178 3/8	72	HP/RIFLE	APPEL	GENE	281
PERRY	1	165 3/8	91	HP/RIFLE	SCHOLL	DUANE	477
PETTIS	1	200 7/8	95	HP/RIFLE	KEMPKER	STEVE	62
	2	188 6/8	91	HP/RIFLE	TETER	MARK R.	148
	3	178 3/8	90	HP/RIFLE	LUETJEN	ROBERT	281
	4	177 4/8	94	HP/RIFLE	SCHMUTZ	GEORGE	294
	5	163 3/8	90	HP/RIFLE	WALTERS	JIM	494
	6	161 2/8	88	HP/RIFLE	THIERFELDER	CHRIS	519
PHELPS	1	194 2/8	86	HP/RIFLE	BRAIDLOW	DOUG	98
	2	186 3/8	59	HP/RIFLE	YOWELL	RAYMOND	176
	3	181 7/8	91	HP/RIFLE	MACORMIC	DOUG	229
	4	178 0/8	73	HP/RIFLE	LEWIS	MICHAEL	288
	5	166 1/8	82	HP/RIFLE	THORPE	ERNEST	469
	6	164 4/8	69	HP/RIFLE	WATSON	REX	485
	7	162 3/8	84	HP/RIFLE	POUND	DAVID	506
	8	160 2/8	94	HP/RIFLE	WASSILAK	TOM	533
PIKE	1	221 4/8	91	HP/RIFLE	SCHANKS	BILLY J.	11
	2	204 1/8	95	HP/RIFLE	JEFFRIES	ROBERT	42
	3	196 7/8	85	HP/RIFLE	GROTE	HARRY	82
	4	194 2/8	80	BOW	KNOWLES	WILLIAM E.	98
	5	189 0/8	92	PICK-UP	DRURY	TOMMY	144
	6	187 1/8	67	HP/RIFLE	WINTERBOWER	WILLIAM	165
	7	186 0/8	90	BOW	BOSTON	BILLY	180
	8	184 0/8	78	HP/RIFLE	HAGEMEIER	GARY E.	206
	9	181 2/8	87	PICK-UP	JOE'S JUG		240
	10	177 5/8	85	HP/RIFLE	RUDD	FREDRICK	292
	11	175 2/8	92	HP/RIFLE	KALLASH	KENNETH	321
	12	170 0/8	77	HP/RIFLE	INGRAM	BOB	423
PLATTE	1	208 3/8	91	PICK-UP	HENSON	GREG	28
	2	202 0/8	91	HP/RIFLE	RICHARDSON	STEVEN	51
	3	195 2/8	89	PICK-UP	UTZ	JEFF	91
	4	187 3/8	85	HP/RIFLE	ROWE	JOHN	162
POLK	1	170 5/8	85	HP/RIFLE	AYRES	PERRY	408
PULASKI	1	192 7/8	73	HP/RIFLE	LAWSON	BILL	111
	2	184 4/8	72	HP/RIFLE	MELTON	JOHN W.	199
	3	179 1/8	76	HP/RIFLE	GLAWSON	MICHAEL	267
	4	174 2/8	72	HP/RIFLE	DOYLE	ROY LEE	337
	5	165 0/8	83	HP/RIFLE	RANSOM	CHARLES R.	481
	6	160 6/8	72	HP/RIFLE	YORK	DARREL J.	524
PUTNAM	1	199 6/8	78	HP/RIFLE	HORNADY	DAVE	69
	2	195 3/8	91	HP/RIFLE	VALENTINE	JASON	89
	3	192 5/8	95	BOW	MURCHISON	TIMOTHY N.	113
	4	191 4/8	89	HP/RIFLE	COWAN	WADE	122
	5	187 0/8	87	HP/RIFLE	RENNELLS	JOSH	168
	6	185 7/8	88	HP/RIFLE	SMITH	PAUL	181
	7	185 3/8	90	HP/RIFLE	MILBURN	CHRISTINA	187
	8	181 5/8	92	HP/RIFLE	MAHONEY	RANDY V.	232
	9	176 0/8	81	HP/RIFLE	DUNKIN	GREG D.	310
	10	173 5/8	96	M/L	REAM	JOE	348
	11	172 6/8	92	HP/RIFLE	STRINGER	ALLAN	366

MISSOURI SHOW-ME BIG BUCKS CLUB RECORDS OF WHITETAIL DEER BY COUNTY, NON-TYP

COUNTY	COUNTY RANK	SCORE	YEAR TAKEN	WEAPON	HUNTER	FIRST NAME	STATE RANK
PUTNAM	11	172 6/8	94	HP/RIFLE	BURNS	KRIS	366
	13	165 5/8	95	HP/RIFLE	GRAY	JEFF	474
	14	161 0/8	83	HP/RIFLE	REAM, JR.	DALE H.	521
RALLS	1	174 2/8	94	HP/RIFLE	HARDY	STEVE	337
RANDOLPH	1	185 3/8	95	HP/RIFLE	McCAWLEY	MIKE	187
	2	184 6/8	68	HP/RIFLE	BELZER	R.L.	196
	3	181 1/8	96	BOW	PALMATORY	DONNIE LEE	242
	4	180 0/8	77	HP/RIFLE	HUDSON	RANDY	254
	5	179 0/8	94	HP/RIFLE	HENDRIX	SHIRLEY	270
	6	175 1/8	76	HP/RIFLE	JOHNSON	GEORGE	325
	7	167 2/8	89	BOW	SPRINGS	RON	460
	8	162 4/8	92	HP/RIFLE	AKINS	ROBERT P.	505
RAY	1	186 7/8	92	HP/RIFLE	BROWN	BOB	169
	2	186 2/8	88	HP/RIFLE	PIERCE	DAVID L.	179
	3	170 0/8	73	HP/RIFLE	WHITE	ALLEN	423
REYNOLDS	1	186 3/8	96	HP/RIFLE	LARAMORE	DANNY	176
	2	160 4/8	95	HP/RIFLE	MARTIN	JOHN W.	527
	3	159 1/8	96	HP/RIFLE	BARTON	QUINTON	538
SALINE	1	204 3/8	60	HP/RIFLE	POINTER	WILLIAM	40
	2	197 0/8	86	PICK-UP	BARTLETT	TOMMY	81
	3	191 0/8	88	HP/RIFLE	STEDING	LARRY	127
	4	185 0/8	83	HP/RIFLE	WISSMAN, JR.	GLEN	192
	5	180 5/8	95	HP/RIFLE	HAYSLIP	JAMES W.	247
	6	179 2/8	91	HP/RIFLE	BLAKE	HAROLD	263
	7	178 3/8	92	HP/RIFLE	O'BRYAN	ROBBIE	281
	8	172 1/8	86	HP/RIFLE	BLUMHORST	ANTHONY	378
	9	165 6/8	92	HP/RIFLE	MORTON	PHILLIP	473
	10	163 0/8	91	HP/RIFLE	RILEY, JR.	DONALD	496
	11	162 7/8	95	HP/RIFLE	HAMILTON	KURT K.	501
SCHUYLER	1	201 5/8	94	HP/RILFE	PAILEY	WAYNE	55
	2	195 5/8	95	HP/RIFLE	FARLEY	JOE	87
	3	180 6/8	60	HP/RIFLE	BLUE	BASIL	243
SCOTLAND	1	189 7/8	73	HP/RIFLE	GUFFEY	DICK	136
	2	185 5/8	84	BOW	SMITH	CHARLES L.	185
	3	180 6/8	85	BOW	SIMPSON	STEVE	243
	4	179 7/8	89	HP/RIFLE	MARTIN	DALE W.	256
	5	179 5/8	95	HP/RIFLE	DOTSON	DAN	259
	6	178 3/8	64	HP/RIFLE	FRANKLIN	PAUL R.	281
	7	172 7/8	88	HP/RIFLE	HUGHES	BOB	365
	8	172 5/8	78	HP/RIFLE	BLAKE	CAROLYN	369
	9	171 3/8	86	HP/RIFLE	FOX	EDWIN	389
	10	171 1/8	82	HP/RIFLE	WHITAKER	RICHARD D.	392
SHELBY	1	192 2/8	71	HP/RIFLE	PARSONS	LINDELL	115
	2	182 3/8	96	HP/RIFLE	CARR	RODNEY A.	224
	3	182 1/8	87	HP/RIFLE	OTTO	WILLARD	228
	4	175 6/8	67	HP/RIFLE	FISHER	BILL	315
	5	174 3/8	96	HP/RIFLE	HENDRIX	ROGER	335
	6	170 0/8	74	HP/RIFLE	McWILLIAMS	DAVID	423
ST. CHARLES	1	187 4/8	66	HP/RIFLE	DETJEN	JOHN	161
	2	187 1/8	94	HP/RIFLE	STRAUSS	MARK	165
	3	184 1/8	62	BOW	STELZER	LARRY D.	204
	4	179 3/8	82	HP/RIFLE	SCHIPPER	RONALD H.	261
	5	173 7/8	81	HP/RIFLE	STREET	MELVIN	344
ST. CLAIR	1	205 1/8	74	HP/RIFLE	PIPER	CARROLL W.	38
	2	189 7/8	76	HP/RIFLE	CRAWFORD	BILLY G.	136
	3	170 7/8	92	HP/RIFLE	PIEPMEIER	LISA	397
ST. FRANCOIS	1	199 4/8	84	HP/RIFLE	HULL	HENRY A.	72
	2	185 0/8	95	HP/RIFLE	JONES	BRUCE L.	192
	3	181 5/8	89	HP/RIFLE	ISGRIG	GENE	232

COUNTY	COUNTY RANK	SCORE	YEAR TAKEN	WEAPON	HUNTER	FIRST NAME	STATE RANK
ST. FRANCOIS	4	180 0/8	86	HP/RIFLE	BROWN	PAUL W.	254
ST. LOUIS	1	333 7/8	81	PICK-UP	BECKMAN	HELLAND	1
	2	192 7/8	94	HP/RIFLE	LUETHAUSER	SCOTT	111
	3	191 7/8	95	HP/RIFLE	DAUSTER	DAVID	118
	4	191 1/8	96	BOW	WERGES	GENE	125
	5	181 5/8	91	HP/RIFLE	HETH	DAVID	232
	6	178 4/8	93	HP/RIFLE	SMITH	ORLANDO A.	276
	7	178 3/8	81	HP/RIFLE	WRIGHT	CECIL	281
	8	176 6/8	94	HP/RIFLE	HELLWEG, III	NORBERT A.	303
	9	176 5/8	89	HP/RIFLE	GRELLNER	RICHARD A.	305
	10	173 5/8	89	BOW	BRANSON	MICHAEL M.	348
	11	173 1/8	92	HP/RIFLE	GEVERMUEHLE	RAY	359
	12	161 4/8	96	HP/RIFLE	LEUTHAUSER	SCOTT	516
STE. GENEIEVE	1	195 5/8	53	HP/RIFLE	WEILER	MARTIN	87
	2	187 5/8	64	HP/RIFLE	VOLZ	KARL	160
	3	183 4/8	90	HP/RIFLE	CARRON	JIM	211
	4	179 7/8	81	HP/RIFLE	DEMARCO	VINCENT	256
	5	178 2/8	73	HP/RIFLE	SHELTON	GLENN	286
	6	173 3/8	96	HP/RIFLE	HURST	CHARLES E.	354
	7	168 7/8	57	HP/RIFLE	HUCK, SR.	JOE	442
	8	168 0/8	88	HP/RIFLE	REECE	CHARLES E.	451
	9	164 4/8	91	HP/RIFLE	ETLING	KATHY	485
STONE	1	160 1/8	76	HP/RIFLE	WILLIAMS	ELSIE	534
SULLIVAN	1	228 2/8	92	HP/RIFLE	HUGHES	BRIAN W.	5
	2	196 1/8	95	HP/RIFLE	WALKER	CARROLL	85
	3	193 0/8	84	HP/RIFLE	HUGHES	GEORGE	108
	4	184 5/8	89	HP/RIFLE	GOOCH	MARTY	197
	5	183 2/8	90	HP/RIFLE	COURTNEY	LONNIE	216
	6	171 7/8	94	HP/RIFLE	STEPHENSON	JOSH	381
	7	170 7/8	95	HP/RIFLE	VAN VELZER	DWAYNE	397
	8	170 6/8	90	HP/RIFLE	CASON	CHERI	403
TANEY	1	164 5/8	90	HP/RIFLE	WALKER	LLOYD	483
TEXAS	1	179 2/8	59	HP/RIFLE	AMBURN	BILL	263
	2	175 3/8	69	HP/RIFLE	BURCH	DON	321
	3	169 6/8	72	HP/RIFLE	MITCHELL	EVERETT	429
	4	169 3/8	80	BOW	BELEW	DON	433
	5	169 2/8	84	HP/RIFLE	ADEY	FREDDIE	434
	6	169 0/8	70	HP/RIFLE	NELSON	LARRY	438
	7	163 4/8	51	HP/RIFLE	LANIER	WAYNE	492
	7	163 4/8	81	HP/RIFLE	NOEL	BOBBY	492
	9	162 1/8	92	HP/RIFLE	PARKER	ROBERT D.	509
VERNON	1	181 6/8	91	HP/RIFLE	YOUNT	TIM	230
	2	168 0/8	86	HP/RIFLE	ROBINSON	BILL	451
	3	166 4/8	73	HP/RIFLE	YURK	BILL	464
WARREN	1	223 7/8	59	HP/RIFLE	WILLIAMS	JAMES	8
	2	194 7/8	82	BOW	JONES	DENNIS	94
	3	193 6/8	71	HP/RIFLE	TONIOLI, SR.	JERRY L.	105
	4	188 6/8	95	HP/RIFLE	BLAIR	JESSE	148
	5	182 3/8	74	HP/RIFLE	FORBIS	GERALD F.	224
	6	177 2/8	80	HP/RIFLE	HELLE	CHARLES E.	299
	7	175 4/8	71	HP/RIFLE	DOLL	RANSOM A.	319
	7	175 4/8	94	HP/RIFLE	HINCH	MARK	319
	9	158 7/8	96	HP/RIFLE	MARSCHEL	JASON	539
WASHINGTON	1	195 2/8	91	HP/RIFLE	RATH	ROBERT	91
	2	168 2/8	94	HP/RIFLE	PRATT, JR.	DEL A.	448
	3	163 0/8	82	HP/RIFLE	MERCER	RONNIE	496
	4	162 3/8	92	HP/RIFLE	HIGGINS	STEVEN A.	506
	5	161 2/8	65	HP/RIFLE	NELSON	JAMES B.	519
WAYNE	1	201 4/8	92	HP/RIFLE	HAYS	DAVID	58

MISSOURI SHOW-ME BIG BUCKS CLUB RECORDS OF WHITETAIL DEER BY COUNTY, NON-TYP

COUNTY	COUNTY RANK	SCORE	YEAR TAKEN	WEAPON	HUNTER	FIRST NAME	STATE RANK
WAYNE	2	195 0/8	89	HP/RIFLE	SICG	JOYCE	93
	3	188 0/8	72	HP/RIFLE	KYRO	JAMES	158
	4	175 7/8	86	HP/RIFLE	CHANDLER	STEVE L.	312
	5	175 1/8	88	BOW	WHITTLEY, JR.	JESSE	325
	6	169 2/8	93	HP/RIFLE	DODD	KEVIN	434
	7	164 6/8	87	HP/RIFLE	COOK	JAY	482
WORTH	1	215 5/8	74	HP/RIFLE	MILLER & NONNENAN	BURTON & REGAN	18
	2	197 1/8	82	HP/RIFLE	KINDER	GARY	77
	3	172 1/8	94	HP/RIFLE	ATKISON	RICK	378
	4	171 0/8	83	HP/RIFLE	McGHEE	DAVID	393

THE ETHICS OF THE HUNT

by

JEFF BERINGER

WILDLIFE STAFF BIOLOGIST

MISSOURI DEPARTMENT OF CONSERVATION

remember my first experience with ethics as they related to hunting. I grew up in rural Wisconsin, started
king on farms at a very young age, and spent my spare time exploring the woods, lakes and fields
und our house. One day a friend and I were killing birds with our BB guns - a daily summer routine while
ting for the cut hay to dry so it could be raked, baled, and stacked in the barn. This activity was accepted
und the farm as we killed house sparrows and starlings that like to roost, nest and defecate in the barn.
ir activities made the hay less palatable to the cattle and they sometimes carried diseases. We were the
rminators. House sparrows and starling were wary quarry though, and by mid summer we could not get
in 50 yards of the survivors. We soon moved away from the barn lots to the woodlots where the birds
e more approachable. Notice I said birds here because we sometimes changed the rules and shot any
that sat still. We knew this was no longer damage control but justified our actions because the birds
e so plentiful. But mostly we didn't think about our actions. One day after killing a song sparrow, I was
iring it when an old lady (probably the property owner and probably not that old) appeared and noticed
bird and the BB guns. She gave my friend and me one hell- of-a-lecture and because we were not yet
ky teenagers, we listened. I forgot much of what she said but I do remember her making a good case for
killing something unless you intended to eat it. We continued our damage control work on house spar-
s and starlings but killed no more song birds for "sport" that summer. During the following summer I
essed a little and occasionally killed a song bird, chipmunk or red squirrel but began to feel guilty about
ng an animal's life for no reason. At age 11, I took a hunter's safety class and part of the class covered
ter ethics. The difference between right and wrong ethical choices became more clear. My hunter ethics
e evolving. Throughout my teenage years I had a few lapses - mostly due to peer pressure. I partici-
d in what I would now consider unethical behavior, road hunting grouse, sky busting ducks, baiting
r. These activities were totally legal where I grew up, nevertheless, they gain the hunter an unfair advan-
e or had a high likelihood of injuring and not retrieving game. The more I learned about the animals I
sued the more I respected them and the harder it became for me to take them unfairly.

ot that I didn't continue to hunt. Wild game was a staple throughout college and is for my family today. I
k I just set a little higher standard for myself these days. I'm a little more particular about whom I hunt
and how we hunt. I generally won't hunt birds without a dog and spend more time searching for cripples
don't take low percentage shots. I spend more time scouting for deer than I do hunting for them. I am
erally a successful hunter but I can still enjoy a hunt for the content, not the act of reducing game to
session. I have a couple of sons now and desperately want them to be hunters and fishermen, woods-
and naturalists. But I hope they can become ethical outdoorsmen/hunters without having to go through
or 10 year evolution. I think they can, I just hope they have the opportunity.

oday the public is scrutinizing hunter actions; like it or not we are in a fishbowl setting. It used to be that
ers were the only ones that used the outdoors, but today we have hikers, mountain bikers, rock climb-
bird watchers and a multitude of other competitors or companions - depending on your perspective. The
eotypical hunter is no longer depicted as the great taker of game, the knowledgeable woodsman

and the careful conservationist as we'd like to be thought. In fact, I can't remember the last time I saw a T sitcom or movie that depicted a hunter in what I would consider a favorable role. Hunting and killing animals isn't a party, and people that think it is have a lot to learn. As hunters it is our responsibility to set things right through our actions and the policing of our own ranks. I have little doubt that the greatest threat to hunting is from our inability to "clean up our own act" as hunters. If we ignore or overlook unethical behaviors and take no action to stop or change them, then we are inviting public condemnation which will further restrict hunting.

The anti-hunting faction often gives human characteristics to wild animals and this strategy often works to turn the uninformed public against hunting. My observations as a biologist and hunter suggest there is one major difference between humans and other animals - humans have a conscience. Instinct drives animals to eat, breed, and survive. I do not believe they fear death as humans do. I do not think they feel guilt, remorse or sadness. The human conscience is what ethics is all about.

So what constitutes an ethical hunter and ethical behavior while in the field? What follows is a list of what I consider to be important ethical topics. Ethics, like religion or politics, can be a very personal belief My views expressed here are personal beliefs and others may have arguments against some of them.

Know and obey wildlife laws. Familiarity with wildlife laws is just one responsibility of a hunter. Knowing wildlife laws will keep good hunters from embarrassing situations. Study fish and wildlife laws like you will be tested on them. Reread them each year, note any changes, and always carry a regulations pamphlet in your hunting vehicle or hunting coat. That way, if you are unsure, you can check the regulations. Hunting requires a clear head and if you are worrying about regulations you are not hunting well.

Hunters sometimes complain about the complexity of regulations. Hunting regulations have become more complicated to accommodate the interests of diverse hunter groups. Also wildlife management has progressed and some species can now be managed with more precision using knowledge gained from scientific studies. For example, today we have deer hunters who specialize in archery, muzzleloaders, modern firearms, hand guns etc. and each of these specialists wants to hunt deer their way. In many cases we have created special seasons for these enthusiasts. Multiple season provide an abundance of recreational opportunity but also make regulations more complex.

State and federal wildlife laws impose some ethics when setting bag limits, hunting hours and method restrictions. Sometimes, however, regional traditions, habitats, and game abundance may influence acceptable hunting methods and laws. For example using dogs to hunt deer would probably be viewed as unethical behavior by most Missourians. However, this is an important deer hunting method in some southern states. Deer doggers take great pride in their ability to plan and forecast the hunt. Land ownership often consists of large plantations where dogs will not readily cross property boundaries and affect other hunters. It is the hunter's responsibility to learn the wildlife laws wherever he or she resides or visit The southern deer hunter that releases a pack of dogs on the opening day of deer season in Missouri would not fare will on the legal or ethical side. But neither would the Missouri deer hunter who attempts t hunt deer from a tree stand in Michigan where it is illegal. When traveling to another state or country to hunt make sure you are familiar with local laws.

Know and follow hunter safety guidelines. Carrying a loaded firearm and taking an animal's life are tremendous responsibilities. Missouri requires hunter safety training for anyone born after *January 1, 1967*. Although hunter safety is a cornerstone of education for hunters, safety education is a continuing process. Hunting safely requires vigilance and a constant awareness of your surroundings. You must be mentally prepared when hunting. It is not a good idea to be thinking about work or an argument you may have had with friend. Hunting requires quick clear decisions. For this reason there is never a place for drugs or alcohol while hunting. Inexperienced hunters should hunt with friends or family under controlled conditions until they have developed an awareness of what it takes to hunt safely. Often novice hunters will not recognize potentially dangerous situations. The ethical hunter will take the time to share his or her experiences and safety tips with novice hunters.

Hunting safely for experienced hunters requires that they use common sense and not take unnecessary risks. Any experienced hunter knows better than to hunt from a tree stand without a safety belt or to climb a tree with a loaded firearm. Yet every year people are hurt of killed from these kinds of self inflicted injuries. Make sure you are familiar with your firearm or bow. Hunters who borrow or purchase a firearm should spend several days shooting to become comfortable with it. Old habits can be hard to break, and a strange gun with a safety in a new spot can be annoying and, at times dangerous. Certainly part of the lure of hunting is the excitement associated with taking game, but this excitement should never replace common sense.

Being physically fit will help enhance hunting experiences and reduce the risk of injury. Physically fit people are clearer thinkers and will be less likely to get into life threatening situations. Hunting can be hard work. Fit hunters can spend more hours afield and tolerate adverse weather better. Fit hunters are more likely to stay on the trail of a wounded animal and more likely to take steady aim after an arduous stalk. Busting through brush all day while quail hunting or bragging out a deer can be physically exhausting. These activities can be an enjoyable part of the hunt if you are in shape. The value and ethics of the hunting experience deteriorates when hunters resort to using vehicles and gadgets to substitute for stamina and fitness.

Treat landowners with respect. In Missouri, 93% of all land is privately owned. Although some hunters use only public land, most hunters rely on the generosity of landowners for places to hunt. When asking a landowner to hunt, you must make a credible and sincere attempt to win their trust. You must convince them that you are an honest and ethical hunter and that they can trust you. Try to look at it from the landowner's perspective. Allowing a person to hunt on your property isn't a light decision. Generally the landowner has nothing to gain by allowing you to hunt. Many landowners live on their property, have livestock, or other valuable commodities and your presence may disrupt their normal routine. If a landowner allows you to hunt, they are saying that they trust you - don't let them down.

I have found the best time to approach landowners is well before the hunting season and when they are not too busy. Many farmers live on their land and a good time to approach them is during summer after the crops are planted but before harvest. Absentee landowners often visit their land on weekends or their home addresses can be found in plat books. A personal visit is always better than a phone call or letter. You should introduce yourself, tell them where you live, and what you would like to hunt on their lands. For instance, asking to bowhunt for deer during December is very specific and the landowner knows what he is committing to. If you gain access to someone's land, ask them where they would like you to park and if they want to be notified each time you hunt. Some landowners will want notification every time you hunt and others will give you more free reign. Often landowners will give you more freedom after they have gotten to know you. Many landowners are interested in your hunting success and appreciate hunting reports. If you are successful, sharing your harvest with the landowner is a great way to show your appreciation for hunting rights. Helping farmers put up hay or mend fence or offering to help with other chores will ensure your access to his land in the future.

Respect the land and wildlife. Ethical hunters treat the wildlands they visit and the animals they hunt with respect. Respect comes from a better understanding and appreciation of wildlife and the environments in which they live. Just as most Americans would never litter on a national monument or show disrespect to war veterans or our flag, hunters should never forget the importance of respecting nature and the gifts we take from it. Hunters should tread lightly, many primitive campers have a motto of leaving a campsite in better shape than it was before they used it. Why shouldn't hunters adopt and follow a similar policy?

Things like picking up litter etc. go without saying but what about not using your 4-wheel drive truck when you will leave big ruts in the woods. Old permanent tree stands that are not being used could easily be torn down. Picking up spent bullet casings and not leaving the paper backing from your transportation tag laying in the woods are small but important examples of things to remember.

Part of respecting the land involves learning about habitats and the animals you as a hunter pursue each fall. Think for a moment about what separates the best hunters you know from the rest. It is not the size of the buck they kill, for there have been countless big bucks killed by inexperienced hunters. What makes a good deer hunter is their knowledge about deer. Just as being good at tennis or chess requires practice and planning, being a good, ethical hunter, requires practice. Serious, ethical hunters take the time to know about their quarry. They know what they eat, and can identify these foods when in the woods. They know when deer breed, migrate, have young and disperse. We can learn much of this knowledge from books and videos but nothing can replace the knowledge gained from spending time in the woods. Experience makes for confident, relaxed hunters. Spend time in the woods throughout the year and you will learn that deer, for example, make trails in March and April that they seldom use in October and November. Finding the ridges that contain acorn laden oaks in September will probably payoff when trying to find deer in late October.

Respecting wildlife also means hunting under conditions that do not give the hunter an unfair advantage. Canned hunts in which animals are released shortly before being killed by "hunters," shooting animals over bait, hunting inside fenced areas where animals movements are restricted or funneled, locating animals with vehicles or aircraft, and competitive hunts are considered unethical by many hunters. There may be other hunting situations that approach or cross the line of fair chase and each hunter must decide if taking an animal under there circumstances is ethical. For many, shooting a turkey off the roost is not considered ethical. Some methods of driving and shooting deer are not conducive with a quality hunt. I remember getting into a covey of quail once and scattering them in a small field where the dogs were sure to find the bulk of them. We found the covey late in the evening as a snow storm was beginning. My partner and I decided to leave the covey alone so the birds could get back together before nightfall and the incoming storm. My friend and I would certainly have experienced some good quail shooting and dog work had we pursued the quail, but we both felt good about our decision. These types of situations and decisions cannot be legislated by state or federal laws and are one of the dilemmas of hunting. Ethical hunters who follow their conscience will make the right choices.

Develop shooting skills. The ethical hunter is a well-practiced hunter, both in the field and on the rifle or bow range. The importance of developing shooting skills cannot be overemphasized. The crack shot is a crack shot because he has fired hundreds of rounds through his gun and knows what he is capable of hitting - or missing. There is no excuse for wounding a deer because you took a shot in heavy cover or beyond your effective range. As important as being a skilled shooter is knowing your weapon's limitation under all circumstances. Shooting at a known distance on a rifle range is vastly different from shooting under low light or windy conditions. The trajectory of the bullet or arrow will influence the importance of knowing the exact distance. Practice estimating distances while in the woods and fields. Improperly estimating the distance from the shooter to the quarry accounts for many missed or wounded animals. Animals in the woods often appear farther away than they really are. Shooting up or downhill or from an elevated blind will influence bullet or arrow placement. Many rifles and bows will shoot relatively flat to a certain yardage without the shooter having to compensate. You can learn these facts by studying ballistic charts or when at the target range. Some hunters mark known distances around their stands with wooden stakes or flagging.

We owe it to the animal to make the kill quick and clean. When in doubt don't shoot. Taking a low percentage shot will, at best, result in a clean miss but also may result in wounding your quarry. People sometimes take desperation shots because they have not seen game and are frustrated, are overly ompetitive, or have a chance at an exceptional animal. Hunting is not a competition, don't get caught up whether you "got your deer yet". If you think about it, by not risking a miss or wounding shot, you are not erting the animal to your presence and the chances of that animal moving closer to you immediately or ometime during the day are good.

Experienced hunters learn to read the behavior of their quarry. A white-tail deer may raise its tail to efecate and not be alarmed, it may swish it side to side while calmly feeding but when it raises its tail and uts its ear's back it is ready to bolt. A shot at this time is risky, especially with a bow. By studying the ternal anatomy of deer and other game the ethical hunter will be better able to place the bullet or arrow in e vitals for a quick clean kill. This is what every hunter should strive for. There may be a time, however, nen the most practiced and calculating hunter will make a poor shot. The deer may have flinched or there ay have been an unnoticed twig between you and the deer that deflected your bullet. Whatever the ason you have wounded an animal and this fact now becomes your primary focus. Exactly what hap-ened can be hard to reconstruct but if you return to your stand and take a moment to re-live the incident your mind, you can probably determine what happened, or at least make an educated guess. From your and determine where the deer was standing and the last place you saw it. Look for hair or blood on the ound where the deer was standing, these will give you an idea of where the deer was hit. Sometimes ood is not present immediately and it will take some careful tracking. Tracking a wounded deer will take your woodsmanship skills, knowledge about the land and character. As Aldo Leopold stated "a peculiar tue in wildlife ethics is that the hunter ordinarily has no gallery to applaud or disapprove of his conduct. natever his acts, they are dictated by his own conscience, rather than a mob of onlookers." Giving up on wounded deer is your call; there are no umpired to cry foul. The ethical hunter will make a good faith ort and, if he fails to find his quarry he will know it wasn't for lack of trying. I know some hunters that lude unretrieved animals in their bag limits.

Take care of your harvest. Successful hunters should take care when dressing, transporting, and ocessing their game. Consuming wild game is as big a part of the hunt as stalking and shooting. Hunting not target practice on live animals. There seems to be some confusion among the press and nonhunting olic about this matter. Some believe that sport hunting consists of shooting animals for the sport but not ng them otherwise. Nothing could be further from the truth. Some so-called hunters have tarnished the age of all hunters by participating in events like pigeon or prairie dog shoots where the animals are shot d left to lay. As an ethical hunter you should use everything you can from your harvested gift from na-e. Wild game is the ultimate health food but for those without a taste for venison, Missouri's "Share the rvest" program enables hunters to donate harvested deer to needy families. Deer hides can be sold for ther, the tails of deer and squirrels make good flies for fishing and some archers collect turkey feathers be used for fletching on arrows. When disposing of the unusable portions of game do so in a respectful nner. Returning bones, feathers and fur to the wild rather than sending them to a landfill or dumping m in a roadside ditch will help complete the ecological cycle.

e sensitive to others. Yes the golden rule even applies to hunting. Hunting isn't a competitive sport there are times and situations when competition can arise. Generally the first person to a blind, tree, or e has claim to that area and the ethical hunter will give them a wide berth. However not all hunters will ow this unwritten code of ethics and sometimes a conflict may arise over a particular spot. The best ution is to move to another location and try to make the best of the remaining hunt. No ones likes con-itations; this is especially true in the field. By moving to another spot you avoid any mishaps that could the outdoor experience. Aggressive, pushy hunters may be the same folks who tailgate and cut you off the freeway. As tempting as it is to get even, don't do it. You are only lowering yourself to their low idards and some of these unstable folks are best avoided. On the other hand, courtesy is contagious perhaps the hunter will recognize your good gesture and do the same for you next time.

As hunters, we need to be sensitive and courteous to other hunters and to the nonhunting public. Hunting gear and clothing should be reserved for hunting and scouting. However proud you are of being a hunter, others may be offended if you walk into a grocery store dressed in blaze orange clothing with a big hunting knife strapped to your belt. Besides, the foreign odors you pick up on your hunting clothing will not enhance your ability to hunt deer. When transporting game do so conservatively. You may be proud of the big buck you just took, but the appropriate way to transport your deer is with the truck tailgate up. Consider that your actions as a hunter may influence public opinion about hunters. If you are respectful and considerate then people you meet will equate those traits with hunters. Of course, the opposite is also true.

A large portion of the public is not opposed to hunting - if it is done with care and the harvest is used. Their views are not strong though and poor behavior by hunters could change their minds. Ethical hunters need not only follow the rules set by conservation agencies but they must follow their conscience. Some groups oppose hunting altogether and would ban all hunting if they could. When the question is who has greater impact on the worlds resources I believe ethical hunters have the moral high ground. The biggest thing that separates hunters from the nonhunting public is that we take direct responsibility for the animals we kill. Our meat doesn't come wrapped in clear plastic with purple inspection stamps and spoil dates. The animals we kill don't spend their lives behind electric fences or confined in station, fed a food mixture laden with growth hormones, and antibiotics, dewormed, debeaked, dehorned and artificially bred. Dying is not easy in nature and the deer killed by the well-placed bullet or broadhead dies quickly and more humanely than its counterparts. Hunters who take wild game locally use less natural resources (gasoline, feed grain, electricity) than vegetarian who buys groceries grown in irrigated fields and trucked to markets thousands of miles away. Hunting is the most ecologically sound, and is probably the most humane way to grow and take animals - when it is done ethically. Ethical hunters have a deeper understanding of wildlife, its habits and biology. They posses woodsmanship skills that cannot be learned from books or videos and they respect the land and themselves. They are proud of their passion -- and their behaviors will influence the future of hunting.

The beginning of a new day

LARRY ZACH
AWARDS AND HONORS

Selected six times as *'Artist of the Year'* by conservation groups in his home state of Iowa.

Designed the 1984 *Iowa Duck Stamp.*

Selected as one of the *'Top 20 Most Popular Artists'* in the nation for 1992. U.S. Art, Feb. 1993.

Broken Solitude - Whitetail was picked as one of the *'Top 20 Most Popular Prints'* for 1992. U.S. Art, Feb. 1993.

Featured in *Artist Profile* in the June, 1993 issue of U.S. Art.

Artwork has appeared on the covers of eighteen magazines including *Oak Ridge Monarch* on the March, 1995 issue of Outdoor Life.

Designed the 1995 *Arkansas Turkey Stamp and Print.*

Selected as one of the *'Top 10 Hottest New Artists'* in the nation. Informart magazine, Jan. 1995.

Created the winning designs for the 1995 and 1996 Iowa Wildlife Federation belt buckle contests.

Designed the print, *Prairie Pair - Bobolinks*, for use as a cover on a new book, the Iowa Breeding Bird Atlas, © 1996.

Selected as *'Artist of the Year'* for the Iowa Elk Breeders in 1997.

Selected as *'Artist of the Year'* for the National Wild Turkey Federation in 1997 and designed the 1997 *National Turkey Stamp and Print.*

Selected to design the *Iowa Habitat Stamps* for 1997, 1998 and 1999.

November Frost

Old Rivals

Winter Sunrise

1997 Iowa Habitat Stamp

Broken Solitude

Autumn Encounter

194

MEASURING ANTLERS AND

MISSOURI'S WHITETAIL DEER

by

DALE H. REAM, JR.
DIRECTOR OF RECORDS
MISSOURI SHOW-ME BIG BUCKS CLUB

When looking at trophy whitetail antlers, we automatically think; "what will it score". Most of the time, the final score, om the Boone and Crockett Club scoring system, which the Missouri Show-Me Big Bucks Club has written permission use, is a bonus. Especially if it is high enough to make the Missouri Big Bucks Club minimum at 140 typical or 155 non-oical. This chapter is about measuring whitetail antlers and the measurers that measurer them. The final score of any ophy antler is the criteria in determining trophy antler status.

The Missouri Show-Me Big Bucks Club recognizes two categories, for record keeping purposes, for the whitetail deer, oical and non-typical. Typical category is for whitetail deer antlers with no abnormal points or very few abnormal ints. Non-typical category is for whitetail deer antlers with several abnormal points.

Official measurements cannot be taken until the antlers have air dried for at least 60 days after the animal was killed. or a point to be counted as a measurable point in whitetail antlers, it must be exactly one inch long and at one inch, length ist exceed width by any amount, or anywhere in the structure of the point, length will exceed width (after one inch) by y mount, then it is a point.

Normal points generally arise from the top of the main am and are usually paired on the opposite side. Generally, tler points up to or just beyond the H-4 circumference are ired with points on the opposite beam. Although you have several normal points towards the end of the main am on one side and not on the other, but would still be unted as normal points, on the side that they are on. A uitetail antler can have unlimited amount of normal points, t generally has no more than 8 per side. On rare occasions, ormal point or points that throw off the symmetry balance m right side to the left side (generally between the H-1 ough the H-4 circumference area) by being located ween the other normal points, and are not located on the er side, can be scored as abnormal points.

Abnormal points are located off the side or bottom of the in beams, or off other points. And as mentioned above, be between normal points on top of the main beam.

Each antler has a right and left side, holding the antlers

A big non-typical whitetail buck starting to shed velvet

in your hands with the end of the main beams protruding away from you, the right beam should be in your right hand an the left beam in your left hand. Both typical and non-typical antlers have a right and left side. A non-typical is scored th same way as a typical antler, except the abnormal points on a non-typical are added into the final score. On a typical score th abnormal points are deducted from the final score. Typical antlers have none or every few inches of abnormal points. Non-typica antlers have several inches of abnormal points.

All measurements are taken in inches. In whitetail deer, to the nearest 1/8 of an inch. Which means, if the measurement falls on a 1/16 mark, you go up to the next 1/8 inch. But, if the measurement falls just short of a 1/16 mark you go back to the next 1/8 inch mark.

The basic tools used in measuring whitetail antlers are: 1/4 inch steel ringend tape, used for circumference measurements and can also be used for length measurements; a compound bow cable with a rivet attached on one end, used for all length measurements, an alligator clip is used to mark the end of measurement; a folding carpenters rule with 6" slide on one end, used to take inside spread if antler main beams are parallel. Tip to tip spread of the end of main beams and greatest spread; a 36" or 48" steel ruler is used for measuring the length of the compound bow cable (1/16th mark must be

Taking does is a must for all trophy hunters, for quality deer management

present); one or two 36" levels with wood block claps or c-clamps, claps are used to hold levels at right angles for th greatest spread measurement (you can also use a straight wall as one right angle and one level for the other right angle 2 carpenters squares 2 foot long, used to determine right angles and used to take inside spread if main beams are n parallel; a graphic ruler, inches in 16th, is helpful in determining point definition; also you will need a soft lead pencil and clipboar

Hunting is a family affair, here uncle Joe Ream helps his nephew BradReam with his buck. Being with family and friends is what hunting is all about.

If you want to try your hand at measuring, the first thing you need to do is to acquire an official score sheet from the Boone and Crockett Club. You will need to know the category of whitetail deer you are going to measurer, either typical or non-typical.

The measuring equipment mentioned above is what an official measurer would use. If you want to try and measure your trophy antlers you can get by with the 1/4 steel tape. Are you ready to start, on the back of the Boone and Crockett score sheet are instructions about each measurement taken. Read it before you start.

I'm going to go through this the way I measure whitetail antlers. Some measurers may start in a different location, but this is how I'm going to start. I will use a series of steps startir 1 and will add the corresponding letter and numbers from the official Boone and Crockett score form.

1. Mark off all points. All points originate from either the main beam or off other points. Take your 1/4 inch steel tape o

compound bow cable, place it along the bottom side of the point being drawn off. This will separate it from the main beam or from another point. Draw a line using a lead pencil on the bottom side of the tape or cable.

2. (Box B). Next we will take the tip to tip spread of the main beams. There are two measurements that show conformation of antlers and are not added into the final score. These are (B) tip to tip spread, and (C) greatest spread. Tip to tip spread is taken from the center of one main beam tip to the center of the other main beam tip, using your folding carpenters ruler with 6" slide at one end. All measurements are recorded in inches to the nearest 1/8 inch. Record this measurement in box B.

3. (F). Length of main beams. In measuring a white-tail antler I always start with the right side and take all measurements on that side before I do the left side. I prefer to use a compound bow cable to take all length measurements, to find the lenght of the cable I use a 36" steel ruler with 1/16" increments. To start the measurement of the right main beam, you must first determine where to start it from. Do this by positioning and turning the right antler to where the right burr (the burr is the very first part of the antler that sets on top of the pedestal) covers the burr on the left main beam. Looking at the right antler, locate the bottom of the right antler burr, find the center or middle of this burr. This is the place where your measurement will begin or end. You can measure the main beam from the center of the burr to the tip of the main beam, or from the tip of the main beam to the center of the burr. I start at the center of the burr and stay in the center of the main beam, up and around where it curves out and forward. Following this contour, stay in the center of the main beam and maintain this flow in the center to the tip of the main beam. The tip may be very pointed, or some what rounded like your thumb. This measurement is taken to the mid-point of the rounding, or center most part of the point. The end of the main beams are counted as points when counting total points, but are not measured as separate points because the end of the main beams are measured in the length of main beam measurement, which we have just completed. To record the right main beam measurement go to column 2, right antler, line F and enter the length in inches to nearest 1/8", for example: 25 2/8.

A normal point is defined as, it generally raises from the top of the main beam and is usually paired on the

Jim Fitzgerald with Jerry Calvert state record bow kill 181 5/8 typical form Chariton County.

B&C measurer Gary Webber, measuring a big 8 point rack. Monica Hunt recording for Gary, Monica does the calligraphy on all the Big Bucks certificates

John W. Rhea II big 12 point rack, scoring 185 3/8 typical B&C points. Taken in Harrison County.

opposite side. Generally up to and just beyond the H-4 circumference towards the end of the main beam you can have several normal unpaired points on one main beam that may not be on the other main beam. These points would still be normal points on that side. All points are measured on its longest side, but never on the edges of a point.

4. Length of the first point, called G-1 and referred to sometimes as the brow point. The G-1 point is always the G-1 point. If it is absent or to short to make point requirement, it is still the G-1 in location. Indicate this circumstance on the score sheet, line G-1, column 2, as "0 0/8" if it is to short or if broken off. Enter a - in the proper space if totally absent. This is done to indicate that a point was there, but did not make point requirement, or its non-existence. Go ahead and measure the G-1, always measure a point on its longest side, on brow points it could be either side. Normally a point that is curved inward or outward, the outer curvature is generally the longest.

Sometimes you can have split or multiple brow points. In these cases each point must meet point requirement and you must determine if each point originates from the main beam or off the other point. Common base points share the same base area coming off the main beam. For a common base points to be counted as individual points there must be a figure 8 at the base of the points (a figure 8 must be clearly visible on both sides). If both points are determined to be a figure 8 than both points will be measured from the base line to the tip of the point. You can only have one normal brow point choose which one pairs best with the opposite G-1 point, then the other points is abnormal and entered in the upper

Kevin Elsea with his 207 2/8 non-typical from Adair County. This set of antlers score 195 net on its typical frame.

B&C measurer Joe Ream with Larry Higgins 207 7/8 non-typical rack. This impressive rack score 184 0/8 net on its typical frame.

Jesse Perry took this monster buck in Pettis County, scoring 190 3/8 typical points.

Wes Seaton took this buck in Putnam County, scoring 179 5/8 B&C points.

198

ght corner of the score form. If you decide that they are not common base points, then one point will be the parent
int and the other or others points are drawn off as separate abnormal points. Whitetail antlers frequently have multiple
ow points. You have now determined the normal G-1 or brow point, you have measured it and now ready to record
is measurement. Remember we are doing the right side first, record this measurement in the box G-1, column 2, right
tler, for example: 5 6/8

5. Length of all remaining normal points on the right main beam. Take the remaining point or points and measure
em as we have just done on the G-1 point, and record them in the proper boxes right antler(G-2, G-3, G-4, ect.).

6. We are now ready to start our circumference measurements. There are always 4 circumference measurements on

Scott Looney , B&C typical 187 6/8, from ClintonCounty, taken in 1994

ch main beam. To take this measurement use your 1/4"
g-end tape. You always start at the burr and proceed toward
e end of the main beam. H-1 circumference measurement is
ken at the smallest place between the burr and the G-1 point.
e H-2 circumference is taken between the G-1 and G-2 points.
e H-3 Circumference measurement is taken between the G-2
d G-3 points. The H-4 Circumference measurement is taken
tween the G-3 and G-4 Points. All measurements are taken in
hes to the nearest 1/8", at the smallest place between points.
cord all measurements in their proper boxes on the score form.
e are still on the right side.

Sometimes certain problems arise pertaining to circum-
ences measurements. If the G-1 point would happen to be
ally absent, no bump or any indication that a point ever
sted, then you would take H-1 and H-2 in the same mea-
ement, at the smallest place between the burr and the G-2
int. If the G-1 is broken and the remaining point material
ll not measure 1" long, or at 1", length will not exceed
dth by any amount or anywhere in the length of this point,
gth will not exceed width by any amount, then you still
e the H-1 circumference as if it was a point and H-2 would
taken at the smallest place between this point and the G-2
nt.

Surpose your deer antlers is an 8 pointer, with 4 normal
nts on each main beam (remember the end of the main
m is counted as a point, but is not measured as a point,
ause it is measured in the main beam length). With no G-
oint present you have no place between points to mea-
e. In this case you already have the G-3 point drawn off,
have separated it from the main beam with the lead pen-
mark. Find the center of the G-3 at the base line where it
rawn off (sometimes it is helpful to go up about halfway
the G-3 point and locate he center at this point, then fol-
this line back to the top of the main beam). Now that we
e the center of the G-3 point located, take your 1/4" steel
e and lay it vertical creating a right angle from this center
rk
the G-3 point, to the bottom of the main beam. Now

Jason Valentine, B&C non-typical 195 2/8, taken in Putnam County 1991

draw a line against the 1/4' steel tape. Measure from this line to end of the main beam, divide the length of this measurement in half. This distance will be where you will take the H-4 circumference. If a trophy antler would happen to be a 6 pointer, with two normal points per side and the end of main beam, then do the same procedure as described above on the G-3 point, and apply it to the G-2 point. Again 1/2 of this distance is where you would take the H-3 and H-4 circumferences. There is always four circumference measurements taken.

7. Measuring abnormal points. The top right part of the score form is where abnormal points are recorded. We have already marked off all points earlier, and have mesured all normal points. In measuring abnormal points you always start at the burr, then proceed up around the main beam to the tip of the main beam. Make all recordings on the score form in this manner for abnormal points.

The right side should be completed. Now follow the same procedures for the left side of the antler.

8. Greatest spread. This is where the levels come in or a right angle straight wall and one level, with c-clamp. Place one side of the antlers (right or left) up to the wall, with the other side protruding away from the wall. Keep the skull plate of the antlers parallel and at a right angle to the wall. Place the level up to the widest point on the outside of the antler. Take this measurement with the folding carpenters rule with the 6" extension. Place the ruler at a right angle and parallel to the center of the antler skull, between the wall and the level, using the slide part of the ruler as needed. Record this measurement in box C - greatest spread.

9. All measurements should be complete. Now record total number of points: Right and Left sides (I always start with the right side first). Do this by going to the last normal point measured and start counting up, including the main beam tip, then go to the abnormal points and add those in the right side. Record them in box A: number of points on right antler. Do the left side the same way and record them in the box for: number of points left antler.

10. Adding up columns and subtracting the difference between the right and left sides. Notice that inside spread is recorded in three places: 1) "D" inside spread of main beams; 2) inside spread credit may equal but not exceed the length of the longest main beam. If the inside spread has not exceeded the longest main beam then enter it in that box. But inside spread has exceeded the longest main beam, then enter the longest main beam length in this box; 3) carry the last figure down to the "totals" box, column 1 (lower left side of the score form).

Dave Hornady antlers scoring 199 6/8 nontypical B&C points, the brow tines on this buck measured over 14 inch long. Taken in Putnam County

Jack Hollingsworth state record non-typical bow kill scoring 199 6/8 poir taken in Jackson County in 1989.

Next, add up the right column 2, then add up the left column 3. Enter this number where it says: TOTALS. If your [troph]y is a typical with some abnomal points, add the right [and] left side abnormal points. You should have subtotals for [bo]th right and left sides. Now, add the abnormal points to[get]her and you should have a total for line E. Carry this total [to] E down to line E below (E. total length of abnormal points, [col]umn 4 difference). Add the entire difference column 4, de[riv]ing at a total for this column. If your trophy is a non-typical [yo]u will have several inches of abnormal points, this score [she]et will be different. Abnormal points on a non-typical score [for]m are added into the final score, and are not listed in the [dif]ference column. Abnormal points are totaled in the column [E.]abnormal points, carry this total down to the bottom left [sid]e of the score form to where is says: ADD LINE E TO[TA]L. Abnormal points are added into the final score on a non[typ]ical antlers. You will add them later into the final score. [Re]member, abnormal points on a typical score form are de[duc]ted. On a non-typical score form, abnormal points are added [int]o the final score.

[In] column 4 difference, substract the difference for the right [and] left sides. Example: if the Rt main beam was 25 6/8 inches [lon]g, the Lt main beam was 24 7/8 inches long, the difference [wou]ld be 7/8 of an inch. Do this through the entire column, [the]n add to get the total. You should now have totals in col[umn]s: 1, 2, 3, and 4.

[1]1. Adding for a final score. Add columns: 1, 2, and 3, to [giv]e you a subtotal. This subtotal (columns: 1, 2, and 3) is [refer]red to as gross typical score. On a typical score form, line [E is] added into the difference, column 4. On a non-typical [scor]e form it is not, but is added into the final score (titled, [E.]line E total). We are going to do a typical antler first, then [no]n-typical antler. As stated above add columns: 1, 2, and 3. [Thi]s will give you a subtotal (referred to as gross typical score). [Nex]t substract column 4. Now you have the final typical score.

[O]n a non-typical score form you add columns: 1, 2, and 3. [This] will give you a subtotal (referred to as gross typical score). [The]n substract column 4, now you have your subtotal. Next, [add] line E total. This gives you the final score for a non-typi[cal a]ntler.

[12]. Filling out the hunter information part of the score form. [First] give the exact locality where killed, means: county and [state] where taken. Second, date killed, including month, day, [year]. Next Hunter; name of the person who killed the deer. [Curr]ent owner; the person currently owning the antlers. Your [tele]phone number; this is necessary if further information is [need]ed. Current owner's address; street or box number, city,

Jeanette and Tracy Dunkin, with Jeanette's trophy whitetail buck.

Kelly valentine with her trophy, scoring 144 0/8 B&C points. Taken in Putnam County, 1995

Clint Ream with his first whitetail buck, taken in 1991. Clint was 8 years old in this picture. Sometimes a trophy is in the eyes of the beholder!

zip code. If a guide was used list guide's name and address. Remarks section is for any abnormalities of unique qualities of th antler being measured. Last but not least, upper right hand corner of the score form, kind of deer, in Missouri it would t Whitetail.

On the back top part of the official score sheet is for the official measurer to record the date, location of where measureme took place and signature of the official measurer, plus their I.D. number (this I.D. number greatly helps in recording the trophi entered). The line for witness, is to witness the official measurer signature.

At the bottom of the back page of the official score form is the FAIR CHASE STATEMENT. This is to be dated ar signed by the hunter for the trophy just measured. This signature must be witnessed by either a notary public, or the offic measurer that measured this trophy. Note: this is for hunter taken trophies.

This completes the official score form. If you have measured your trophy and it makes the minimum for the Missou Show-Me Big Bucks Club at 140 typical or 155 non-typical or better. To enter a trophy into the state records, it will ne to measured by an official measurer for the Missouri Show-Me Big Bucks Club. The Big Bucks Club accepts scо sheets of trophy whitetail deer that have been measured by official measurers for the following clubs: The Boone a Crockett Club; the Pope and Young Club; the Longhunters Society; the Missouri Show-Me Big Bucks Club; and A chery Big Bucks of Missouri. To enter your trophy antlers

mail the original score form, (if your trophy qualifies for B&C, P&Y, LHS, they require the original score form, we do accept good copies in these situations) photo of trophy, and entry fee; the entry fee is $17.00 plus $3.00 for mailings (the Big Buck Club is non-profit and relies on entry fees and items sold to club members to run the club). Mail to:

Missouri Show-Me Big Bucks Club
POB 9
Unionville, MO 63565-0009

Official Measurers for the Missouri Show-Me Big Bucks Club, measuring at DJ' Kirksville Missouri in 1990. lt to rt: Charlie Montague, Arnold Vest, Lee Smith, Dale F Ream, Jr. and Joe Ream.

Carrol Walker, non-typical 196 1/8 B&C points, taken in Sullivan County.

Paul Smith three beam buck scored 185 7/8 non-typical B&C points, take Putnam County, 1988

OFFICIAL MEASURERS

folks that measure our trophies could be our next door neighbor, or a person who lives in our city or county. ut official measurers no record keeping program could fulfill it obligations, as a record keeping program. What you his 1st Record Book for the Missouri Show-Me Big Club was made possible by these folks, along with the club members, oporters. As the Director of Records for the Missouri Show-Me Big Bucks Club, I want to **"thank"** each measurer that has currently measuring. These dedicated measurers are hunters and outdoor enthusiast themselves, who puts in hundred of ach year measuring trophies for hunters, they receive no pay, they do it for the love of the outdoors,

the camaraderie with other measurers and hunters. But for the **Majestic Whitetail Deer.**

rds of hunting activities is a record of our heritage here ouri. Without records many of our hunting activities phies would be forgotten. Without records many of the ophies and hunters listed in this first record book , have slipped away and been forgotten.

p to us (hunters) to maintain and preserve our hunting e for today, tomorrow and on into the future. To sustain e and forests so future generations of hunters will have to explore and game to hunt. To keep records of game nd memories of hunting experiences. We must always ble, yet firm and adhere to our heritage of hunting.

Jerry Kennedy, with his Scotland buck taken in 1990, scored 181 2/8 B&C typical points.

Oitker, 13 yrs. old, with an 8 pt. buck, taken in Dekalb County. This young took this trophy with a bow, November 6, 1994.

B&C measurer Joe Ream, with his 1996 trophy, scoring 173 5/8 non-typical. Taken with a muzzleloader in Putnam County.

Big Buck measure Tracy Dunkin presnts Kirby Matthews with a hunting knife at the 1996 Deer Classic. The Knife was donated by: Tom Rowland

Tracy Dunkin presents John R. Neal a Knight Wolverine Muzzleloading Rifle at the Missouri Deer classic, 1996. Donated by: Modern Muzzleloading ,Inc

Curtis Riley, typical 167 7/8, Putnam County

Steve Krueger, non-typcial 199 5/8, Boone County

Randy Tucker, typical 170 4/8, Sullivan County

Tracy Fritchey, typical 177 7/8, Boone County

RECORD KEEPING CLUBS IN

NORTH AMERICA

for

WHITETAIL DEER

⌐sted below are national record keeping organizations. Also state record keeping programs that border around Mis-⌐, what the recording fees are, (all states bordering Missouri, the record keeping programs are keep by the conserva-⌐gencies in there state) and minimum entries for whitetial deer. I mention this because when you see free on some of the ⌐ering states entry fees, it is free to the hunter, but paid for by the taxpayers.

⌐e and Crockett Club; Old Milwaukee Depot; 250 Station Drive; Missoula, MT. 59801-2753. Phone number: 406/⌐1888. Director or records, Jack Reneau. (all weapons and found trophies) Minimums for the All-Time Record Book: ⌐ypical, 195 non-typical. Minimums for the Awards Record Book: 160 typical, 185 non-typical. Entry fee $25.00. National ⌐am.

⌐and Young Club; Box 548; Chatfield, MN. 55923. Phone number: 507/867-4144. Director of Records, Glenn Hisey. ⌐taken trophies only) Minimums for entry: 125 typical, 155 non-typical. Entry fees $25.00. National Program.

⌐onghunters Society; POB 67; Friendship, IN. 47021. Phone number: 812/667-5231. Director of Records, Joyce ⌐. (muzzleloader weapons only) Minimums for entry: 130 typical, 160 non-typical. Entry fees $25.00. National Program.

⌐American Shed Hunters Club; 5750 W. 139th St.; Savage, MN 65378. Phone number: 612/447-8900. Director of ⌐ds, Jeff LeBaron. (shed antlers only) Minimums for entry: 60 typical, 70 non-typical. Entry fee, single shed $5.00., matched ⌐10.00. National Program.

⌐uri Show-Me Big Bucks Club; POB 9; Unionville, MO 63565-0009. Phone number: 660/947-3650. Director of ⌐ds, Dale H. Ream, Jr. (all weapons and found trophies) Minimum for entry: 140 typical, 155 non-typical. Entry fee $17.00 ⌐.00 for mailings. State Program.

⌐ry Big Bucks of Missouri; 209 Jefferson St.; Greenfield, MO 65661. Phone number: 417/637-2467. Director of ⌐ds, Chuck Myers. (bow taken only) Minimuns for entry: 100 typical, 125 non-typical. Entry fee $10.00 first entry, ⌐each additional entry. $3.00 a year membership dues. State Program.

⌐Department of Natural Resources; Iowa Trophy Deer Records; Wallace State Office Bldg.; Des Moines, IA. 50319-⌐Phone number: 515/281-4815. Director of Reords, Jim Zohrer. (all weapons) Minimums for entry: gun - 150 typi-⌐n - 170 non-typical, bow - 135 typical, bow- 155 non-typical. Entry fee none. State Program.

⌐s Department of Natural Resources; Big Buck Recognition Program; 524 S. Second St.; Springfield, IL. 62701. ⌐number: 217/785-5091. Director of Records, Constituency Services (all weapons) Minimums for entry: gun - 140 typical, ⌐60 non-typical, bow - 115 typical, bow - 130 non-typical. Entry fee none. State Program.

Kansas Big Game Recognition Program; Rt 2 Box 54 A; Pratt, KS 67124. Phone number: 316/672-5911. Director Records, Mike Miller. (all weapons) Minimuns for entry: gun - 135 typical, gun - 150 non-typical, bow - 115 typic bow - 120 non-typical. Entry fees none. State Program.

Nebraska Big Game Program; 2200 N. 33rd St.; Lincoln, NE. 68503. Phone number: 402/471-0641. Director of Reco Randy Stutheit. (all weapons) Minimuns for entry: gun- 150 typical, gun - 160 non-typical, bow - 125 typical, bow - non-typical, muzzleloader - 140 typical, muzzleloader 155 non-typical. Entry fees none. State Program.

Oklahoma City Curtis Awards Program; Game Division; 11801 N Lincoln Blvd.; Oklahoma City, OK. 73105. Phone num 405/521-2739. Director of Records, Mike Shaw. (all weapons) Minimuns for entry: 135 typical, 150 non-typical. Entry none. State Program.

Arkansas Trophy Deer; POB 629; Magnolia, AR. 71753. Phone number: 870/234-4706. Director of Records, Doughty and Ken Young. (all weapons) Minimuns for entry: 125 based and up, trophy listings all weapons, 150 typi 160 non-typical. Entry Fee unknown. State Program.

Tennessee Deer Registry; POB 40747; Nashville, TN. 37204. Phone number: 615/781-6612. Director of Records, Layton. (all weapons) Minimuns for entry: gun - 140 typical, gun - 165 non-typical, bow - 115 typical, bow - 140 typcial. Entry fee none. State Program.

Kentucky Deer Registry. Phone number 606/824-7507. Director of Records, John Phillips. National Records. State Prog

Michael Garrett buck scoring 168 1/8 typical , Harrison County

Nick Michael holding Josh Rennels Buck ,186 6/8 non-typical ,putnam Co

David Vanraden, 168 2/8 typical, Linn Co.

Jerry Goodin, 166 5/8 typical, Mercer Co.

Gary Snell buck, scoring 190 6/8 non-typical, Cape Girardeau Co.

James Michell buck scoring 169 2/8 typical, Maries Co.

Derrick Powell buck scoring 161 5/8 typical, Henry Co.

Thomas Ham buck scoring 166 3/8 typical, Montgomery Co.

Jessie Blair buck scoring 188 6/8 non-typical, Warren Co.

Stephen Kropf buck scoring 160 6/8, Greene Co.

J.R. Noe buck scoring 163 6/8 typical, Grundy Co.

Dallas Chipps buck scoring 169 1/8 typical, Texas Co.

James Hines buck scoring 167 6/8 typical
Sullivan County

Steven Richardson buck scoring 202 5/8
non-typical, Platte Co.

Jeff Trent, Junior Trent with Glen Trent antlers s
ing 169 4/8 typical, Putnam County

Brandon Young buck scoring 163 4/8 typical
Putnam County

Bill Morris buck scoring 162 7/8 typical
Linn County

Wade Cowan buck scoring 191 4/8 non-typic
Putnam County

Official Measurer Jim Fitzgerald and his buck
scoring 167 4/8 typcial, Linn County

Joe Ream buck scoring 155 2/8 typical
Putnam County

John West buck scoring 196 1/8 non-typical
Laclede County

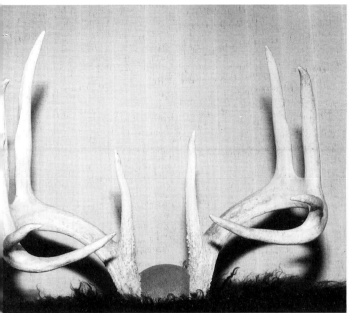

Merrill Willey, 157 1/8 typical, Shelby County

Roscoe L. Simmons, 150 2/8 typical, Oregon County

Larry Tuttle, 174 6/8 non-typical, Grundy County

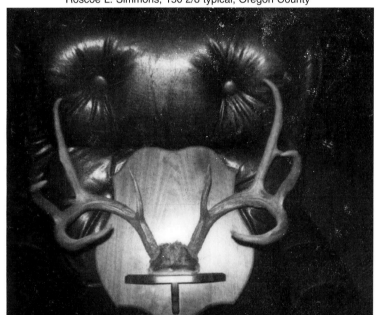

J.R. Temmen, 144 5/8 typical, Osage County

Jackson D. Sanders, 140 1/8 typical, Henry County

John O. Richeson, 141 4/8 typical, Franklin County

209

Dwight Roberts, 141 6/8 typical, Polk County

Judy A. Retherford, 151 2/8 typical, Montgomery Co.

Jeff Schultz, 152 4/8 typical, Lewis County

Richard Tefertiller, 155 5/8 typical, Barton County

George Valley, 160 6/8 typical, Crawford County

Walter Pritchard, 196 5/8 non-typical, Newton C

Dennis Maggart, 165 5/8 typical, Sullivan County

John Rummel, 142 2/8 typical, Cedar County

Richard Ray, 150 4/8 typical, Barton Coun

210

nan Grass, 140 0/8 typical, Cape Girardeau Co.

Roger Eason, 146 4/8 typical, Cedar County

Wis Esther, 149 6/8 typical, Laclede County

erry Fisher, 152 2/8 typical, Andrew County

Lisa Piepmeier, 170 7/8 non-typical, St. Clair County

Richard Peterson, 144 5/8 typical, Laclede County

illit Clark, 142 0/8 typical, Pulaski County

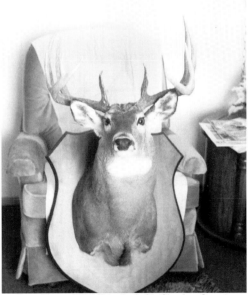
Gary Dyer, 155 0/8 typical, St. Charles County

Kenneth Dickinson, 152 5/8 typical, Laclede County

211

William Crist, 160 4/8 typical, Saline County

Andy Core, 140 2/8 typical, Pulsoski County

Edmon Bruce, 140 2/8 typical, Crawford Cou

Billy Alcorn, 161 4/8 typical, Webster County

Dan Baker, 145 3/8 typical, Franklin County

Derek Bax, 159 4/8 typical, Lawrence Coun

Charles Oney, 145 5/8 typical, Barry County

Don Burch, 175 3/8 non-typical, Texas County

Wesley Willis, 143 1/8 typical, Morgan Cou

lvin Nida, 149 2/8 typical, Henry County

Barney Johnson, 167 0/8 non-typical, Jefferson Co.

Bobbie Kerns, 161 5/8 non-typical, Henry County

nael Harsell, 160 0/8 typical, Knox County

Kenneth Lucius, 145 0/8 typical, Cedar County

John Martin, 160 4/8 typical, Reynolds County

Montgomery, 142 6/8 typical, Pettis County

Marvin Lentz, 183 4/8 typical, Chariton County

Heath Hulsey, 155 0/8 typical, St. Clair County

213

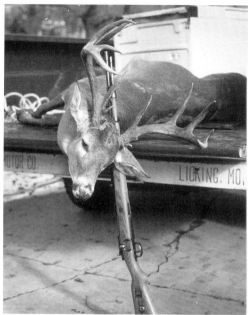
Everett Mitchell, 169 6/8 non-typical, Texas County

Matt Narzinski, 144 2/8 typical, Callaway County

Roy Juergens, 148 7/8 typical, Carter Count

Billy Schanks, 221 4/8 non-typical, Pike County

William Richardson, 164 3/8 typical, Saline County

P/u,Richard Harris, 201 0/8 non-typical, Jasper

Randy Wilson, 163 7/8 typical, Moniteau County

George Cross, 144 7/8 typical, Crawford County

Michael James, 169 0/8 typical, Ray Count

214

enneth Hiatte, 152 2/8 typical, Montgomery Co.

Raymond Sparks, 151 4/8 typical, Caldwell County

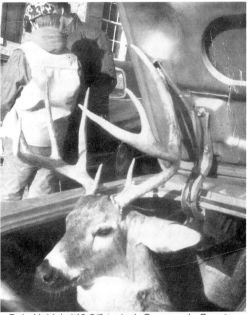

Dale Heidel, 142 5/8 typical, Gasconade County

ldie Freeman, 150 5/8 typical, Ripley County

Ed Clemmons, 153 0/8 typical, Ray County

Mark Hass, 150 7/8 typical, Callaway County

Dennis Curran, 157 0/8 typical, Holt County

Craig Todd, 150 4/8 typical, Lewis County

Alan Blomberg, 149 2/8 typical, Miller County

Keith Koehler, 156 1/8 typical, St. Charles County

George Koppelmann, 152 0/8 typical, Franklin Co.

Barry Denson, 154 7/8 typical, Henry County

Ernie Douglas, 162 1/8 typical, Morgan County

John Worley, 152 6/8 typical, Camdon County

Ralph Bowman, 162 6/8 typical, Monroe Cour

Francis Wood, 180 1/8 non-typical, Livingston Co.

William Winterbower, 187 1/8 non-typical, Pike Co.

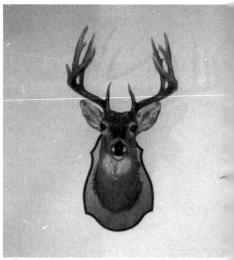
Roy Whanger, 150 5/8 typical, Callaway Cou

ald Schipper, 179 3/8 non-typ, St. Charles Co.

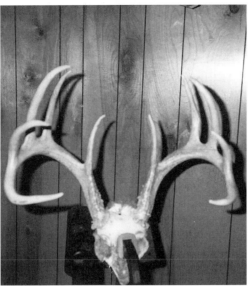

Brad Smart, 141 4/8 typical, Henry County

Claude Tracy, 166 4/8 non-typical, Greene County

rald Schulte, 160 0/8 typical, Montgomery Co.

James Seay, 158 6/8 typical, Lewis County

Barney Johnson, 167 0/8 typical, Jefferson County

e Johnson, 160 4/8 non-typical, Cass County

Clayton Knepp, 142 0/8 typical, St. Clair County

Clayton Kline, 168 7/8 typical, Knox County

Dale Martin, 179 7/8 non-typical, Scotland County

Gary Hilton, 151 6/8 typical, Christian County

Dee Smith, 149 2/8 typical, Laclede County

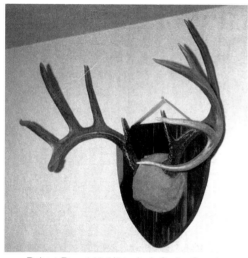

Robert Roy, 141 1/8 typical, Cedar County

Eddie Nevils, 145 4/8 typical, Johnson County

Darrell Hobbs, 145 5/8 typical, Cape Girardeau

Wayne Church, 145 7/8 typical, Benton County

Brian Giles, 140 3/8 typical, Benton County

Martin Weiler, 195 5/8 non-typ, Ste. Geneieve

Marty Gooch, 184 5/8 non-typical, Sullivan County

Mark Clinton, 150 6/8 typcial, Bates County

Steve Hendricks, 141 4/8 typical, St. Clair County

Jerry Balke, 152 6/8 typical, Pettis County

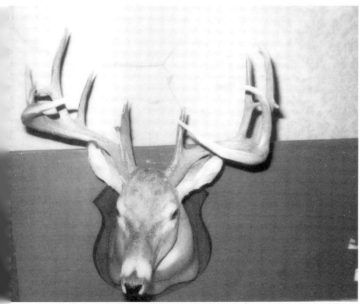

Darren Ball, 163 7/8 typical, Monroe County

Judith M. Noe, 151 2/8 typical, Mercer County

Deonne Marshall, 146 2/8 typical, St. Clair County

Donald Dutton, 148 5/8 typical, Clay County

Tommy Garnett, 179 0/8 typical, Monroe County

Steve Hardy, 174 2/8 non-typical, Ralls County

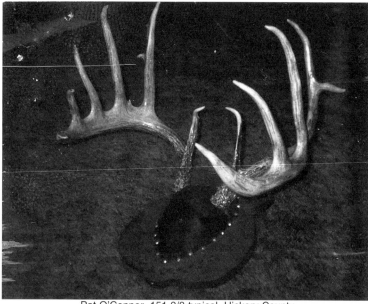

Pat O'Connor, 151 2/8 typical, Hickory County

Steve Graves, 140 2/8 typical, Benton County

Milda Gerschefske, 143 7/8 typical, Gasconade County

Marvin Null, 161 4/8 typical, Bates County

Glenn Shelton, 178 2/8 non-typical, Ste. Geneieve County

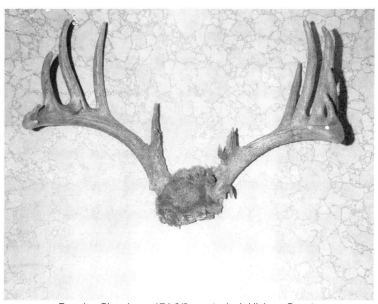

Douglas Chambers, 174 3/8 non-typical, Hickory County

Pick-Up, 170 4/8 typical, Saline County, owner Terry Lovekamp

Pick-Up, 174 5/8 typical, Boone County, owner Terry Lovekamp

221

Larry Poppa, 205 7/8 non-typical, Atchison County, owner Terry Lovekamp

Clint Easley, 205 7/8 non-typical, Macon County, owner Terry Lovekamp

Evelyn Priebe, 223 4/8 non-typical, Clark County, owner Terry Lovekamp

Pick-Up, 259 1/8 non-typical, Jackson County, owner Terry Lovekamp

MISSOURI SHOW-ME BIG BUCKS CLUB OFFICIAL MEASURERS

STATE	COUNTY	FIRST NAME	LAST NAME	CITY	CLUBS MEASURER FOR
MO	ADAIR	BILL	FARLEY	KIRKSVILLE	MO/SMBBC,ABBoM
		SHUAN	KLINGSMITH	GREEN CASTLE	MO/SMBBC,ABBoM
		ANTHONY P.	MIHALEVICH	KIRKSVILLE	P&Y,LHS,MO/SMBBC,ABBoM
		BILL	OTTEN	KIRKSVILLE	MO/SMBBC,ABBoM
		ROGER	PEECHER	KIRKSVILLE	MO/SMBBC,ABBoM
		DONNIE	WAYBILL	KIRKSVILLE	MO/SMBBC,ABBoM
	ANDREW	BOB	MOLSBEE	SAVANNAH	MO/SMBBC,ABBoM
		ROGER E.	WOLKEN	SAVANNAH	MO/SMBBC,ABBoM
	ATCHISON	RICHARD	SPERBER	ROCK PORT	MO/SMBBC,ABBoM
	AUDRAIN	RANDY	KRIEGEL	MEXICO	MO/SMBBC,ABBoM
	BARTON	TODD	PAYNE	LAMAR	MO/SMBBC,ABBoM
		JERRY M.	WORLEY	LAMAR	P&Y,MO/SMBBC,ABBoM
	BATES	KENNY	GABRIEL	BUTLER	MO/SMBBC,ABBoM
	BENTON	MARVIN R.	FERGUSON	LINCOLN	MO/SMBBC,ABBoM
	BOONE	TINA S.	BROOKE	COLUMBIA	MO/SMBBC,ABBOM
		R. SCOTT	BRUNDAGE	COLUMBIA	MO/SMBBC
		JIM	COOK	COLUMBIA	MO/SMBBC,ABBoM
		TOM	MARSHALL	COLUMBIA	MO/SMBBC,ABBoM
		DAVID	MEGAHAN	COLUMBIA	MO/SMBBC,ABBoM
		JOHN	MEYER	COLUMBIA	MO/SMBBC,ABBoM
		WAYNE R.	PORATH	COLUMBIA	B&C,P&Y,LHS,MO/SMBBC,ABBoM
		JOHN H.	SCHULZ	COLUMBIA	MO/SMBBC,ABBoM
	BUCHANAN	RICHARD	BOHANAN	ST. JOSEPH	MO/SMBBC,ABBoM
		BILL	BRAVO	ST. JOSEPH	MO/SMBBC,ABBoM
		DOUG	CLEMONS	ST. JOSEPH	MO/SMBBC,ABBoM
		BILL	COVERDELL	ST. JOSEPH	MO/SMBBC,ABBoM
		ED	EVANS	AGENCY	MO/SMBBC,ABBoM
		STEVEN	GOBEN	ST. JOSEPH	MO/SMBBC,ABBoM
		KEVIN	HANSON	ST. JOSEPH	MO/SMBBC,ABBoM
		CAROL	HARTIG	ST. JOSEPH	MO/SMBBC,ABBoM
		MIKE	McMILLIAN	ST. JOSEPH	MO/SMBBC,ABBoM
		BRUCE	RICHARDSON	ST. JOSEPH	MO/SMBBC,ABBoM
		TIM D.	RIPPERGER	ST. JOSEPH	MO/SMBBC,ABBoM
	BUTLER	GAYLE	KINGERY	POPLAR BLUFF	MO/SMBBC,ABBOM
	CALDWELL	LEWIS	BROWNING	AUXVASSE	MO/SMBBC,ABBoM
		DENNIS L.	CRANE	FULTON	MO/SMBBC,ABBoM
	CALLAWAY	JEFF	GIBONEY	FULTON	MO/SMBBC,ABBoM
		JOSEPH E.	McCRAY	FULTON	MO/SMBBC,ABBoM
	CAMDEN	REX	MARTENSEN	CAMDENTON	MO/SMBBC,ABBoM
		RICHARD	ROBBINS	LAKE OZARK	MO/SMBBC,ABBoM
		EDGAR	WEBB	CAMDENTON	MO/SMBBC,ABBoM
	CAPE GIRARDEAU	DEVIN	AMELUNKE	JACKSON	MO/SMBBC,ABBoM
		ROCKY D.	HAYES	CAPE GIRARDEAU	MO/SMBBC,ABBoM
		MIKE	KAHLE	JACKSON	MO/SMBBC,ABBoM
		GARY	NEWCOMB	CAPE GIRARDEAU	MO/SMBBC,ABBoM
		BRUCE	SCHEETER	CAPE GIRARDEAU	MO/SMBBC,ABBoM
		STEPHEN J.	WILSON	JACKSON	MO/SMBBC,ABBoM
	CARROLL	MARTIN	BROOKE	NORBORNE	MO/SMBBC,ABBoM
	CARTER	DAVID	NANCE	GRANDIN	P&Y,MO/SMBBC,ABBoM
	CEDAR	JIM	CARGILL	EL DORADO SPRINGS	MO/SMBBC,ABBoM
		CARL	CONWAY	EL DORADO SPRINGS	MO/SMBBC,ABBoM
		QUENTON	WALSH	EL DORADO SPRINGS	MO/SMBBC,ABBoM
	CHARITON	JOHN	WEIMER	SALISBURY	MO/SMBBC,ABBoM
	CHRISTIAN	R. DALE	DORTCH	OZARK	P&Y,MO/SMBBC,ABBoM
	CLADWELL	DEREK	COLE	RAYTOWN	MO/SMBBC,ABBoM
	CLARK	NEIL	ACKLIE	KAHOKA	MO/SMBBC,ABBoM
		DAVID	RIGGS	KAHOKA	MO/SMBBC,ABBoM
	CLAY	RICK	ALLEY	KANSAS CITY	MO/SMBBC,ABBoM
		GLEN	BARTON	EXCELSIOR SPRINGS	MO/SMBBC,ABBoM
		STEVE	CORDLE	GLADSTONE	MO/SMBBC,ABBoM
		JEFF	UTZ	SMITHVILLE	MO/SMBBC,ABBoM
		HARLAD "SONNY"	WELLS	LIBERTY	MO/SMBBC,ABBoM
	CLINTON	PAUL MITCH	HOOVER	PLATTSBURG	MO/SMBBC,ABBoM
	COLE	LARRY	HAGER	JEFFERSON CITY	MO/SMBBC,ABBoM
		DAN P.	HOLLINGSWORTH	JEFFERSON CITY	P&Y,MO/SMBBC,ABBoM
		LAWRENCE	REDEL	JEFFERSON CITY	B&C,P&Y,LHS,MO/SMBBC,ABBoM
		OLLIE	TORGERSON	JEFFERSON CITY	MO/SMBBC,ABBoM
	COOPER	H.A.	NIXON	WOOLDRIDGE	MO/SMBBC,ABBoM
	CRAWFORD	ROBIN G.	BRANDENBURG	STEELVILLE	MO/SMBBC,ABBoM
		TERRY W.	DAUGHTREY	SULLIVAN	MO/SMBBC,ABBoM
		CHARLES L.	GRIFFIN	SULLIVAN	MO/SMBBC,ABBoM
		DAVE	IVES	CUBA	MO/SMBBC,ABBoM
		CONRAD L.	MALLADY	SULLIVAN	MO/SMBBC,ABBoM
		THOMAS M.	STROTHER, III	SULLIVAN	MO/SMBBC,ABBoM
	DADE	CHARLES A.	MYERS	GREENFIELD	P&Y,MO/SMBBC,ABBoM
		HARRY A.	TANKESLEY, JR.	GREENFIELD	MO/SMBBC,ABBoM

224

STATE	COUNTY	FIRST NAME	LAST NAME	CITY	CLUBS MEASURER FOR
MO	DAVIESS	VAUGHN B.	WALTERS	GALLATIN	MO/SMBBC,ABBoM
	DE KALB	JOE	CAMPBELL	CLARKSDALE	MO/SMBBC,ABBoM
		KYLE	CARROLL	MAYSVILLE	MO/SMBBC,ABBoM
		JAMES W.	MARTIN	WEATHERBY	P&Y,LHS,MO/SMBBC,ABBoM
	DENT	JERRY D.	ELLIOTT	SALEM	MO/SMBBC,ABBoM
		DAVID A.	NICHOLS	SALEM	MO/SMBBC,ABBoM
	FRANKLIN	GORDON L.	JARVIS	WASHINGTON	MO/SMBBC,ABBoM
		WILLIAM	KOHNE	SULLIVAN	B&C,P&Y,LHS,MO/SMBBC,ABBoM
		WARREN W.	WIEDEMANN	NEW HAVEN	MO/SMBBC,ABBoM
	GASCONADE	TODD	ABERNATHY	BLAND	MO/SMBBC,ABBoM
		KEVIN	BRYANT	HERMANN	MO/SMBBC,ABBoM
		RON	WEST	OWENSVILLE	MO/SMBBC,ABBoM
	GASCOONADE	WILLIE	ROETHEMEYER	ROSEBUD	MO/SMBBC,ABBoM
	GENTRY	RANDY	ARNDT	ALBANY	MO/SMBBC,ABBoM
		DAVID F.	WELLS	ALBANY	MO/SMBBC,ABBoM
	GREENE	DARYL E.	BILLINGS	SPRINGFIELD	MO/SMBBC,ABBoM
		RICHARD	FLINT	WILLARD	B&C,LHS,MO/SMBBC,ABBoM
		WAYNE	GENDRON	SPRINGFIELD	MO/SMBBC,ABBoM
		W. CREED	MILLSAPS	SPRINGFIELD	MO/SMBBC,ABBoM
		BILL	PHILLIPS	SPRINGFIELD	MO/SMBBC,ABBoM
		CARL	WEST	SPRINGFIELD	MO/SMBBC,ABBoM
	GRUNDY	LEE	SMITH	TRENTON	P&Y,LHS,MO/SMBBC,ABBoM
	HARRISON	WILLIAM	LENHART	BETHANY	MO/SMBBC,ABBoM
	HENRY	BARRY	DENISON	BROWNINGTON	MO/SMBBC,ABBoM
		TERRY	FINDER	CLINTON	MO/SMBBC,ABBoM
		DENNIS J.	MEYERS	CLINTON	MO/SMBBC,ABBoM
		MIKE	NORTHINGTON	WINDSOR	MO/SMBBC,ABBoM
	HOLT	BRIAN	KUNKEL	MOUND CITY	MO/SMBBC,ABBoM
		RUSSELL L.	SHIFFLETT	MOUND CITY	MO/SMBBC,ABBoM
	HOWELL	VICKI	CHRITTON-MYERS	WILLOW SPRINGS	MO/SMBBC,ABBOM
	JACKSON	MARC J.	BOWEN	BLUE SPRINGS	B&C,P&Y,MO/SMBBC,ABBoM
		DANIEL L.	JOHNSON	BLUE SPRINGS	P&Y,LHS,MO/SMBBC,ABBoM
		JAMES S.	MARTIN	INDEPENDENCE	B&C,P&Y,LHS,MO/SMBBC,ABBoM
		MICK	McQUINN	INDEPENDENCE	MO/SMBBC,ABBoM
		JOE	MONTELEONE	KANSAS CITY	MO/SMBBC,ABBoM
		PAT	O'CONNOR	RAYTOWN	MO/SMBBC,ABBoM
		ROGER	SPARKS	INDEPENDENCE	MO/SMBBC,ABBoM
		MYRAL	WATSON	BLUE SPRINGS	MO/SMBBC,ABBoM
	JASPER	DENNIS	PAGE	ORONOGO	MO/SMBBC,ABBoM
		JEFF	RIESENMY	JOPLIN	MO/SMBBC,ABBoM
	JEFFERSON	BOB H.	MINNER	DESOTO	MO/SMBBC,ABBoM
		JAMES E.	MRAZ	FENTON	P&Y,MO/SMBBC,ABBoM
	LAFAYETTE	CHRIS W.	CAPPS	LEXINGTON	MO/SMBBC,ABBoM
	LINCOLN	JAY D.	HURD	EOLIA	MO/SMBBC,ABBoM
	LINN	JIM	FITZGERALD	NEW BOSTON	P&Y,LHS,MO/SMBBC,ABBoM
		MARTIN	MARKS	MEADVILLE	B&C,P&Y,LHS,MO/SMBBC,ABBoM
		D. JEFF	PURCELL	BROOKFIELD	MO/SMBBC,ABBoM
		ROBLEY	SANDERS	BROOKFIELD	MO/SMBBC,ABBoM
	LIVINGSTON	KYLE	HIBNER	CHILLICOTHE	MO/SMBBC,ABBoM
		JAMES C.	TAYLOR	UTICA	MO/SMBBC,ABBoM
	MACON	JOHN	COOK	MACON	MO/SMBBC,ABBoM
	MADISON	CORY	TIEFENAUER	FREDERICKTOWN	MO/SMBBC,ABBOM
	MARIES	PATRICK J.	MASEK	VIENNA	MO/SMBBC,ABBoM
	MARION	DAN	JANES	HANNIBAL	P&Y,MO/BBC,ABBoM
	McDONALD	BRAD	BUTLER	JOPLIN	MO/SMBBC,ABBoM
	MILLER	JAMES L.	PHILLIPS	BRUMLEY	MO/SMBBC,ABBoM
	MONITEAU	JOHN	McPHERSON	CALIFORNIA	MO/SMBBC,ABBoM
		WAYNE	MURI	JAMESTOWN	MO/SMBBC,ABBoM
		LARRY	STRICKFADEN	CALIFORNIA	MO/SMBBC,ABBoM
	MONROE	HAROLD W.	HITCHCOCK	PARIS	MO/SMBBC,ABBOM
	MONTGOMERY	GENE	TUMA	MONTGOMERY CITY	MO/SMBBC,ABBoM
	MORGAN	DEAN	EVANS	GRAVOIS MILLS	MO/SMBBC,ABBoM
		THOMAS J.	HAMILTON	VERSAILLES	MO/SMBBC,ABBoM
		KURT	HEISLER	VERSAILLES	MO/SMBBC,ABBoM
		MAX	MIDDLETON	VERSAILLES	MO/SMBBC,ABBoM
	NODAWAY	LARRY	DAVISON	HOPKINS	MO/SMBBC,ABBoM
		EDWARD J.	HIGDON	MARYVILLE	MO/SMBBC,ABBoM
	OSAGE	JERRY	ABERNATHY	BLAND	P&Y,MO/SMBBC,ABBoM
		MARK J.	HAVILAND	LINN	MO/SMBBC,ABBoM
		RUSSELL	TITUS	LOOSE CREEK	MO/SMBBC,ABBoM
	OZARK	DANNY	BILLINGS	NOBLE	MO/SMBBC,ABBoM
	PERRY	MATTHEW	REED	PERRYVILLE	MO/SMBBC,ABBoM
	PETTIS	JIM	GEBHART	SMITHTON	MO/SMBBC,ABBoM
	PHELPS	LARRY G.	EVANS	ST. JAMES	MO/SMBBC,ABBoM
		STEPHEN	ZAP	ROLLA	MO/SMBBC,ABBoM
	PIKE	DON	BARNES	BOWLING GREEN	P&Y,MO/SMBBC,ABBoM

225

MISSOURI SHOW-ME BIG BUCKS CLUB OFFICIAL MEASURERS

STATE	COUNTY	FIRST NAME	LAST NAME	CITY	CLUBS MEASURER FOR
MO	PIKE	JOHN H.	DETJEN	FRANKFORD	B&C,P&Y,LHS,MO/SMBBC,ABBoM
		VICKY	GRAVER	BOWLING GREEN	MO/SMBBC,ABBoM
		LOWELL	MILLER	BOWLING GREEN	MO/SMBBC,ABBoM
	PLATTE	STEVEN W.	NICHOLS	PLATTE CITY	MO/SMBBC,ABBoM
		DOUGLAS J.	YEAGER	PLATTE CITY	MO/SMBBC,ABBoM
	POLK	RON	SCURLOCK	BOLIVAR	MO/SMBBC,ABBoM
	PULASKI	JIM	BRAITHWAIT	RICHLAND	B&C,LHS,MO/SMBBC,ABBoM
		RUSSELL L.	ROST	WAYNESVILLE	MO/SMBBC,ABBoM
	PUTNAM	LARRY	HACKNEY	UNIONVILLE	MO/SMBBC,ABBoM,IA/BBC
		SCOTT M.	INGERSOLL	UNIONVILLE	MO/SMBBC,ABBoM,IA/BBC
		BRADLEY DALE	REAM	UNIONVILLE	MO/SMBBC,ABBoM
		JOE	REAM	UNIONVILLE	B&C,P&Y,LHS,MO/SMBBC,ABBoM,IA/BBC,IL/
		CLINT HENRY	REAM	UNIONVILLE	MO/SMBBC,ABBoM
		DALE H.	REAM, JR.	UNIONVILLE	B&C,P&Y,LHS,MO/SMBBC,ABBoM,IA/BBC,IL/
		GERALD W.	WEBBER	UNIONVILLE	B&C,P&Y,LHS,MO/SMBBC,ABBoM,IA/BBC,IL/
	RALLS	STEVEN A.	HARDY	NEW LONDON	P&Y,MO/SMBBC,ABBoM
		RUSSELL	SMITH	NEW LONDON	MO/SMBBC,ABBoM
	RANDOLPH	PAUL	JEFFRIES	MOBERLY	MO/SMBBC,ABBoM
		GENE	SIMMERMAN	MOBERLY	MO/SMBBC,ABBoM
	RAY	GEORGE L.	HISER	EXCELSIOR SPRINGS	MO/SMBBC,ABBoM
	SALINE	DAVID	CRAMER	MARSHALL	MO/SMBBC,ABBoM
		TOM	DAVIDSON	MARSHALL	MO/SMBBC,ABBoM
		ANTHONY	EDDY	SLATER	MO/SMBBC,ABBoM
		PAUL	HILGEDICK	MARSHALL	MO/SMBBC,ABBoM
	SCHUYLER	RANDY D.	FOWLER	QUEEN CITY	MO/SMBBC,ABBoM
		BOB	FREMON	LANCASTER	MO/SMBBC,ABBoM
		RICHARD	SAPP	QUEEN CITY	MO/SMBBC,ABBoM
	SCOTLAND	MICHAEL	WAGNER	MEMPHIS	MO/SMBBC,ABBoM
	SHELBY	RUSTY D.	GANDER	SHELBYVILLE	MO/SMBBC,ABBoM
		BILL	MAYS	SHELBINA	MO/SMBBC,ABBoM
		JAMIE	McWILLIAMS	LEANARD	MO/SMBBC,ABBoM
	ST. CHARLES	RANDY	COOPER	ST. CHARLES	MO/SMBBC,ABBoM
		MARTY	MARLER	ST. PETERS	MO/SMBBC,ABBoM
		KERRY	MISCHE	ST. CHARLES	MO/SMBBC,ABBoM
		DAN	SCHULTE	ST. PETERS	MO/SMBBC,ABBoM
	ST. FRANCOIS	RONNIE	GADBERRY	ST. MARY	P&Y,LHS,MO/SMBBC,ABBoM
		DONALD P.	ROPER	FARMINGTON	B&C,P&Y,LHS,IL/BBC,MO/SMBBC,ABBoM
	ST. LOUIS	VIC	HEINCKER	ST. LOUIS	MO/SMBBC,ABBoM
		JIM	HOLDENRIED	OAKVILLE	P&Y,LHS,MO/SMBBC,ABBoM
		CARL	SCHWARZ	ST. LOUIS	P&Y,MO/SMBBC,ABBoM
		PAUL C.	SCHWARZ (DECEASED)	ST. LOUIS	B&C,P&Y,LHS,MO/SMBBC,ABBoM
		GREG	STIPPEC	ST. LOUIS	MO/SMBBC,ABBoM
	STE. GENEVIEVE	STEVE & CHERYL	BARKER	STE. GENEVIEVE	MO/SMBBC,ABBoM
		RAY	JOGGERST	STE. GENEVIEVE	MO/SMBBC,ABBoM
		KEITH W.	LINDSEY	STE. GENEVIEVE	MO/SMBBC,ABBoM
	STODDARD	TED	DINKINS	DEXTER	MO/SMBBC,ABBoM
	STONE	DECATUR	MITCHELL	CRANE	MO/SMBBC,ABBoM
	SULLIVAN	HEATH	HALLEY	GREEN CITY	P&Y,MO/SMBBC,ABBoM
	TEXAS	NEIL B.	JONES	BUCYRUS	MO/SMBBC,ABBoM
		STEVE	WILLIAMS	HOUSTON	MO/SMBBC,ABBoM
	VERNON	LARRY D.	ABRAHAM	NEVADA	B&C,P&Y,LHS,MO/SMBBC,ABBoM
		DARRELL	ADAMS	MOUNDVILLE	MO/SMBBC,ABBoM
		ROGER	HENSLEY	NEVADA	P&Y,ABBoM,MO/SMBBC
	WARREN	BARBARA	BOSCHERT	WARRENTON	MO/SMBBC,ABBoM
		MICHAEL	MEYER	MARTHASVILLE	MO/SMBBC,ABBoM
	WASHINGTON	DUANE A.	BUCHANAN	POTOSI	MO/SMBBC,ABBoM
	WAYNE	THOMAS E.	TONEY	PIEDMONT	MO/SMBBC,ABBoM
	WEBSTER	DAVID	McDANIEL	MARSHFIELD	MO/SMBBC,ABBoM
	WORTH	JULIA	KOLLITZ	GRANT CITY	MO/SMBBC,ABBoM
KS	JOHNSON	CALVIN	BAUMGARTEN	OLATHE	P&Y,MO/SMBBC,ABBoM
IL	ADAMS	ROCKY	MERREIGHN	QUINCY	IL/BBP,MO/SMBBC,ABBOM
		GREGORY A.	NIXON	QUINCY	P&Y,LHS,MO/SMBBC
	FAYETTE	MIKE	KISTLER	BROWNSTOWN	B&C,P&Y,LHS,IL/BBP,MO/SMBBC,ABBOM
	MACON	TIM	WALMSLEY	DECATOR	B&C,P&Y,LHS,IL/BBC,MO/SMBBC,ABBOM
	SCHUYLER	TOM	GROVER	RUSHVILLE	B&C,P&Y,LHS,IL/BBP,MO/SMBBC,ABBOM
IA	APPANOOSE	RANDY	McPHERREN	UNIONVILLE	B&C,P&Y,LHS,MO/SMBBC,ABBoM,IA/BBC
	BOONE	BILL	BUNGER	MADRID	B&C,P&Y,LHS,IA/BBC,MO/SMBBC,ABBoM
	POLK	KEVIN	FREYMILLER	DES MOINES	B&C,P&Y,LHS,MO/SMBBC,ABBoM,IA/BBC,II
	POTTAWATTAMIE	DOUG	CLAYTON	COUNCIL BLUFFS	B&C,P&Y,LHS,IA/BBC,MO/SMBBC,ABBoM
	WAPELLO	ARNOLD	VEST	OTTUMWA	B&C,P&Y,LHS,MO/SMBBC,ABBoM,IA/BBC,II
	WASHINGTON	DON	PFEIFFER	WASHINGTON	B&C,P&Y,LHS,IA/BBC,MO/SMBBC,ABBoM
	WOODBURY	MICHAEL W.	McKENNA	SALIX	P&Y,LHS,MO/SMBBC,ABBoM,IA/BBC
CA	PUTNAM	TRACY W.	DUNKIN	FRESNO	MO/SMBBC,ABBoM

MISSOURI SHOW-ME BIG BUCKS CLUB

LISTING BY COUNTY ALL ENTRIES

T - TYPICAL - NT - NON-TYPICAL

MISSOURI SHOW-ME BIG BUCKS CLUB

ENTRIES 160 TYPICAL, 185 NON-TYPICAL, BOONE AND CROCKETT POINTS

T - IS FOR TYPICAL; NT - IS FOR NON-TYPICAL

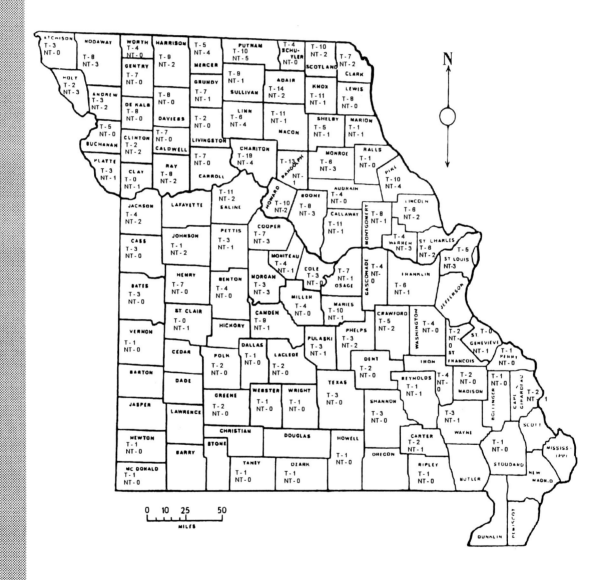

2   Folio copy

MISSOURI SHOW-ME BIG BUCKS CLUB

ENTRIES 170 TYPICAL, 195 NON-TYPCIAL, BOONE AND CROCKETT POINTS

T - IS FOR TYPICALS, NT - IS FOR NON-TYPICALS

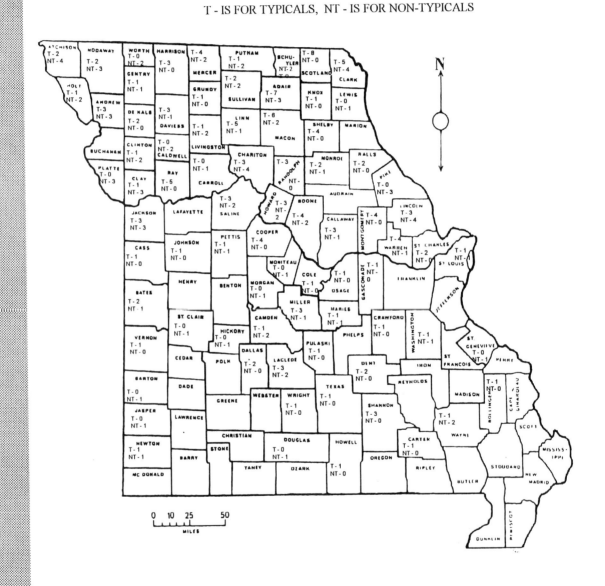

```
                    MISSOURI SHOW-ME BIG BUCKS CLUB
--------------------------------------------------------------------
YEAR, NUMBER OF ANTLERED DEER TAKEN IN MISSOURI, ANTLERED
DEER ENTERED THAT YEAR, PERCENT OF ANTLERED DEER ENTERED
--------------------------------------------------------------------

YEAR      NUMBER OF BUCKS TAKEN      BUCKS ENTERED      PERCENT
----      ---------------------      -------------      -------
1981           31,721                     77            0.242741
1982           38,097                    130            0.341234
1983           40,452                    108            0.266983
1984           47,067                    116            0.246457
1985           43,109                    129            0.299241
1986           50,073                    171            0.299616
1987           72,323                    169            0.233673
1988           71,846                    201            0.279765
1989           78,233                    195            0.249255
1990           76,937                    221            0.287248
1991           65,567                    224            0.341635
1992           75,500                    212            0.280794
1993           76,337                    163            0.213526
1994           83,048                    198            0.238416
1995           97,868                    291            0.297339
1996           94,990                    185            0.194757
1997          NO DATA

--------------------------------------------------------------------
```

The figures, number of bucks harvested were provided by
the Missouri Department of Conservation.

The 1996 figures will change after the Missouri Deer
Classic in 1997.

If you want to take a trophy buck that qualifies for the
Missouri Show-Me Big Bucks Club (140 typical - 155
non-typical), you must let the button bucks, 1 1/2 year
old, and 2 1/2 year old bucks walk!

If you want meat most adult doe deer will field dress as
much (or in most cases will field dress more) as any 1 1/2
or 2 1/2 year old buck that ever lived.

MISSOURI SHOW-ME BIG BUCKS CLUB

BREAK DOWN OF TYPICAL AND NON-TYPICAL ENTRIES

TYPICAL		NON-TYPICAL	
140 - 149 7/8 = 1098	***	155 - 169 7/8 = 113	
150 - 159 7/8 = 1295	***	170 - 184 7/8 = 233	
160 - 169 7/8 = 462	***	185 - 194 7/8 = 102	
170 - 179 7/8 = 115	***	195 - 219 7/8 = 82	
180 - 189 7/8 = 37	***	220 - 239 7/8 = 8	
190 - 199 7/8 = 4	***	240 - 259 7/8 = 2	
200 - > = 1	***	260 - > = 1	

MINIMUMS FOR MISSOURI BIG BUCKS 140 TYPICAL - 155 NON-T
(takes rifle, bow, muzzleloader, pistol, pick-ups)

MINIMUMS FOR BOONE & CROCKETT ALL-TIME 170 TYP - 195 NON-T
(takes rifle, bow, muzzleloader, pistol, pick-ups)

MINIMUMS FOR B&C AWARDS BOOK 160 TYPICAL - 185 NON-TYPICAL
(takes rifle, bow, muzzleloader, pistol, pick-ups)

MINIMUMS FOR POPE AND YOUNG 125 TYPICAL - 155 NON-TYPICAL
(takes bow)

MINIMUMS FOR LONGHUNTERS SOCIETY 130 TYP - 160 NON-TYP
(takes muzzleloader)

MINIMUMS FOR ARCHERY BIG BUCKS OF MO.- 100 TYP - 125 NON-T
(takes bow)

(takes - means the weapon used in hunting, each record
keeping program records animals taken with that weapon)

MISSOURI

SHOW-ME

BIG BUCKS CLUB

RECORDS OF WHITETAIL DEER

IN MISSOURI

AS RANKED IN THE STATE

TYPICAL & NON-TYPICAL

by

DALE H. REAM, JR.

MISSOURI SHOW-ME BIG BUCKS CLUB RECORDS OF WHITETAIL DEER BY STATE, TYPICAL

STATE RANK	SCORE	COUNTY	YEAR TAKEN	INCHES TYPICAL R	L	INSIDE SPREAD	INCHES ABNORMAL	LENGTH MAIN BEAM R	L	NUMBER POINTS R	L	HUNTER	FIRST NAME	OWNER	FIRST NAME
1	205 0/8	RANDOLPH	71	92 7/8	96 5/8	24 2/8	0	26 6/8	25 4/8	6	6	GIBSON	LARRY	MISSOURI BIG	BUCKS CLUB
2	199 4/8	CLARK	69	97 2/8	92 7/8	20 0/8	1 4/8	27 2/8	26 2/8	8	5	BRUNK	JEFFREY	SAME	
3	193 4/8	LINN	96	104 1/8	88 2/8	19 4/8	1 2/8	29 5/8	30 2/8	6	5	KEARNS	TIM J.	SAME	
4	190 3/8	PETTIS	86	88 7/8	91 1/8	20 4/8	1 3/8	27 0/8	26 7/8	6	7	PERRY	JESSE A.	SAME	
5	190 0/8	CALLAWAY	95	83 5/8	94 0/8	23 4/8	0	25 0/8	24 7/8	7	7	BARKS	BEN	SAME	
6	189 5/8	VERNON	96	91 6/8	86 3/8	17 7/8	0	28 0/8	27 3/8	7	6	GUINN	BRAD	AMER.NAT.MUSEUM	FISH & WILDLIFE
7	187 6/8	SHELBY	84	88 7/8	86 0/8	18 5/8	1 7/8	25 1/8	25 2/8	7	6	WILLEY	RODNEY	SAME	
7	187 6/8	CLINTON	94	86 2/8	85 5/8	21 0/8	1 4/8	29 7/8	29 6/8	5	6	LOONEY	SCOTT E.	SAME	
9	187 2/8	SCOTLAND	71	86 5/8	91 3/8	19 4/8	4 6/8	26 0/8	26 2/8	6	8	BERHORST	ROBIN	SAME	
10	187 1/8	ST. LOUIS	72	88 0/8	88 6/8	19 7/8	0	28 2/8	28 5/8	5	6	TUCKER	MACK	SAME	
10	187 1/8	COOPER	74	88 1/8	88 1/8	19 4/8	2 5/8	26 4/8	26 5/8	6	7	DITTO	JOE	SAME	
10	187 1/8	MERCER	86	85 6/8	87 3/8	18 7/8	0	27 7/8	28 3/8	5	5	SUMMERS	BOB	SAME	
13	186 7/8	ATCHISON	68	89 3/8	93 2/8	19 1/8	5 2/8	27 7/8	27 2/8	7	8	MOODY	MIKE	SAME	
13	186 7/8	PHELPS	76	91 6/8	95 0/8	20 1/8	1 2/8	25 6/8	26 4/8	6	7	LANCASTER		FRANKLIN	DAN
13	186 7/8	ANDREW	89	83 4/8	86 0/8	20 5/8	0	26 3/8	26 7/8	5	5	TILL	KENNETH	SAME	
16	186 2/8	LACLEDE	72	85 0/8	88 1/8	22 4/8	1 4/8	25 0/8	25 4/8	6	7	OGLE	LARRY	SAME	
17	186 0/8	CARTER	63	90 2/8	85 3/8	18 6/8	0	26 6/8	26 7/8	6	6	GOGGIN	RICHARD N.	SAME	
18	185 5/8	DALLAS	86	88 3/8	86 4/8	19 2/8	2 5/8	25 2/8	25 4/8	7	6	HEADINGS	JAMES	SAME	
19	185 4/8	SHELBY	88	84 2/8	85 7/8	19 4/8	1 2/8	25 5/8	26 0/8	6	5	PARSONS	RONALD L.	SAME	
20	185 3/8	HARRISON	95	83 5/8	85 2/8	19 5/8	0	26 3/8	27 0/8	6	6	RHEA II	JOHN W.	SAME	
21	184 5/8	PHELPS	88	85 0/8	85 0/8	15 7/8	0	27 2/8	27 0/8	5	5	DAVIDSON	DON	SAME	
21	184 5/8	DALLAS	92	85 4/8	87 1/8	18 0/8	1 5/8	25 2/8	25 4/8	5	7	GARNER	LYNN	SAME	
23	183 4/8	CHARITON	68	83 6/8	95 0/8	18 2/8	0	26 6/8	26 6/8	5	6	LENTZ	MARVIN	SAME	
24	182 4/8	WARREN	68	88 3/8	83 5/8	18 4/8	1 6/8	27 0/8	26 6/8	7	5	TANNER	DONALD L.	SAME	
24	182 4/8	PHELPS	89	84 0/8	88 6/8	16 2/8	0	26 0/8	25 2/8	5	5	DAVIDSON	DON	SAME	
26	182 2/8	PHELPS	96	90 7/8	85 7/8	19 6/8	0	29 1/8	28 6/8	6	6	GABEL	DAVE	SAME	
27	182 1/8	LINCOLN	88	81 0/8	83 1/8	22 1/8	0	27 0/8	26 7/8	5	5	MUDD	DAVID	SAME	
27	182 1/8	BOONE	94	84 6/8	80 1/8	22 1/8	0	26 5/8	25 7/8	6	6	MILLER	JEFF L.	SAME	
27	182 1/8	ADAIR	96	83 7/8	87 2/8	23 1/8	7 0/8	28 2/8	27 4/8	7	8	LUSHER	SELBY	SAME	
30	181 5/8	CASS	91	84 5/8	85 5/8	19 6/8	1 1/8	23 6/8	24 3/8	7	7	WATSON	WILLIAM MARTI	SAME	
30	181 5/8	CHARITON	91	84 3/8	87 4/8	19 3/8	0	23 5/8	24 2/8	7	7	CALVERT	JERRY	SAME	
30	181 5/8	ADAIR	92	89 6/8	85 6/8	18 2/8	6 1/8	25 6/8	25 4/8	9	6	SIMONSON	L.D.	SAME	

MISSOURI SHOW-ME BIG BUCKS CLUB RECORDS OF WHITETAIL DEER BY STATE, TYPICAL

STATE RANK	SCORE	COUNTY	YEAR TAKEN	INCHES TYPICAL R	L	INSIDE SPREAD	INCHES ABNORMAL	LENGTH MAIN BEAM R	L	NUMBER POINTS R	L	HUNTER	FIRST NAME	OWNER	FIRST NAME
33	181 4/8	PIKE	87	89 6/8	89 6/8	20 6/8	7 4/8	26 2/8	27 6/8	6	6	PENROD	RALPH	SAME	
34	181 2/8	SCOTLAND	89	81 6/8	85 7/8	20 6/8	2 2/8	27 7/8	28 2/8	5	6	KENNEDY	JERRY	SAME	
35	181 0/8	DAVIESS	75	83 1/8	84 5/8	18 4/8	0	27 5/8	26 4/8	5	5	OLIPHANT	F.D.	SAME	
35	181 0/8	ADAIR	92	89 2/8	96 7/8	20 6/8	7 2/8	27 6/8	26 6/8	9	7	HILL	MIKE	SAME	
37	180 7/8	MARIES	94	81 1/8	80 4/8	23 7/8	0	27 4/8	27 6/8	6	6	BILYEU	JESSE MATT	SAME	
38	180 4/8	ANDREW	67	84 7/8	83 2/8	17 2/8	1 0/8	23 5/8	24 4/8	6	5	ASHLEY	VIRGIL M.	SAME	
38	180 4/8	PLATTE	87	87 0/8	86 3/8	23 1/8	9 1/8	23 4/8	24 1/8	8	7	MARTIN	JIM	SAME	
40	180 2/8	LINN	70	84 5/8	84 7/8	20 5/8	6 7/8	26 3/8	25 7/8	6	7	BURCH	E.L.	SAME	
41	180 1/8	PHELPS	73	84 4/8	80 6/8	20 1/8	0	26 4/8	26 5/8	6	6	HAGENHOFF	BILLY	SAME	
41	180 1/8	CHARITON	82	84 5/8	82 4/8	15 7/8	0	27 0/8	26 0/8	5	5	PEARMAN	RICKY	SAME	
43	179 6/8	MACON	88	88 3/8	80 5/8	19 0/8	0	27 1/8	25 5/8	5	5	YOUNG	JOHN W.	SAME	
44	179 5/8	SHANNON	89	81 1/8	89 3/8	21 2/8	2 5/8	24 6/8	25 0/8	7	7	FRY	ROBERT K.	SAME	
44	179 5/8	PUTNAM	92	84 1/8	82 4/8	21 0/8	2 1/8	28 6/8	27 6/8	6	5	SEATON	WES	SAME	
46	179 4/8	MACON	95	85 0/8	86 7/8	15 2/8	0	26 3/8	24 4/8	5	6	RICKWA	MARK	SAME	
47	179 1/8	SCOTLAND	85	82 5/8	84 5/8	22 3/8	6 2/8	25 7/8	25 6/8	6	6	SMITH	DAVID ROY	SAME	
47	179 1/8	RALLS	92	83 7/8	84 4/8	19 4/8	4 7/8	25 1/8	25 4/8	8	7	FAHLE	STEVE	SAME	
49	179 0/8	MONROE	88	83 4/8	81 3/8	21 0/8	0	26 2/8	26 5/8	5	5	GARNETT	TOMMY	SAME	
50	178 0/8	CLARK	66	83 2/8	81 1/8	21 6/8	0	26 7/8	27 2/8	6	6	COURTNEY	ALLEN L.	SAME	
51	177 7/8	BOONE	94	84 6/8	83 2/8	18 3/8	2 0/8	27 3/8	27 0/8	6	7	FRITCHEY	TRACY	SAME	
51	177 7/8	BATES	95	88 2/8	84 0/8	18 7/8	6 6/8	27 4/8	27 2/8	7	6	WHITE	DAN	SAME	
53	177 6/8	CLARK	85	82 0/8	82 7/8	19 0/8	0	24 3/8	23 5/8	5	5	NOBLE	BILLIE	SAME	
53	177 6/8	OSAGE	95	82 0/8	80 6/8	21 4/8	0	25 3/8	25 4/8	6	6	LANGFORD	CHUCK	SAME	
55	177 1/8	CLARK	93	82 5/8	83 3/8	17 7/8	0	22 3/8	24 2/8	6	6	BANASZEK	JOHN	SAME	
56	177 0/8	MACON	91	82 7/8	78 7/8	19 6/8	0	26 1/8	25 1/8	6	6	FREEMAN	W.R.	SAME	
57	176 7/8	ANDREW	95	79 4/8	79 3/8	22 5/8	0	25 0/8	25 2/8	6	6	MADDOX	BRIAN	SAME	
58	176 6/8	LACLEDE	76	83 1/8	81 2/8	22 3/8	1 7/8	28 6/8	28 0/8	5	5	SULLIVAN	CHARLES	SAME	
58	176 6/8	JACKSON	96	82 7/8	79 7/8	20 0/8	0	29 1/8	28 5/8	6	5	WILLIAMS	CHARLES	SAME	
60	176 3/8	WRIGHT	86	82 7/8	83 2/8	20 2/8	4 1/8	25 1/8	25 3/8	5	7	NAPIER	MIKE	SAME	
61	176 1/8	JOHNSON	90	78 3/8	83 3/8	23 5/8	3 2/8	27 1/8	27 4/8	6	5	STEPHENS	JAMES	SAME	
62	176 0/8	SCOTLAND	72	81 3/8	77 2/8	21 6/8	0	26 7/8	26 2/8	5	5	MORTON	JIMMY	SAME	
63	176 0/8	JACKSON	95	79 3/8	82 1/8	21 4/8	0	25 5/8	25 3/8	6	6	HIESBERGE	MICHAEL A.	SAME	
63	176 0/8	MONTGOMERY	96	85 1/8	84 0/8	19 0/8	7 6/8	27 0/8	27 0/8	7	8	KNOEPFLEIN	DAVE	SAME	

MISSOURI SHOW-ME BIG BUCKS CLUB RECORDS OF WHITETAIL DEER BY STATE, TYPICAL

STATE RANK	SCORE	COUNTY	YEAR TAKEN	INCHES TYPICAL R	L	INSIDE SPREAD	INCHES ABNORMAL	LENGTH MAIN BEAM R	L	NUMBER POINTS R	L	HUNTER	FIRST NAME	OWNER	FIRST NAME
65	175 4/8	HOLT	62	79 7/8	80 3/8	21 2/8	0	25 6/8	25 4/8	5	5	SCHAEFFER	ORRIE L.	SAME	
66	175 3/8	DENT	82	81 1/8	80 7/8	18 2/8	1 1/8	26 4/8	26 0/8	7	6	UMHOEFER	KEN	SAME	
67	175 1/8	COLE	95	82 2/8	86 5/8	19 7/8	6 2/8	26 6/8	29 0/8	6	6	BRUEMMER	BRIAN	SAME	
68	175 0/8	HARRISON	74	79 4/8	78 5/8	19 6/8	0	23 2/8	24 0/8	5	5	GRAHAM	CARL	SAME	
68	175 0/8	MONTGOMERY	76	80 3/8	83 5/8	19 7/8	2 5/8	26 2/8	25 3/8	6	7	WOODRUFF, JR.	RICHARD	SAME	
70	174 7/8	DAVIESS	86	83 3/8	85 6/8	17 6/8	7 1/8	25 0/8	25 0/8	7	8	HOOVER	BRANDON	SAME	
71	174 6/8	HOWARD	85	80 6/8	81 4/8	24 5/8	6 5/8	26 3/8	25 0/8	5	7	ALLPHIN	DAVID	SAME	
71	174 6/8	SHANNON	92	80 7/8	83 3/8	21 3/8	3 1/8	24 6/8	26 3/8	5	6	LINDSEY	SCOTT	SAME	
73	174 5/8	GASCONADE	74	85 6/8	81 7/8	17 1/8	2 2/8	22 5/8	23 2/8	7	7	GRIFFITH	DANNY	SAME	
73	174 5/8	DEKALB	88	83 5/8	85 6/8	17 2/8	7 1/8	26 0/8	26 3/8	7	8	HOOVER	MONTE	SAME	
73	174 5/8	RAY	90	85 6/8	83 3/8	20 4/8	7 1/8	28 6/8	28 0/8	6	9	BALES	DENNIS B.	SAME	
73	174 5/8	DENT	90	80 3/8	84 7/8	16 7/8	0	23 3/8	23 5/8	5	5	WYLIE	THOMAS P.	SAME	
73	174 5/8	BOONE	95	87 5/8	80 0/8	19 7/8	5 2/8	28 4/8	28 1/8	6	6	LOVEKAMP	TERRY L.	SAME	
78	174 3/8	CLARK	65	84 4/8	83 0/8	17 7/8	7 2/8	26 2/8	25 6/8	6	6	PRUETT	DICK	SAME	
78	174 3/8	KNOX	72	80 1/8	78 4/8	23 5/8	3 2/8	28 1/8	26 7/8	6	5	SIMMONS	JON	SAME	
78	174 3/8	MONTGOMERY	77	80 0/8	88 5/8	21 6/8	5 3/8	26 4/8	27 0/8	6	9	DIXON	DARREN D.	SAME	
78	174 3/8	NEWTON	94	84 1/8	80 4/8	16 3/8	1 0/8	26 1/8	25 5/8	7	6	WOLFE	SCOTT	SAME	
82	174 2/8	MACON	59	76 7/8	77 0/8	23 0/8	0	26 0/8	25 7/8	5	5	RUNNELS	ALVIN	SAME	
83	174 1/8	CALLAWAY	68	83 4/8	86 5/8	16 6/8	4 1/8	25 0/8	25 0/8	8	7	LAFON	JAC	SAME	
84	174 0/8	COOPER	88	82 3/8	82 7/8	18 1/8	5 7/8	26 3/8	26 6/8	8	7	SCHLUP	MIKE	SAME	
84	174 0/8	RANDOLPH	95	79 3/8	83 0/8	20 2/8	5 0/8	25 1/8	26 3/8	8	6	SEINER	ROGER	SAME	
86	173 7/8	SALINE	71	85 4/8	88 3/8	19 4/8	1 5/8	24 5/8	26 0/8	5	5	DICKEY	WILLIAM	SAME	
86	173 7/8	TEXAS	81	79 4/8	74 1/8	25 5/8	0	27 2/8	26 2/8	7	5	BELEW	DON	SAME	
86	173 7/8	LINN	91	80 4/8	77 7/8	21 2/8	1 1/8	25 2/8	25 2/8	5	6	SIMPSON	DANNY	SAME	
89	173 5/8	GENTRY	69	78 7/8	84 5/8	18 3/8	1 6/8	25 2/8	25 4/8	5	8	OBERBECK	WILLIAN F. (BILL)	SAME	
89	173 5/8	JACKSON	95	76 6/8	81 6/8	25 3/8	1 2/8	30 1/8	30 0/8	6	5	SYTKOWSKI	MIKE	SAME	
89	173 5/8	WARREN	95	80 5/8	85 5/8	19 3/8	5 2/8	24 5/8	26 7/8	6	5	SKELTON	GLENN	SAME	
92	173 4/8	NODAWAY	87	87 3/8	82 3/8	20 3/8	8 5/8	27 5/8	28 1/8	7	6	HART	GARY	SAME	
92	173 4/8	MILLER	96	79 7/8	86 1/8	22 7/8	1 5/8	23 3/8	28 1/8	6	6	BERRY	STEVE	SAME	
94	173 3/8	MACON	69	77 2/8	77 3/8	22 3/8	0	24 6/8	25 0/8	6	6	WHITE	RICHARD	SAME	
95	173 2/8	WARREN	80	77 0/8	82 0/8	23 5/8	4 3/8	26 7/8	28 5/8	6	6	LEY	JEROME	SAME	
95	173 2/8	ADAIR	86	85 2/8	86 4/8	19 0/8	6 2/8	27 2/8	26 7/8	7	6	HATFIELD	ERIC	SAME	

MISSOURI SHOW-ME BIG BUCKS CLUB RECORDS OF WHITETAIL DEER BY STATE, TYPICAL

STATE RANK	SCORE	COUNTY	YEAR TAKEN	INCHES TYPICAL R	INCHES TYPICAL L	INSIDE SPREAD	INCHES ABNORMAL	LENGTH MAIN BEAM R	LENGTH MAIN BEAM L	NUMBER POINTS R	NUMBER POINTS L	HUNTER	FIRST NAME	OWNER	FIRST NAME
97	173 1/8	SHELBY	81	78 6/8	83 2/8	19 5/8	3 6/8	26 5/8	27 6/8	7	6	LIGHT	WILLIAM	SAME	
97	173 1/8	RALLS	88	78 2/8	79 4/8	20 2/8	2 5/8	27 4/8	27 1/8	5	4	JAMES	LES	SAME	
97	173 1/8	LINCOLN	92	82 0/8	80 0/8	17 0/8	3 7/8	26 0/8	25 6/8	7	6	NARUP, DDS	DANIEL A.	SAME	
100	173 0/8	MERCER	65	80 2/8	82 4/8	16 2/8	2 4/8	23 7/8	24 5/8	7	6	CLAPHAM	CODA	SAME	
100	173 0/8	HOWARD	78	77 7/8	79 2/8	21 7/8	1 1/8	28 0/8	28 2/8	7	6	BANNING	RAY	SAME	
100	173 0/8	ADAIR	82	78 7/8	80 2/8	20 0/8	0	24 4/8	25 5/8	6	6	PINKERTON	DENNIS E.	SAME	
100	173 0/8	CLAY	96	91 7/8	82 0/8	19 4/8	7 2/8	25 4/8	27 1/8	9	8	BRESHEARS	NEAL B.	SAME	
104	172 7/8	ST. CHARLES	80	79 3/8	77 1/8	20 3/8	0	23 4/8	23 6/8	5	5	SATTLER	NOBERT J.	SAME	
105	172 4/8	COOPER	60	78 3/8	86 0/8	20 0/8	1 4/8	29 6/8	28 6/8	5	7	KUEN	DALE	SAME	
105	172 4/8	NODAWAY	85	78 6/8	78 6/8	19 6/8	0	23 6/8	24 6/8	6	6	DAVISON	LARRY	SAME	
107	172 3/8	MONROE	67	79 6/8	77 6/8	19 5/8	1 6/8	26 0/8	26 2/8	6	5	BRAY	CLARK E.	SAME	
107	172 3/8	MERCER	88	78 7/8	86 6/8	16 2/8	1 1/8	26 4/8	26 7/8	5	7	SIMPSON	JARIN	SAME	
109	172 2/8	BOLLINGER	66	79 0/8	80 7/8	18 2/8	0	25 7/8	25 6/8	5	5	FORNKAHL	HADLEY E.	SAME	
109	172 2/8	MERCER	93	78 2/8	86 2/8	18 0/8	0	24 2/8	25 4/8	6	6	HOLT	BRAD	SAME	
111	172 1/8	MILLER	92	78 5/8	80 3/8	19 3/8	4 2/8	25 2/8	26 3/8	6	6	BELL	JIM	SAME	
112	172 0/8	RANDOLPH	68	78 5/8	79 0/8	21 7/8	5 1/8	25 0/8	25 2/8	5	6	SIMMERMAN	GENE	SAME	
112	172 0/8	RAY	78	83 4/8	80 6/8	15 0/8	1 2/8	26 2/8	25 3/8	7	6	LINDLEY	DWIGHT	SAME	
112	172 0/8	PIKE	88	88 6/8	80 2/8	18 3/8	0	24 1/8	26 0/8	6	5	HIPES	MARK R.	SAME	
112	172 0/8	CALLAWAY	90	79 6/8	79 3/8	15 6/8	0	23 7/8	23 5/8	5	5	QUICK	LARRY	SAME	
112	172 0/8	DEKALB	91	81 6/8	82 6/8	19 3/8	8 1/8	24 2/8	24 7/8	10	5	DAVIS	DEAN	SAME	
117	171 7/8	SCOTLAND	84	74 5/8	75 4/8	24 1/8	0	26 2/8	26 4/8	5	5	SMITH	DAVID	SAME	
118	171 5/8	CRAWFORD	82	77 3/8	86 4/8	17 3/8	0	26 0/8	25 6/8	5	5	GLASER	CHRIS	GLASER	FRED
118	171 5/8	DAVIESS	92	80 7/8	79 5/8	18 4/8	2 5/8	24 2/8	22 7/8	6	5	DEWEESE	DAVE	SAME	
120	171 4/8	SCOTLAND	89	79 1/8	83 1/8	18 6/8	3 0/8	26 4/8	25 2/8	6	6	ROBESON	HARRY	SAME	
121	171 3/8	WASHINGTON	87	81 3/8	81 5/8	18 0/8	3 5/8	23 1/8	23 0/8	6	5	BOUSE	JERRY	SAME	
121	171 3/8	HOWARD	92	81 1/8	86 2/8	18 5/8	5 0/8	26 4/8	26 6/8	6	8	POWELL	DERRICK	SAME	
123	171 2/8	RAY	82	77 6/8	77 4/8	21 4/8	0	26 6/8	26 2/8	5	5	HIGHTOWER	RON	SAME	
123	171 2/8	LINN	92	78 3/8	78 7/8	19 6/8	2 2/8	25 0/8	25 4/8	5	6	MUELLER	BRYAN	SAME	
123	171 2/8	LINCOLN	92	79 6/8	77 3/8	17 2/8	0	24 0/8	23 5/8	6	6	NORTON	NEIL	SAME	
123	171 2/8	SALINE	95	77 6/8	80 3/8	18 4/8	0	25 7/8	26 7/8	5	5	EDWARDS	JEFFREY E.	SAME	
127	171 1/8	LIVINGSTON	86	87 1/8	77 4/8	20 1/8	1 6/8	28 5/8	26 6/8	6	6	WEST	RICHARD	SAME	
127	171 1/8	WARREN	90	77 6/8	81 3/8	20 4/8	1 5/8	28 3/8	28 2/8	5	7	CASPER	JIM	SAME	

MISSOURI SHOW-ME BIG BUCKS CLUB RECORDS OF WHITETAIL DEER BY STATE, TYPICAL

STATE RANK	SCORE	COUNTY	YEAR TAKEN	INCHES TYPICAL R	L	INSIDE SPREAD	INCHES ABNORMAL	LENGTH MAIN BEAM R	L	NUMBER POINTS R	L	HUNTER	FIRST NAME	OWNER	FIRST NAME
129	171 0/8	RAY	66	0	0	0	0	0	0	0	0	SIEGEL	DALE	SAME	
129	171 0/8	SULLIVAN	72	79 2/8	78 0/8	16 0/8	0	25 3/8	25 1/8	5	5	HARVEY, JR.	FORNEY	SAME	
129	171 0/8	PIKE	82	85 6/8	80 6/8	16 4/8	3 0/8	27 3/8	25 5/8	6	6	HOLDENRIED	JIM	SAME	
129	171 0/8	CHRISTIAN	83	82 1/8	79 4/8	15 6/8	0	25 2/8	24 0/8	5	5	HERNDON	MELBA	SAME	
129	171 0/8	SCOTLAND	94	76 6/8	80 5/8	19 6/8	0	27 1/8	27 3/8	5	6	ANDERSON	RICK	SAME	
134	170 7/8	ADAIR	85	84 5/8	85 2/8	19 4/8	6 5/8	26 6/8	25 6/8	7	7	HATFIELD	ERIC	SAME	
134	170 7/8	WAYNE	89	77 7/8	80 5/8	17 7/8	2 4/8	25 5/8	25 7/8	6	8	BOSTIC	DARRELL	SAME	
136	170 6/8	HOWELL	74	79 0/8	77 5/8	20 0/8	2 2/8	27 2/8	26 4/8	6	6	WOODSON	ROY	SAME	
137	170 5/8	SHANNON	71	82 6/8	77 5/8	18 1/8	2 2/8	26 2/8	26 2/8	6	6	BLAND	GARRY	SAME	
137	170 5/8	ATCHISON	80	78 6/8	86 1/8	18 2/8	1 5/8	26 7/8	25 4/8	5	7	MUNSEY	ROY	SAME	
137	170 5/8	GRUNDY	88	80 0/8	79 0/8	18 5/8	3 2/8	27 3/8	27 7/8	6	6	WEATHERS	MICHAEL C.	SAME	
140	170 4/8	LINN	76	76 1/8	79 3/8	20 0/8	0	25 3/8	24 5/8	5	5	SPAINHOUR	DONALD	SAME	
140	170 4/8	SULLIVAN	81	78 2/8	80 6/8	19 0/8	3 6/8	25 1/8	25 1/8	6	5	TUCKER	RANDY	SAME	
140	170 4/8	LACLEDE	86	78 7/8	80 7/8	18 7/8	6 1/8	26 7/8	26 5/8	5	6	SHERRER	KEITH D.	SAME	
140	170 4/8	SALINE	94	82 6/8	82 0/8	21 5/8	11 3/8	27 4/8	27 6/8	9	8	PICK-UP		LOVEKAMP	TERRY L.
144	170 3/8	MILLER	71	82 5/8	77 3/8	19 3/8	1 6/8	25 6/8	25 1/8	7	6	JOHNSON	RAY	SAME	
144	170 3/8	CAMDEN	80	82 3/8	82 5/8	15 2/8	5 1/8	25 7/8	24 7/8	7	5	GREEN III	TREY	SAME	
144	170 3/8	COOPER	90	79 5/8	79 5/8	17 7/8	5 0/8	27 2/8	27 1/8	6	7	BINNIE	JIM	SAME	
144	170 3/8	HARRISON	91	78 2/8	78 6/8	17 3/8	0	26 1/8	26 1/8	5	5	GENTRY	GLEN	SAME	
148	170 2/8	MACON	92	79 7/8	78 7/8	17 0/8	0	27 0/8	27 2/8	5	5	DEWEESE	RENEE	SAME	
148	170 2/8	ST. CHARLES	94	83 3/8	82 3/8	21 4/8	6 0/8	27 0/8	26 3/8	8	7	VEHIGE	LEROY	SAME	
150	170 1/8	PULASKI	86	77 5/8	84 4/8	21 5/8	0	25 7/8	25 7/8	6	6	ADKINS	CHUCK	SAME	
151	170 0/8	BATES	69	82 7/8	82 0/8	17 4/8	2 4/8	26 4/8	26 5/8	7	5	ROSIER	GARY	SAME	
151	170 0/8	SHELBY	73	85 1/8	75 2/8	19 6/8	0	26 3/8	24 5/8	5	5	GANDER	RUSTY D.	SAME	
151	170 0/8	SCOTLAND	74	79 3/8	76 4/8	20 6/8	0	24 3/8	23 2/8	5	5	YOUNG	CHESTER JAMES	SAME	
151	170 0/8	RAY	87	81 2/8	78 3/8	17 2/8	1 0/8	24 1/8	23 5/8	6	7	KING	LARRY	SAME	
151	170 0/8	MONTGOMERY	88	80 4/8	76 0/8	18 7/8	1 0/8	27 7/8	26 4/8	5	6	MASKEY	KENNETH	SAME	
151	170 0/8	ADAIR	89	84 4/8	84 1/8	19 1/8	5 1/8	25 7/8	26 0/8	6	7	YANTIS	DONNIE	SAME	
151	170 0/8	BOONE	91	78 7/8	79 2/8	16 3/8	2 7/8	25 7/8	26 1/8	7	5	BARROWS	NORMAN	SAME	
158	169 6/8	JACKSON	86	76 6/8	76 6/8	20 6/8	0	25 0/8	25 1/8	5	5	TROTTER	BRYAN	SAME	
159	169 5/8	SALINE	94	79 3/8	75 2/8	20 1/8	0	25 7/8	24 1/8	5	5	RAMEY	BILL	SAME	
160	169 4/8	PUTNAM	60	84 4/8	79 3/8	16 2/8	1 2/8	26 4/8	26 2/8	6	6	TRENT	GLEN	SAME	

MISSOURI SHOW-ME BIG BUCKS CLUB RECORDS OF WHITETAIL DEER BY STATE, TYPICAL

STATE RANK	SCORE	COUNTY	YEAR TAKEN	INCHES TYPICAL R	L	INSIDE SPREAD	INCHES ABNORMAL	LENGTH MAIN BEAM R	L	NUMBER POINTS R	L	HUNTER	FIRST NAME	OWNER	FIRST NAME
160	169 4/8	BENTON	68	81 5/8	79 0/8	17 5/8	2 1/8	22 4/8	22 4/8	5	5	BYBEE	L.J.	SAME	
162	169 3/8	CALDWELL	91	83 7/8	77 4/8	18 5/8	2 0/8	25 3/8	23 3/8	6	6	ROBESON	MIKE	SAME	
163	169 2/8	SCOTLAND	67	79 7/8	73 0/8	23 2/8	0	27 5/8	26 6/8	5	5	PARRIS	ADREN	SAME	
163	169 2/8	MARIES	80	79 0/8	78 1/8	18 0/8	0	23 6/8	23 4/8	6	6	MITCHELL	JAMES	SAME	
163	169 2/8	CLARK	89	74 1/8	78 6/8	21 4/8	0	25 5/8	26 1/8	5	5	BUTLER	KENNY	SAME	
166	169 1/8	PETTIS	84	77 2/8	75 6/8	19 7/8	0	25 3/8	24 4/8	5	5	MEYER	ALVIN J.	SAME	
166	169 1/8	TEXAS	90	83 5/8	82 1/8	17 2/8	6 1/8	24 3/8	24 0/8	10	8	CHIPPS	DALLAS	SAME	
166	169 1/8	ST. CHARLES	90	76 7/8	81 6/8	19 1/8	1 2/8	26 2/8	27 5/8	5	6	HOPEN	PAUL	SAME	
166	169 1/8	HENRY	95	77 7/8	80 1/8	19 1/8	2 4/8	25 2/8	25 6/8	6	7	WHEELER	KENT	SAME	
170	169 0/8	KNOX	71	80 6/8	83 2/8	17 2/8	0	24 7/8	27 4/8	5	5	MEEK	EDWARD M.	SAME	
170	169 0/8	MONTGOMERY	77	79 6/8	78 6/8	16 4/8	0	27 0/8	27 4/8	5	5	SPENO	SAM J.	SAME	
170	169 0/8	RAY	96	79 1/8	76 4/8	19 4/8	0	23 4/8	23 1/8	5	5	JAMES	MICHAEL	SAME	
173	168 7/8	KNOX	82	80 5/8	78 3/8	20 3/8	3 0/8	25 0/8	25 1/8	5	6	KLINE	CLAYTON	SAME	
174	168 6/8	COOPER	78	83 4/8	78 0/8	21 5/8	5 5/8	27 3/8	27 5/8	7	6	BURNETT	GUY	SAME	
174	168 6/8	IRON	82	79 1/8	74 4/8	21 2/8	1 4/8	26 0/8	25 0/8	5	5	WIGGER	MARK	SAME	
174	168 6/8	HENRY	86	79 5/8	78 7/8	19 0/8	5 2/8	27 0/8	26 3/8	5	7	NORMAN	LYMAN	NORMAN	ANITA
174	168 6/8	CALDWELL	89	77 4/8	77 3/8	21 0/8	0	24 2/8	24 1/8	5	5	KELLETT	DANIEL T.	SAME	
174	168 6/8	MONTGOMERY	94	77 0/8	81 6/8	18 0/8	1 2/8	23 0/8	25 0/8	5	6	VANBOOVEN	DAVE	SAME	
179	168 5/8	PIKE	74	76 1/8	78 0/8	22 1/8	0	27 4/8	25 6/8	5	5	STROOT	EDWARD	SAME	
179	168 5/8	CARTER	79	76 7/8	78 0/8	17 2/8	1 3/8	25 4/8	25 4/8	5	6	LEACH	LEWIN	SAME	
181	168 4/8	CHARITON	67	74 7/8	78 6/8	21 5/8	1 5/8	26 4/8	27 0/8	6	5	MONTAGUE	CHARLES	DECEASED	
181	168 4/8	HOWELL	68	79 3/8	77 0/8	20 3/8	2 5/8	26 2/8	25 3/8	6	5	HOFF	GERRY	SAME	
181	168 4/8	GREENE	91	76 5/8	76 7/8	19 4/8	0	24 0/8	23 5/8	5	5	ANDREWS	DON	SAME	
184	168 3/8	HENRY	76	78 4/8	78 4/8	16 1/8	2 2/8	23 7/8	23 4/8	7	6	MORAN	DARRELL	SAME	
184	168 3/8	PUTNAM	76	73 6/8	77 0/8	23 2/8	0	26 7/8	26 0/8	5	5	BRANSCOMB	BRIAN	SAME	
184	168 3/8	ADAIR	78	78 2/8	77 2/8	23 3/8	6 2/8	24 7/8	24 0/8	5	6	CONLEY	ROGER	SAME	
184	168 3/8	WORTH	81	77 6/8	73 7/8	21 5/8	0	27 4/8	27 1/8	6	6	NIGH, JR.	WESLEY	SAME	
184	168 3/8	REYNOLDS	90	76 3/8	84 6/8	19 2/8	1 3/8	25 4/8	25 5/8	6	6	SUTTON	RANDY	SAME	
184	168 3/8	CRAWFORD	93	77 5/8	77 3/8	21 1/8	0	24 1/8	25 1/8	6	5	TURNBOUGH	GLENWOOD	SAME	
190	168 2/8	CALLAWAY	63	78 4/8	78 7/8	20 2/8	2 2/8	23 1/8	23 6/8	8	6	BENSON	RUSSELL	SAME	
190	168 2/8	OSAGE	86	77 4/8	77 0/8	18 2/8	0	21 6/8	22 4/8	6	6	GRANNEMANN	MARK	SAME	
190	168 2/8	LINN	94	78 7/8	83 0/8	19 5/8	6 3/8	28 1/8	27 6/8	7	5	VANRADEN	DAVID	SAME	

MISSOURI SHOW-ME BIG BUCKS CLUB RECORDS OF WHITETAIL DEER BY STATE, TYPICAL

STATE RANK	SCORE	COUNTY	YEAR TAKEN	INCHES TYPICAL R	INCHES TYPICAL L	INSIDE SPREAD	INCHES ABNORMAL	LENGTH MAIN BEAM R	LENGTH MAIN BEAM L	NUMBER POINTS R	NUMBER POINTS L	HUNTER	FIRST NAME	OWNER	FIRST NAME
193	168 1/8	HARRISON	93	79 3/8	85 4/8	19 3/8	3 4/8	26 6/8	27 6/8	7	6	GARRETT	MICHAEL C.	SAME	
194	168 0/8	JACKSON	84	75 7/8	81 2/8	23 0/8	3 2/8	23 4/8	26 0/8	6	6	ALLEN	RON	SAME	
194	168 0/8	IRON	89	74 4/8	78 5/8	19 2/8	0	26 3/8	26 3/8	6	6	BUTERY	SCOTT	SAME	
194	168 0/8	SULLIVAN	90	75 2/8	80 2/8	21 4/8	1 4/8	28 3/8	28 7/8	6	5	HINES	JAMES E.	SAME	
197	167 7/8	BUCHANAN	62	80 3/8	77 2/8	15 7/8	0	26 1/8	26 6/8	5	5	COOK	DWAYNE	SAME	
197	167 7/8	PIKE	73	79 4/8	80 3/8	19 5/8	3 4/8	28 5/8	29 2/8	6	7	DEWEY	LESTER	SAME	
197	167 7/8	PUTNAM	80	75 7/8	77 4/8	20 1/8	0	25 1/8	24 1/8	6	6	RILEY	CURTIS	SAME	
197	167 7/8	OZARK	82	75 7/8	81 2/8	18 7/8	0	25 4/8	24 3/8	5	6	JENKINS	REX E.	SAME	
197	167 7/8	HOWARD	87	75 5/8	76 4/8	18 5/8	0	24 1/8	24 1/8	5	5	TAYLOR	R.W.	SAME	
197	167 7/8	LEWIS	89	80 1/8	81 1/8	18 4/8	8 7/8	24 3/8	25 1/8	7	8	MULLEN	SCOTT	SAME	
197	167 7/8	DEKALB	94	78 4/8	78 4/8	20 5/8	4 2/8	31 0/8	30 2/8	6	5	STAHL	HANK	SAME	
204	167 6/8	MERCER	67	78 1/8	75 7/8	18 0/8	0	24 1/8	25 1/8	5	5	BARNETT	ALLEN R.	SAME	
205	167 5/8	SULLIVAN	69	75 0/8	78 6/8	18 7/8	0	25 7/8	25 7/8	5	5	MICHAEL	KENNETH L.	MICHAEL	BRYON
205	167 5/8	ADAIR	72	75 5/8	76 3/8	22 4/8	1 7/8	27 0/8	26 7/8	5	6	ASHER	JERRY	SAME	
205	167 5/8	NODAWAY	78	76 7/8	79 1/8	19 1/8	2 6/8	26 2/8	26 7/8	6	6	BALDWIN	LARRY	SAME	
205	167 5/8	CLARK	80	74 3/8	74 7/8	19 6/8	0	25 0/8	24 5/8	5	5	BINGHAM	ED	SAME	
205	167 5/8	MONROE	82	78 1/8	78 2/8	18 7/8	4 6/8	26 0/8	25 4/8	6	6	BIRD	JERRY	SAME	
205	167 5/8	HOWARD	84	80 3/8	76 6/8	17 1/8	3 0/8	23 7/8	22 6/8	5	7	PROCTOR	MIKE	SAME	
205	167 5/8	ST. LOUIS	87	76 1/8	74 5/8	20 3/8	0	25 4/8	26 1/8	5	5	MEYER	MERVIN J.	SAME	
205	167 5/8	PIKE	95	77 5/8	77 6/8	17 5/8	0	24 2/8	24 6/8	5	5	RICHARDSON	GUY H.	SAME	
213	167 4/8	ADAIR	80	77 2/8	74 7/8	19 2/8	0	26 0/8	26 2/8	5	5	SCHEMPP	JIMMY K.	SAME	
213	167 4/8	BOONE	86	82 5/8	79 7/8	17 5/8	5 3/8	22 1/8	20 5/8	8	7	CALDWELL	SCOTT	SAME	
213	167 4/8	LINN	91	76 5/8	80 6/8	18 0/8	0	25 7/8	25 1/8	5	6	FITZGERALD	JIM	SAME	
213	167 4/8	SCHUYLER	95	77 1/8	77 2/8	17 0/8	0	26 2/8	25 3/8	6	5	CHANCE	LARRY	SAME	
217	167 3/8	PUTNAM	81	84 3/8	77 4/8	18 1/8	0	23 7/8	24 5/8	6	6	SMITH	EARL	SAME	
217	167 3/8	CHARITON	88	72 6/8	78 7/8	21 5/8	0	23 0/8	24 0/8	5	6	SHARP	RONALD	SAME	
217	167 3/8	MONROE	92	75 1/8	80 2/8	19 5/8	0	28 1/8	27 6/8	6	6	McMURDO	WES	SAME	
217	167 3/8	OSAGE	95	78 3/8	78 3/8	14 4/8	1 1/8	23 3/8	23 6/8	5	6	MORFELD	SCOTT	SAME	
221	167 2/8	PUTNAM	77	79 6/8	77 0/8	19 7/8	1 3/8	25 3/8	23 1/8	5	6	MICHAEL	MONTE	SAME	
221	167 2/8	COOPER	83	79 2/8	81 5/8	19 3/8	8 3/8	26 1/8	27 0/8	7	6	ROBERTSON	DAN	SAME	
221	167 2/8	LACLEDE	89	79 3/8	82 2/8	21 6/8	11 0/8	27 2/8	27 4/8	7	10	KRUEGER	ELDAR R.	SAME	
221	167 2/8	AUDRAIN	90	78 3/8	80 5/8	16 7/8	4 5/8	25 2/8	24 6/8	6	7	WHALEN	LARRY	SAME	

MISSOURI SHOW-ME BIG BUCKS CLUB RECORDS OF WHITETAIL DEER BY STATE, TYPICAL

STATE RANK	SCORE	COUNTY	YEAR TAKEN	INCHES TYPICAL R	INCHES TYPICAL L	INSIDE SPREAD	INCHES ABNORMAL	LENGTH MAIN BEAM R	LENGTH MAIN BEAM L	NUMBER POINTS R	NUMBER POINTS L	HUNTER	FIRST NAME	OWNER	FIRST NAME
225	167 1/8	CLARK	87	75 5/8	72 7/8	24 7/8	0	27 5/8	27 0/8	5	5	MOHR	CHAD	SAME	
225	167 1/8	DEKALB	92	80 3/8	81 3/8	22 4/8	2 7/8	27 5/8	28 1/8	6	6	WEIGAND	KENDALL	SAME	
227	166 7/8	RANDOLPH	75	79 5/8	81 7/8	16 0/8	4 7/8	24 6/8	26 0/8	7	7	SCOTT	STEVE	SAME	
227	166 7/8	MARIES	82	86 7/8	77 6/8	22 6/8	9 5/8	29 0/8	26 6/8	6	7	VERHOFF	PAUL	SAME	
227	166 7/8	HICKORY	83	72 2/8	74 6/8	24 2/8	1 5/8	25 5/8	26 0/8	5	6	DRISKILL	JEFF	SAME	
230	166 7/8	GENTRY	89	80 7/8	80 6/8	16 0/8	2 1/8	23 4/8	23 2/8	6	7	DIERENFELDT	CLARENCE	SAME	
230	166 7/8	LEWIS	93	79 7/8	72 5/8	21 5/8	0 0/8	26 0/8	25 2/8	6	5	ELLISON	JOHN	SAME	
230	166 7/8	NODAWAY	95	77 7/8	76 4/8	17 7/8	1 6/8	24 6/8	25 0/8	6	7	HOLTMAN	STEVE	SAME	
230	166 7/8	CLARK	95	76 0/8	80 6/8	17 2/8	1 5/8	25 5/8	27 2/8	6	5	THOMSON	MARY F.	SAME	
230	166 7/8	RANDOLPH	96	77 3/8	75 2/8	17 5/8	0	23 0/8	23 4/8	5	5	CRUTCHFIELD	ART	SAME	
235	166 6/8	CHARITON	90	75 7/8	77 7/8	16 6/8	0	24 6/8	24 7/8	5	5	BERTSCH	DAVID C.	SAME	
235	166 6/8	GASCONADE	90	78 3/8	80 3/8	16 6/8	1 0/8	24 5/8	25 0/8	7	6	APPRILL	CURT	SAME	
235	166 6/8	SHANNON	94	76 7/8	77 1/8	18 2/8	0	24 4/8	22 3/8	5	6	ELLIOT	LARRY	LINDSEY	SCOTT
238	166 5/8	CHARITON	67	77 3/8	76 3/8	20 1/8	1 0/8	28 2/8	25 1/8	7	6	KLINE	LARRY	KLINE	LAWRENCE G.
238	166 5/8	CARROLL	73	76 5/8	79 1/8	21 0/8	3 1/8	26 7/8	26 0/8	5	7	HUNDLEY	RONNIE	SAME	
238	166 5/8	ADAIR	87	0	0	0	0 0/8	0	0	0	0	ELFRINK	DAN	SAME	
238	166 5/8	MERCER	88	72 7/8	76 1/8	21 7/8	0 0/8	26 7/8	26 7/8	5	5	GOODIN	JERRY	SAME	
238	166 5/8	BATES	90	80 6/8	76 6/8	24 2/8	10 1/8	27 4/8	26 4/8	7	7	MORELAND	DALLAS	SAME	
238	166 5/8	DEKALB	94	84 1/8	75 6/8	16 7/8	0	25 0/8	24 2/8	6	5	NIECE	PAUL	SAME	
244	166 4/8	BUCHANAN	82	79 6/8	76 3/8	21 3/8	3 3/8	28 1/8	27 5/8	6	6	FIMPLE	MIKE	SAME	
244	166 4/8	SHANNON	83	78 6/8	77 6/8	18 2/8	1 6/8	23 6/8	22 6/8	7	6	GEORGE	DENVER D.	SAME	
244	166 4/8	KNOX	87	79 1/8	79 3/8	17 7/8	3 3/8	25 6/8	25 4/8	6	8	MAUZY	TOM	SAME	
244	166 4/8	RIPLEY	91	76 3/8	74 2/8	18 2/8	0	25 6/8	25 4/8	5	5	McGOWAN	JACK	SAME	
244	166 4/8	CALDWELL	92	75 6/8	75 1/8	19 2/8	0	26 4/8	25 7/8	6	6	HUNTER	RON	SAME	
249	166 3/8	WASHINGTON	49	75 1/8	83 1/8	17 5/8	0	26 5/8	26 2/8	5	6	ROUSAN	BERN	SAME	
249	166 3/8	IRON	83	76 5/8	77 4/8	18 6/8	3 1/8	25 4/8	26 4/8	5	6	CLIBURN	JAMES	SAME	
249	166 3/8	DAVIESS	88	78 3/8	78 4/8	17 2/8	4 3/8	25 1/8	25 1/8	6	7	KLINE	HOMER	SAME	
249	166 3/8	LACLEDE	88	76 3/8	75 1/8	17 5/8	0	25 5/8	25 2/8	5	5	MOYERS	GERALD D.	SAME	
249	166 3/8	MONTGOMERY	90	79 7/8	78 7/8	18 5/8	7 6/8	28 2/8	27 2/8	7	7	HAM	THOMAS	SAME	
249	166 3/8	TEXAS	90	81 7/8	77 7/8	17 3/8	0	27 2/8	26 4/8	6	5	PAMPERIEN	GREG	SAME	
255	166 2/8	PIKE	75	77 7/8	77 2/8	20 3/8	0	26 2/8	27 5/8	5	5	NICOSIA	RAYMOND	SAME	
255	166 2/8	CAMDEN	79	75 2/8	75 6/8	16 2/8	0	21 6/8	21 6/8	6	6	WOLFE	NELLIE JANE	SAME	

MISSOURI SHOW-ME BIG BUCKS CLUB RECORDS OF WHITETAIL DEER BY STATE, TYPICAL

STATE RANK	SCORE	COUNTY	YEAR TAKEN	INCHES TYPICAL R	L	INSIDE SPREAD	INCHES ABNORMAL	LENGTH MAIN BEAM R	L	NUMBER POINTS R	L	HUNTER	FIRST NAME	OWNER	FIRST NAME
255	166 2/8	VERNON	90	75 5/8	79 3/8	16 2/8	0	26 1/8	25 6/8	4	4	BRANNAN	ERWIN		SAME
255	166 2/8	CHARITON	95	78 2/8	82 0/8	20 0/8	8 4/8	26 3/8	25 4/8	7	6	MILONSKI	MIKE C.		SAME
259	166 1/8	SULLIVAN	82	77 2/8	76 5/8	19 1/8	3 4/8	25 5/8	25 5/8	6	5	GLIDEWELL	GREG		SAME
259	166 1/8	ST. CHARLES	89	78 3/8	79 3/8	19 4/8	5 1/8	26 3/8	26 3/8	6	8	VAILS	GARY		SAME
259	166 1/8	BOONE	93	75 1/8	74 2/8	20 3/8	0	25 3/8	26 2/8	5	5	HARMON	SCOTT		SAME
262	166 0/8	SHELBY	70	85 0/8	80 1/8	21 0/8	10 6/8	28 4/8	28 1/8	5	5	HAMMOND	JACK		SAME
262	166 0/8	ADAIR	74	75 5/8	77 3/8	18 2/8	0	26 7/3	26 1/8	5	5	DANIELS	NELSON		SAME
262	166 0/8	SCOTLAND	81	74 3/8	73 7/8	19 6/8	0	26 6/3	26 5/8	5	5	HYDE	ROY C.		SAME
262	166 0/8	ANDREW	86	72 5/8	76 0/8	21 4/8	0	23 7/8	23 5/8	5	5	SHIFFLETT	RANDY		SAME
262	166 0/8	CALLAWAY	88	77 1/8	80 4/8	16 2/8	4 4/8	24 2/8	24 6/8	7	6	WURM	TIM		SAME
262	166 0/8	MILLER	92	78 1/8	78 1/8	20 0/8	0	26 6/8	25 6/8	5	7	CASTEN	BRUCE		SAME
262	166 0/8	DAVIESS	95	77 2/8	78 1/8	19 4/8	0	26 0/8	26 2/8	6	6	LEWALLEN	GARY		SAME
269	165 7/8	FRANKLIN	80	75 2/8	76 4/8	17 1/8	0	24 5/8	25 0/8	5	5	REITZ	CARL J.		SAME
269	165 7/8	RAY	82	78 2/8	74 4/8	21 6/8	4 5/8	26 1/8	25 0/8	6	5	JOY	RICHARD P.	MODERN	MUZZLELOADING
269	165 7/8	MADISON	94	77 1/8	76 6/8	20 1/8	2 6/8	24 5/8	24 4/8	6	5	HELM	TONY JOE		SAME
269	165 7/8	MACON	95	73 7/8	75 4/8	19 1/8	0	27 4/8	28 5/8	5	5	PHILLIPS	JOHN A.		SAME
273	165 6/8	DAVIESS	73	80 7/8	74 5/8	21 2/8	0	26 4/8	25 6/8	5	5	HELDENBRAND	GERALD		SAME
273	165 6/8	CHARITON	92	79 4/8	77 6/8	16 6/8	0	22 7/8	23 2/8	6	6	HAGANS	ROBERT		SAME
273	165 6/8	HARRISON	94	75 0/8	74 2/8	20 0/8	0	26 3/8	26 3/8	5	5	FERREE	CLARK		SAME
276	165 5/8	RANDOLPH	66	78 6/8	79 2/8	20 1/8	0	25 2/8	26 1/8	5	5	MESSER	DAVID		SAME
269	165 5/8	RANDOLPH	77	77 2/8	80 0/8	22 0/8	7 5/8	24 7/8	24 2/8	5	7	RICKERTSEN	CHRIS M.		SAME
269	165 5/8	PHELPS	79	80 1/8	76 2/8	19 6/8	6 3/8	26 1/8	25 7/8	9	7	BLACK	STEVE		SAME
269	165 5/8	WARREN	85	81 3/8	78 1/8	17 7/8	0	24 2/8	24 4/8	6	5	GILDEHAUS	JAMES H.		SAME
269	165 5/8	GENTRY	86	80 3/8	77 7/8	18 6/8	7 5/8	24 5/8	24 6/8	7	6	BYRANT	JIM		SAME
269	165 5/8	SULLIVAN	90	75 2/8	76 3/8	17 6/8	1 3/8	23 2/8	24 2/8	5	6	MAGGART	DENNIS		SAME
269	165 5/8	FRANKLIN	90	74 6/8	76 5/8	19 5/8	0	25 5/8	25 2/8	5	5	FELLER	KEVIN		SAME
283	165 4/8	CHARITON	79	76 2/8	78 7/8	20 6/8	6 4/8	22 4/8	22 4/8	7	7	BURRIS	OWEN		SAME
283	165 4/8	KNOX	82	77 7/8	78 6/8	19 2/8	5 2/8	25 1/8	25 6/8	5	5	BOES	BRUCE		SAME
283	165 4/8	ATCHISON	88	81 3/8	75 7/8	19 2/8	4 2/8	28 5/8	26 3/8	7	6	HOWELL	MIKE		SAME
283	165 4/8	MACON	93	78 1/8	74 6/8	17 6/8	1 4/8	25 2/8	24 4/8	6	5	STEVENS	TONY		SAME
283	165 4/8	CHARITON	94	75 2/8	74 5/8	19 4/8	0	25 0/8	24 7/8	5	5	GIOVANINI	MICHAEL D.		SAME
288	165 3/8	LEWIS	67	76 4/8	74 3/8	24 2/8	1 3/8	28 4/8	28 1/8	5	6	HUDNUT	GILVIA B.		SAME

MISSOURI SHOW-ME BIG BUCKS CLUB RECORDS OF WHITETAIL DEER BY STATE, TYPICAL

STATE RANK	SCORE	COUNTY	YEAR TAKEN	INCHES TYPICAL R	L	INSIDE SPREAD	INCHES ABNORMAL	LENGTH MAIN BEAM R	L	NUMBER POINTS R	L	HUNTER	FIRST NAME	OWNER	FIRST NAME
288	165 3/8	CAPE GIRARDEAU	87	75 3/8	76 1/8	17 3/8	0	23 1/8	22 2/8	5	5	BURGFELD	LAWSON	SAME	
288	165 3/8	GRUNDY	89	74 3/8	79 1/8	16 7/8	0	25 0/8	25 3/8	5	5	HARRIS	CLAUDE	SAME	
288	165 3/8	MONROE	93	76 5/8	77 0/8	18 6/8	3 1/8	26 4/8	25 6/8	6	6	MEIER	LARRY	SAME	
288	165 3/8	HARRISON	95	75 6/8	76 2/8	19 1/8	0	25 4/8	24 0/8	5	5	SCHNEIDER	ROBERT S.	SAME	
293	165 2/8	SHELBY	66	73 2/8	73 1/8	22 7/8	0	25 0/8	23 4/8	5	5	CALDWELL	JAMES R.	SAME	
293	165 2/8	BUCHANAN	85	80 1/8	79 0/8	19 5/8	6 1/8	24 3/8	25 3/8	8	8	FARRELL	JAY	SAME	
293	165 2/8	PIKE	89	76 5/8	79 5/8	19 6/8	3 0/8	25 4/8	26 1/8	6	6	HENDERSON	JAMES	SAME	
296	165 1/8	FRANKLIN	46	79 1/8	77 2/8	20 1/8	3 0/8	27 0/8	25 7/8	5	6	WILSON	JAMES F.	SAME	
296	165 1/8	HARRISON	74	77 4/8	78 0/8	19 5/8	3 6/8	26 6/8	26 0/8	7	6	MAXWELL	ROGER L.	SAME	
296	165 1/8	PLATTE	91	74 4/8	76 1/8	18 1/8	0	25 4/8	24 7/8	5	5	STEWART	MICHAEL	SAME	
299	165 0/8	SHELBY	78	79 1/8	81 5/8	16 2/8	4 2/8	26 0/8	24 0/8	5	6	ELLIOTT	JACKSON D.	SAME	
299	165 0/8	MARIES	84	73 0/8	73 0/8	24 4/8	2 0/8	25 0/8	25 3/8	6	5	GRUBER	ROBERT W.	SAME	
299	165 0/8	ATCHISON	89	73 5/8	75 5/8	19 2/8	0	25 1/8	25 1/8	4	4	REOADES	VERNIE	SAME	
299	165 0/8	MILLER	92	74 0/8	76 5/8	19 0/8	0	24 4/8	24 6/8	5	5	MOSELEY	RANDY B.	SAME	
303	164 7/8	NODAWAY	72	81 0/8	84 3/8	15 6/8	10 7/8	26 2/8	26 6/8	7	7	McKEE	ROBERT	SAME	
303	164 7/8	HARRISON	85	77 5/8	71 4/8	22 1/8	0	26 5/8	26 5/8	5	4	ROBERTSON	JUNIOR	SAME	
303	164 7/8	CALLAWAY	86	76 0/8	81 5/8	16 6/8	1 5/8	23 5/8	23 4/8	7	7	QUICK	BOB	SAME	
303	164 7/8	PIKE	95	75 2/8	75 7/8	21 1/8	2 4/8	25 5/8	25 5/8	7	5	KIMBRO	BILL	SAME	
307	164 6/8	MILLER	54	77 2/8	74 6/8	19 4/8	3 6/8	26 0/8	26 1/8	7	5	ROBINETT	OSBY L.	RICHARDSON	TIM
307	164 6/8	SHELBY	71	75 0/8	80 0/8	17 4/8	2 0/8	24 7/8	24 4/8	6	5	PETERS	DONALD H.	SAME	
307	164 6/8	ST. CHARLES	74	72 0/8	72 5/8	24 6/8	0	25 3/8	25 7/8	4	4	HEALEY, JR.	COL. CR	SAME	
307	164 6/8	OSAGE	89	76 5/8	78 7/8	20 0/8	6 2/8	23 2/8	23 2/8	6	5	KAISER	MARK A.	SAME	
307	164 6/8	GRUNDY	89	77 2/8	80 2/8	19 2/8	5 2/8	23 7/8	25 0/8	6	6	TODD	RANDALL	SAME	
307	164 6/8	CALLAWAY	93	82 3/8	80 2/8	18 1/8	6 7/8	25 0/8	25 1/8	8	7	JUNGERMANN	GARY	SAME	
313	164 5/8	SULLIVAN	81	72 1/8	76 7/8	20 3/8	0	25 6/8	25 6/8	5	5	MURPHY	MARK D.	SAME	
313	164 5/8	PHELPS	81	75 7/8	78 6/8	17 3/8	0	23 5/8	24 5/8	6	6	MAXWELL	WAYNE	SAME	
313	164 5/8	CARROLL	84	73 1/8	78 2/8	21 0/8	1 4/8	25 4/8	26 4/8	6	5	GOEDEKE	RANDY	SAME	
313	164 5/8	CAMDEN	89	74 1/8	77 6/8	17 5/8	2 2/8	27 7/8	27 7/8	5	6	CAPPS	LESTER	SAME	
313	164 5/8	POLK	95	74 1/8	75 7/8	18 1/8	0	25 4/8	25 4/8	6	6	BUCKNER	LLOYD	SAME	
313	164 5/8	PLATTE	95	77 1/8	72 4/8	19 5/8	0	24 6/8	23 7/8	5	5	HIATT	CHRIS	SAME	
319	164 4/8	CHARITON	70	75 0/8	77 4/8	20 3/8	1 7/8	22 3/8	22 7/8	6	5	JOHNSON	WILLIAM	DECEASED	
319	164 4/8	MONITEAU	76	79 0/8	78 0/8	16 7/8	0	24 5/8	23 3/8	6	5	HICKAM	J.R.	SAME	

MISSOURI SHOW-ME BIG BUCKS CLUB RECORDS OF WHITETAIL DEER BY STATE, TYPICAL

STATE RANK	SCORE	COUNTY	YEAR TAKEN	INCHES TYPICAL R	INCHES TYPICAL L	INSIDE SPREAD	INCHES ABNORMAL	LENGTH MAIN BEAM R	LENGTH MAIN BEAM L	NUMBER POINTS R	NUMBER POINTS L	HUNTER	FIRST NAME	OWNER	FIRST NAME
319	164 4/8	CLARK	86	78 3/8	82 1/8	19 3/8	4 5/8	25 7/8	26 1/8	7	5	REDDING	JERRY	SAME	
319	164 4/8	PETTIS	87	75 0/8	75 0/8	20 4/8	0	24 4/8	25 4/8	6	6	TEMPLETON	LARRY	SAME	
319	164 4/8	CHARITON	88	74 2/8	77 4/8	18 0/8	0	25 1/8	25 4/8	5	5	DUNIVENT	SEAN	SAME	
319	164 4/8	DENT	89	75 2/8	75 4/8	19 0/8	0	22 5/8	23 1/8	5	5	BOOKER	LYNDELL	SAME	
319	164 4/8	COOPER	92	78 0/8	78 7/8	19 1/8	6 3/8	26 0/8	26 4/8	7	6	PAINTER	BOB	SAME	
319	164 4/8	OSAGE	94	77 2/8	73 7/8	17 2/8	0	25 1/8	24 7/8	5	5	ROESLEIN	DERRICK	SAME	
319	164 4/8	MACON	94	74 3/8	79 1/8	17 6/8	1 1/8	24 4/3	24 1/8	6	5	WISDOM	GEORGE W.	SAME	
328	164 3/8	COLE	87	80 6/8	76 5/8	16 0/8	1 2/8	25 3/8	22 4/8	5	6	LEPPER	CURTIS A.	SAME	
328	164 3/8	CLARK	89	75 0/8	76 1/8	19 1/8	0	26 3/8	25 4/8	5	5	BERHORST	ALAN	SAME	
328	164 3/8	SALINE	92	76 4/8	75 3/8	17 7/8	0	24 4/8	25 0/8	5	5	RICHARDSON	WILLIAM L.	SAME	
328	164 3/8	AUDRAIN	95	73 5/8	79 0/8	18 1/8	0	23 6/8	24 2/8	5	6	QUALLS	DAVE	SAME	
332	164 2/8	MACON	77	76 0/8	73 7/8	20 4/8	1 0/8	27 2/8	25 4/8	6	5	DEMORY	LLOYD	SAME	
332	164 2/8	RANDOLPH	79	72 5/8	75 0/8	21 3/8	1 5/8	24 4/8	25 2/8	6	5	CATER	JERRY	SAME	
332	164 2/8	CARTER	82	77 3/8	74 7/8	19 2/8	0	26 6/8	27 2/8	5	5	GOLDSCHMIDT	A.L.	SAME	
332	164 2/8	CALLAWAY	83	75 5/8	77 3/8	17 4/8	0	25 4/8	25 4/8	6	5	UNDERWOOD	LARRY	SAME	
332	164 2/8	WARREN	85	75 6/8	74 5/8	20 0/8	0	25 3/8	25 2/8	5	5	HANDLANG	MELVIN	SAME	
332	164 2/8	CRAWFORD	87	81 1/8	78 1/8	19 1/8	6 2/8	24 7/8	26 5/8	7	6	LARUE	PHIL	SAME	
332	164 2/8	LIVINGSTON	87	76 3/8	74 2/8	18 0/8	0	24 4/8	25 0/8	5	5	THOMPSON	MARK E.	SAME	
332	164 2/8	DAVIESS	89	76 0/8	77 0/8	16 7/8	2 5/8	25 1/8	24 3/8	6	6	MORT	KENNETH	SAME	
332	164 2/8	GENTRY	91	74 1/8	74 7/8	19 2/8	0	25 6/8	25 7/8	5	6	WILLIAMS	LLOYD	SAME	
332	164 2/8	MONTGOMERY	94	76 2/8	78 0/8	18 4/8	4 2/8	24 4/8	25 0/8	7	5	GROSSE	BEN	SAME	
332	164 2/8	RAY	95	74 5/8	75 6/8	17 0/8	0	24 3/8	24 4/8	5	5	PRUITT	DOUG	SAME	
332	164 2/8	HENRY	96	75 6/8	74 4/8	16 6/8	0	23 3/8	23 4/8	5	5	WILLIAMS	RONALD	SAME	
332	164 2/8	HENRY	96	74 4/8	74 3/8	19 6/8	0	25 2/8	25 6/8	5	5	MILLER, JR.	LARRY G.	SAME	
345	164 1/8	BOONE	80	76 7/8	72 6/8	19 1/8	0	25 2/8	25 0/8	6	5	WYATT	CHRISTOPHER	SAME	
345	164 1/8	LEWIS	83	76 6/8	79 3/8	16 6/8	3 0/8	26 6/8	25 0/8	5	5	EWING	L. DALE	SAME	
345	164 1/8	CALLAWAY	92	73 5/8	74 7/8	18 5/8	0	24 7/8	24 3/8	5	5	RAILTON, JR.	EDGAR J.	SAME	
345	164 1/8	ADAIR	93	74 2/8	75 6/8	17 6/8	1 1/8	24 6/8	24 5/8	5	6	BAUMGARTNER	RODNEY	SAME	
349	164 0/8	MONITEAU	74	75 4/8	75 1/8	19 4/8	1 6/8	25 4/8	26 2/8	6	6	McPHERSON	JOHN	SAME	
349	164 0/8	RANDOLPH	75	75 3/8	74 0/8	19 4/8	1 4/8	23 6/8	24 0/8	6	6	THOMAS	JAMES	SAME	
349	164 0/8	MARIES	83	79 2/8	78 1/8	15 3/8	5 3/8	24 0/8	24 5/8	5	7	POGUE	JOHN	SAME	
349	164 0/8	ST. FRANCOIS	89	75 0/8	72 1/8	22 5/8	1 3/8	25 4/8	26 2/8	5	6	HENSON	SHARON	SAME	

MISSOURI SHOW-ME BIG BUCKS CLUB RECORDS OF WHITETAIL DEER BY STATE, TYPICAL

STATE RANK	SCORE	COUNTY	YEAR TAKEN	INCHES TYPICAL R	L	INSIDE SPREAD	INCHES ABNORMAL	LENGTH MAIN BEAM R	L	NUMBER POINTS R	L	HUNTER	FIRST NAME	OWNER	FIRST NAME
349	164 0/8	LINN	89	79 1/8	76 4/8	16 6/8	4 6/8	26 2/8	25 6/8	7	6	YARDLEY	BRADY	SAME	
349	164 0/8	DEKALB	89	72 1/8	79 1/8	18 6/8	0	26 7/8	27 0/8	4	5	FURGESON	ARLEY	SAME	
349	164 0/8	HOLT	92	75 6/8	80 1/8	17 6/8	0	23 4/8	22 6/8	5	6	MONTGOMERY	EDWARD	SAME	
356	163 7/8	CARROLL	72	79 4/8	72 2/8	18 1/8	0	26 2/8	26 2/8	5	5	MANSFIELD	HAROLD G.	SAME	
356	163 7/8	MONROE	83	80 4/8	83 2/8	21 1/8	9 6/8	26 6/8	27 6/8	9	7	BALL	DARREN	SAME	
356	163 7/8	COLE	84	77 7/8	83 6/8	18 1/8	8 6/8	24 0/8	24 4/8	9	7	LISTER	RICK	SAME	
356	163 7/8	MONITEAU	86	77 1/8	86 3/8	16 1/8	4 2/8	24 1/8	23 0/8	5	7	WILSON	RANDY	SAME	
356	163 7/8	HOWARD	87	76 7/8	79 5/8	16 1/8	0	24 1/8	25 4/8	5	6	HUGGANS	MIKE	SAME	
356	163 7/8	CALLAWAY	88	74 0/8	75 6/8	17 3/8	0	23 3/8	23 5/8	5	5	PRETTYMAN	MARK	SAME	
356	163 7/8	TEXAS	89	74 1/8	74 4/8	20 5/8	2 4/8	25 6/8	25 2/8	5	7	NEUGEBAUER	LONNIE	SAME	
356	163 6/8	ST. LOUIS	71	85 4/8	74 7/8	18 7/8	1 0/8	26 3/8	22 7/8	6	5	KNIGHT	VEARL	SAME	
363	163 6/8	PIKE	73	76 3/8	75 7/8	19 5/8	3 5/8	27 5/8	29 4/8	6	4	MILAN	PHILLIP	SAME	
363	163 6/8	WRIGHT	80	75 5/8	75 5/8	16 4/8	0	26 0/8	26 6/8	5	5	WHITE	TONY	SAME	
363	163 6/8	CLINTON	85	80 4/8	75 3/8	18 6/8	0	24 4/8	23 1/8	5	5	MICK	DENNIS	SAME	
363	163 6/8	PLATTE	95	75 1/8	75 1/8	19 6/8	0	25 3/8	24 4/8	5	5	BASH	JEFF	SAME	
368	163 5/8	GRUNDY	83	77 0/8	73 5/8	19 1/8	0	28 1/8	26 1/8	5	5	COPELAND	KENNETH A.	SAME	
368	163 5/8	JACKSON	85	79 5/8	80 0/8	19 4/8	9 1/8	25 1/8	25 4/8	6	8	SHOTTON, JR.	CHARLES C.	SAME	
368	163 5/8	SHANNON	86	76 7/8	77 4/8	19 5/8	7 0/8	22 6/8	22 4/8	5	7	REYNOLDS	PAUL	SAME	
368	163 5/8	CHARITON	93	73 7/8	75 3/8	18 5/8	0	23 7/8	24 0/8	5	6	PATTERSON	FRED	SAME	
368	163 5/8	SCOTLAND	94	75 7/8	76 4/8	16 2/8	3 1/8	24 0/8	24 2/8	6	5	WATKINS	DALE E.	SAME	
373	163 4/8	CHARITON	74	77 1/8	77 5/8	18 2/8	5 6/8	25 0/8	24 5/8	6	6	ROBERTS, SR.	VIC	SAME	
373	163 4/8	MONITEAU	81	73 6/8	76 4/8	19 1/8	2 7/8	24 5/8	25 0/8	5	6	WHITE	CHRIS	SAME	
373	163 4/8	SCOTLAND	84	73 1/8	76 6/8	20 2/8	0	23 7/8	24 7/8	5	6	BRANDRIFF	RAYMOND E.	SAME	
373	163 4/8	HOWARD	90	73 7/8	73 5/8	19 0/8	0	24 0/8	24 3/8	5	5	BREWSTER	JIM	SAME	
373	163 4/8	MACON	91	72 3/8	73 7/8	21 2/8	0 0/8	24 5/8	23 7/8	5	5	ALLEN	CALVIN	SAME	
378	163 3/8	BOONE	73	77 6/8	78 1/8	18 4/8	6 7/8	26 2/8	26 4/8	6	6	THOMPSON	CHESTER	SAME	
378	163 3/8	ADAIR	74	77 2/8	78 3/8	20 1/8	0	27 0/8	27 5/8	4	5	CAMERON	MIKE	SAME	
378	163 3/8	NODAWAY	89	84 6/8	80 3/8	17 4/8	6 7/8	28 4/8	26 7/8	5	8	DAVISON	JEFF	SAME	
378	163 3/8	RAY	94	72 1/8	75 6/8	22 5/8	0	25 7/8	26 4/8	5	5	HAYES	KERRY	SAME	
378	163 3/8	GRUNDY	94	75 5/8	78 2/8	16 7/8	0	23 6/8	23 7/8	5	5	NICHOLS	RONALD S.	SAME	
383	163 2/8	WARREN	59	80 6/8	78 1/8	19 0/8	3 0/8	25 0/8	26 5/8	7	6	AVERY	ALTON	SAME	
383	163 2/8	KNOX	67	77 2/8	79 1/8	18 6/8	7 4/8	26 6/8	26 6/8	6	5	PARTON	BOBBY DEAN	SAME	

STATE RANK	SCORE	COUNTY	YEAR TAKEN	INCHES TYPICAL R	L	INSIDE SPREAD	INCHES ABNORMAL	LENGTH MAIN BEAM R	L	NUMBER POINTS R	L	HUNTER	FIRST NAME	OWNER	FIRST NAME
383	163 2/8	BOONE	73	77 4/8	79 1/8	18 6/8	5 2/8	24 7/8	26 2/8	6	5	WELLS	JAMES K.	SAME	
383	163 2/8	MACON	77	73 1/8	75 3/8	17 4/8	0	24 1/8	24 3/8	5	5	KOGER	RICHARD	SAME	
383	163 2/8	MILLER	81	74 1/8	77 5/8	15 6/8	0	27 1/8	26 2/8	5	5	KINDER	JIM	SAME	
383	163 2/8	RALLS	82	75 6/8	74 2/8	19 4/8	1 2/8	24 5/8	25 4/8	5	6	FORD	FRANKIE	SAME	
383	163 2/8	WORTH	85	71 5/8	73 3/8	21 4/8	0	27 2/8	28 1/8	5	5	SPICER	GARY	SAME	
383	163 2/8	MERCER	90	79 0/8	77 1/8	17 4/8	5 0/8	25 7/8	26 5/8	5	7	TRAVIS	DAMON K.	SAME	
383	163 2/8	BUCHANAN	91	76 6/8	75 2/8	17 2/8	0	26 4/8	27 3/8	5	5	DONALDSON	JEFF	SAME	
392	163 1/8	WAYNE	67	74 3/8	72 7/8	19 7/8	0	24 6/8	25 2/8	5	5	FOX	JAMES	SAME	
393	163 0/8	SALINE	73	73 6/8	76 2/8	20 2/8	0	25 7/8	25 1/8	5	5	OWENS	STEVEN	SAME	
393	163 0/8	RANDOLPH	77	74 2/8	74 0/8	18 1/8	1 5/8	25 4/8	25 2/8	5	6	JOHNSON	GEORGE	SAME	
393	163 0/8	MERCER	83	75 3/8	77 1/8	18 2/8	0	26 2/8	27 0/8	6	5	NELSON	TRACY	SAME	
393	163 0/8	HARRISON	84	78 0/8	73 6/8	18 2/8	0	25 6/8	25 7/8	6	5	GIBSON	DONALD	SAME	
393	163 0/8	BENTON	85	74 0/8	77 4/8	18 0/8	0	24 2/8	24 3/8	5	5	THOMAS	ROBERT	SAME	
393	163 0/8	MARIES	86	76 6/8	75 6/8	14 0/8	0	21 1/8	20 5/8	5	5	HEMPE	JOHN E.	SAME	
393	163 0/8	HENRY	86	75 5/8	75 5/8	16 3/8	1 3/8	24 3/8	24 6/8	6	5	SOELDNER	JAMES	SAME	
393	163 0/8	HICKORY	86	77 5/8	74 3/8	17 2/8	0	25 2/8	24 0/8	5	6	PEARSON	GARY	SAME	
393	163 0/8	CARROLL	88	78 7/8	77 2/8	17 0/8	0	24 0/8	23 0/8	6	5	WEBB	JARED E.	SAME	
393	163 0/8	CHARITON	89	74 0/8	73 5/8	18 3/8	0	25 4/8	25 0/8	5	5	STILL	EDDIE	SAME	
393	163 0/8	POLK	90	74 6/8	78 0/8	21 7/8	5 3/8	27 2/8	27 5/8	6	6	WELLS	STACY	SAME	
393	163 0/8	HOWARD	91	72 1/8	77 3/8	22 2/8	0	27 1/8	27 6/8	5	5	NICHOLS	KEITH	SAME	
393	163 0/8	CALDWELL	96	75 7/8	76 3/8	17 0/8	2 0/8	24 5/8	26 2/8	5	6	ANDERSON	JEFFREY B.	SAME	
406	162 7/8	MACON	76	72 4/8	75 6/8	19 7/8	0	22 7/8	23 0/8	5	6	PIKE	FRANK	SAME	
406	162 7/8	MACON	88	76 0/8	75 4/8	16 0/8	4 7/8	24 3/8	24 5/8	8	7	WOOD	JERRY	SAME	
406	162 7/8	HOWARD	93	76 7/8	75 4/8	18 7/8	5 4/8	26 7/8	26 4/8	8	6	KAYLOR	JAY	SAME	
406	162 7/8	CASS	93	83 4/8	85 5/8	18 4/8	11 1/8	27 6/8	28 4/8	8	6	GOOSEY	RICK W.	SAME	
406	162 7/8	LINN	94	76 4/8	77 4/8	18 6/8	4 3/8	23 1/8	23 0/8	6	7	MORRIS	BILL	SAME	
411	162 6/8	FRANKLIN	84	73 5/8	77 4/8	17 7/8	0	25 0/8	24 6/8	5	5	KRIEFALL	DAN	SAME	
411	162 6/8	CLINTON	88	70 5/8	73 2/8	21 6/8	0	23 1/8	23 1/8	5	5	NORTON	DAVID	SAME	
411	162 6/8	WAYNE	89	75 6/8	75 6/8	18 4/8	5 0/8	26 4/8	26 7/8	7	6	STANFILL	RICK	SAME	
411	162 6/8	GRUNDY	90	75 3/8	81 2/8	16 1/8	1 3/8	26 4/8	26 2/8	4	6	NOE	J.R.	SAME	
411	162 6/8	CAMDEN	91	72 6/8	77 0/8	17 4/8	0	24 5/8	24 7/8	5	5	SCHMITT	BOB	SAME	
411	162 6/8	MONROE	96	77 2/8	73 5/8	18 7/8	2 7/8	26 2/8	25 7/8	6	5	BOWMAN	RALPH	SAME	

STATE RANK	SCORE	COUNTY	YEAR TAKEN	INCHES TYPICAL R	L	INSIDE SPREAD	INCHES ABNORMAL	LENGTH MAIN BEAM R	L	NUMBER POINTS R	L	HUNTER	FIRST NAME	OWNER	FIRST NAME
417	162 5/8	RAY	59	73 1/8	72 0/8	19 7/8	0	24 7/8	24 3/8	5	5	WRIGHT	PAUL	WRIGHT	SHERMAN
417	162 5/8	HARRISON	69	76 2/8	81 2/8	19 2/8	5 1/8	25 3/8	25 0/8	7	5	HILLYARD	LARRY	SAME	
417	162 5/8	LEWIS	70	73 5/8	75 2/8	17 1/8	0	24 4/8	25 4/8	5	5	SIMMONS	ART	SAME	
417	162 5/8	SULLIVAN	71	70 5/8	77 3/8	21 7/8	0	25 4/8	25 5/8	5	5	BOWE	LLOYD	SAME	
417	162 5/8	BOLLINGER	72	83 1/8	75 5/8	19 3/8	3 5/8	22 2/8	22 3/8	6	7	GOCKEL, JR.	JOE	SAME	
417	162 5/8	RANDOLPH	75	73 4/8	74 2/8	19 7/8	0	26 5/8	27 0/8	5	4	RICHARDS	MR.	MYERS	DAN
417	162 5/8	FRANKLIN	79	75 7/8	74 6/8	20 5/8	6 0/8	24 0/8	24 4/8	7	5	VAN LEER	DAN	SAME	
417	162 5/8	PUTNAM	84	75 3/8	85 3/8	19 2/8	2 7/8	28 2/8	28 5/8	6	5	PICKETT	DAVID	SAME	
417	162 5/8	MORGAN	85	76 0/8	75 7/8	20 3/8	0	25 3/8	23 0/8	6	6	AVEY	JEFFREY	SAME	
417	162 5/8	ST. CHARLES	85	74 1/8	73 3/8	19 7/8	0	27 2/8	27 4/8	5	5	HEILIGER	ROLAND	SAME	
417	162 5/8	LIVINGSTON	90	76 6/8	78 4/8	15 1/8	0	27 1/8	27 0/8	5	5	THOMPSON	CLARENCE	SAME	
417	162 5/8	HOWARD	91	73 5/8	78 0/8	21 4/8	5 5/8	26 3/8	26 2/8	6	7	POWELL	DERRICK	SAME	
417	162 5/8	PUTNAM	94	81 7/8	77 1/8	16 4/8	6 7/8	27 1/8	25 5/8	7	10	YOUNG	BRANDON	SAME	
417	162 5/8	KNOX	96	78 2/8	80 6/8	18 5/8	10 0/8	25 6/8	25 5/8	5	7	PERRIGO	DOUG	SAME	
431	162 4/8	RAY	70	77 3/8	75 0/8	23 2/8	3 0/8	29 0/8	28 0/8	6	5	OFFUTT	SAM	SAME	
431	162 4/8	CRAWFORD	71	84 2/8	72 3/8	18 4/8	0	25 7/8	26 2/8	6	5	MOUTRAY	TERRY	SAME	
431	162 4/8	MARIES	73	78 2/8	78 5/8	18 5/8	8 1/8	23 4/8	23 4/8	7	7	THOMAS	GREG	SAME	
431	162 4/8	PUTNAM	78	77 3/8	73 7/8	24 6/8	5 6/8	26 2/8	26 3/8	6	7	LARUE	LLOYD	SAME	
431	162 4/8	ADAIR	79	78 7/8	82 6/8	24 2/8	12 4/8	25 4/8	25 7/8	6	8	LEDFORD	STEVE	SAME	
431	162 4/8	COOPER	85	76 6/8	76 2/8	19 2/8	6 4/8	23 7/8	22 3/8	6	5	THURMAN	DENNIS	SAME	
431	162 4/8	GENTRY	87	72 2/8	72 6/8	21 0/8	0	26 0/8	25 6/8	4	4	BUERKY	GARY	SAME	
431	162 4/8	ST. LOUIS	92	77 4/8	76 4/8	17 4/8	0	24 3/8	24 6/8	6	6	LEUTHAUSER	SCOTT	SAME	
439	162 3/8	NODAWAY	59	0	0	0	0	0	0	0	0	ADKINS	FRANKLIN T.	DECEASED	
439	162 3/8	SULLIVAN	67	73 5/8	75 6/8	16 5/8	0	23 1/8	24 0/8	5	5	JEFFRIES	EDWIN	SAME	
439	162 3/8	MACON	70	73 0/8	75 4/8	17 5/8	0	24 6/8	24 7/8	5	5	WILLIAMS	DWIGHT	SAME	
439	162 3/8	MERCER	71	71 1/8	74 2/8	20 1/8	0	23 3/8	23 2/8	5	5	THOMPSON	E.J.	SAME	
439	162 3/8	TANEY	74	76 2/8	73 3/8	17 5/8	0	27 7/8	27 7/8	5	5	NEWBERRY	DAVID	SAME	
439	162 3/8	CHARITON	76	73 5/8	75 5/8	18 3/8	0	24 4/8	24 1/8	5	5	JOHNSON	SAM	SAME	
439	162 3/8	SALINE	78	75 6/8	78 0/8	18 0/8	6 1/8	25 4/8	25 4/8	7	7	CRAMER	DAVID L.	SAME	
439	162 3/8	JACKSON	86	77 5/8	72 6/8	18 0/8	0	24 2/8	24 3/8	6	6	COOKSTON	STEVE	SAME	
439	162 3/8	MARIES	93	73 5/8	76 7/8	16 7/8	0	23 6/8	24 6/8	6	5	MESSERSMITH	RICHARD	SAME	
439	162 3/8	HOWARD	94	74 2/8	81 6/8	19 6/8	1 5/8	27 2/8	27 6/8	6	6	DOBSON	KEVIN	SAME	

MISSOURI SHOW--ME BIG BUCKS CLUB RECORDS OF WHITETAIL DEER BY STATE, TYPICAL

STATE RANK	SCORE	COUNTY	YEAR TAKEN	INCHES TYPICAL R	L	INSIDE SPREAD	INCHES ABNORMAL	LENGTH MAIN BEAM R	L	NUMBER POINTS R	L	HUNTER	FIRST NAME	OWNER	FIRST NAME
439	162 3/8	BENTON	95	77 0/8	81 4/8	18 5/8	0	25 7/8	24 7/8	6	6	KESTNER	MARK	SAME	
439	162 3/8	PUTNAM	96	72 6/8	74 6/8	20 7/8	3 0/8	26 6/8	27 5/8	4	6	HABERBERGER	MARK E.	SAME	
451	162 2/8	SULLIVAN	73	74 7/8	73 7/8	17 4/8	1 4/8	25 3/8	25 4/8	6	5	CREASON	JOHN	SAME	
451	162 2/8	BUCHANAN	75	80 7/8	76 4/8	19 4/8	4 4/8	27 0/8	28 0/8	5	5	DONALDSON	FRED	SAME	
451	162 2/8	CALLAWAY	82	73 4/8	71 4/8	20 6/8	0	27 0/8	25 2/8	5	5	THOMAS	RANDY	SAME	
451	162 2/8	SCOTLAND	85	77 0/8	80 1/8	17 7/8	9 1/8	24 3/8	24 4/8	7	7	McBEE	JIM L.	SAME	
455	162 1/8	MADISON	83	78 0/8	77 4/8	19 0/8	9 1/8	27 5/8	26 4/8	8	8	MORICE	VIRGIL C.	SAME	
455	162 1/8	WARREN	88	77 2/8	74 3/8	18 1/8	0	25 0/8	25 4/8	7	6	KLEWEIS	ED	SAME	
455	162 1/8	WORTH	88	77 4/8	79 5/8	19 2/8	6 3/8	25 2/8	26 2/8	5	8	LYNCH	MIKE	SAME	
455	162 1/8	SCOTLAND	90	77 4/8	76 2/8	19 3/8	5 2/8	25 0/8	24 5/8	7	6	POHLERS	MIKE	SAME	
455	162 1/8	GENTRY	90	84 2/8	76 7/8	20 5/8	9 2/8	29 4/8	30 1/8	7	6	PARMAN	MARK	SAME	
455	162 1/8	MORGAN	91	72 6/8	77 1/8	18 3/8	0	23 4/8	24 5/8	5	5	DOUGLAS	ERNIE	SAME	
455	162 1/8	COLE	96	77 2/8	74 3/8	17 4/8	1 1/8	24 0/8	24 6/8	7	6	RACKERS	CARL	SAME	
462	162 0/8	LINCOLN	60	73 6/8	73 6/8	21 0/8	0	24 7/8	26 0/8	5	5	STARKEY	ROBERT	SAME	
462	162 0/8	ADAIR	81	74 7/8	77 6/8	13 4/8	0	21 4/8	22 6/8	5	5	MAGNESS	MIKE	SAME	
462	162 0/8	PIKE	86	73 2/8	71 4/8	18 6/8	0	24 7/8	24 5/8	5	5	DROSTE	LOUIS N.	SAME	
462	162 0/8	DEKALB	92	70 6/8	72 5/8	25 2/8	1 4/8	25 7/8	24 3/8	6	5	CROWLEY	DOYLE	SAME	
462	162 0/8	KNOX	96	79 7/8	80 3/8	17 3/8	8 3/8	28 7/8	29 0/8	6	9	LINDEMANN	STEVE	SAME	
467	161 7/8	PULASKI	53	73 6/8	75 6/8	19 5/8	2 0/8	24 2/8	25 6/8	5	6	SHOCKLEY	JOSEPH C.	SAME	
467	161 7/8	FRANKLIN	54	78 7/8	77 6/8	17 2/8	6 6/8	27 0/8	27 6/8	7	6	KOPPELMANN	TERRY	SAME	
467	161 7/8	MARION	87	74 3/8	74 1/8	16 5/8	0	23 4/8	24 4/8	5	5	SCHAEFER	JAMES	SAME	
467	161 7/8	CARROLL	88	74 5/8	76 4/8	20 5/8	0	24 4/8	25 5/8	5	5	MOORE	RAYMOND	DECEASED	
467	161 7/8	DEKALB	89	75 3/8	75 2/8	19 0/8	2 3/8	26 2/8	26 4/8	5	6	OWEN III	SAM	SAME	
467	161 7/8	SALINE	90	72 1/8	73 1/8	20 1/8	0	25 0/8	25 2/8	5	5	ALFREY	ROBERT	SAME	
467	161 7/8	DEKALB	91	79 6/8	77 1/8	18 4/8	8 7/8	24 0/8	24 2/8	9	5	COURTNEY	CHAD	SAME	
467	161 7/8	SALINE	94	76 6/8	79 4/8	15 3/8	0	23 4/8	24 0/8	6	6	NELSON	ED	SAME	
467	161 7/8	MONTGOMERY	94	74 0/8	73 5/8	19 5/8	0	23 4/8	23 3/8	5	5	ROSNER	MARK	SAME	
476	161 6/8	SCOTLAND	66	69 6/8	74 6/8	22 4/8	0	23 3/8	24 4/8	5	5	CHANCE	KEITH	SAME	
476	161 6/8	RANDOLPE	74	72 1/8	76 6/8	19 4/8	0	25 4/8	24 4/8	5	5	BROWNING	EDDIE	SAME	
476	161 6/8	SALINE	81	78 2/8	74 0/8	18 0/8	0	23 4/8	24 0/8	5	4	LAND	VIRGIL A.	SAME	
476	161 6/8	LINCOLN	86	75 6/8	74 4/8	15 2/8	0	25 6/8	23 4/8	5	5	NEUSUS	JACK	SAME	
476	161 6/8	LINCOLN	88	73 1/8	71 6/8	20 2/8	0	24 6/8	25 1/8	5	5	SITZE	RICHARD	SAME	

MISSOURI SHOW-ME BIG BUCKS CLUB RECORDS OF WHITETAIL DEER BY STATE, TYPICAL

STATE RANK	SCORE	COUNTY	YEAR TAKEN	INCHES TYPICAL R	L	INSIDE SPREAD	INCHES ABNORMAL	LENGTH MAIN BEAM R	L	NUMBER POINTS R	L	HUNTER	FIRST NAME	OWNER	FIRST NAME
476	161 6/8	SALINE	90	78 3/8	72 5/8	18 4/8	0	25 0/8	26 0/8	5	5	EDMONDS	PAUL	SAME	
476	161 6/8	WORTH	90	74 0/8	75 3/8	18 4/8	2 0/8	24 1/8	24 3/8	6	5	JAMES	DUANE	SAME	
476	161 6/8	RANDOLPH	92	77 5/8	77 2/8	20 2/8	4 4/8	28 3/8	28 5/8	6	5	BLOCK	NEIL	SAME	
476	161 6/8	HARRISON	92	77 4/8	76 6/8	15 4/8	0 0/8	23 4/8	23 4/8	5	5	MEEKS	BOB	SAME	
476	161 6/8	RANDOLPH	96	76 5/8	72 5/8	18 0/8	0	23 4/8	23 0/8	5	5	CONGER	KERRY	SAME	
486	161 5/8	HICKORY	66	73 2/8	75 7/8	17 0/8	1 1/8	23 0/8	24 5/8	6	6	HEARE	CHARLES E.	SAME	
486	161 5/8	NODAWAY	74	77 2/8	76 1/8	19 5/8	2 6/8	24 7/8	26 0/8	6	6	HILSABECK	ED	SAME	
486	161 5/8	PIKE	80	75 7/8	76 6/8	18 6/8	6 2/8	28 0/8	29 4/8	6	5	PRESTON	ROGER	SAME	
486	161 5/8	LINCOLN	83	74 2/8	74 0/8	16 5/8	0	25 6/8	25 4/8	5	5	BRAUNGARDT	JASON	SAME	
486	161 5/8	LEWIS	86	71 5/8	72 6/8	22 0/8	0	26 5/8	25 4/8	5	5	MASON	GENE	SAME	
486	161 5/8	DEKALB	88	74 3/8	76 7/8	18 3/8	3 2/8	24 0/8	24 6/8	7	5	MARTIN	JIM W.	SAME	
486	161 5/8	CHARITON	89	76 3/8	78 0/8	18 2/8	8 1/8	24 4/8	24 2/8	6	9	FULLINGTON	DON	SAME	
493	161 4/8	WEBSTER	67	71 7/8	79 3/8	20 6/8	1 6/8	26 4/8	25 5/8	7	5	ALCORN	BILLY J.	SAME	
493	161 4/8	BENTON	72	78 0/8	73 2/8	18 4/8	2 6/8	24 1/8	23 4/8	5	7	ROGERS	DUANE	SAME	
493	161 4/8	HARRISON	78	73 5/8	75 4/8	17 2/8	0	24 7/8	24 2/8	5	5	BOOTHE	WAYNE	SAME	
493	161 4/8	GASCONADE	78	75 6/8	75 5/8	17 6/8	1 4/8	22 4/8	23 5/8	6	5	HAVENER	DELBERT	SAME	
493	161 4/8	BATES	81	75 3/8	74 0/8	20 7/8	5 1/8	25 3/8	23 7/8	5	7	NULL	MARVIN	SAME	
493	161 4/8	CAMDEN	86	73 1/8	72 2/8	18 6/8	1 3/8	23 0/8	22 2/8	5	6	GOLDSBERRY	DAVID	SAME	
493	161 4/8	AUDRAIN	89	79 3/8	73 0/8	19 0/8	4 0/8	26 7/8	25 1/8	6	7	HENDRIX	WILLIAM	SAME	
493	161 4/8	ADAIR	90	76 7/8	78 6/8	16 4/8	2 2/8	25 2/8	24 1/8	7	6	ZEIGLER	LEON	SAME	
493	161 4/8	HOWARD	94	72 7/8	71 6/8	19 0/8	0	25 2/8	25 1/8	5	5	PRENTZLER	LARRY RAY	SAME	
493	161 4/8	OSAGE	95	74 5/8	76 6/8	19 1/8	1 1/8	24 1/8	25 1/8	6	7	TITUS	RUSSELL	SAME	
503	161 3/8	CHARITON	60	73 6/8	77 7/8	20 5/8	3 0/8	26 1/8	24 7/8	6	6	PENNINGTON	MARION	SAME	
503	161 3/8	COOPER	80	75 7/8	77 5/8	15 7/8	3 6/8	24 2/8	25 1/8	5	4	BRENGARTH	FRANCIS	SAME	
503	161 3/8	CHARITON	80	80 5/8	76 3/8	18 4/8	4 7/8	24 2/8	24 6/8	6	9	POPE	GARY	SAME	
503	161 3/8	OSAGE	80	76 5/8	78 2/8	17 0/8	4 1/8	24 0/8	25 2/8	6	6	WEBER	ROGER	SAME	
503	161 3/8	GRUNDY	81	81 4/8	86 7/8	13 2/8	11 7/8	26 1/8	26 2/8	8	9	STAMPER	JUNIOR	SAME	
503	161 3/8	KNOX	86	71 2/8	73 7/8	18 7/8	0	25 6/8	25 4/8	5	5	DIXSON	DALE	SAME	
503	161 3/8	ADAIR	89	75 1/8	73 6/8	21 0/8	3 7/8	26 5/8	26 6/8	7	5	MOYER	ANN	SAME	
503	161 3/8	KNOX	95	76 3/8	75 6/8	18 5/8	4 2/8	26 4/8	27 6/8	6	4	McARTHUR	BRAD	SAME	
503	161 3/8	JOHNSON	95	78 3/8	76 4/8	17 5/8	7 4/8	27 0/8	27 1/8	6	7	SHEETS	JIM	SAME	
512	161 2/8	CALLAWAY	74	74 0/8	78 1/8	16 6/8	0	24 3/8	24 2/8	5	5	UNDERWOOD	LARRY	SAME	

251

STATE RANK	SCORE	COUNTY	YEAR TAKEN	INCHES TYPICAL R	INCHES TYPICAL L	INSIDE SPREAD	INCHES ABNORMAL	LENGTH MAIN BEAM R	LENGTH MAIN BEAM L	NUMBER POINTS R	NUMBER POINTS L	HUNTER	FIRST NAME	OWNER	FIRST NAME
512	161 2/8	CAPE GIRARDEAU	84	72 6/8	74 5/8	19 0/8	0	25 1/8	25 2/8	5	5	BEUSSICK	PHILIP J.	SAME	
512	161 2/8	AUDRAIN	88	78 0/8	75 5/8	18 4/8	6 2/8	26 4/8	25 6/8	6	6	DAY	JOHN	SAME	
512	161 2/8	SCOTLAND	88	72 1/8	72 7/8	19 2/8	0	24 1/8	24 7/8	5	5	HARLAN	ROGER	SAME	
512	161 2/8	LEWIS	89	82 2/8	82 2/8	16 0/8	10 4/8	23 6/8	23 2/8	7	9	FOUST	LONNIE	SAME	
512	161 2/8	ADAIR	90	72 2/8	75 0/8	18 2/8	0	24 7/8	26 1/8	5	5	HUGHES	BRIAN W.	SAME	
512	161 2/8	CARROLL	90	73 5/8	72 6/8	19 0/8	1 6/8	26 6/8	25 6/8	6	5	DAVIES	DANNY	SAME	
512	161 2/8	HENRY	91	73 0/8	73 7/8	19 0/8	0	24 1/8	24 2/8	6	6	POWELL	JIM	SAME	
512	161 2/8	LEWIS	72	84 3/8	73 3/8	20 3/8	0	24 2/8	23 0/8	6	5	PENN	LARRY	SAME	
520	161 1/8	HOLT	74	76 1/8	75 2/8	16 3/8	0	24 1/8	25 3/8	6	6	TURNER	BRUCE	SAME	
520	161 1/8	SALINE	83	72 7/8	73 4/8	18 2/8	1 3/8	22 6/8	23 3/8	6	5	LEATHERS	MARK	SAME	
520	161 1/8	MACON	83	79 1/8	69 6/8	21 7/8	0	25 6/8	25 7/8	5	4	CARNAHAN	MAURIEDA	SAME	
520	161 1/8	HICKORY	87	73 4/8	75 4/8	19 4/8	1 5/8	25 1/8	26 4/8	5	6	DORMAN	MARVIN L.	SAME	
520	161 1/8	CALDWELL	88	73 6/8	75 3/8	15 5/8	0	22 2/8	22 5/8	5	5	MYERS	GARY	SAME	
520	161 1/8	PERRY	88	80 4/8	74 4/8	19 7/8	9 0/8	26 2/8	26 0/8	6	6	RENAUD	DARYL	SAME	
520	161 1/8	ADAIR	94	78 0/8	80 3/8	18 5/8	7 4/8	26 2/8	26 0/8	7	8	FIXX	VIVAN	SAME	
520	161 1/8	ATCHISON	95	78 3/8	80 4/8	20 2/8	8 7/8	26 3/8	28 0/8	8	6	GROFF	GREG	SAME	
520	161 1/8	BOONE	96	74 5/8	74 1/8	17 3/8	0	23 4/8	22 6/8	6	6	SCHULTE	LARRY	SAME	
530	161 0/8	SCOTLAND	71	79 3/8	75 4/8	18 2/8	6 4/8	25 4/8	23 6/8	7	6	WAGNER	MICHAEL E.	SAME	
530	161 0/8	SHELBY	77	70 6/8	72 2/8	20 4/8	0	25 0/8	25 0/8	5	5	LONG	DAVID	SAME	
530	161 0/8	SCHUYLER	83	72 3/8	74 7/8	17 0/8	0	22 6/8	23 3/8	5	5	GIBSON	DEAN	SAME	
530	161 0/8	LINCOLN	84	82 2/8	76 2/8	20 2/8	7 2/8	25 5/8	23 5/8	6	8	WELLS	RON	SAME	
530	161 0/8	STODDARD	95	73 0/8	74 7/8	20 4/8	0	27 0/8	25 3/8	5	5	LANDEWEE	PAUL F.	SAME	
535	160 7/8	WASHINGTON	66	71 2/8	72 6/8	23 2/8	2 7/8	25 6/8	26 5/8	5	7	PENNOCK	NORBERT	SAME	
535	160 7/8	WASHINGTON	69	78 1/8	74 7/8	15 7/8	0	23 4/8	24 3/8	6	5	CLANTON	BYRON	SAME	
535	160 7/8	ADAIR	70	82 6/8	72 3/8	19 5/8	0	26 0/8	26 3/8	5	4	HUTCHESON	RUSSEL	SAME	
535	160 7/8	ST. CHARLES	76	73 4/8	73 1/8	17 1/8	0	24 1/8	23 6/8	5	5	SCHULTE	DANIEL D.	SAME	
535	160 7/8	GENTRY	79	75 6/8	81 4/8	18 4/8	6 0/8	24 2/8	25 0/8	6	9	JENSEN	JOE	SAME	
535	160 7/8	MONTGOMERY	87	76 3/8	81 6/8	15 5/8	1 0/8	27 5/8	26 4/8	5	6	ALVAREZ	DENNIS	SAME	
535	160 7/8	CALLAWAY	91	73 6/8	74 2/8	14 7/8	0	25 1/8	24 7/8	5	5	ATTERBERRY	TIM	SAME	
535	160 7/8	LINN	91	72 6/8	76 0/8	17 3/8	0 0/8	24 7/8	25 3/8	5	6	BURNS	KEVIN	SAME	
543	160 6/8	WASHINGTON	62	73 1/8	71 4/8	18 0/8	0	24 2/8	23 7/8	5	5	SUMPTER	MONROE	SAME	
543	160 6/8	DALLAS	69	78 0/8	75 4/8	15 7/8	4 3/8	25 2/8	23 1/8	6	6	EVANS	JERRY	SAME	

MISSOURI SHOW-ME BIG BUCKS CLUB RECORDS OF WHITETAIL DEER BY STATE, TYPICAL

STATE RANK	SCORE	COUNTY	YEAR TAKEN	INCHES TYPICAL R	INCHES TYPICAL L	INSIDE SPREAD	INCHES ABNORMAL	LENGTH MAIN BEAM R	LENGTH MAIN BEAM L	NUMBER POINTS R	NUMBER POINTS L	HUNTER	FIRST NAME	OWNER	FIRST NAME
543	160 6/8	CHRISTIAN	69	73 7/8	80 3/8	18 0/8	2 6/8	25 0/8	24 4/8	4	5	SHIPMAN	FARRIS	SAME	
543	160 6/8	MARIES	77	76 3/8	72 1/8	17 0/8	2 0/8	25 0/8	23 6/8	5	5	BENNEKE	ANTHONY	SAME	
543	160 6/8	CRAWFORD	82	77 0/8	79 1/8	19 1/8	6 5/8	21 7/8	23 0/8	7	9	VALLEY	GEORGE	SAME	
543	160 6/8	HOWARD	87	71 2/8	76 5/8	21 5/8	2 5/8	24 6/8	24 3/8	5	8	WOOD	ROB	SAME	
543	160 6/8	PHELPS	90	73 6/8	73 7/8	16 2/8	0	22 4/8	22 2/8	5	5	DEUSER	RICHARD	SAME	
543	160 6/8	SCHUYLER	92	79 1/8	74 5/8	18 3/8	6 1/8	26 6/8	26 6/8	7	6	SUMMERS	JOE	SAME	
543	160 6/8	CHARITON	93	74 2/8	79 2/8	18 1/8	5 1/8	26 5/8	26 6/8	6	8	POPE	ROGER	SAME	
543	160 6/8	GREENE	95	85 1/8	75 6/8	19 2/8	3 6/8	28 0/8	27 6/8	5	6	KROPF	STEPHEN	SAME	
553	160 5/8	PULASKI	54	73 1/8	70 0/8	21 7/8	1 2/8	26 5/8	26 2/8	6	5	CHAMBERS	HERBERT	SAME	
553	160 5/8	MONROE	69	71 1/8	69 5/8	21 5/8	0	27 4/8	26 7/8	4	4	YUSKO	ANDREW	SAME	
553	160 5/8	MONTGOMERY	87	82 0/8	81 3/8	15 6/8	10 7/8	24 1/8	24 4/8	8	8	WAELDER	KEVIN	SAME	
553	160 5/8	RANDOLPH	88	69 2/8	71 7/8	24 3/8	0	28 0/8	26 7/8	4	4	POLLARD	MARK W.	SAME	
553	160 5/8	CAMDEN	88	73 7/8	72 1/8	19 3/8	0	23 7/8	25 3/8	5	5	STENSON	LEROY	SAME	
553	160 5/8	MACON	90	74 3/8	80 2/8	17 5/8	0	25 5/8	25 5/8	5	6	LENZINI, JR.	JOHN	SAME	
553	160 5/8	PULASKI	94	73 0/8	74 6/8	21 5/8	5 6/8	26 0/8	26 4/8	6	7	KOECHLING	RICHARD	SAME	
560	160 4/8	CAMDEN	81	71 6/8	70 6/8	19 0/8	0	23 3/8	23 3/8	5	5	DORF	MICHAEL P.	SAME	
560	160 4/8	NODAWAY	83	72 4/8	71 7/8	19 1/8	0	26 3/8	27 1/8	5	5	WALLACE	DICK	SAME	
560	160 4/8	RAY	85	77 0/8	74 0/8	19 2/8	0	24 4/8	25 3/8	5	5	KIRK	DOUGLAS	SAME	
560	160 4/8	RANDOLPH	85	79 7/8	75 3/8	20 1/8	1 1/8	24 2/8	23 5/8	8	5	HAYES	ROY	SAME	
560	160 4/8	DAVIESS	87	70 0/8	74 7/8	21 0J/8	00	24 4/8	25 0/8	5	5	BOYD	SAM	SAME	
560	160 4/8	WAYNE	88	75 0/8	78 2/8	19 1/8	1 3/8	27 3/8	27 2/8	6	4	ROACH	CARL	SAME	
560	160 4/8	COOPER	90	79 1/8	75 0/8	20 4/8	9 2/8	26 0/8	24 0/8	6	9	WOOD	TOM	SAME	
560	160 4/8	PUTNAM	90	72 6/8	73 0/8	20 5/8	1 5/8	27 7/8	26 3/8	5	6	TORREY	MARK	SAME	
560	160 4/8	OSAGE	92	73 5/8	72 0/8	18 2/8	0	25 1/8	24 3/8	5	5	LUECKE	LEON	SAME	
560	160 4/8	SALINE	92	75 2/8	78 2/8	19 3/8	1 1/8	25 6/8	25 6/8	6	6	CRIST	WILLIAM E.	SAME	
560	160 4/8	DAVIESS	92	74 4/8	76 0/8	21 4/8	9 0/8	24 5/8	25 0/8	8	6	BROWN	JOHN T.	SAME	
560	160 4/8	GRUNDY	94	74 0/8	79 5/8	18 4/8	0	26 1/8	27 0/8	5	5	KASEY	JAMES	SAME	
560	160 4/8	SALINE	95	76 7/8	76 5/8	21 2/8	11 6/8	25 6/8	26 4/8	6	7	EVANS	BRAD	SAME	
560	160 4/8	LINN	96	75 4/8	72 0/8	17 0/8	0	25 6/8	25 3/8	5	5	ATKINSON	CAMDEN	SAME	
574	160 3/8	SCOTLAND	70	70 7/8	75 2/8	20 2/8	0	25 2/8	24 5/8	5	5	SHELLEY	LARRY	SAME	
574	160 3/8	IRON	73	72 0/8	72 5/8	19 5/8	0	24 1/8	25 2/8	5	5	STEWART	JAMES	SAME	
574	160 3/8	DENT	83	70 3/8	73 4/8	20 5/8	0	24 2/8	24 0/8	5	5	CONLEY	CHRIS	SAME	

253

MISSOURI SHOW-ME BIG BUCKS CLUB RECORDS OF WHITETAIL DEER BY STATE, TYPICAL

STATE RANK	SCORE	COUNTY	YEAR TAKEN	INCHES TYPICAL R	INCHES TYPICAL L	INSIDE SPREAD	INCHES ABNORMAL	LENGTH MAIN BEAM R	LENGTH MAIN BEAM L	NUMBER POINTS R	NUMBER POINTS L	HUNTER	FIRST NAME	OWNER	FIRST NAME
574	160 3/8	KNOX	87	75 4/8	76 7/8	20 5/8	7 6/8	26 3/8	26 5/8	5	6	HOOD	LARRY	SAME	
574	160 3/8	DAVIESS	88	79 1/8	80 2/8	19 2/8	2 7/8	26 5/8	26 6/8	7	6	BOWMAN	BRENT	SAME	
574	160 3/8	CARROLL	93	94 2/8	73 3/8	17 6/8	1 3/8	24 5/8	23 6/8	8	6	DREW	GARY C.	SAME	
574	160 3/8	SULLIVAN	94	77 0/8	76 2/8	19 1/8	4 4/8	23 0/8	23 5/8	6	9	GLIDEWELL	BRANDON	SAME	
574	160 3/8	CHARITON	94	79 7/8	78 1/8	15 5/8	8 4/8	25 4/8	26 4/8	6	7	GROSVENOR	CHARLES H.	SAME	
574	160 3/8	LINCOLN	95	74 5/8	76 0/8	15 0/8	1 7/8	25 0/8	24 4/8	6	5	CREECH	SCOTT	SAME	
574	160 3/8	CASS	96	71 3/8	74 3/8	20 1/8	2 0/8	24 7/8	24 7/8	5	6	ATKINSON	MARVIN	SAME	
574	160 2/8	ST. LOUIS	68	74 3/8	76 0/8	19 2/8	4 4/8	24 6/8	24 6/8	6	5	WATTS	THEODORE C.	SAME	
584	160 2/8	DAVIESS	71	72 3/8	71 3/8	19 4/8	0	23 0/8	22 6/8	5	5	STOUT	CLAUDE	SAME	
584	160 2/8	PETTIS	82	76 0/8	71 5/8	17 0/8	0	25 2/8	24 2/8	5	5	LAWTON	ARTHUR	SAME	
584	160 2/8	NEWTON	82	74 2/8	81 2/8	16 0/8	2 6/8	22 6/8	24 3/8	5	6	REYNOLDS	HARLAN	SAME	
584	160 2/8	CAMDEN	86	73 2/8	70 3/8	21 2/8	0	23 3/8	23 4/8	6	6	BEASLEY	WADE	SAME	
584	160 2/8	MARIES	87	74 5/8	72 2/8	18 6/8	2 6/8	24 7/8	24 7/8	6	6	YORK	DARREL J.	SAME	
584	160 2/8	CALDWELL	88	80 5/8	79 6/8	18 2/8	11 4/8	26 6/8	28 4/8	8	8	CAMPBELL	SCOTT	SAME	
584	160 2/8	BATES	88	76 4/8	79 1/8	19 5/8	5 3/8	26 4/8	27 1/8	7	6	LEEMASTERS	MIKE	SAME	
584	160 2/8	McDONALD	89	74 5/8	71 6/8	17 2/8	0	25 3/8	25 1/8	5	5	BRIXEY	WILLARD	SAME	
584	160 2/8	ANDREW	90	77 2/8	82 5/8	19 2/8	13 4/8	27 2/8	28 4/8	6	6	SHEETS	NINA	SAME	
584	160 2/8	MARIES	92	72 5/8	71 6/8	18 0/8	0	22 6/3	22 1/8	5	5	SEYMORE	MURL	SAME	
584	160 2/8	MORGAN	92	72 7/8	74 5/8	20 2/8	3 6/8	23 4/3	25 0/8	5	6	BRUNJES	MARK	SAME	
584	160 2/8	ST. LOUIS	92	80 2/8	71 6/8	17 6/8	0	27 0/8	25 4/8	6	5	SHELTON	ERIC	SAME	
584	160 2/8	CASS	94	76 5/8	71 0/8	19 0/8	0	26 2/8	25 1/8	5	5	GARRETT	DONNY	SAME	
584	160 2/8	GASCONADE	95	71 0/8	77 2/8	19 6/8	1 4/8	26 4/8	27 0/8	6	5	GOODMAN	RICK	SAME	
599	160 1/8	CLARK	65	70 3/8	73 2/8	19 7/8	0	24 3/8	24 1/8	5	5	ACKLIE	NEAL	SAME	
599	160 1/8	ST. FRANCOIS	67	69 7/8	69 1/8	21 3/8	2 0/8	25 0/8	25 0/8	5	5	SMITH	JAMES	SAME	
599	160 1/8	NODAWAY	82	75 4/8	70 7/8	21 6/8	1 3/8	28 1/8	27 7/8	4	5	AUFERT	CHARLES	SAME	
599	160 1/8	CALLAWAY	85	72 0/8	75 4/8	18 7/8	1 4/8	25 7/8	26 1/8	6	6	BACKER, SR.	FORREST	SAME	
599	160 1/8	ST. CHARLES	87	74 2/8	78 5/8	21 2/8	6 5/8	26 2/8	25 4/8	5	5	FITZPATRICK	MAURICE	SAME	
599	160 1/8	PIKE	94	77 5/8	82 6/8	19 2/8	10 0/8	25 0/8	25 2/8	7	5	BURNER	MATT	SAME	
605	160 0/8	BOONE	66	70 7/8	74 0/8	21 7/8	1 7/8	25 6/8	26 7/8	5	4	PENBERTHY	LARRY	SAME	
605	160 0/8	RAY	67	73 2/8	71 2/8	21 0/8	0	25 0/8	24 0/8	5	5	WRIGHT	DALE	SAME	
605	160 0/8	MONTGOMERY	71	73 4/8	72 4/8	16 6/8	0	25 5/8	24 6/8	5	5	SCHULTE	GERALD	SAME	
605	160 0/8	GREENE	72	70 6/8	73 5/8	19 6/8	0	25 5/8	25 1/8	5	5	ROBERTS	MIKE	SAME	

254

MISSOURI SHOW-ME BIG BUCKS CLUB RECORDS OF WHITETAIL DEER BY STATE, TYPICAL

STATE RANK	SCORE	COUNTY	YEAR TAKEN	INCHES TYPICAL R	L	INSIDE SPREAD	INCHES ABNORMAL	LENGTH MAIN BEAM R	L	NUMBER POINTS R	L	HUNTER	FIRST NAME	OWNER	FIRST NAME
605	160 0/8	GASCONADE	75	74 3/8	72 4/8	16 4/8	0	22 6/8	22 4/8	5	5	FRICKE	VIRGIL	SAME	
605	160 0/8	CRAWFORD	77	74 4/8	75 1/8	17 0/8	2 4/8	23 5/8	24 7/8	6	6	HUBLER	JOE	SAME	
605	160 0/8	ANDREW	79	73 5/8	80 0/8	17 2/8	3 0/8	26 5/8	27 3/8	6	5	HORN	BILL	SAME	
605	160 0/8	CAMDEN	80	72 0/8	72 6/8	16 0/8	0	21 0/8	21 2/8	5	5	FREDERICK	GARY	SAME	
605	160 0/8	CALDWELL	80	72 4/8	74 4/8	19 2/8	2 0/8	24 3/8	24 1/8	6	5	SWEENEY	GREG	MCDANIEL	JOHNNY
605	160 0/8	CAMDEN	82	74 3/8	73 1/8	16 2/8	0	22 0/8	22 5/8	5	5	WILLIAMS	JACK	SAME	
605	160 0/8	COOPER	84	73 4/8	70 4/8	20 0/8	0	23 0/8	22 3/8	5	5	SMITH	NANCY	SAME	
605	160 0/8	BOONE	91	72 7/8	71 4/8	18 2/8	0	24 4/8	24 6/8	5	5	RAY	LARRY	SAME	
605	160 0/8	KNOX	93	74 4/8	72 5/8	19 3/8	2 5/8	24 4/8	24 5/8	5	6	HARSELL	MICHAEL	SAME	
605	160 0/8	GENTRY	94	75 3/8	83 6/8	18 6/8	7 6/8	24 5/8	26 3/8	9	7	LEDBETTER	CURTIS	SAME	
605	160 0/8	SCHUYLER	95	70 3/8	72 3/8	20 2/8	0 0/8	24 5/8	26 1/8	5	5	LEWIS	WILLIAM R.	SAME	
620	159 7/8	WASHINGTON	57	73 3/8	73 1/8	17 1/8	0	26 4/8	26 1/8	4	4	MASON	GEORGE	DECEASED	
620	159 7/8	FRANKLIN	63	75 3/8	73 1/8	18 7/8	3 5/8	24 0/8	23 6/8	5	6	SCHUTTENBERG	THEODORE T.	SAME	
620	159 7/8	CHARITON	86	71 4/8	73 6/8	18 5/8	0	24 7/8	25 4/8	4	4	ARGETSINGER	BRIAN D.	SAME	
620	159 7/8	CALDWELL	88	69 7/8	72 2/8	20 7/8	0	23 4/8	23 2/8	5	6	FIELDS	RICHARD	SAME	
620	159 7/8	LINCOLN	88	72 1/8	72 2/8	18 5/8	0	22 0/8	22 5/8	5	5	OWENS	BILL	SAME	
620	159 7/8	RANDOLPH	89	72 1/8	74 2/8	19 4/8	2 3/8	23 5/8	23 7/8	5	6	RICKERTSEN	CHRIS M.	SAME	
620	159 7/8	RANDOLPH	90	76 2/8	73 4/8	18 5/8	0	24 5/8	25 1/8	5	5	STOEBE	DONNIE	SAME	
620	159 7/8	BATES	93	70 5/8	75 3/8	19 3/8	0	26 2/8	27 0/8	5	5	BOARD	BRIAN E.	SAME	
628	159 6/8	MERCER	75	72 3/8	74 3/8	15 2/8	0	23 2/8	25 2/8	5	5	SHAFFER	REVA L.	SAME	
628	159 6/8	PHELPS	82	79 4/8	74 2/8	17 7/8	4 7/8	23 3/8	23 3/8	7	6	SPENCER	ALLEN C.	SAME	
628	159 6/8	BENTON	83	70 2/8	73 1/8	20 2/8	0	23 5/8	24 0/8	5	5	KREISLER	DILLARD	SAME	
628	159 6/8	GASCONADE	85	72 3/8	71 7/8	19 2/8	0	22 6/8	23 4/8	4	4	RUWWE	CLYDE	SAME	
628	159 6/8	CASS	87	71 2/8	73 5/8	17 6/8	0	26 5/8	26 6/8	4	4	RUPARD	ROGER E.	SAME	
628	159 6/8	GASCONADE	87	74 4/8	74 6/8	18 6/8	8 0/8	24 4/8	24 4/8	0	0	THEISSEN	DANNY	SAME	
628	159 6/8	BOONE	88	71 5/8	78 1/8	20 2/8	3 6/8	23 6/8	25 6/8	5	7	MUELLER	GARY	SAME	
628	159 6/8	ANDREW	88	71 5/8	74 4/8	18 2/8	0	24 4/8	24 2/8	5	5	MANN	ROGER	SAME	
628	159 6/8	BATES	89	71 5/8	71 3/8	18 6/8	0	26 0/8	26 1/8	4	4	CLIFTON	DANNY	SAME	
628	159 6/8	HARRISON	89	73 7/8	76 1/8	19 7/8	3 1/8	24 2/8	24 0/8	6	6	RICHARDSON	JERRY	SAME	
628	159 6/8	CLINTON	89	73 0/8	73 4/8	17 0/8	0	28 1/8	27 7/8	5	5	CAIN	MICHAEL	SAME	
628	159 6/8	PETTIS	92	72 2/8	72 2/8	18 2/8	0	26 3/8	27 1/8	5	5	CORNINE	GARY	SAME	
628	159 6/8	GRUNDY	94	73 4/8	76 0/8	17 0/8	1 0/8	24 7/8	24 6/8	5	6	RICKETTS	BOB	SAME	

MISSOURI SHOW-ME BIG BUCKS CLUB RECORDS OF WHITETAIL DEER BY STATE, TYPICAL

STATE RANK	SCORE	COUNTY	YEAR TAKEN	INCHES TYPICAL R	INCHES TYPICAL L	INSIDE SPREAD	INCHES ABNORMAL	LENGTH MAIN BEAM R	LENGTH MAIN BEAM L	NUMBER POINTS R	NUMBER POINTS L	HUNTER	FIRST NAME	OWNER	FIRST NAME
641	159 5/8	COOPER	62	72 3/8	76 4/8	19 0/8	2 1/8	25 1/8	24 1/8	6	5	JEWETT	GILL	SAME	
641	159 5/8	CALLAWAY	72	76 2/8	74 3/8	18 6/8	3 3/8	27 0/8	25 1/8	7	5	WEKENBORG	THOMAS L.	SAME	
641	159 5/8	SCHUYLER	77	74 2/8	71 0/8	19 5/8	1 0/8	26 1/8	26 0/8	6	5	WHEELER	TERRY	SAME	
641	159 5/8	PUTNAM	79	79 3/8	76 4/8	18 1/8	0	25 3/8	25 5/8	5	5	FISHER	MARK	SAME	
641	159 5/8	HOLT	81	73 3/8	74 4/8	17 7/8	1 4/8	22 7/8	22 6/8	6	5	ARNDT	RANDY	SAME	
641	159 5/8	SCOTLAND	84	72 5/8	72 5/8	18 3/8	0	24 5/8	24 6/8	6	6	ADAMS	JOHN W.	SAME	
641	159 5/8	GREENE	86	73 0/8	73 4/8	16 5/8	0	23 2/8	23 6/8	4	4	BENNETT	MARK	SAME	
641	159 5/8	DADE	87	80 4/8	76 7/8	17 5/8	3 0/8	27 2/8	25 2/8	6	6	BARTHOLOMEW	EDWARD	SAME	
641	159 5/8	KNOX	87	72 7/8	75 5/8	19 1/8	3 4/8	23 3/8	25 0/8	5	6	KLOCKE	MARK RALPH	SAME	
641	159 5/8	CLARK	91	70 5/8	73 5/8	24 6/8	4 1/8	24 7/8	25 4/8	7	6	WILKINSON, JR.	PHIL E.	SAME	
641	159 5/8	HARRISON	92	75 0/8	76 2/8	13 5/8	1 0/8	24 2/3	24 6/8	5	6	VANDEVENDER	KEITH	SAME	
641	159 5/8	MORGAN	94	74 3/8	73 4/8	18 3/8	0	24 7/3	24 3/8	5	5	WALSH	JEFF	SAME	
641	159 5/8	MILLER	94	74 3/8	73 6/8	20 0/8	4 1/8	23 6/8	22 7/8	8	7	SCHULTE	WAYNE	SAME	
654	159 4/8	CALDWELL	74	72 7/8	76 5/8	22 5/8	0	26 0/8	27 0/8	6	6	SHELTON	J.T.	SAME	
654	159 4/8	SCOTLAND	76	69 6/8	74 7/8	21 4/8	0	26 4/8	25 7/8	4	5	YORK	DARRELL	SAME	
654	159 4/8	COOPER	82	70 7/8	68 7/8	22 6/8	0	24 2/8	24 1/8	5	5	JOBE	CARL	SAME	
654	159 4/8	NEWTON	84	72 7/8	75 0/8	18 0/8	1 2/8	24 2/8	24 1/8	7	6	VERMILLION	BOB	SAME	
654	159 4/8	PETTIS	86	71 1/8	76 3/8	19 0/8	0	25 2/8	24 3/8	5	5	SIMON	BOB	SAME	
654	159 4/8	CALLAWAY	88	74 1/8	72 7/8	16 0/8	0	24 1/8	25 0/8	5	5	MEINHARDT	SHAWN	SAME	
654	159 4/8	ST. CLAIR	90	76 0/8	72 7/8	15 6/8	0	26 5/8	26 5/8	5	5	MOORE	CHARLES L.	SAME	
654	159 4/8	SULLIVAN	90	72 6/8	71 6/8	18 6/8	0	23 6/8	24 2/8	5	5	HOCKER	ROGER	SAME	
654	159 4/8	REYNOLDS	90	72 4/8	72 7/8	18 0/8	0	25 3/8	25 4/8	5	5	COWIN	RANDY L.	SAME	
654	159 4/8	LAWRENCE	94	71 6/8	75 6/8	17 0/8	0	23 5/8	23 6/8	5	5	BAX	DEREK A.	SAME	
654	159 4/8	RAY	95	77 1/8	76 4/8	17 7/8	3 1/8	24 4/8	25 0/8	7	5	TEMPLETON	EDDIE	SAME	
665	159 3/8	FRANKLIN	40	73 3/8	74 7/8	18 1/8	1 4/8	21 7/8	24 2/8	7	6	BRUEGGEMANN	ADOLPH	SAME	
665	159 3/8	ADAIR	66	72 5/8	72 3/8	20 3/8	0	25 7/8	24 5/8	5	5	BRAGG	PAUL	SAME	
665	159 3/8	MONTGOMERY	78	72 7/8	76 2/8	16 5/8	0	24 2/8	22 7/8	5	5	DEVLIN	GENE	SAME	
665	159 3/8	RALLS	80	77 7/8	75 5/8	19 2/8	8 3/8	25 4/8	25 1/8	7	8	RILEY	HARRY L.	SAME	
665	159 3/8	PUTNAM	83	73 0/8	73 4/8	17 7/8	0	24 2/8	23 6/8	5	5	LARUE	LLOYD	SAME	
665	159 3/8	CAPE GIRARDEAU	88	74 1/8	77 5/8	20 3/8	6 6/8	25 2/8	26 1/8	7	7	HINDMAN	KIM	SAME	
665	159 3/8	DAVIESS	91	72 4/8	73 3/8	20 3/8	2 6/8	26 2/8	26 4/8	6	5	FULLER	NORMA C.	SAME	
665	159 3/8	RANDOLPH	93	77 1/8	72 4/8	16 1/8	0	22 6/8	22 1/8	5	5	WILSON	DARRELL	SAME	

MISSOURI SHOW-ME BIG BUCKS CLUB RECORDS OF WHITETAIL DEER BY STATE, TYPICAL

STATE RANK	SCORE	COUNTY	YEAR TAKEN	INCHES TYPICAL R	L	INSIDE SPREAD	INCHES ABNORMAL	LENGTH MAIN BEAM R	L	NUMBER POINTS R	L	HUNTER	FIRST NAME	OWNER	FIRST NAME
665	159 3/8	CLARK	95	72 7/8	74 3/8	20 6/8	2 3/8	27 3/8	26 7/8	5	6	STURM	ROCKY	SAME	
665	159 3/8	COOPER	96	72 0/8	73 1/8	20 5/8	1 2/8	25 3/8	24 5/8	6	5	VOSS	ALLEN A.	SAME	
675	159 2/8	ATCHISON	74	78 6/8	75 4/8	17 5/8	7 1/8	27 1/8	26 1/8	6	8	SCHOMBURG	WARREN	SAME	
675	159 2/8	FRANKLIN	74	74 1/8	73 0/8	18 4/8	0	25 2/8	25 0/8	6	5	HAID	DANNY	SAME	
675	159 2/8	HARRISON	79	74 1/8	75 5/8	19 4/8	6 0/8	24 6/8	24 4/8	7	6	McBROOM	JAMES K.	SAME	
675	159 2/8	HOWARD	81	75 0/8	69 5/8	20 6/8	0	27 1/8	26 4/8	5	4	BUCK	DEAN	SAME	
675	159 2/8	CALDWELL	84	74 5/8	74 0/8	15 7/8	0	23 4/8	23 0/8	5	5	MYERS	GARY	SAME	
675	159 2/8	GASCONADE	89	79 1/8	72 2/8	16 5/8	1 5/8	27 3/8	25 6/8	5	5	AHONEN	JOHN	SAME	
675	159 2/8	GASCONADE	89	72 5/8	73 4/8	17 0/8	0	24 0/8	24 4/8	5	5	OLDFATHER	RAY	SAME	
675	159 2/8	CHARITON	90	77 3/8	73 7/8	17 1/8	3 7/8	23 1/8	22 1/8	5	6	WRIGHT	GARY	SAME	
675	159 2/8	CARROLL	93	70 4/8	71 5/8	19 2/8	0	23 6/8	23 2/8	5	5	PARKER	JAMES	SAME	
675	159 2/8	MONROE	94	71 2/8	73 3/8	18 2/8	0	25 3/8	24 5/8	5	5	LEHENBAUER	BOB	SAME	
675	159 2/8	LINCOLN	96	75 0/8	75 5/8	18 2/8	3 4/8	24 7/8	25 6/8	6	6	CHARTRAND	LONNIE	SAME	
675	159 2/8	GASCONADE	UNK	72 0/8	72 3/8	19 6/8	0	26 0/8	26 7/8	5	5	WEST	RON	SAME	
675	159 1/8	SCHUYLER	74	70 5/8	71 3/8	22 1/8	0	22 1/8	22 3/8	5	5	FREMON	W.G.	SAME	
687	159 1/8	SCOTLAND	76	72 7/8	74 2/8	16 7/8	2 4/8	23 4/8	23 1/8	5	6	BARICKMAN	TOM	SAME	
687	159 1/8	MACON	80	71 0/8	73 7/8	18 5/8	0	24 7/8	24 3/8	5	5	HOUPT	CARL	SAME	
687	159 1/8	CHARITON	84	74 4/8	71 4/8	20 7/8	1 2/8	22 2/8	21 2/8	5	6	WARD	ROBERT	SAME	
687	159 1/8	MONTGOMERY	86	76 4/8	75 1/8	21 1/8	9 1/8	25 0/8	25 4/8	7	6	SCHLANKER	FRANK	SAME	
687	159 1/8	MERCER	89	72 7/8	77 4/8	17 0/8	0	23 2/8	24 4/8	6	6	RALSTON	MIKE	SAME	
687	159 1/8	HOLT	91	78 7/8	75 0/8	19 6/8	3 3/8	26 0/8	26 1/8	6	6	DEGENHARDT	JOHN	SAME	
687	159 1/8	WARREN	94	79 3/8	71 1/8	17 7/8	0	27 6/8	25 6/8	5	5	KLEIMAN	KENNETH M.	SAME	
695	159 0/8	ADAIR	59	69 6/8	75 0/8	21 2/8	0	23 1/8	24 7/8	5	5	DOUGLAS	LEON	SAME	
695	159 0/8	MONROE	73	73 4/8	74 5/8	17 1/8	2 7/8	26 2/8	26 2/8	5	6	BOZOIAN	DR. HARRY	SAME	
695	159 0/8	TEXAS	76	72 5/8	73 3/8	17 0/8	0	25 0/8	25 0/8	5	5	FUNK	DAVID	SAME	
695	159 0/8	DAVIESS	76	72 2/8	70 5/8	20 6/8	0	23 6/8	24 4/8	5	5	SALMON	RALPH	SAME	
695	159 0/8	SHELBY	80	76 6/8	74 4/8	15 0/8	3 2/8	25 3/8	24 1/8	5	6	COLLINS	JIM	SAME	
695	159 0/8	ST. CHARLES	82	73 1/8	81 0/8	16 4/8	1 2/8	24 2/8	23 7/8	5	6	BOLLMANN	JEFF	SAME	
695	159 0/8	HOLT	82	69 0/8	71 4/8	21 6/8	0	26 4/8	26 2/8	5	5	MUNYAN	LARRY	SAME	
695	159 0/8	DENT	86	79 0/8	77 3/8	15 4/8	4 2/8	23 7/8	24 5/8	6	5	KEENEY	ED	SAME	
695	159 0/8	BOONE	86	70 1/8	73 6/8	19 2/8	0	21 4/8	24 1/8	5	5	SHAWVER	CHARLES	SAME	
695	159 0/8	CRAWFORD	86	75 7/8	70 5/8	19 0/8	1 2/8	23 3/8	22 6/8	5	6	WILMESHERR	STANLEY	SAME	

MISSOURI SHOW-ME BIG BUCKS CLUB RECORDS OF WHITETAIL DEER BY STATE, TYPICAL

STATE RANK	SCORE	COUNTY	YEAR TAKEN	INCHES TYPICAL R	L	INSIDE SPREAD	INCHES ABNORMAL	LENGTH MAIN BEAM R	L	NUMBER POINTS R	L	HUNTER	FIRST NAME	OWNER	FIRST NAME
695	159 0/8	SCOTLAND	88	78 0/8	76 1/8	18 7/8	7 7/8	24 2/8	24 2/8	6	6	HURST	TONY	SAME	
695	159 0/8	SALINE	89	73 6/8	71 4/8	17 3/8	1 1/8	25 0/8	25 0/8	5	6	GARR	MARK	SAME	
695	159 0/8	PUTNAM	91	73 4/8	71 4/8	18 4/8	0	24 4/8	24 6/8	5	5	RYERSON	RICK L.	SAME	
695	159 0/8	WARREN	92	81 4/8	72 7/8	17 6/8	0	23 3/8	22 4/8	6	6	KREPS	STEVE	SAME	
695	159 0/8	MONTGOMERY	93	75 4/8	82 5/8	21 7/8	7 7/8	27 0/8	27 2/8	8	6	GRIMES	STEVE	SAME	
695	159 0/8	ST. LOUIS	94	73 1/8	76 6/8	16 5/8	3 7/8	24 7/8	25 1/8	6	5	KREIENKAMP	STEVE	SAME	
695	159 0/8	RAY	94	71 3/8	77 4/8	18 4/8	0	27 4/8	27 1/8	5	5	HOLDER	KELLY D.	SAME	
712	158 7/8	MACON	73	71 6/8	70 6/8	21 7/8	0	24 0/8	25 0/8	5	5	BURKHART	VERN	SAME	
712	158 7/8	CLARK	80	80 1/8	73 6/8	20 2/8	5 3/8	24 1/8	23 6/8	6	7	COCHENOUR	GERALD	SAME	
712	158 7/8	AUDRAIN	80	78 5/8	73 2/8	17 4/8	3 1/8	23 2/8	23 7/8	6	7	SMITH	LARRY D.	SAME	
712	158 7/8	CALLAWAY	81	74 5/8	77 7/8	18 1/8	5 4/8	26 0/8	24 6/8	6	7	NEAL	LARRY	SAME	
712	158 7/8	FRANKLIN	87	73 7/8	71 6/8	17 5/8	0	23 2/8	22 7/8	5	5	LAWRENCE	TINA M.	SAME	
712	158 7/8	HENRY	88	72 4/8	71 5/8	22 1/8	4 0/8	26 7/8	26 1/8	6	5	RUCKER	LAVERNE	SAME	
712	158 7/8	OSAGE	90	76 6/8	77 4/8	14 7/8	4 0/8	22 0/8	21 4/8	7	7	COX	MIKE	SAME	
719	158 6/8	SCOTLAND	65	72 7/8	72 0/8	19 0/8	0	23 1/8	22 6/8	6	6	HOLTON	ROBERT E.	SAME	
719	158 6/8	DAVIESS	71	74 2/8	70 1/8	21 6/8	0	24 4/8	26 1/8	5	5	IDDINGS	ED	SAME	
719	158 6/8	PIKE	73	76 3/8	73 4/8	17 7/8	4 7/8	27 2/8	27 3/8	6	5	NOBLE	JOHN R.	SAME	
719	158 6/8	CALDWELL	73	83 4/8	73 3/8	18 6/8	3 4/8	23 0/8	23 2/8	7	7	TITTLE	GARY	SAME	
719	158 6/8	BARRY	75	73 1/8	71 6/8	18 1/8	2 1/8	23 0/8	23 0/8	6	5	FAIRCHILD	PAUL	SAME	
719	158 6/8	MILLER	83	83 3/8	73 2/8	18 0/8	4 6/8	24 4/8	24 4/8	7	9	GRAVES	TOM	SAME	
719	158 6/8	BARRY	85	71 5/8	71 0/8	18 4/8	1 0/8	23 2/8	23 1/8	5	6	THOMAS	CLYDE L.	SAME	
719	158 6/8	MONROE	87	76 1/8	77 3/8	16 2/8	6 0/8	22 2/8	22 4/8	6	5	WHEELER	MIKE	SAME	
719	158 6/8	DENT	87	70 3/8	69 5/8	22 2/8	0	24 0/8	24 6/8	5	5	HINKLE	CARL	SAME	
719	158 6/8	SCOTLAND	88	74 1/8	79 0/8	16 0/8	5 4/8	22 4/8	22 7/8	5	7	YOUNG	DAVID	SAME	
719	158 6/8	GENTRY	88	73 0/8	71 5/8	18 0/8	0	23 6/8	22 4/8	5	5	SUTTON	ROBERT	SAME	
719	158 6/8	ST. CHARLES	88	76 4/8	77 6/8	22 2/8	10 5/8	25 3/8	27 0/8	7	7	COLYER	JOHN D.	SAME	
719	158 6/8	LEWIS	90	74 2/8	72 7/8	18 4/8	4 0/8	24 1/8	24 2/8	6	8	SEAY	JAMES H.	SAME	
719	158 6/8	CARROLL	90	72 0/8	74 7/8	20 4/8	3 2/8	26 0/8	27 0/8	6	5	AVERSMAN	DONALD	SAME	
719	158 6/8	MORGAN	96	71 0/8	71 1/8	19 0/8	0	23 0/8	23 2/8	5	5	NOLTING	JEFF	SAME	
719	158 6/8	CHARITON	96	79 4/8	74 6/8	16 4/8	1 4/8	21 0/8	21 2/8	6	7	GOOCH	JERRY	SAME	
735	158 5/8	BARRY	87	74 1/8	74 2/8	15 4/8	2 5/8	24 1/8	23 5/8	6	6	THURMAN	RICHARD	SAME	
735	158 5/8	ANDREW	93	71 7/8	75 0/8	17 6/8	2 1/8	24 4/8	24 3/8	6	6	FLORA	PATTY	SAME	

MISSOURI SHOW-ME BIG BUCKS CLUB RECORDS OF WHITETAIL DEER BY STATE, TYPICAL

STATE RANK	SCORE	COUNTY	YEAR TAKEN	INCHES TYPICAL R	L	INSIDE SPREAD	INCHES ABNORMAL	LENGTH MAIN BEAM R	L	NUMBER POINTS R	L	HUNTER	FIRST NAME	OWNER	FIRST NAME
735	158 5/8	TEXAS	93	75 0/8	73 7/8	15 7/8	1 6/8	24 1/8	25 0/8	6	5	SCANTLIN	DAVID	SAME	
735	158 5/8	WASHINGTON	95	70 6/8	70 6/8	19 7/8	0	25 6/8	25 6/8	5	5	JOHNSON	JEFFREY	SAME	
739	158 4/8	RANDOLPH	59	72 6/8	71 7/8	20 4/8		23 3/8	25 5/8	6	6	CHISM	ROBERT	SAME	
739	158 4/8	CAPE GIRARDEAU	66	70 6/8	71 1/8	18 4/8	0	22 6/8	22 3/8	5	5	JONES	EUGENE	SAME	
739	158 4/8	SCOTLAND	67	71 4/8	77 5/8	19 4/8	0	26 0/8	26 0/8	5	5	HOSKINSON	BILL	SAME	
739	158 4/8	RANDOLPH	69	71 3/8	71 4/8	20 4/8	1 0/8	26 0/8	26 3/8	5	4	BOWDEN	DANNY	SAME	
739	158 4/8	GENTRY	82	74 2/8	71 2/8	16 6/8	0	24 2/8	23 1/8	5	5	YOUNG	RANDALL	SAME	
739	158 4/8	OZARK	84	73 0/8	72 5/8	17 2/8	1 1/8	23 5/8	25 0/8	5	6	HIXON	RAY	SAME	
739	158 4/8	WARREN	84	71 6/8	72 2/8	21 2/8	0	23 5/8	25 1/8	6	5	GERARD	TRAVIS	SAME	
739	158 4/8	MONROE	86	70 4/8	70 1/8	18 6/8	0	26 7/8	26 7/8	4	4	McMORRIS	JAMES R.	SAME	
739	158 4/8	ST. CHARLES	86	74 7/8	72 4/8	15 4/8	0	25 0/8	24 7/8	5	5	BUEKER	HARLAN	SAME	
739	158 4/8	ADAIR	87	76 2/8	81 3/8	17 0/8	4 0/8	25 3/8	25 0/8	9	6	CLAY	TERRY	SAME	
739	158 4/8	COLE	87	71 5/8	74 5/8	17 0/8	0	25 0/8	25 0/8	5	5	SCHEPERLE	RAY	SAME	
739	158 4/8	MONROE	89	77 2/8	76 4/8	19 6/8	5 2/8	27 5/8	26 6/8	6	5	RENCH	STEVE L.	SAME	
739	158 4/8	MARIES	95	71 7/8	72 5/8	19 4/8	0	27 1/8	27 4/8	5	4	BOYD	PATRICK J.	SAME	
739	158 4/8	KNOX	96	70 0/8	74 7/8	22 0/8	0	23 0/8	24 3/8	5	6	HETTINGER	RUSSELL	SAME	
739	158 3/8	PIKE	67	0	0	0	0	0	0	0	0	SHOTTEN	CHARLES	SAME	
753	158 3/8	HARRISON	70	75 6/8	73 5/8	21 1/8	6 0/8	23 3/8	23 5/8	8	7	LEWIS	ERNIE	SAME	
753	158 3/8	SCOTLAND	78	76 4/8	74 1/8	17 6/8	3 7/8	23 4/8	22 7/8	6	6	FRANKLIN	PAUL R.	SAME	
753	158 3/8	CALLAWAY	81	71 1/8	73 7/8	17 3/8	0	24 6/8	24 6/8	5	5	BURRE	KELLY	SAME	
753	158 3/8	SCOTLAND	88	71 0/8	74 3/8	16 3/8	0	21 2/8	21 2/8	6	5	BAIR	DOUG	SAME	
753	158 3/8	CARTER	91	68 1/8	67 2/8	25 5/8	0	26 5/8	26 3/8	4	4	LINDSEY	SCOTT	SAME	
753	158 3/8	JACKSON	93	71 1/8	77 5/8	21 2/8	4 0/8	27 6/8	27 3/8	5	7	GARRETSON	SHAYNE	SAME	
753	158 3/8	DENT	94	75 5/8	77 7/8	16 5/8	2 4/8	21 4/8	22 0/8	7	7	LIGHT	HERSHEL	SAME	
753	158 3/8	PUTNAM	95	76 2/8	73 0/8	17 7/8	1 4/8	23 3/8	22 2/8	7	5	COWIE	KAREN	SAME	
753	158 3/8	CHARITON	96	71 0/8	71 3/8	18 1/8	0	23 5/8	24 1/8	5	5	HALL	REV. RICKY L.	SAME	
763	158 2/8	CHARITON	59	70 3/8	71 1/8	20 6/8	0	23 0/8	24 0/8	5	5	WOHLGEMUTH	VERNON	SAME	
763	158 2/8	MARION	61	82 6/8	71 0/8	16 2/8	0	26 7/8	25 6/8	6	4	McELWEE	BURYL	SAME	
763	158 2/8	HARRISON	77	71 3/8	71 7/8	19 0/8	0	24 7/8	25 3/8	5	5	BENNETT	CARL	SAME	
763	158 2/8	OSAGE	82	73 3/8	72 0/8	18 5/8	2 1/8	23 7/8	22 6/8	5	6	BOLTEN	DELBERT	SAME	
763	158 2/8	LINCOLN	83	78 2/8	80 6/8	17 4/8	6 4/8	26 2/8	27 7/8	8	7	PORTER	RAY	SAME	
763	158 2/8	COLE	87	75 7/8	74 4/8	21 2/8	0	23 1/8	23 3/8	6	6	CROCKER	DENNY	SAME	

MISSOURI SHOW-ME BIG BUCKS CLUB RECORDS OF WHITETAIL DEER BY STATE, TYPICAL

STATE RANK	SCORE	COUNTY	YEAR TAKEN	INCHES TYPICAL R	INCHES TYPICAL L	INSIDE SPREAD	INCHES ABNORMAL	LENGTH MAIN BEAM R	LENGTH MAIN BEAM L	NUMBER POINTS R	NUMBER POINTS L	HUNTER	FIRST NAME	OWNER	FIRST NAME
763	158 2/8	AUDRAIN	87	74 3/8	74 1/8	18 1/8	2 1/8	23 4/8	25 7/8	6	5	DUNGAN	TERRY	SAME	
763	158 2/8	RAY	87	79 3/8	75 6/8	19 6/8	8 2/8	27 4/8	26 2/8	5	9	WHITE	BRAD	SAME	
763	158 2/8	SHELBY	88	70 6/8	73 1/8	17 6/8	0	26 0/8	26 0/8	4	5	MCEWEN	RANDY	SAME	
763	158 2/8	CALLAWAY	89	72 5/8	73 1/8	19 2/8	3 0/8	22 4/8	22 4/8	7	6	SUTTON	DOYLE	SAME	
763	158 2/8	GRUNDY	90	77 1/8	78 5/8	20 2/8	6 4/8	28 3/8	27 4/8	8	6	REED	ALLAN D.	SAME	
763	158 2/8	CALLAWAY	93	72 5/8	70 5/8	18 2/8	0	22 3/8	22 4/8	5	6	BROWNE	CHRIS	SAME	
763	158 2/8	WAYNE	95	78 4/8	78 2/8	15 6/8	6 4/8	23 7/8	24 6/8	7	5	ROSE	LARRY E.	SAME	
763	158 2/8	GASCONADE	95	70 6/8	72 2/8	20 0/8	2 0/8	25 4/8	25 6/8	6	5	TUSCHHOFF	RAYMOND	SAME	
777	158 1/8	SHELBY	67	72 2/8	74 3/8	17 5/8	0	24 0/8	23 7/8	5	5	BOUDREAU	WILLIAM L.	SAME	
777	158 1/8	MARIES	67	73 0/8	72 1/8	19 6/8	1 1/8	26 0/8	23 5/8	5	6	HONSE	HENRY	SAME	
777	158 1/8	BENTON	71	71 4/8	71 7/8	19 5/8	0	25 1/8	25 0/8	5	4	PERRY	E.R.	SAME	
777	158 1/8	GENTRY	75	82 0/8	75 4/8	22 7/8	9 0/8	25 1/8	27 7/8	6	8	DARNELL	KEVIN	SAME	
777	158 1/8	PERRY	77	75 7/8	76 1/8	14 6/8	3 5/8	21 7/8	20 4/8	5	7	WELKER	ROBERT	SAME	
777	158 1/8	HARRISON	82	83 2/8	74 7/8	19 5/8	11 6/8	26 4/8	26 3/8	6	6	BENNETT	FRED	SAME	
777	158 1/8	KNOX	86	70 0/8	70 0/8	21 3/8	0	26 3/8	26 0/8	5	5	MASTERS	GARY	SAME	
777	158 1/8	HARRISON	89	77 6/8	75 6/8	17 0/8	6 5/8	25 2/8	26 2/8	5	8	HILL	JARALD R.	SAME	
777	158 1/8	SCOTLAND	92	74 3/8	71 5/8	17 7/8	0	24 7/8	22 6/8	5	5	LEWIS	ROGER W.	SAME	
777	158 1/8	REYNOLDS	93	77 6/8	72 4/8	15 4/8	2 1/8	24 3/8	24 3/8	7	6	VOLNER	CLINTON S.	SAME	
777	158 1/8	SCHUYLER	96	72 1/8	72 1/8	16 3/8	0	24 1/8	24 3/8	5	5	BAILEY	MIKE C.	SAME	
788	158 0/8	HARRISON	63	75 7/8	72 7/8	18 4/8	5 4/8	25 5/8	24 6/8	6	8	BROWN	CLARENCE R.	SAME	
788	158 0/8	CALLAWAY	70	73 2/8	71 5/8	17 5/8	1 3/8	24 6/8	24 7/8	5	6	WYMAN	DANNY	SAME	
788	158 0/8	WARREN	73	70 5/8	71 3/8	18 2/8	0	25 6/8	25 2/8	5	5	BIERBAUM	EMMET W.	SAME	
788	158 0/8	CLARK	76	74 7/8	73 1/8	19 5/8	5 5/8	24 0/8	24 5/8	7	6	SMITH	ALBERT	SAME	
788	158 0/8	NEWTON	78	71 5/8	74 3/8	16 0/8	0	24 0/8	23 7/8	5	5	LUMMIS	PERRY	SAME	
788	158 0/8	STE. GENEIEVE	80	72 3/8	72 1/8	17 0/8	2 0/8	24 4/8	24 4/8	0	0	DRURY	KEITH	SAME	
788	158 0/8	DADE	85	71 0/8	76 7/8	18 2/8	0	23 6/8	23 3/8	5	6	MYERS	CHARLES A.	SAME	
788	158 0/8	SULLIVAN	86	70 2/8	69 4/8	18 2/8	0	22 3/8	23 1/8	5	5	MARTIN	CHARLES	SAME	
788	158 0/8	RAY	89	75 2/8	80 5/8	17 3/8	1 5/8	23 3/8	25 3/8	5	7	BELLIS	RAYMOND L.	SAME	
788	158 0/8	MERCER	89	70 2/8	70 3/8	22 0/8	0	23 1/8	24 0/8	5	5	EAKES	JASON	SAME	
788	158 0/8	COOPER	90	73 2/8	72 4/8	18 4/8	3 2/8	23 6/8	23 3/8	6	7	KOLLER	SCOTT	SAME	
788	158 0/8	SALINE	91	79 2/8	74 1/8	16 4/8	0	22 2/8	23 4/8	5	5	WISE	K. WAYNE	SAME	
788	158 0/8	PIKE	92	72 1/8	71 7/8	16 6/8	0	23 4/8	23 2/8	5	5	BROWN	KENNETH	SAME	

MISSOURI SHOW-ME BIG BUCKS CLUB RECORDS OF WHITETAIL DEER BY STATE, TYPICAL

STATE RANK	SCORE	COUNTY	YEAR TAKEN	INCHES TYPICAL R	L	INSIDE SPREAD	INCHES ABNORMAL	LENGTH MAIN BEAM R	L	NUMBER POINTS R	L	HUNTER	FIRST NAME	OWNER	FIRST NAME
788	158 0/8	BOONE	92	72 3/8	74 7/8	18 4/8	2 0/8	25 1/8	25 3/8	5	6	WISE	MIKE	SAME	
788	158 0/8	LINCOLN	93	70 5/8	71 5/8	18 4/8	1 0/8	22 2/8	22 1/8	6	5	GNADE	MARK	SAME	
788	158 0/8	CLARK	95	71 7/8	75 0/8	17 2/8	1 4/8	23 0/8	22 4/8	6	5	MORSE	BILL	SAME	
788	158 0/8	MILLER	96	71 5/8	76 0/8	19 7/8	3 5/8	23 2/8	23 4/8	6	7	HOWSER	EDWARD A.	SAME	
788	158 0/8	DAVIESS	96	71 0/8	71 0/8	18 4/8	0	24 2/8	23 7/8	5	5	LEE	MELVIN	SAME	
806	157 7/8	CAPE GIRARDEAU	59	69 3/8	72 1/8	22 5/8	0	25 5/8	24 2/8	5	6	BOREN	ROLAND	BOREN	MRS. ROLAND
806	157 7/8	BOONE	86	73 6/8	74 4/8	19 1/8	1 0/8	26 5/8	27 2/8	5	6	HAGANS	ROBERT	SAME	
806	157 7/8	LINCOLN	87	74 4/8	73 4/8	17 7/8	3 0/8	25 6/8	27 1/8	5	6	MCCARTNEY	GARY	SAME	
806	157 7/8	MONROE	88	71 1/8	86 7/8	17 5/8	0	23 2/8	24 4/8	5	6	MAYES	BILL	SAME	
806	157 7/8	DEKALB	89	78 2/8	86 5/8	18 5/8	9 4/8	25 6/8	22 7/8	5	8	YOUNG	LARRY	SAME	
806	157 7/8	CHARITON	94	69 7/8	72 6/8	18 1/8	0	27 0/8	27 0/8	5	5	LAUHOFF	GREG	SAME	
812	157 6/8	ADAIR	73	73 1/8	71 0/8	18 6/8	0	27 0/8	26 1/8	5	5	FLEAK	DAVID	SAME	
812	157 6/8	MARIES	79	80 1/8	76 3/8	16 7/8	7 3/8	25 0/8	25 7/8	7	6	MARSHALL	TOM	SAME	
812	157 6/8	RALLS	86	71 2/8	75 5/8	15 6/8	0	23 0/8	24 2/8	5	5	FIEDLER	DAVE	SAME	
812	157 6/8	GREENE	88	69 3/8	73 7/8	19 1/8	0	25 0/8	26 1/8	5	5	ANDREWS	DON M.	SAME	
812	157 6/8	SCOTLAND	88	76 1/8	76 4/8	17 5/8	8 1/8	24 2/8	24 6/8	7	8	HOLT	MARK	SAME	
812	157 6/8	BOONE	90	73 4/8	74 0/8	18 1/8	3 7/8	24 1/8	24 1/8	6	5	THORNHILL	CURTIS	SAME	
812	157 6/8	DEKALB	92	71 3/8	72 2/8	18 2/8	0	24 6/8	24 2/8	5	5	ELLIS	JEREMY	SAME	
812	157 6/8	BENTON	92	73 3/8	80 2/8	16 0/8	2 0/8	23 5/8	23 2/8	7	8	OWEN	RODNEY	SAME	
812	157 6/8	MORGAN	96	74 1/8	70 3/8	18 2/8	0	24 6/8	24 2/8	5	5	SHULTZ	GENE	SAME	
821	157 5/8	BENTON	77	77 4/8	77 3/8	16 4/8	8 6/8	25 2/8	24 0/8	6	7	VAN NATTA, SR.	JAMES E.	SAME	
821	157 5/8	SCOTLAND	83	71 6/8	76 4/8	15 3/8	0	22 0/8	22 6/8	5	6	SMITH	DAVID	SAME	
821	157 5/8	SCOTLAND	86	69 4/8	72 0/8	19 7/8	1 0/8	25 0/8	25 3/8	6	5	VASSHOLZ	FRITZ	SAME	
821	157 5/8	FRANKLIN	87	71 6/8	68 6/8	22 3/8	0	23 0/8	23 3/8	5	5	NOVOTNEY	WILLIAM R.	SAME	
821	157 5/8	JOHNSON	87	77 4/8	75 2/8	17 3/8	7 6/8	26 6/8	26 1/8	6	7	STEPHENS	JAMES	SAME	
821	157 5/8	WAYNE	89	70 4/8	70 6/8	21 3/8	0	26 0/8	26 1/8	5	6	BOWLING	ROD	SAME	
821	157 5/8	MONROE	90	74 0/8	74 0/8	19 1/8	0	22 3/8	24 2/8	5	6	WILLINGHAM	RAY	SAME	
821	157 5/8	PUTNAM	91	75 4/8	73 6/8	18 2/8	5 7/8	25 0/8	24 6/8	7	6	BUSHNELL	TONY	SAME	
821	157 5/8	CASS	93	74 6/8	77 3/8	18 6/8	8 1/8	25 0/8	24 5/8	7	7	MCCALL	WILLIAM E.	SAME	
821	157 5/8	LEWIS	94	72 7/8	71 4/8	19 0/8	2 3/8	27 4/8	26 5/8	5	6	HITTLER	TRACY	SAME	
821	157 5/8	CALLAWAY	94	77 3/8	74 6/8	19 2/8	7 3/8	23 5/8	23 7/8	6	7	WALLACE	JAMES O.	SAME	
821	157 5/8	MACON	96	73 4/8	72 3/8	17 5/8	0	24 0/8	25 0/8	5	5	BOND	DWAYNE	SAME	

MISSOURI SHOW-ME BIG BUCKS CLUB RECORDS OF WHITETAIL DEER BY STATE, TYPICAL

STATE RANK	SCORE	COUNTY	YEAR TAKEN	INCHES TYPICAL R	L	INSIDE SPREAD	INCHES ABNORMAL	LENGTH MAIN BEAM R	L	NUMBER POINTS R	L	HUNTER	FIRST NAME	OWNER	FIRST NAME
833	157 4/8	HARRISON	71	74 3/8	75 0/8	18 5/8	3 7/8	25 0/8	25 3/8	5	8	WHITE	JIM	SAME	
833	157 4/8	RAY	71	72 3/8	75 0/8	19 0/8	4 2/8	24 4/8	26 0/8	5	6	BEARD	ELBERT	SAME	
833	157 4/8	NODAWAY	72	71 3/8	72 2/8	21 5/8	3 3/8	23 1/8	22 6/8	6	6	McGINNESS	J.D.	SAME	
833	157 4/8	SALINE	74	73 0/8	73 6/8	20 0/8	5 2/8	25 3/8	27 0/8	4	5	VAUGHAN	GREGORY L.	SAME	
833	157 4/8	MORGAN	82	78 7/8	77 7/8	14 7/8	5 5/8	25 2/8	24 7/8	8	5	SANDERS	GRACE	MEGAHAN	DAVID
833	157 4/8	HOLT	84	75 1/8	77 2/8	16 0/8	0	24 6/8	26 1/8	6	5	RAMSAY	TERRY	SAME	
833	157 4/8	PLATTE	85	71 0/8	75 7/8	19 2/8	2 4/8	25 3/8	25 4/8	5	5	CALLEHAN	MELVIN	SAME	
833	157 4/8	SCHUYLER	86	79 7/8	73 6/8	18 2/8	3 4/8	21 6/8	21 2/8	6	7	WEBSTER III	THOMAS M.	SAME	
833	157 4/8	MILLER	88	72 0/8	75 5/8	17 6/8	3 4/8	22 4/8	23 0/8	7	7	DUNCAN	TIM	SAME	
833	157 4/8	JOHNSON	89	72 2/8	72 2/8	22 6/8	0	23 3/8	23 6/8	5	5	STEPHENS	JAMES	SAME	
833	157 4/8	CAMDEN	89	73 7/8	79 0/8	20 1/8	8 5/8	27 5/8	27 1/8	5	7	HEISLEN	DALE	SAME	
833	157 4/8	PLATTE	91	69 4/8	72 5/8	19 0/8	0	23 2/8	24 2/8	5	5	ASHPAUGH	JAMES W.	SAME	
833	157 4/8	HENRY	93	71 7/8	70 4/8	18 4/8	0	24 6/8	24 3/8	5	5	McCALMON	KEVIN	SAME	
833	157 4/8	PUTNAM	96	71 3/8	72 4/8	16 0/8	0	22 5/8	22 7/8	5	5	HALLEY	HEATH	SAME	
833	157 4/8	WORTH	96	75 2/8	79 1/8	18 2/8	5 6/8	23 2/8	26 3/8	7	7	MERCER	MARVIN	SAME	
848	157 3/8	HOWELL	68	67 6/8	69 0/8	23 1/8	0	26 0/8	25 7/8	5	5	SMITH	DR. H.D.	ACKLIN	ROBERT L.
848	157 3/8	CARTER	77	72 2/8	72 7/8	16 3/8	1 0/8	21 5/8	22 0/8	6	5	REDMAN	JOHN	SAME	
848	157 3/8	HICKORY	82	77 4/8	72 5/8	20 2/8	4 3/8	27 0/8	28 0/8	7	5	FLESHMAN	WILLIAM	SAME	
848	157 3/8	SHELBY	83	73 4/8	69 3/8	19 5/8	0	26 7/8	26 0/8	5	5	GORDON	DWAYNE	SAME	
848	157 3/8	PIKE	86	70 3/8	73 2/8	17 5/8	0	24 2/8	24 4/8	5	5	LAWRENCE	GREG	SAME	
853	157 2/8	WAYNE	63	70 4/8	71 3/8	18 6/8	0	23 5/8	23 6/8	5	5	WILDERMAN	WILLIAM	SAME	
853	157 2/8	PULASKI	76	68 5/8	69 6/8	20 4/8	0	24 5/8	26 0/8	5	5	LOGAN	ROBERT	SAME	
853	157 2/8	CALLAWAY	78	77 2/8	71 2/8	18 6/8	0	25 4/8	26 2/8	6	5	BODE	GERALD	SAME	
853	157 2/8	LACLEDE	78	72 1/8	72 4/8	17 2/8	0	26 0/8	27 2/8	5	5	TAGGART	KEITH	SAME	
853	157 2/8	CLAY	87	70 3/8	76 7/8	19 0/8	0	26 0/8	25 6/8	5	5	RUKAVINA	BILLY J.	SAME	
853	157 2/8	HOLT	88	72 7/8	74 3/8	20 3/8	2 1/8	25 2/8	25 6/8	5	6	BERENDZEN	JAY	SAME	
853	157 2/8	DEKALB	88	75 5/8	75 2/8	22 7/8	7 5/8	24 6/8	24 1/8	7	6	LAWSON	MIKE	SAME	
853	157 2/8	GENTRY	88	70 7/8	74 2/8	16 4/8	0	21 4/8	21 1/8	6	6	HENRY	MARK	SAME	
853	157 2/8	LINN	91	72 5/8	75 4/8	17 4/8	0	21 2/8	22 4/8	5	5	ROSANBALM	LARRY	SAME	
853	157 2/8	CHARITON	95	74 1/8	82 0/8	17 0/8	2 0/8	26 2/8	25 4/8	4	6	IGO	SAMUEL DAVID	SAME	
853	157 2/8	ADAIR	96	70 6/8	70 3/8	20 4/8	0	25 5/8	25 5/8	5	5	ROHDE	WILLIAM A.	SAME	
864	157 1/8	MACON	59	74 4/8	86 5/8	18 5/8	2 4/8	26 3/8	25 3/8	5	7	EASLEY	RAY	SAME	

MISSOURI SHOW-ME BIG BUCKS CLUB RECORDS OF WHITETAIL DEER BY STATE, TYPICAL

STATE RANK	SCORE	COUNTY	YEAR TAKEN	INCHES TYPICAL R	L	INSIDE SPREAD	INCHES ABNORMAL	LENGTH MAIN BEAM R	L	NUMBER POINTS R	L	HUNTER	FIRST NAME	OWNER	FIRST NAME
864	157 1/8	MILLER	60	0	0	0	0	0	0	0	0	PEMORTON	OSCAR D.	MEREDITH	GENE
864	157 1/8	SHELBY	60	73 2/8	72 1/8	16 1/8	0	23 3/8	24 4/8	5	5	WILLEY	MERRILL	SAME	
864	157 1/8	JASPER	76	78 4/8	74 6/8	16 0/8	5 7/8	25 7/8	24 3/8	6	9	MORT	RICHARD B.	SAME	
864	157 1/8	OSAGE	80	72 5/8	72 2/8	17 1/8	0	26 3/8	25 7/8	5	5	PFAHL	RICHARD	SAME	
864	157 1/8	CLINTON	80	76 4/8	75 3/8	17 6/8	7 1/8	25 6/8	24 6/8	6	6	NORTON	DAVID	SAME	
864	157 1/8	HOLT	84	80 7/8	74 3/8	16 6/8	7 1/8	26 4/8	24 5/8	6	7	SQUAW CREEK	NWR	NAT.WILDLIFE	REFUGE
864	157 1/8	PUTNAM	90	72 3/8	74 6/8	18 6/8	5 5/8	24 1/8	25 1/8	7	6	TUCKER	MATT	SAME	
864	157 1/8	CRAWFORD	92	75 7/8	71 6/8	17 1/8	2 4/8	21 5/8	22 1/8	6	5	MARNATI	FATHER (LOUIS)	SAME	
864	157 1/8	PERRY	93	69 2/8	73 5/8	21 4/8	1 5/8	24 6/8	26 0/8	6	5	DENNINGER	STANLEY	SAME	
864	157 1/8	HENRY	96	70 4/8	71 0/8	18 5/8	0	24 5/8	24 1/8	6	6	BUTLER	JAMES	SAME	
864	157 0/8	HARRISON	67	70 3/8	72 0/8	19 0/8	0	24 5/8	26 2/8	5	5	DAVIS	MARCO	DECEASED	
875	157 0/8	HOLT	70	71 2/8	71 7/8	19 0/8	0	21 6/8	23 2/8	5	5	CURRAN	DENNIS	SAME	
875	157 0/8	McDONALD	71	71 0/8	72 7/8	16 0/8	0	23 0/8	22 4/8	5	5	MITCHELL	NEAL	SAME	
875	157 0/8	CEDAR	71	70 2/8	73 4/8	19 2/8	1 2/8	25 2/8	24 6/8	5	5	HARVEY	GENE	HARVEY	BEN
875	157 0/8	WARREN	73	70 6/8	72 2/8	17 0/8	0	23 4/8	23 7/8	5	5	EDWARDS	NORMAN J.	SAME	
875	157 0/8	SULLIVAN	74	71 2/8	71 7/8	19 0/8	0	25 4/8	25 2/8	5	5	WHEELER	TERRY	WHEELER	MIKE
875	157 0/8	LIVINGSTON	84	72 6/8	69 1/8	21 6/8	0	23 6/8	23 3/8	6	6	MOORE	RICKY	SAME	
875	157 0/8	COOPER	84	75 4/8	75 5/8	16 5/8	4 6/8	24 0/8	24 3/8	7	7	PENNINGTON	LEROY	SAME	
875	157 0/8	SALINE	88	73 7/8	76 4/8	18 2/8	0	25 2/8	25 4/8	5	5	HUNTER	DAVID	SAME	
875	157 0/8	OSAGE	88	76 5/8	74 6/8	18 7/8	9 1/8	24 1/8	21 5/8	6	9	REYNOLDS	DENNIS	SAME	
875	157 0/8	SHANNON	88	74 0/8	72 1/8	17 3/8	1 3/8	25 7/8	26 4/8	6	5	LINDSEY	ROGER	SAME	
875	157 0/8	HOLT	88	69 6/8	75 0/8	20 0/8	0	25 6/8	27 3/8	4	4	BLANKENSHIP	GLEN	SAME	
875	157 0/8	CALLAWAY	89	71 5/8	72 1/8	18 0/8	0	22 1/8	22 0/8	5	5	REVELLE	JOEL	SAME	
875	157 0/8	DAVIESS	92	70 5/8	73 2/8	22 6/8	6 4/8	24 6/8	25 4/8	7	5	HOLCOMB	STEVE	SAME	
875	157 0/8	SCHUYLER	94	75 3/8	77 1/8	13 7/8	1 0/8	23 5/8	23 4/8	6	7	McCORMICK	DONALD L.	SAME	
875	157 0/8	LINN	95	68 7/8	70 6/8	21 0/8	0	25 4/8	25 0/8	4	4	GREGORY	WALTER D.	SAME	
875	157 0/8	SULLIVAN	95	70 4/8	73 6/8	19 6/8	0	26 0/8	24 5/8	5	5	GROFF	RODNEY S.	SAME	
875	157 0/8	ADAIR	95	75 4/8	75 3/8	17 0/8	6 6/8	26 4/8	25 1/8	7	8	HOFFLAND	SCOTT A.	SAME	
893	156 7/8	BOONE	80	68 2/8	70 2/8	18 1/8	0	23 6/8	25 1/8	5	5	McCLINTOCH	WAYNE	SAME	
893	156 7/8	CLARK	82	71 0/8	73 3/8	16 6/8	1 1/8	25 0/8	24 7/8	6	5	MORTON	DON	SAME	
893	156 7/8	BOONE	85	71 5/8	71 5/8	21 3/8	0	24 6/8	27 1/8	4	4	MITCHELL	GARY	SAME	
893	156 7/8	COLE	86	72 5/8	74 3/8	15 3/8	0	23 2/8	22 5/8	5	5	SWANIGAN	GENE	SAME	

263

MISSOURI SHOW-ME BIG BUCKS CLUB RECORDS OF WHITETAIL DEER BY STATE, TYPICAL

STATE RANK	SCORE	COUNTY	YEAR TAKEN	INCHES TYPICAL R	L	INSIDE SPREAD	INCHES ABNORMAL	LENGTH MAIN BEAM R	L	NUMBER POINTS R	L	HUNTER	FIRST NAME	OWNER	FIRST NAME
893	156 7/8	OSAGE	90	70 4/8	70 4/8	22 0/8	3 3/8	23 4/8	22 4/8	6	6	HURST	DANNY		SAME
893	156 7/8	CRAWFORD	92	76 4/8	71 3/8	18 5/8	0	27 6/8	26 4/8	5	5	GILLESPIE	RANDY		SAME
893	156 7/8	SALINE	95	70 0/8	75 0/8	20 2/8	3 1/8	22 2/8	23 0/8	6	6	VOGL	KENNETH		SAME
900	156 6/8	FRANKLIN	79	71 2/8	71 3/8	16 0/8	0	25 4/8	24 6/8	5	5	FRANKENBERG	DONALD		SAME
900	156 6/8	CHARITON	80	70 2/8	76 6/8	21 2/8	0	25 4/8	26 6/8	6	6	MITCHELL	LARRY		SAME
900	156 6/8	LINCOLN	81	74 3/8	78 3/8	20 6/8	11 0/8	25 7/8	25 2/8	4	8	HEITMAN	GERALD		SAME
900	156 6/8	PUTNAM	81	70 2/8	69 5/8	21 6/8	0	23 5/8	23 7/8	5	5	SMITH	PAUL W.		SAME
900	156 6/8	OREGON	83	71 1/8	69 6/8	19 2/8	0	25 4/8	24 1/8	5	5	VESTAL	JACK		SAME
900	156 6/8	LINCOLN	83	72 0/8	73 3/8	18 5/8	4 5/8	22 0/8	22 5/8	6	6	EICHLER	KEN		SAME
900	156 6/8	COOPER	85	70 5/8	69 2/8	21 6/8	0	24 6/8	25 7/8	5	5	PRICE	JEFF		SAME
900	156 6/8	MILLER	85	74 0/8	72 3/8	17 2/8	0	26 0/8	23 4/8	5	5	MYERS	BILL		SAME
900	156 6/8	CLINTON	88	74 0/8	76 4/8	15 0/8	5 6/8	25 2/8	25 2/8	6	5	GRIFFIN	BEN		SAME
900	156 6/8	FRANKLIN	88	72 7/8	72 6/8	18 5/8	0	23 0/8	23 5/8	5	6	ROTHWEIL	GERALD A.		SAME
900	156 6/8	MACON	96	70 7/8	71 5/8	16 6/8	0	21 3/8	21 5/8	5	5	BASLER	ERIC J.		SAME
911	156 5/8	LINCOLN	58	82 0/8	73 7/8	19 2/8	9 1/8	24 7/8	25 4/8	9	7	NIEHOFF	JOE		SAME
911	156 5/8	TEXAS	65	75 5/8	71 7/8	22 7/8	0	27 0/8	23 5/8	6	6	SULLINS	HAROLD		SAME
911	156 5/8	CLINTON	70	72 2/8	75 3/8	18 2/8	0	23 4/8	23 3/8	5	6	KISKY	DON		SAME
911	156 5/8	BOONE	79	71 3/8	72 2/8	21 4/8	2 3/8	25 3/8	26 2/8	5	6	COOK	LARRY		SAME
911	156 5/8	PLATTE	81	68 3/8	76 0/8	19 1/8	1 4/8	24 3/8	24 4/8	6	7	FREEMYER	BILL		SAME
911	156 5/8	PLATTE	82	71 5/8	70 4/8	19 3/8	0	25 0/8	25 0/8	5	5	WHEELER	STEVE		SAME
911	156 5/8	BOONE	87	72 3/8	72 2/8	16 7/8	0	26 2/8	26 2/8	5	5	NICHOLS	HAROLD		SAME
911	156 5/8	COOPER	88	74 0/8	71 1/8	18 5/8	0	24 7/8	24 1/8	6	5	STRECK	CHRIS		SAME
911	156 5/8	JACKSON	89	69 6/8	70 0/8	19 5/8	0	24 3/8	24 5/8	5	5	COLLINS	JAMES E.		SAME
911	156 5/8	CHARITON	91	74 1/8	74 6/8	16 3/8	3 4/8	25 3/8	25 6/8	6	6	LEONARD	NATHAN		SAME
911	156 5/8	CALDWELL	93	74 4/8	75 1/8	16 6/8	4 5/8	24 2/8	25 2/8	7	8	MCCALLISTER	TOM		SAME
911	156 5/8	SCOTLAND	95	73 3/8	71 4/8	18 5/8	2 0/8	24 6/8	25 1/8	6	5	STOTT	TRAVIS		SAME
911	156 5/8	SALINE	96	70 4/8	73 6/8	24 1/8	7 4/8	26 2/8	27 1/8	6	6	DAVIS	GERRY D.		SAME
911	156 5/8	MADISON	96	70 7/8	69 3/8	18 7/8	0	22 6/8	22 7/8	6	5	SCHMIDT	DANIEL D.		SAME
925	156 4/8	WASHINGTON	69	69 0/8	74 1/8	19 4/8	0	24 5/8	24 7/8	5	6	PHIPPS	LEE		SAME
925	156 4/8	HOLT	73	74 3/8	75 4/8	16 4/8	3 6/8	21 1/8	22 0/8	7	5	DYE	ROBERT L.		SAME
925	156 4/8	KNOX	76	74 1/8	72 2/8	17 2/8	0	23 6/8	25 3/8	5	5	HITCHCOCK	ROBERT		SAME
925	156 4/8	MACON	84	74 3/8	74 1/8	17 6/8	7 2/8	23 4/8	23 4/8	8	6	HOBBY	CHARLES		SAME

MISSOURI SHOW-ME BIG BUCKS CLUB RECORDS OF WHITETAIL DEER BY STATE, TYPICAL

STATE RANK	SCORE	COUNTY	YEAR TAKEN	INCHES TYPICAL R	L	INSIDE SPREAD	INCHES ABNORMAL	LENGTH MAIN BEAM R	L	NUMBER POINTS R	L	HUNTER	FIRST NAME	OWNER	FIRST NAME
925	156 4/8	SALINE	85	75 4/8	87 6/8	17 0/8	3 6/8	25 5/8	23 6/8	0	0	BOSSALLER	ELDON	SAME	
925	156 4/8	PLATTE	85	69 6/8	72 7/8	17 6/8	0	26 0/8	26 1/8	5	5	STACKHOUSE	GUY	SAME	
925	156 4/8	CLARK	85	75 2/8	83 4/8	16 5/8	6 7/8	23 7/8	23 5/8	5	7	BROOKS	BRIAN	SAME	
925	156 4/8	MACON	86	68 6/8	69 7/8	20 2/8	0	25 1/8	26 5/8	4	4	MEYER	DALE	SAME	
925	156 4/8	MARIES	86	72 7/8	74 7/8	16 4/8	2 4/8	24 2/8	25 0/8	6	7	BUCKOWITZ	ART	SAME	
925	156 4/8	MONTGOMERY	87	69 4/8	80 4/8	18 0/8	0	26 2/8	27 2/8	4	5	KICKER	ROBERT	SAME	
925	156 4/8	HARRISON	88	72 0/8	69 4/8	19 4/8	0	24 7/8	23 6/8	5	5	MCBROOM	CHRIS	SAME	
925	156 4/8	MARIES	89	75 6/8	75 5/8	15 6/8	8 0/8	22 4/8	21 6/8	6	6	WILES	GARY	SAME	
925	156 4/8	MONTGOMERY	89	70 0/8	74 0/8	18 0/8	0	25 0/8	25 2/8	5	5	DEBENPORT	ROGER G.	SAME	
925	156 4/8	AUDRAIN	93	75 1/8	75 2/8	16 4/8	5 6/8	25 3/8	26 6/8	7	4	LYNN	ROY E.	SAME	
925	156 4/8	PIKE	93	72 7/8	80 7/8	19 1/8	2 5/8	25 4/8	24 5/8	6	9	GROTE	BOBBY	SAME	
940	156 3/8	HARRISON	67	71 0/8	70 5/8	18 5/8	0	23 0/8	21 4/8	5	5	HENDERSON	JERRY	SAME	
940	156 3/8	CLARK	73	72 6/8	74 1/8	20 1/8	5 2/8	24 0/8	24 4/8	7	7	BRUNK	ARNOLD	SAME	
940	156 3/8	CLAY	75	72 6/8	69 6/8	17 1/8	0	23 3/8	23 1/8	5	5	CLEVENGER	KEN	SAME	
940	156 3/8	BOLLINGER	79	72 5/8	68 5/8	19 3/8	0	26 1/8	25 4/8	4	4	ASLINGER	HARLOD G.	SAME	
940	156 3/8	GASCONADE	79	71 5/8	73 4/8	18 0/8	1 3/8	22 7/8	21 4/8	5	7	GOODMAN	JERRY L.	SAME	
940	156 3/8	CALLAWAY	83	69 7/8	72 7/8	17 3/8	0	24 1/8	24 3/8	5	5	BURRE	KELLY	SAME	
940	156 3/8	SCOTLAND	84	69 3/8	70 2/8	22 1/8	0	23 4/8	24 3/8	4	4	SMITH	DAVID	SAME	
940	156 3/8	CALLAWAY	86	74 6/8	71 7/8	16 4/8	3 1/8	23 6/8	23 4/8	6	6	MCGRATH	MARK	SAME	
940	156 3/8	GASCONADE	86	78 2/8	73 6/8	18 2/8	7 4/8	24 6/8	25 2/8	6	6	BRANDT	EUGENE E.	SAME	
940	156 3/8	LINCOLN	89	70 3/8	70 1/8	18 5/8	0	24 2/8	24 2/8	5	5	BRAUNGARDT	GARY	SAME	
940	156 3/8	SHANNON	93	71 3/8	71 5/8	17 1/8	0	23 6/8	23 1/8	5	5	LINDSEY	SCOTT	SAME	
940	156 3/8	SCOTT	95	74 2/8	69 1/8	18 1/8	0	26 7/8	26 6/8	4	4	DANIELS	TIMOTHY L.	SAME	
940	156 3/8	MORGAN	96	71 3/8	77 1/8	16 4/8	2 5/8	23 4/8	23 5/8	6	6	HOLSTEN	YRONNE	SAME	
953	156 2/8	CALLAWAY	58	69 7/8	69 7/8	19 6/8	1 0/8	25 0/8	25 7/8	5	5	WINDSOR	O.V.	SAME	
953	156 2/8	PIKE	63	73 2/8	75 5/8	19 4/8	2 6/8	24 2/8	24 0/8	7	6	MORRIS	GEORGE	SAME	
953	156 2/8	LAFAYETTE	71	70 5/8	71 5/8	22 0/8	1 0/8	23 7/8	24 5/8	5	5	BUESING	MERLE	SAME	
953	156 2/8	KNOX	76	74 7/8	72 3/8	18 6/8	2 5/8	27 0/8	25 7/8	5	5	HAMILTON	MELVIN	SAME	
953	156 2/8	MONITEAU	83	73 5/8	74 3/8	17 4/8	7 0/8	24 1/8	23 7/8	6	7	FARRIS	NICK	SAME	
953	156 2/8	JASPER	84	70 1/8	71 5/8	19 6/8	1 1/8	24 6/8	25 0/8	6	5	WREN	JEFF	SAME	
953	156 2/8	LEWIS	86	74 5/8	69 5/8	21 0/8	0	25 6/8	25 6/8	5	5	MILLER	RICHARD D.	SAME	
953	156 2/8	CALLAWAY	87	70 0/8	72 2/8	17 6/8	0	24 1/8	23 6/8	5	6	BECKERMAN	SCOTT	SAME	

265

MISSOURI SHOW-ME BIG BUCKS CLUB RECORDS OF WHITETAIL DEER BY STATE, TYPICAL

STATE RANK	SCORE	COUNTY	YEAR TAKEN	INCHES TYPICAL R	INCHES TYPICAL L	INSIDE SPREAD	INCHES ABNORMAL	LENGTH MAIN BEAM R	LENGTH MAIN BEAM L	NUMBER POINTS R	NUMBER POINTS L	HUNTER	FIRST NAME	OWNER	FIRST NAME
953	156 2/8	RAY	90	72 2/8	71 2/8	19 4/8	0	24 6/8	24 6/8	5	5	HEWITT	WESLEY	SAME	
953	156 2/8	GRUNDY	91	72 2/8	73 3/8	21 1/8	5 1/8	25 1/8	24 7/8	5	9	HALL	TIM	SAME	
953	156 2/8	PLATTE	93	75 3/8	68 5/8	19 6/8	0	27 0/8	26 3/8	5	4	HEYDINGER	JEFF	SAME	
953	156 2/8	DAVIESS	93	70 1/8	71 0/8	19 4/8	2 2/8	25 6/8	26 4/8	4	6	STEWART	JERRY	SAME	
953	156 2/8	SHANNON	95	73 2/8	75 2/8	16 0/8	3 0/8	23 0/8	22 7/8	6	5	LINDSEY	SCOTT	SAME	
953	156 2/8	LINCOLN	95	71 0/8	70 0/8	19 0/8	1 0/8	26 2/8	26 2/8	6	5	HURD	J.D.	SAME	
953	156 2/8	ST. LOUIS	72	77 2/8	71 5/8	16 5/8	1 4/8	26 5/8	26 0/8	6	4	DELANEY	DAVE	SAME	
967	156 1/8	CALLAWAY	76	71 6/8	70 0/8	19 3/8	0	27 0/8	26 5/8	5	5	FERGUSON	JAMES F.	SAME	
967	156 1/8	MERCER	78	67 4/8	73 6/8	22 3/8	1 2/8	25 2/8	27 1/8	5	4	EASTIN	CURTIS	SAME	
967	156 1/8	WASHINGTON	86	71 4/8	70 0/8	19 1/8	2 2/8	24 7/8	23 6/8	6	5	HARNESS	WAYNE	SAME	
967	156 1/8	SULLIVAN	86	70 1/8	73 5/8	22 0/8	1 5/8	23 1/8	23 4/8	6	6	GANN	KENNY	SAME	
967	156 1/8	CAMDEN	88	69 6/8	70 7/8	19 5/8	1 4/8	27 5/8	27 3/8	5	4	BRAILE	ED	SAME	
967	156 1/8	GENTRY	89	69 3/8	69 1/8	19 1/8	0	23 7/8	23 6/8	5	5	LAU	ROGER	SAME	
967	156 1/8	COOPER	90	73 7/8	69 5/8	20 1/8	0	25 5/8	25 4/8	5	4	COOK	MIKE	SAME	
967	156 1/8	JOHNSON	90	70 5/8	67 6/8	21 5/8	0	26 2/8	25 7/8	5	5	JACKSON	JOHN	SAME	
967	156 1/8	CALDWELL	91	80 0/8	70 3/8	18 3/8	1 4/8	27 6/8	27 0/8	6	4	STANLEY	BOB D.	SAME	
967	156 1/8	ANDREW	92	71 3/8	72 4/8	18 0/8	2 3/8	24 4/8	24 4/8	6	6	LANCE	RONNIE	SAME	
967	156 1/8	WARREN	94	74 1/8	74 2/8	17 4/8	2 5/8	25 4/8	26 0/8	6	6	COX	PAUL R.	SAME	
967	156 1/8	ST. CHARLES	94	72 3/8	74 5/8	16 4/8	2 3/8	25 5/8	25 1/8	6	6	KOEHLER	KEITH	SAME	
967	156 1/8	SALINE	95	71 7/8	71 5/8	18 7/8	0	26 5/8	25 2/8	4	4	ZINN	TOMMY D.	SAME	
981	156 0/8	HOWARD	59	70 6/8	73 4/8	18 2/8	0	25 2/8	23 5/8	5	5	AHOLT	ROY	SAME	
981	156 0/8	STE. GENEVIEVE	71	70 4/8	71 7/8	17 4/8	2 0/8	22 7/8	23 3/8	6	5	MANION	JAMES C.	SAME	
981	156 0/8	BARRY	71	71 6/8	76 1/8	18 6/8	3 0/8	22 0/8	23 4/8	6	5	TOWE	TED	SAME	
981	156 0/8	ST. CHARLES	72	69 5/8	72 0/8	20 4/8	0	24 4/8	24 0/8	5	5	HERGERG	RANDALL O.	SAME	
981	156 0/8	LINCOLN	85	69 7/8	71 1/8	18 6/8	0	24 0/8	24 2/8	5	5	BOWERS	BRUCE	SAME	
981	156 0/8	WORTE	85	71 7/8	70 2/8	19 4/8	0	23 6/3	22 4/8	4	4	SASSANI	KOUROS	SAME	
981	156 0/8	PUTNAM	86	77 3/8	75 0/8	19 4/8	6 0/8	25 6/3	22 7/8	7	6	GADBERRY	RONNIE	SAME	
981	156 0/8	CAMDEN	87	73 4/8	72 5/8	17 4/8	3 4/8	24 5/8	25 0/8	6	6	YAEGER	WILLIAM	SAME	
981	156 0/8	NODAWAY	88	77 6/8	75 3/8	18 5/8	7 5/8	25 7/8	25 0/8	7	8	PEVE	BOB	SAME	
981	156 0/8	MONTGOMERY	91	72 1/8	72 0/8	15 6/8	0	25 3/8	24 4/8	5	5	HAYES	GARY	SAME	
981	156 0/8	ATCHISON	91	71 1/8	74 0/8	17 5/8	1 1/8	23 1/8	22 4/8	5	6	SLENKER	TIM	SAME	
981	156 0/8	SCHUYLER	91	71 4/8	72 5/8	16 6/8	1 6/8	23 7/8	24 0/8	5	6	BAILEY	WAYNE	SAME	

STATE RANK	SCORE	COUNTY	YEAR TAKEN	INCHES TYPICAL R	L	INSIDE SPREAD	INCHES ABNORMAL	LENGTH MAIN BEAM R	L	NUMBER POINTS R	L	HUNTER	FIRST NAME	OWNER	FIRST NAME
981	156 0/8	SULLIVAN	96	72 2/8	75 4/8	16 0/8	2 4/8	22 6/8	22 3/8	6	6	ANDERS, SR.	GARY	SAME	
994	155 7/8	MACON	75	73 1/8	75 1/8	20 2/8	8 3/8	24 6/8	24 2/8	7	6	AMEDEI	JOHN	SAME	
994	155 7/8	OSAGE	80	72 6/8	73 1/8	14 3/8		24 5/8	23 3/8	5	5	MONROE	JERRY	SAME	
994	155 7/8	OZARK	82	68 3/8	72 1/8	19 7/8		23 1/8	23 1/8	5	5	BLACKBURN	JIMMY JOE	SAME	
994	155 7/8	MONITEAU	84	71 1/8	73 0/8	16 3/8		25 2/8	24 3/8	5	5	HOBACK	DENNIS H.	SAME	
994	155 7/8	CALLAWAY	85	71 3/8	70 4/8	18 5/8	1 0/8	24 6/8	24 4/8	6	5	SCHINDLER	DON	SAME	
994	155 7/8	ST. FRANCOIS	88	74 3/8	72 7/8	18 3/8	5 0/8	24 5/8	25 0/8	6	7	MAY	MATTHEW	SAME	
994	155 7/8	CAPE GIRARDEAU	91	76 5/8	75 6/8	20 7/8	7 4/8	27 7/8	29 0/8	7	8	LIVINGSTON	GARRETT	SAME	
994	155 7/8	RANDOLPH	93	76 6/8	73 3/8	15 7/8	6 4/8	26 5/8	25 3/8	7	6	RICE	JAMES	SAME	
994	155 7/8	JEFFERSON	94	72 5/8	70 4/8	20 5/8		25 5/8	26 4/8	5	4	ASELMAN	JAMES	SAME	
994	155 7/8	CARROLL	95	71 4/8	80 2/8	19 0/8	2 7/8	23 4/8	24 4/8	5	6	GREGG	RUSSELL	SAME	
1004	155 6/8	STE. GENEIEVE	62	81 1/8	80 6/8	16 7/8	6 7/8	28 4/8	28 2/8	6	9	STEARNS	KEN	SAME	
1004	155 6/8	PHELPS	67	0		0	0	0	0	0	0	GOLLAHON	JOHN P.	SAME	
1004	155 6/8	CHARITON	76	68 6/8	68 3/8	22 6/8		24 4/8	24 6/8	5	5	MILLER	MARK	SAME	
1004	155 6/8	JOHNSON	79	73 3/8	70 2/8	22 0/8	2 2/8	27 4/8	25 4/8	4	5	CORBETT	DWAYNE	SAME	
1004	155 6/8	WARREN	84	70 4/8	69 2/8	17 6/8		24 4/8	24 0/8	5	5	NICKS	DEAN	SAME	
1004	155 6/8	ST. LOUIS	84	75 0/8	70 3/8	19 2/8	4 2/8	24 0/8	23 0/8	6	6	ECKSTEIN	MARTIN H.	SAME	
1004	155 6/8	DENT	87	78 1/8	70 5/8	18 3/8	1 3/8	22 7/8	24 1/8	6	5	WARDEN	DARREL	SAME	
1004	155 6/8	ST. CHARLES	88	69 2/8	73 2/8	18 4/8		21 3/8	22 1/8	5	5	BURBES	JERRY	SAME	
1004	155 6/8	CALLAWAY	89	76 4/8	77 0/8	17 4/8	8 2/8	23 6/8	25 4/8	6	7	GIBONEY	JEFF	SAME	
1004	155 6/8	PIKE	90	70 0/8	70 1/7	18 6/8		25 5/8	25 7/8	5	5	MORRIS	SEAN	SAME	
1004	155 6/8	DEKALB	90	75 0/8	74 7/8	19 7/8	8 5/8	26 7/8	28 5/8	6	6	LESLIE	LLOYD A.	SAME	
1004	155 6/8	STODDARD	90	71 5/8	72 2/8	15 6/8		21 7/8	22 5/8	6	6	HEDSPETH	LINUEL	SAME	
1004	155 6/8	CALLAWAY	91	69 3/8	73 4/8	18 6/8		22 7/8	23 0/8	5	6	NEELY	STANLEY B.	SAME	
1004	155 6/8	HOLT	92	74 7/8	72 7/8	19 7/8	8 1/8	24 0/8	22 3/8	6	6	BARKER	CARROL	SAME	
1004	155 6/8	PUTNAM	92	71 3/8	68 0/8	20 6/8		25 3/8	25 2/8	5	5	BRYAN	MIKE	SAME	
1004	155 6/8	HARRISON	92	72 2/8	70 4/8	19 0/8	1 4/8	20 4/8	20 0/8	5	6	JAMES	JERRY	SAME	
1004	155 6/8	LACLEDE	92	73 1/8	73 3/8	17 5/8	3 3/8	24 6/8	25 5/8	6	5	McCANN	ROY	SAME	
1004	155 6/8	ST. LOUIS	93	85 1/8	78 5/8	16 7/8	5 3/8	24 0/8	24 2/8	7	5	WHITTENBERG	ALAN E.	SAME	
1004	155 6/8	BOLLINGER	95	71 0/8	72 2/8	16 2/8		24 0/8	24 4/8	5	5	WELKER	DALE	SAME	
1023	155 5/8	LEWIS	70	68 6/8	74 0/8	18 1/8		23 5/8	23 5/8	5	5	SPARKS	RILEY P.	SAME	
1023	155 5/8	PIKE	71	80 1/8	77 0/8	14 0/8	6 7/8	17 5/8	18 7/8	8	6	SPARKS	CHARLES F.	SAME	

MISSOURI SHOW-ME BIG BUCKS CLUB RECORDS OF WHITETAIL DEER BY STATE, TYPICAL

STATE RANK	SCORE	COUNTY	YEAR TAKEN	INCHES TYPICAL R	L	INSIDE SPREAD	INCHES ABNORMAL	LENGTH MAIN BEAM R	L	NUMBER POINTS R	L	HUNTER	FIRST NAME	OWNER	FIRST NAME
1023	155 5/8	TEXAS	77	72 3/8	74 1/8	16 3/8	0	24 5/8	22 4/8	5	5	HANCOCK	JERRY	SAME	
1023	155 5/8	CALLAWAY	78	74 6/8	74 5/8	16 4/8	3 7/8	25 6/8	25 2/8	5	7	BUSKEN	LEONARD	SAME	
1023	155 5/8	HARRISON	79	72 7/8	70 5/8	15 5/8	0	22 4/8	22 2/8	6	6	BENNETT	DAVID O.	SAME	
1023	155 5/8	PHELPS	79	72 1/8	72 2/8	18 1/8	2 4/8	25 7/8	24 5/8	6	5	PONZER	BRUCE	SAME	
1023	155 5/8	BARTON	80	70 3/8	71 6/8	16 7/8	0	23 5/8	23 5/8	5	5	TEFERTILLER	RICHARD	SAME	
1023	155 5/8	OZARK	82	75 1/8	74 7/8	19 3/8	9 2/8	23 6/8	24 0/8	8	7	JAMES	IVAN	SAME	
1023	155 5/8	HARRISON	83	79 4/8	75 5/8	17 5/8	8 6/8	23 6/8	23 4/8	5	7	JEANES	CHARLES	SAME	
1023	155 5/8	HARRISON	85	67 4/8	70 2/8	20 5/8	0	26 1/8	26 2/8	4	4	ALLEN	WAYNE	SAME	
1023	155 5/8	PULASKI	86	73 3/8	73 5/8	20 3/8	6 2/8	25 4/8	25 6/8	7	5	AGEE	BRUCE	SAME	
1023	155 5/8	LEWIS	86	74 3/8	71 1/8	17 1/8	2 4/8	24 1/8	23 1/8	6	5	McDONALD	JAMES	SAME	
1023	155 5/8	SALINE	89	69 2/8	80 1/8	19 1/8	0	22 5/8	24 0/8	6	6	ENGLAND	LARRY	SAME	
1023	155 5/8	OSAGE	94	70 7/8	73 6/8	16 3/8	0	23 5/8	24 6/8	5	5	VOSS	ADRIAN	SAME	
1023	155 5/8	CAPE GIRARDEAU	94	66 2/8	67 6/8	24 3/8	0	25 4/8	26 2/8	4	4	FARROW	MIKE	SAME	
1023	155 5/8	PERRY	94	72 6/8	75 6/8	19 4/8	8 1/8	24 7/8	25 4/8	7	6	PETZOLDT	TROY	SAME	
1023	155 5/8	MONTGOMERY	95	72 3/8	71 6/8	16 1/8	1 6/8	25 3/8	26 0/8	6	5	SULLIVAN	KEVIN P.	SAME	
1040	155 4/8	WARREN	67	75 3/8	71 6/8	17 6/8	1 2/8	23 6/8	25 0/8	5	6	ELLIS	D.C.	SAME	
1040	155 4/8	IRON	68	72 0/8	72 3/8	18 2/8	0	23 5/8	23 7/8	5	5	RONEY	CHARLES G.	SAME	
1040	155 4/8	HARRISON	71	71 3/8	73 0/8	22 2/8	0	28 4/8	26 6/8	4	4	HALE	ROBERT E.	SAME	
1040	155 4/8	BENTON	75	75 0/8	72 0/8	20 2/8	0	25 7/8	24 6/8	5	5	BEYER	DAN	SAME	
1040	155 4/8	CARROLL	82	68 2/8	69 1/8	23 6/8	0	25 1/8	24 6/8	5	5	RODENBURG	CHARLES	SAME	
1040	155 4/8	HICKORY	85	69 7/8	69 2/8	20 4/8	0	24 1/8	23 2/8	4	4	WEYER	TOM	SAME	
1040	155 4/8	JACKSON	87	77 1/8	71 3/8	16 4/8	0	25 1/8	24 4/8	6	5	SHOTTON, JR.	CHARLES C.	SAME	
1040	155 4/8	CALDWELL	88	74 0/8	71 0/8	17 0/8	0	24 0/8	22 3/8	5	5	KAVANAUGH	MATT	SAME	
1040	155 4/8	WORTH	89	76 6/8	72 0/8	15 4/8	0	27 0/8	24 6/8	5	5	VON GEYSO	FRANK	SAME	
1040	155 4/8	HOWARD	90	71 0/8	72 3/8	18 0/8	2 2/8	23 2/8	24 6/8	6	5	REAGAN	DEAN	SAME	
1040	155 4/8	SULLIVAN	91	77 6/8	77 4/8	13 5/8	3 7/8	25 5/3	24 7/8	6	5	HIGH	DUANE	HIGH	BRIAN
1040	155 4/8	SHANNON	92	70 5/8	72 4/8	18 0/8	1 2/8	26 3/3	26 0/8	4	6	STROTHER	LARRY M.	SAME	
1040	155 4/8	ADAIR	93	72 5/8	72 5/8	17 5/8	1 1/8	26 0/3	25 2/8	5	6	ERWIN	MIKE	SAME	
1040	155 4/8	HOWARD	93	71 1/8	75 7/8	15 7/8	2 1/8	24 0/3	23 6/8	6	6	SIMS	NORMAN L.	SAME	
1040	155 4/8	ADAIR	93	71 3/8	69 2/8	19 2/8	1 0/8	22 4/8	22 3/8	6	5	HOMAN, JR.	KENNETH	SAME	
1040	155 4/8	LINCOLN	94	73 3/8	76 2/8	18 4/8	4 0/8	24 1/8	23 6/8	6	5	STEPHENS	CARLIS	SAME	
1040	155 4/8	CALLAWAY	95	70 0/8	72 0/8	15 4/8	0	22 4/8	22 4/8	5	5	HARTSOCK	ALAN L.	SAME	

MISSOURI SHOW-ME BIG BUCKS CLUB RECORDS OF WHITETAIL DEER BY STATE, TYPICAL

STATE RANK	SCORE	COUNTY	HUNTER	YEAR TAKEN	INCHES TYPICAL R	INCHES TYPICAL L	INSIDE SPREAD	INCHES ABNORMAL	LENGTH MAIN BEAM R	LENGTH MAIN BEAM L	NUMBER POINTS R	NUMBER POINTS L	FIRST NAME	OWNER	FIRST NAME
1040	155 4/8	WARREN	MOORE	96	70 0/8	72 5/8	18 0/8	0	24 5/8	24 4/8	5	5	CECIL M.	SAME	
1040	155 4/8	CALLAWAY	WEBB	96	72 5/8	71 2/8	17 5/8	1 1/8	23 6/8	25 1/8	6	5	JAMES	SAME	
1059	155 3/8	WORTH	THURMAN	72	75 4/8	70 0/8	17 1/8	1 2/8	24 0/8	23 4/8	6	4	DAVID	SAME	
1059	155 3/8	ADAIR	EASLEY	72	76 6/8	74 4/8	15 3/8	0	23 5/8	23 5/8	6	5	GARY L.	SAME	
1059	155 3/8	SCHUYLER	FREMON	76	74 7/8	76 3/8	19 3/8	10 4/8	25 1/8	25 1/8	9	7	BOB	SAME	
1059	155 3/8	CRAWFORD	HEMSATH	82	69 4/8	71 1/8	18 5/8	1 0/8	23 4/8	24 2/8	6	5	DON	SAME	
1059	155 3/8	ADAIR	FLOYD	87	74 6/8	75 4/8	20 2/8	7 1/8	26 0/8	26 1/8	7	7	TRAVIS	SAME	
1059	155 3/8	PUTNAM	WILLIAMS	88	72 4/8	76 2/8	18 4/8	2 1/8	25 6/8	26 6/8	5	6	LAWRENCE	SAME	
1059	155 3/8	PETTIS	MORRISON	91	69 6/8	74 7/8	15 3/8	1 0/8	21 6/8	23 7/8	5	6	JOHN D.	SAME	
1059	155 3/8	LIVINGSTON	SHILT	95	74 2/8	77 4/8	16 7/8	7 0/8	24 2/8	24 1/8	6	6	JOE D.	SAME	
1059	155 3/8	ST. FRANCOIS	CALLAHAN	95	71 1/8	71 1/8	18 1/8	1 0/8	24 6/8	25 4/8	6	5	LARRY	SAME	
1068	155 2/8	MARIES	HONSE	67	71 5/8	73 6/8	17 5/8	2 7/8	25 6/8	25 5/8	6	6	WESLEY	SAME	
1068	155 2/8	ATCHISON	GRIMES	70	72 4/8	71 5/8	17 6/8	0	22 5/8	24 2/8	5	5	HAROLD	SAME	
1068	155 2/8	MACON	BRADLEY	73	80 5/8	72 3/8	22 0/8	10 6/8	28 6/8	29 0/8	8	6	HAROLD	SAME	
1068	155 2/8	KNOX	MORROW	73	74 4/8	74 6/8	18 4/8	3 4/8	20 0/8	24 4/8	6	6	ELVIN RAY	MORROW	JEFF
1068	155 2/8	PHELPS	MONTGOMERY	73	70 1/8	70 5/8	17 0/8	0	24 0/8	23 4/8	5	5	CLYDE	SAME	
1068	155 2/8	PULASKI	SHELDEN	77	72 6/8	75 4/8	19 0/8	7 0/8	24 2/8	24 0/8	6	7	WILLIAM J.	SAME	
1068	155 2/8	SCOTLAND	HATFIELD	79	72 4/8	73 4/8	15 2/8	0	21 4/8	21 3/8	6	6	RODNEY	SAME	
1068	155 2/8	GASCONADE	PETERS	82	71 4/8	69 2/8	17 6/8	0	24 0/8	23 0/8	5	5	RAYMOND A.	SAME	
1068	155 2/8	CHARITON	BATTAGLIA	84	73 5/8	71 2/8	16 2/8	2 6/8	23 4/8	23 0/8	6	6	ANTHONY	SAME	
1068	155 2/8	STE. GENEIEVE	DAVITZ	87	68 6/8	73 5/8	18 2/8	0	23 5/8	24 4/8	6	5	KERMITH C.	SAME	
1068	155 2/8	CLARK	YATES	88	70 2/8	77 3/8	19 0/8	0	26 0/8	26 1/8	5	5	STEVEN	SAME	
1068	155 2/8	MONROE	HAYS	88	72 5/8	74 3/8	15 4/8	0	22 2/8	21 6/8	5	6	DON LEO	SAME	
1068	155 2/8	ADAIR	YOUNG	88	69 2/8	70 0/8	20 4/8	0	25 7/8	25 2/8	5	5	BURT	SAME	
1068	155 2/8	CHARITON	MONNIG	89	69 7/8	71 0/8	19 6/8	0	25 6/8	24 4/8	5	5	CHARLIE	SAME	
1068	155 2/8	MACON	SIMMONS	90	75 4/8	70 2/8	19 4/8	3 6/8	25 4/8	25 6/8	6	6	STEVEN	SAME	
1068	155 2/8	PUTNAM	REAM	90	70 7/8	72 2/8	18 2/8	0	23 6/8	23 5/8	5	5	JOE	SAME	
1068	155 2/8	CALDWELL	SWINDLER	91	75 4/8	76 3/8	17 0/8	2 0/8	25 2/8	26 4/8	6	7	DARREN	SAME	
1068	155 2/8	PETTIS	ANNERSON	91	69 2/8	70 7/8	17 2/8	0	25 6/8	26 4/8	4	4	SAM	SAME	
1068	155 2/8	PIKE	McINTURFF	91	74 2/8	73 0/8	21 6/8	3 6/8	23 1/8	24 3/8	8	6	JOHN P.	SAME	
1068	155 2/8	CHARITON	GORDON	92	71 3/8	69 5/8	19 3/8	1 2/8	25 4/8	24 3/8	6	5	CHARLES	SAME	
1068	155 2/8	ATCHISON	KUHNS	92	69 3/8	71 7/8	17 6/8	0	22 4/8	22 3/8	6	6	JEFF	SAME	

MISSOURI SHOW-ME BIG BUCKS CLUB RECORDS OF WHITETAIL DEER BY STATE, TYPICAL

STATE RANK	SCORE	COUNTY	YEAR TAKEN	INCHES TYPICAL R	INCHES TYPICAL L	INSIDE SPREAD	INCHES ABNORMAL	LENGTH MAIN BEAM R	LENGTH MAIN BEAM L	NUMBER POINTS R	NUMBER POINTS L	HUNTER	FIRST NAME	OWNER	FIRST NAME
1068	155 2/8	ADAIR	95	72 4/8	71 0/8	17 1/8	2 1/8	24 6/8	25 0/8	6	5	MORROW	MARTY	SAME	
1068	155 2/8	ST. CHARLES	95	71 3/8	69 5/8	17 4/8	0	24 4/8	24 4/8	5	5	KORTZEDORY	MICHAEL	SAME	
1091	155 1/8	MADISON	64	78 6/8	74 7/8	19 2/8	8 3/8	24 4/8	23 7/8	5	4	GANN	KENNETH	SAME	
1091	155 1/8	CEDAR	70	70 4/8	73 4/8	17 5/8	0	26 3/8	27 3/8	5	5	UNDERWOOD	WESLEY	SAME	
1091	155 1/8	NODAWAY	72	71 2/8	69 6/8	18 5/8	2 2/8	23 0/8	23 2/8	6	5	DAVISON	LARRY	SAME	
1091	155 1/8	ATCHISON	72	72 7/8	68 2/8	21 3/8	0	26 3/8	25 2/8	5	5	HULETT	DAVID	SAME	
1091	155 1/8	GENTRY	81	70 5/8	68 5/8	22 3/8	2 2/8	25 3/8	26 2/8	6	5	WALLACE	RICHARD	SAME	
1091	155 1/8	TEXAS	81	69 6/8	72 6/8	17 5/8	0	24 1/8	23 3/8	5	5	SULLINS	NARVEL	SAME	
1091	155 1/8	LIVINGSTON	84	72 5/8	77 4/8	18 6/8	6 7/8	26 1/8	27 2/8	6	8	BUSWELL	DENNIS	SAME	
1091	155 1/8	PLATTE	89	75 2/8	71 2/8	14 5/8	0	25 3/8	25 3/8	6	5	SHAFER	SCOTT	SAME	
1091	155 1/8	CAPE GIRARDEAU	91	69 5/8	73 3/8	19 3/8	1 2/8	24 7/8	25 0/8	6	5	AINSWORTH	JOE	SAME	
1091	155 1/8	SULLIVAN	92	71 5/8	70 6/8	18 7/8	0	25 7/8	25 0/8	5	5	GUION	LONNIE	SAME	
1091	155 1/8	JACKSON	95	73 1/8	72 4/8	18 3/8	0	24 6/8	24 0/8	5	5	STEPHENS	JAMES	SAME	
1102	155 0/8	GREENE	70	73 7/8	68 2/8	20 4/8	0	24 0/8	24 2/8	5	4	JOHNSON	RICHARD	SAME	
1102	155 0/8	SCOTLAND	73	69 3/8	69 2/8	19 6/8	0	24 3/8	25 3/8	4	4	BUNCH	JOHN	SAME	
1102	155 0/8	SCOTLAND	74	67 6/8	71 5/8	23 4/8	0	25 6/8	26 2/8	4	5	ARNOLD	JUDY	SAME	
1102	155 0/8	ST. CHARLES	81	72 3/8	72 2/8	17 3/8	3 1/8	22 5/8	21 5/8	6	5	DYER	GARY J.	SAME	
1102	155 0/8	FRANKLIN	81	72 3/8	72 0/8	18 6/8	3 4/8	24 4/8	24 3/8	7	6	OVERSCHMIDT	VERNON	SAME	
1102	155 0/8	ST. CLAIR	82	71 4/8	72 6/8	17 0/8	4 4/8	24 4/8	24 4/8	5	5	HULSEY	HEATH	SAME	
1102	155 0/8	SHELBY	83	70 7/8	75 3/8	18 6/8	2 0/8	25 6/8	26 5/8	5	5	BLAINE	REESE	SAME	
1102	155 0/8	CLARK	86	75 0/8	77 1/8	15 1/8	7 3/8	25 1/8	25 1/8	5	8	CAMPBELL	JOHN	SAME	
1102	155 0/8	SHANNON	87	70 0/8	71 3/8	20 1/8	1 3/8	25 7/8	24 7/8	5	6	VERMILLION	RAY	SAME	
1102	155 0/8	ST. CHARLES	87	77 0/8	71 6/8	21 0/8	4 4/8	25 4/8	27 3/8	6	4	RAGSDALE	ROGER	SAME	
1102	155 0/8	JACKSON	88	69 0/8	71 2/8	19 7/8	0	23 7/8	23 2/8	5	5	HARRIS	LYNN	SAME	
1102	155 0/8	CALLAWAY	92	68 6/8	71 4/8	18 4/8	0	23 5/8	23 2/8	5	5	CLARK	LARRY J.	SAME	
1102	155 0/8	MONTGOMERY	93	72 3/8	71 4/8	14 2/8	0	26 4/8	25 2/8	4	4	HAM	RICHARD	SAME	
1102	155 0/8	BARRY	95	73 1/8	72 2/8	15 2/8	0	24 4/8	24 5/8	5	5	DODSON	JOHN	SAME	
1102	155 0/8	AUDRAIN	95	76 5/8	73 5/8	14 2/8	1 4/8	23 0/8	22 7/8	6	8	HEADINGS	SANFORD O.	SAME	
1102	155 0/8	WORTH	96	70 0/8	71 1/8	17 0/8	0	24 4/8	25 0/8	5	5	DeFREECE	SHAWN E.	SAME	
1118	154 7/8	KNOX	64	74 3/8	71 2/8	16 3/8	0	22 0/8	23 2/8	5	5	COLE	WILLARD C.	SAME	
1118	154 7/8	BARRY	67	71 2/8	72 0/8	17 3/8	0	21 2/8	22 7/8	6	6	PRIER	WINFRED	SAME	
1118	154 7/8	MACON	69	76 1/8	72 4/8	23 1/8	8 2/8	26 0/8	24 6/8	6	6	LARSON	ALBERT	SAME	

STATE RANK	SCORE	COUNTY	YEAR TAKEN	INCHES TYPICAL R	L	INSIDE SPREAD	INCHES ABNORMAL	LENGTH MAIN BEAM R	L	NUMBER POINTS R	L	HUNTER	FIRST NAME	OWNER	FIRST NAME
1118	154 7/8	WASHINGTON	73	74 3/8	72 2/8	16 3/8	3 0/8	24 6/8	22 6/8	6	6	BISHOP	DEAN R.	SAME	
1118	154 7/8	DADE	85	72 1/8	70 5/8	17 6/8	0	23 3/8	22 2/8	5	5	KING	BILL	SAME	
1118	154 7/8	MERCER	89	70 3/8	71 6/8	15 3/8	0	23 6/8	24 3/8	5	5	DeMOSS	KENNETH	SAME	
1118	154 7/8	BOONE	90	74 0/8	72 4/8	17 3/8	3 0/8	24 6/8	24 3/8	5	5	LOVELESS	JIM	SAME	
1118	154 7/8	JACKSON	92	68 7/8	75 7/8	18 3/8	1 0/8	23 6/8	25 3/8	7	6	SCHLEIF	JOHN T.	SAME	
1118	154 7/8	BATES	92	70 7/8	67 5/8	19 5/8	0	23 5/8	23 4/8	5	5	VANGORDON	JOHN L.	SAME	
1118	154 7/8	HENRY	94	74 4/8	74 4/8	19 4/8	7 3/8	28 0/8	26 6/8	6	6	DENISON	BARRY	SAME	
1118	154 7/8	DAVIESS	94	70 1/8	71 1/8	18 2/8	1 1/8	23 3/8	23 0/8	5	6	STIGALL	GENE	SAME	
1118	154 7/8	BENTON	95	71 5/8	73 1/8	19 7/8	2 2/8	26 1/8	26 0/8	7	5	MEYER	DENNIS	SAME	
1130	154 6/8	ATCHISON	60	70 1/8	70 4/8	18 0/8	0	24 7/8	23 5/8	5	5	COOK	JIM	SAME	
1130	154 6/8	BENTON	68	69 6/8	68 6/8	22 2/8	1 1/8	24 2/8	23 3/8	5	5	O'CONNOR	PAT	SAME	
1130	154 6/8	SCOTLAND	79	67 7/8	71 2/8	19 6/8	0	23 2/8	23 7/8	5	5	GUNDY	MICHELE	SAME	
1130	154 6/8	BARTON	80	72 0/8	68 2/8	21 7/8	3 1/8	24 2/8	23 2/8	6	6	BRUMMETT	DAVE M.	SAME	
1130	154 6/8	CAPE GIRARDEAU	83	67 3/8	73 0/8	21 4/8	0	27 7/8	28 2/8	5	5	SEIBEL	HARRY H.	SAME	
1130	154 6/8	WASHINGTON	85	72 1/8	71 3/8	18 6/8	0	22 4/8	22 2/8	5	5	LANDS	PAUL	SAME	
1130	154 6/8	SULLIVAN	86	73 7/8	81 0/8	17 2/8	3 0/8	26 6/8	25 0/8	6	7	GILVIN	JOE	SAME	
1130	154 6/8	CALLAWAY	87	69 0/8	74 7/8	19 0/8	1 2/8	22 3/8	22 3/8	5	7	CONNER	ALLEN	SAME	
1130	154 6/8	WORTH	89	71 5/8	70 0/8	17 4/8	0	22 5/8	22 4/8	5	5	LYNCH	LESLIE	SAME	
1130	154 6/8	CAPE GIRARDEAU	89	69 4/8	69 0/8	20 0/8	0	27 7/8	27 1/8	4	4	FEE	BRUCE A.	SAME	
1130	154 6/8	HOWELL	90	70 5/8	67 3/8	20 6/8	0	22 3/8	22 1/8	5	5	SPENCER	SCOTT	SAME	
1130	154 6/8	PUTNAM	91	78 4/8	72 5/8	16 4/8	0	23 2/8	23 7/8	5	5	O'BRIEN	MATTHEW DAVID	SAME	
1130	154 6/8	PUTNAM	92	71 3/8	74 5/8	16 4/8	0	23 5/8	23 0/8	4	5	LARUE	LLOYD	SAME	
1130	154 6/8	MILLER	95	73 6/8	73 1/8	16 1/8	4 7/8	25 0/8	24 6/8	6	5	WILDER	KERRY	SAME	
1130	154 6/8	GRUNDY	95	69 6/8	70 2/8	18 3/8	2 1/8	24 3/8	24 1/8	4	4	STILES	W.J.	SAME	
1130	154 6/8	CLINTON	96	70 3/8	70 5/8	18 4/8	0	23 6/8	23 2/8	6	5	FEIGHERT	LUKE	SAME	
1146	154 5/8	SALINE	66	68 4/8	74 0/8	19 3/8	0	25 4/8	25 2/8	4	4	NORMAN	VINCE	SAME	
1146	154 5/8	BOONE	72	71 4/8	69 2/8	17 1/8	0	23 0/8	22 5/8	5	5	STORM	DEAN	SAME	
1146	154 5/8	GENTRY	77	72 2/8	71 6/8	19 5/8	1 2/8	27 1/8	27 0/8	7	7	GILLESPIE	CRAIG	SAME	
1146	154 5/8	PERRY	84	69 1/8	69 3/8	21 1/8	0	26 1/8	26 1/8	5	5	WEBER	JAMESON	SAME	
1146	154 5/8	PLATTE	86	69 4/8	70 2/8	19 6/8	1 3/8	25 5/8	27 0/8	4	4	PERKINS	ANDREW	SAME	
1146	154 5/8	CRAWFORD	87	68 3/8	70 2/8	18 7/8	0	24 7/8	24 5/8	5	5	PAYNE	NORMAN	SAME	
1146	154 5/8	SHELBY	89	70 5/8	67 4/8	19 5/8	0	24 0/8	23 3/8	5	5	LARRICK	JOHN L.	SAME	

271

MISSOURI SHOW-ME BIG BUCKS CLUB RECORDS OF WHITETAIL DEER BY STATE, TYPICAL

STATE RANK	SCORE	COUNTY	YEAR TAKEN	INCHES TYPICAL R	L	INSIDE SPREAD	INCHES ABNORMAL	LENGTH MAIN BEAM R	L	NUMBER POINTS R	L	HUNTER	FIRST NAME	OWNER	FIRST NAME
1146	154 5/8	CASS	89	75 1/8	77 2/8	16 4/8	2 7/8	24 1/8	23 4/8	5	8	RAYMOND	DAVID	SAME	
1146	154 5/8	MONROE	90	78 3/8	73 5/8	18 1/8	0	26 1/8	25 1/8	6	5	STROPPEL	CALVIN	SAME	
1146	154 5/8	CARROLL	91	77 1/8	74 3/8	15 3/8	0	23 7/8	23 3/8	5	5	PATTERSON	AVA	SAME	
1146	154 5/8	RALLS	91	72 5/8	71 3/8	13 7/8	0	20 6/8	20 1/8	6	6	SMITH	TROY M.	SAME	
1146	154 5/8	CALLAWAY	91	70 2/8	71 1/8	17 1/8	0	24 0/8	24 0/8	5	5	TRACY	JIM	SAME	
1146	154 5/8	SALINE	91	69 4/8	68 6/8	20 1/8	0	23 5/8	24 6/8	5	5	PLUMMER	CHARLES L.	SAME	
1146	154 5/8	BOONE	92	76 4/8	75 7/8	17 3/8	0	24 2/8	24 1/8	8	6	McKEE	DANNY	SAME	
1146	154 5/8	HARRISON	94	71 3/8	69 5/8	19 1/8	0	24 7/8	25 6/8	5	4	LEWIS, III	ROY EVERETT	SAME	
1146	154 5/8	COOPER	95	70 0/8	71 7/8	15 7/8	0	22 6/8	23 0/8	5	5	SPENCE	TERRY	SAME	
1146	154 5/8	GASCONADE	96	78 1/8	74 5/8	16 2/8	4 5/8	25 7/8	26 0/8	7	6	BOLAND	JEFFREY J.	SAME	
1146	154 5/8	NODAWAY	96	70 4/8	68 2/8	18 5/8	0	23 6/8	23 5/8	5	5	HARDEN	MAX	SAME	
1164	154 4/8	GASCONADE	58	0	0	0	0	0	0	0	0	MOTTER	MARION	SAME	
1164	154 4/8	DAVIESS	68	69 0/8	72 7/8	20 0/8	0	24 0/8	23 5/8	5	5	MORT	K.H.	SAME	
1164	154 4/8	FRANKLIN	74	72 0/8	72 7/8	19 1/8	6 1/8	23 2/8	23 5/8	6	5	BRUEGGEMANN	KENNETH R.	SAME	
1164	154 4/8	ST. CLAIR	76	69 1/8	70 1/8	21 1/8	3 5/8	23 1/8	23 3/8	5	5	BROWN	LARRY	SAME	
1164	154 4/8	LINCOLN	84	74 0/8	70 4/8	17 4/8	2 0/8	23 5/8	23 7/8	5	6	HUPP	JERRY	SAME	
1164	154 4/8	GREENE	86	71 3/8	70 6/8	15 4/8	1 0/8	24 4/8	25 0/8	6	5	LAMBERT	BRENT	SAME	
1164	154 4/8	KNOX	87	72 3/8	72 4/8	16 6/8	0	26 1/8	26 3/8	5	5	SCHRAGE	JERRY L.	SAME	
1164	154 4/8	RANDOLPH	89	68 7/8	69 4/8	20 0/8	0	24 6/8	24 3/8	5	5	HUDSON	RANDY	SAME	
1164	154 4/8	MADISON	90	72 7/8	79 6/8	19 2/8	10 4/8	26 1/8	26 3/8	8	8	TRIPP	GABRIEL W.	SAME	
1164	154 4/8	CHARITON	91	71 1/8	76 6/8	17 6/8	0	24 1/8	24 1/8	4	5	GIBSON	BEN	SAME	
1174	154 3/8	HOWELL	74	67 2/8	74 7/8	19 7/8	0	24 1/8	25 1/8	4	5	HIGHLEY	DANNY	SAME	
1174	154 3/8	JASPER	80	77 3/8	73 2/8	17 4/8	5 3/8	23 6/8	21 6/8	7	6	CROUCH	LARRY	SAME	
1174	154 3/8	JOHNSON	83	74 7/8	73 1/8	18 5/8	5 0/8	22 5/8	24 6/8	5	6	ADAMS	DALE	SAME	
1174	154 3/8	FRANKLIN	84	69 2/8	69 1/8	18 7/8	0	24 0/8	24 0/8	5	5	PILGRAM	PHIL	SAME	
1174	154 3/8	NEWTON	87	70 5/8	72 2/8	18 2/8	1 1/8	25 6/8	25 4/8	5	6	MAYBERRY	TOM	SAME	
1174	154 3/8	MACON	88	69 0/8	71 0/8	17 7/8	0	24 7/8	25 0/8	5	5	SMITH	KEN	SAME	
1174	154 3/8	SALINE	88	68 4/8	73 7/8	18 6/8	0	25 0/8	25 4/8	5	5	NORMAN	NOEL	SAME	
1174	154 3/8	HARRISON	89	72 3/8	77 5/8	15 1/8	1 2/8	23 1/8	21 6/8	5	7	WRIGHT	TOBY	SAME	
1174	154 3/8	SULLIVAN	89	71 4/8	73 4/8	20 5/8	8 0/8	26 5/3	27 0/8	7	8	SCHROCK	JERRY L.	SAME	
1174	154 3/8	MERCER	90	69 1/8	68 7/8	19 1/8	0	25 1/3	24 5/8	5	5	KEEN	MICHAEL J.	SAME	
1174	154 3/8	MONTGOMERY	94	72 0/8	75 1/8	18 5/8	5 0/8	24 6/3	25 0/8	5	6	UTHLAUT	RONALD	SAME	

MISSOURI SHOW-ME BIG BUCKS CLUB RECORDS OF WHITETAIL DEER BY STATE, TYPICAL

STATE RANK	SCORE	COUNTY	YEAR TAKEN	INCHES TYPICAL R	INCHES TYPICAL L	INSIDE SPREAD	INCHES ABNORMAL	LENGTH MAIN BEAM R	LENGTH MAIN BEAM L	NUMBER POINTS R	NUMBER POINTS L	HUNTER	FIRST NAME	OWNER	FIRST NAME
1174	154 3/8	SULLIVAN	95	77 7/8	73 2/8	16 5/8	8 0/8	25 1/8	24 7/8	5	6	CUNNINGHAM	WESLEY	SAME	
1186	154 2/8	HARRISON	67	67 1/8	69 5/8	20 2/8	0	24 5/8	25 4/8	5	5	FORDYCE	MAX	SAME	
1186	154 2/8	GASCONADE	69	76 2/8	72 2/8	18 2/8	9 7/8	24 4/8	24 7/8	10	6	ENKE	ARTHUR	SAME	
1186	154 2/8	OSAGE	71	73 1/8	68 6/8	17 0/8	0	24 3/8	24 0/8	5	5	GAULT	HAROLD E.	SAME	
1186	154 2/8	McDONALD	76	73 1/8	75 1/8	14 2/8	2 6/8	21 1/8	23 4/8	7	6	LYSTER	CLINT	SAME	
1186	154 2/8	LINCOLN	77	67 7/8	73 5/8	19 0/8	0	26 0/8	25 6/8	5	5	BRIGGS	GARY E.	SAME	
1186	154 2/8	RANDOLPH	80	70 7/8	70 0/8	17 6/8	0	24 5/8	23 5/8	5	5	THOMAS	FRANK	SAME	
1186	154 2/8	BOONE	85	67 2/8	70 4/8	21 6/8	0	26 1/8	26 2/8	5	6	SMALLWOOD	DON	SAME	
1186	154 2/8	WARREN	87	71 7/8	77 6/8	16 3/8	4 2/8	21 5/8	22 3/8	6	8	BALLMANN	MARK A.	SAME	
1186	154 2/8	LIVINGSTON	87	65 6/8	65 7/8	23 0/8	0	23 0/8	22 7/8	5	5	MILLER	FOREST D.	SAME	
1186	154 2/8	CRAWFORD	87	87 3/8	76 5/8	17 1/8	12 4/8	23 6/8	24 2/8	9	8	OGLE	STEVE	SAME	
1186	154 2/8	HOWARD	89	71 0/8	70 1/8	21 2/8	0	27 0/8	27 0/8	5	5	CAIN	RICKY	SAME	
1186	154 2/8	ANDREW	90	74 /8	74 5/8	20 4/8	7 4/8	24 2/8	24 4/8	8	5	FISHER	JERRY	SAME	
1186	154 2/8	LINCOLN	90	68 5/8	70 1/8	17 2/8	0	22 4/8	22 4/8	5	5	SHOCKLEE	DERON A.	SAME	
1186	154 2/8	DEKALB	90	69 3/8	69 6/8	20 5/8	2 7/8	23 1/8	22 1/8	6	5	MARTIN	JIM W.	SAME	
1186	154 2/8	OSAGE	91	68 4/8	71 1/8	18 2/8	0	25 0/8	24 6/8	5	5	STUCKEY	MARK	SAME	
1186	154 2/8	DEKALB	91	73 3/8	73 4/8	18 0/8	5 6/8	23 4/8	23 4/8	7	9	MARTIN	JIM W.	SAME	
1186	154 2/8	COOPER	93	68 5/8	69 5/8	20 2/8	0	27 2/8	27 0/8	4	4	WOOD	TOM	SAME	
1186	154 2/8	ANDREW	94	71 4/8	70 7/8	18 4/8	1 0/8	23 0/8	24 4/8	5	6	KENDALL	BEN	SAME	
1186	154 2/8	WASHINGTON	95	68 4/8	69 0/8	20 0/8	0	26 5/8	27 4/8	4	4	SITZES	JAMIE E.	SAME	
1186	154 2/8	MORGAN	95	77 6/8	74 0/8	16 2/8	7 0/8	24 5/8	25 3/8	8	6	WOHLT	GEORGE H.	SAME	
1186	154 2/8	ST. LOUIS	96	69 7/8	68 2/8	18 4/8	0	27 6/8	27 4/8	4	4	WIGGINS	JESSIE	SAME	
1207	154 1/8	RANDOLPH	66	72 5/8	73 7/8	20 3/8	0	23 3/8	24 2/8	5	7	WAGNER	DAVID	SAME	
1207	154 1/8	ANDREW	69	72 1/8	76 2/8	16 6/8	4 7/8	25 7/8	25 2/8	6	5	SMITH	JERRY	SAME	
1207	154 1/8	BARRY	71	69 2/8	70 2/8	19 0/8	2 5/8	21 2/8	21 2/8	7	6	RENFRO	CLEO	SAME	
1207	154 1/8	MERCER	73	72 0/8	68 6/8	17 7/8	0	21 5/8	21 5/8	6	5	HERIFORD	ART	SAME	
1207	154 1/8	RALLS	80	69 3/8	74 2/8	19 1/8	2 6/8	26 0/8	26 2/8	6	6	COUCH	BILL	SAME	
1207	154 1/8	TEXAS	81	71 1/8	71 0/8	16 1/8	0	25 1/8	25 0/8	5	5	MENDENHALL	MIKE	SAME	
1207	154 1/8	ATCHISON	83	73 4/8	78 6/8	17 6/8	9 7/8	20 5/8	20 7/8	6	7	HARMON	BRITT	SAME	
1207	154 1/8	PETTIS	89	73 3/8	74 5/8	16 7/8	5 6/8	26 6/8	24 7/8	5	5	ELLISON	RONNIE	SAME	
1207	154 1/8	ST. CHARLES	89	70 0/8	70 3/8	21 1/8	0	25 6/8	26 0/8	4	4	STEPHENS	CARLIS	SAME	
1207	154 1/8	GENTRY	90	78 3/8	74 0/8	17 7/8	9 4/8	27 4/8	26 7/8	8	8	ANGLE	STEVE	SAME	

STATE RANK	SCORE	COUNTY	YEAR TAKEN	INCHES TYPICAL R	L	INSIDE SPREAD	INCHES ABNORMAL	LENGTH MAIN BEAM R	L	NUMBER POINTS R	L	HUNTER	FIRST NAME	OWNER	FIRST NAME
1207	154 1/8	CALLAWAY	91	69 2/8	70 6/8	18 1/8	0	24 1/8	26 4/8	5	5	MORRIS	ROBBY	SAME	
1207	154 1/8	CAMDEN	93	80 4/8	73 0/8	17 2/8	6 7/8	27 2/8	25 4/8	8	5	MURPHY	JACK	SAME	
1219	154 0/8	CALLAWAY	72	71 7/8	75 4/8	20 7/8	7 3/8	27 2/8	26 0/8	9	8	WILDEISEN	ORVILLE	SAME	
1219	154 0/8	GRUNDY	73	68 7/8	70 4/8	19 4/8	1 6/8	25 7/8	25 6/8	5	6	THOGMARTIN	LEROY	SAME	
1219	154 0/8	LINCOLN	79	72 2/8	71 7/8	15 5/8	3 5/8	24 5/8	25 1/8	6	7	WOMMACK	DAVE	SAME	
1219	154 0/8	LACLEDE	80	71 1/8	73 0/8	18 0/8	5 4/8	23 7/8	24 4/8	6	9	WILSON	WALLACE	SAME	
1219	154 0/8	LEWIS	81	68 5/8	70 3/8	17 4/8	0	23 4/8	23 4/8	5	5	BARICKMAN	TOM	SAME	
1219	154 0/8	CLINTON	82	73 7/8	71 4/8	19 4/8	4 2/8	24 6/8	22 4/8	7	6	BURNETT	SHAWN	SAME	
1219	154 0/8	RANDOLPH	82	72 3/8	71 1/8	19 4/8	1 2/8	24 0/8	25 4/8	6	5	WATKINS	FLOYD	SAME	
1219	154 0/8	CARROLL	83	74 4/8	70 6/8	16 5/8	4 5/8	24 1/8	24 3/8	7	6	ADKISON	DALE	SAME	
1219	154 0/8	GASCONADE	83	72 5/8	70 0/8	15 6/8	0	23 6/8	23 0/8	5	5	OLIVER	DELTON	SAME	
1219	154 0/8	MERCER	84	79 2/8	75 1/8	18 4/8	5 6/8	21 6/8	24 1/8	7	6	BIERLE	JEFF	SAME	
1219	154 0/8	NODAWAY	86	72 0/8	69 1/8	16 4/8	0	23 4/8	22 4/8	5	5	FARRELL	STEVEN	SAME	
1219	154 0/8	NODAWAY	88	76 3/8	72 2/8	19 5/8	7 5/8	23 4/8	23 7/8	8	5	OWENS	RICHARD	SAME	
1219	154 0/8	HENRY	91	68 7/8	70 3/8	20 4/8	1 2/8	25 0/8	25 7/8	5	4	HULL	MATTHEW L.	SAME	
1219	154 0/8	BARTON	92	73 1/8	71 5/8	16 2/8	0	23 2/8	21 2/8	6	5	EHLERS	KIM C.	SAME	
1219	154 0/8	GASCONADE	93	74 1/8	73 7/8	17 4/8	4 6/8	24 3/8	23 7/8	5	5	MASTERS	GARY	SAME	
1219	154 0/8	MORGAN	94	69 0/8	69 7/8	18 2/8	1 2/8	24 7/8	24 4/8	5	5	ROSS	MICHAEL E.	SAME	
1219	154 0/8	DOUGLAS	95	67 5/8	68 4/8	20 6/8	0	25 3/8	25 0/8	4	4	McPHERSON	JEFF	SAME	
1219	154 0/8	DEKALB	95	70 2/8	70 0/8	18 4/8	3 4/8	25 6/8	26 0/8	6	5	MARTIN	JIM W.	SAME	
1219	154 0/8	PETTIS	95	68 7/8	69 7/8	18 4/8	0	26 0/8	27 0/8	7	4	RAY	GEORGE W.	SAME	
1238	153 7/8	AUDRAIN	71	71 0/8	69 2/8	19 4/8	2 1/8	23 3/8	23 1/8	4	5	ROBERTS	BOB	SAME	
1238	153 7/8	MONTGOMERY	73	73 5/8	72 3/8	17 1/8	4 0/8	24 5/8	23 7/8	7	6	SCHULTE	GERALD	SAME	
1238	153 7/8	BOONE	76	73 1/8	70 6/8	18 5/8	0	25 7/8	25 5/8	4	5	THORNHILL	STEVE	SAME	
1238	153 7/8	DENT	78	69 4/8	70 7/8	17 1/8	0	22 3/8	23 5/8	5	5	GULLET	RANDY	SAME	
1238	153 7/8	HOWELL	79	68 4/8	72 0/8	18 1/8	0	24 2/8	24 7/8	5	5	COLLINS	JIM	SAME	
1238	153 7/8	MACON	84	72 3/8	72 2/8	17 2/8	4 0/8	25 4/8	25 0/8	7	5	HEPWORTH	BERNARD	SAME	
1238	153 7/8	LINCOLN	86	72 3/8	68 0/8	21 1/8	1 6/8	22 7/8	22 5/8	5	6	KENNEDY, JR.	RICHARD J.	SAME	
1238	153 7/8	PETTIS	86	68 5/8	70 3/8	18 1/8	0	24 0/8	24 5/8	5	5	HOLTGERWE	RICHARD	SAME	
1238	153 7/8	CARROLL	88	70 7/8	69 5/8	16 5/8	0	24 0/8	24 6/8	5	5	BUCKNER II	JOHN	SAME	
1238	153 7/8	RALLS	88	73 4/8	75 6/8	19 2/8	8 1/8	25 0/8	24 3/8	6	7	UNDERWOOD	BOB	SAME	
1238	153 7/8	RAY	88	72 2/8	71 5/8	16 4/8	1 3/8	23 4/8	23 7/8	5	6	KIRK	CHRISTOPHER	SAME	

274

MISSOURI SHOW-ME BIG BUCKS CLUB RECORDS OF WHITETAIL DEER BY STATE, TYPICAL

STATE RANK	SCORE	COUNTY	YEAR TAKEN	INCHES TYPICAL R	INCHES TYPICAL L	INSIDE SPREAD	INCHES ABNORMAL	LENGTH MAIN BEAM R	LENGTH MAIN BEAM L	NUMBER POINTS R	NUMBER POINTS L	HUNTER	FIRST NAME	OWNER	FIRST NAME
1238	153 7/8	AUDRAIN	88	72 5/8	72 4/8	16 3/8	0	22 2/8	21 7/8	6	6	SIMS	SCOTT W.	SAME	
1238	153 7/8	VERNON	89	68 2/8	73 5/8	19 7/8	0	25 4/8	26 6/8	4	5	ROBINSON	BILL	SAME	
1238	153 7/8	SULLIVAN	89	69 5/8	74 6/8	18 0/8	1 7/8	23 4/8	22 7/8	5	7	WHITLOCK	MARCUS	SAME	
1238	153 7/8	DENT	92	72 7/8	71 5/8	16 2/8	2 7/8	72 7/8	71 5/8	5	6	DANZ	DARA	SAME	
1238	153 7/8	ADAIR	92	71 0/8	71 3/8	17 1/8	0	23 5/8	23 4/8	5	5	JOHNSON	JERRY	SAME	
1238	153 7/8	BATES	92	71 2/8	70 2/8	15 7/8	0	26 1/8	26 3/8	4	4	TILLERY	HOWARD	SAME	
1238	153 7/8	PHELPS	94	73 2/8	72 1/8	16 5/8	0	22 6/8	23 2/8	5	5	MACORMIC	JIM	SAME	
1256	153 6/8	OZARK	66	70 0/8	70 1/8	19 1/8	2 5/8	25 2/8	24 1/8	5	6	PIPIN	DON A.	SAME	
1256	153 6/8	HARRISON	70	73 1/8	74 1/8	20 0/8	8 6/8	24 4/8	23 4/8	6	7	HARDING	MARVIN	SAME	
1256	153 6/8	CALLAWAY	73	72 6/8	77 7/8	17 0/8	9 1/8	22 5/8	22 5/8	7	7	BUSKEN	LEONARD	SAME	
1256	153 6/8	HOWELL	76	71 5/8	70 7/8	16 7/8	1 2/8	23 1/8	24 4/8	6	5	HOWELL	EARL	SAME	
1256	153 6/8	GENTRY	76	69 4/8	76 1/8	18 5/8	1 3/8	23 6/8	24 4/8	6	6	RENO	RAYMOND	SAME	
1256	153 6/8	PIKE	79	64 7/8	70 2/8	24 0/8	0	26 6/8	28 1/8	4	4	STUMBAUGH	KEVIN	SAME	
1256	153 6/8	STODDARD	80	68 5/8	69 2/8	19 6/8	2 2/8	23 2/8	23 5/8	5	6	BARTON	GARY	SAME	
1256	153 6/8	WAYNE	82	70 1/8	71 2/8	19 2/8	0	26 6/8	24 7/8	4	4	RUNNELS	LINDELL	SAME	
1256	153 6/8	COOPER	83	70 4/8	70 2/8	19 0/8	0	23 1/8	21 1/8	6	6	MADDOX	RAYMOND	SAME	
1256	153 6/8	CHARITON	84	71 6/8	73 4/8	21 5/8	5 1/8	28 0/8	24 7/8	8	6	RODGERS	BILL	SAME	
1256	153 6/8	DAVIESS	85	66 1/8	68 1/8	22 4/8	0	24 0/8	23 7/8	5	5	COLLINS	DENNIS	SAME	
1256	153 6/8	DADE	86	74 1/8	68 3/8	18 1/8	1 1/8	25 5/8	25 0/8	6	5	TEFERTILLER	LARRY	SAME	
1256	153 6/8	DENT	92	67 1/8	71 2/8	19 4/8	0	24 6/8	24 6/8	4	4	PORDORSKI	JEROME L.	SAME	
1256	153 6/8	MONTGOMERY	93	70 6/8	72 4/8	19 5/8	4 1/8	25 4/8	24 5/8	5	7	CARTEE	GREG	SAME	
1256	153 6/8	ADAIR	94	73 5/8	70 6/8	17 5/8	2 1/8	22 2/8	22 4/8	7	6	NOVINGER	GLEN	SAME	
1256	153 6/8	CHARITON	95	77 2/8	72 6/8	18 2/8	2 0/8	24 0/8	23 3/8	6	4	SMITH	PHILLIP	SAME	
1256	153 6/8	GASCONADE	96	69 3/8	68 1/8	19 0/8	0	24 1/8	24 1/8	6	5	BUSCHMANN	ALFRED	SAME	
1273	153 5/8	SHELBY	69	73 0/8	71 2/8	19 2/8	3 1/8	23 5/8	25 6/8	5	6	SMOOT	RONALD C.	SAME	
1273	153 5/8	MACON	74	72 1/8	68 5/8	18 0/8	1 1/8	23 4/8	23 2/8	5	6	POWELL	GARY R.	SAME	
1273	153 5/8	LEWIS	79	69 0/8	70 4/8	18 3/8	0	24 3/8	25 1/8	5	5	McCUTCHAN	DENNIS	SAME	
1273	153 5/8	OZARK	79	71 4/8	68 3/8	22 1/8	3 2/8	23 4/8	24 4/8	7	5	ROBERTSON	HENRY	SAME	
1273	153 5/8	LIVINGSTON	80	67 6/8	70 7/8	20 6/8	1 1/8	24 3/8	24 6/8	5	6	COLEMAN	FRED	SAME	
1273	153 5/8	RANDOLPH	83	73 7/8	69 7/8	16 2/8	3 0/8	24 3/8	26 2/8	6	5	WOODY	CLAYTON	SAME	
1273	153 5/8	BOONE	84	71 5/8	72 0/8	15 5/8	0	25 6/8	24 2/8	6	5	GARRETT	JACK	SAME	
1273	153 5/8	NODAWAY	85	67 2/8	68 5/8	20 3/8	0	23 7/8	24 4/8	5	5	ANDREWS	RONALD	SAME	

MISSOURI SHOW-ME BIG BUCKS CLUB RECORDS OF WHITETAIL DEER BY STATE, TYPICAL

STATE RANK	SCORE	COUNTY	YEAR TAKEN	INCHES TYPICAL R	L	INSIDE SPREAD	INCHES ABNORMAL	LENGTH MAIN BEAM R	L	NUMBER POINTS R	L	HUNTER	FIRST NAME	OWNER	FIRST NAME
1273	153 5/8	HARRISON	86	69 6/8	71 2/8	17 7/8	0	22 3/8	21 4/8	5	5	BURNS	MITCHELL	SAME	
1273	153 5/8	HOWARD	87	74 3/8	80 0/8	18 5/8	12 4/8	25 0/8	25 7/8	8	9	KOLKS	BOB	SAME	
1273	153 5/8	DAVIESS	88	69 5/8	67 2/8	21 1/8	1 0/8	25 2/8	24 6/8	5	4	WIDEMAN	JOEL	SAME	
1273	153 5/8	SALINE	90	77 7/8	69 3/8	19 3/8	0	23 0/8	23 5/8	5	4	MURDOCK	JIM	SAME	
1273	153 5/8	LACLEDE	92	78 3/8	77 5/8	17 2/8	5 7/8	23 6/8	25 4/8	6	6	TAGGART	KEITH	SAME	
1273	153 5/8	CHARITON	93	68 6/8	72 2/8	16 5/8	0	22 1/8	22 2/8	5	5	HOWARD	BOB	SAME	
1287	153 4/8	CALDWELL	66	71 3/8	74 7/8	17 1/8	1 1/8	24 4/8	22 5/8	4	6	DEWEESE	CECIL	SAME	
1287	153 4/8	WARREN	69	0	0	0	0	0	0	0	0	TANNER	DONALD L.	SAME	
1287	153 4/8	WARREN	69	72 4/8	72 3/8	17 5/8	4 5/8	22 5/8	23 7/8	7	5	SZACHNIESKI	BARRY	SAME	
1287	153 4/8	MONROE	70	68 0/8	68 6/8	20 2/8	0	22 7/8	24 0/8	5	5	GILLIAM	ROBERT J.	SAME	
1287	153 4/8	MERCER	71	69 1/8	82 2/8	21 0/8	5 4/8	25 5/8	25 4/8	4	6	HODGES	FRANK D.	SAME	
1287	153 4/8	OSAGE	72	74 6/8	73 0/8	17 5/8	5 5/8	23 6/8	24 5/8	6	7	WATERS	JAMES	SAME	
1287	153 4/8	CLINTON	74	70 4/8	68 0/8	19 4/8	0	25 3/8	25 0/8	5	5	MILLER	RONNIE	SAME	
1287	153 4/8	RAY	76	69 3/8	70 4/8	19 1/8	2 2/8	25 1/8	26 5/8	6	5	MYNATT	LARRY	SAME	
1287	153 4/8	COLE	77	77 4/8	68 7/8	16 0/8	0	24 4/E	24 5/8	5	4	KLIETHENMES	LEON	SAME	
1287	153 4/8	CHARITON	80	71 5/8	76 0/8	18 1/8	1 3/8	24 3/8	24 0/8	7	6	LENTZ	LINDY	SAME	
1287	153 4/8	CALLAWAY	80	69 7/8	72 6/8	14 6/8	0	22 5/8	22 4/8	5	5	GIBONEY	MARVIN	SAME	
1287	153 4/8	ST. CLAIR	82	68 2/8	71 0/8	18 0/8	0	23 0/3	22 4/8	5	5	HARRIS	JACK T.	SAME	
1287	153 4/8	CHARITON	86	67 7/8	76 2/8	17 6/8	0	22 6/3	24 5/8	5	6	SMITH	TOM	SAME	
1287	153 4/8	HARRISON	88	73 3/8	71 5/8	18 5/8	3 7/8	24 5/8	25 3/8	6	5	CLARK	ROBERT W.	SAME	
1287	153 4/8	WARREN	88	71 5/8	72 6/8	14 4/8	0	22 2/8	21 4/8	5	5	ENGEMANN	DAVID	SAME	
1287	153 4/8	TEXAS	89	70 2/8	69 0/8	18 6/8	0	25 2/8	24 0/8	4	4	TUNE	ROGER	SAME	
1287	153 4/8	RIPLEY	91	73 7/8	76 3/8	21 1/8	7 3/8	26 2/8	26 4/8	6	7	YORK	LYLE D.	SAME	
1287	153 4/8	RANDOLPH	91	72 3/8	72 3/8	17 2/8	4 2/8	23 5/8	24 1/8	5	7	MONTGOMERY	HAROLD	SAME	
1287	153 4/8	BOONE	91	73 3/8	74 1/8	19 1/8	2 7/8	23 5/8	24 4/8	6	6	DOMETRORCH	BRENT	SAME	
1287	153 4/8	SCOTLAND	94	69 5/8	70 6/8	16 4/8	0	23 6/8	24 3/8	5	5	CREEK	ALLEN W.	SAME	
1287	153 4/8	ATCHISON	94	71 5/8	71 3/8	16 0/8	0	24 1/8	23 4/8	5	5	AVRETT	MIKE	SAME	
1287	153 4/8	PUTNAM	95	71 5/8	69 4/8	16 4/8	0	22 0/8	21 6/8	5	5	BURNS	KRIS	SAME	
1287	153 4/8	HARRISON	96	70 1/8	74 6/8	15 7/8	1 7/8	23 1/8	24 0/8	4	5	HILLYARD	TODD	SAME	
1310	153 3/8	HOWARD	72	69 6/8	70 1/8	16 7/8	1 2/8	23 4/8	23 4/8	6	4	HILGEDICK	GLENN	SAME	
1310	153 3/8	TEXAS	75	69 0/8	69 6/8	21 7/8	0	25 4/8	24 4/8	5	5	OGDON	CARL	SAME	
1310	153 3/8	PULASKI	81	68 6/8	74 6/8	16 3/8	0	24 0/8	23 6/8	5	5	SCOTT	ROBERT W.	SAME	

MISSOURI SHOW-ME BIG BUCKS CLUB RECORDS OF WHITETAIL DEER BY STATE, TYPICAL

STATE RANK	SCORE	COUNTY	YEAR TAKEN	INCHES TYPICAL R	L	INSIDE SPREAD	INCHES ABNORMAL	LENGTH MAIN BEAM R	L	NUMBER POINTS R	L	HUNTER	FIRST NAME	OWNER	FIRST NAME
1310	153 3/8	RALLS	82	69 6/8	70 5/8	17 7/8	0	24 7/8	24 4/8	5	6	LONG	RONALD L.	SAME	
1310	153 3/8	MACON	83	68 6/8	72 5/8	20 1/8	3 2/8	26 7/8	27 2/8	5	5	ALBRIGHT	MICHAEL KEITH	SAME	
1310	153 3/8	GRUNDY	87	71 3/8	73 0/8	20 3/8	6 2/8	24 0/8	23 0/8	5	6	SCHMIDT	GERALD	SAME	
1310	153 3/8	SULLIVAN	89	69 3/8	66 7/8	22 1/8	0	23 4/8	24 1/8	5	5	MILDWARD	RICHARD L.	SAME	
1310	153 3/8	MONTGOMERY	90	71 6/8	68 0/8	18 1/8	0	25 5/8	25 7/8	5	5	CULLOM	DAVID	SAME	
1310	153 3/8	HARRISON	91	71 0/8	67 6/8	18 1/8	0	24 1/8	23 0/8	4	4	CHANDLER	ROBERT L.	SAME	
1310	153 3/8	SCOTLAND	91	72 3/8	73 2/8	15 3/8	2 0/8	24 1/8	22 1/8	6	5	DAVIS	JOHN	SAME	
1310	153 3/8	CLARK	92	68 6/8	69 1/8	16 7/8	0	22 5/8	22 6/8	5	5	ALDERTON	RRIAN	SAME	
1310	153 3/8	SALINE	92	73 3/8	72 6/8	16 7/8	5 6/8	24 0/8	25 1/8	6	5	KNOX	ROBERT	SAME	
1310	153 3/8	SALINE	93	70 1/8	72 4/8	18 2/8	0	23 2/8	24 3/8	5	5	DOHERTY	TOM	SAME	
1310	153 3/8	ATCHISON	94	70 5/8	70 6/8	17 5/8	2 0/8	25 6/8	25 5/8	6	6	WENNIHAN	JOHN	SAME	
1310	153 3/8	CARROLL	95	71 5/8	77 0/8	17 7/8	2 0/8	23 6/8	23 2/8	6	7	GUGLIELEMENCCI	CRAIG	SAME	
1310	153 3/8	RANDOLPH	96	70 2/8	67 7/8	19 5/8	0	23 2/8	24 2/8	5	5	COLLEY	TERRY	SAME	
1310	153 3/8	NEW MADRID	96	67 4/8	69 1/8	21 1/8	0	27 1/8	26 4/8	4	4	SIMMONS	FLOYD	SAME	
1310	153 2/8	CRAWFORD	55	73 6/8	72 4/8	18 6/8	6 4/8	25 4/8	23 4/8	5	6	HELLE	FRANK E.	SAME	
1327	153 2/8	ADAIR	72	72 3/8	68 4/8	18 4/8	0	24 5/8	24 7/8	5	4	WADDILL	ELLIS	SAME	
1327	153 2/8	MARIES	74	69 2/8	73 1/8	19 0/8	0	19 4/8	23 3/8	5	5	KERR	ROBERT	SAME	
1327	153 2/8	DAVIESS	74	81 0/8	73 3/8	17 0/8	9 2/8	25 3/8	25 0/8	8	7	ROGERS	DAVID	SAME	
1327	153 2/8	MONROE	74	73 3/8	74 2/8	17 7/8	2 7/8	23 7/8	26 1/8	5	6	DIXSON	MICHAEL R.	SAME	
1327	153 2/8	LEWIS	75	71 0/8	73 1/8	17 2/8	5 2/8	26 2/8	25 7/8	8	8	PINSON	KENNETH R.	SAME	
1327	153 2/8	MACON	76	69 2/8	73 0/8	16 0/8	1 0/8	22 2/8	22 1/8	6	6	BANE	ARTHUR	SAME	
1327	153 2/8	ATCHISON	78	68 6/8	69 2/8	18 4/8	1 2/8	25 2/8	24 7/8	5	4	JENSEN	JANET	SAME	
1327	153 2/8	DALLAS	82	68 6/8	71 3/8	19 2/8	2 6/8	25 0/8	25 1/8	5	5	REED	DAVE	SAME	
1327	153 2/8	SCOTLAND	84	69 2/8	71 4/8	20 1/8	4 1/8	26 0/8	26 0/8	8	6	YOUNG	DAVID	SAME	
1327	153 2/8	ADAIR	87	70 5/8	70 2/8	15 0/8	0	21 4/8	21 4/8	5	5	MOOTS	FERREL A.	SAME	
1327	153 2/8	OREGON	90	77 2/8	75 5/8	14 4/8	5 7/8	23 3/8	24 2/8	7	7	SUTTON	DONALD	SAME	
1327	153 2/8	SULLIVAN	90	70 6/8	72 2/8	15 0/8	0	23 6/8	24 0/8	5	6	FOSTER	RUSSELL A.	SAME	
1327	153 2/8	PUTNAM	92	71 0/8	69 5/8	18 4/8	1 4/8	24 1/8	23 3/8	6	5	KOTTWITZ	ANDREW	SAME	
1327	153 2/8	KNOX	94	69 3/8	71 4/8	16 0/8	0	24 1/8	24 3/8	5	5	BERGMAN	DAVID	SAME	
1327	153 2/8	MACON	94	72 2/8	70 7/8	19 3/8	5 3/8	25 5/8	26 0/8	6	5	SLOAN	KENT	SAME	
1327	153 2/8	COOPER	94	71 2/8	74 5/8	15 4/8	2 4/8	24 6/8	25 2/8	6	5	KNEDGEN	DARRELL J.	SAME	
1344	153 1/8	ADAIR	79	67 6/8	71 6/8	17 5/8	0	24 2/8	25 3/8	4	4	COY	ELDON	SAME	

MISSOURI SHOW-ME BIG BUCKS CLUB RECORDS OF WHITETAIL DEER BY STATE, TYPICAL

STATE RANK	SCORE	COUNTY	YEAR TAKEN	INCHES TYPICAL R	L	INSIDE SPREAD	INCHES ABNORMAL	LENGTH MAIN BEAM R	L	NUMBER POINTS R	L	HUNTER	FIRST NAME	OWNER	FIRST NAME
1344	153 1/8	NODAWAY	81	68 1/8	67 0/8	22 1/8	0	25 0/8	25 4/8	4	4	McINTYRE	BASIL	SAME	
1344	153 1/8	ATCHISON	81	69 5/8	69 4/8	19 3/8	1 6/8	25 5/8	26 4/8	6	5	LONG	RALPH	SAME	
1344	153 1/8	LINN	84	72 6/8	69 1/8	16 5/8	0	22 0/8	21 7/8	5	5	SCHUENEMAN	LESTER	SAME	
1344	153 1/8	CAPE GIRARDEAU	85	74 0/8	69 1/8	16 4/8	1 5/8	25 0/8	23 3/8	6	5	LOWES	PAUL	SAME	
1344	153 1/8	JASPER	87	74 2/8	74 4/8	17 7/8	8 0/8	24 0/8	23 6/8	6	8	WEBB	JIM	SAME	
1344	153 1/8	AUDRAIN	89	69 6/8	68 4/8	19 5/8	0	23 1/8	24 2/8	5	5	LYBARGER	DWAYNE	SAME	
1344	153 1/8	SULLIVAN	91	72 2/8	70 1/8	18 3/8	0	25 5/8	25 7/8	5	5	WILCOX	WILLIAM B.	SAME	
1344	153 1/8	SALINE	92	24 4/8	25 1/8	18 3/8	5 0/8	24 4/8	25 1/8	6	7	GREEN	KEITH	SAME	
1344	153 1/8	DOUGLAS	92	70 3/8	70 4/8	14 5/8	0	24 4/8	24 4/8	5	5	SCHINDLER	WILLIAM C.	SAME	
1344	153 1/8	SCOTLAND	96	68 6/8	72 4/8	22 2/8	5 7/8	26 6/8	26 6/8	5	6	DeNOON	BILL	SAME	
1355	153 0/8	RAY	70	70 5/8	66 6/8	21 0/8	0	25 0/8	25 1/8	5	5	CLEMMONS	ED	SAME	
1355	153 0/8	HICKORY	71	71 1/8	74 0/8	16 1/8	4 3/8	26 0/8	25 7/8	7	6	HOCKMAN	ARNOLD	SAME	
1355	153 0/8	AUDRAIN	84	73 0/8	70 1/8	16 5/8	1 5/8	22 0/8	21 5/8	5	6	BEABOUT	RANDY	SAME	
1355	153 0/8	RAY	86	69 3/8	75 1/8	21 1/8	4 5/8	27 2/8	26 5/8	8	6	LAMAR	DON	SAME	
1355	153 0/8	MACON	87	72 6/8	77 5/8	17 3/8	2 3/8	26 1/8	26 4/8	5	5	RICHARDSON	BOBBY	SAME	
1355	153 0/8	SCOTLAND	88	69 5/8	73 2/8	19 3/8	3 1/8	23 6/8	22 6/8	6	5	BRADLEY	BOBBY R.	SAME	
1355	153 0/8	PUTNAM	88	68 2/8	69 2/8	19 6/8	1 0/8	24 6/8	24 1/8	5	6	HURLEY	LARRY	SAME	
1355	153 0/8	BOONE	89	74 1/8	71 5/8	15 2/8	3 0/8	24 6/3	25 7/8	5	7	BEAN	WILLIAM	SAME	
1355	153 0/8	DAVIESS	89	65 1/8	66 5/8	24 6/8	0	25 3/8	24 0/8	6	5	RENFRO	DAVID	SAME	
1355	153 0/8	KNOX	90	74 5/8	68 6/8	17 2/8	0	25 6/8	25 0/8	6	5	TAYLOR	KEVIN	SAME	
1355	153 0/8	PUTNAM	91	73 4/8	74 4/8	15 6/8	4 4/8	23 1/8	22 6/8	6	7	LARUE	JOYCE	SAME	
1355	153 0/8	AUDRAIN	93	70 4/8	70 4/8	18 4/8	0	24 3/8	23 7/8	5	5	CAMPBELL	RICK	SAME	
1355	153 0/8	MONROE	93	69 6/8	71 5/8	16 0/8	0	24 0/8	23 4/8	5	5	PEIRICK	TOM	SAME	
1355	153 0/8	GASCONADE	93	72 5/8	70 6/8	19 0/8	4 4/8	23 3/8	22 5/8	7	7	ROST	ED	SAME	
1355	153 0/8	WARREN	95	72 1/8	71 2/8	20 1/8	6 7/8	28 1/8	27 2/8	5	7	JOERLING	GENE	SAME	
1370	152 7/8	MERCER	72	70 0/8	70 3/8	17 3/8	3 4/8	26 4/8	27 0/8	5	5	CLEM	VELDON T.	SAME	
1370	152 7/8	CALLAWAY	77	74 5/8	70 5/8	17 7/8	5 0/8	27 3/8	27 0/8	7	7	DOERHOFF	GREGORY	SAME	
1370	152 7/8	DAVIESS	78	66 7/8	69 0/8	21 7/8	0	22 7/8	23 2/8	6	6	MOORE	MIKE	SAME	
1370	152 7/8	WORTH	79	68 6/8	68 7/8	19 5/8	0	23 1/8	23 4/8	4	4	STEVENS	PREN	SAME	
1370	152 7/8	MARIES	85	71 2/8	75 3/8	20 3/8	10 0/8	23 2/8	25 7/8	6	8	GADDY	LYNN	SAME	
1370	152 7/8	CALLAWAY	85	68 4/8	69 0/8	20 6/8	2 1/8	25 2/8	25 0/8	5	4	DANUSER	JERRY	SAME	
1370	152 7/8	MACON	85	68 0/8	70 1/8	19 6/8	0	27 4/8	28 3/8	5	4	SMEDLEY	LARRY	SAME	

MISSOURI SHOW-ME BIG BUCKS CLUB RECORDS OF WHITETAIL DEER BY STATE, TYPICAL

STATE RANK	SCORE	COUNTY	YEAR TAKEN	INCHES TYPICAL R	L	INSIDE SPREAD	INCHES ABNORMAL	LENGTH MAIN BEAM R	L	NUMBER POINTS R	L	HUNTER	FIRST NAME	OWNER	FIRST NAME
1370	152 7/8	HOWELL	87	69 0/8	70 5/8	16 7/8	0	25 1/8	24 5/8	5	5	HOWARD	GLENN	SAME	
1370	152 7/8	DEKALB	87	67 5/8	68 5/8	20 1/8	0	25 1/8	26 0/8	4	4	MARTIN	JIM W.	SAME	
1370	152 7/8	RANDOLPH	87	69 3/8	70 0/8	16 0/8	0	23 5/8	23 6/8	5	5	WHITE	STEPHEN C.	SAME	
1370	152 7/8	RAY	89	69 2/8	68 7/8	19 7/8	0	24 3/8	25 1/8	5	4	DICKEY	LLOYD A.	SAME	
1370	152 7/8	CAPE GIRARDEAU	91	72 3/8	69 7/8	18 0/8	3 1/8	23 4/8	24 1/8	6	5	VINES	BOB	SAME	
1370	152 7/8	ADAIR	95	69 7/8	72 0/8	19 1/8	0	27 1/8	27 3/8	5	5	KLUG	KEVIN L.	SAME	
1370	152 7/8	CHARITON	96	69 7/8	72 2/8	16 4/8	1 3/8	24 2/8	23 2/8	5	6	BLACKWELL	ROD	SAME	
1370	152 7/8	NODAWAY	96	68 6/8	69 5/8	16 5/8	0	24 2/8	24 2/8	4	4	WILHELM	JIM	SAME	
1385	152 6/8	MONROE	73	71 6/8	70 2/8	17 1/8	1 7/8	22 6/8	21 7/8	5	6	MINOR	FRED	SAME	
1385	152 6/8	HOWELL	75	69 3/8	67 6/8	18 4/8	0	20 4/8	20 4/8	5	5	WOMACK	JERRY	SAME	
1385	152 6/8	PERRY	79	76 4/8	75 4/8	19 6/8	0	24 3/8	22 6/8	7	7	AUSTIN	PAUL	SAME	
1385	152 6/8	CAMDEN	82	68 6/8	70 2/8	17 2/8	0	23 4/8	23 2/8	5	5	WORLEY	JOHN	SAME	
1385	152 6/8	SCOTLAND	85	78 0/8	75 3/8	14 6/8	11 0/8	22 7/8	22 5/8	7	8	ROBINSON	RON	SAME	
1385	152 6/8	WASHINGTON	86	71 4/8	71 5/8	16 5/8	1 7/8	24 7/8	23 2/8	6	5	RIGEL	BILL	SAME	
1385	152 6/8	HOWARD	87	70 3/8	70 2/8	17 0/8	1 2/8	24 1/8	23 3/8	5	6	LEISURE, JR.	BAXTER	SAME	
1385	152 6/8	COLE	87	69 0/8	66 3/8	20 4/8	0	26 3/8	26 4/8	4	4	OUSLEY	HAROLD	SAME	
1385	152 6/8	SHELBY	87	71 2/8	71 0/8	21 4/8	7 0/8	22 0/8	22 5/8	6	7	MAYES	BILL	SAME	
1385	152 6/8	CAPE GIRARDEAU	89	68 3/8	69 6/8	19 4/8	0	25 2/8	24 7/8	4	4	ABERNATHY	GERELD	SAME	
1385	152 6/8	PETTIS	91	75 2/8	71 1/8	16 6/8	1 0/8	23 4/8	24 0/8	6	6	BALKE	JERRY M.	SAME	
1385	152 6/8	ATCHISON	93	69 2/8	69 1/8	16 2/8	0	22 6/8	22 4/8	5	5	HOWELL	BILL	SAME	
1385	152 6/8	AUDRAIN	93	71 1/8	72 3/8	16 4/8	0	21 6/8	23 0/8	6	6	BURNS	GLEN E.	SAME	
1385	152 6/8	REYNOLDS	93	72 0/8	69 3/8	16 1/8	1 7/8	24 4/8	23 6/8	5	6	HALL	ELVIS	SAME	
1399	152 5/8	CALLAWAY	57	73 5/8	69 0/8	19 1/8	1 0/8	23 4/8	24 3/8	6	5	WINDSOR	O.V.	SAME	
1399	152 5/8	RALLS	59	68 4/8	69 1/8	19 7/8	1 4/8	23 5/8	24 5/8	6	5	CURLESS	DONALD	SAME	
1399	152 5/8	TEXAS	67	66 7/8	66 0/8	21 7/8	0	24 4/8	23 6/8	4	4	JORDAN	BUD	SAME	
1399	152 5/8	WARREN	67	70 0/8	72 2/8	16 6/8	3 1/8	25 2/8	24 7/8	7	5	JOERLING	LAWRENCE	SAME	
1399	152 5/8	CHARITON	69	71 1/8	69 0/8	19 1/8	2 6/8	28 2/8	28 0/8	4	5	BLOSS	GARY	SAME	
1399	152 5/8	WASHINGTON	72	68 1/8	68 6/8	21 5/8	2 6/8	24 7/8	25 0/8	6	6	GROSS	ARTHUR B.	SAME	
1399	152 5/8	PHELPS	72	68 3/8	70 5/8	16 7/8	0	22 1/8	22 0/8	5	5	GANN	E.E.	SAME	
1399	152 5/8	LINN	73	73 1/8	72 6/8	17 4/8	6 5/8	23 1/8	23 5/8	5	6	SCHUENEMAN	LESTER	SAME	
1399	152 5/8	GENTRY	74	72 4/8	70 1/8	18 1/8	0	24 2/8	25 1/8	7	5	DARNELL	KEVIN	SAME	
1399	152 5/8	LINN	76	73 4/8	68 0/8	17 5/8	0	24 1/8	23 2/8	5	5	GANN	ROBERT	GANN	DANNY

STATE RANK	SCORE	COUNTY	YEAR TAKEN	INCHES TYPICAL R	INCHES TYPICAL L	INSIDE SPREAD	INCHES ABNORMAL	LENGTH MAIN BEAM R	LENGTH MAIN BEAM L	NUMBER POINTS R	NUMBER POINTS L	HUNTER	FIRST NAME	OWNER	FIRST NAME
1399	152 5/8	BENTON	78	69 7/8	69 2/8	17 1/8	0	24 5/8	23 6/8	5	5	HOSTERMAN	LARRY	SAME	
1399	152 5/8	LACLEDE	81	70 7/8	72 3/8	18 3/8	1 2/8	22 3/8	23 6/8	6	6	DICKINSON	KENNETH LEE	SAME	
1399	152 5/8	HARRISON	83	72 2/8	72 3/8	16 4/8	3 5/8	23 2/8	25 0/8	6	6	FRAME	DAVID	SAME	
1399	152 5/8	ST. CHARLES	84	68 2/8	69 6/8	18 7/8	0	22 2/8	22 3/8	5	5	COLYER	JOE	SAME	
1399	152 5/8	PULASKI	84	71 2/8	70 1/8	16 5/8	0	24 2/8	25 2/8	5	5	HAGE	RICHARD	SAME	
1399	152 5/8	BARRY	84	71 0/8	73 6/8	19 0/8	7 5/8	26 2/8	28 0/8	7	7	UTTER	CARMEN W.	SAME	
1399	152 5/8	MACON	87	70 3/8	70 2/8	18 0/8	2 1/8	20 5/8	21 3/8	6	5	HULL	MARTIN	SAME	
1399	152 5/8	SCOTLAND	88	68 6/8	71 6/8	15 7/8	0	25 0/8	25 5/8	5	5	GUNDY	KEVIN	SAME	
1399	152 5/8	REYNOLDS	89	72 1/8	69 0/8	15 5/8	0	23 1/8	23 5/8	6	5	TURNER	TERRY G.	SAME	
1399	152 5/8	WAYNE	89	77 3/8	67 7/8	19 3/8	0	27 2/8	25 3/8	5	5	CRUTCHFIELD	WINFRED	SAME	
1399	152 5/8	PUTNAM	90	71 6/8	70 4/8	19 1/8	1 4/8	25 5/8	24 1/8	5	6	VIGGERS	LEE	SAME	
1399	152 5/8	ADAIR	92	71 5/8	73 3/8	16 7/8	3 4/8	27 5/8	25 5/8	5	6	IVIE	MICHAEL	SAME	
1399	152 5/8	PHELPS	95	69 7/8	68 3/8	18 7/8	0	24 7/8	24 3/8	5	5	YELTON	RICHARD	SAME	
1399	152 5/8	SALINE	95	68 0/8	68 3/8	19 5/8	0	24 2/8	24 3/8	4	4	CRAWFORD	CHARLES	SAME	
1423	152 4/8	CRAWFORD	53	70 2/8	70 4/8	15 6/8	0	22 2/8	22 7/8	5	5	LEA	WILLIAM L.	SAME	
1423	152 4/8	NEWTON	54	69 1/8	66 5/8	22 2/8	0	24 1/8	25 1/8	5	5	GRANE	JOHN R.	SAME	
1423	152 4/8	CRAWFORD	64	70 6/8	75 6/8	21 2/8	0	24 0/8	27 1/8	5	5	MABE, JR.	RICHARD	SAME	
1423	152 4/8	LIVINGSTON	67	0	0	0	0	0	0	0	0	YOS	RAYBURN	SAME	
1423	152 4/8	McDONALD	67	70 6/8	68 0/8	17 4/8	0	24 0/8	24 3/8	5	5	HARPER	ROYCE	SAME	
1423	152 4/8	MACON	69	68 5/8	70 3/8	17 2/8	0	22 4/8	22 2/8	6	6	MILLER	CHARLES K.	SAME	
1423	152 4/8	CHARITON	74	68 4/8	67 6/8	18 6/8	0	25 6/8	25 4/8	5	5	BELT	BOB H.	SAME	
1423	152 4/8	PUTNAM	77	67 4/8	70 7/8	18 2/8	0	22 5/8	24 5/8	4	4	SUMMERS	JIM	SAME	
1423	152 4/8	KNOX	78	67 7/8	70 1/8	21 1/8	1 5/8	22 6/8	23 0/8	5	6	SCHUSTER	IRVIN E.	SAME	
1423	152 4/8	GENTRY	80	70 5/8	72 5/8	17 4/8	0	23 3/8	23 7/8	6	6	DOOLITTLE	BILL	SAME	
1423	152 4/8	BATES	82	73 6/8	66 2/8	20 2/8	0	22 5/8	21 4/8	5	5	BURCH	BRETT	SAME	
1423	152 4/8	LEWIS	83	78 5/8	75 4/8	19 7/8	11 5/8	25 1/8	25 3/8	6	6	SCHULTZ	JEFF	SAME	
1423	152 4/8	NODAWAY	84	70 1/8	71 5/8	18 2/8	0	22 1/8	23 4/8	5	5	GRAHAM	GALEN	SAME	
1423	152 4/8	CALLAWAY	84	67 6/8	68 0/8	19 2/8	0	23 0/8	23 3/8	5	5	ORSO	TOM	SAME	
1423	152 4/8	CALLAWAY	84	69 4/8	73 4/8	17 2/8	2 2/8	21 5/8	22 2/8	6	6	SEBASTIAN	BRIAN	SAME	
1423	152 4/8	KNOX	86	74 0/8	68 3/8	18 4/8	0	26 5/8	25 5/8	5	4	BRUMBAUGH	DAVID A.	SAME	
1423	152 4/8	PLATTE	86	69 6/8	70 4/8	15 5/8	0	23 1/8	23 5/8	5	5	WHITE	STEPHEN C.	SAME	
1423	152 4/8	NODAWAY	86	77 0/8	77 0/8	15 0/8	12 6/8	21 5/8	21 5/8	7	8	DURBIN	FRANCIS	SAME	

MISSOURI SHOW-ME BIG BUCKS CLUB RECORDS OF WHITETAIL DEER BY STATE, TYPICAL

STATE RANK	SCORE	COUNTY	YEAR TAKEN	INCHES TYPICAL R	INCHES TYPICAL L	INSIDE SPREAD	INCHES ABNORMAL	LENGTH MAIN BEAM R	LENGTH MAIN BEAM L	NUMBER POINTS R	NUMBER POINTS L	HUNTER	FIRST NAME	OWNER	FIRST NAME
1423	152 4/8	CHARITON	87	76 3/8	71 4/8	17 0/8	0	25 1/8	25 4/8	5	5	SCHMITT	CLARENCE	SAME	
1423	152 4/8	RALLS	88	68 4/8	70 3/8	17 4/8	0	20 3/8	20 5/8	5	5	MURPHY	DONALD W.	SAME	
1423	152 4/8	ADAIR	89	68 5/8	70 3/8	16 4/8	0	23 2/8	23 2/8	5	5	BEATTY	LEONARD	SAME	
1423	152 4/8	SULLIVAN	89	71 2/8	73 7/8	21 1/8	3 1/8	23 6/8	24 1/8	5	7	OTTO	ART	SAME	
1423	152 4/8	CHARITON	89	67 7/8	67 2/8	20 2/8	0	24 6/8	25 2/8	4	4	HURT	RANDY	SAME	
1423	152 4/8	CARROLL	90	66 5/8	68 0/8	19 2/8	0	25 4/8	26 2/8	4	4	OWEN	HEATH THOMAS	SAME	
1423	152 4/8	WARREN	91	70 2/8	74 0/8	16 4/8	0	23 5/8	24 7/8	5	5	JONES	MICHAEL R.	SAME	
1423	152 4/8	CAPE GIRARDEAU	92	66 4/8	68 2/8	21 0/8	0	24 0/8	24 3/8	4	4	ALLEN	JEREL	SAME	
1423	152 4/8	WORTH	93	75 2/8	71 2/8	14 2/8	4 0/8	23 1/8	23 0/8	6	6	ALLEN	RICHARD	SAME	
1423	152 4/8	SALINE	94	67 6/8	70 1/8	20 4/8	2 2/8	25 7/8	26 1/8	5	5	KLASING	JAMES	SAME	
1423	152 4/8	SALINE	94	68 6/8	67 4/8	20 0/8	0	22 6/8	23 0/8	5	5	LOESING	THOMAS	SAME	
1423	152 4/8	MILLER	94	72 1/8	73 6/8	14 2/8	0	19 0/8	19 2/8	5	5	MYERS	JIM J.	SAME	
1453	152 3/8	CAMDEN	67	71 6/8	68 2/8	18 1/8	0	28 6/8	24 4/8	4	4	RAMSEY	JAMES E.	SAME	
1453	152 3/8	SHELBY	70	68 2/8	66 5/8	19 7/8	0	25 7/8	25 0/8	4	4	RESA	ED	SAME	
1453	152 3/8	SCOTLAND	70	75 2/8	75 6/8	19 4/8	6 7/8	24 0/8	25 1/8	6	6	SLAYTON	TIM	SAME	
1453	152 3/8	HOLT	70	77 5/8	69 7/8	21 5/8	0	28 2/8	28 0/8	6	5	COTTON	GEORGE	SAME	
1453	152 3/8	MONROE	73	70 5/8	74 6/8	18 5/8	0	26 2/8	25 7/8	4	5	ABBOT	JOE	SAME	
1453	152 3/8	CLARK	76	69 5/8	67 4/8	18 1/8	0	23 6/8	22 7/8	5	5	STEWART	BILL F.	SAME	
1453	152 3/8	WARREN	82	71 3/8	72 2/8	17 2/8	4 1/8	25 2/8	25 3/8	5	7	DUFRENNE	KENNY	SAME	
1453	152 3/8	CARROLL	84	69 3/8	68 5/8	18 7/8	1 4/8	23 2/8	23 0/8	5	6	KIRKHOLM	MARK	SAME	
1453	152 3/8	GASCONADE	85	70 2/8	68 2/8	17 7/8	1 6/8	23 0/8	22 5/8	5	6	HAWKINS	JOHN	SAME	
1453	152 3/8	MONTGOMERY	85	68 0/8	69 1/8	16 7/8	0	22 7/8	23 1/8	5	5	RUPPEL	RUSSELL	SAME	
1453	152 3/8	CASS	86	67 4/8	70 0/8	19 1/8	0	26 4/8	25 7/8	4	4	HOCKER	GORDON	SAME	
1453	152 3/8	CLAY	88	68 4/8	69 7/8	21 1/8	4 4/8	27 2/8	27 2/8	6	6	BALDWIN	TRACY	SAME	
1453	152 3/8	SCOTLAND	88	67 5/8	68 4/8	18 5/8	0	24 6/8	24 1/8	5	5	TAGUE	DIANE	SAME	
1453	152 3/8	HENRY	89	74 7/8	71 3/8	16 2/8	5 5/8	24 1/8	23 2/8	6	6	CLAUNCH	DAVID	SAME	
1453	152 3/8	CAPE GIRARDEAU	91	68 2/8	75 2/8	17 5/8	0	25 0/8	24 1/8	5	5	RUCH	LARRY F.	SAME	
1453	152 3/8	HENRY	93	68 6/8	68 6/8	18 1/8	0	25 6/8	25 5/8	5	5	COOK	PHIL G.	SAME	
1469	152 2/8	WARREN	59	72 6/8	74 6/8	21 3/8	11 1/8	25 2/8	25 0/8	8	8	PLACKEMEIER	ROY	SAME	
1469	152 2/8	LINN	68	70 0/8	68 2/8	21 0/8	3 4/8	24 0/8	24 7/8	6	5	MARTENS	C.E.	SAME	
1469	152 2/8	HARRISON	71	69 2/8	72 7/8	19 6/8	3 0/8	23 6/8	22 5/8	6	6	COMER	GORDON	SAME	
1469	152 2/8	HOWARD	74	71 1/8	75 0/8	19 4/8	8 0/8	25 3/8	25 4/8	7	7	SUNDERLAND	WOODROW	SAME	

STATE RANK	SCORE	COUNTY	YEAR TAKEN	INCHES TYPICAL R	L	INSIDE SPREAD	INCHES ABNORMAL	LENGTH MAIN BEAM R	L	NUMBER POINTS R	L	HUNTER	FIRST NAME	OWNER	FIRST NAME
1469	152 2/8	LINCOLN	77	69 5/8	67 5/8	17 2/8	0	22 5/8	22 3/8	5	5	SOMMER	RICHARD	SAME	
1469	152 2/8	MONTGOMERY	79	69 0/8	74 2/8	17 2/8	0	25 0/8	25 0/8	6	6	HIATTE	KENNETH	SAME	
1469	152 2/8	CHARITON	79	73 6/8	69 7/8	16 0/8	0	23 2/8	20 6/8	5	5	LINEBAUGH	DEBORAH	SAME	
1469	152 2/8	ADAIR	84	69 0/8	69 4/8	18 2/8	2 6/8	23 3/8	23 2/8	5	6	FARLEY	BILL	SAME	
1469	152 2/8	CASS	84	67 0/8	69 1/8	18 2/8	0	24 7/8	25 1/8	4	4	HOOK	GEORGE E.	SAME	
1469	152 2/8	CLARK	85	67 4/8	70 1/8	19 0/8	0	24 0/8	23 2/8	5	5	DUNNING	MIKE	SAME	
1469	152 2/8	SULLIVAN	88	72 0/8	69 6/8	19 5/8	4 1/8	25 6/8	26 1/8	7	6	SMITH	BRUCE	SAME	
1469	152 2/8	ST. CLAIR	88	77 3/8	72 1/8	18 0/8	7 6/8	25 2/8	26 0/8	6	7	BURCHETT	TRAVIS L.	SAME	
1469	152 2/8	BOONE	89	68 2/8	69 0/8	19 1/8	1 1/8	23 4/8	25 1/8	5	6	BERGSIEKER	VERNON	SAME	
1469	152 2/8	POLK	90	73 4/8	69 0/8	19 4/8	0	23 2/8	23 4/8	7	5	CAMPBELL	TOM	SAME	
1469	152 2/8	PIKE	90	69 3/8	68 5/8	17 6/8	0	22 2/8	23 3/8	4	4	SCHUMAN	FRED A.	SAME	
1469	152 2/8	SCHUYLER	90	73 4/8	69 0/8	19 1/8	3 3/8	26 4/8	25 7/8	7	5	PIERCEALL	JIM	SAME	
1469	152 2/8	DEKALB	91	72 4/8	70 6/8	17 2/8	0	24 1/8	25 4/8	5	5	MALLEN	SCOTT	SAME	
1469	152 2/8	ANDREW	92	69 6/8	68 3/8	17 2/8	0	24 6/8	23 4/8	5	5	BARNETT	TIM	SAME	
1469	152 2/8	RIPLEY	92	70 7/8	68 1/8	19 2/8	0	22 4/8	20 5/8	6	6	KEEL	BRUCE	SAME	
1469	152 2/8	MARION	93	69 0/8	68 6/8	19 0/8	0	25 1/8	23 6/8	5	5	MILLER	PHILLIP	SAME	
1469	152 2/8	JASPER	94	71 6/8	72 5/8	16 3/8	2 5/8	22 3/8	23 0/8	6	6	BYNUM	THERON D.	SAME	
1469	152 2/8	WARREN	94	69 5/8	70 2/8	15 0/8	0	23 7/8	23 4/8	5	5	FENSOM	JOHN	SAME	
1469	152 2/8	DENT	95	70 6/8	67 4/8	17 6/8	0	22 3/8	22 0/8	5	5	TODD	ANDY	SAME	
1469	152 2/8	WAYNE	95	69 4/8	69 0/8	17 6/8	0	22 6/8	22 7/8	5	5	WATKINS	CARL L.	SAME	
1493	152 1/8	FRANKLIN	51	69 5/8	71 7/8	18 7/8	0	22 7/8	24 0/8	5	5	SCHROEDER	DON	SAME	
1493	152 1/8	MORGAN	58	72 6/8	75 4/8	19 3/8	11 6/8	24 1/8	24 6/8	7	6	PARRISH	ROBERT	SAME	
1493	152 1/8	CLARK	70	68 7/8	68 7/8	17 5/8	1 2/8	21 5/8	21 3/8	6	5	COURTNEY	ALLEN L.	SAME	
1493	152 1/8	PHELPS	73	70 6/8	69 7/8	17 0/8	1 7/8	24 7/8	24 3/8	5	6	RHODES	ROCKY	SAME	
1493	152 1/8	ANDREW	81	74 7/8	70 0/8	16 3/8	4 2/8	23 5/8	23 2/8	5	6	HOSKINS	ROBERT	SAME	
1493	152 1/8	ADAIR	82	70 6/8	73 0/8	17 7/8	4 2/8	26 6/8	26 5/8	5	4	LEDFORD	OWEN	SAME	
1493	152 1/8	BARTON	83	69 5/8	73 3/8	16 7/8	0	24 6/8	24 5/8	4	5	BICKFORD	JERRY	SAME	
1493	152 1/8	REYNOLDS	83	67 3/8	71 1/8	18 3/8	0	22 4/8	22 2/8	5	5	SMITH	RICHARD	SAME	
1493	152 1/8	MILLER	83	69 4/8	74 3/8	18 1/8	1 2/8	22 2/8	23 3/8	6	5	GROOSE	CHRIS	SAME	
1493	152 1/8	PETTIS	86	70 2/8	69 1/8	17 4/8	1 2/8	25 0/8	24 1/8	5	6	RHODUS, JR.	LEWIS M.	SAME	
1493	152 1/8	WAYNE	87	72 2/8	65 5/8	18 0/8	0	23 4/8	24 1/8	5	5	VANNOY	MARVIN	SAME	
1493	152 1/8	CLINTON	87	69 7/8	76 4/8	16 4/8	4 1/8	25 2/8	26 3/8	6	6	WATERS	CHARLES	SAME	

MISSOURI SHOW-ME BIG BUCKS CLUB RECORDS OF WHITETAIL DEER BY STATE, TYPICAL

STATE RANK	SCORE	COUNTY	YEAR TAKEN	INCHES TYPICAL R	L	INSIDE SPREAD	INCHES ABNORMAL	LENGTH MAIN BEAM R	L	NUMBER POINTS R	L	HUNTER	FIRST NAME	OWNER	FIRST NAME
1493	152 1/8	COOPER	88	74 3/8	71 3/8	20 6/8	4 7/8	24 1/8	25 3/8	6	6	ROOT	RODGER	SAME	
1493	152 1/8	SULLIVAN	89	69 1/8	69 6/8	19 7/8	2 4/8	26 1/8	26 0/8	5	5	PARKS	DOUG	SAME	
1493	152 1/8	WRIGHT	90	70 3/8	70 7/8	14 7/8	0	24 5/8	24 6/8	4	4	FLAKE	DAVID	SAME	
1493	152 1/8	REYNOLDS	90	68 2/8	69 7/8	17 1/8	0	23 2/8	23 3/8	5	5	RANEY	CARL	SAME	
1493	152 1/8	CALDWELL	92	72 1/8	70 6/8	15 1/8	0	24 5/8	22 2/8	5	5	CREWS	BILL	SAME	
1493	152 1/8	ADAIR	92	76 2/8	72 3/8	17 5/8	5 4/8	24 7/8	26 3/8	8	6	SPARKS	ROBERT	SAME	
1493	152 1/8	CALLAWAY	92	71 5/8	68 0/8	17 1/8	0	24 1/8	24 3/8	5	5	WEKENBORG	TOM	SAME	
1493	152 1/8	DENT	92	69 3/8	69 5/8	17 3/8	0	22 2/8	23 3/8	5	5	RUTLEDGE	LAWRENCE J.	SAME	
1493	152 1/8	LINCOLN	95	71 3/8	70 1/8	22 1/8	4 2/8	22 4/8	22 4/8	7	6	DIETIKER	STEVE	SAME	
1493	152 1/8	MADISON	95	68 3/8	74 4/8	17 1/8	0	24 2/8	23 7/8	5	6	BROOKS	DALE B.	SAME	
1493	152 1/8	ANDREW	95	73 2/8	69 6/8	18 4/8	5 3/8	24 3/8	24 2/8	5	6	JONES	RICHARD	SAME	
1493	152 1/8	ADAIR	96	71 3/8	68 5/8	19 2/8	3 5/8	22 5/8	22 1/8	7	5	STEWART	RYAN	SAME	
1493	152 1/8	PETTIS	96	67 5/8	70 4/8	18 5/8	0	22 5/8	24 1/8	5	5	RHODUS III	LEWIS M.	SAME	
1493	152 1/8	HARRISON	96	78 2/8	74 5/8	18 0/8	9 3/8	26 1/8	24 6/8	6	7	NICHOLLS	KENT	SAME	
1519	152 0/8	MORGAN	55	72 6/8	73 7/8	17 4/8	4 0/8	26 4/8	26 0/8	6	7	GILL	CLYDE	SAME	
1519	152 0/8	WARREN	57	69 5/8	67 3/8	19 0/8	1 4/8	25 4/8	24 6/8	6	5	WEST	IRVIN G.	SAME	
1519	152 0/8	BUCHANAN	60	72 7/8	72 6/8	17 6/8	0	25 7/8	24 6/8	6	5	MARRIOTT	RODGER	SAME	
1519	152 0/8	FRANKLIN	63	74 2/8	70 2/8	17 4/8	1 0/8	24 5/8	22 0/8	5	6	KOPPELMANN, JR.	GEORGE H.	SAME	
1519	152 0/8	GASCONADE	69	66 5/8	70 3/8	21 0/8	0	25 1/8	25 4/8	4	4	APPRILL	MELVIN	SAME	
1519	152 0/8	OSAGE	70	67 0/8	69 1/8	19 0/8	0	22 2/8	22 7/8	5	5	ADKINS	GENE	SAME	
1519	152 0/8	McDONALD	70	69 5/8	68 5/8	18 2/8	2 0/8	25 4/8	24 6/8	6	5	MURRAY	JAMES B.	SAME	
1519	152 0/8	GASCONADE	72	70 0/8	69 6/8	16 4/8	0	22 5/8	23 0/8	5	5	POSEY	STEVEN A.	SAME	
1519	152 0/8	RANDOLPH	72	66 7/8	80 4/8	20 4/8	0	26 4/8	25 5/8	4	5	O'BRYAN	DAN	SAME	
1519	152 0/8	MERCER	75	74 2/8	70 6/8	20 5/8	7 0/8	24 0/8	24 2/8	7	8	MOORE	RICHARD	SAME	
1519	152 0/8	MERCER	75	71 6/8	72 3/8	14 0/8	0	22 6/8	21 0/8	5	5	GEORGE	JERRY	SAME	
1519	152 0/8	MONITEAU	76	68 5/8	67 6/8	19 4/8	0	27 0/8	27 2/8	5	5	NIVENS	NORMAN	SAME	
1519	152 0/8	SCOTLAND	78	66 7/8	67 1/8	18 6/8	0	25 2/8	25 2/8	4	4	TRIPLETT	BOB	SAME	
1519	152 0/8	AUDRAIN	80	68 2/8	73 2/8	17 2/8	0	23 5/8	23 6/8	4	5	TERRY	JEFF	SAME	
1519	152 0/8	OREGON	81	68 0/8	69 2/8	17 6/8	0	21 4/8	21 0/8	5	5	BARTON	GARY	SAME	
1519	152 0/8	SCOTLAND	82	69 5/8	68 6/8	18 3/8	0	25 7/8	23 6/8	5	5	KICE	JAMIE	SAME	
1519	152 0/8	BENTON	86	70 0/8	70 7/8	16 5/8	1 1/8	23 7/8	22 7/8	5	6	BACON	DALLAS	SAME	
1519	152 0/8	SCHUYLER	87	70 0/8	65 5/8	22 2/8	0	25 3/8	24 2/8	5	4	BYRN	BRIAN	SAME	

MISSOURI SHOW-ME BIG BUCKS CLUB RECORDS OF WHITETAIL DEER BY STATE, TYPICAL

STATE RANK	SCORE	COUNTY	YEAR TAKEN	INCHES TYPICAL R	L	INSIDE SPREAD	INCHES ABNORMAL	LENGTH MAIN BEAM R	L	NUMBER POINTS R	L	HUNTER	FIRST NAME	OWNER	FIRST NAME
1519	152 0/8	LINCOLN	88	71 5/8	71 6/8	15 6/8	1 0/8	25 2/8	24 1/8	5	5	CONNETT	SQUIRE	SAME	
1519	152 0/8	LIVINGSTON	88	77 1/8	69 7/8	19 3/8	4 3/8	24 1/8	25 1/8	5	5	SMITH	ROGER	SAME	
1519	152 0/8	SALINE	88	78 2/8	71 0/8	19 2/8	8 2/8	22 2/8	22 3/8	9	9	KELLEY	JOHN	SAME	
1519	152 0/8	LINCOLN	89	71 0/8	69 4/8	17 4/8	0	27 0/8	26 3/8	5	5	THOMPSON, JR.	DONALD E.	SAME	
1519	152 0/8	ATCHISON	90	74 0/8	75 1/8	17 5/8	8 7/8	22 5/8	23 7/8	8	7	GEBHARDS	RAYMOND	SAME	
1519	152 0/8	AUDRAIN	92	69 1/8	70 0/8	17 7/8	1 0/8	25 4/8	25 3/8	5	6	PEAK	PAUL	SAME	
1519	152 0/8	CAPE GIRARDEAU	92	69 1/8	72 6/8	20 4/8	0	26 0/8	24 2/8	4	5	BROWN	CHARLES	SAME	
1519	152 0/8	WARREN	93	71 2/8	72 3/8	17 2/8	4 1/8	23 4/8	23 2/8	6	7	FEHLINGS	SCOTT	SAME	
1519	152 0/8	LACLEDE	93	69 4/8	74 1/8	15 0/8	0	22 4/8	22 0/8	5	5	HARRIS	JOHN M.	SAME	
1519	152 0/8	MERCER	94	72 3/8	67 7/8	20 5/8	3 3/8	27 4/8	26 4/8	6	6	SLAUGHTER	DAVID	SAME	
1519	152 0/8	PUTNAM	95	67 6/8	69 1/8	19 2/8	0	24 1/8	24 2/8	5	5	PARKER	MICHAEL	SAME	
1519	152 0/8	WAYNE	96	68 2/8	70 5/8	17 0/8	0	24 7/8	24 4/8	4	4	GOLDBECK	MIKE	SAME	
1519	152 0/8	PHELPS	96	72 0/8	75 6/8	18 6/8	10 6/8	23 2/8	24 3/8	6	6	WASSILAK	JIM	SAME	
1550	151 7/8	IRON	64	77 4/8	73 1/8	18 5/8	9 6/8	23 4/8	25 0/8	7	9	RONALD	ARTHUR L.	SAME	
1550	151 7/8	ST. CLAIR	69	70 2/8	71 3/8	16 7/8	1 4/8	22 2/8	23 2/8	5	6	FLETCHER	DONALD W.	SAME	
1550	151 7/8	MONROE	71	75 2/8	73 0/8	18 4/8	3 5/8	28 1/8	26 7/8	7	6	BOZOIAN	STEVE	SAME	
1550	151 7/8	CALLAWAY	80	70 5/8	69 6/8	18 3/8	1 2/8	24 3/8	25 1/8	5	6	CRANE	DENNIS	SAME	
1550	151 7/8	BOLLINGER	80	68 5/8	72 7/8	14 7/8	0	23 5/8	25 2/8	5	5	CLEMENTS	RALPH	SAME	
1550	151 7/8	CARROLL	82	72 1/8	69 1/8	17 5/8	0	24 6/3	25 4/8	5	4	SHERWOOD	WILLIAM G.	SAME	
1550	151 7/8	BOONE	85	73 2/8	72 0/8	18 5/8	7 2/8	26 5/3	26 5/8	7	5	ALLEN	JOHN	SAME	
1550	151 7/8	MILLER	86	68 6/8	72 2/8	16 7/8	0	22 0/8	21 6/8	5	6	BOWMAN	CHUCK	SAME	
1550	151 7/8	HENRY	86	75 3/8	73 5/8	16 4/8	9 1/8	24 0/8	23 4/8	8	7	KEDIGH	BILL	SAME	
1550	151 7/8	JOHNSON	86	67 5/8	70 7/8	17 5/8	0	24 2/8	24 2/8	5	5	BALDWIN	IRA	SAME	
1550	151 7/8	SCOTLAND	90	70 0/8	67 6/8	17 5/8	0	24 4/8	24 3/8	5	5	MCVEIGH	KEN	SAME	
1550	151 7/8	SCHUYLER	93	68 1/8	71 2/8	18 5/8	2 2/8	22 5/8	23 5/8	6	6	PARSONS	CHARLIE	SAME	
1550	151 7/8	SCOTLAND	93	73 6/8	67 6/8	17 3/8	0	26 2/8	25 7/8	5	4	SCHUMACHER	DAN	SAME	
1550	151 7/8	DAVIESS	94	70 3/8	71 2/8	17 4/8	2 3/8	23 4/8	22 2/8	6	6	MYERS	JOHN	SAME	
1550	151 7/8	KNOX	94	73 5/8	70 7/8	15 5/8	4 0/8	22 6/8	22 3/8	7	7	COULTER	TERRY	SAME	
1550	151 7/8	OSAGE	96	69 5/8	69 1/8	16 3/8	0	23 1/8	23 1/8	5	5	HENDRIX	GENEVIEVE	SAME	
1566	151 6/8	SHANNON	62	68 1/8	68 5/8	20 7/8	2 3/8	23 1/8	23 5/8	5	6	HOWELL	GORDON	SAME	
1566	151 6/8	FRANKLIN	70	69 4/8	74 2/8	15 4/8	0	24 2/8	23 5/8	5	5	MYRICK	AVERY	SAME	
1566	151 6/8	CHRISTIAN	70	69 7/8	67 6/8	16 4/8	0	22 6/8	22 5/8	4	4	HILTON	GARY	SAME	

STATE RANK	SCORE	COUNTY	YEAR TAKEN	INCHES TYPICAL R	L	INSIDE SPREAD	INCHES ABNORMAL	LENGTH MAIN BEAM R	L	NUMBER POINTS R	L	HUNTER	FIRST NAME	OWNER	FIRST NAME
1566	151 6/8	CALLAWAY	78	70 7/8	71 0/8	15 4/8	0	22 2/8	23 1/8	5	5	SPATAFORA	JOE	SAME	
1566	151 6/8	NEWTON	82	71 7/8	75 1/8	17 4/8	4 2/8	23 5/8	22 6/8	6	6	SHOBE	BOB	SAME	
1566	151 6/8	PIKE	84	74 1/8	65 4/8	21 4/8	0	25 4/8	25 3/8	5	5	BOULWARE	DEAN	SAME	
1566	151 6/8	LAWRENCE	85	74 1/8	72 4/8	15 7/8	6 1/8	23 2/8	22 4/8	7	7	JOHNSON	LARRY	SAME	
1566	151 6/8	LIVINGSTON	86	69 2/8	71 3/8	18 1/8	1 1/8	25 1/8	24 4/8	5	5	CARLSON	DOROTHY	SAME	
1566	151 6/8	DAVIESS	88	67 4/8	67 5/8	19 6/8	0	24 5/8	25 3/8	4	4	REYNOLDS	RUSSELL	SAME	
1566	151 6/8	SCOTLAND	88	69 1/8	71 3/8	17 1/8	2 7/8	24 5/8	24 4/8	4	5	MEINHARDT	MIKE	SAME	
1566	151 6/8	ADAIR	90	66 5/8	71 4/8	19 0/8	0	24 2/8	24 2/8	5	5	RUBLE	ROBERT	SAME	
1566	151 6/8	HARRISON	90	69 5/8	75 6/8	20 0/8	0	26 3/8	28 1/8	4	5	ALLEN	WAYNE	SAME	
1566	151 6/8	MERCER	90	67 1/8	69 4/8	18 1/8	0	22 5/8	23 5/8	4	4	CRAIG	DARRYL D.	SAME	
1566	151 6/8	PUTNAM	92	72 6/8	70 7/8	16 5/8	5 3/8	23 2/8	23 3/8	6	7	LARUE	LLOYD	SAME	
1566	151 6/8	SALINE	92	78 3/8	73 4/8	16 5/8	9 1/8	24 5/8	24 2/8	8	8	O'BRYAN	ROBBIE	SAME	
1566	151 6/8	MERCER	93	68 3/8	75 3/8	19 1/8	3 5/8	23 3/8	25 0/8	6	6	BAKER	ROBERT	SAME	
1566	151 6/8	DENT	93	68 2/8	72 6/8	15 2/8	0	22 2/8	22 3/8	5	5	JONES	MARK B.	SAME	
1566	151 6/8	JEFFERSON	95	72 7/8	69 5/8	15 6/8	0	24 7/8	25 0/8	5	5	RAMSEY	JAMES H.	SAME	
1566	151 6/8	OSAGE	96	67 3/8	67 4/8	19 6/8	0	23 1/8	22 3/8	5	5	FICK	PATRICK J.	SAME	
1566	151 6/8	RANDOLPH	96	71 7/8	73 4/8	17 4/8	5 6/8	24 2/8	24 6/8	6	6	DALE	ROY	SAME	
1566	151 6/8	CARTER	68	67 5/8	67 4/8	17 7/8	0	23 6/8	23 4/8	5	5	SEYMOUR	MICHAEL J.	SAME	
1586	151 5/8	MARIES	69	69 3/8	65 5/8	21 1/8	0	23 0/8	22 3/8	5	5	HELTON	ROGER	SAME	
1586	151 5/8	ST. LOUIS	71	70 2/8	66 2/8	22 2/8	1 5/8	25 6/8	25 6/8	5	5	SIDWELL	WILLIAM E.	SAME	
1586	151 5/8	STONE	75	67 5/8	68 4/8	18 3/8	0	23 7/8	24 2/8	5	5	BLADES	WAYNE	SAME	
1586	151 5/8	JACKSON	76	74 6/8	71 6/8	19 5/8	7 4/8	25 0/8	25 0/8	5	6	GIESEKE	MIKE DAVID	SAME	
1586	151 5/8	CALLAWAY	76	67 2/8	66 0/8	20 5/8	1 0/8	25 4/8	25 4/8	5	4	CUNO	LARRY	SAME	
1586	151 5/8	CALLAWAY	77	69 2/8	68 7/8	17 3/8	0	24 6/8	25 5/8	4	4	LONG	STEVEN	SAME	
1586	151 5/8	MONTGOMERY	79	74 3/8	82 0/8	14 2/8	7 5/8	24 2/8	25 5/8	8	6	LANG	MIKE	SAME	
1586	151 5/8	KNOX	80	69 0/8	68 4/8	17 3/8	0	23 2/8	23 2/8	6	6	EASLEY	LEROY	SAME	
1586	151 5/8	DOUGLAS	82	67 6/8	67 4/8	21 0/8	0	23 4/8	24 2/8	5	5	DUCKWORTH	RANDY	SAME	
1586	151 5/8	MONROE	82	67 5/8	67 6/8	19 1/8	0	23 4/8	23 0/8	5	5	MAGRUDER	MIKE	SAME	
1586	151 5/8	SCOTLAND	82	67 0/8	74 4/8	18 7/8	0	25 2/8	24 6/8	5	5	HOSKINSON	BILL	SAME	
1586	151 5/8	SCOTLAND	83	67 0/8	67 1/8	19 3/8	0	23 6/8	24 0/8	4	4	AUSTIN	JOHN	SAME	
1586	151 5/8	HOLT	84	75 1/8	72 5/8	15 7/8	0	25 2/8	22 3/8	5	5	REYNOLDS	JERRY	SAME	
1586	151 5/8	JACKSON	85	65 5/8	67 3/8	23 3/8	1 4/8	24 6/8	25 1/8	5	4	OSBORN	ROY A.	DECEASED	

MISSOURI SHOW-ME BIG BUCKS CLUB RECORDS OF WHITETAIL DEER BY STATE, TYPICAL

STATE RANK	SCORE	COUNTY	YEAR TAKEN	INCHES TYPICAL R	L	INSIDE SPREAD	INCHES ABNORMAL	LENGTH MAIN BEAM R	L	NUMBER POINTS R	L	HUNTER	FIRST NAME	OWNER	FIRST NAME
1586	151 5/8	BENTON	86	73 6/8	75 1/8	16 4/8	4 3/8	25 7/8	28 2/8	6	8	MEDLOCK	JOHNNY	SAME	
1586	151 5/8	GASCONADE	86	70 3/8	68 5/8	15 7/8	0	23 7/8	23 7/8	5	5	WILLIAMS	ED	WEST	RON
1586	151 5/8	RALLS	87	80 6/8	73 6/8	18 2/8	9 7/8	26 2/8	26 5/8	7	4	WEST	ALLEN	SAME	
1586	151 5/8	MILLER	88	67 2/8	68 6/8	18 3/8	0	22 0/8	21 6/8	5	5	BAX	ANTHONY	SAME	
1586	151 5/8	ST. CLAIR	90	71 2/8	77 1/8	18 4/8	8 3/8	24 3/8	23 7/8	6	7	LOCKRIDGE	ROBIN	SAME	
1586	151 5/8	ADAIR	90	68 4/8	69 7/8	19 4/8	1 7/8	25 3/8	25 0/8	6	5	WILSON	CHRIS	SAME	
1586	151 5/8	TEXAS	91	71 1/8	69 5/8	18 0/8	2 5/8	24 1/8	23 1/8	6	5	WELLS	DON	SAME	
1586	151 5/8	MACON	92	71 2/8	73 4/8	17 7/8	0	23 7/8	25 3/8	5	6	BARRON	GREGG	SAME	
1586	151 5/8	HOWARD	92	71 3/8	68 0/8	16 5/8	1 0/8	23 0/8	23 0/8	5	6	CARTON	JOHN	SAME	
1586	151 5/8	MONTGOMERY	93	71 0/8	70 5/8	17 7/8	4 6/8	21 6/8	22 5/8	5	6	WALTON	SCOTT	SAME	
1586	151 5/8	LEWIS	94	68 4/8	69 1/8	16 3/8	0	23 4/8	24 2/8	5	5	SHUMAN	MARK	SAME	
1586	151 5/8	ADAIR	95	69 6/8	73 4/8	18 0/8	1 3/8	22 5/8	24 0/8	6	5	PARTIN	GAROLD	SAME	
1613	151 4/8	OSAGE	63	68 4/8	69 4/8	18 0/8	1 0/8	24 4/8	24 1/8	6	5	BODE	FRED F.	SAME	
1613	151 4/8	CRAWFORD	63	69 4/8	67 4/8	17 2/8	0	22 5/8	22 3/8	5	5	SHOEMAKE	BOB	SAME	
1613	151 4/8	ANDREW	72	74 3/8	71 2/8	21 3/8	10 7/8	25 7/8	25 3/8	7	8	DEGENHARDT	JOHN	SAME	
1613	151 4/8	MACON	78	73 0/8	72 4/8	18 1/8	3 5/8	27 3/8	25 1/8	6	6	WILSON	JIM	SAME	
1613	151 4/8	WRIGHT	81	66 2/8	69 4/8	20 0/8	0	23 7/8	24 0/8	5	5	DUDLEY	JAMES L.	SAME	
1613	151 4/8	BOONE	82	69 2/8	70 3/8	17 5/8	1 5/8	23 3/8	22 4/8	5	6	CRANE	MURIEL	SAME	
1613	151 4/8	CALDWELL	83	68 2/8	79 4/8	17 2/8	1 2/8	24 7/8	25 1/8	5	5	SPARKS	RAYMOND W.	SAME	
1613	151 4/8	RAY	83	68 7/8	70 3/8	18 0/8	2 0/8	22 6/8	21 5/8	6	5	ALBRECHT	DONALD	SAME	
1613	151 4/8	LINCOLN	84	71 1/8	72 1/8	16 4/8	4 0/8	24 0/3	24 0/8	7	5	DETJEN	BRYON	SAME	
1613	151 4/8	CARROLL	84	70 6/8	70 0/8	17 3/8	3 1/8	24 1/3	23 5/8	6	6	MORITZ	LEE	SAME	
1613	151 4/8	OSAGE	84	69 1/8	69 6/8	18 0/8	0	24 2/8	26 2/8	5	5	FITZPATRICK	WAYNE	SAME	
1613	151 4/8	SULLIVAN	85	68 2/8	71 3/8	21 7/8	1 5/8	23 0/8	22 4/8	6	6	GANN	KENNY	SAME	
1613	151 4/8	LINN	86	68 6/8	68 3/8	19 0/8	0	24 5/8	24 2/8	4	4	CLAIBORNE	JAMES	SAME	
1613	151 4/8	CRAWFORD	86	71 3/8	73 7/8	19 5/8	2 7/8	24 5/8	24 3/8	6	8	KELLER	RANDY	SAME	
1613	151 4/8	CRAWFORD	87	70 2/8	68 4/8	18 0/8	1 5/8	25 6/8	25 2/8	4	5	ROBERTSON	VERNON	SAME	
1613	151 4/8	SCOTLAND	88	67 6/8	67 4/8	18 0/8	0	24 2/8	23 7/8	4	4	ARNOLD	DAVID L.	SAME	
1613	151 4/8	HOLT	88	69 3/8	69 0/8	16 7/8	2 1/8	22 7/8	22 5/8	5	6	RASMIC	MIKE	SAME	
1613	151 4/8	RAY	88	71 2/8	69 7/8	19 4/8	0	23 6/8	25 1/8	5	5	KIRK	DOUGLAS	SAME	
1613	151 4/8	LEWIS	90	67 7/8	66 1/8	19 6/8	0	24 7/8	25 0/8	5	5	EMRICK	BLAINE	SAME	
1613	151 4/8	ATCHISON	94	72 2/8	71 7/8	18 1/8	6 3/8	25 6/8	25 0/8	6	6	WATKINS	TRAVIS	SAME	

MISSOURI SHOW-ME BIG BUCKS CLUB RECORDS OF WHITETAIL DEER BY STATE, TYPICAL

STATE RANK	SCORE	COUNTY	YEAR TAKEN	INCHES TYPICAL R	L	INSIDE SPREAD	INCHES ABNORMAL	LENGTH MAIN BEAM R	L	NUMBER POINTS R	L	HUNTER	FIRST NAME	OWNER	FIRST NAME
1613	151 4/8	BENTON	95	68 6/8	74 0/8	17 0/8	0	26 5/8	26 1/8	4	5	PENNINGTON, JR.	JIM	SAME	
1613	151 4/8	MARION	95	68 1/8	69 3/8	18 2/8	0	23 4/8	23 4/8	5	6	BOHRER	RYAN	SAME	
1613	151 4/8	LINN	96	70 3/8	71 7/8	20 1/8	5 7/8	25 2/8	23 7/8	6	7	PAULUS	JOHN	SAME	
1613	151 4/8	PHELPS	96	72 5/8	77 5/8	18 1/8	9 1/8	26 5/8	28 5/8	7	7	KINSLOW	ARNOLD W.	SAME	
1637	151 3/8	GRUNDY	70	75 5/8	68 7/8	19 1/8	0	25 4/8	26 2/8	5	4	GIBSON	WESLEY	GIBSON	JEFF
1637	151 3/8	HOLT	76	72 2/8	74 7/8	17 2/8	2 3/8	23 1/8	22 6/8	5	8	SCARBROUGH	FRANK	SAME	
1637	151 3/8	AUDRAIN	78	72 7/8	72 0/8	18 4/8	9 5/8	23 0/8	23 2/8	6	7	BRANSTETTER	BOB	SAME	
1637	151 3/8	COOPER	78	71 2/8	71 1/8	18 4/8	5 5/8	24 1/8	23 4/8	7	5	RENTSCHLER	DAVID	SAME	
1637	151 3/8	ADAIR	78	68 1/8	68 0/8	19 0/8	1 1/8	24 6/8	24 3/8	5	4	ELLIS	WAYNE	SAME	
1637	151 3/8	PIKE	80	69 7/8	70 1/8	19 7/8	0	24 1/8	25 1/8	5	4	MUFF	EDWARD	SAME	
1637	151 3/8	DEKALB	81	69 4/8	75 6/8	18 6/8	6 7/8	27 1/8	28 0/8	6	4	SIMMONS	JACKIE	SAME	
1637	151 3/8	CAMDEN	84	67 7/8	66 7/8	18 5/8	0	25 6/8	25 2/8	4	4	SHRAUGER, JR.	RUSSELL	SAME	
1637	151 3/8	ST. LOUIS	85	71 3/8	70 1/8	18 1/8	0	26 0/8	24 5/8	5	4	LEUTHAUSER	RONALD	SAME	
1637	151 3/8	COOPER	88	69 5/8	72 1/8	18 7/8	5 2/8	24 1/8	24 2/8	7	5	JEWETT	JEFF	SAME	
1637	151 3/8	PULASKI	90	68 4/8	68 6/8	17 6/8	1 5/8	25 7/8	25 7/8	5	4	SHELDEN	MARK	SAME	
1637	151 3/8	LIVINGSTON	91	65 6/8	69 5/8	20 1/8	0	23 1/8	23 2/8	5	5	BUCKNER	E.W.	SAME	
1637	151 3/8	COOPER	91	68 3/8	69 2/8	18 1/8	0	22 7/8	22 6/8	5	5	MEYER	RICK E.	SAME	
1637	151 3/8	CHARITON	92	71 7/8	71 7/8	14 0/8	2 1/8	23 7/8	22 6/8	6	6	BERTSCH	DAVID C.	SAME	
1637	151 3/8	SALINE	95	68 1/8	72 3/8	22 3/8	0	24 5/8	25 6/8	6	6	PARRISH	ROBERT	SAME	
1637	151 3/8	MONTGOMERY	95	69 2/8	71 4/8	14 1/8	0	22 6/8	23 0/8	5	5	SHELTON	DOUG	SAME	
1637	151 3/8	RAY	95	73 6/8	77 6/8	18 4/8	10 3/8	25 1/8	24 6/8	7	11	HIATT	PHILLIP R.	SAME	
1637	151 3/8	SALINE	95	72 2/8	72 5/8	17 6/8	8 5/8	22 0/8	23 1/8	6	6	EDDY	JOE	SAME	
1637	151 3/8	DENT	96	68 6/8	68 1/8	16 5/8	0	25 6/8	25 4/8	5	5	LAPLANT	MARK	SAME	
1656	151 2/8	HICKORY	60	75 2/8	72 7/8	17 6/8	3 4/8	23 0/8	23 4/8	7	6	O'CONNOR	PAT	SAME	
1656	151 2/8	SCOTLAND	71	75 2/8	76 2/8	17 7/8	9 1/8	23 7/8	22 4/8	6	7	HILPERT	GARY	SAME	
1656	151 2/8	KNOX	71	69 1/8	67 0/8	17 2/8	0	26 1/8	26 1/8	4	4	HUSE	RICKY	SAME	
1656	151 2/8	LEWIS	73	69 5/8	73 2/8	19 7/8	6 3/8	25 7/8	25 4/8	8	5	STEWART	EDWARD L.	SAME	
1656	151 2/8	BOONE	74	70 2/8	73 0/8	16 4/8	3 6/8	23 4/8	23 2/8	6	6	HUFFMAN	FRANK	SAME	
1656	151 2/8	MERCER	77	68 3/8	73 6/8	17 4/8	1 2/8	23 6/8	23 6/8	5	5	NOE	JUDITH M.	SAME	
1656	151 2/8	DAVIESS	78	77 0/8	68 2/8	17 4/8	0	25 2/8	25 1/8	5	4	GARDNER	ALBERT	SAME	
1656	151 2/8	OSAGE	81	71 4/8	69 0/8	16 2/8	0	71 4/8	69 0/8	5	5	BRANDT	URBAN	SAME	
1656	151 2/8	GASCONADE	81	68 1/8	72 7/8	15 0/8	0	23 6/8	26 0/8	5	5	SEAMON	TIM	SAME	

MISSOURI SHOW-ME BIG BUCKS CLUB RECORDS OF WHITETAIL DEER BY STATE, TYPICAL

STATE RANK	SCORE	COUNTY	YEAR TAKEN	INCHES TYPICAL R	L	INSIDE SPREAD	INCHES ABNORMAL	LENGTH MAIN BEAM R	L	NUMBER POINTS R	L	HUNTER	FIRST NAME	OWNER	FIRST NAME
1656	151 2/8	ADAIR	83	69 5/8	70 3/8	19 4/8	0	23 4/8	25 3/8	5	5	STEWART	RON	SAME	
1656	151 2/8	DEKALB	83	64 1/8	68 4/8	23 0/8	0	24 4/8	24 4/8	5	5	HILL	DON	SAME	
1656	151 2/8	MARION	84	67 5/8	69 0/8	19 0/8	0	22 2/8	23 0/8	5	5	BLOMBERG	CHRIS	SAME	
1656	151 2/8	LEWIS	85	70 6/8	67 0/8	18 0/8	0	23 6/8	22 6/8	5	5	ST. CLAIR	STEVE	SAME	
1656	151 2/8	MORGAN	86	67 4/8	71 1/8	18 0/8	0	24 0/8	23 6/8	5	5	KNUTH	KENNY	SAME	
1656	151 2/8	HENRY	86	69 0/8	68 0/8	17 6/8	0	23 4/8	22 4/8	5	5	SMITKA	BILL	SAME	
1656	151 2/8	RAY	87	70 3/8	70 4/8	16 6/8	0	22 1/8	22 4/8	5	6	ESTES	NOAH	SAME	
1656	151 2/8	PERRY	87	72 6/8	74 7/8	17 5/8	5 1/8	25 0/8	23 7/8	5	5	STENGEL	TOM	SAME	
1656	151 2/8	CLARK	87	73 1/8	70 7/8	17 4/8	0	24 2/8	25 4/8	6	4	FIFE	FRED R.	SAME	
1656	151 2/8	RAY	87	71 2/8	69 4/8	15 0/8	0	23 0/8	24 2/8	5	5	HICKS	LARRY	SAME	
1656	151 2/8	MONTGOMERY	88	67 1/8	69 7/8	20 4/8	0	25 0/8	23 4/8	5	5	RETHERFORD	JUDY	SAME	
1656	151 2/8	BATES	88	66 5/8	67 7/8	20 0/8	0	28 0/8	27 7/8	4	4	ANDULA	RAY	SAME	
1656	151 2/8	COOPER	90	71 6/8	67 7/8	20 4/8	4 6/8	25 6/8	25 5/8	5	5	HOFSTETTER	ROSS	SAME	
1656	151 2/8	GRUNDY	90	70 6/8	8 1/8	17 4/8	0	23 2/8	23 2/8	6	5	HUGHES	TIM	SAME	
1656	151 2/8	ST. LOUIS	90	74 2/8	73 6/8	18 0/8	7 0/8	25 4/8	24 0/8	6	5	RUFFINO	PHIL	SAME	
1656	151 2/8	CRAWFORD	91	70 6/8	68 0/8	15 6/8	0	24 2/8	23 7/8	5	5	LEM	TOM	SAME	
1656	151 2/8	HOWARD	91	68 6/8	69 1/8	17 4/8	0	22 3/8	22 4/8	5	5	SENTER	DANIEL LEE	SAME	
1656	151 2/8	RAY	91	66 3/8	64 7/8	21 6/8	0	24 2/8	24 0/8	5	5	BROCK	WADE	SAME	
1656	151 2/8	RANDOLPH	92	66 5/8	68 5/8	19 6/8	0	24 4/8	24 2/8	5	5	BATES	JOHN F.	SAME	
1656	151 2/8	RAY	92	70 0/8	70 5/8	17 4/8	0	23 0/8	24 0/8	5	5	HOLTZCLAW	TONY	SAME	
1656	151 2/8	JASPER	92	71 6/8	73 6/8	14 3/8	4 3/8	23 2/8	23 6/8	7	7	SMITH	GREG	SAME	
1656	151 2/8	CALLAWAY	92	70 2/8	68 3/8	16 2/8	0	24 2/8	23 6/8	5	5	VARNADORE	TRACY	SAME	
1656	151 2/8	DAVIESS	93	70 6/8	79 5/8	20 1/8	8 1/8	26 3/8	25 6/8	5	5	HIGHTREE	JOHN	SAME	
1656	151 2/8	GENTRY	95	73 4/8	73 6/8	16 1/8	8 1/8	25 0/8	25 1/8	7	6	SCHRADER	FRED	SAME	
1656	151 2/8	DAVIESS	95	67 4/8	72 4/8	17 2/8	0	24 1/8	24 7/8	5	5	CARTER	SCOTT	SAME	
1656	151 1/8	RALLS	64	71 5/8	69 4/8	19 5/8	0	25 3/8	24 3/8	5	5	PEERY	TOMMY	SAME	
1690	151 1/8	SULLIVAN	67	72 1/8	73 0/8	18 0/8	3 5/8	27 1/8	25 2/8	5	5	SAYRE	PHILLIP	SAME	
1690	151 1/8	ADAIR	71	70 2/8	70 1/8	18 4/8	3 7/8	22 3/8	23 4/8	7	5	TRANSANO	EDDY	SAME	
1690	151 1/8	SHELBY	73	69 4/8	69 0/8	16 1/8	0	23 3/8	23 6/8	5	5	BROWN	NOBLE	SAME	
1690	151 1/8	MARIES	75	69 1/8	82 0/8	16 5/8	3 6/8	22 1/8	23 7/8	6	8	SCHEULEN	DANIEL	SAME	
1690	151 1/8	HARRISON	77	70 0/8	73 4/8	15 2/8	1 7/8	25 3/8	24 5/8	5	6	DEVER	GUS	SAME	
1690	151 1/8	PETTIS	77	71 4/8	70 4/8	17 4/8	2 1/8	22 2/8	23 1/8	6	6	TAYLOR	CHESTER	SAME	

MISSOURI SHOW-ME BIG BUCKS CLUB RECORDS OF WHITETAIL DEER BY STATE, TYPICAL

STATE RANK	SCORE	COUNTY	YEAR TAKEN	INCHES TYPICAL R	L	INSIDE SPREAD	INCHES ABNORMAL	LENGTH MAIN BEAM R	L	NUMBER POINTS R	L	HUNTER	FIRST NAME	OWNER	FIRST NAME
1690	151 1/8	DAVIESS	79	66 5/8	70 1/8	17 7/8	0	22 4/8	22 4/8	5	5	LEE	MICHAEL	SAME	
1690	151 1/8	BATES	82	70 2/8	68 3/8	19 5/8	0	26 0/8	27 5/8	5	5	WILSON	WILLIAM J.	SAME	
1690	151 1/8	DEKALB	86	73 7/8	70 0/8	18 2/8	4 1/8	25 0/8	24 2/8	6	7	LEIVAN	NEAL	SAME	
1690	151 1/8	PHELPS	86	71 2/8	78 5/8	17 4/8	3 7/8	25 5/8	26 1/8	5	5	DAVIS	DOUG	SAME	
1690	151 1/8	LIVINGSTON	86	67 6/8	69 0/8	16 6/8	0	22 6/8	23 1/8	5	5	MENEELY	HOWARD	SAME	
1690	151 1/8	LINN	87	71 1/8	69 6/8	18 4/8	3 7/8	25 5/8	26 5/8	6	5	CAMPBELL	KEITH	SAME	
1690	151 1/8	BOONE	87	84 3/8	67 7/8	19 3/8	0	23 /48	23 4/8	6	4	SHELTON	SAM	SAME	
1690	151 1/8	JEFFERSON	88	74 6/8	69 6/8	16 3/8	0	22 0/8	23 2/8	5	5	NORTH	STEVE	SAME	
1690	151 1/8	ADAIR	88	70 3/8	68 3/8	19 4/8	2 7/8	20 7/8	20 5/8	6	6	TUGGLE	TOMMY	SAME	
1690	151 1/8	ST. CHARLES	90	69 1/8	75 7/8	20 4/8	3 7/8	28 4/8	27 6/8	5	6	HALE	GREG	SAME	
1690	151 1/8	CHARITON	90	68 4/8	71 1/8	18 3/8	1 0/8	24 1/8	24 0/8	5	6	WOMACK	ROBERT	SAME	
1690	151 1/8	IRON	91	74 1/8	72 4/8	17 4/8	6 5/8	21 7/8	22 2/8	7	8	HARTWICK	CHARISSE	SAME	
1690	151 1/8	OSAGE	93	68 5/8	68 7/8	18 4/8	3 3/8	22 5/8	22 3/8	7	5	BERHORST	JACOB	SAME	
1690	151 1/8	ST. LOUIS	93	69 6/8	68 0/8	16 7/8	0	21 4/8	22 0/8	5	5	HILL	WILLAIM H.	SAME	
1690	151 1/8	AUDRAIN	93	68 1/8	74 7/8	16 2/8	1 3/8	25 4/8	26 0/8	5	6	GRAWE	MIKE	SAME	
1690	151 1/8	COOPER	93	76 6/8	71 0/8	15 5/8	4 0/8	24 3/8	23 5/8	5	6	MARTIN	STEVE W.	SAME	
1690	151 1/8	TEXAS	94	69 4/8	76 3/8	17 7/8	3 6/8	23 7/8	23 0/8	7	5	KIRKMAN	CARLOSS	SAME	
1690	151 1/8	PHELPS	95	69 5/8	69 3/8	17 1/8	2 0/8	21 4/8	22 4/8	5	6	FABICK, III	JOHN	SAME	
1715	151 0/8	CEDAR	74	71 4/8	71 7/8	18 2/8	0	24 3/8	22 5/8	5	5	MONTGOMERY	FARREL	SAME	
1715	151 0/8	HARRISON	76	69 2/8	68 0/8	18 2/8	1 2/8	21 4/8	21 1/8	5	6	BAYLESS	ROGER	SAME	
1715	151 0/8	MARIES	76	69 7/8	71 6/8	15 3/8	2 1/8	24 4/8	24 4/8	6	5	WELLER	JERRY	SAME	
1715	151 0/8	HENRY	79	73 4/8	74 6/8	17 4/8	6 0/8	24 0/8	24 4/8	6	7	PARKS	BOB	SAME	
1715	151 0/8	CARTER	82	72 1/8	70 2/8	17 0/8	1 0/8	22 7/8	18 4/8	6	7	BUTLER	HAROLD	SAME	
1715	151 0/8	COOPER	83	68 2/8	68 0/8	19 6/8	0	24 5/8	24 0/8	5	5	HECKMAN	HAROLD	SAME	
1715	151 0/8	DAVIESS	84	72 1/8	71 2/8	15 1/8	4 1/8	24 6/8	24 5/8	7	6	STRAIN	SCOTT	SAME	
1715	151 0/8	SCOTLAND	88	69 6/8	65 6/8	19 4/8	0	27 3/8	26 3/8	4	4	ANDERSON	STEVE	SAME	
1715	151 0/8	BENTON	88	71 3/8	68 5/8	15 6/8	0	23 5/8	22 4/8	5	5	LEGG	RITA F.	SAME	
1715	151 0/8	HARRISON	88	67 4/8	70 0/8	16 4/8	0	26 2/8	26 2/8	4	4	MCGINNES	DEAN	SAME	
1715	151 0/8	MORGAN	89	68 0/8	68 6/8	19 6/8	0	23 4/8	22 5/8	5	5	MCCURRY	L.O.	SAME	
1715	151 0/8	GENTRY	89	70 2/8	70 2/8	18 2/8	1 6/8	26 6/8	25 2/8	5	6	MCFADDEN	MIKE	SAME	
1715	151 0/8	MARIES	93	68 4/8	72 0/8	16 0/8	0	21 7/8	22 0/8	6	7	STEVENS, SR.	ROBERT L.	SAME	
1715	151 0/8	CHARITON	93	70 7/8	69 2/8	16 6/8	3 6/8	23 6/8	23 5/8	7	5	SUNDERLAND	HARDIN	SAME	

MISSOURI SHOW-ME BIG BUCKS CLUB RECORDS OF WHITETAIL DEER BY STATE, TYPICAL

STATE RANK	SCORE	COUNTY	YEAR TAKEN	INCHES TYPICAL R	INCHES TYPICAL L	INSIDE SPREAD	INCHES ABNORMAL	LENGTH MAIN BEAM R	LENGTH MAIN BEAM L	NUMBER POINTS R	NUMBER POINTS L	HUNTER	FIRST NAME	OWNER	FIRST NAME
1715	151 0/8	CALLAWAY	93	69 4/8	67 2/8	18 0/8	0	23 6/8	23 7/8	5	5	WILSON	MONICA	SAME	
1715	151 0/8	GASCONADE	95	68 7/8	69 2/8	15 0/8	0	23 5/8	24 4/8	5	5	MEHRHOFF	KEN	SAME	
1715	151 0/8	SALINE	95	79 4/8	68 5/8	20 4/8	6 6/8	28 6/8	28 4/8	6	6	MURPHY	STEVE	SAME	
1715	151 0/8	SHELBY	95	69 4/8	74 3/8	17 5/8	5 1/8	22 2/8	23 0/8	6	6	HAWKINS	KENNY	SAME	
1715	151 0/8	MORGAN	96	70 5/8	70 1/8	16 6/8	0	24 7/8	23 0/8	5	5	SUTTON	BOB	SAME	
1734	150 7/8	McDONALD	58	68 4/8	69 6/8	17 5/8	0	23 1/8	23 6/8	6	6	JOHNSON	JACK	SAME	
1734	150 7/8	JEFFERSON	67	69 6/8	67 5/8	18 5/8	0	23 2/8	24 0/8	5	5	COOPER	AUSTIN	SAME	
1734	150 7/8	FRANKLIN	68	66 3/8	69 5/8	18 1/8	0	23 6/8	23 7/8	5	5	WEBB	BENTON	WEBB	ELSIE
1734	150 7/8	CAMDEN	71	75 0/8	73 0/8	18 7/8	3 0/8	26 0/8	24 0/8	6	6	ESTHER	W.S.	SAME	
1734	150 7/8	CARROLL	77	70 5/8	71 4/8	19 5/8	0	20 0/8	23 2/8	7	7	MOORE	DEARL	SAME	
1734	150 7/8	RAY	85	68 7/8	66 7/8	18 5/8	0	23 4/8	24 1/8	5	5	BARNETT	J.E.	SAME	
1734	150 7/8	DAVIESS	85	66 3/8	69 7/8	18 1/8	0	23 7/8	25 0/8	4	4	POLEYN	SHANE	SAME	
1734	150 7/8	JASPER	85	74 3/8	73 1/8	16 6/8	5 5/8	26 3/8	26 6/8	4	8	McWILLIAMS	ELMER	SAME	
1734	150 7/8	SALINE	87	71 0/8	68 0/8	17 1/8	0	24 4/8	25 2/8	5	5	COPELAND	DAVID	SAME	
1734	150 7/8	WAYNE	87	73 1/8	73 4/8	17 6/8	8 5/8	26 5/8	26 4/8	7	6	GREEN	DALE	SAME	
1734	150 7/8	HOWARD	87	66 4/8	69 5/8	17 7/8	0	24 7/8	26 1/8	5	5	BRAITHWAIT	JIM	SAME	
1734	150 7/8	OSAGE	87	70 4/8	72 7/8	17 0/8	5 1/8	21 0/8	21 3/8	6	6	RUSH	ALBERT	SAME	
1734	150 7/8	DAVIESS	88	72 0/8	73 3/8	17 1/8	0	23 7/8	24 6/8	7	5	TEEL	BRIAN	SAME	
1734	150 7/8	HARRISON	91	64 4/8	70 3/8	21 7/8	0	23 1/8	23 3/8	5	5	MITCHELL	JUSTIN	SAME	
1734	150 7/8	MERCER	91	71 7/8	71 0/8	16 4/8	2 5/8	24 0/8	22 6/8	6	5	SHARP	CHRIS	SAME	
1734	150 7/8	PIKE	92	71 2/8	69 7/8	16 3/8	0	19 7/8	18 5/8	5	5	HOLTSMAN	LLOYD	SAME	
1734	150 7/8	CALLAWAY	94	67 5/8	67 6/8	17 5/8	0	22 5/8	22 4/8	6	5	HAAS	MARK	SAME	
1734	150 7/8	MARION	94	66 4/8	68 5/8	18 7/8	0	21 7/8	22 6/8	5	5	BELL, JR.	DONALD E.	SAME	
1734	150 7/8	DENT	94	70 3/8	68 2/8	18 5/8	0	22 3/3	22 4/8	6	6	WHITAKER	RUSSELL	SAME	
1734	150 7/8	SULLIVAN	94	66 6/8	67 0/8	19 5/8	0	23 0/3	22 7/8	5	5	LAWSON	DALE	SAME	
1734	150 7/8	CRAWFORD	95	68 4/8	71 0/8	16 3/8	1 0/8	23 4/8	24 5/8	6	5	COLE	BRITT L.	SAME	
1734	150 7/8	MONTGOMERY	95	71 5/8	69 1/8	15 4/8	1 3/8	23 3/8	24 1/8	5	6	ROBINSON	JoANN	SAME	
1756	150 6/8	HARRISON	70	67 4/8	71 3/8	17 0/8	1 2/8	23 3/8	24 3/8	5	4	HARDING	SAMMIE	SAME	
1756	150 6/8	NEWTON	76	68 1/8	65 3/8	20 2/8	0	23 1/8	22 5/8	5	5	ELBRADER	DENNIS R.	SAME	
1756	150 6/8	STONE	81	67 4/8	66 6/8	20 1/8	2 3/8	23 1/8	23 2/8	5	5	SCHULZ	EARL	SAME	
1756	150 6/8	GENTRY	83	87 2/8	72 1/8	16 2/8	7 6/8	25 2/8	24 2/8	6	6	HENSLEY	JOHN	SAME	
1756	150 6/8	BOONE	84	70 6/8	72 6/8	17 5/8	6 1/8	24 2/8	24 4/8	7	6	DOUGLAS	JOE	SAME	

STATE RANK	SCORE	COUNTY	YEAR TAKEN	INCHES TYPICAL R	L	INSIDE SPREAD	INCHES ABNORMAL	LENGTH MAIN BEAM R	L	NUMBER POINTS R	L	HUNTER	FIRST NAME	OWNER	FIRST NAME
1756	150 6/8	MACON	84	75 3/8	73 3/8	16 4/8	7 1/8	24 0/8	23 5/8	7	6	CLEMENS	JOE	SAME	
1756	150 6/8	PETTIS	84	68 6/8	71 5/8	16 6/8	0	23 2/8	23 1/8	6	6	LEFTWICH	JEFF	SAME	
1756	150 6/8	RANDOLPH	84	66 3/8	71 0/8	19 4/8	0	23 7/8	23 5/8	5	5	MAUPIN	ALLEN	SAME	
1756	150 6/8	PIKE	85	68 6/8	67 7/8	16 6/8	0	23 7/8	23 3/8	5	5	ROBINSON	STEVEN	SAME	
1756	150 6/8	GENTRY	85	70 4/8	69 0/8	19 0/8	0	24 1/8	25 0/8	5	5	LIPPARD	MIKE	SAME	
1756	150 6/8	SALINE	85	71 7/8	73 5/8	18 3/8	5 7/8	23 0/8	22 6/8	6	7	RHODES	CHESTER	SAME	
1756	150 6/8	NODAWAY	85	66 3/8	66 0/8	20 6/8	0	26 7/8	26 6/8	4	4	DAVISON	JEFF	SAME	
1756	150 6/8	TANEY	85	70 3/8	67 5/8	16 4/8	0	24 2/8	24 2/8	5	5	HOLIDAY	LARRY	SAME	
1756	150 6/8	MORGAN	86	69 2/8	67 6/8	16 0/8	0	22 4/8	22 4/8	5	5	MITCHELL	CHARLEY	SAME	
1756	150 6/8	CARROLL	87	72 0/8	70 1/8	15 2/8	0	21 7/8	20 7/8	5	5	BARTLETT, JR.	ROY E.	SAME	
1756	150 6/8	GASCONADE	87	69 5/8	71 2/8	16 4/8	0	26 2/8	24 7/8	4	5	WEHMEYER	RUSSELL	SAME	
1756	150 6/8	SALINE	87	77 7/8	72 1/8	19 1/8	11 0/8	25 3/8	26 1/8	6	8	SCOTT	WILLIAM W.	SAME	
1756	150 6/8	CHARITON	88	74 6/8	69 7/8	17 0/8	4 4/8	26 2/8	25 3/8	7	7	ERICKSON	TEDDY	SAME	
1756	150 6/8	HENRY	88	75 0/8	66 6/8	17 6/8	0	23 5/8	23 2/8	5	4	BAILEY	JOE	SAME	
1756	150 6/8	HARRISON	88	67 1/8	69 2/8	20 4/8	2 0/8	25 4/8	25 6/8	4	5	KELLEY	BRIAN	SAME	
1756	150 6/8	BATES	89	68 1/8	68 7/8	18 7/8	0	23 1/8	22 3/8	5	5	CLINTON	MARK E.	SAME	
1756	150 6/8	CRAWFORD	89	69 3/8	68 3/8	16 2/8	0	22 3/8	22 7/8	5	5	LOGAN	CLAY	SAME	
1756	150 6/8	CASS	90	71 2/8	71 3/8	19 1/8	6 5/8	27 0/8	25 4/8	5	6	HEAPER	C.W.	SAME	
1756	150 6/8	HOWARD	90	70 0/8	67 4/8	17 4/8	0	21 6/8	22 2/8	5	5	FINLEY	JOHN	SAME	
1756	150 6/8	WRIGHT	90	71 3/8	68 0/8	17 2/8	0	25 2/8	23 7/8	4	4	DODSON	EDWIN	SAME	
1756	150 6/8	VERNON	91	68 2/8	66 3/8	19 6/8	0	26 0/8	26 4/8	4	4	FOX	SCOTT R.	SAME	
1756	150 6/8	SALINE	91	73 7/8	70 6/8	14 6/8	0	23 7/8	24 0/8	5	4	EVANS	JEFF	SAME	
1756	150 6/8	MACON	92	72 0/8	70 3/8	14 6/8	0	23 6/8	24 5/8	5	5	BRISCOE	JOHN	SAME	
1756	150 6/8	LIVINGSTON	94	68 1/8	65 7/8	20 0/8	0	25 4/8	26 0/8	4	4	ROMESBURG	ROY	SAME	
1756	150 6/8	MORGAN	94	71 1/8	71 3/8	18 7/8	6 7/8	24 1/8	23 7/8	6	7	BONDURANT	STEVE	SAME	
1756	150 6/8	DAVIESS	95	70 3/8	78 1/8	18 6/8	0	23 0/8	23 4/8	5	6	COULSON	STAN	SAME	
1756	150 6/8	ST. CHARLES	95	69 7/8	66 7/8	18 4/8	0	23 7/8	23 6/8	4	4	OSTMANN	WILLIAM G. (BILL)	SAME	
1756	150 6/8	SCHUYLER	96	69 0/8	69 6/8	18 0/8	0	24 7/8	23 1/8	5	6	ANDERSON	BRIAN N.	SAME	
1789	150 5/8	CALLAWAY	65	68 2/8	71 5/8	17 5/8	1 6/8	22 0/8	26 1/8	6	5	WHANGER	ROY	SAME	
1789	150 5/8	SHELBY	72	66 7/8	67 7/8	18 1/8	0	21 7/8	21 7/8	5	5	CLINE	VICTOR R.	SAME	
1789	150 5/8	VERNON	72	70 6/8	72 5/8	22 2/8	2 5/8	28 3/8	26 6/8	6	6	GASTEL	K.J.	SAME	
1789	150 5/8	PIKE	75	67 5/8	67 2/8	17 7/8	0	23 6/8	24 0/8	4	4	HUCKSTEP, JR.	RICHARD	SAME	

MISSOURI SHOW-ME BIG BUCKS CLUB RECORDS OF WHITETAIL DEER BY STATE, TYPICAL

STATE RANK	SCORE	COUNTY	YEAR TAKEN	INCHES TYPICAL R	INCHES TYPICAL L	INSIDE SPREAD	INCHES ABNORMAL	LENGTH MAIN BEAM R	LENGTH MAIN BEAM L	NUMBER POINTS R	NUMBER POINTS L	HUNTER	FIRST NAME	OWNER	FIRST NAME
1789	150 5/8	HOLT	75	67 0/8	66 7/8	17 7/8	0	25 0/8	25 2/8	5	5	McGUIRE	BILL	SAME	
1789	150 5/8	BOONE	76	67 4/8	67 0/8	18 1/8	0	24 6/8	24 3/8	4	4	PHILLIPS	BOB	SAME	
1789	150 5/8	DAVIESS	76	68 6/8	71 5/8	19 6/8	4 5/8	23 6/8	22 6/8	5	8	BASSETT	JERRY	SAME	
1789	150 5/8	NODAWAY	80	69 7/8	69 7/8	16 4/8	2 5/8	22 1/8	22 2/8	6	5	LINDSTRON	C.B.	SAME	
1789	150 5/8	RIPLEY	82	67 7/8	74 2/8	22 3/8	6 2/8	25 1/8	25 1/8	7	7	FREEMAN	ELDIE T.	SAME	
1789	150 5/8	CALLAWAY	84	68 2/8	66 3/8	19 1/8	0	24 0/8	23 4/8	5	5	BARTON	OVA	SAME	
1789	150 5/8	DEKALB	85	76 3/8	70 6/8	16 3/8	0	24 3/8	23 7/8	6	5	ALLAN	DAVE	SAME	
1789	150 5/8	PIKE	85	67 6/8	69 5/8	17 3/8	0	24 7/8	25 6/8	4	4	WHEELER	CHRIS	SAME	
1789	150 5/8	LINN	86	68 1/8	67 3/8	19 7/8	0	23 6/8	23 2/8	6	5	ATKINSON	PAUL H.	SAME	
1789	150 5/8	NEWTON	86	70 5/8	68 5/8	17 1/8	1 6/8	23 6/8	22 7/8	5	6	KING	TONY	SAME	
1789	150 5/8	PUTNAM	88	69 0/8	68 0/8	19 3/8	0	21 4/8	22 2/8	6	5	MITCHELL	DANNIE	SAME	
1789	150 5/8	MONITEAU	88	68 7/8	71 2/8	15 7/8	0	22 6/8	22 4/8	5	6	HOWARD	KENNETH R.	SAME	
1789	150 5/8	MACON	89	70 1/8	68 5/8	14 3/8	0	22 2/8	22 4/8	5	5	AKINS	ROBERT P.	SAME	
1789	150 5/8	CALLAWAY	90	71 0/8	67 6/8	18 7/8	0	26 3/8	25 2/8	5	5	McVEIGH	DAVID	SAME	
1789	150 5/8	STE. GENEIEVE	90	67 7/8	67 1/8	19 5/8	0	23 1/8	22 7/8	5	5	GEGG	NORMAN	SAME	
1789	150 5/8	DAVIESS	91	69 6/8	69 0/8	17 6/8	2 1/8	23 3/8	24 2/8	5	6	THOMPSON	HOWARD K.	SAME	
1789	150 5/8	BOLLINGER	92	67 2/8	67 4/8	18 1/8	1 0/8	22 3/8	22 6/8	5	6	GLAUS	STACEY	SAME	
1789	150 5/8	MONITEAU	95	71 7/8	69 1/8	15 3/8	1 0/8	25 2/8	25 4/8	7	5	BIERI	JASON	SAME	
1811	150 4/8	ST. CLAIR	59	77 1/8	72 2/8	18 6/8	10 0/8	25 1/8	25 1/8	0	0	BOUGH	JOHN	SAME	
1811	150 4/8	RANDOLPH	72	68 0/8	69 3/8	17 0/8	0	21 6/8	23 1/8	5	5	WOGOMON	GERALD	SAME	
1811	150 4/8	PIKE	72	72 1/8	69 0/8	17 4/8	0	24 4/8	24 0/8	6	5	SCHULZ	CLIFF	SAME	
1811	150 4/8	KNOX	74	67 4/8	75 2/8	22 0/8	5 6/8	25 1/8	25 1/8	6	8	LAY	KEITH	SAME	
1811	150 4/8	ANDREW	76	70 3/8	75 3/8	17 2/8	3 6/8	23 5/8	22 4/8	6	6	MORAN, SR.	ROBERT L.	SAME	
1811	150 4/8	BOONE	82	72 4/8	68 6/8	15 6/8	0	24 0/8	22 5/8	5	5	HINES	ROGER	SAME	
1811	150 4/8	LEWIS	84	69 0/8	70 4/8	15 4/8	0	23 2/8	23 0/8	5	5	TODD	CRAIG	SAME	
1811	150 4/8	LINCOLN	87	70 2/8	70 4/8	17 4/8	2 5/8	21 7/8	23 0/8	5	5	HERMANN	STEVE	SAME	
1811	150 4/8	BATES	89	74 4/8	70 0/8	14 0/8	1 2/8	23 0/8	23 6/8	6	5	WILEY	CHAD	SAME	
1811	150 4/8	MILLER	89	76 6/8	73 4/8	18 1/8	11 5/8	26 3/8	24 2/8	6	6	FRITCHEY, JR.	LARRY	SAME	
1811	150 4/8	ST. CLAIR	90	68 3/8	71 3/8	14 6/8	0	22 7/8	22 4/8	5	5	HAMILTON	JEFF	SAME	
1811	150 4/8	LINN	90	67 6/8	66 4/8	19 6/8	0	25 0/8	25 5/8	4	4	FITZGERALD	JIM	SAME	
1811	150 4/8	BARRY	90	71 4/8	71 3/8	15 7/8	3 5/8	24 6/8	23 4/8	6	7	SHOCKLEY	MICHAEL	SAME	
1811	150 4/8	GASCONADE	90	71 3/8	73 6/8	18 6/8	9 2/8	25 0/8	24 4/8	6	6	TRAUB	ROBERT	SAME	

MISSOURI SHOW-ME BIG BUCKS CLUB RECORDS OF WHITETAIL DEER BY STATE, TYPICAL

STATE RANK	SCORE	COUNTY	YEAR TAKEN	INCHES TYPICAL R	INCHES TYPICAL L	INSIDE SPREAD	INCHES ABNORMAL	LENGTH MAIN BEAM R	LENGTH MAIN BEAM L	NUMBER POINTS R	NUMBER POINTS L	HUNTER	FIRST NAME	OWNER	FIRST NAME
1811	150 4/8	ADAIR	91	67 6/8	70 0/8	18 4/8	0	21 6/8	24 0/8	5	5	PHILLIPS	RICHARD	SAME	
1811	150 4/8	ADAIR	91	76 1/8	69 2/8	16 6/8	2 6/8	23 4/8	23 6/8	7	7	RECKNER	CUB	SAME	
1811	150 4/8	PERRY	92	71 4/8	66 7/8	20 1/8	1 3/8	26 3/8	27 1/8	6	5	WEITH	STANLEY	SAME	
1811	150 4/8	DENT	92	69 5/8	66 6/8	23 2/8	4 4/8	26 5/8	26 1/8	7	5	GREEN	MICHAEL	SAME	
1811	150 4/8	LEWIS	93	68 7/8	68 7/8	21 7/8	3 1/8	23 4/8	23 7/8	6	6	ASKEW	LARRY	SAME	
1811	150 4/8	BARTON	93	66 3/8	75 2/8	19 2/8	0	25 0/8	24 7/8	4	5	RAY	RICHARD	SAME	
1811	150 4/8	HOWARD	94	71 5/8	69 6/8	19 3/8	4 7/8	24 0/8	24 0/8	6	8	BOSTON	KEVIN	SAME	
1811	150 4/8	MACON	95	72 2/8	69 6/8	17 3/8	4 1/8	23 2/8	23 7/8	6	4	TAYLOR	JAMES	SAME	
1811	150 4/8	CHARITON	95	68 3/8	68 1/8	19 0/8	0	25 3/8	24 4/8	5	5	ATKINSON	STEVEN S.	SAME	
1811	150 4/8	CAMDEN	73	68 6/8	67 1/8	16 5/8	0	22 7/8	23 0/8	5	5	THOMAS	LARRY D.	SAME	
1811	150 4/8	HARRISON	79	69 1/8	68 0/8	16 5/8	0	23 0/8	22 5/8	5	5	HUSKEY	LARRY	SAME	
1834	150 3/8	CRAWFORD	81	70 3/8	69 0/8	16 6/8	1 7/8	22 6/8	23 0/8	5	6	VAUGHN	LAURA	SAME	
1834	150 3/8	COOPER	82	72 6/8	69 6/8	19 4/8	8 5/8	24 7/8	24 5/8	8	6	POTTER	RANDY	SAME	
1834	150 3/8	JACKSON	83	68 7/8	70 0/8	17 2/8	2 1/8	25 1/8	25 0/8	5	5	THOMEY	MARVIN	SAME	
1834	150 3/8	SHELBY	84	71 6/8	69 5/8	14 7/8	2 6/8	22 4/8	22 7/8	5	6	BICHSEL	DAVID	SAME	
1834	150 3/8	BENTON	84	66 4/8	67 0/8	18 7/8	0	24 6/8	24 1/8	5	5	PRITCHETT	MERLIN L.	SAME	
1834	150 3/8	KNOX	86	75 1/8	69 7/8	17 7/8	4 2/8	24 2/8	25 5/8	6	5	BOECKMAN	TERRY	SAME	
1834	150 3/8	HARRISON	86	69 3/8	70 5/8	20 6/8	6 7/8	24 3/8	25 0/8	7	6	PARKHURST	DOYLE	SAME	
1834	150 3/8	CAMDEN	91	68 3/8	65 6/8	18 7/8	0	23 0/8	22 5/8	5	5	MCDANIEL	BRUCE	SAME	
1834	150 3/8	CLINTON	91	77 7/8	71 0/8	20 1/8	11 0/8	23 2/8	22 6/8	8	5	REYNOLDS	MELVIN	SAME	
1834	150 3/8	RAY	92	69 6/8	68 3/8	16 1/8	0	22 0/8	21 2/8	5	5	KING	JOHNNIE	SAME	
1834	150 3/8	MACON	92	66 3/8	71 0/8	18 3/8	0	26 0/8	26 3/8	5	5	MCELROY	KEVIN D.	SAME	
1834	150 3/8	GRUNDY	92	70 3/8	73 0/8	17 4/8	3 5/8	24 0/8	22 4/8	7	7	KOENIG	EDDIE	SAME	
1834	150 3/8	TEXAS	94	72 2/8	70 5/8	17 6/8	7 5/8	26 3/8	26 2/8	8	7	SMITH	RODNEY T.	SAME	
1834	150 3/8	PETTIS	94	67 6/8	67 0/8	19 1/8	0	23 7/8	23 3/8	5	5	AKER	STEVEN	SAME	
1834	150 3/8	CALLAWAY	94	71 7/8	75 6/8	15 7/8	6 6/8	23 4/8	22 4/8	6	6	COGORNO	GENE	SAME	
1834	150 3/8	BOONE	96	66 6/8	66 7/8	18 5/8	1 2/8	23 4/8	23 2/8	5	4	THORNHILL	CURTIS	SAME	
1834	150 3/8	CALLAWAY	96	71 0/8	68 6/8	20 0/8	4 3/8	23 1/8	23 0/8	9	5	ROESNER	GREG	SAME	
1853	150 2/8	HARRISON	67	68 0/8	69 4/8	17 2/8	0	27 6/8	27 3/8	4	4	PRESTON	RAYMOND	SAME	
1853	150 2/8	CHARITON	71	67 1/8	76 5/8	19 2/8	0	25 1/8	24 2/8	5	6	GORDON	WILLIAM	SAME	
1853	150 2/8	RALLS	72	72 7/8	68 1/8	18 0/8	2 0/8	24 0/8	23 7/8	5	7	FENDRICK	DICK	SAME	
1853	150 2/8	ADAIR	74	65 6/8	68 3/8	20 2/8	0	25 2/8	24 6/8	5	5	FLOWERS	JIM	SAME	

MISSOURI SHOW-ME BIG BUCKS CLUB RECORDS OF WHITETAIL DEER BY STATE, TYPICAL

STATE RANK	SCORE	COUNTY	YEAR TAKEN	INCHES TYPICAL R	L	INSIDE SPREAD	INCHES ABNORMAL	LENGTH MAIN BEAM R	L	NUMBER POINTS R	L	HUNTER	FIRST NAME	OWNER	FIRST NAME
1853	150 2/8	OREGON	77	70 0/8	68 3/8	16 4/8	0	22 3/8	22 3/8	6	6	SIMMONS	ROSCOE	SAME	
1853	150 2/8	LACLEDE	78	71 3/8	74 2/8	16 3/8	2 3/8	22 1/8	22 5/8	5	6	FREDERICK	BILL	SAME	
1853	150 2/8	SCOTLAND	79	68 7/8	66 7/8	20 7/8	1 7/8	24 2/8	24 3/8	5	6	SPARKS	JOHN R.	SAME	
1853	150 2/8	CHARITON	81	70 2/8	69 4/8	16 2/8	0	24 3/8	23 2/8	6	6	PARKER	RONNIE	SAME	
1853	150 2/8	ADAIR	85	66 7/8	68 6/8	19 0/8	0	23 5/8	24 6/8	4	4	WOMACK	WILLIAM	SAME	
1853	150 2/8	PIKE	86	69 2/8	69 2/8	15 0/8	0	24 1/8	23 0/8	4	4	HENDERSON	CURTIS	SAME	
1853	150 2/8	RAY	87	68 5/8	75 7/8	16 4/8	3 4/8	21 4/8	23 5/8	6	6	BRANHAM	KENDALL	SAME	
1853	150 2/8	PERRY	87	67 7/8	69 1/8	16 6/8	0	22 1/8	22 4/8	5	5	GUTH	ED	SAME	
1853	150 2/8	PUTNAM	88	71 7/8	67 5/8	17 7/8	2 3/8	25 6/8	24 4/8	5	4	LARUE	LLOYD	SAME	
1853	150 2/8	CASS	88	69 3/8	65 6/8	20 0/8	0	28 5/8	28 6/8	4	4	VIAR	FRED W.	SAME	
1853	150 2/8	GASCONADE	88	66 5/8	66 6/8	20 0/8	0	26 2/8	27 6/8	4	4	FREDRICK	MAYNARD	SAME	
1853	150 2/8	TEXAS	88	72 4/8	68 1/8	15 6/8	0	23 7/8	23 7/8	5	4	UMKNOWN		KOPP	RONALD F.
1853	150 2/8	HOWARD	90	66 0/8	71 0/8	18 4/8	0	24 0/8	25 2/8	5	5	CUNDIFF	RICKY	SAME	
1853	150 2/8	PUTNAM	90	68 2/8	66 3/8	19 2/8	0	25 1/8	24 4/8	4	4	LARUE	LOYD	SAME	
1853	150 2/8	CLINTON	91	67 2/8	67 2/8	21 2/8	0	23 0/8	22 7/8	6	6	BOSLEY	DAVID	SAME	
1853	150 2/8	PUTNAM	91	70 0/8	69 7/8	16 1/8	3 1/8	22 2/8	22 3/8	6	5	DEFREITAS	JACK	SAME	
1853	150 2/8	CHARITON	91	67 4/8	68 5/8	24 2/8	7 0/8	23 0/8	24 2/8	6	7	BLALOCK	BRUCE	SAME	
1853	150 2/8	CLINTON	93	71 4/8	69 3/8	15 0/8	2 4/8	22 6/8	22 5/8	5	6	VOGT	DOUG	SAME	
1853	150 2/8	REYNOLDS	93	71 6/8	66 2/8	19 6/8	0	23 3/8	22 4/8	5	5	HEDGER	JOHN	SAME	
1853	150 2/8	DAVIESS	94	69 3/8	74 0/8	15 2/8	0	22 2/8	22 4/8	5	5	COX	RALPH	SAME	
1853	150 2/8	DENT	94	65 1/8	66 7/8	20 2/8	0	24 1/8	24 1/8	5	5	DILLON	TOM M.	SAME	
1853	150 2/8	DENT	95	70 7/8	70 1/8	18 0/8	3 2/8	23 6/8	23 2/8	6	6	SCHNARR	LARRY	SAME	
1879	150 1/8	HARRISON	67	70 1/8	70 4/8	18 5/8	5 5/8	23 2/8	24 1/8	6	6	GIBSON	NORMAN L.	SAME	
1879	150 1/8	LINCOLN	74	69 5/8	72 1/8	17 3/8	3 0/8	21 0/8	21 1/8	6	6	CREECH	MIKE	SAME	
1879	150 1/8	PLATTE	81	69 7/8	72 4/8	18 1/8	0	25 2/8	22 6/8	5	5	COONS	RICHARD	SAME	
1879	150 1/8	PHELPS	81	71 1/8	88 4/8	17 4/8	9 5/8	27 0/8	27 2/8	7	9	JOHNSON	LEONARD	SAME	
1879	150 1/8	GASCONADE	82	68 4/8	67 6/8	18 7/8	1 6/8	23 4/8	22 2/8	6	5	SPURGEON	JERRY L.	SAME	
1879	150 1/8	MARIES	82	69 1/8	73 1/8	16 7/8	3 4/8	22 6/8	22 4/8	6	7	HEMMINGHAUS	JOHN	SAME	
1879	150 1/8	WARREN	85	69 5/8	67 7/8	18 1/8	0	22 2/8	23 1/8	6	5	SMITH	DWAIN	SAME	
1879	150 1/8	DEKALB	85	69 0/8	68 0/8	17 2/8	1 7/8	25 6/8	25 6/8	4	5	GAISER	ROGER E.	SAME	
1879	150 1/8	JOHNSON	86	68 4/8	67 5/8	19 1/8	0	23 0/8	22 7/8	5	5	SLAUGHTER	STEVEN	SAME	
1879	150 1/8	GRUNDY	87	70 2/8	68 2/8	17 1/8	0	24 0/8	25 0/8	5	4	McDANIEL	RONALD	SAME	

STATE RANK	SCORE	COUNTY	YEAR TAKEN	INCHES TYPICAL R	L	INSIDE SPREAD	INCHES ABNORMAL	LENGTH MAIN BEAM R	L	NUMBER POINTS R	L	HUNTER	FIRST NAME	OWNER	FIRST NAME
1879	150 1/8	CHARITON	90	65 6/8	68 3/8	19 7/8	0	25 4/8	26 0/8	4	4	LINSCOTT	DUANE R.	SAME	
1879	150 1/8	SHELBY	91	74 7/8	74 2/8	17 4/8	7 1/8	24 5/8	23 3/8	6	8	BUCKMAN	MIKE	SAME	
1879	150 1/8	ADAIR	91	66 4/8	71 0/8	17 1/8	0	24 7/8	24 7/8	5	5	BAUMGARTNER	RODNEY	SAME	
1879	150 1/8	COOPER	91	79 0/8	68 5/8	15 6/8	1 3/8	25 6/8	26 4/8	5	5	GREER	JACK	SAME	
1879	150 1/8	RALLS	93	69 1/8	66 1/8	21 6/8	3 4/8	24 6/8	24 6/8	4	5	RIEDINGER	REGGIE	SAME	
1879	150 1/8	SHELBY	95	70 3/8	67 7/8	17 5/8	0	22 7/8	23 2/8	5	5	SMOOT	DOUG	SAME	
1879	150 1/8	ANDREW	95	68 5/8	68 4/8	17 1/8	3 0/8	23 1/8	23 0/8	6	5	COX	TONY	SAME	
1879	150 1/8	CHARITON	96	69 0/8	69 1/8	17 7/8	1 2/8	21 5/8	22 7/8	5	6	MOREHEAD	DANNY H.	SAME	
1879	150 0/8	CAMDEN	58	0	0	0	0	0	0	0	0	SMENTKOWSKI	A.J.	SAME	
1897	150 0/8	TEXAS	65	72 3/8	67 3/8	15 2/8	0	22 4/8	24 2/8	5	4	LEADFORD	GLEN	SAME	
1897	150 0/8	RAY	70	67 6/8	70 2/8	15 2/8	0	25 0/8	25 0/8	5	5	IMGARTEN	FRED	SAME	
1897	150 0/8	PLATTE	71	75 1/8	73 3/8	18 5/8	12 3/8	22 5/8	22 4/8	8	8	CHAPIN	LOREN L.	SAME	
1897	150 0/8	FRANKLIN	71	68 1/8	70 5/8	19 2/8	0	22 3/8	24 4/8	5	5	BOLTE	GARY	SAME	
1897	150 0/8	CHARITON	76	67 1/8	68 5/8	17 4/8	0	25 0/8	25 2/8	4	4	RUKAVINA	JOE	SAME	
1897	150 0/8	BOONE	82	69 2/8	67 0/8	20 2/8	1 2/8	24 0/8	23 5/8	6	6	DAWSON	DAVID	SAME	
1897	150 0/8	RALLS	85	70 6/8	72 4/8	16 7/8	5 5/8	23 5/8	24 0/8	6	8	CERNEA	MIKE	SAME	
1897	150 0/8	GRUNDY	87	67 4/8	69 2/8	18 0/8	0	22 1/8	22 0/8	5	5	HILL	BILL	SAME	
1897	150 0/8	BOONE	88	68 1/8	68 1/8	16 5/8	1 1/8	24 1/8	24 3/8	5	6	SCHINDLER	DON	SAME	
1897	150 0/8	ST. CLAIR	88	70 5/8	72 2/8	18 0/8	3 4/8	25 0/8	24 0/8	5	5	HOSTETTER	NELSON L.	SAME	
1897	150 0/8	CALLAWAY	88	68 7/8	70 3/8	17 5/8	3 3/8	22 1/8	22 3/8	7	5	DAWSON	DRAKE Q.	SAME	
1897	150 0/8	LINCOLN	89	70 5/8	69 7/8	13 4/8	1 4/8	23 7/8	23 4/8	5	6	EISENBATH	DAVID C.	SAME	
1897	150 0/8	LIVINGSTON	90	67 0/8	72 7/8	17 0/8	0	21 1/8	22 5/8	5	5	LOLLAR	MIKE	SAME	
1897	150 0/8	LINCOLN	93	69 6/8	65 5/8	19 4/8	0	28 2/8	27 3/8	4	4	MENNEMEYER	ED	SAME	
1897	150 0/8	PIKE	93	69 3/8	72 0/8	16 0/8	1 6/8	24 0/8	23 6/8	7	6	DAVIS, III	JAMES M.	SAME	
1897	150 0/8	CASS	95	68 2/8	68 3/8	17 4/8	0	24 4/8	25 0/8	5	5	AYLER	JERRY	SAME	
1897	150 0/8	CALDWELL	96	68 5/8	73 4/8	15 4/8	0	22 6/8	22 7/8	4	5	RUPERT	SCOTT	SAME	
1915	149 7/8	DENT	61	71 0/8	67 5/8	17 7/8	2 4/8	24 6/8	24 6/8	6	6	ADAMS, JR.	CLIFFORD	SAME	
1915	149 7/8	BATES	73	66 1/8	65 1/8	22 7/8	0	25 2/8	25 2/8	6	6	BETHEL	RONNIE A.	SAME	
1915	149 7/8	JACKSON	74	68 2/8	68 6/8	18 1/8	0	22 7/8	23 1/8	6	6	SHINNEMAN	HOMER	SHINNEMAN	JIM
1915	149 7/8	WASHINGTON	77	69 1/8	70 2/8	16 5/8	0	21 0/8	21 2/8	6	6	RUFKAHR	MIKE	SAME	
1915	149 7/8	RANDOLPH	84	67 0/8	70 6/8	15 3/8	0	23 4/8	24 5/8	5	6	VITT	JOE	SAME	
1915	149 7/8	CAMDEN	86	65 1/8	71 1/8	21 6/8	1 1/8	22 5/8	24 3/8	6	5	KAISER	JOHN	SAME	

MISSOURI SHOW-ME BIG BUCKS CLUB RECORDS OF WHITETAIL DEER BY STATE, TYPICAL

STATE RANK	SCORE	COUNTY	YEAR TAKEN	INCHES TYPICAL R	L	INSIDE SPREAD	INCHES ABNORMAL	LENGTH MAIN BEAM R	L	NUMBER POINTS R	L	HUNTER	FIRST NAME	OWNER	FIRST NAME
1915	149 7/8	ST. LOUIS	86	68 3/8	68 5/8	20 0/8	1 3/8	23 6/8	25 0/8	6	5	HOFFMAN	EARL R.	SAME	
1915	149 7/8	JACKSON	88	71 7/8	68 2/8	17 3/8	0	23 0/8	23 5/8	6	5	EASLEY	TYRON	SAME	
1915	149 7/8	JACKSON	93	71 0/8	81 4/8	16 4/8	4 7/8	23 3/8	24 6/8	6	5	THOMPSON	JOHN	SAME	
1915	149 7/8	JACKSON	94	75 1/8	71 2/8	20 7/8	10 4/8	26 2/8	25 5/8	6	7	BISACCA	MARK	SAME	
1915	149 7/8	CARTER	96	66 2/8	65 0/8	22 3/8	0	25 3/8	23 2/8	5	5	SCHAFER	KELLY	SAME	
1926	149 6/8	BENTON	68	67 3/8	72 0/8	15 4/8	0	22 4/8	23 1/8	5	5	FISHER	BOB	SAME	
1926	149 6/8	LACLEDE	73	69 0/8	71 3/8	17 4/8	0	23 4/8	24 0/8	5	5	ESTHER	W.S.	SAME	
1926	149 6/8	MORGAN	78	72 7/8	72 5/8	14 7/8	6 1/8	22 6/8	22 6/8	6	8	MEYER	HAROLD	SAME	
1926	149 6/8	FRANKLIN	80	69 4/8	71 4/8	21 5/8	5 1/8	27 2/8	27 4/8	6	7	LANDERS	LARRY	SAME	
1926	149 6/8	CAMDEN	82	69 1/8	66 1/8	18 0/8	0	23 1/8	23 0/8	5	5	SHARP	CLIFFORD	SAME	
1926	149 6/8	MONITEAU	82	66 7/8	70 1/8	17 4/8	0	23 4/8	23 1/8	5	5	WYCOFF	LARRY	SAME	
1926	149 6/8	FRANKLIN	86	69 2/8	70 5/8	18 5/8	2 5/8	24 3/8	23 6/8	6	6	BOWEN	GLORIA	SAME	
1926	149 6/8	MONITEAU	88	67 0/8	72 4/8	18 6/8	0	22 7/8	24 2/8	5	5	KUNZE	WAYNE	SAME	
1926	149 6/8	IRON	92	69 1/8	69 4/8	16 7/8	1 1/8	24 4/8	24 7/8	6	5	CAMPBELL	TERESA L.	SAME	
1926	149 6/8	TEXAS	93	70 5/8	68 5/8	17 0/8	0	21 4/8	20 7/8	6	6	QUESENBERRY	BASIL	SAME	
1936	149 6/8	DALLAS	69	70 3/8	67 3/8	16 3/8	0	21 5/8	22 0/8	5	5	ALLEN	JAMES E.	SAME	
1936	149 5/8	WASHINGTON	72	67 1/8	67 3/8	18 5/8	0	22 0/8	22 4/8	5	5	SIMPSON	WILLIS HENRY	SAME	
1936	149 5/8	PHELPS	79	70 0/8	72 0/8	16 4/8	1 2/8	23 3/8	22 4/8	5	7	KLIPFEL	E. ALAN	SAME	
1936	149 5/8	MORGAN	82	74 6/8	68 3/8	20 0/8	2 1/8	23 4/8	24 0/8	5	5	HIBBON	JOHN	SAME	
1936	149 5/8	ST. CHARLES	86	69 0/8	70 5/8	15 0/8	2 1/8	20 5/8	20 2/8	6	7	THOMPSON	DON	SAME	
1936	149 5/8	DADE	87	67 7/8	68 1/8	15 7/8	0	21 6/8	22 0/8	5	5	JOHNSTON	JERRY	SAME	
1936	149 5/8	MORGAN	91	69 3/8	65 1/8	19 3/8	0	25 6/8	25 4/8	5	5	MILLER	DAVID	SAME	
1936	149 5/8	DALLAS	91	70 1/8	68 4/8	20 2/8	4 3/8	70 1/8	68 4/8	6	7	LUTTRELL	BOB	WILSON	BART
1936	149 5/8	DALLAS	91	0	0	0	0	0	0	0	0	WILSON	BART	SAME	
1936	149 5/8	HOWELL	92	71 2/8	69 7/8	15 4/8	3 7/8	24 7/8	25 2/8	7	5	FRENCH	THOMAS E.	SAME	
1936	149 5/8	PHELPS	92	69 1/8	68 0/8	15 5/8	0	22 4/8	22 1/8	5	5	POUND	DAVID	SAME	
1936	149 5/8	CARTER	94	67 2/8	67 5/8	17 1/8	0	23 0/8	22 7/8	5	5	WALKER	PHILLIP DON	SAME	
1936	149 5/8	MORGAN	95	69 6/8	70 0/8	14 7/8	2 4/8	23 3/8	24 1/8	7	5	ROSS	MATT	SAME	
1936	149 4/9	WASHINGTON	77	67 2/8	68 6/8	15 4/8	0	23 0/E	24 0/8	5	5	MERCER	MERLIN	SAME	
1936	149 4/8	HENRY	56	69 6/8	66 1/8	20 6/8	3 2/8	24 3/E	24 3/8	5	6	HAMILTON	MAX C.	SAME	
1936	149 4/8	GASCONADE	67	70 4/8	66 2/8	18 4/8	0	24 0/8	23 4/8	5	5	DUNCAN	LARRY	SAME	
1936	149 4/8	RIPLEY	69	68 3/8	69 6/8	16 0/8	0	23 0/8	22 0/8	5	5	SMITH	LUTHER	SAME	

MISSOURI SHOW-ME BIG BUCKS CLUB RECORDS OF WHITETAIL DEER BY STATE, TYPICAL

STATE RANK	SCORE	COUNTY	YEAR TAKEN	INCHES TYPICAL R	INCHES TYPICAL L	INSIDE SPREAD	INCHES ABNORMAL	LENGTH MAIN BEAM R	LENGTH MAIN BEAM L	NUMBER POINTS R	NUMBER POINTS L	HUNTER	FIRST NAME	OWNER	FIRST NAME
1936	149 4/8	DALLAS	91	67 0/8	65 3/8	19 0/8	0	22 4/8	21 4/8	5	5	WALKER	WADE	SAME	
1936	149 4/8	MARIES	92	74 4/8	69 0/8	16 4/8	0	24 0/8	25 4/8	5	4	BRUNNERT, JR.	DON	SAME	
1936	149 4/8	CASS	93	70 6/8	68 0/8	20 0/8	2 6/8	22 2/8	23 3/8	6	6	THOMAS	DAVID	SAME	
1936	149 4/8	MONROE	93	71 6/8	66 6/8	17 0/8	0	22 7/8	21 6/8	5	5	ASHER	VERNON	SAME	
1936	149 4/8	SALINE	95	69 3/8	70 4/8	17 0/8	2 2/8	23 0/8	23 2/8	5	6	MOBILE	MICHAEL R.	SAME	
1936	149 4/8	BOONE	95	66 5/8	66 2/8	18 4/8	0	23 2/8	23 3/8	5	5	McMANAMA	SCOTT	SAME	
1959	149 3/8	FRANKLIN	60	74 2/8	68 7/8	17 4/8	5 1/8	26 4/8	25 6/8	7	5	UNGER	EDWARD	SAME	
1959	149 3/8	DENT	68	66 4/8	67 0/8	18 6/8	0	24 6/8	24 4/8	5	5	KING	COLLEEN	SAME	
1959	149 3/8	OREGON	76	67 5/8	68 5/8	16 7/8	0	23 1/8	23 7/8	5	5	BARTON	GARY	SAME	
1959	149 3/8	ST. LOUIS	79	73 4/8	67 3/8	18 2/8	3 0/8	22 5/8	21 5/8	6	6	ZERWIG	ALAN	SAME	
1959	149 3/8	BATES	82	74 0/8	68 2/8	18 3/8	2 2/8	23 2/8	23 6/8	5	5	DURST	MIKE	SAME	
1959	149 3/8	WAYNE	84	68 7/8	74 3/8	17 3/8	0	22 1/8	22 4/8	4	5	WILFONG	RAY	SAME	
1959	149 3/8	JOHNSON	86	67 3/8	71 5/8	16 4/8	1 7/8	22 5/8	23 1/8	6	5	BURKE	GARY	SAME	
1959	149 3/8	OREGON	87	69 2/8	68 5/8	20 1/8	1 3/8	24 4/8	22 2/8	6	5	WALKER	GARY	SAME	
1959	149 3/8	TEXAS	89	68 0/8	70 2/8	15 3/8	0	19 4/8	20 7/8	6	6	BUCHHEIT	DENNIS	SAME	
1959	149 3/8	WAYNE	89	70 7/8	67 5/8	19 1/8	1 0/8	23 3/8	25 4/8	6	5	KEPPIER	JOHN	SAME	
1959	149 3/8	MARIES	95	69 3/8	66 1/8	17 3/8	0	23 5/8	23 3/8	5	5	KLEFFNER	DON	SAME	
1959	149 3/8	NODAWAY	95	68 1/8	69 3/8	18 3/8	2 3/8	24 0/8	24 2/8	4	5	FOSTER	WILLIAM L.	SAME	
1959	149 3/8	CLARK	95	66 7/8	67 4/8	20 3/8	0	24 7/8	24 7/8	4	5	ELFRINK	DAVID E.	SAME	
1959	149 3/8	TEXAS	96	68 7/8	68 2/8	17 4/8	4 1/8	23 5/8	23 4/8	7	5	GASTON	DON	SAME	
1973	149 2/8	ST. CLAIR	72	68 0/8	67 3/8	20 0/8	2 2/8	22 4/8	23 4/8	4	5	STODDARD	NELSON	SAME	
1973	149 2/8	LACLEDE	72	68 4/8	72 6/8	20 1/8	3 3/8	24 4/8	24 1/8	5	7	SMITH	DEE	SAME	
1973	149 2/8	MARIES	79	75 3/8	76 7/8	16 3/8	8 5/8	23 4/8	24 4/8	6	7	MOLKENBUR	DAVE	SAME	
1973	149 2/8	JACKSON	84	65 7/8	67 0/8	18 0/8	0	23 6/8	23 4/8	5	5	THOMEY	MARVIN	SAME	
1973	149 2/8	WASHINGTON	85	66 5/8	68 1/8	17 4/8	0	24 1/8	24 1/8	5	5	POLITTE	TERRY	SAME	
1973	149 2/8	JACKSON	85	66 3/8	68 7/8	17 6/8	0	23 2/8	22 5/8	5	5	THOMEY	MARVIN	SAME	
1973	149 2/8	TEXAS	85	67 3/8	71 1/8	15 6/8	0	23 3/8	23 4/8	5	5	LIPSCOMB	ROY	SAME	
1973	149 2/8	TEXAS	87	67 0/8	68 6/8	17 0/8	0	21 6/8	22 0/8	5	5	CARR	RUSSELL	SAME	
1973	149 2/8	COLE	87	67 2/8	68 6/8	15 1/8	0	23 1/8	23 2/8	5	5	ADRIAN	JAMES	SAME	
1973	149 2/8	CASS	88	70 1/8	66 3/8	20 4/8	1 4/8	24 6/8	23 7/8	6	4	HELPHREY	ROGER	SAME	
1973	149 2/8	MILLER	89	66 1/8	68 6/8	19 0/8	0	24 4/8	24 3/8	5	5	BLOMBERG	ALAN	SAME	
1973	149 2/8	McDONALD	91	67 3/8	66 2/8	20 4/8	2 0/8	24 0/8	23 0/8	6	5	WARDEN	SUSAN RAE	SAME	

MISSOURI SHOW-ME BIG BUCKS CLUB RECORDS OF WHITETAIL DEER BY STATE, TYPICAL

STATE RANK	SCORE	COUNTY	YEAR TAKEN	INCHES TYPICAL R	INCHES TYPICAL L	INSIDE SPREAD	INCHES ABNORMAL	LENGTH MAIN BEAM R	LENGTH MAIN BEAM L	NUMBER POINTS R	NUMBER POINTS L	HUNTER	FIRST NAME	OWNER	FIRST NAME
1973	149 2/8	LACLEDE	91	71 0/8	76 5/8	18 6/8	9 2/8	22 2/8	24 3/8	6	6	YOUNG	ROBERT A.	SAME	
1973	149 2/8	HENRY	93	69 1/8	68 2/8	17 0/8	0	24 1/8	24 0/8	4	4	NIDA	CALVIN	SAME	
1973	149 2/8	MONROE	96	68 4/8	66 3/8	17 0/8	0	23 4/8	22 6/8	5	5	WEST	JUSTIN	SAME	
1988	149 1/8	FRANKLIN	63	67 6/8	68 3/8	17 1/8	0	24 3/8	26 5/8	4	4	BRUEGEMANN	PAUL	SAME	
1988	149 1/8	HOWELL	67	71 4/8	78 4/8	16 2/8	10 1/8	23 2/8	25 3/8	6	9	ANSTINE	GERALD	SAME	
1988	149 1/8	TEXAS	73	71 7/8	66 7/8	18 0/8	0	24 0/8	22 6/8	6	5	KEITH	KENNETH J.	SAME	
1988	149 1/8	CARROLL	83	65 6/8	67 3/8	19 1/8	0	23 3/8	23 2/8	5	5	FLOYD	CHARLIE	SAME	
1988	149 1/8	SALINE	86	69 1/8	69 6/8	14 3/8	1 2/8	21 0/8	20 7/8	5	6	MARSH	TOM	SAME	
1988	149 1/8	MADISON	86	67 4/8	69 1/8	16 1/8	0	23 2/8	22 7/8	5	5	HARDING, JR.	JOHN A.	HARDING	BILL
1988	149 1/8	COOPER	89	69 3/8	68 1/8	19 6/8	4 3/8	23 2/8	21 5/8	6	5	PEASE	TOM	SAME	
1988	149 1/8	BOLLINGER	90	74 6/8	70 7/8	19 3/8	4 2/8	23 6/8	23 1/8	6	7	GREER	BRUCE	SAME	
1988	149 1/8	COOPER	93	65 5/8	67 2/8	19 3/8	0	22 7/8	23 3/8	5	5	MILLER	STEVEN	SAME	
1988	149 1/8	SCOTLAND	96	66 0/8	67 4/8	19 1/8	0	23 0/8	23 2/8	5	5	GARNETT	JAMES MICHAEL	SAME	
1998	149 0/8	CAMDEN	62	66 4/8	66 2/8	18 6/8	0	24 7/8	24 7/8	4	4	WOODALL	LESLIE LEE	SAME	
1998	149 0/8	BENTON	74	67 1/8	72 2/8	18 4/8	1 2/8	24 3/8	23 7/8	5	6	NEWKIRK	SCOTTY	SAME	
1998	149 0/8	CAMDEN	74	69 3/8	67 7/8	14 6/8	0	22 4/8	21 6/8	5	7	CAMPBELL, JR.	KEN L.	SAME	
1998	149 0/8	MARIES	81	69 2/8	67 0/8	16 4/8	0	22 2/8	22 6/8	5	5	MAHANEY	BOB	SAME	
1998	149 0/8	PERRY	83	66 7/8	69 3/8	19 2/8	1 4/8	20 0/8	21 5/8	6	5	LEUCKEL	PAUL A.	SAME	
1998	149 0/8	MILLER	83	67 1/8	70 3/8	18 0/8	1 4/8	22 4/8	22 6/8	6	5	PLEMMONS	JIMMIE	SAME	
1998	149 0/8	DOUGLAS	84	68 7/8	68 1/8	16 2/8	0	22 4/8	22 6/8	5	5	JOHNSON	GENE	SAME	
1998	149 0/8	STONE	86	69 6/8	67 5/8	17 6/8	0	24 3/8	23 2/8	5	5	CREEL	TODD	SAME	
1998	149 0/8	WAYNE	87	67 6/8	70 5/8	16 4/8	0	22 7/8	22 6/8	5	5	COX	JEFF	SAME	
1998	149 0/8	PULASKI	87	68 1/8	66 6/8	17 0/8	0	23 2/8	23 7/8	5	5	DOYLE	TOMMY	SAME	
1998	149 0/8	CASS	89	70 5/8	67 7/8	20 2/8	6 6/8	25 0/8	24 6/8	5	6	BROOKS	WILLIAM O.	SAME	
1998	149 0/8	MILLER	91	76 5/8	66 6/8	15 4/8	0	25 1/8	23 7/8	5	5	MINNICK	TROY	SAME	
1998	149 0/8	CEDAR	94	67 6/8	68 5/8	16 6/8	0	21 2/8	22 1/8	5	5	LANE	MIKE	SAME	
1998	149 0/8	HENRY	96	67 1/8	70 0/8	19 4/8	1 6/8	22 7/8	22 5/8	6	6	BAUER	BRETT	SAME	
2012	148 7/8	TEXAS	58	68 4/8	68 1/8	15 5/8	0	22 3/8	23 1/8	5	5	ICE	ELMER	SAME	
2012	148 7/8	PUTNAM	60	67 7/9	63 7/8	23 1/8	0	28 3/8	27 3/8	4	4	CLEM	VELDON T.	SAME	
2012	148 7/8	BATES	65	72 7/8	87 4/8	17 7/8	12 6/8	26 3/8	26 0/8	7	9	HATTON	CHARLIE	SAME	
2012	148 7/8	CARTER	66	68 4/8	67 7/8	17 1/8	0	22 1/8	22 2/8	5	5	JUERGENS	ROY E.	SAME	
2012	148 7/8	PHELPS	66	74 4/8	74 2/8	15 1/8	8 0/8	24 7/8	25 1/8	6	8	WOOLMAN	BILL	SAME	

MISSOURI SHOW-ME BIG BUCKS CLUB RECORDS OF WHITETAIL DEER BY STATE, TYPICAL

STATE RANK	SCORE	COUNTY	YEAR TAKEN	INCHES TYPICAL R	INCHES TYPICAL L	INSIDE SPREAD	INCHES ABNORMAL	LENGTH MAIN BEAM R	LENGTH MAIN BEAM L	NUMBER POINTS R	NUMBER POINTS L	HUNTER	FIRST NAME	OWNER	FIRST NAME
2012	148 7/8	LAFAYETTE	70	68 1/8	66 7/8	18 4/8	0	23 2/8	23 0/8	5	5	LARKIN	THOMAS	SAME	
2012	148 7/8	STE. GENEIEVE	79	64 7/8	73 4/8	19 3/8	0	22 7/8	24 3/8	5	6	VOGEL	EDWIN	SAME	
2012	148 7/8	WAYNE	84	70 4/8	68 4/8	19 0/8	6 1/8	24 1/8	23 5/8	0	0	WELLS	ANDY	SAME	
2012	148 7/8	RIPLEY	94	70 5/8	71 3/8	14 1/8	0	22 1/8	22 7/8	5	5	EDDINGTON	BRAD	SAME	
2012	148 7/8	PLATTE	94	69 1/8	69 4/8	19 3/8	5 0/8	24 2/8	23 5/8	7	6	JAMISON	FRANK	SAME	
2012	148 7/8	SALINE	95	73 4/8	76 1/8	17 2/8	4 7/8	23 3/8	24 5/8	5	7	WISEMAN	JAMES	SAME	
2012	148 7/8	BOONE	96	68 2/8	68 3/8	20 7/8	6 4/8	23 2/8	22 6/8	5	5	KUSTER	JOSEPH W.	SAME	
2024	148 6/8	CAMDEN	54	64 3/8	67 2/8	20 0/8	0	20 6/8	22 0/8	5	5	GREEN	ARNOLD	SAME	
2024	148 6/8	CAPE GIRARDEAU	85	66 4/8	66 3/8	20 0/8	0	24 2/8	23 4/8	5	5	LANDS	DALLAS K.	SAME	
2024	148 6/8	BOLLINGER	88	68 5/8	67 3/8	20 5/8	4 1/8	23 2/8	23 0/8	6	6	ANTHONY	W. SCOTT	SAME	
2024	148 6/8	PETTIS	90	64 7/8	71 3/8	20 6/8	0	23 7/8	23 1/8	5	5	KIZER	KEITH	SAME	
2024	148 6/8	SALINE	94	78 2/8	67 7/8	15 4/8	0	24 5/8	22 4/8	5	4	TUCKER	BRIAN P.	SAME	
2024	148 6/8	WASHINGTON	94	68 5/8	67 0/8	16 2/8	0	23 6/8	23 4/8	5	5	HUBBLE	DAVE	MEDLIN	GERALD
2024	148 6/8	MILLER	94	73 0/8	68 0/8	15 6/8	0	23 6/8	25 2/8	5	5	TIPTON	EDGER	SAME	
2024	148 6/8	BATES	95	66 3/8	67 3/8	19 2/8	0	25 1/8	26 4/8	4	4	TIFFEY	GARY	SAME	
2024	148 6/8	CRAWFORD	95	66 0/8	67 3/8	19 2/8	0	23 7/8	24 1/8	4	4	ORTON	JAMES	SAME	
2024	148 6/8	ST. CHARLES	96	65 2/8	66 0/8	22 0/8	0	26 2/8	26 4/8	4	4	HOLDMEYER	CLARENCE L.	SAME	
2024	148 6/8	RAY	96	70 6/8	67 5/8	17 2/8	0	22 6/8	23 6/8	5	5	KIRK	DOUG	SAME	
2035	148 5/8	JEFFERSON	62	65 2/8	68 4/8	18 0/8	0	24 4/8	24 7/8	5	5	BRINLEY	CLYDE H.	SAME	
2035	148 5/8	HOWELL	68	67 7/8	67 5/8	16 3/8	0	24 0/8	23 5/8	5	5	HENDRIX, Jr.	JOHN	SAME	
2035	148 5/8	GASCONADE	71	67 1/8	66 3/8	17 5/8	0	22 0/8	22 2/8	5	5	SWOBODA	M.F.	SAME	
2035	148 5/8	NEWTON	77	71 2/8	68 3/8	15 5/8	0	22 4/8	21 3/8	6	6	BINGHAM	DALE	SAME	
2035	148 5/8	ST. CHARLES	80	68 4/8	77 7/8	20 5/8	5 2/8	22 2/8	25 2/8	6	6	DAVIDSON	EDWARD J.	SAME	
2035	148 5/8	STE. GENEIEVE	82	66 6/8	72 7/8	16 3/8	0	24 5/8	25 0/8	5	6	GEARY	GEORGE	SAME	
2035	148 5/8	DENT	90	72 7/8	68 3/8	16 7/8	1 0/8	23 7/8	25 2/8	6	5	CAMPBELL	TONY	SAME	
2035	148 5/8	BENTON	90	66 6/8	68 1/8	16 4/8	0	23 1/8	23 1/8	5	5	LEGG	RITA	SAME	
2035	148 5/8	CLAY	91	69 5/8	68 3/8	18 5/8	2 4/8	23 4/8	22 6/8	8	7	DUTTON	DONALD	SAME	
2035	148 5/8	COOPER	92	70 0/8	71 1/8	18 7/8	2 2/8	24 0/8	24 4/8	5	5	FERGUSON	ALAN	SAME	
2035	148 5/8	ST. LOUIS	92	74 3/8	71 3/8	15 4/8	3 1/8	22 5/8	21 3/8	7	7	WISNIEWSKI	JAY	SAME	
2035	148 5/8	CHARITON	95	67 5/8	65 2/8	19 3/8	0	22 0/8	22 3/8	5	5	WOMACK	MIKE	SAME	
2035	148 5/8	CRAWFORD	95	72 2/8	69 0/8	15 7/8	2 0/8	25 1/8	25 2/8	6	6	PAYNE	MARK	SAME	
2048	148 4/8	MORGAN	68	75 2/8	68 5/8	21 2/8	7 6/8	27 2/8	25 7/8	7	6	EARNEST, JR.	L.M.	SAME	

STATE RANK	SCORE	COUNTY	YEAR TAKEN	INCHES TYPICAL R	INCHES TYPICAL L	INSIDE SPREAD	INCHES ABNORMAL	LENGTH MAIN BEAM R	LENGTH MAIN BEAM L	NUMBER POINTS R	NUMBER POINTS L	HUNTER	FIRST NAME	OWNER	FIRST NAME
2048	148 4/8	BENTON	75	68 0/8	68 2/8	17 6/8	0	23 0/8	21 4/8	5	5	FISHER	BOB	SAME	
2048	148 4/8	SALINE	75	73 3/8	67 0/8	16 6/8	0	26 1/8	25 4/8	5	5	HIGHBARGER	RONALD	SAME	
2048	148 4/8	DOUGLAS	81	67 0/8	72 4/8	16 2/8	0	26 0/8	25 1/8	5	5	DODSON	DAVID	SAME	
2048	148 4/8	OREGON	83	71 6/8	66 1/8	16 6/8	0	21 1/8	20 7/8	5	5	ALSUP	BRENT	SAME	
2048	148 4/8	JEFFERSON	85	68 0/8	67 6/8	18 6/8	0	21 2/8	20 2/8	7	7	MONTGOMERY	KENNETH A.	SAME	
2048	148 4/8	WASHINGTON	85	67 7/8	67 1/8	16 6/8	0	23 3/8	23 6/8	5	5	CHRISTOPHER	ROBERT	SAME	
2048	148 4/8	MILLER	87	66 5/8	68 5/8	19 7/8	0	22 1/8	21 4/8	6	6	WALL	CLARK	SAME	
2048	148 4/8	GREENE	87	66 2/8	66 5/8	18 6/8	0	24 6/8	24 7/8	5	5	SCHREINER	CLIFF	SAME	
2048	148 4/8	COOPER	95	67 0/8	64 7/8	17 4/8	0	23 6/8	23 6/8	5	5	DUVALL	TWILLA D.	SAME	
2048	148 4/8	ST. LOUIS	95	67 4/8	67 3/8	20 0/8	0	24 4/8	24 0/8	5	5	BAUER	DONALD J.	SAME	
2048	148 4/8	MERCER	96	67 5/8	69 2/8	17 6/8	0	23 2/8	22 5/8	6	6	FINNEY	GRAG	SAME	
2060	148 3/8	MORGAN	66	71 0/8	66 7/8	17 7/8	1 0/8	25 2/8	23 5/8	5	6	JONES	JOHN E.	SAME	
2060	148 3/8	CRAWFORD	70	67 1/8	69 2/8	16 5/8	0	21 4/8	22 6/8	5	5	McMILLEN	ROBERT	SAME	
2060	148 3/8	PETTIS	76	64 4/8	71 2/8	22 6/8	2 7/8	24 2/8	24 2/8	5	5	SHACKLES	ROBERT L.	SAME	
2060	148 3/8	MORGAN	82	71 0/8	68 2/8	18 1/8	0	23 2/8	22 3/8	6	6	VOGT	STEVE	SAME	
2060	148 3/8	MADISON	86	67 0/8	63 3/8	21 1/8	0	22 6/8	23 6/8	5	5	THOMAS	DONALD M.	SAME	
2060	148 3/8	MILLER	87	66 7/8	70 3/8	17 3/8	0	23 7/8	22 3/8	6	6	GOLDEN	EARL	SAME	
2060	148 3/8	STODDARD	90	67 2/8	69 5/8	18 7/8	2 4/8	25 5/8	24 5/8	4	5	BARNFIELD	CLINT	SAME	
2060	148 3/8	MONITEAU	90	67 0/8	69 0/8	17 7/8	0	23 6/8	22 4/8	4	5	BURLINGAME	PHILLIP	SAME	
2060	148 3/8	FRANKLIN	92	67 0/8	68 2/8	17 3/8	1 4/8	22 2/8	21 7/8	5	6	KOPP	GERALD E.	SAME	
2060	148 3/8	WARREN	94	66 6/8	72 1/8	19 6/8	1 5/8	25 0/8	24 7/8	6	6	CASPER	JIM	SAME	
2060	148 3/8	MACON	96	66 6/8	68 6/8	19 0/8	1 3/8	24 3/8	23 6/8	5	6	HERRMANN	STEVE	SAME	
2071	148 2/8	PERRY	60	69 0/8	71 4/8	15 2/8	0	23 4/8	23 0/8	6	6	VINSON	HAROLD D.	SAME	
2071	148 2/8	MARIES	73	66 5/8	75 6/8	18 4/8	0	24 2/8	24 7/8	4	5	JONES	RALPH	SAME	
2071	148 2/8	CAMDEN	79	69 5/8	70 4/8	18 0/8	0	19 7/8	22 5/8	7	6	PRYOR	TERRY	SAME	
2071	148 2/8	ST. CLAIR	83	67 5/8	71 5/8	18 4/8	3 2/8	25 2/8	24 7/8	6	5	QUICK	LARRY GENE	SAME	
2071	148 2/8	PERRY	84	70 0/8	69 7/8	16 4/8	0	22 4/8	23 0/8	6	7	KOENIG	ALAN	SAME	
2071	148 2/8	MADISON	86	66 0/8	68 1/8	16 6/8	0	21 7/8	22 1/8	4	4	PHILIPPS	THOMAS E.	SAME	
2071	148 2/8	WASHINGTON	87	67 6/8	67 1/8	19 2/8	0	25 0/8	25 4/8	5	5	JACOX	RANDY	SAME	
2071	148 2/8	ST. CLAIR	87	66 5/8	66 4/8	19 4/8	0	22 6/8	22 4/8	5	5	WILLIAMS	ROBERT D.	SAME	
2071	148 2/8	CALLAWAY	88	68 4/8	71 1/8	21 3/8	3 1/8	24 4/8	24 3/8	4	6	MASCHGER	JERRY	SAME	
2071	148 2/8	MONITEAU	88	68 3/8	69 0/8	15 2/8	1 6/8	22 1/8	21 5/8	5	6	WOLFRUM	GAIL E.	SAME	

STATE RANK	SCORE	COUNTY	YEAR TAKEN	INCHES TYPICAL R	L	INSIDE SPREAD	INCHES ABNORMAL	LENGTH MAIN BEAM R	L	NUMBER POINTS R	L	HUNTER	FIRST NAME	OWNER	FIRST NAME
2071	148 2/8	DENT	89	66 6/8	63 0/8	22 2/8	0	24 4/8	24 4/8	4	4	ENKE	GILBERT	SAME	
2071	148 2/8	PERRY	91	68 5/8	67 0/8	16 6/8	0	23 1/8	20 7/8	5	5	BALL	PAM	SAME	
2071	148 2/8	MONITEAU	91	71 2/8	69 1/8	18 2/8	1 4/8	26 3/8	25 7/8	5	5	REDDEN	CHARLES	SAME	
2071	148 2/8	ANDREW	94	69 5/8	70 2/8	16 6/8	3 2/8	22 1/8	22 5/8	7	5	PFLUGRADT	LARRY	SAME	
2071	148 2/8	MONTGOMERY	95	70 3/8	65 5/8	17 6/8	0	23 3/8	22 1/8	5	5	KNOEPFLEIN	JACK	SAME	
2071	148 2/8	OSAGE	95	69 1/8	69 4/8	15 6/8	4 4/8	24 4/8	24 5/8	4	5	ROESLEIN	RUDI	SAME	
2071	148 2/8	CALLAWAY	96	71 1/8	73 3/8	15 6/8	4 2/8	22 6/8	22 7/8	6	6	JORDAN	SCOTT	SAME	
2071	148 2/8	CHRISTIAN	68	64 1/8	62 7/8	22 3/8	0	24 1/8	23 5/8	5	5	STAFFORD	DALE	SAME	
2088	148 1/8	MARIES	71	68 6/8	68 2/8	18 7/8	0	27 0/8	24 3/8	4	5	SAPPINGTON	BILLY	SAME	
2088	148 1/8	OSAGE	78	69 6/8	69 0/8	16 7/8	1 4/8	25 3/8	25 6/8	6	5	WEBER	ROGER	SAME	
2088	148 1/8	WRIGHT	79	66 3/8	73 2/8	18 4/8	3 1/8	25 2/8	25 6/8	4	5	TURNER	LARRY	SAME	
2088	148 1/8	SCOTT	81	65 5/8	66 3/8	19 3/8	0	22 4/8	23 4/8	4	4	MILLER	JOHN	SAME	
2088	148 1/8	HICKORY	81	71 5/8	73 0/8	16 2/8	7 1/8	23 2/8	23 3/8	6	6	MATTHEWS	KIRBY	SAME	
2088	148 1/8	CAPE GIRARDEAU	81	65 1/8	72 1/8	18 1/8	0	26 2/8	26 2/8	4	5	BROWN	ALBERT	SAME	
2088	148 1/8	HICKORY	87	70 6/8	66 2/8	18 2/8	2 5/8	22 6/8	22 3/8	6	5	LANGTON	DAVID	SAME	
2088	148 1/8	DENT	87	67 3/8	69 1/8	18 3/8	3 6/8	22 3/8	23 0/8	6	6	DIEM	FRED	MAJOR	DONALD
2088	148 1/8	MILLER	87	68 4/8	70 1/8	15 3/8	2 2/8	20 3/8	20 5/8	5	6	MORGAN	ANTHONY	SAME	
2088	148 1/8	POLK	89	67 1/8	67 0/8	15 7/8	0	22 4/8	22 2/8	5	5	ELLIS	KENNETH N.	SAME	
2088	148 1/8	PULASKI	89	68 1/8	68 2/8	19 1/8	4 7/8	23 4/8	23 4/8	7	5	DOYLE	ROY LEE	SAME	
2088	148 1/8	MONITEAU	92	70 0/8	66 2/8	18 5/8	3 0/8	25 3/8	24 7/8	4	5	BARNETT	TERRY	SAME	
2101	148 0/8	CRAWFORD	49	65 6/8	66 6/8	20 0/8	0	22 6/8	23 4/8	5	5	FARRIS	HAROLD	SAME	
2101	148 0/8	CRAWFORD	60	66 1/8	75 1/8	18 2/8	8 6/8	24 5/8	24 6/8	6	8	PETERSON	PAUL F.	SAME	
2101	148 0/8	COOPER	73	70 5/8	69 4/8	19 3/8	5 3/8	24 3/8	22 3/8	8	6	SCHUPP	BILL	SAME	
2101	148 0/8	FRANKLIN	81	67 7/8	66 3/8	16 4/8	0	22 6/8	22 1/8	5	5	DIMMETT	RONALD	SAME	
2101	148 0/8	DADE	82	64 5/8	65 4/8	20 6/8	0	22 4/8	23 0/8	5	5	HEDRICK	RON	SAME	
2101	148 0/8	FRANKLIN	86	64 4/8	68 6/8	19 6/8	0	22 4/8	22 5/8	5	5	HELLING	ROLLIN	SAME	
2101	148 0/8	PERRY	86	71 7/8	69 4/8	14 2/8	0	24 0/8	23 1/8	5	5	TUCKER	JIM	SAME	
2101	148 0/8	FRANKLIN	86	67 3/8	65 6/8	17 4/8	0	23 5/8	24 4/8	4	4	VAN WINKLE	RICHARD	SAME	
2101	148 0/8	VERNON	89	72 0/8	67 1/8	16 6/8	0	25 5/8	25 7/8	4	4	MOONEY II	TOM R.	SAME	
2101	148 0/8	MORGAN	91	66 5/8	67 3/8	18 6/8	0	23 5/8	24 4/8	5	5	SIMMONS	DAVID	SAME	
2101	148 0/8	MORGAN	92	64 4/8	69 0/8	21 4/8	0	23 5/8	24 1/8	5	5	MARRIOTT	PHILLIP C.	SAME	
2101	148 0/8	JACKSON	93	76 4/8	68 5/8	20 1/8	2 3/8	24 7/8	24 1/8	6	5	SCHUBERT	CHESTER	SAME	

STATE RANK	SCORE	COUNTY	YEAR TAKEN	INCHES TYPICAL R	L	INSIDE SPREAD	INCHES ABNORMAL	LENGTH MAIN BEAM R	L	NUMBER POINTS R	L	HUNTER	FIRST NAME	OWNER	FIRST NAME
2101	148 0/8	GASCONADE	95	69 3/8	71 6/8	16 3/8	2 7/8	24 6/8	24 6/8	6	5	WEHMEYER	JANIE	SAME	
2114	147 7/8	PHELPS	57	70 5/8	70 6/8	15 2/8	5 5/8	22 4/8	22 0/8	8	7	DESHURLEY	REX	DESHURLEY	JOE
2114	147 7/8	SALINE	74	69 1/8	68 2/8	20 6/8	5 3/8	23 0/8	23 2/8	6	6	LAND	BOB	SAME	
2114	147 7/8	MONITEAU	83	67 5/8	66 5/8	15 5/8	0	21 3/8	21 4/8	5	5	PORTER	LANNY	SAME	
2114	147 7/8	ST. LOUIS	83	67 4/8	68 2/8	16 3/8	0	22 3/8	21 7/8	5	5	BERGMANN	DAVID	SAME	
2114	147 7/8	JASPER	84	69 3/8	69 3/8	16 1/8	2 2/8	22 0/8	22 6/8	6	7	CLINE	GAYLE	SAME	
2114	147 7/8	VERNON	86	66 3/8	69 2/8	16 7/8	1 2/8	22 5/8	22 6/8	6	5	PARRISH	KEVIN	SAME	
2114	147 7/8	OSAGE	88	64 5/8	66 0/8	18 5/8	0	22 6/8	22 7/8	4	4	VOSS	DEREK A.	SAME	
2114	147 7/8	OREGON	89	67 2/8	64 1/8	20 7/8	0	24 5/8	23 3/8	5	5	EMERY	MIKE	SAME	
2114	147 7/8	WASHINGTON	89	71 6/8	71 2/8	15 4/8	5 5/8	23 1/8	23 5/8	8	7	MEDLIN	GREGORY D.	SAME	
2114	147 7/8	ST. CLAIR	90	69 7/8	67 7/8	17 2/8	1 1/8	24 4/8	24 0/8	6	5	BRAY	RICK	SAME	
2114	147 7/8	BOLLINGER	92	64 1/8	68 2/8	19 5/8	0	24 4/8	25 6/8	4	4	WESBECHER	RONNIE	SAME	
2114	147 7/8	HOWARD	95	75 4/8	73 6/8	17 4/8	14 1/8	23 5/8	24 4/8	7	7	WESTHUES	GEORGIA	SAME	
2126	147 6/8	FRANKLIN	66	66 5/8	66 1/8	20 2/8	0	25 3/8	23 6/8	5	5	DOOR	NEIL	SAME	
2126	147 6/8	FRANKLIN	75	68 0/8	65 6/8	19 2/8	0	23 5/8	22 7/8	6	5	WILSON	JOHN	SAME	
2126	147 6/8	SHANNON	79	64 3/8	69 3/8	21 4/8	1 4/8	20 0/8	21 4/8	6	5	SEARCY	DONALD D.	SAME	
2126	147 6/8	CEDAR	85	68 3/8	64 5/8	18 6/8	0	24 3/8	23 5/8	4	4	RUTLEDGE	TOM	SAME	
2126	147 6/8	CAMDEN	86	69 3/8	69 1/8	14 6/8	1 2/8	25 1/8	24 4/8	5	6	WHITMORE	BILLY	SAME	
2126	147 6/8	COLE	87	65 5/8	67 6/8	16 4/8	0	23 5/8	24 4/8	4	4	HUFF	ROBERT	SAME	
2126	147 6/8	CAMDEN	88	65 5/8	67 4/8	18 0/8	0	23 4/8	22 7/8	5	5	JENNINGS	LENN	SAME	
2126	147 6/8	TEXAS	89	71 4/8	68 5/8	14 5/8	2 1/8	22 5/8	20 5/8	6	7	GIVENS	GARY	SAME	
2126	147 6/8	OSAGE	92	70 1/8	67 5/8	14 6/8	0	22 4/8	21 6/8	5	5	HAFLEY	SAM	SAME	
2126	147 6/8	REYNOLDS	92	66 7/8	70 0/8	17 0/8	0	25 7/8	24 4/8	5	5	MARTIN	ROCKY	SAME	
2126	147 6/8	RIPLEY	94	70 3/8	69 2/8	19 0/8	1 2/8	24 6/8	24 4/8	6	6	MUSE	STEVEN E.	SAME	
2126	147 6/8	WASHINGTON	96	66 6/8	66 3/8	18 3/8	1 1/8	23 7/8	23 1/8	5	6	GOODSON	KELLY E.	SAME	
2138	147 5/8	DENT	68	67 0/8	66 7/8	18 6/8	1 1/8	22 4/8	23 3/8	5	6	WILDT	AL	SAME	
2138	147 5/8	WARREN	68	66 6/8	70 1/8	17 1/8	0	23 4/8	23 6/8	5	6	CASPER	TIMOTHY W.	SAME	
2138	147 5/8	CAMDEN	72	71 4/8	65 4/8	18 5/8	0	25 2/8	24 2/8	5	4	WESTFALL	DAN	SAME	
2138	147 5/8	STONE	73	69 7/8	68 4/8	17 1/8	2 6/8	22 5/8	23 5/8	6	5	RICE	JOE	SAME	
2138	147 5/8	TANEY	73	66 4/8	65 7/8	22 5/8	0	24 2/8	24 2/8	5	5	ROSSNER	HERMAN	SAME	
2138	147 5/8	CRAWFORD	82	65 0/8	72 6/8	18 5/8	1 0/8	26 7/8	26 3/8	4	4	LOGAN	ROBERT R.	SAME	
2138	147 5/8	CALLAWAY	83	67 6/8	68 7/8	19 0/8	3 5/8	24 3/8	23 4/8	5	6	BEVL	DALE	SAME	

MISSOURI SHOW-ME BIG BUCKS CLUB RECORDS OF WHITETAIL DEER BY STATE, TYPICAL

STATE RANK	SCORE	COUNTY	YEAR TAKEN	INCHES TYPICAL R	L	INSIDE SPREAD	INCHES ABNORMAL	LENGTH MAIN BEAM R	L	NUMBER POINTS R	L	HUNTER	FIRST NAME	OWNER	FIRST NAME
2138	147 5/8	BENTON	85	71 0/8	74 4/8	17 4/8	9 1/8	24 2/8	23 5/8	6	7	SWEENEY	GREG	SAME	
2138	147 5/8	MARIES	86	66 5/8	70 0/8	14 7/8	0	25 6/8	26 5/8	4	4	BARNHART	JOHN	SAME	
2138	147 5/8	HICKORY	91	70 0/8	69 4/8	16 4/8	6 1/8	22 2/8	22 2/8	6	5	PALMER	FORREST A.	SAME	
2148	147 4/8	TANEY	81	67 7/8	70 3/8	16 4/8	2 0/8	22 3/8	22 2/8	5	6	OUSLEY	CHUCK	SAME	
2148	147 4/8	HENRY	87	66 4/8	68 1/8	16 2/8	0	22 5/8	22 3/8	5	5	DENNIS	CARY	SAME	
2148	147 4/8	IRON	88	65 2/8	66 4/8	18 0/8	0	23 5/8	23 3/8	5	5	JENKINS, JR.	MARVIN	SAME	
2148	147 4/8	CRAWFORD	89	68 3/8	65 1/8	20 4/8	2 0/8	23 7/8	24 3/8	6	5	FARRIS	RICK	SAME	
2148	147 4/8	HENRY	90	65 3/8	65 2/8	20 6/8	0	26 2/8	25 7/8	4	4	SWATERS	BILL	SAME	
2148	147 4/8	COLE	94	67 1/8	69 3/8	16 2/8	0	23 4/8	23 1/8	5	6	BOESSEN	ANTHONY N.	SAME	
2148	147 4/8	SALINE	96	74 1/8	73 2/8	17 7/8	1 1/8	26 5/8	24 1/8	4	6	ROGERS	TIM	SAME	
2155	147 3/8	OZARK	67	66 0/8	68 6/8	20 5/8	2 0/8	25 4/8	25 2/8	4	6	MCNEIL	BERT	SAME	
2155	147 3/8	OSAGE	75	64 6/8	66 3/8	19 3/8	0	24 4/8	23 6/8	5	5	KOELHER	WILLIAM	SAME	
2155	147 3/8	MORGAN	83	66 7/8	69 3/8	17 3/8	2 0/8	21 6/8	22 3/8	5	6	HALL	GARY	SAME	
2155	147 3/8	JACKSON	84	69 7/8	71 2/8	12 7/8	1 0/8	22 0/8	22 3/8	7	5	THOMEY	MARVIN	SAME	
2155	147 3/8	WASHINGTON	85	72 1/8	71 4/8	16 7/8	9 4/8	23 0/8	22 3/8	6	6	BUST	JOE	SAME	
2155	147 3/8	MORGAN	88	70 1/8	70 1/8	17 0/8	4 5/8	22 6/8	23 6/8	7	7	DITTO	JOE	SAME	
2155	147 3/8	MILLER	91	70 1/8	70 2/8	16 6/8	8 7/8	22 4/8	22 3/8	6	6	PEMBERTON	DAVID	SAME	
2155	147 3/8	VERNON	91	64 6/8	65 0/8	21 1/8	0	23 6/8	24 3/8	4	4	MCGRATH	FRANK	SAME	
2155	147 3/8	STE. GENEIEVE	91	67 2/8	68 2/8	18 2/8	3 1/8	26 2/8	25 6/8	4	5	HICKMAN	DALE	SAME	
2155	147 3/8	COLE	93	68 1/8	72 5/8	15 7/8	2 2/8	26 1/8	25 3/8	4	6	WHEELER	STEVE	SAME	
2155	147 3/8	HENRY	93	73 3/8	71 1/8	16 4/8	5 7/8	23 0/8	21 2/8	7	6	CANNON	JEREMY	SAME	
2155	147 3/8	KNOX	95	67 2/8	70 4/8	17 5/8	4 4/8	22 3/8	23 4/8	5	6	SCHULTZ	RANDALL	SAME	
2167	147 2/8	NEWTON	67	65 2/8	69 1/8	16 6/8	0	22 2/8	22 5/8	4	4	WELSH	TOM	SAME	
2167	147 2/8	OREGON	68	70 7/8	68 0/8	14 2/8	0	22 2/8	22 2/8	5	5	BRUMLEY	DONALD	SAME	
2167	147 2/8	VERNON	79	69 0/8	66 6/8	16 0/8	0	26 0/8	26 0/8	5	4	COUCH	PHIL	SAME	
2167	147 2/8	STE. GENEIEVE	85	68 4/8	69 4/8	16 4/8	4 2/8	21 5/8	22 4/8	7	7	HILL	CHRIS L.	SAME	
2167	147 2/8	CRAWFORD	86	66 3/8	68 4/8	19 0/8	1 4/8	22 3/8	22 2/8	5	6	HARTLEY	DR. DENNIS	SAME	
2167	147 2/8	CRAWFORD	86	67 5/8	67 7/8	17 2/8	0	23 0/8	21 3/8	5	5	DOTSON	DANIEL	SAME	
2167	147 2/8	CAPE GIRARDEAU	87	70 7/8	68 6/8	17 2/8	1 5/8	24 1/8	23 7/8	5	5	SMITH	TIM B.	SAME	
2167	147 2/8	CRAWFORD	88	67 6/8	69 3/8	14 4/8	0	22 2/8	22 4/8	5	5	PIAZZA	LARRY	SAME	
2167	147 2/8	SALINE	89	72 4/8	73 7/8	16 2/8	1 6/8	23 2/8	23 7/8	7	7	KLASING	JERRY	SAME	
2167	147 2/8	TANEY	89	70 4/8	67 1/8	18 1/8	4 1/8	24 0/8	24 2/8	8	5	COFFELT	JIM	SAME	

303

MISSOURI SHOW-ME BIG BUCKS CLUB RECORDS OF WHITETAIL DEER BY STATE, TYPICAL

STATE RANK	SCORE	COUNTY	YEAR TAKEN	INCHES TYPICAL R	INCHES TYPICAL L	INSIDE SPREAD	INCHES ABNORMAL	LENGTH MAIN BEAM R	LENGTH MAIN BEAM L	NUMBER POINTS R	NUMBER POINTS L	HUNTER	FIRST NAME	OWNER	FIRST NAME
2167	147 2/8	SALINE	92	69 1/8	68 0/8	17 1/8	2 1/8	23 6/8	22 6/8	5	6	DRISKELL	JOHN E.	SAME	
2167	147 2/8	WASHINGTON	92	67 7/8	66 4/8	19 5/8	2 7/8	23 0/8	23 5/8	5	7	MEDLIN	GREGORY D.	SAME	
2167	147 2/8	HOWARD	93	72 5/8	73 2/8	15 1/8	5 3/8	23 5/8	21 4/8	8	6	MAXFIELD	DAVID	SAME	
2167	147 2/8	LAWRENCE	94	73 3/8	65 0/8	17 6/8	0	25 1/8	24 6/8	5	4	GRAFF	JASON	SAME	
2167	147 2/8	GASCONADE	95	66 6/8	72 7/8	15 6/8	0	24 4/8	23 4/8	5	5	HABERBERGER	DAVID	SAME	
2167	147 2/8	HARRISON	96	64 6/8	69 7/8	18 2/8	0	22 5/8	24 0/8	5	5	GARRETT	MARVIN	SAME	
2167	147 2/8	DENT	47	64 7/8	67 4/8	18 5/8	1 2/8	22 1/8	23 2/8	6	5	KAHRS	JAMES W.	SAME	
2183	147 1/8	SHANNON	61	69 3/8	68 1/8	15 5/8	0	22 1/8	22 0/8	6	6	HEDRICK	RON	SAME	
2183	147 1/8	BENTON	71	71 2/8	70 1/8	17 2/8	7 5/8	26 1/8	26 2/8	5	5	CHANCE	BILL	SAME	
2183	147 1/8	TEXAS	81	69 4/8	67 4/8	18 7/8	0	21 6/8	22 2/8	5	5	CAMPBELL	HERBERT	CAMPBELL	JEFF
2183	147 1/8	BENTON	82	64 5/8	64 3/8	21 1/8	0	25 6/8	25 7/8	4	4	KNOX	ARNOLD	SAME	
2183	147 1/8	OSAGE	83	65 7/8	68 0/8	15 7/8	0	21 2/8	21 0/8	5	5	BACON	AARON	SAME	
2183	147 1/8	FRANKLIN	85	64 4/8	67 5/8	19 1/8	0	21 4/8	23 6/8	4	4	WARGIN, SR.	RICHARD W.	SAME	
2183	147 1/8	CASS	88	69 2/8	73 0/8	19 1/8	9 6/8	24 0/8	24 3/8	7	6	HAMBLIN	RICHARD	SAME	
2183	147 1/8	LACLEDE	88	67 0/8	70 1/8	20 7/8	6 4/8	22 1/8	22 7/8	6	5	FULKERSON	BRUCE	SAME	
2183	147 1/8	CALLAWAY	90	65 0/8	73 4/8	17 5/8	0	24 7/8	25 1/8	4	5	UNDERWOOD	LARRY	SAME	
2183	147 1/8	GASCONADE	91	67 4/8	68 4/8	15 1/8	0	23 7/8	24 4/8	5	5	GIEDINGHAGEN	KURT	SAME	
2183	147 1/8	VERNON	93	69 5/8	66 7/8	16 5/8	0	22 6/8	24 0/8	5	5	BOGART	LARRY D.	SAME	
2195	147 0/8	TEXAS	55	69 1/8	75 3/8	15 1/8	1 5/8	25 2/8	24 2/8	5	5	STILLEY	VAUGHN	SAME	
2195	147 0/8	CRAWFORD	69	66 1/8	66 7/8	15 6/8	0	23 4/8	23 7/8	5	5	LAFFERTY	JOHN	SAME	
2195	147 0/8	HICKORY	72	70 0/8	69 3/8	19 2/8	0	25 2/8	24 7/8	6	6	MERTGEN	JULIA	SAME	
2195	147 0/8	CEDAR	75	23 2/8	22 7/8	16 3/8	1 1/8	23 2/8	22 7/8	5	6	BURNS	ROBBIN	SAME	
2195	147 0/8	STE. GENEIEVE	77	67 1/8	64 7/8	17 4/8	0	24 7/8	25 0/8	4	4	BOYER	VIRGIL	SAME	
2195	147 0/8	MORGAN	80	70 2/8	66 3/8	20 1/8	0	24 2/8	22 1/8	5	5	HEIMSOTH	MARK D.	SAME	
2195	147 0/8	JACKSON	83	72 1/8	69 2/8	17 6/8	3 0/8	22 4/8	24 0/8	7	6	McCURRY	L.O.	SAME	
2195	147 0/8	JOHNSON	86	66 2/8	68 6/8	16 0/8	0	21 0/8	23 0/8	5	5	MEADS	WAYNE	SAME	
2195	147 0/8	CEDAR	86	65 1/8	75 4/8	19 2/8	1 2/8	22 5/8	24 0/8	6	8	BARNARD	DAVID	SAME	
2195	147 0/8	GASCONADE	88	68 0/8	66 2/8	17 6/8	0	21 5/8	22 2/8	5	5	WHITTALL	STEVE	SAME	
2195	147 0/8	CAMDEN	88	68 2/8	67 5/8	18 0/8	0	23 1/8	23 0/8	5	5	ARNONE	GUY	SAME	
2195	147 0/8	IRON	89	68 6/8	64 3/8	18 2/8	0	23 4/8	23 1/8	5	5	INMAN	BYRON B.	SAME	
2195	147 0/8	PHELPS	89	65 4/8	69 0/8	17 2/8	0	22 0/8	21 5/8	6	5	CARROLL	DEREK	SAME	
2195	147 0/8	LAFAYETTE	91	69 1/8	66 2/8	22 3/8	3 7/8	26 7/8	24 6/8	4	6	KRAUS	KEN	SAME	

MISSOURI SHOW-ME BIG BUCKS CLUB RECORDS OF WHITETAIL DEER BY STATE, TYPICAL

STATE RANK	SCORE	COUNTY	YEAR TAKEN	INCHES TYPICAL R	INCHES TYPICAL L	INSIDE SPREAD	INCHES ABNORMAL	LENGTH MAIN BEAM R	LENGTH MAIN BEAM L	NUMBER POINTS R	NUMBER POINTS L	HUNTER	FIRST NAME	OWNER	FIRST NAME
2195	147 0/8	JOHNSON	91	64 0/8	68 0/8	19 4/8	0	19 4/8	19 4/8	6	6	SMITH	WILLIAM E.	SAME	
2195	147 0/8	CAPE GIRARDEAU	91	63 6/8	65 5/8	20 0/8	0	25 6/8	26 1/8	4	4	WALLIS	WILLIAM E.	SAME	
2195	147 0/8	CALLAWAY	91	74 3/8	69 4/8	16 4/8	4 2/8	22 6/8	22 4/8	7	6	BARKS	BEN	SAME	
2195	147 0/8	MONITEAU	91	67 1/8	68 3/8	15 0/8	0	22 0/8	21 2/8	5	5	FLEISCHMANN	GARY	SAME	
2195	147 0/8	MONTGOMERY	95	70 2/8	71 1/8	15 6/8	6 2/8	24 5/8	24 3/8	6	6	GRAVE	DOUG	SAME	
2214	146 7/8	CRAWFORD	55	64 7/8	66 5/8	17 7/8	0	23 1/8	23 2/8	5	5	McCOY	JOHN RILEY	McCOY	ERIC
2214	146 7/8	FRANKLIN	69	66 2/8	67 7/8	19 3/8	0	23 5/8	23 5/8	5	5	ANDERSON	DENNIS	SAME	
2214	146 7/8	PHELPS	72	66 3/8	69 6/8	16 5/8	0	23 5/8	23 1/8	5	5	WATSON	DONALD LEROY	SAME	
2214	146 7/8	MORGAN	72	71 0/8	76 6/8	17 0/8	9 1/8	21 0/8	25 2/8	6	6	ZIMMERMAN	ELWOOD	SAME	
2214	146 7/8	STE. GENEVIEVE	73	66 7/8	67 6/8	19 5/8	0	24 3/8	23 6/8	6	6	HUCK	JEFFREY PAUL	SAME	
2214	146 7/8	SALINE	84	67 4/8	64 0/8	21 3/8	0	24 2/8	23 6/8	5	5	VOGL	KENNETH	SAME	
2214	146 7/8	ST. CHARLES	85	68 1/8	66 5/8	16 6/8	1 7/8	24 2/8	23 0/8	5	4	DUNKMANN	DWAIN	SAME	
2214	146 7/8	WARREN	86	69 5/8	67 1/8	19 6/8	3 5/8	24 0/8	23 5/8	6	6	KESSELHEIM	JEFF	SAME	
2214	146 7/8	HENRY	87	66 5/8	71 3/8	17 4/8	3 1/8	23 0/8	23 0/8	6	6	BAILEY	DANNY	SAME	
2214	146 7/8	TEXAS	87	64 7/8	64 5/8	21 1/8	0	22 3/8	20 3/8	5	5	GOINS	RICK	SAME	
2214	146 7/8	LAFAYETTE	91	68 4/8	67 2/8	19 1/8	0	24 2/8	23 1/8	5	5	RUNNELS	TRACY	SAME	
2225	146 6/8	REYNOLDS	60	66 1/8	64 2/8	19 2/8	1 0/8	24 7/8	24 6/8	5	5	CARR	DICK	SAME	
2225	146 6/8	JOHNSON	76	65 7/8	68 1/8	17 2/8	0	23 7/8	23 1/8	4	4	BRACKEN	CHARLES E.	SAME	
2225	146 6/8	OSAGE	77	65 7/8	67 6/8	16 0/8	0	21 7/8	21 4/8	5	5	TOWNLEY	STEVEN	SAME	
2225	146 6/8	CHRISTIAN	79	68 6/8	65 5/8	18 1/8	2 1/8	24 2/8	24 2/8	5	6	LINDSEY	DAVID L.	SAME	
2225	146 6/8	PHELPS	82	66 5/8	65 5/8	17 6/8	0	23 1/8	23 6/8	5	5	LANE	RONNIE	SAME	
2225	146 6/8	SHANNON	84	72 0/8	73 0/8	17 4/8	8 4/8	25 6/8	26 3/8	8	7	YOUNG	CHUCK	SAME	
2225	146 6/8	VERNON	86	72 0/8	73 6/8	14 6/8	9 6/8	22 2/8	23 6/8	7	6	BURRELL	JEFF	SAME	
2225	146 6/8	CALLAWAY	90	67 1/8	65 1/8	17 6/8	0	25 5/8	25 6/8	5	5	SPURGEON	DAVID D.	SAME	
2225	146 6/8	ST. CLAIR	95	67 1/8	68 7/8	17 4/8	0	22 7/8	24 5/8	4	4	GENGLER	MIKE	SAME	
2225	146 6/8	STODDARD	96	64 0/8	66 6/8	20 2/8	0	23 3/8	22 6/8	5	5	REYNOLDS	DON	SAME	
2235	146 5/8	COOPER	73	65 4/8	65 0/8	18 7/8	0	22 4/8	22 4/8	5	5	WALTHER	ERNIE	SAME	
2235	146 5/8	COLE	84	66 0/8	70 2/8	16 5/8	1 6/8	24 3/8	24 4/8	6	5	STUCKEY	NORMAN	SAME	
2235	146 5/8	CLARK	86	71 3/8	78 1/8	16 2/8	10 1/8	24 3/8	24 3/8	8	8	COURTNEY	ALLEN L.	SAME	
2235	146 5/8	SALINE	87	73 6/8	72 0/8	18 1/8	8 6/8	26 4/8	27 0/8	8	6	SYLVESTER	LEON	SAME	
2235	146 5/8	PULASKI	87	70 1/8	70 1/8	17 7/8	4 6/8	22 1/8	23 5/8	6	6	ENTWISTLE	KENNETH P.	SAME	
2235	146 5/8	HENRY	94	68 1/8	66 0/8	18 3/8	0	26 0/8	25 1/8	4	4	GOTH	BRETT	SAME	

MISSOURI SHOW-ME BIG BUCKS CLUB RECORDS OF WHITETAIL DEER BY STATE, TYPICAL

STATE RANK	SCORE	COUNTY	YEAR TAKEN	INCHES TYPICAL R	L	INSIDE SPREAD	INCHES ABNORMAL	LENGTH MAIN BEAM R	L	NUMBER POINTS R	L	HUNTER	FIRST NAME	OWNER	FIRST NAME
2235	146 5/8	CASS	94	72 5/8	74 2/8	18 6/8	11 3/8	26 4/8	25 3/8	8	6	GARDNER	JOHN S.	SAME	
2242	146 4/8	FRANKLIN	62	67 5/8	71 0/8	18 0/8	4 0/8	25 7/8	26 0/8	6	6	FRIZZELL	CHRISTOPHER	SAME	
2242	146 4/8	PULASKI	75	67 1/8	71 7/8	14 6/8		23 2/8	23 3/8	5	5	HELFRICH	DR. LORING R.	SAME	
2242	146 4/8	PERRY	79	64 3/8	66 6/8	18 0/8		24 0/8	24 1/8	4	4	THOMPSON	QUINTIN	SAME	
2242	146 4/8	CEDAR	80	65 5/8	66 2/8	18 0/8		23 6/8	23 7/8	4	4	EASON	ROGER	SAME	
2242	146 4/8	PULASKI	84	65 5/8	69 5/8	18 0/8		26 1/8	25 1/8	5	6	BELL	IRVIN G.	SAME	
2242	146 4/8	BENTON	89	70 4/8	66 0/8	17 4/8		22 4/8	23 4/8	5	5	BAIN	RICK	SAME	
2242	146 4/8	COOPER	89	66 6/8	68 2/8	16 6/8		20 3/8	19 5/8	5	5	FRIEDRICH	JERRY	SAME	
2242	146 4/8	CAMDEN	92	67 2/8	67 1/8	18 1/8	3 1/8	23 4/8	24 2/8	5	6	ABBOTT	CEANN	SAME	
2242	146 4/8	COOPER	93	66 7/8	66 6/8	16 2/8		22 4/8	22 5/8	5	5	AGGELER	LYLE	SAME	
2242	146 4/8	KNOX	95	66 1/8	71 4/8	18 0/8		24 3/8	24 7/8	4	5	DENT	DALE	SAME	
2252	146 3/8	BENTON	69	67 2/8	65 4/8	18 1/8		23 3/8	24 1/8	5	5	COOPER	LOUIS A.	SAME	
2252	146 3/8	MARIES	75	66 7/8	67 4/8	19 5/8		24 4/8	23 6/8	6	5	WEST	JOSEPH	SAME	
2252	146 3/8	TEXAS	76	66 6/8	65 4/8	18 4/8	1 1/8	24 6/8	24 7/8	5	5	BARTON	ELMER	SAME	
2252	146 3/8	BATES	76	68 1/8	66 1/8	20 2/8	1 7/8	25 4/8	26 7/8	5	4	LEFEVRE	RANDY	SAME	
2252	146 3/8	MISSISSIPPI	83	66 5/8	65 1/8	17 3/8		21 7/8	22 0/8	5	5	DUENNE, JR.	HENRY	SAME	
2252	146 3/8	ST. LOUIS	84	66 4/8	68 1/8	17 5/8	1 2/8	24 0/8	24 1/8	6	5	CHRISTIE	DAN	SAME	
2252	146 3/8	OZARK	88	68 3/8	65 1/8	20 2/8	2 5/8	23 4/8	22 4/8	6	7	ROGERS	RON	SAME	
2252	146 3/8	STE. GENEIEVE	89	68 7/8	66 1/8	20 4/8	3 3/8	22 6/8	23 5/8	8	7	FOLKERTS	WIL A.	SAME	
2252	146 3/8	GASCONADE	89	65 3/8	63 0/8	20 5/8		25 2/8	25 1/8	4	4	APPRILL	KENNETH	SAME	
2252	146 3/8	COLE	89	77 0/8	73 7/8	14 5/8	7 2/8	23 0/8	19 4/8	9	8	STROESSNER	BILL	SAME	
2252	146 3/8	MORGAN	91	66 5/8	67 0/8	15 5/8		23 1/8	23 6/8	5	5	HOLEM	LURLEEN	SAME	
2252	146 3/8	HARRISON	93	69 0/8	73 7/8	18 4/8	7 7/8	24 3/8	24 0/8	6	9	CRAIG	VERNON L.	SAME	
2252	146 3/8	PHELPS	94	66 0/8	67 5/8	17 3/8		25 2/8	23 6/8	5	5	FEELER	GARY	SAME	
2252	146 3/8	ST. LOUIS	96	63 4/8	65 2/8	19 5/8		22 1/8	22 3/8	5	5	GILL	BUTCH	SAME	
2266	146 2/8	CARTER	37	66 7/8	65 6/8	16 4/8		21 3/8	22 0/8	5	5	LEBARON	FRANK	DECEASED	
2266	146 2/8	PERRY	80	68 4/8	64 6/8	17 4/8		23 4/8	21 7/8	5	5	HAERTLING	CLINTON	SAME	
2266	146 2/8	COOPER	80	68 3/8	65 4/8	16 0/8		24 1/8	23 7/8	5	5	MEYER	ALVIN J.	SAME	
2266	146 2/8	BOLLINGER	86	75 4/8	67 5/8	17 7/8	4 7/8	24 0/8	24 5/8	5	6	MYRACLE	JERRY	SAME	
2266	146 2/8	DALLAS	87	65 7/8	68 5/8	19 5/8	3 5/8	24 1/8	24 1/8	6	7	RAMBO	LYNETTE	SAME	
2266	146 2/8	WAYNE	88	64 6/8	64 2/8	18 2/8		23 0/8	23 1/8	5	5	GROOM	VIRGIL E.	SAME	
2266	146 2/8	BENTON	91	78 3/8	69 0/8	18 0/8	7 0/8	24 0/8	23 2/8	7	6	KEPHART	ARMOND R.	SAME	

STATE RANK	SCORE	COUNTY	YEAR TAKEN	INCHES TYPICAL R	L	INSIDE SPREAD	INCHES ABNORMAL	LENGTH MAIN BEAM R	L	NUMBER POINTS R	L	HUNTER	FIRST NAME	OWNER	FIRST NAME
2266	146 2/8	MARIES	92	67 7/8	70 0/8	15 1/8	2 5/8	24 4/8	24 7/8	4	6	SINDEN, JR.	WILLIAM R.	SAME	
2266	146 2/8	CRAWFORD	93	64 6/8	66 6/8	18 6/8	0	23 1/8	23 5/8	5	5	BASS	STEPHEN	SAME	
2266	146 2/8	GASCONADE	94	64 6/8	67 0/8	17 0/8	0	22 2/8	22 1/8	4	4	ISAAK	STEVE	SAME	
2266	146 2/8	OSAGE	95	67 1/8	67 3/8	16 4/8	0	23 1/8	21 5/8	5	5	WULFF	JEROME H.	SAME	
2266	146 2/8	CAMDEN	95	65 3/8	66 1/8	16 0/8	0	23 2/8	24 2/8	4	4	STEWARD	ROBERT L.	SAME	
2266	146 2/8	CAMDEN	95	64 7/8	65 1/8	18 4/8	0	23 7/8	23 2/8	5	5	ACKERSON	ART	SAME	
2266	146 2/8	HICKORY	95	67 1/8	69 3/8	17 7/8	4 1/8	23 4/8	23 3/8	5	5	JOHNSON	PAM	SAME	
2266	146 2/8	ST. CLAIR	95	65 7/8	65 0/8	21 0/8	0	25 6/8	26 1/8	4	4	MARSHALL	DEONNE	SAME	
2281	146 1/8	CAPE GIRARDEAU	65	60 6/8	68 3/8	23 7/8	0	26 4/8	27 0/8	4	5	RIDINGS	CHARLES	SAME	
2281	146 1/8	OSAGE	73	67 2/8	67 2/8	18 2/8	3 7/8	23 4/8	23 6/8	8	5	OTTO	DAVE	SAME	
2281	146 1/8	PERRY	77	70 7/8	66 6/8	15 7/8	2 6/8	24 1/8	22 4/8	6	5	COFFELT	CHARLES E.	SAME	
2281	146 1/8	ST. LOUIS	86	68 5/8	65 5/8	16 5/8	0	21 6/8	22 0/8	5	5	GUEMMER	GERALD	SAME	
2281	146 1/8	BOLLINGER	90	67 2/8	66 7/8	16 3/8	0	22 6/8	22 1/8	5	5	PRUETT	BILLY	SAME	
2281	146 1/8	ST. CHARLES	92	67 5/8	72 3/8	16 2/8	4 0/8	26 3/8	26 4/8	7	5	HAMRICK	BENJAMIN F.	SAME	
2281	146 1/8	OREGON	93	70 4/8	66 0/8	19 1/8	0	24 1/8	24 6/8	5	4	PARROTT	WOODROW	SAME	
2281	146 1/8	BENTON	94	67 6/8	66 6/8	14 3/8	0	20 6/8	19 4/8	5	5	COX	DAVID	SAME	
2281	146 1/8	PHELPS	95	67 5/8	69 3/8	16 1/8	0	22 0/8	23 0/8	5	6	PLANK	ROBERT	SAME	
2281	146 1/8	PHELPS	71	65 5/8	65 0/8	17 4/8	0	18 7/8	19 4/8	5	5	FRUEH	BOB	SAME	
2290	146 0/8	WAYNE	75	67 1/8	68 0/8	19 2/8	0	21 6/8	20 7/8	7	5	ROPER	DONALD P.	SAME	
2290	146 0/8	FRANKLIN	81	67 3/8	64 7/8	17 6/8	0	22 4/8	23 2/8	5	5	PALMER	KEVIN	SAME	
2290	146 0/8	GASCONADE	84	68 1/8	66 7/8	15 0/8	2 6/8	21 4/8	21 4/8	5	5	WEHRLE	HOWARD	SAME	
2290	146 0/8	PERRY	85	73 1/8	66 3/8	16 0/8	0	24 2/8	24 1/8	7	6	SCHROETER	JERRY	SAME	
2290	146 0/8	PHELPS	85	66 1/8	70 1/8	16 6/8	0	23 6/8	23 7/8	5	5	BLACK	LOGAN	SAME	
2290	146 0/8	CAPE GIRARDEAU	89	68 6/8	68 3/8	17 2/8	6 4/8	22 0/8	21 6/8	0	0	WILKENS	JANET	SAME	
2290	146 0/8	MARIES	90	69 1/8	64 6/8	19 0/8	1 6/8	22 1/8	22 1/8	6	5	SKOUBY	JUDY	SAME	
2290	146 0/8	RAY	94	65 1/8	72 1/8	16 6/8	0	24 3/8	24 6/8	5	5	KIRK	DOUGLAS	SAME	
2290	146 0/8	SALINE	95	66 7/8	65 5/8	16 4/8	0	22 6/8	23 2/8	4	4	RAMEY	BILL	SAME	
2290	146 0/8	COOPER	95	69 0/8	66 4/8	18 2/8	0	24 4/8	26 2/8	5	4	GRAPES	MIKE	SAME	
2290	146 0/8	GASCONADE	95	68 1/8	71 2/8	14 5/8	4 1/8	21 0/8	22 4/8	5	7	McGEE	TRAVIS H.	SAME	
2302	145 7/8	MARIES	72	69 0/8	64 6/8	19 1/8	0	25 1/8	23 6/8	5	5	RAMSEY	GABE	SAME	
2302	145 7/8	GASCONADE	72	67 2/8	67 4/8	20 0/8	5 5/8	24 7/8	24 3/8	4	5	SPURGEON	DOYLE	SAME	
2302	145 7/8	BENTON	78	65 6/8	63 0/8	22 4/8	1 3/8	25 3/8	24 3/8	6	5	CHURCH	WAYNE	SAME	

STATE RANK	SCORE	COUNTY	YEAR TAKEN	INCHES TYPICAL R	L	INSIDE SPREAD	INCHES ABNORMAL	LENGTH MAIN BEAM R	L	NUMBER POINTS R	L	HUNTER	FIRST NAME	OWNER	FIRST NAME
2302	145 7/8	TANEY	82	65 5/8	66 7/8	18 3/8	2 7/8	21 7/8	22 0/8	6	6	McINTURFF	RON	SAME	
2302	145 7/8	MONITEAU	89	68 5/8	68 0/8	17 0/8	4 5/8	26 7/8	27 3/8	5	5	JENKINS	DANIEL R.	SAME	
2302	145 7/8	LACLEDE	95	69 1/8	68 1/8	16 2/8	4 5/8	22 6/8	22 1/8	5	6	HARRIS	JOHN M.	SAME	
2302	145 7/8	WAYNE	95	65 3/8	72 3/8	17 2/8	1 3/8	23 6/8	24 1/8	5	5	FRYMIRE	JACKIE	SAME	
2302	145 7/8	REYNOLDS	95	62 2/8	64 3/8	21 7/8	0	21 7/8	22 0/8	5	5	SMITH	DARREL	SAME	
2302	145 7/8	HOLT	96	66 1/8	66 4/8	16 5/8	0	24 0/8	23 6/8	5	5	CUNNINGHAM	MIKE	SAME	
2311	145 6/8	WASHINGTON	69	65 2/8	74 0/8	16 2/8	0	23 0/8	25 1/8	5	5	MERCER	CURTIS D.	SAME	
2311	145 6/8	CAMDEN	71	66 6/8	66 2/8	19 0/8	0	23 7/8	22 5/8	4	4	FRANKS	CHARLES	SAME	
2311	145 6/8	PETTIS	72	69 2/8	67 6/8	18 2/8	2 0/8	26 2/8	25 5/8	6	5	CATON	MARVIN E.	SAME	
2311	145 6/8	SALINE	76	65 0/8	68 1/8	17 3/8	1 1/8	23 5/8	24 4/8	6	5	JOHNSON	KENNETH E.	SAME	
2311	145 6/8	TEXAS	77	69 4/8	71 0/8	15 5/8	6 1/8	25 6/8	25 7/8	6	7	ICE	RONALD	SAME	
2311	145 6/8	CHRISTIAN	78	64 1/8	67 6/8	17 4/8	0	23 4/8	24 0/8	5	5	ROUSSELL	PHILLIP	SAME	
2311	145 6/8	HOWELL	80	64 7/8	65 1/8	16 2/8	0	21 6/8	21 7/8	4	4	DOCK	FRED W.	SAME	
2311	145 6/8	NEWTON	85	66 5/8	66 0/8	15 0/8	0	23 6/8	24 0/8	5	5	HORNOR	CURTIS	SAME	
2311	145 6/8	CAMDEN	91	66 6/8	66 6/8	14 2/8	0	20 3/8	20 5/8	5	5	SCHAFFNER	BRYAN C.	SAME	
2311	145 6/8	LAFAYETTE	91	71 4/8	70 5/8	14 4/8	4 6/8	23 1/8	22 0/8	6	7	WODRICH	DARRELL	SAME	
2311	145 6/8	PULASKI	94	65 2/8	67 4/8	20 0/8	0	24 6/8	24 3/8	4	5	CLARK	GARY	SAME	
2311	145 6/8	JACKSON	94	70 4/8	68 1/8	18 4/8	6 0/8	21 6/8	21 7/8	5	6	STAHL	JEFF	SAME	
2311	145 6/8	MACON	95	65 6/8	68 4/8	16 4/8	0	25 3/8	24 6/8	5	5	REPLOGLE	EVAN W.	SAME	
2324	145 5/8	WASHINGTON	58	69 6/8	69 0/8	17 0/8	7 3/8	23 2/8	22 6/8	6	8	RUSSELL	RICHARD	SAME	
2324	145 5/8	NEWTON	65	63 1/8	64 3/8	20 7/8	0	23 0/8	24 2/8	4	4	COOPER	DAVID F.	SAME	
2324	145 5/8	NEWTON	85	68 7/8	71 1/8	17 7/8	7 6/8	25 0/8	24 4/8	8	5	SWARTZ	GARY	SAME	
2324	145 5/8	BENTON	86	68 3/8	65 1/8	16 5/8	0	22 4/8	22 1/8	5	5	ANDREWS	RICHARD	SAME	
2324	145 5/8	MORGAN	88	65 2/8	65 5/8	16 5/8	0	21 6/8	22 5/8	5	5	BORTS	JOANN	SAME	
2324	145 5/8	CAPE GIRARDEAU	95	69 4/8	64 5/8	20 7/8	4 4/8	24 2/8	23 0/8	5	5	HOBBS	DARRELL W.	SAME	
2324	145 5/8	SCOTLAND	96	65 4/8	65 3/8	17 5/8	0	21 4/8	20 7/8	5	5	HOLT	BRANDON	SAME	
2331	145 4/8	PULASKI	69	66 5/8	63 4/8	21 5/8	1 5/8	24 0/8	24 3/8	5	5	MYERS	J.D.	SAME	
2331	145 4/8	HOWELL	72	67 5/8	72 3/8	15 1/8	4 1/8	24 0/8	23 6/8	6	7	BERZINA	JIM	SAME	
2331	145 4/8	COOPER	77	66 6/8	66 1/8	14 6/8	0	21 4/8	21 7/8	5	5	SIECKMANN	TERRY	SAME	
2331	145 4/8	PETTIS	80	72 4/8	68 2/8	15 4/8	4 2/8	22 0/8	21 0/8	7	6	NEVILS	EDDIE R.	SAME	
2331	145 4/8	OZARK	82	65 1/8	66 5/8	21 3/8	3 7/8	24 4/8	24 7/8	7	6	HORINE	BRUCE	SAME	
2331	145 4/8	LAWRENCE	84	65 2/8	63 2/8	19 4/8	0	25 2/8	24 1/8	4	4	HAMM	MELVIN	SAME	

MISSOURI SHOW-ME BIG BUCKS CLUB RECORDS OF WHITETAIL DEER BY STATE, TYPICAL

STATE RANK	SCORE	COUNTY	YEAR TAKEN	INCHES TYPICAL R	L	INSIDE SPREAD	INCHES ABNORMAL	LENGTH MAIN BEAM R	L	NUMBER POINTS R	L	HUNTER	FIRST NAME	OWNER	FIRST NAME
2331	145 4/8	KNOX	85	69 1/8	66 2/8	15 1/8	0	22 5/8	22 7/8	5	5	HOUSE	BOYD	SAME	
2331	145 4/8	GASCONADE	86	66 2/8	66 4/8	15 4/8	0	21 2/8	21 4/8	4	4	SCHNEIDER	JAMES	SCHNEIDER	BOB
2331	145 4/8	JEFFERSON	87	68 7/8	65 1/8	17 0/8	0	24 6/8	22 2/8	5	5	NORTH	STEVE	SAME	
2331	145 4/8	JOHNSON	87	72 4/8	73 2/8	17 6/8	9 4/8	24 4/8	24 0/8	6	7	PETTY	HOMER	SAME	
2331	145 4/8	OZARK	90	65 7/8	66 7/8	13 6/8	0	20 0/8	20 7/8	5	5	POORE	DAVID	SAME	
2331	145 4/8	JASPER	91	67 4/8	69 0/8	16 6/8	2 0/8	22 2/8	23 4/8	6	5	PIERCE	EDDY G.	SAME	
2331	145 4/8	MILLER	92	66 2/8	66 1/8	15 6/8	0	24 4/8	24 3/8	5	5	PHILLIPS	PATSY J.	SAME	
2331	145 4/8	ATCHISON	94	69 0/8	68 2/8	16 7/8	7 3/8	23 1/8	22 6/8	5	4	WOOTEN	LARRY D.	SAME	
2331	145 4/8	SALINE	95	69 5/8	66 2/8	15 0/8	2 0/8	22 3/8	21 0/8	5	6	WISEMAN	SAM	SAME	
2331	145 4/8	HARRISON	95	66 6/8	64 3/8	17 2/8	0	22 4/8	22 2/8	5	5	HAGEN	MICHAEL J.	SAME	
2331	145 4/8	HOWARD	95	65 3/8	67 0/8	16 3/8	0	22 4/8	22 3/8	5	5	HILGEDICK	GLENN	SAME	
2331	145 4/8	CARROLL	96	72 6/8	66 5/8	17 4/8	3 5/8	24 2/8	24 7/8	5	5	WILCOX	MARK	SAME	
2331	145 4/8	HARRISON	96	64 0/8	68 1/8	18 2/8	0	21 0/8	23 4/8	5	5	EASTON	STEVE	SAME	
2331	145 3/8	PHELPS	65	65 3/8	68 6/8	15 3/8	0	20 4/8	22 0/8	5	5	WATSON	RAY	SAME	
2350	145 3/8	PERRY	72	67 7/8	65 1/8	15 5/8	0	21 1/8	21 0/8	5	5	MEYER	JOE	MEYER	LEO
2350	145 3/8	BOLLINGER	87	68 7/8	66 4/8	17 3/8	5 0/8	24 6/8	24 6/8	6	5	ENDERLE	RON	SAME	
2350	145 3/8	GASCONADE	90	65 5/8	63 6/8	20 1/8	0	24 0/8	22 0/8	5	5	SCHULTE	JUDY	SAME	
2350	145 3/8	JOHNSON	91	70 2/8	68 6/8	19 2/8	10 3/8	26 1/8	25 5/8	8	4	LENZ	EDWARD	SAME	
2350	145 3/8	FRANKLIN	92	67 6/8	66 0/8	16 5/8	3 2/8	20 4/8	20 2/8	6	6	BAKER	DAN	SAME	
2350	145 3/8	CAPE GIRARDEAU	93	65 3/8	68 5/8	21 4/8	6 3/8	23 2/8	23 6/8	4	5	KLINGEMAN	PHIL	SAME	
2350	145 3/8	CAMDEN	93	63 6/8	67 2/8	19 3/8	0	21 7/8	23 0/8	5	5	FRY	EDDIE	SAME	
2350	145 3/8	CRAWFORD	95	65 7/8	65 1/8	17 3/8	0	21 5/8	20 6/8	5	5	ISOM	BRIAN	SAME	
2350	145 3/8	BARRY	95	67 1/8	67 6/8	17 1/8	1 2/8	25 0/8	24 5/8	7	5	CRAIN	R. STEVEN	SAME	
2350	145 3/8	ST. LOUIS	96	64 4/8	65 7/8	20 1/8	0	23 4/8	22 7/8	5	5	MCCONNELL	DAVID	SAME	
2361	145 2/8	GASCONADE	50	67 0/8	64 7/8	21 1/8	2 3/8	27 2/8	28 2/8	6	6	LANGENDOERFER	AUGUST	FRICKE	VIRGIL
2361	145 2/8	TEXAS	74	72 4/8	71 2/8	17 1/8	1 3/8	24 1/8	24 0/8	6	6	BATES	KENNETH	SAME	
2361	145 2/8	McDONALD	74	74 0/8	68 6/8	14 5/8	6 5/8	24 0/8	22 5/8	6	5	WASMAN	BOBBY	SAME	
2361	145 2/8	CRAWFORD	80	69 2/8	72 7/8	18 4/8	11 0/8	24 4/8	24 1/8	9	6	WEBER	MIKE	SAME	
2361	145 2/8	VERNON	82	65 4/8	73 3/8	19 6/8	1 2/8	24 3/8	23 5/8	5	5	ARTHUR	LAWANNA	SAME	
2361	145 2/8	CAMDEN	82	66 3/8	68 7/8	17 1/8	3 3/8	24 2/8	24 2/8	7	4	HANKS	GLEN	SAME	
2361	145 2/8	COOPER	82	67 0/8	71 3/8	20 4/8	3 6/8	25 0/8	25 0/8	5	5	REAGAN	DARRIN	SAME	
2361	145 2/8	FRANKLIN	88	65 5/8	65 4/8	17 0/8	0	23 0/8	23 5/8	5	5	HUSSEY	KEN	SAME	

MISSOURI SHOW-ME BIG BUCKS CLUB RECORDS OF WHITETAIL DEER BY STATE, TYPICAL

STATE RANK	SCORE	COUNTY	YEAR TAKEN	INCHES TYPICAL R	L	INSIDE SPREAD	INCHES ABNORMAL	LENGTH MAIN BEAM R	L	NUMBER POINTS R	L	HUNTER	FIRST NAME	OWNER	FIRST NAME
2361	145 2/8	DENT	89	65 4/8	67 4/8	17 4/8	0	22 3/8	22 5/8	5	5	ADAMS	MARVIN	SAME	
2361	145 2/8	DENT	89	67 7/8	70 7/8	16 7/8	4 3/8	23 2/8	23 5/8	5	6	SCHAFER	JOHN L.	SAME	
2361	145 2/8	MARIES	89	65 2/8	65 /68	16 0/8	0	22 4/8	23 5/8	5	5	KLEFNER	DON	SAME	
2361	145 2/8	COOPER	90	68 7/8	66 5/8	17 1/8	2 3/8	24 1/8	24 0/8	6	4	THIESSEN	RONDA	SAME	
2361	145 2/8	MARIES	95	67 2/8	65 7/8	14 6/8	0	19 7/8	20 1/8	5	5	SCHWEER	JEFF	SAME	
2361	145 2/8	SALINE	95	69 6/8	70 0/8	12 4/8	2 0/8	22 2/8	23 2/8	6	5	HURSMAN	TONY	SAME	
2361	145 2/8	DALLAS	95	66 0/8	68 1/8	17 0/8	0	22 6/8	24 4/8	5	5	HOSTETLER	MARION	SAME	
2361	145 2/8	MACON	95	71 1/8	65 3/8	18 1/8	1 5/8	24 0/8	24 7/8	6	4	BALDWIN	PORTER	SAME	
2361	145 2/8	PUTNAM	96	69 0/8	67 0/8	19 3/8	4 3/8	23 3/8	23 5/8	6	5	REAM, JR.	DALE H.	SAME	
2361	145 2/8	MACON	96	68 4/8	73 0/8	19 2/8	0	24 5/8	24 5/8	4	6	SIZEMORE	DONNIE	SAME	
2379	145 1/8	PIKE	67	70 7/8	67 2/8	18 0/8	6 0/8	21 2/8	21 4/8	6	7	MARTIN	EDDIE E.	SAME	
2379	145 1/8	BARRY	71	67 1/8	66 7/8	14 5/8	0	22 4/8	22 7/8	5	5	DAVIS	DOYLE	SAME	
2379	145 1/8	SALINE	79	65 2/8	71 0/8	15 5/8	0	24 5/8	24 7/8	4	6	RAYL	ALAN	SAME	
2379	145 1/8	SALINE	79	71 5/8	69 4/8	18 6/8	7 7/8	25 1/8	24 4/8	7	7	TENNILL	RONNIE	SAME	
2379	145 1/8	PERRY	85	67 1/8	68 7/8	17 3/8	5 6/8	21 2/8	21 5/8	6	5	STUEVE	DAVID	SAME	
2379	145 1/8	PHELPS	88	66 0/8	69 4/8	17 5/8	3 2/8	22 1/8	21 4/8	6	7	FITZGERALD	SEAN	SAME	
2379	145 1/8	SALINE	89	68 7/8	69 4/8	17 4/3	5 1/8	22 0/8	21 3/8	5	6	BRADSHAW	DON	SAME	
2379	145 1/8	OZARK	90	63 7/8	64 7/8	18 7/8	0	24 6/3	24 5/8	4	4	BEACH	JERRY	SAME	
2379	145 1/8	MILLER	91	75 6/8	73 6/8	14 6/8	13 3/8	24 3/8	24 0/8	6	8	VESTAL	TIM	SAME	
2379	145 1/8	SHANNON	93	64 7/8	66 0/8	17 1/8	0	22 7/8	22 2/8	5	5	LANHAM	BUD	SAME	
2379	145 1/8	SHANNON	94	66 5/8	69 4/8	16 1/8	0	24 4/8	23 4/8	4	5	FOSTER	TERRY	SAME	
2379	145 1/8	KNOX	96	65 0/8	68 5/8	16 1/8	0	21 5/8	21 5/8	5	5	HOUSE	BOYD	SAME	
2391	145 0/8	FRANKLIN	56	65 0/8	68 3/8	20 0/8	2 7/8	26 1/8	26 7/8	5	5	WEBB	BENTON	WEBB	ELSIE
2391	145 0/8	LACLEDE	64	76 2/8	68 6/8	19 3/8	3 3/8	26 7/8	25 5/8	6	6	MANION	ED	SAME	
2391	145 0/8	COLE	77	70 0/8	70 0/8	17 1/8	1 3/8	22 1/8	21 7/8	7	6	JEAGER	JOHN	SAME	
2391	145 0/8	WRIGHT	78	66 3/8	72 0/8	19 0/8	2 2/8	23 6/8	25 2/8	6	5	WILLIAMS	GARRY	SAME	
2391	145 0/8	OZARK	78	67 7/8	66 5/8	15 4/8	0	24 2/8	24 2/8	6	6	McDANIEL	MICHAEL	SAME	
2391	145 0/8	PERRY	78	63 3/8	66 4/8	19 0/8	0	24 1/8	24 2/8	5	5	HUBER	LARRY M.	SAME	
2391	145 0/8	CRAWFORD	83	71 2/8	66 5/8	71 2/8	1 2/8	22 3/8	21 0/8	6	5	HEDRICK	DAVID	SAME	
2391	145 0/8	SALINE	86	64 4/8	65 0/8	19 0/8	0	23 0/8	24 1/8	4	4	MORTON	LARRY	SAME	
2391	145 0/8	OSAGE	86	64 1/8	62 6/8	19 4/8	0	25 6/8	25 6/8	4	4	BUDNIK	STEVEN	SAME	
2391	145 0/8	MARIES	87	69 4/8	64 3/8	20 3/8	1 3/8	24 2/8	24 4/8	6	4	NOBLETT	DENNIS	SAME	

STATE RANK	SCORE	COUNTY	YEAR TAKEN	INCHES TYPICAL R	INCHES TYPICAL L	INSIDE SPREAD	INCHES ABNORMAL	LENGTH MAIN BEAM R	LENGTH MAIN BEAM L	NUMBER POINTS R	NUMBER POINTS L	HUNTER	FIRST NAME	OWNER	FIRST NAME
2391	145 0/8	HENRY	87	65 4/8	65 7/8	18 0/8	0	25 4/8	26 0/8	4	4	HEANY	RANDY	SAME	
2391	145 0/8	GASCONADE	88	68 2/8	69 6/8	15 4/8	6 4/8	21 4/8	21 4/8	5	6	PEARSON	DOUG	SAME	
2391	145 0/8	MISSISSIPPI	91	72 0/8	64 2/8	18 6/8	0	24 5/8	25 6/8	6	4	DILL	DEE	SAME	
2391	145 0/8	CEDAR	92	68 0/8	65 7/8	15 5/8	1 5/8	25 0/8	24 6/8	5	4	LUCIUS	KENNETH	SAME	
2391	145 0/8	CRAWFORD	92	69 6/8	69 5/8	15 1/8	0	21 7/8	21 2/8	6	5	MARTIN	A.B.	SAME	
2391	145 0/8	CALLAWAY	92	71 4/8	71 5/8	19 7/8	11 1/8	23 7/8	20 7/8	7	7	UNDERWOOD	LARRY	SAME	
2391	145 0/8	SALINE	93	65 6/8	69 0/8	17 2/8	3 4/8	22 1/8	22 0/8	6	7	HARRIS	DARREN	SAME	
2391	145 0/8	CHARITON	94	75 2/8	67 6/8	16 1/8	4 1/8	23 7/8	22 5/8	5	6	PALMER	TERRY	SAME	
2391	145 0/8	CARTER	94	69 7/8	66 4/8	16 2/8	0	22 1/8	21 4/8	5	5	PAYNE	BERT	SAME	
2391	145 0/8	CARTER	95	75 1/8	67 4/8	17 4/8	4 0/8	23 1/8	24 6/8	6	6	BARNETT	SAM	SAME	
2391	145 0/8	MORGAN	96	65 4/8	70 2/8	15 4/8	1 5/8	22 4/8	23 2/8	6	5	MILLER	BRIAN S.	SAME	
2412	144 7/8	CRAWFORD	50	64 5/8	66 3/8	17 3/8	0	21 6/8	21 2/8	5	5	CROSS	GEORGE	SAME	
2412	144 7/8	CEDAR	59	63 4/8	65 6/8	21 3/8	0	23 1/8	23 0/8	4	5	MOON	ORAN B.	SAME	
2412	144 7/8	WASHINGTON	77	63 0/8	73 6/8	18 7/8	0	23 0/8	24 0/8	5	5	WORLEY	LARRY	SAME	
2412	144 7/8	PETTIS	80	66 6/8	64 3/8	18 5/8	0	21 6/8	20 2/8	5	5	CHARLES	LYONEL	SAME	
2412	144 7/8	DALLAS	82	64 3/8	66 3/8	18 1/8	0	22 7/8	22 4/8	5	5	MORGANS	GREG	SAME	
2412	144 7/8	FRANKLIN	84	64 6/8	68 5/8	20 0/8	2 3/8	24 3/8	26 1/8	4	5	JOHNSON	GERALD	SAME	
2412	144 7/8	STE. GENEIEVE	86	68 0/8	69 4/8	16 5/8	2 4/8	22 4/8	21 6/8	8	5	VOLMAR	LINDA	SAME	
2412	144 7/8	OSAGE	90	64 4/8	68 6/8	18 1/8	2 2/8	23 0/8	23 0/8	5	6	FINOCCHIARO, SR.	ROBERT	SAME	
2412	144 7/8	MARIES	92	66 5/8	64 6/8	17 3/8	0	21 4/8	20 5/8	5	5	STUEKEN	ROGER	SAME	
2412	144 7/8	McDONALD	92	66 6/8	67 7/8	14 5/8	0	22 7/8	22 3/8	5	5	ANDERSON	RANDY	SAME	
2412	144 7/8	ST. CLAIR	92	69 6/8	66 1/8	19 5/8	7 0/8	24 4/8	23 0/8	6	6	BOURLAND	SHEILA M.	SAME	
2412	144 7/8	OREGON	95	64 2/8	72 0/8	17 7/8	0	27 1/8	25 7/8	5	5	HOLLIS	RICK	LINDSEY	SCOTT
2412	144 7/8	ST. FRANCOIS	95	70 0/8	67 4/8	15 0/8	3 1/8	21 4/8	22 4/8	6	5	TEDDER	JESSE MICHAEL	SAME	
2425	144 6/8	FRANKLIN	49	63 5/8	68 6/8	23 6/8	0	23 7/8	26 5/8	4	4	MEYER	R.A.	SAME	
2425	144 6/8	GASCONADE	63	76 5/8	63 3/8	20 1/8	0	25 7/8	25 4/8	5	4	LANDOLT	BOB	SAME	
2425	144 6/8	ST. FRANCOIS	71	63 5/8	66 7/8	17 6/8	0	24 4/8	25 5/8	4	4	STROUP	JUNIOR C.	SAME	
2425	144 6/8	MACON	76	65 7/8	76 6/8	19 3/8	5 7/8	22 6/8	23 7/8	6	7	KEUNE	RONALD	SAME	
2425	144 6/8	COLE	79	65 7/8	67 1/8	14 6/8	0	23 0/8	23 7/8	5	5	MELLER	KEITH	SAME	
2425	144 6/8	WRIGHT	79	65 1/8	68 1/8	15 2/8	0	20 4/8	22 0/8	5	5	HYLTON	LLOYD	SAME	
2425	144 6/8	SHANNON	82	69 4/8	65 5/8	16 0/8	0	22 7/8	23 0/8	5	4	COOLEY	SHAWN	SAME	
2425	144 6/8	FRANKLIN	89	70 7/8	68 7/8	15 4/8	5 2/8	23 2/8	23 2/8	7	6	SCHMELZ	JOHN J.	SAME	

311

MISSOURI SHOW-ME BIG BUCKS CLUB RECORDS OF WHITETAIL DEER BY STATE, TYPICAL

STATE RANK	SCORE	COUNTY	YEAR TAKEN	INCHES TYPICAL R	L	INSIDE SPREAD	INCHES ABNORMAL	LENGTH MAIN BEAM R	L	NUMBER POINTS R	L	HUNTER	FIRST NAME	OWNER	FIRST NAME
2425	144 6/8	DOUGLAS	90	72 1/8	70 7/8	15 1/8	7 3/8	25 6/8	26 0/8	7	7	MOORE	HAROLD E.	SAME	
2425	144 6/8	IRON	91	64 7/8	64 3/8	17 2/8	0	24 7/8	25 3/8	5	5	AUBUCHON	BARRY	SAME	
2425	144 6/8	GASCONADE	92	66 4/8	65 6/8	20 0/8	0	21 3/8	24 0/8	5	4	SCHWINKE	ELDORE W.	SAME	
2425	144 6/8	HICKORY	92	67 2/8	71 5/8	19 2/8	8 6/8	22 3/8	23 2/8	7	6	ROARK	KATHLEEN	SAME	
2425	144 6/8	CEDAR	93	63 2/8	63 2/8	20 0/8	0	25 7/8	25 4/8	4	4	BRAKE	RALPH	SAME	
2425	144 6/8	PERRY	94	67 0/8	68 1/8	15 2/8	2 0/8	22 7/8	22 4/8	6	7	HAGAN	ROBERT H.	SAME	
2425	144 6/8	MORGAN	94	71 5/8	73 1/8	18 1/8	11 5/8	23 1/8	22 6/8	7	8	MAHNKEN	KEVIN	SAME	
2425	144 6/8	BATES	95	67 4/8	71 4/8	16 0/8	3 2/8	23 3/8	24 6/8	6	6	SIMMS	DOUG	SAME	
2425	144 6/8	RIPLEY	96	66 1/8	65 4/8	18 4/8	0	25 4/8	25 5/8	5	5	WHISNAT	PETE	SAME	
2442	144 5/8	STE. GENEIEVE	52	66 5/8	65 7/8	17 2/8	1 1/8	22 1/8	22 6/8	5	5	GYURICA	PHILLIP	SAME	
2442	144 5/8	OSAGE	58	69 5/8	70 5/8	17 2/8	9 5/8	24 1/8	23 7/8	7	7	BACKES	HUBERT	SAME	
2442	144 5/8	CAPE GIRARDEAU	67	77 2/8	67 6/8	17 3/8	5 2/8	25 1/8	22 6/8	7	6	DRAKE	PAUL	SAME	
2442	144 5/8	STE. GENEIEVE	67	64 7/8	65 4/8	18 5/8	0	22 3/8	22 7/8	5	5	HOLLIS	DORRIS C.	SAME	
2442	144 5/8	OSAGE	68	67 6/8	66 1/8	18 7/8	1 4/8	24 2/8	25 6/8	4	5	TEMMEN	J.R.	SAME	
2442	144 5/8	FRANKLIN	74	66 5/8	65 5/8	22 6/8	1 1/8	21 4/8	25 1/8	6	5	MOLL	RON	SAME	
2442	144 5/8	LACLEDE	81	67 2/8	66 4/8	14 3/8	0	21 4/8	21 4/8	4	4	PETERSON	RICHARD	SAME	
2442	144 5/8	COOPER	83	0	0	0	0	0	0	0	0	QUINT	JOHN	SAME	
2442	144 5/8	MONITEAU	87	71 2/8	70 2/8	16 1/8	7 6/8	23 5/8	23 1/8	6	7	HEES	DAVID	SAME	
2442	144 5/8	McDONALD	88	65 1/8	66 5/8	15 7/8	0	22 3/8	21 7/8	5	5	STARCHMAN	RON	SAME	
2442	144 5/8	BENTON	88	63 3/8	66 0/8	19 7/8	0	23 0/8	22 2/8	5	5	TAGTMEYER	VIRGIL	SAME	
2442	144 5/8	CAMDEN	89	63 4/8	67 3/8	18 7/8	0	23 2/8	24 3/8	5	5	CARROLL	KENNY	SAME	
2442	144 5/8	CAMDEN	90	68 0/8	65 3/8	15 7/8	0	21 7/8	22 5/8	5	5	MOORE	DENNIS	SAME	
2442	144 5/8	PETTIS	90	68 1/8	73 2/8	18 7/8	5 4/8	22 6/8	21 5/8	6	7	ARNETT	RICHARD	SAME	
2442	144 5/8	HENRY	94	64 3/8	65 2/8	18 3/8	0	21 0/8	22 3/8	5	5	SIMMERMON	RENEE	SAME	
2442	144 5/8	CAPE GIRARDEAU	96	68 1/8	67 4/8	16 5/8	0	25 2/8	24 2/8	5	5	FORD	MICHAEL	SAME	
2442	144 5/8	CHARITON	96	64 7/8	66 7/8	17 6/8	1 3/8	23 4/8	25 6/8	6	6	ODOWD	BRADLEY	SAME	
2459	144 5/8	PHELPS	51	66 3/8	65 0/8	16 0/8	0	23 4/8	23 4/8	5	5	FEELER	GALE	FEELER	MRS. JERRY G.
2459	144 4/8	DADE	73	68 4/8	63 7/8	17 6/8	0	23 0/8	22 6/8	5	5	HEMBREE	JOHN	SAME	
2459	144 4/8	COOPER	82	67 6/8	66 3/8	14 4/8	1 0/8	21 2/8	21 0/8	5	5	RILEY	CHRIS WAYNE	SAME	
2459	144 4/8	LAWRENCE	84	61 3/8	68 7/8	21 6/8	0	24 2/8	24 6/8	5	5	CLAYTON	JERRY	SAME	
2459	144 4/8	HENRY	85	71 3/8	68 3/8	16 7/8	4 1/8	23 3/8	23 1/8	7	5	NORTHINGTON	MIKE	SAME	
2459	144 4/8	CAMDEN	88	68 0/8	67 4/8	17 2/8	4 2/8	22 0/8	21 0/8	5	7	PROPST	KEVIN	SAME	

MISSOURI SHOW-ME BIG BUCKS CLUB RECORDS OF WHITETAIL DEER BY STATE, TYPICAL

STATE RANK	SCORE	COUNTY	YEAR TAKEN	INCHES TYPICAL R	L	INSIDE SPREAD	INCHES ABNORMAL	LENGTH MAIN BEAM R	L	NUMBER POINTS R	L	HUNTER	FIRST NAME	OWNER	FIRST NAME
2459	144 4/8	ST. CLAIR	88	68 3/8	66 3/8	18 6/8	0	21 6/8	24 6/8	5	5	FARRIS	JAY	SAME	
2466	144 3/8	IRON	67	64 4/8	65 4/8	16 3/8	0	23 0/8	23 1/8	4	4	POINSETT	CHARLES	SAME	
2466	144 3/8	OZARK	72	65 0/8	64 7/8	16 5/8	0	21 0/8	20 7/8	4	4	LOSCHKY	DAVID	SAME	
2466	144 3/8	OZARK	73	66 6/8	67 6/8	17 5/8	3 6/8	23 5/8	23 1/8	5	6	ROBERTS	JIM	SAME	
2466	144 3/8	OSAGE	77	66 2/8	67 7/8	15 1/8	0	23 2/8	22 7/8	5	5	SCHELL	GARY	SAME	
2466	144 3/8	MORGAN	80	0	0	0	0	0	0	0	0	RIGHT	MAXRY L.	SAME	
2466	144 3/8	MORGAN	80	64 7/8	66 2/8	16 3/8	0	23 6/8	24 3/8	5	5	YOUNG	GARY L.	SAME	
2466	144 3/8	JOHNSON	83	66 1/8	65 0/8	18 2/8	1 3/8	23 4/8	22 6/8	5	6	BYERS	JOHN	SAME	
2466	144 3/8	BENTON	84	63 4/8	65 0/8	18 1/8	0	22 6/8	23 0/8	5	5	FINDLEY	STEVE	SAME	
2466	144 3/8	CRAWFORD	84	64 2/8	68 1/8	18 7/8	3 6/8	22 1/8	22 0/8	8	5	SCOTT	LONNIE	SAME	
2466	144 3/8	OSAGE	87	66 7/8	70 4/8	15 6/8	3 3/8	24 7/8	25 0/8	5	5	BAX	CHRIS C.	SAME	
2466	144 3/8	PERRY	87	65 7/8	62 6/8	20 5/8	0	25 7/8	23 2/8	4	4	KIRN	BRENT	SAME	
2466	144 3/8	MARIES	89	64 3/8	64 2/8	20 5/8	0	24 0/8	25 7/8	4	4	TOEBBEN	MIKE	SAME	
2466	144 3/8	MADISON	89	65 1/8	67 7/8	18 5/8	1 2/8	23 7/8	22 3/8	5	7	MOWRY	CHRIS	SAME	
2466	144 3/8	REYNOLDS	90	65 3/8	64 1/8	19 6/8	3 5/8	23 2/8	23 1/8	5	6	CROCKER	APRIL	SAME	
2466	144 3/8	DENT	90	73 3/8	70 6/8	19 4/8	10 1/8	21 2/8	23 5/8	11	8	FISHER	ANDREW C.	SAME	
2466	144 3/8	MONITEAU	92	64 5/8	67 6/8	17 3/8	0	23 0/8	23 7/8	6	6	PAYNE	COLE	SAME	
2466	144 3/8	TEXAS	96	66 4/8	67 3/8	15 2/8	1 7/8	20 7/8	21 3/8	5	6	LINDSEY	ROGER S.	SAME	
2483	144 2/8	MORGAN	66	67 1/8	65 6/8	18 1/8	4 4/8	24 4/8	22 4/8	6	4	VIEBROCK	BOB	SAME	
2483	144 2/8	WASHINGTON	77	62 4/8	66 2/8	19 2/8	0	25 3/8	25 4/8	5	5	PHILLIPS	G.D.	SAME	
2483	144 2/8	SHANNON	84	64 1/8	64 7/8	16 4/8	0	20 2/8	20 6/8	5	5	DEBLOIS	DOUG	SAME	
2483	144 2/8	ST. CLAIR	87	64 3/8	64 6/8	17 0/8	0	20 7/8	20 7/8	5	5	COLLINS	DONALD	SAME	
2483	144 2/8	JACKSON	88	64 6/8	66 2/8	19 0/8	1 0/8	22 4/8	21 5/8	6	5	VAN RADEN	DAVID	SAME	
2483	144 2/8	MARIES	89	65 7/8	64 5/8	15 5/8	0	21 6/8	21 5/8	5	5	BELL	FRANZ	SAME	
2483	144 2/8	CAPE GIRARDEAU	89	72 2/8	66 1/8	15 4/8	0	22 2/8	23 1/8	5	4	SAWYER	DEAN	SAME	
2483	144 2/8	BARTON	90	69 2/8	69 6/8	18 3/8	4 7/8	25 4/8	25 4/8	7	6	RANDALL	RODNEY	SAME	
2483	144 2/8	GASCONADE	92	64 1/8	67 7/8	16 2/8	0	25 5/8	25 6/8	4	4	BARCH	RON	SAME	
2483	144 2/8	JACKSON	92	70 0/8	67 4/8	20 0/8	4 4/8	26 0/8	23 6/8	6	7	GARRETSON	SHAYNE	SAME	
2483	144 2/8	HENRY	93	68 2/8	71 6/8	16 6/8	3 6/8	23 4/8	22 6/8	5	6	KENNEY	DOUG	SAME	
2483	144 2/8	MILLER	93	70 4/8	69 0/8	16 1/8	9 5/8	21 5/8	21 5/8	7	8	LUTTRELL	TONY RAY	SAME	
2483	144 2/8	CALLAWAY	93	70 5/8	69 2/8	13 4/8	5 6/8	21 7/8	22 1/8	7	5	NARZINSKI	MATTHEW L.	SAME	
2483	144 2/8	MORGAN	94	64 0/8	65 4/8	22 1/8	5 3/8	24 5/8	24 5/8	6	7	WRIGHT	LESTER	SAME	

MISSOURI SHOW-ME BIG BUCKS CLUB RECORDS OF WHITETAIL DEER BY STATE, TYPICAL

STATE RANK	SCORE	COUNTY	YEAR TAKEN	INCHES TYPICAL R	L	INSIDE SPREAD	INCHES ABNORMAL	LENGTH MAIN BEAM R	L	NUMBER POINTS R	L	HUNTER	FIRST NAME	OWNER	FIRST NAME
2483	144 2/8	CHARITON	96	72 1/8	76 7/8	14 4/8	10 4/8	22 4/8	21 2/8	7	6	BROKKS	SCOTT	SAME	
2498	144 1/8	GASCONADE	74	69 2/8	64 4/8	16 5/8	0	21 5/8	21 3/8	5	5	SPURGEON	DON	SAME	
2498	144 1/8	FRANKLIN	79	64 5/8	64 6/8	20 1/8	2 2/8	23 6/8	24 4/8	5	4	TIMLIN	WILLIAM J.	TIMLIN	PATRICK & WANDA
2498	144 1/8	PERRY	80	64 6/8	64 3/8	18 5/8	0	22 4/8	21 1/8	5	5	SCHMIDT	BRAD	SAME	
2498	144 1/8	HOLT	82	65 5/8	64 0/8	16 1/8	0	21 1/8	21 1/8	5	5	BULLOCK	LEONARD	SAME	
2498	144 1/8	PERRY	85	62 2/8	61 2/8	21 7/8	0	22 6/8	22 5/8	4	4	HECHT	MIKE	SAME	
2498	144 1/8	DENT	86	64 2/8	67 0/8	19 5/8	2 4/8	21 6/8	23 4/8	7	5	CARTY	LARRY	SAME	
2498	144 1/8	SALINE	86	65 2/8	68 2/8	16 5/8	0	26 2/8	25 2/8	5	5	BLEDSOE	RICK	SAME	
2498	144 1/8	BARTON	88	65 5/8	66 0/8	18 3/8	0	23 3/8	24 4/8	4	4	HAGENSICKER	JAMES M.	SAME	
2498	144 1/8	BENTON	88	73 6/8	66 1/8	17 3/8	3 0/8	24 4/8	22 0/8	6	6	POWELL	CURTIS A.	SAME	
2498	144 1/8	ST. CLAIR	89	67 7/8	64 2/8	17 7/8	0	24 5/8	23 5/8	5	4	HUTTON	OLIVER	SAME	
2498	144 1/8	HOWELL	92	61 7/8	69 5/8	20 7/8	0	20 7/8	24 7/8	4	4	GROSZE	GARY	SAME	
2498	144 1/8	SALINE	92	64 6/8	65 1/8	16 3/8	0	21 6/8	21 6/8	5	5	MALTER	JUSTIN	SAME	
2498	144 1/8	KNOX	93	64 0/8	71 3/8	16 1/8	0	22 1/8	23 2/8	5	5	DAVIS	DONNIE L.	SAME	
2498	144 1/8	COOPER	93	66 3/8	66 3/8	17 1/8	3 4/8	21 1/8	21 4/8	6	6	WESSING	JEFF	SAME	
2498	144 1/8	MONITEAU	96	65 6/8	67 6/8	15 7/8	0	20 6/8	21 4/8	5	5	KUNZE	WAYNE	SAME	
2498	144 1/8	TEXAS	96	66 6/8	68 7/8	16 3/8	0	22 5/8	23 4/8	5	5	STONE	DONALD	SAME	
2514	144 0/8	DOUGLAS	57	67 0/8	66 0/8	14 4/8	0	23 0/8	22 4/8	5	5	CAIN	HAROLD L.	SAME	
2514	144 0/8	OSAGE	71	65 1/8	69 1/8	17 6/8	0	24 7/8	25 5/8	4	4	NILGES	LAWRENCE G.	SAME	
2514	144 0/8	LACLEDE	72	64 3/8	63 4/8	18 2/8	0	24 5/8	24 5/8	4	4	McMURDO	MIKE	SAME	
2514	144 0/8	DALLAS	73	66 1/8	63 7/8	20 0/8	3 6/8	24 7/8	23 6/8	5	5	GILLHAM	MIKE	SAME	
2514	144 0/8	MORGAN	78	70 4/8	72 7/8	16 1/8	7 1/8	24 4/8	24 5/8	7	9	WHITE	LORAN	SAME	
2514	144 0/8	SALINE	79	66 1/8	65 5/8	14 0/8	0	21 6/8	21 3/8	5	5	BRUNS	LESLIE	SAME	
2514	144 0/8	CRAWFORD	80	69 1/8	66 4/8	18 6/8	4 3/8	23 5/8	23 3/8	6	6	SAPPINGTON	COLIN	SAME	
2514	144 0/8	OZARK	82	64 1/8	64 2/8	18 4/8	0	23 3/8	22 4/8	5	4	FREEMAN	DAVID	SAME	
2514	144 0/8	ST. FRANCOIS	85	64 0/8	67 5/8	16 2/8	0	21 1/8	21 1/8	5	5	BYERS	TED R.	SAME	
2514	144 0/8	GASCONADE	85	66 4/8	66 2/8	15 4/8	0	20 6/8	21 2/8	5	5	FRICKE	DENNIS	SAME	
2514	144 0/8	NEW MADRID	85	64 7/8	67 7/8	19 2/8	3 6/8	24 2/8	23 6/8	6	5	DANIELS	AVERA	SAME	
2514	144 0/8	PERRY	87	65 6/8	66 5/8	17 6/8	0	22 3/8	22 7/8	5	5	PETZOLDT	MARVIN P.	SAME	
2514	144 0/8	SALINE	89	69 0/8	66 1/8	14 2/8	1 6/8	21 7/8	21 3/8	5	6	ADAMS	BILL	SAME	
2514	144 0/8	POLK	91	65 1/8	68 3/8	16 2/8	0	22 1/8	22 3/8	5	5	PAXSON	BRUCE	SAME	
2514	144 0/8	MARIES	92	67 6/8	66 7/8	17 3/8	3 3/8	24 5/8	24 0/8	5	5	RAGAN	DONALD G.	SAME	

STATE RANK	SCORE	COUNTY	YEAR TAKEN	INCHES TYPICAL R	L	INSIDE SPREAD	INCHES ABNORMAL	LENGTH MAIN BEAM R	L	NUMBER POINTS R	L	HUNTER	FIRST NAME	OWNER	FIRST NAME
2514	144 0/8	BOLLINGER	94	68 6/8	65 5/8	13 2/8	0	21 1/8	21 3/8	5	5	BROSHUIS	RICK	SAME	
2514	144 0/8	LAFAYETTE	94	67 7/8	66 2/8	16 0/8	0	22 1/8	21 5/8	5	5	BEUMER	DEAN	SAME	
2514	144 0/8	SCOTLAND	95	67 7/8	67 3/8	16 5/8	1 1/8	22 0/8	23 1/8	6	6	SMALL	MICHAEL	SAME	
2514	144 0/8	GRUNDY	95	64 2/8	65 6/8	18 5/8	2 3/8	20 1/8	21 0/8	6	6	CREASON	RICHARD	SAME	
2533	143 7/8	GASCONADE	63	69 5/8	68 5/8	19 3/8	0	25 0/8	26 1/8	7	7	AHLBON	B.G.	SAME	
2533	143 7/8	GASCONADE	76	68 5/8	65 5/8	21 0/8	7 5/8	26 0/8	25 0/8	5	5	GERSCHEFSKE	MILDA	SAME	
2533	143 7/8	COOPER	76	65 6/8	65 6/8	16 7/8	0	22 7/8	23 5/8	4	4	FRIEDRICH	ALFRED	SAME	
2533	143 7/8	CAPE GIRARDEAU	76	67 5/8	67 1/8	19 7/8	0	21 2/8	21 2/8	6	6	ZIEGLER	JEROME	SAME	
2533	143 7/8	MARIES	82	65 4/8	67 1/8	15 1/8	0	23 2/8	23 3/8	5	5	RAGAN	ROGER	SAME	
2533	143 7/8	CRAWFORD	86	67 7/8	66 3/8	17 7/8	0	20 3/8	21 1/8	6	5	SMITH	FRANCIS L.	SAME	
2533	143 7/8	FRANKLIN	87	66 5/8	69 1/8	20 0/8	6 3/8	25 0/8	25 0/8	6	5	SMITH	ROBERT D.	SAME	
2533	143 7/8	CAMDEN	89	66 3/8	73 6/8	17 4/8	5 1/8	23 4/8	24 5/8	5	8	CARTWRIGHT	JOHN	SAME	
2533	143 7/8	RIPLEY	89	64 6/8	66 1/8	18 7/8	1 2/8	23 2/8	23 5/8	6	5	BYERS	TED R.	SAME	
2533	143 7/8	LACLEDE	89	66 7/8	66 7/8	17 0/8	1 3/8	24 1/8	22 2/8	6	5	YOUNG	ROBERT A.	SAME	
2533	143 7/8	TEXAS	90	68 3/8	68 6/8	14 4/8	4 5/8	23 5/8	24 0/8	8	5	YOAKUM	DELMAR	SAME	
2533	143 7/8	PETTIS	90	66 6/8	66 0/8	18 5/8	2 6/8	24 0/8	22 2/8	5	6	PARKHURST	ROBERT RICHARD	SAME	
2533	143 7/8	PETTIS	91	64 0/8	70 0/8	18 3/8	0	26 3/8	25 7/8	4	5	ELLISON	RUSTY	SAME	
2533	143 7/8	CARTER	92	67 5/8	66 6/8	15 4/8	0	21 4/8	22 1/8	5	5	POGUE	RANDY	SAME (DOE DEER)	
2533	143 7/8	JASPER	93	62 6/8	66 6/8	19 7/8	0	25 3/8	24 7/8	4	5	PIERCE	ED	SAME	
2533	143 7/8	HENRY	95	68 6/8	66 6/8	19 4/8	5 5/8	23 5/8	23 5/8	6	6	KIELY	JAMES	SAME	
2533	143 7/8	GENTRY	95	65 1/8	68 1/8	14 3/8	0	22 2/8	23 1/8	5	5	CRAWFORD	BRYON	SAME	
2550	143 6/8	FRANKLIN	72	67 0/8	66 1/8	16 6/8	0	21 1/8	22 5/8	5	5	VOSS	RUDOLPH	SAME	
2550	143 6/8	HOWELL	72	64 1/8	67 7/8	18 0/8	0	24 6/8	24 0/8	4	4	BRADDISH	RICK	SAME	
2550	143 6/8	SHANNON	72	65 7/8	67 4/8	14 4/8	0	23 0/8	22 2/8	5	5	REIMINGER	DAVE	SAME	
2550	143 6/8	BARTON	75	64 7/8	66 1/8	15 2/8	1 0/8	21 0/8	22 4/8	6	6	VANGILDER	RANDY	SAME	
2550	143 6/8	DOUGLAS	76	65 3/8	65 2/8	17 6/8	0	20 6/8	20 2/8	5	5	RHOADS	JOHNNY	SAME	
2550	143 6/8	GREENE	79	64 1/8	64 3/8	19 4/8	0	23 3/8	22 3/8	5	5	LASSLEY	DELBERT	SAME	
2550	143 6/8	NEW MADRID	83	67 7/8	70 5/8	16 1/8	1 1/8	25 3/8	24 5/8	5	6	JAMES	RILEY	SAME	
2550	143 6/8	MARIES	86	63 6/8	64 1/8	17 0/8	0	24 2/8	24 2/8	4	4	FRITCHEY	JUSTIN D.	SAME	
2550	143 6/8	WARREN	86	66 6/8	65 1/8	19 5/8	2 3/8	22 7/8	23 3/8	6	5	CASPER	JIM	SAME	
2550	143 6/8	BENTON	88	65 4/8	66 6/8	15 4/8	0	22 2/8	21 1/8	5	5	SEDGWICK	BILLY T.	SAME	
2550	143 6/8	HICKORY	88	64 2/8	66 0/8	18 7/8	1 1/8	23 6/8	23 6/8	6	5	PUMMILL	LAURA	SAME	

MISSOURI SHOW-ME BIG BUCKS CLUB RECORDS OF WHITETAIL DEER BY STATE, TYPICAL

STATE RANK	SCORE	COUNTY	YEAR TAKEN	INCHES TYPICAL R	L	INSIDE SPREAD	INCHES ABNORMAL	LENGTH MAIN BEAM R	L	NUMBER POINTS R	L	HUNTER	FIRST NAME	OWNER	FIRST NAME
2550	143 6/8	PHELPS	92	64 3/8	64 6/8	18 6/8	0	22 4/8	23 0/8	5	5	BURNS	EARL	SAME	
2550	143 6/8	MILLER	92	62 0/8	64 1/8	19 6/8	0	25 0/8	25 4/8	4	4	STONER	MIKE	SAME	
2550	143 6/8	LACLEDE	93	63 7/8	68 4/8	19 2/8	0	24 4/8	23 3/8	5	5	TREMBLER	JOEL	SAME	
2564	143 5/8	PULASKI	67	70 4/8	72 0/8	14 1/8	9 4/8	22 4/8	22 4/8	8	8	BARCLAY	JAMES B.	SAME	
2564	143 5/8	CAPE GIRARDEAU	68	65 6/8	65 2/8	18 1/8	0	23 0/8	22 4/8	5	5	SCHATTAUER	LLOYD	SAME	
2564	143 5/8	MILLER	74	69 4/8	69 5/8	18 5/8	10 4/8	24 5/8	24 6/8	6	7	RACKERS	STANLEY	SAME	
2564	143 5/8	LACLEDE	75	64 5/8	65 4/8	17 3/8	0	22 1/8	22 7/8	5	5	SULLIVAN	CHARLES	SAME	
2564	143 5/8	FRANKLIN	81	64 4/8	67 4/8	17 3/8	1 0/8	23 6/8	23 0/8	5	6	COOK, JR.	JOSEPH M.	SAME	
2564	143 5/8	MONITEAU	81	64 6/8	69 1/8	19 5/8	1 4/8	25 3/8	25 7/8	5	5	LITTLE	HEATH	SAME	
2564	143 5/8	COOPER	82	64 2/8	67 7/8	17 0/8	1 7/8	22 3/8	23 2/8	5	4	FARRIS	DAN	SAME	
2564	143 5/8	WASHINGTON	89	66 7/8	64 4/8	15 3/8	0	24 1/8	23 3/8	4	4	FRANKLIN	ALAN D.	SAME	
2564	143 5/8	SALINE	91	63 2/8	66 7/8	19 3/8	0	23 3/8	25 0/8	5	5	McDANIEL	CRAIG	SAME	
2564	143 5/8	BARRY	91	66 2/8	64 1/8	18 7/8	3 2/8	23 3/8	23 4/8	5	5	ONEY	CHARLES E.	SAME	
2564	143 5/8	PUTNAM	92	66 4/8	70 4/8	19 3/8	6 0/8	24 4/8	24 2/8	4	7	PERKINS	BRIAN LEE	SAME	
2564	143 5/8	ST. FRANCOIS	92	68 4/8	66 2/8	17 1/8	0	22 5/8	23 1/8	5	5	FREEMAN	DENNIS P.	SAME	
2564	143 5/8	PETTIS	95	71 0/8	65 3/8	15 5/8	0	22 5/8	23 0/8	6	5	JEFFERIS	DAVID	SAME	
2577	143 4/8	TEXAS	73	73 0/8	66 4/8	17 0/8	3 4/8	27 1/8	25 7/8	6	5	OGDON	CARL	SAME	
2577	143 4/8	MADISON	74	67 7/8	71 2/8	15 4/8	0	20 7/8	22 1/8	5	5	PALUBIAK	GARY	SAME	
2577	143 4/8	GASCONADE	79	64 4/8	74 0/8	18 4/8	0	26 0/8	31 0/8	4	5	SCHNEIDER	JIM	SCHNEIDER	JAMES
2577	143 4/8	ST. LOUIS	82	68 6/8	63 0/8	19 2/8	0	25 3/8	22 4/8	4	4	BERGMANN	DAVID	SAME	
2577	143 4/8	BOLLINGER	85	63 5/8	63 1/8	18 4/8	0	24 0/8	24 0/8	4	4	MORGAN	SCOTT	SAME	
2577	143 4/8	TEXAS	86	65 4/8	67 7/8	15 6/8	0	22 7/8	24 7/8	5	5	FRAMPTON	LLOYD	FRAMPTON	MICHEEL
2577	143 4/8	PETTIS	88	65 3/8	66 6/8	17 0/8	0	25 6/8	24 1/8	4	5	DOVE	JAMES J.	SAME	
2577	143 4/8	ANDREW	90	62 7/8	64 4/8	20 3/8	1 4/8	23 5/8	24 0/8	6	5	WOLF, JR.	BILL	SAME	
2577	143 4/8	GREENE	93	63 7/8	64 6/8	19 0/8	0	23 6/8	23 2/8	5	5	BARNHOUSE	JEFFERY L.	SAME	
2577	143 4/8	SULLIVAN	95	66 1/8	63 2/8	17 4/8	0	24 0/8	23 7/8	5	5	McDONALD	AARON	SAME	
2577	143 4/8	BARRY	95	66 3/8	65 2/8	17 4/8	1 0/8	26 4/8	24 5/8	5	4	RENKOSKI	DENNIS	SAME	
2577	143 4/8	OSAGE	95	71 1/8	68 3/8	15 4/8	1 4/8	21 4/8	22 3/8	5	6	OLIGSCHLAEGER	TIM	SAME	
2577	143 4/8	PERRY	96	64 1/8	64 6/8	18 6/8	0	24 1/8	22 4/8	5	4	RELLERGERT	DAVID L.	SAME	
2577	143 4/8	ANDREW	96	65 6/8	65 7/8	17 6/8	0	23 6/8	23 3/8	4	5	DEERING	SHANE	SAME	
2591	143 3/8	MADISON	71	68 7/8	68 4/8	20 1/8	8 4/8	25 1/8	22 7/8	5	5	SCHULTZ	BILL	SAME	
2591	143 3/8	WASHINGTON	71	68 1/8	66 2/8	16 3/8	3 6/8	22 4/8	22 7/8	6	5	SULLENTROP	HOWARD	SAME	

MISSOURI SHOW-ME BIG BUCKS CLUB RECORDS OF WHITETAIL DEER BY STATE, TYPICAL

STATE RANK	SCORE	COUNTY	YEAR TAKEN	INCHES TYPICAL R	L	INSIDE SPREAD	INCHES ABNORMAL	LENGTH MAIN BEAM R	L	NUMBER POINTS R	L	HUNTER	FIRST NAME	OWNER	FIRST NAME	STATE FIRST NAME
2591	143 3/8	MONITEAU	80	62 5/8	65 6/8	18 5/8	0	22 4/8	24 0/8	4	4	DIETZEL	JOHN	SAME		
2591	143 3/8	WASHINGTON	82	63 4/8	64 0/8	19 3/8	0	24 5/8	24 2/8	5	5	STACK	DEAN R.	SAME		
2591	143 3/8	LACLEDE	85	65 0/8	64 5/8	16 3/8	0	23 0/8	23 0/8	5	5	RAINES	MIKE	SAME		
2591	143 3/8	DENT	86	68 1/8	68 5/8	19 7/8	6 0/8	20 6/8	21 5/8	5	7	BATSCHELET	DON	SAME		
2591	143 3/8	TANEY	91	66 4/8	65 0/8	20 3/8	2 4/8	24 1/8	24 0/8	5	5	HAMMONS	GEORGE	SAME		
2598	143 2/8	HOWELL	72	63 0/8	64 6/8	19 2/8	0	23 1/8	24 2/8	5	5	JOHNSON	BILL	SAME		
2598	143 2/8	FRANKLIN	74	67 0/8	68 7/8	17 7/8	7 3/8	26 3/8	26 1/8	4	6	KLOEPPEL	RAYMOND J.	SAME		
2598	143 2/8	WARREN	79	64 6/8	66 2/8	17 0/8	0	22 4/8	22 1/8	5	5	MASCHGER	JERRY	SAME		
2598	143 2/8	PHELPS	84	65 1/8	66 6/8	15 4/8	0	24 3/8	23 7/8	4	4	DARLINGTON	ROBERT	SAME		
2598	143 2/8	MARIES	85	62 2/8	68 0/8	20 6/8	0	24 1/8	24 4/8	4	5	WEBER	PAUL A.	SAME		
2598	143 2/8	GASCONADE	85	65 3/8	65 3/8	15 0/8	0	21 4/8	21 2/8	5	5	SCHNEIDER	JIM AND BOB	SAME		
2598	143 2/8	SHANNON	87	64 0/8	63 0/8	17 4/8	0	22 1/8	21 4/8	5	5	BLAND	GARY	LINDSAY	SCOTT	
2598	143 2/8	GREENE	87	68 0/8	64 1/8	15 2/8	0	23 3/8	23 4/8	5	5	FLETCHER	RICK	SAME		
2598	143 2/8	MARIES	87	68 3/8	68 2/8	15 2/8	2 6/8	24 4/8	25 2/8	5	6	RIDENHOUR	DANNEY	SAME		
2598	143 2/8	VERNON	90	63 0/8	64 5/8	19 2/8	0	23 0/8	22 0/8	5	5	ANDERS	ED	SAME		
2598	143 2/8	MORGAN	91	65 4/8	66 0/8	15 4/8	0	23 0/8	22 5/8	5	5	McPHERSON	MARTIN	SAME		
2598	143 2/8	TEXAS	91	66 6/8	69 0/8	19 6/8	7 6/8	25 2/8	24 7/8	7	6	LUTZ	THOMAS	SAME		
2598	143 2/8	FRANKLIN	92	66 3/8	63 3/8	16 4/8	0	23 4/8	23 0/8	5	5	SCHOWE	BLAKE	SAME		
2598	143 2/8	ST. FRANCOIS	93	67 7/8	68 0/8	15 0/8	3 2/8	21 0/8	21 5/8	7	7	STOTLER	HOMER	SAME		
2598	143 2/8	POLK	93	66 0/8	67 5/8	16 4/8	0	22 2/8	24 3/8	5	5	DURYEE	JIM	SAME		
2598	143 2/8	MILLER	94	66 4/8	65 5/8	18 6/8	1 6/8	23 5/8	21 2/8	6	5	HERIGON	NATHAN	SAME		
2598	143 2/8	WASHINGTON	96	67 0/8	66 3/8	17 6/8	3 2/8	24 7/8	24 4/8	6	6	CLICK	BRYAN	SAME		
2615	143 1/8	McDONALD	67	64 1/8	64 4/8	17 1/8	0	23 1/8	22 5/8	5	5	WELLESLEY	ALLAN	SAME		
2615	143 1/8	PERRY	73	63 4/8	63 6/8	22 1/8	0	23 6/8	22 4/8	4	5	BURROUGHES	LARRY	SAME		
2615	143 1/8	ST. CLAIR	80	65 1/8	63 1/8	17 7/8	0	24 6/8	25 0/8	4	4	BARNES	KIRBY W.	SAME		
2615	143 1/8	ST. LOUIS	82	63 4/8	65 1/8	17 3/8	0	23 3/8	24 1/8	4	4	SARTORS	DANNY	SAME		
2615	143 1/8	MARIES	84	68 0/8	63 0/8	19 1/8	0	24 7/8	23 2/8	5	4	FRITCHEY	CARL	SAME		
2615	143 1/8	OSAGE	86	71 3/8	67 6/8	17 7/8	10 0/8	24 7/8	24 4/8	7	6	SCHAEFER	RON	SAME		
2615	143 1/8	COOPER	87	66 0/8	67 3/8	15 7/8	0	23 3/8	23 5/8	5	5	GREER	JACK	SAME		
2615	143 1/8	SALINE	88	64 4/8	66 6/8	18 7/8	0	25 2/8	23 3/8	5	5	EDDY	ALAN	SAME		
2615	143 1/8	ST. CLAIR	89	63 7/8	64 0/8	19 5/8	0	22 7/8	21 6/8	5	5	SHOUSE	MARK	SAME		
2615	143 1/8	MORGAN	91	67 1/8	67 7/8	15 1/8	0	24 4/8	22 4/8	5	5	WILLIS	WISLEY DALE	SAME		

STATE RANK	SCORE	COUNTY	YEAR TAKEN	INCHES TYPICAL R	L	INSIDE SPREAD	INCHES ABNORMAL	LENGTH MAIN BEAM R	L	NUMBER POINTS R	L	HUNTER	FIRST NAME	OWNER	FIRST NAME
2615	143 1/8	STE. GENEIEVE	95	68 1/8	66 7/8	14 6/8	2 1/8	23 3/8	22 3/8	6	5	VOGT	RICHARD	SAME	
2626	143 0/8	BOLLINGER	64	65 4/8	65 4/8	18 6/8	0	24 0/8	23 3/8	4	5	ROPER	RONNIE D.	SAME	
2626	143 0/8	PERRY	68	68 5/8	67 1/8	16 2/8	5 2/8	24 2/8	23 7/8	7	7	MARTIN	ROBERT L.	SAME	
2626	143 0/8	SCOTLAND	71	72 7/8	70 2/8	19 0/8	3 6/8	23 6/8	26 0/8	6	5	CHILDRESS	SCOTT	SAME	
2626	143 0/8	SHANNON	72	67 5/8	63 4/8	16 6/8	0	24 6/8	23 7/8	5	5	ARTHUR	TED	SAME	
2626	143 0/8	MARIES	78	67 0/8	65 1/8	17 0/8	1 4/8	23 7/8	24 3/8	5	5	BUTLER	DOUG	SAME	
2626	143 0/8	PERRY	78	66 2/8	66 2/8	17 2/8	4 4/8	22 0/8	22 6/8	6	6	LIX, JR.	LOUIS	SAME	
2626	143 0/8	DENT	86	68 6/8	65 7/8	18 1/8	3 5/8	22 3/8	22 0/8	6	7	MARTI	DAVID	SAME	
2626	143 0/8	MILLER	86	65 7/8	65 6/8	18 4/8	3 0/8	23 6/8	23 0/8	6	6	WILSON	JERRY	SAME	
2626	143 0/8	CASS	86	64 5/8	63 5/8	20 0/8	0	26 4/8	25 7/8	5	4	WHITLOCK	HARRY	SAME	
2626	143 0/8	SALINE	91	67 3/8	62 7/8	17 2/8	0	25 2/8	23 4/8	4	4	ALDREDGE	LARRY	SAME	
2626	143 0/8	TEXAS	91	62 7/8	68 2/8	18 4/8	0	20 6/8	20 2/8	5	6	JUNG	STANLEY V.	SAME	
2626	143 0/8	RIPLEY	92	63 5/8	64 3/8	18 0/8	0	24 3/8	24 2/8	4	4	TROTTER	JESSE	SAME	
2626	143 0/8	VERNON	93	64 4/8	65 6/8	17 4/8	0	22 7/8	22 7/8	5	6	NEWTON	BILL W.	SAME	
2626	143 0/8	SULLIVAN	94	64 2/8	65 1/8	15 6/8	0	19 6/8	20 5/8	5	5	HALTERMAN	KEN	SAME	
2626	143 0/8	DALLAS	96	67 7/8	70 3/8	15 2/8	4 4/8	24 1/8	24 0/8	6	6	SWEANEY	JAMES A.	SAME	
2641	142 7/8	PHELPS	69	64 5/8	65 4/8	17 3/8	0	22 0/8	20 7/8	6	6	COX	ROBERT	SAME	
2641	142 7/8	JACKSON	72	64 4/8	64 0/8	16 3/8	0	20 2/8	21 0/8	5	5	COX	GARY	SAME	
2641	142 7/8	OSAGE	82	63 5/8	65 2/8	16 5/8	0	24 4/8	24 0/8	4	4	LUECKE	DEAN	SAME	
2641	142 7/8	CARTER	92	64 7/8	63 4/8	17 7/8	0	23 0/8	23 2/8	5	5	WILKINS	BILL	SAME	
2641	142 7/8	TEXAS	93	64 2/8	64 2/8	17 7/8	0	23 0/8	23 5/8	5	5	TAYLOR	ARLAN	SAME	
2641	142 7/8	MADISON	94	65 3/8	65 2/8	17 4/8	3 3/8	23 6/8	23 4/8	4	5	SHY	JUNIOR	SAME	
2647	142 6/8	OSAGE	78	62 6/8	69 1/8	17 4/8	0	22 7/8	22 6/8	4	5	VOSS	HERBERT H.	SAME	
2647	142 6/8	CAMDEN	79	68 0/8	63 0/8	20 3/8	2 5/8	23 2/8	23 0/8	6	6	EDWARDS	JOE DAVID	SAME	
2647	142 6/8	PHELPS	79	64 3/8	65 1/8	14 6/8	0	21 5/8	21 5/8	5	5	BURNS	WILSON	SAME	
2647	142 6/8	PETTIS	79	61 7/8	74 3/8	23 0/8	2 0/8	23 2/8	24 5/8	4	4	MONTGOMERY	JAMES	SAME	
2647	142 6/8	OSAGE	81	68 5/8	63 7/8	19 2/8	0	23 0/8	23 5/8	4	4	MATTHEWS	JAMES	SAME	
2647	142 6/8	MARIES	82	64 5/8	69 0/8	20 2/8	0	23 2/8	25 4/8	5	4	KLEFNER	MIKE	SAME	
2647	142 6/8	FRANKLIN	84	62 7/8	65 5/8	18 4/8	2 6/8	20 7/8	21 6/8	6	6	TERSCHLUSE	MARVIN	SAME	
2647	142 6/8	COLE	84	64 1/8	65 0/8	17 2/8	0	20 5/8	21 2/8	5	5	SCHNEIDER	GARY	SAME	
2647	142 6/8	SHANNON	87	65 3/8	65 0/8	16 0/8	0	24 4/8	24 0/8	5	5	STUCKEY	F. DAVID	SAME	
2647	142 6/8	CRAWFORD	87	67 0/8	61 0/8	21 2/8	0	22 6/8	22 3/8	5	5	MOUTRAY	TERRY	SAME	

STATE RANK	SCORE	COUNTY	YEAR TAKEN	INCHES TYPICAL R	L	INSIDE SPREAD	INCHES ABNORMAL	LENGTH MAIN BEAM R	L	NUMBER POINTS R	L	HUNTER	FIRST NAME	OWNER	FIRST NAME
2647	142 6/8	WAYNE	87	62 7/8	69 7/8	18 1/8	1 1/8	23 5/8	25 5/8	5	5	TONEY	MIKE	SAME	
2647	142 6/8	ST. CLAIR	89	62 7/8	62 7/8	19 6/8	1 2/8	25 0/8	24 5/8	4	5	ABBOTT	ELMER	SAME	
2647	142 6/8	MACON	96	62 0/8	62 0/8	21 6/8	0	22 3/8	21 6/8	5	5	MILLIRON	STEVE	SAME	
2660	142 5/8	CARTER	71	67 7/8	63 6/8	21 1/8	0	23 1/8	22 2/8	5	5	BARDWELL	VINCE	SAME	
2660	142 5/8	GASCONADE	72	65 0/8	66 6/8	14 5/8	0	22 1/8	22 2/8	5	5	HEIDEL	DALE	SAME	
2660	142 5/8	CAMDEN	76	67 4/8	64 2/8	17 7/8	0	24 5/8	23 6/8	5	5	BLANKENSHIP	LILBURN F.	SAME	
2660	142 5/8	STE. GENEIEVE	79	69 7/8	68 1/8	18 6/8	8 5/8	21 3/8	21 1/8	5	5	JOKERST	GENE	SAME	
2660	142 5/8	COOPER	82	66 0/8	72 1/8	15 0/8	4 3/8	25 0/8	25 0/8	6	7	PFEIFFER	LOGAN	SAME	
2660	142 5/8	HENRY	82	65 6/8	63 1/8	17 1/8	0	23 1/8	22 2/8	5	5	CARNEY	KENT	SAME	
2660	142 5/8	SALINE	85	64 5/8	64 7/8	17 1/8	0	23 2/8	24 2/8	5	4	SLEEPER	RANDY	SAME	
2660	142 5/8	ST. FRANCOIS	86	67 6/8	65 3/8	15 3/8	2 6/8	21 4/8	21 7/8	6	5	COLLINS	ROGER	SAME	
2660	142 5/8	JOHNSON	87	63 7/8	71 2/8	18 5/8	0	22 1/8	22 6/8	4	5	MORRIS	HUGH	SAME	
2660	142 5/8	TEXAS	87	62 7/8	64 4/8	17 7/8	0	20 4/8	20 5/8	5	5	JAUDES	KIRK A.	SAME	
2660	142 5/8	LACLEDE	87	66 6/8	69 7/8	15 4/8	5 3/8	27 7/8	27 6/8	6	5	UDER	KENNY	SAME	
2660	142 5/8	CAPE GIRARDEAU	87	64 2/8	69 3/8	17 1/8	0	23 4/8	22 2/8	4	5	WIBBENMEYER	LES	SAME	
2660	142 5/8	OSAGE	89	66 5/8	64 4/8	15 1/8	0	21 6/8	20 7/8	5	5	PFAHL	EDWARD	SAME	
2660	142 5/8	MARION	90	64 4/8	67 5/8	18 3/8	2 6/8	22 7/8	23 0/8	6	6	CARSON	BOB	SAME	
2660	142 5/8	MONITEAU	90	66 1/8	67 1/8	15 5/8	1 2/8	21 6/8	23 0/8	6	6	LIGHT	KEVIN	SAME	
2660	142 5/8	OZARK	93	64 7/8	63 0/8	18 5/8	0	22 2/8	22 1/8	5	5	COLEMAN	R. DENNIS	SAME	
2660	142 5/8	PETTIS	95	64 7/8	63 7/8	21 2/8	2 7/8	22 5/8	23 2/8	6	6	ELLISON	RANDY	SAME	
2660	142 5/8	LINCOLN	95	65 0/8	67 5/8	18 5/8	0	23 6/8	23 3/8	4	5	MUDD	BILLY	SAME	
2678	142 4/8	OSAGE	70	65 6/8	65 4/8	17 3/8	1 3/8	21 4/8	21 2/8	5	6	LUECKE	KENNY	SAME	
2678	142 4/8	STE. GENEIEVE	82	63 0/8	67 5/8	17 2/8	0	24 4/8	26 2/8	5	5	BREWSTER	JOE	SAME	
2678	142 4/8	LACLEDE	82	66 6/8	61 1/8	20 2/8	0	25 0/8	23 7/8	5	5	WALLANDER	JACK	SAME	
2678	142 4/8	OZARK	82	66 7/8	65 3/8	14 6/8	0	23 0/8	24 2/8	5	5	HARTGRAVES	JIMMIE	SAME	
2678	142 4/8	LACLEDE	84	64 2/8	62 0/8	21 0/8	1 4/8	22 0/8	22 2/8	6	5	BAKER	BOBBY	SAME	
2678	142 4/8	ST. FRANCOIS	88	0	0	0	0	0	0	0	0	DAVIS	GARY	SAME	
2678	142 4/8	TEXAS	88	67 7/8	63 1/8	18 2/8	0	23 3/8	23 3/8	5	5	McCARTER	W. GENE	SAME	
2678	142 4/8	OZARK	88	63 7/8	66 2/8	18 4/8	0	21 3/8	23 3/8	5	4	LLOYD, JR.	JOHN A.	SAME	
2678	142 4/8	CAMDEN	88	62 7/8	63 2/8	20 5/8	0	22 5/8	23 0/8	4	4	STEELE	ROBERT C.	SAME	
2678	142 4/8	SALINE	89	70 2/8	72 0/8	16 5/8	11 5/8	21 4/8	21 5/8	6	7	ZIMMERSCHIED	BRIAN	SAME	
2678	142 4/8	SHANNON	90	66 6/8	67 0/8	18 7/8	3 1/8	25 6/8	26 3/8	6	6	BLAND	BOBBY W.	SAME	

MISSOURI SHOW-ME BIG BUCKS CLUB RECORDS OF WHITETAIL DEER BY STATE, TYPICAL

STATE RANK	SCORE	COUNTY	YEAR TAKEN	INCHES TYPICAL R	INCHES TYPICAL L	INSIDE SPREAD	INCHES ABNORMAL	LENGTH MAIN BEAM R	LENGTH MAIN BEAM L	NUMBER POINTS R	NUMBER POINTS L	HUNTER	FIRST NAME	OWNER	FIRST NAME
2678	142 4/8	MORGAN	94	70 0/8	63 7/8	18 7/8	3 7/8	24 7/8	63 7/8	5	6	WOOLERY	WALTER	SAME	
2678	142 4/8	BARTON	96	65 2/8	64 1/8	18 2/8	0	23 2/8	20 7/8	5	5	GORDON, IV	DAVID P.	SAME	
2691	142 3/8	GASCONADE	52	64 5/8	75 5/8	14 6/8	0	22 6/8	22 2/8	5	6	BAUR	FRANK E.	SAME	
2691	142 3/8	GASCONADE	68	63 2/8	67 3/8	15 7/8	0	23 4/8	23 5/8	5	5	FRANKENBERG	ALAN	SAME	
2691	142 3/8	COOPER	68	62 0/8	62 6/8	22 1/8	0	24 7/8	23 1/8	4	4	RINACKE	ERV	SAME	
2691	142 3/8	CAMDEN	69	65 0/8	63 3/8	17 7/8	0	20 1/8	19 6/8	5	5	JOHNSON	RON	SAME	
2691	142 3/8	LINCOLN	80	63 2/8	70 7/8	17 1/8	0	24 6/8	25 6/8	4	5	TWELLMAN	RON	SAME	
2691	142 3/8	GASCONADE	81	64 6/8	64 1/8	17 1/8	0	22 6/8	23 6/8	4	4	MUELLER	TIM	SAME	
2691	142 3/8	PHELPS	82	66 0/8	66 0/8	17 0/8	0	20 6/8	21 4/8	5	5	CLIFTON, SR.	DAVID N.	SAME	
2691	142 3/8	ST. CLAIR	85	64 0/8	66 3/8	20 0/8	2 3/8	21 5/8	23 7/8	4	6	HARRIS	JACK T.	SAME	
2691	142 3/8	HENRY	86	74 2/8	66 3/8	17 4/8	5 3/8	23 6/8	23 4/8	8	6	HILLS	RUSSELL	DENISON	BARRY
2691	142 3/8	FRANKLIN	91	81 7/8	67 7/8	17 6/8	3 5/8	23 3/8	15 2/8	6	7	DIMMETT	RONALD	SAME	
2701	142 2/8	OREGON	57	77 0/8	66 0/8	16 2/8	0	21 7/8	21 7/8	6	6	CLINE	GLEN	SAME	
2701	142 2/8	DALLAS	63	66 2/8	65 7/8	18 3/8	2 5/8	21 3/8	20 3/8	5	8	REED	DALE	SAME	
2701	142 2/8	HENRY	70	62 5/8	61 6/8	20 2/8	0	23 0/8	22 4/8	4	4	BAILEY	W.E. (BILL)	SAME	
2701	142 2/8	MILLER	73	67 7/8	71 1/8	15 4/8	1 2/8	20 7/8	21 5/8	5	6	STRANGE	JACK	SAME	
2701	142 2/8	CEDAR	80	64 4/8	63 4/8	15 4/8	0	23 2/8	23 2/8	5	5	RUMMEL	JOHN	SAME	
2701	142 2/8	MONITEAU	82	65 6/8	68 6/8	14 2/8	2 2/8	19 6/8	20 7/8	6	6	GOLLADAY	AL	SAME	
2701	142 2/8	TEXAS	91	65 0/8	63 4/8	16 4/8	0	22 0/8	22 1/8	6	5	STAFFORD	KEN	SAME	
2701	142 2/8	MONITEAU	93	67 6/8	68 0/8	15 7/8	5 7/8	23 4/8	23 0/8	6	7	ZIEHMER	ROBERT L.	SAME	
2709	142 1/8	TEXAS	59	61 0/8	66 0/8	23 7/8	0	24 5/8	26 6/8	4	5	AUSTIN	LARRY B.	SAME	
2709	142 1/8	FRANKLIN	59	67 6/8	73 6/8	17 1/8	5 6/8	24 2/8	24 2/8	5	9	VOSS	ROBERT	SAME	
2709	142 1/8	JEFFERSON	60	70 3/8	66 6/8	18 2/8	0	23 4/8	24 7/8	5	5	HARPER	WILLIAM W.	SAME	
2709	142 1/8	IRON	69	71 2/8	64 3/8	20 0/8	5 7/8	22 7/8	23 2/8	7	6	MERKEL	LARRY	SAME	
2709	142 1/8	OSAGE	71	65 6/8	62 6/8	18 0/8	0	24 7/8	24 5/8	4	4	HOFFMAN	CHARLES	SAME	
2709	142 1/8	HENRY	75	64 0/8	64 1/8	16 6/8	0	24 6/8	25 6/8	4	4	KIDWELL	DON	SAME	
2709	142 1/8	PHELPS	80	64 6/8	64 0/8	16 5/8	0	22 2/8	21 7/8	5	5	PIAZZA	GEORGE	SAME	
2709	142 1/8	CRAWFORD	82	62 4/8	71 0/8	18 7/8	0	23 5/8	23 0/8	5	5	IVES	DAVE	SAME	
2709	142 1/8	MERCER	82	68 2/8	64 2/8	18 4/8	4 5/8	22 2/8	22 2/8	7	4	MARTIN	JAMES W.	SAME	
2709	142 1/8	COOPER	85	66 4/8	67 0/8	17 6/8	5 1/8	23 2/8	23 4/8	6	7	PRICE	JEFF	SAME	
2709	142 1/8	TEXAS	88	63 2/8	64 5/8	17 7/8	1 2/8	23 5/8	24 1/8	6	5	RHODES	JONATHAN	SAME	
2709	142 1/8	SALINE	89	71 6/8	64 0/8	17 5/8	1 2/8	22 1/8	23 0/8	7	5	UNDERWOOD	JERRY	SAME	

MISSOURI SHOW-ME BIG BUCKS CLUB RECORDS OF WHITETAIL DEER BY STATE, TYPICAL

STATE RANK	SCORE	COUNTY	YEAR TAKEN	INCHES TYPICAL R	INCHES TYPICAL L	INSIDE SPREAD	INCHES ABNORMAL	LENGTH MAIN BEAM R	LENGTH MAIN BEAM L	NUMBER POINTS R	NUMBER POINTS L	HUNTER	FIRST NAME	OWNER	FIRST NAME
2709	142 1/8	LACLEDE	94	70 5/8	67 7/8	16 4/8	1 1/8	24 1/8	22 5/8	6	5	LEMERY	GARY	SAME	
2709	142 1/8	ST. LOUIS	95	68 6/8	71 4/8	17 1/8	7 2/8	24 0/8	23 6/8	6	7	WERGES	ROBERT O.	SAME	
2709	142 1/8	PUTNAM	95	70 6/8	69 5/8	14 7/8	6 0/8	23 1/8	23 3/8	7	6	PEARSON	BOBBY	SAME	
2709	142 1/8	DENT	96	67 4/8	65 5/8	14 7/8		23 3/8	23 1/8	4	4	MORTON, SR.	RONALD D.	SAME	
2725	142 0/8	MARIES	72	71 0/8	61 7/8	18 6/8	0	26 3/8	24 5/8	5	4	PERKINS	ROBERT	SAME	
2725	142 0/8	MARIES	72	63 0/8	63 0/8	17 5/8	0	20 0/8	20 1/8	5	5	REDEL	LAWRENCE	SAME	
2725	142 0/8	SALINE	74	67 1/8	66 2/8	14 2/8	0	21 1/8	21 3/8	5	4	HOLLINGSWORTH	KENNY K.	SAME	
2725	142 0/8	PULASKI	74	63 7/8	63 5/8	17 2/8	0	22 4/8	23 2/8	4	4	CLARK	WILLIT B.	SAME	
2725	142 0/8	PERRY	75	64 0/8	64 4/8	15 6/8	0	20 6/8	21 4/8	5	5	HOOD	JAMES L.	SAME	
2725	142 0/8	COOPER	77	62 7/8	65 3/8	18 5/8	1 1/8	22 7/8	23 6/8	6	5	HURST	ROBBIE	SAME	
2725	142 0/8	LACLEDE	81	64 1/8	62 5/8	18 4/8	0	24 1/8	22 7/8	4	4	HILTON	DELMAR	SAME	
2725	142 0/8	TEXAS	83	66 6/8	66 4/8	17 0/8	2 2/8	22 0/8	22 2/8	5	6	SHEPPARD	EDWARD F.	SAME	
2725	142 0/8	ST. CLAIR	83	71 0/8	63 5/8	17 3/8	2 1/8	23 6/8	24 0/8	5	5	KNEPP	CLAYTON M.	SAME	
2725	142 0/8	FRANKLIN	85	63 1/8	62 2/8	19 6/8	0	22 7/8	21 7/8	4	4	FIGGEMEIER	KENNETH M.	SAME	
2725	142 0/8	MONITEAU	86	67 6/8	63 0/8	16 2/8	0	23 4/8	23 2/8	6	5	ENOWSKI	BOB	SAME	
2725	142 0/8	SALINE	88	65 4/8	61 5/8	19 6/8	0	24 6/8	23 4/8	4	4	STEDING	ED	SAME	
2725	142 0/8	HENRY	90	67 1/8	71 0/8	18 7/8	8 3/8	23 5/8	23 7/8	6	7	HOLMGREN	CHRISTOPHER	SAME	
2725	142 0/8	SALINE	90	63 7/8	63 2/8	17 2/8	0	23 2/8	23 4/8	5	5	LARUE	DALE	SAME	
2725	142 0/8	STE. GENEIEVE	90	63 6/8	68 6/8	18 2/8	0	22 2/8	20 3/8	6	6	McCLANAHAN	ROBERT	SAME	
2725	142 0/8	MARIES	92	64 6/8	64 3/8	16 2/8	0	23 1/8	23 0/8	5	5	ALEXANDER	MICHAEL	SAME	
2725	142 0/8	MONITEAU	92	62 3/8	63 3/8	18 4/8	0	20 5/8	20 3/8	5	5	DOWELL, JR.	HARLAN	SAME	
2725	142 0/8	COOPER	93	63 2/8	67 4/8	16 0/8	0	25 1/8	26 2/8	4	4	CLEVENGER	MICHAEL	SAME	
2725	142 0/8	BARTON	95	63 7/8	66 7/8	18 0/8	3 0/8	23 7/8	25 1/8	6	5	FRIEDEN	KURT	SAME	
2725	142 0/8	COOPER	95	67 7/8	65 1/8	15 5/8	1 5/8	23 1/8	22 0/8	6	5	WESSING	JEFF	SAME	
2725	142 0/8	LACLEDE	95	65 4/8	66 2/8	15 4/8	0	21 6/8	66 2/8	5	5	VANDERHOEF	WILLIAM C.	SAME	
2725	142 0/8	MACON	96	67 6/8	66 0/8	15 2/8	1 2/8	22 4/8	22 0/8	6	5	BOGEART, JR.	ROBERT L.	SAME	
2747	141 7/8	MORGAN	68	65 5/8	63 0/8	15 6/8	0	20 0/8	19 6/8	5	5	LANGEWISCH	HARRY	SAME	
2747	141 7/8	LACLEDE	82	67 2/8	65 0/8	16 3/8	0	23 0/8	21 4/8	5	5	FUGITT	BOB	SAME	
2747	141 7/8	CAMDEN	85	63 1/8	67 5/8	17 3/8	0	23 6/8	23 6/8	4	5	WEST	STEVE	SAME	
2747	141 7/8	BENTON	90	66 6/8	66 7/8	15 5/8	0	22 2/8	21 3/8	6	5	WYATT	MICHAEL W.	SAME	
2747	141 7/8	OSAGE	91	66 5/8	63 0/8	17 5/8	0	23 4/8	23 3/8	4	4	BOEN, III	JAMES M.	SAME	
2747	141 7/8	CALLAWAY	91	66 3/8	63 6/8	18 2/8	1 3/8	22 1/8	23 1/8	5	5	UNDERWOOD	LARRY	SAME	

STATE RANK	SCORE	COUNTY	YEAR TAKEN	INCHES TYPICAL R	L	INSIDE SPREAD	INCHES ABNORMAL	LENGTH MAIN BEAM R	L	NUMBER POINTS R	L	HUNTER	FIRST NAME	OWNER	FIRST NAME
2747	141 7/8	FRANKLIN	93	65 4/8	67 1/8	18 6/8	4 1/8	24 4/8	23 5/8	6	6	BORGMEYER	GREG	SAME	
2747	141 7/8	JASPER	95	63 5/8	69 0/8	15 5/8	0	21 5/8	23 0/8	5	5	TILLMAN	DAVID L.	SAME	
2747	141 7/8	OSAGE	95	62 6/8	63 5/8	16 3/8	0	20 4/8	20 7/8	5	5	REHAGEN	RON	SAME	
2756	141 6/8	STE. GENEIEVE	61	70 4/8	67 5/8	21 0/8	3 0/8	24 2/8	25 3/8	5	5	KINKEAD	TERRY	SAME	
2756	141 6/8	VERNON	66	64 3/8	65 5/8	16 6/8	0	24 2/8	24 6/8	5	5	JENKINS	MIKE	SAME	
2756	141 6/8	FRANKLIN	66	65 5/8	65 1/8	18 1/8	2 5/8	21 0/8	21 0/8	6	5	ROWDEN	WALTER M.	SAME	
2756	141 6/8	McDONALD	71	68 2/8	63 1/8	15 6/8	0	20 3/8	19 7/8	6	5	MICHAEL	RICHARD	SAME	
2756	141 6/8	FRANKLIN	72	64 7/8	63 5/8	15 6/8	0	22 4/8	22 6/8	5	5	YOUNG	HARLAN	SAME	
2756	141 6/8	TEXAS	80	66 1/8	63 1/8	18 0/8	0	23 4/8	23 0/8	5	5	BONNER	JOE	SAME	
2756	141 6/8	POLK	80	63 7/8	64 1/8	15 2/8	0	23 5/8	24 1/8	4	4	ROBERTS	DWIGHT	SAME	
2756	141 6/8	MARIES	82	64 7/8	67 0/8	18 0/8	0	24 3/8	24 0/8	5	5	KOEHLER	FRANK	SAME	
2756	141 6/8	JEFFERSON	84	63 3/8	64 1/8	16 6/8	0	23 7/8	23 0/8	4	4	SULLIVAN	ALONZO	SAME	
2756	141 6/8	SALINE	86	65 3/8	66 7/8	19 2/8	0	23 2/8	23 6/8	5	6	KRUGER	DARRYL	SAME	
2756	141 6/8	CASS	88	63 0/8	66 1/8	17 0/8	1 0/8	23 1/8	24 4/8	6	5	BEARD	ED	SAME	
2756	141 6/8	BOLLINGER	93	67 6/8	71 1/8	16 2/8	8 0/8	20 4/8	22 2/8	7	6	CLINGINGSMITH	DONALD L.	SAME	
2756	141 6/8	VERNON	95	63 2/8	62 2/8	17 4/8	0	23 1/8	22 6/8	5	5	MASON	CLEM V.	SAME	
2756	141 6/8	HENRY	95	71 4/8	66 5/8	14 2/8	1 2/8	21 6/8	22 7/8	6	6	FELLHOELTER	CURTIS	SAME	
2756	141 6/8	CASS	96	66 2/8	68 1/8	16 0/8	0	23 5/8	22 5/8	5	5	DEMPSEY	STEVE	SAME	
2756	141 6/8	RALLS	96	67 5/8	72 3/8	17 2/8	6 0/8	23 4/8	23 2/8	5	5	BURNETT	BOB	SAME	
2772	141 5/8	OSAGE	67	67 1/8	68 7/8	17 6/8	6 5/8	22 3/8	22 0/8	5	6	RADEMANN	ELMER	SAME	
2772	141 5/8	WASHINGTON	75	65 6/8	65 1/8	16 1/8	0	22 1/8	22 0/8	5	5	KLOPPE	ROWAN R.	SAME	
2772	141 5/8	SALINE	82	63 0/8	67 4/8	17 3/8	0	25 3/8	24 4/8	4	4	MASTERS	NORMAN	SAME	
2772	141 5/8	COOPER	82	65 2/8	63 3/8	17 7/8	0	24 4/8	23 3/8	5	5	REAMS	LARRY	SAME	
2772	141 5/8	ST. FRANCOIS	83	66 7/8	63 0/8	15 5/8	0	24 2/8	23 1/8	4	4	WALKER	DARREN R.	SAME	
2772	141 5/8	PULASKI	84	62 6/8	64 5/8	17 3/8	0	21 3/8	20 4/8	5	5	DICKENS	TERRY	SAME	
2772	141 5/8	SALINE	88	64 5/8	63 1/8	17 7/8	0	22 0/8	23 0/8	5	5	THIEL	DON	SAME	
2772	141 5/8	ST. CLAIR	90	63 6/8	63 4/8	19 1/8	0	23 2/8	24 5/8	4	4	DEITCH	BOBBY	SAME	
2772	141 5/8	OSAGE	90	67 6/8	69 5/8	18 1/8	8 6/8	23 5/8	23 0/8	7	7	SMITH	STEPHEN C.	SAME	
2772	141 5/8	SALINE	91	66 6/8	70 4/8	15 4/8	1 7/8	22 1/8	22 5/8	4	6	KNOX	MIKE	SAME	
2772	141 5/8	STE. GENEIEVE	94	65 2/8	66 6/8	15 1/8	1 2/8	21 4/8	21 2/8	6	5	CLUKIES	PAUL A.	SAME	
2772	141 5/8	WRIGHT	95	67 4/8	73 7/8	13 3/8	0	24 3/8	23 0/8	5	6	THRONE	CURTIS	SAME	
2772	141 5/8	PETTIS	96	62 2/8	70 4/8	18 5/8	0	25 0/8	25 4/8	5	6	TYLAR	RICK	SAME	

MISSOURI SHOW-ME BIG BUCKS CLUB RECORDS OF WHITETAIL DEER BY STATE, TYPICAL

STATE RANK	SCORE	COUNTY	YEAR TAKEN	INCHES TYPICAL R	L	INSIDE SPREAD	INCHES ABNORMAL	LENGTH MAIN BEAM R	L	NUMBER POINTS R	L	HUNTER	FIRST NAME	OWNER	FIRST NAME
2772	141 5/8	DAVIESS	96	69 5/8	65 6/8	14 5/8	2 0/8	20 3/8	19 4/8	7	6	HULLINGER, JR.	LAWSON H.	SAME	
2772	141 5/8	CALDWELL	96	64 7/8	64 2/8	15 7/8	0	19 6/8	20 0/8	5	5	JONES	GAYLEN D.	SAME	
2787	141 4/8	CRAWFORD	45	66 2/8	70 1/8	18 2/8	8 4/8	20 2/8	21 3/8	7	6	LEA	WILLIAM L.	SAME	
2787	141 4/8	OREGON	71	62 3/8	61 6/8	19 2/8	0	21 2/8	21 2/8	5	5	PARROTT	WOODROW	SAME	
2787	141 4/8	FRANKLIN	77	62 3/8	66 1/8	23 2/8	6 2/8	22 0/8	24 5/8	6	5	RICHESON	JOHN O.	SAME	
2787	141 4/8	HENRY	81	67 5/8	63 4/8	15 6/8	0	23 3/8	21 3/8	5	5	SMART	BRAD	SAME	
2787	141 4/8	PULASKI	82	64 6/8	63 2/8	16 0/8	0	21 2/8	20 6/8	5	5	CHAPMAN	MATT	SAME	
2787	141 4/8	ST. CLAIR	83	63 0/8	62 7/8	17 2/8	0	23 3/8	23 2/8	5	5	HENDRICKS	STEVE	SAME	
2787	141 4/8	LAFAYETTE	85	62 7/8	64 0/8	16 6/8	0	24 5/8	24 6/8	4	4	KEY	MIKE	SAME	
2787	141 4/8	GASCONADE	86	63 2/8	61 0/8	21 0/8	0	25 4/8	24 4/8	4	4	APPRILL	KENNETH	SAME	
2787	141 4/8	GREENE	86	62 2/8	66 3/8	16 7/8	0	24 3/8	24 7/8	4	4	PULLEY	TOM	SAME	
2787	141 4/8	DENT	86	66 4/8	67 2/8	18 3/8	6 3/8	24 5/8	24 2/8	6	4	FISHER	ANDREW C.	SAME	
2787	141 4/8	CAPE GIRARDEAU	87	63 7/8	69 5/8	15 6/8	0	22 3/8	22 0/8	5	5	SLINKARD	THOMAS E.	SAME	
2787	141 4/8	SALINE	88	70 6/8	64 2/8	17 2/8	0	24 5/8	25 1/8	5	4	MALTER	TOM	SAME	
2787	141 4/8	IRON	88	61 7/8	66 1/8	19 4/8	0	24 1/8	23 5/8	5	5	TIEFENAUER	LARRY L.	SAME	
2787	141 4/8	SALINE	89	66 1/8	62 1/8	17 4/8	0	21 0/8	21 0/8	5	5	DRAFFEN	WILLIAM	SAME	
2787	141 4/8	PERRY	90	64 4/8	64 1/8	19 2/8	0	21 7/8	23 7/8	5	5	KIRN	NELSON E.	SAME	
2787	141 4/8	ST. CLAIR	90	61 6/8	62 5/8	20 3/8	0	22 6/8	23 4/8	5	5	WILLIAMSON	JIM	SAME	
2787	141 4/8	CASS	90	64 7/8	65 6/8	16 4/8	0	25 1/8	24 5/8	5	5	MOORE	SHERRI	SAME	
2787	141 4/8	GASCONADE	91	69 4/8	64 3/8	20 4/8	1 2/8	23 3/8	22 3/8	6	5	EPPLE	GLENNON	SAME	
2787	141 4/8	LAFAYETTE	91	66 5/8	62 3/8	17 4/8	0	21 5/8	20 0/8	5	5	LIMBACK	WILLIAM	SAME	
2787	141 4/8	SALINE	91	65 2/8	61 5/8	19 4/8	0	26 0/8	25 6/8	5	5	McMASTERS, JR.	JOHNNY	SAME	
2787	141 4/8	SALINE	92	64 3/8	67 4/8	16 2/8	0	22 0/8	22 3/8	4	5	KRUGER	DARRYL	SAME	
2787	141 4/8	BENTON	94	64 6/8	63 7/8	17 5/8	2 1/8	24 1/8	24 5/8	6	5	GERLT	LONNIE J.	SAME	
2787	141 4/8	MORGAN	94	63 0/8	62 7/8	18 4/8	0	22 7/8	22 7/8	5	5	WENIG	ROBERT D.	SAME	
2787	141 4/8	MARIES	95	62 3/8	64 5/8	17 6/8	0	20 0/8	21 4/8	5	5	BUSCHMANN	RICK	SAME	
2787	141 4/8	STE. GENEVIEVE	95	71 7/8	70 3/8	16 3/8	13 1/8	23 4/8	22 0/8	7	8	JOKERST	DAVID L.	SAME	
2812	141 3/8	JEFFERSON	54	68 6/8	62 4/8	18 3/8	0	25 3/8	25 7/8	4	4	HAYES	DONNELL E.	SAME	
2812	141 3/8	TANEY	76	63 2/8	63 0/8	16 5/8	0	23 2/8	22 7/8	4	4	HANNAH	RICK	SAME	
2812	141 3/8	SALINE	87	66 3/8	66 2/8	19 1/8	2 0/8	24 4/8	24 2/8	5	5	WISKUR	DOYLE	SAME	
2812	141 3/8	STE. GENEVIEVE	88	66 3/8	64 7/8	14 3/8	0	22 2/8	21 4/8	5	5	VINCENT	DAVID A.	SAME	
2812	141 3/8	COLE	88	64 0/8	66 4/8	19 5/8	2 2/8	21 6/8	21 4/8	6	6	DISTLER	DON	SAME	

MISSOURI SHOW-ME BIG BUCKS CLUB RECORDS OF WHITETAIL DEER BY STATE, TYPICAL

STATE RANK	SCORE	COUNTY	YEAR TAKEN	INCHES TYPICAL R	L	INSIDE SPREAD	INCHES ABNORMAL	LENGTH MAIN BEAM R	L	NUMBER POINTS R	L	HUNTER	FIRST NAME	OWNER	FIRST NAME
2812	141 3/8	PETTIS	89	61 7/8	63 5/8	18 7/8	0	22 1/8	23 2/8	5	5	WILLIAMS	RONNIE	SAME	
2812	141 3/8	LACLEDE	89	62 3/8	69 3/8	18 4/8	0	23 6/8	22 7/8	5	5	SULLIVAN	BRANDON	SAME	
2812	141 3/8	JACKSON	91	63 1/8	65 7/8	15 5/8	0	21 3/8	21 2/8	5	5	HOOD	WENDELL E.	SAME	
2812	141 3/8	PERRY	92	63 5/8	64 2/8	19 3/8	0	24 6/8	23 2/8	4	4	ROLLET	DAVID F.	SAME	
2812	141 3/8	ST. LOUIS	92	62 0/8	65 6/8	18 1/8	0	24 2/8	24 2/8	4	5	LEUTHAUSER	RONALD	SAME	
2812	141 3/8	PETTIS	92	66 4/8	68 0/8	14 1/8	4 4/8	22 3/8	23 4/8	7	6	LORENZ	TRAVIS G.	SAME	
2812	141 3/8	LACLEDE	93	63 2/8	63 5/8	16 7/8	0	24 1/8	23 6/8	4	4	PATTON	MARY	SAME	
2812	141 3/8	WASHINGTON	95	64 7/8	68 7/8	17 1/8	0	22 7/8	23 5/8	4	5	O'NEAL, JR.	JIMMY J.	SAME	
2812	141 3/8	VERNON	95	70 2/8	63 4/8	16 6/8	1 3/8	25 5/8	23 5/8	6	5	GRUENHAGEN	ARON	SAME	
2812	141 3/8	WAYNE	96	64 0/8	66 3/8	18 2/8	1 1/8	21 4/8	25 1/8	5	6	LOAFMAN	BYRON	SAME	
2812	141 3/8	KNOX	96	65 5/8	64 3/8	16 3/8	0	22 0/8	23 3/8	5	5	DAVIS	DONNIE L.	SAME	
2828	141 2/8	PHELPS	71	67 7/8	63 2/8	18 4/8	0	23 2/8	23 5/8	5	5	MYERS	NICK D.	SAME	
2828	141 2/8	OSAGE	72	69 5/8	71 7/8	15 3/8	5 7/8	22 5/8	24 3/8	6	7	KOENIGSFELD	ANDREW	SAME	
2828	141 2/8	GASCONADE	73	69 2/8	62 6/8	15 6/8	0	21 4/8	21 4/8	4	4	BINKHOLDER	MICHAEL	SAME	
2828	141 2/8	PULASKI	76	68 5/8	69 6/8	17 6/8	9 2/8	24 1/8	24 1/8	7	7	HUTTON	RANDALL	SAME	
2828	141 2/8	COOPER	78	63 7/8	60 5/8	20 4/8	0	24 3/8	23 0/8	4	4	JOHNSTON	RAY	SAME	
2828	141 2/8	SHELBY	81	68 0/8	64 3/8	14 3/8	1 3/8	20 7/8	21 0/8	6	5	McWILLIAMS	JAMIE	SAME	
2828	141 2/8	BENTON	82	63 7/8	62 3/8	18 2/8	0	22 6/8	21 6/8	5	5	JEFFRIES	CLINTON	SAME	
2828	141 2/8	CARTER	82	65 1/8	63 3/8	17 0/8	0	23 2/8	21 6/8	5	5	SONTHEIMER	MICHAEL C.	SAME	
2828	141 2/8	OSAGE	83	66 2/8	62 1/8	20 0/8	1 4/8	23 2/8	21 5/8	5	6	McFADDEN	RALPH	SAME	
2828	141 2/8	CARTER	83	63 6/8	63 5/8	17 0/8	0	20 6/8	22 0/8	5	5	LAYTON	JEFF	SAME	
2828	141 2/8	COLE	87	66 0/8	66 3/8	17 4/8	1 0/8	21 4/8	22 4/8	6	5	BINKLEY	BILL	SAME	
2828	141 2/8	BARTON	87	67 5/8	65 7/8	17 3/8	3 1/8	22 2/8	21 1/8	8	7	LAFON	WAYNE	SAME	
2828	141 2/8	WAYNE	89	65 4/8	65 0/8	15 0/8	0	25 1/8	24 5/8	5	4	DENKINS	BILL	SAME	
2828	141 2/8	CRAWFORD	90	65 6/8	72 6/8	16 3/8	3 5/8	21 2/8	22 3/8	6	7	SAMMELMAN	MIKE	SAME	
2828	141 2/8	CARTER	92	64 6/8	64 0/8	15 2/8	0	22 2/8	22 0/8	5	5	BENEDICK	BOB	SAME	
2828	141 2/8	BENTON	95	62 3/8	66 1/8	17 4/8	0	23 1/8	23 7/8	5	5	HADDOCK	SAM	SAME	
2844	141 1/8	CAMDEN	66	62 6/8	63 1/8	17 3/8	0	23 3/8	23 7/8	5	5	GROVES	DAVID	SAME	
2844	141 1/8	MADISON	67	65 1/8	66 1/8	18 7/8	0	25 1/8	24 0/8	4	4	HENSON	IRA	SAME	
2844	141 1/8	CEDAR	67	65 7/8	67 2/8	16 5/8	3 0/8	21 6/8	21 3/8	5	6	ROY	ROBERT L.	SAME	
2844	141 1/8	COOPER	72	64 7/8	68 3/8	16 6/8	1 1/8	26 0/8	24 6/8	6	5	FISHER	CLAUDE	FISHER	HUTH
2844	141 1/8	McDONALD	73	74 4/8	72 7/8	13 7/8	10 2/8	22 0/8	23 0/8	9	8	RING	GERALD	SAME	

MISSOURI SHOW-ME BIG BUCKS CLUB RECORDS OF WHITETAIL DEER BY STATE, TYPICAL

STATE RANK	SCORE	COUNTY	YEAR TAKEN	INCHES TYPICAL R	L	INSIDE SPREAD	INCHES ABNORMAL	LENGTH MAIN BEAM R	L	NUMBER POINTS R	L	HUNTER	FIRST NAME	OWNER	FIRST NAME
2844	141 1/8	CAPE GIRARDEAU	78	66 5/8	66 6/8	18 7/8	0	21 4/8	22 0/8	6	6	ZIEGLER	JEROME	SAME	
2844	141 1/8	CRAWFORD	82	64 3/8	63 1/8	17 5/8	0	22 0/8	22 2/8	5	5	JEPSEN	PAUL	SAME	
2844	141 1/8	MILLER	82	69 3/8	69 5/8	19 6/8	6 5/8	23 0/8	23 2/8	6	7	SCHINSA	MICHAEL	SAME	
2844	141 1/8	MORGAN	83	65 6/8	63 6/8	16 7/8	2 6/8	21 1/8	21 1/8	5	6	SCHRECK	LARRY	SAME	
2844	141 1/8	SALINE	85	66 3/8	70 0/8	16 6/8	3 2/8	21 3/8	21 3/8	6	6	ADCOCK	WAYNE	SAME	
2844	141 1/8	STODDARD	86	66 2/8	64 3/8	16 3/8	1 2/8	22 5/8	22 1/8	6	5	HARDIN	RICK	SAME	
2844	141 1/8	MONITEAU	86	61 5/8	63 2/8	19 7/8	0	23 4/8	23 4/8	4	4	YORK	WAYNE	SAME	
2844	141 1/8	CHRISTIAN	87	63 3/8	64 3/8	19 3/8	2 2/8	21 5/8	22 1/8	5	7	KUENZ	STEVE	SAME	
2844	141 1/8	CAMDEN	87	64 5/8	72 7/8	17 3/8	5 3/8	24 2/8	24 6/8	5	6	PATTON	TOMMY	SAME	
2844	141 1/8	LACLEDE	88	66 2/8	65 1/8	18 3/8	2 0/8	24 1/8	22 0/8	6	5	MASSEY	DENNIS	SAME	
2844	141 1/8	SALINE	89	62 5/8	63 4/8	17 2/8	0	25 0/8	26 2/8	4	4	HARE	PHIL	SAME	
2844	141 1/8	COOPER	89	67 3/8	68 1/8	19 2/8	8 5/8	21 4/8	22 2/8	6	7	THURMAN	TROY	SAME	
2844	141 1/8	MONITEAU	92	64 6/8	67 2/8	16 3/8	1 4/8	19 7/8	20 5/8	5	6	HEES	DAVID	SAME	
2844	141 1/8	PETTIS	96	65 1/8	63 1/8	20 3/8	1 2/8	23 3/8	24 1/8	5	5	WHITLOW	JOSEPH E.	SAME	
2863	141 0/8	HICKORY	66	63 1/8	65 3/8	18 1/8	3 3/8	22 3/8	23 0/8	4	6	MOORE	LAWSON P.	SAME	
2863	141 0/8	OSAGE	68	67 7/8	67 0/8	17 0/8	9 0/8	21 6/8	22 0/8	6	6	SANDBOTHE	EDWARD	SAME	
2863	141 0/8	OREGON	70	69 2/8	66 1/8	16 7/8	4 7/8	22 5/8	22 5/8	6	6	MILLER	WILLIAM M.	SAME	
2863	141 0/8	FRANKLIN	74	63 5/8	65 7/8	20 1/8	0	25 6/8	24 4/8	6	5	STACK	DOYLE	SAME	
2863	141 0/8	MARIES	79	67 2/8	65 0/8	17 6/8	0	23 6/8	24 4/8	5	5	WILSON	BOB J.	SAME	
2863	141 0/8	ST. LOUIS	82	69 6/8	67 7/8	16 2/8	5 6/8	22 2/8	20 6/8	8	7	WILES	JACK	SAME	
2863	141 0/8	GASCONADE	82	65 4/8	67 4/8	16 1/8	6 1/8	21 4/8	22 2/8	7	6	GORMAN	BRAD	SAME	
2863	141 0/8	VERNON	84	60 4/8	64 5/8	22 0/8	0	25 0/8	24 0/8	4	4	MORLAN	ED	SAME	
2863	141 0/8	FRANKLIN	85	62 6/8	65 2/8	19 0/8	0	24 1/8	25 1/8	4	4	NULL	KURT A.	SAME	
2863	141 0/8	STODDARD	87	62 5/8	62 6/8	18 2/8	0	23 0/8	23 1/8	5	5	PAGE	GAVIN	SAME	
2863	141 0/8	CAPE GIRARDEAU	87	62 5/8	65 6/8	17 0/8	1 0/8	21 4/8	21 0/8	5	6	SLINKARD	RICHARD	SAME	
2863	141 0/8	SALINE	93	66 7/8	62 6/8	17 6/8	1 2/8	20 3/8	20 3/8	7	5	McGUIRE	RICK	SAME	
2863	141 0/8	MORGAN	93	62 5/8	64 5/8	18 6/8	0	23 5/8	22 4/8	5	5	NOLTING	RONNIE	EDGAR	TRENT P.
2863	141 0/8	COOPER	95	69 0/8	66 6/8	18 0/8	5 3/8	26 0/8	26 0/8	4	6	LOESING	MARK	SAME	
2877	140 7/8	OSAGE	67	68 4/8	67 4/8	16 5/8	5 7/8	23 3/8	22 4/8	9	7	DICKNEITE	DENNIS	SAME	
2877	140 7/8	MARIES	72	65 1/8	65 5/8	15 7/8	0	24 7/8	24 0/8	5	5	CORDSMEYER, JR.	ELMER	SAME	
2877	140 7/8	DENT	73	73 3/8	67 2/8	15 6/8	9 3/8	25 3/8	24 6/8	7	6	JONES	BUFORD	SAME	
2877	140 7/8	WAYNE	78	63 1/8	65 2/8	15 3/8	0	21 3/8	22 1/8	5	5	NEAL	JERRY	SAME	

MISSOURI SHOW-ME BIG BUCKS CLUB RECORDS OF WHITETAIL DEER BY STATE, TYPICAL

STATE RANK	SCORE	COUNTY	YEAR TAKEN	INCHES TYPICAL R	INCHES TYPICAL L	INSIDE SPREAD	INCHES ABNORMAL	LENGTH MAIN BEAM R	LENGTH MAIN BEAM L	NUMBER POINTS R	NUMBER POINTS L	HUNTER	FIRST NAME	OWNER	FIRST NAME
2877	140 7/8	COLE	78	65 4/8	69 0/8	16 7/8	0	22 2/8	21 0/8	4	5	HEMMEL	CHARLES	SAME	
2877	140 7/8	FRANKLIN	79	65 6/8	74 0/8	17 7/8	4 4/8	24 4/8	22 4/8	6	5	STRAATMAN	AL J.	SAME	
2877	140 7/8	BENTON	82	63 3/8	62 5/8	17 1/8	0	22 6/8	21 3/8	5	5	VAUGHAN	ROBERT	SAME	
2877	140 7/8	ST. LOUIS	82	68 4/8	64 6/8	19 7/8	0	22 0/8	21 7/8	6	5	REPP	JACK	SAME	
2877	140 7/8	COOPER	83	66 0/8	66 7/8	15 3/8	1 4/8	21 7/8	21 5/8	5	6	JOBE	BRIAN	SAME	
2877	140 7/8	NEWTON	83	62 5/8	66 3/8	20 1/8	3 6/8	24 2/8	24 1/8	6	5	GARCIA	JEFF	SAME	
2877	140 7/8	WASHINGTON	84	66 0/8	69 4/8	14 4/8	4 1/8	21 3/8	21 2/8	6	6	WILLIAMS	JOHN	SAME	
2877	140 7/8	MARIES	87	63 5/8	63 6/8	17 5/8	0	23 7/8	22 7/8	4	4	GEMMING	DON	SAME	
2877	140 7/8	GENTRY	87	63 1/8	64 7/8	16 0/8	1 1/8	23 4/8	23 7/8	5	4	RODERIQUE	CAROL	SAME	
2877	140 7/8	SALINE	88	63 6/8	65 4/8	17 2/8	2 5/8	23 4/8	23 1/8	4	5	MASTERS	NORMAN	SAME	
2877	140 7/8	SULLIVAN	93	61 5/8	75 2/8	17 5/8	0	24 7/8	25 2/8	4	6	SCHOONOVER	TOM	SAME	
2877	140 7/8	OSAGE	94	65 5/8	70 1/8	15 7/8	0	23 2/8	22 1/8	4	5	DIAL	KEITH	SAME	
2877	140 7/8	LAFAYETTE	95	73 4/8	63 4/8	19 3/8	3 0/8	25 0/8	23 1/8	7	4	WILLIAMS	CHARLES	SAME	
2877	140 7/8	PUTNAM	96	60 7/8	64 6/8	19 1/8	0	22 4/8	23 1/8	4	5	MARVIN	WADE	SAME	
2895	140 6/8	ST. LOUIS	61	66 0/8	63 3/8	18 4/8	2 6/8	21 0/8	21 2/8	6	7	ZERWIG	RAYMOND	SAME	
2895	140 6/8	HENRY	65	65 3/8	63 3/8	17 0/8	0	25 1/8	24 4/8	5	4	TIRMAN	JERRY	REYNOLDS	JERRY
2895	140 6/8	MADISON	68	62 6/8	63 4/8	21 6/8	0	25 1/8	25 1/8	4	4	REICHERT	GEORGE	SAME	
2895	140 6/8	FRANKLIN	83	61 1/8	65 4/8	19 6/8	0	23 4/8	25 3/8	5	4	LAWRENCE	MIKE	SAME	
2895	140 6/8	GREENE	83	64 7/8	67 7/8	20 3/8	8 3/8	24 2/8	24 0/8	9	8	BRAY	BRETT	SAME	
2895	140 6/8	PUTNAM	84	61 1/8	61 7/8	17 4/8	2 0/8	24 5/8	25 3/8	5	4	REAM	JOE	SAME	
2895	140 6/8	PERRY	85	64 5/8	64 5/8	15 4/8	0	19 7/8	19 4/8	4	5	STEFFENS	RANDALL R.	SAME	
2895	140 6/8	PUTNAM	86	63 6/8	65 7/8	19 0/8	0	23 4/8	22 1/8	5	5	TORREY	MELODY	SAME	
2895	140 6/8	BARTON	88	64 3/8	63 1/8	16 2/8	0	21 6/8	22 2/8	6	5	FRIEDEN	KURT	SAME	
2895	140 6/8	DENT	88	62 2/8	64 3/8	17 4/8	0	23 4/8	24 0/8	4	4	CAMDEN	RANDY	SAME	
2895	140 6/8	TEXAS	90	62 5/8	65 0/8	18 4/8	0	24 7/8	23 4/8	5	5	VOGELIE	MICHAEL A.	SAME	
2895	140 6/8	KNOX	95	63 5/8	76 7/8	16 4/8	0	23 3/8	23 3/8	4	5	STRANGE	KEVIN	SAME	
2895	140 6/8	CAPE GIRARDEAU	95	60 7/8	61 6/8	19 6/8	0	23 2/8	23 3/8	4	4	REED	ROBERT	SAME	
2908	140 5/8	FRANKLIN	64	64 1/8	67 3/8	18 1/8	5 4/8	23 4/8	23 6/8	6	7	DIAZ	DENNIS	SAME	
2908	140 5/8	NEWTON	68	66 3/8	65 6/8	16 2/8	3 3/8	22 1/8	21 4/8	5	5	LOPRESTI	ANTHONY F.	SAME	
2908	140 5/8	IRON	73	63 6/8	63 7/8	15 1/8	0	20 0/8	19 2/8	5	5	WEADON, JR.	JOE	SAME	
2908	140 5/8	SCOTLAND	73	63 1/8	68 1/8	16 7/8	0	24 5/8	24 3/8	4	5	DAVIS	DARL	SAME	
2908	140 5/8	SALINE	79	66 6/8	61 2/8	18 5/8	0	24 1/8	24 0/8	5	4	TYRE	JIMMIE D.	SAME	

MISSOURI SHOW-ME BIG BUCKS CLUB RECORDS OF WHITETAIL DEER BY STATE, TYPICAL

STATE RANK	SCORE	COUNTY	YEAR TAKEN	INCHES TYPICAL R	L	INSIDE SPREAD	INCHES ABNORMAL	LENGTH MAIN BEAM R	L	NUMBER POINTS R	L	HUNTER	FIRST NAME	OWNER	FIRST NAME
2908	140 5/8	FRANKLIN	83	70 0/8	67 7/8	20 6/8	11 3/8	23 0/8	22 6/8	9	7	CUNNINGHAM	ROBERT W.	SAME	
2908	140 5/8	MONITEAU	84	63 3/8	65 5/8	16 7/8	0	25 2/8	23 6/8	4	4	JONES	GARY	SAME	
2908	140 5/8	HICKORY	85	64 6/8	63 0/8	16 1/8	0	21 6/8	21 1/8	5	5	THOMPSON	FLOYD	SAME	
2908	140 5/8	BATES	85	62 2/8	65 4/8	16 7/8	0	24 2/8	24 0/8	4	4	GOLLADAY	JOHN D.	SAME	
2908	140 5/8	CAPE GIRARDEAU	90	62 4/8	64 2/8	16 3/8	0	23 0/8	23 1/8	5	5	NOLAN	LAURA J.	SAME	
2908	140 5/8	OSAGE	91	74 4/8	69 6/8	19 4/8	5 3/8	23 3/8	23 5/8	6	7	STROPE	MICHAEL R.	SAME	
2908	140 5/8	LINN	94	66 0/8	61 7/8	17 1/8	0	23 3/8	23 1/8	5	5	KOENIGSFELD	RAY	SAME	
2908	140 5/8	NEW MADRID	95	61 4/8	63 0/8	18 7/8	0	25 3/8	25 1/8	4	4	GLAUS	BILL R.	SAME	
2908	140 5/8	ST. CLAIR	95	68 7/8	65 3/8	14 1/8	3 4/8	23 7/8	22 0/8	7	5	SMITH	RANDY	SAME	
2908	140 5/8	MARIES	95	61 2/8	62 6/8	21 5/8	0	23 0/8	22 7/8	5	5	YOUNG	JOHNNIE	SAME	
2908	140 5/8	CRAWFORD	96	63 4/8	65 0/8	15 4/8	0	23 2/8	23 3/8	4	4	HOPWOOD, JR.	EUGENE F.	SAME	
2908	140 5/8	OREGON	96	64 0/8	64 0/8	16 5/8	0	22 1/8	22 4/8	5	5	McFANN	JERRY S.	SAME	
2925	140 4/8	BOLLINGER	65	65 5/8	61 7/8	19 4/8	0	19 6/8	21 0/8	5	5	VANDEVAN	KEN	SAME	
2925	140 4/8	VERNON	82	67 2/8	64 1/8	16 0/8	0	22 2/8	22 4/8	5	5	NELANDER	ED	SAME	
2925	140 4/8	MORGAN	82	68 0/8	63 7/8	16 1/8	2 1/8	22 2/8	22 3/8	6	5	THEISEN	DAVID	SAME	
2925	140 4/8	CRAWFORD	82	60 4/8	62 4/8	20 2/8	0	24 1/8	23 7/8	5	5	SAPPINGTON	COLIN	SAME	
2925	140 4/8	DENT	85	62 6/8	65 5/8	15 3/8	0	21 7/8	22 4/8	5	5	CARTY	LARRY	SAME	
2925	140 4/8	GASCONADE	90	64 0/8	62 3/8	16 6/8	0	23 1/8	21 5/8	4	4	WEHMEYER	RUSSELL	SAME	
2925	140 4/8	CARTER	91	62 7/8	64 0/8	17 0/8	0	21 3/8	20 5/8	5	5	YANCEY	JAMES	SAME	
2925	140 4/8	PULASKI	92	62 0/8	65 1/8	17 4/8	0	21 5/8	22 7/8	4	4	WIGLEY	MARVIN T.	SAME	
2925	140 4/8	SALINE	92	62 7/8	61 7/8	18 0/8	0	21 6/8	22 0/8	4	4	SMITH	LUCAS	SAME	
2925	140 4/8	SCOTT	96	62 5/8	61 3/8	23 0/8	0	24 1/8	23 0/8	4	4	SMITH	KEVIN	SAME	
2935	140 3/8	GASCONADE	45	67 2/8	62 5/8	18 4/8	2 5/8	23 3/8	23 0/8	6	6	QUICK	OREL R.	SAME	
2935	140 3/8	CRAWFORD	57	64 5/8	65 5/8	15 1/8	2 0/8	22 5/8	23 4/8	6	5	BRUCE	EDMON S.	SAME	
2935	140 3/8	TEXAS	69	66 3/8	65 7/8	15 6/8	3 7/8	24 7/8	23 4/8	6	6	DOUGLAS	DAVID	SAME	
2935	140 3/8	HOWELL	73	63 1/8	69 7/8	16 3/8	1 6/8	23 4/8	23 6/8	5	5	EMERICK	W.R.	SAME	
2935	140 3/8	COOPER	75	64 4/8	61 4/8	17 5/8	0	23 3/8	22 5/8	5	5	STEGNER	JOHN	SAME	
2935	140 3/8	STE. GENEIEVE	79	63 0/8	63 7/8	16 5/8	0	22 2/8	23 0/8	5	5	MENGE	DAVID	SAME	
2935	140 3/8	WRIGHT	79	63 3/8	67 1/8	14 7/8	0	21 2/8	21 4/8	5	5	WERKMEISTER	GENE	SAME	
2935	140 3/8	CRAWFORD	81	63 4/8	67 1/8	16 7/8	3 0/8	20 2/8	21 2/8	7	5	SLONE	MIKE	SAME	
2935	140 3/8	LACLEDE	82	61 6/8	65 7/8	16 7/8	0	19 7/8	20 3/8	5	5	HILTON	MATT	SAME	
2935	140 3/8	COOPER	83	63 1/8	65 6/8	15 5/8	0	21 3/8	21 0/8	5	5	IMHOFF	MIKE	SAME	

MISSOURI SHOW-ME BIG BUCKS CLUB RECORDS OF WHITETAIL DEER BY STATE, TYPICAL

STATE RANK	SCORE	COUNTY	YEAR TAKEN	INCHES TYPICAL R	L	INSIDE SPREAD	INCHES ABNORMAL	LENGTH MAIN BEAM R	L	NUMBER POINTS R	L	HUNTER	FIRST NAME	OWNER	FIRST NAME
2935	140 3/8	HENRY	87	64 2/8	65 7/8	15 5/8	1 2/8	22 0/8	22 7/8	5	6	KEDIGH	BILL	SAME	
2935	140 3/8	COOPER	87	65 1/8	69 0/8	19 1/8	0	27 4/8	24 6/8	4	4	HUMFELD	BILL	SAME	
2935	140 3/8	HICKORY	88	63 1/8	70 1/8	17 6/8	1 7/8	23 2/8	24 0/8	4	6	TAYLOR	GENE R.	SAME	
2935	140 3/8	OREGON	89	67 0/8	69 1/8	15 5/8	4 2/8	24 7/8	22 6/8	7	6	COLLICOTT	BILL	SAME	
2935	140 3/8	SHANNON	89	61 2/8	61 4/8	20 6/8	0	24 0/8	24 0/8	4	4	LINDSEY	ROGER	SAME	
2935	140 3/8	GASCONADE	92	68 7/8	70 7/8	18 5/8	11 2/8	25 6/8	26 2/8	5	6	NAGLE	DOUGLAS	SAME	
2935	140 3/8	BENTON	96	66 2/8	63 2/8	19 4/8	2 7/8	23 1/8	23 5/8	5	5	GILES	BRIAN	SAME	
2935	140 3/8	MADISON	64	64 4/8	61 2/8	19 2/8	0	22 5/8	23 0/8	5	4	WHITE	FRED	SAME	
2952	140 2/8	MORGAN	69	66 4/8	64 2/8	14 6/8	1 2/8	19 0/8	19 0/8	5	6	HICKSON	JACK	SAME	
2952	140 2/8	MARIES	75	63 3/8	62 6/8	16 0/8	0	22 5/8	22 2/8	4	4	ROWE	DALE	SAME	
2952	140 2/8	GASCONADE	78	66 3/8	65 3/8	15 4/8	4 0/8	17 4/8	17 4/8	5	5	SCHNEIDER	DONNA	SAME	
2952	140 2/8	PULASKI	80	64 0/8	67 5/8	15 6/8	0	22 3/8	23 0/8	4	5	CORE	ANDY O.	SAME	
2952	140 2/8	TANEY	80	62 2/8	67 6/8	17 5/8	2 3/8	19 2/8	21 2/8	5	6	MCMAHON	JUNIOR	SAME	
2952	140 2/8	JACKSON	83	64 5/8	65 0/8	14 4/8	0	22 6/8	23 2/8	4	4	LANGENSAND	WAYNE C.	SAME	
2952	140 2/8	PHELPS	85	61 3/8	69 1/8	19 7/8	1 1/8	22 0/8	23 2/8	5	6	BARKS	TIM	SAME	
2952	140 2/8	BOLLINGER	85	63 2/8	63 2/8	19 0/8	0	25 4/8	25 1/8	5	4	PROVAZNIK	MICHAEL JOHN	SAME	
2952	140 2/8	BENTON	87	69 3/8	70 3/8	18 0/8	9 2/8	22 0/8	23 3/8	6	7	GRAVES, JR.	STEVE	SAME	
2952	140 2/8	COLE	88	65 5/8	62 7/8	17 0/8	0	26 2/8	24 7/8	4	4	OTT	PAUL G.	SAME	
2952	140 2/8	LACLEDE	88	59 3/8	59 3/8	22 4/8	2 0/8	23 1/8	23 1/8	4	4	MCCORMICK	BRANDON	SAME	
2952	140 2/8	JACKSON	89	65 7/8	64 7/8	14 4/8	0	21 0/8	20 3/8	6	5	TERRY	BOB	SAME	
2952	140 2/8	PETTIS	89	68 5/8	62 2/8	17 4/8	1 6/8	24 1/8	24 0/8	5	5	GATSCHET	MIKE	SAME	
2952	140 2/8	DOUGLAS	91	62 5/8	61 7/8	18 2/8	0	23 5/8	23 4/8	4	4	JOHNSTON	CHARLIE	SAME	
2952	140 2/8	PETTIS	91	64 3/8	65 1/8	15 2/8	1 2/8	21 2/8	20 6/8	6	6	VAUGHAN	HAROLD	SAME	
2952	140 2/8	CARTER	92	67 6/8	64 3/8	20 6/8	8 0/8	23 1/8	22 6/8	7	6	BOTKIN	DALE	SAME	
2952	140 2/8	COOPER	92	68 3/8	64 0/8	15 1/8	1 5/8	23 1/8	21 7/8	5	6	VOSS	ALLEN A.	SAME	
2952	140 2/8	SALINE	93	64 6/8	70 0/8	15 2/8	2 0/8	21 2/8	21 2/8	5	6	JOHNSON	LEON	SAME	
2952	140 2/8	SALINE	93	65 0/8	63 2/8	17 0/8	0	24 0/8	22 0/8	5	5	CROKA	ALVIN	SAME	
2952	140 2/8	POLK	95	66 1/8	62 5/8	15 2/8	0	23 6/8	23 3/8	5	5	EIGSTI	WILLIS	SAME	
2952	140 2/8	PUTNAM	95	63 1/8	61 4/8	20 0/8	0	25 0/8	23 4/8	5	5	GADBERRY	RONNIE	SAME	
2952	140 2/8	HOWARD	95	67 2/8	64 4/8	15 2/8	0	22 4/8	21 6/8	5	5	SUNDERLAND	HARDIN	SAME	
2952	140 2/8	WEBSTER	95	68 4/8	63 3/8	19 2/8	4 0/8	24 5/8	22 6/8	6	7	BIGLEY	JIMMIE L.	SAME	
2952	140 2/8	MARION	95	65 5/8	62 4/8	17 0/8	0	22 4/8	21 6/8	5	5	DAVID	LARRY	SAME	

MISSOURI SHOW-ME BIG BUCKS CLUB RECORDS OF WHITETAIL DEER BY STATE, TYPICAL

STATE RANK	SCORE	COUNTY	YEAR TAKEN	INCHES TYPICAL R	L	INSIDE SPREAD	INCHES ABNORMAL	LENGTH MAIN BEAM R	L	NUMBER POINTS R	L	HUNTER	FIRST NAME	OWNER	STATE FIRST NAME
2952	140 2/8	PERRY	96	61 7/8	63 5/8	18 4/8	0	22 6/8	22 1/8	4	4	PETZOLDT	TOMMY	SAME	
2978	140 1/8	RIPLEY	73	65 5/8	63 1/8	17 5/8	0	21 4/8	21 6/8	6	5	CLAYTON	GILLIE	SAME	
2978	140 1/8	WRIGHT	76	62 3/8	66 3/8	20 6/8	3 7/8	21 0/8	22 2/8	5	5	MARTIN	DON	SAME	
2978	140 1/8	MADISON	79	65 0/8	64 7/8	15 3/8	0	23 5/8	24 7/8	5	5	BOYD	JIM	SAME	
2978	140 1/8	PHELPS	83	61 6/8	63 5/8	17 1/8	0	21 6/8	21 7/8	5	5	SPURGEON	JOHN	SAME	
2978	140 1/8	OZARK	86	65 2/8	65 0/8	16 7/8	0	22 0/8	24 7/8	5	5	COLE	GARY L.	SAME	
2978	140 1/8	SALINE	86	64 3/8	65 7/8	17 0/8	3 7/8	21 7/8	22 3/8	6	5	DAVIS	JERRY	SAME	
2978	140 1/8	FRANKLIN	88	63 3/8	67 3/8	14 6/8	0	22 2/8	22 0/8	6	6	LASCHKE	JOSEPH E.	SAME	
2978	140 1/8	STODDARD	90	63 4/8	64 2/8	15 7/8	0	22 5/8	22 3/8	5	5	WRIGHT	JOHN M.	SAME	
2978	140 1/8	COOPER	90	65 1/8	66 0/8	17 6/8	4 5/8	24 0/8	24 0/8	5	8	YOUNG	KENNY	SAME	
2978	140 1/8	PULASKI	94	62 5/8	61 6/8	18 3/8	0	23 6/8	23 2/8	4	4	THILTGEN	EUGENE	SAME	
2978	140 1/8	PETTIS	95	66 0/8	63 3/8	15 5/8	0	21 7/8	20 4/8	5	5	FISHER	ERIC	SAME	
2978	140 1/8	HENRY	96	65 4/8	61 3/8	19 1/8	1 0/8	22 6/8	23 1/8	5	6	SANDERS	JACKSON D.	SAME	
2978	140 0/8	PULASKI	68	61 2/8	62 2/8	19 3/8	1 1/8	22 4/8	22 6/8	6	5	HEISSERER	FRANK L.	SAME	
2990	140 0/8	OZARK	70	66 5/8	63 5/8	15 3/8	0	24 0/8	25 2/8	5	5	SKAGGS	DON	SAME	
2990	140 0/8	McDONALD	73	66 2/8	62 4/8	16 2/8	0	22 2/8	22 7/8	5	5	BUSH	DR. S.S.	SAME	
2990	140 0/8	GASCONADE	73	66 6/8	66 5/8	17 0/8	4 2/8	24 0/8	23 1/8	7	6	WACKER	JAMES	SAME	
2990	140 0/8	COLE	77	63 7/8	66 0/8	15 2/8	0	22 5/8	22 0/8	6	6	WIEBERG	HENRY	SAME	
2990	140 0/8	GASCONADE	79	70 2/8	71 6/8	19 2/8	8 6/8	23 6/8	23 6/8	5	5	WITTE	LESLIE	SAME	
2990	140 0/8	GASCONADE	79	62 0/8	61 5/8	19 4/8	0	22 4/8	22 4/8	4	4	WATSON	STEVE	SAME	
2990	140 0/8	JACKSON	80	65 0/8	62 6/8	15 0/8	0	23 3/8	22 3/8	5	5	THOMEY	MARVIN	SAME	
2990	140 0/8	BENTON	83	64 6/8	63 0/8	15 6/8	0	20 7/8	21 5/8	5	5	KOLL	RICK	SAME	
2990	140 0/8	HICKORY	87	64 7/8	64 7/8	14 2/8	1 2/8	20 4/8	20 6/8	6	5	GILLOTTE	MICHAEL	SAME	
2990	140 0/8	CAPE GIRARDEAU	89	65 5/8	63 6/8	15 0/8	0	22 1/8	22 0/8	5	5	GRASS	NORMAN	SAME	
2990	140 0/8	WAYNE	89	62 7/8	61 7/8	18 5/8	1 1/8	22 6/8	22 5/8	5	6	LEMMON	JODY	SAME	
2990	140 0/8	CHARITON	89	69 2/8	67 5/8	16 5/8	9 1/8	24 5/8	25 2/8	5	5	RODGERS	BILL	SAME	
2990	140 0/8	CAMDEN	90	65 7/8	71 4/8	18 4/8	4 2/8	18 3/8	23 3/8	5	7	BROWN	PAUL	SAME	
2990	140 0/8	COLE	91	64 1/8	71 1/8	16 7/8	4 5/8	23 3/8	23 5/8	5	6	PLANK	JIM	SAME	
2990	140 0/8	MADISON	92	62 2/8	64 1/8	16 4/8	0	25 0/8	25 0/8	4	4	LOWERY	GREG	SAME	
2990	140 0/8	ST. CLAIR	92	64 0/8	59 7/8	20 2/8	0	26 1/8	24 2/8	4	4	HARPER	WILFORD N.	SAME	
2990	140 0/8	MONITEAU	93	67 0/8	61 6/8	16 6/8	0	23 5/8	23 1/8	5	4	WOLFE	DANNY	SAME	
2990	140 0/8	BOONE	93	67 2/8	64 6/8	18 6/8	6 3/8	23 0/8	22 6/8	8	7	THORNHILL	CURTIS	SAME	

STATE RANK	SCORE	COUNTY	YEAR TAKEN	INCHES TYPICAL R	L	INSIDE SPREAD	INCHES ABNORMAL	LENGTH MAIN BEAM R	L	NUMBER POINTS R	L	HUNTER	FIRST NAME	OWNER	FIRST NAME
2990	140 0/8	LACLEDE	95	64 3/8	64 2/8	15 4/8	0	22 7/8	22 6/8	5	5	MIZER	TIM W.	SAME	
2990	140 0/8	JOHNSON	95	62 3/8	65 3/8	15 2/8	0	22 5/8	22 7/8	4	4	WRIGHT	MELFORD L.	SAME	
2990	140 0/8	CAMDEN	96	66 0/8	65 7/8	15 6/8	0	24 1/8	24 3/8	5	5	HEISLEN	CORY	SAME	
2990	140 0/8	SULLIVAN	96	65 3/8	64 3/8	17 0/8	0	22 5/8	20 4/8	5	5	SHOOP	MARCUS	SAME	

330

MISSOURI SHOW-ME BIG BUCKS CLUB RECORDS OF WHITETAIL DEER BY STATE, NON-TYP

STATE RANK	SCORE	COUNTY	YEAR TAKEN	INCHES TYPICAL R	L	INSIDE SPREAD	INCHES ABNORMAL	LENGTH MAIN BEAM R	L	NUMBER POINTS R	L	HUNTER	FIRST NAME	OWNER	STATE FIRST NAME
1	333 7/8	ST. LOUIS	81	66 2/8	66 3/8	23 3/8	184 0/8	24 1/8	23 3/8	19	25	BECKMAN	HELLAND	MISSOURI MDC	
2	259 5/8	CHARITON	85	91 2/8	96 6/8	20 3/8	58 4/8	26 7/8	26 7/8	14	13	LINSCOTT	DUANE R.	AMER.NAT.MUSEUM	FISH & WILDLIFE
3	259 1/8	JACKSON	96	78 5/8	76 3/8	14 0/8	97 3/8	25 0/8	24 7/8	20	15	LOVEKAMP	TERRY L.	LOVEKAMP	TERRY L.
4	233 1/8	NODAWAY	92	82 5/8	86 0/8	19 5/8	60 0/8	24 4/8	25 3/8	15	12	BARCUS	KEN	SAME	
5	228 2/8	SULLIVAN	92	70 1/8	63 5/8	18 3/8	88 1/8	24 2/8	23 1/8	10	16	HUGHES	BRIAN W.	SAME	
6	226 0/8	MORGAN	62	71 0/8	77 7/8	20 4/8	65 6/8	28 1/8	27 0/8	17	17	SOUSLEY	ART	SAME	
7	225 5/8	LACLEDE	90	82 5/8	83 1/8	16 4/8	49 5/8	25 3/8	25 4/8	11	14	LUTHY	SCOTT	SAME	
8	223 7/8	WARREN	59	83 5/8	84 2/8	21 1/8	38 6/8	24 5/8	25 1/8	13	12	WILLIAMS	JAMES	SAME	
9	223 4/8	CLARK	67	53 2/8	57 4/8	20 2/8	99 6/8	20 3/8	19 5/8	11	15	PRIEBE	EVELYN	LOVEKAMP	TERRY L.
10	223 2/8	ATCHISON	83	85 0/8	85 6/8	24 1/8	42 3/8	26 2/8	28 1/8	11	11	SUTTER	JERRY	SAME	
11	221 4/8	PIKE	91	87 0/8	89 1/8	20 3/8	27 7/8	27 4/8	27 5/8	10	12	SCHANKS	BILLY J.	SAME	
12	219 7/8	MONITEAU	83	76 0/8	78 3/8	21 2/8	50 3/8	25 7/8	26 6/8	18	13	STOKES	BARNEY	SAME	
13	218 6/8	LINCOLN	62	81 5/8	82 2/8	19 7/8	42 0/8	26 0/8	25 1/8	12	9	GUTERMUTH	SYLVESTER	SAME	
14	218 5/8	CHARITON	79	83 1/8	82 7/8	18 4/8	36 7/8	26 2/8	25 6/8	9	11	McSPARREN	STAN	SAME	
15	217 7/8	MARIES	74	93 1/8	87 1/8	21 3/8	30 0/8	27 7/8	28 2/8	10	16	DAKE	GERALD	SAME	
16	217 0/8	LINCOLN	91	84 3/8	77 6/8	19 0/8	50 0/8	27 4/8	25 6/8	11	11	MITTS	PAT D.	SAME	
17	216 6/8	CLAY	91	88 2/8	83 0/8	18 2/8	32 6/8	30 1/8	29 3/8	14	13	THOMEY	MARVIN	SAME	
18	215 5/8	WORTH	74	92 7/8	87 7/8	20 2/8	21 1/8	28 0/8	28 0/8	10	9	MILLER & NONNENAN	BURTON & REGAN	SAME	
19	214 3/8	CLAY	96	67 3/8	79 3/8	17 3/8	63 4/8	24 0/8	24 7/8	15	10	MYNATT II	JERRY W.	SAME	
20	212 7/8	NODAWAY	81	87 7/8	92 3/8	23 7/8	20 0/8	31 2/8	29 6/8	8	10	BARCUS	KENNETH	SAME	
21	212 5/8	BARTON	91	79 1/8	78 0/8	19 6/8	45 5/8	79 1/8	78 0/8	13	13	CRYSTAL	DAVID	SAME	
22	212 0/8	LIVINGSTON	61	74 3/8	76 6/8	18 7/8	53 5/8	24 6/8	21 3/8	5	15	HUGHES	MARSHALL	SAME	
23	211 0/8	MERCER	95	73 4/8	71 5/8	15 3/8	53 1/8	21 4/8	21 6/8	8	11	GRAY	TREVE	SAME	
24	210 7/8	LEWIS	95	78 4/8	79 6/8	18 5/8	37 2/8	25 7/8	26 1/8	10	9	MEAD	RON	SAME	
25	208 7/8	ATCHISON	64	86 2/8	86 5/8	21 6/8	20 1/8	25 1/8	26 0/8	8	11	LEE	KENNETH W.	SAME	
25	208 7/8	BATES	95	75 2/8	74 6/8	19 6/8	43 7/8	26 0/8	25 7/8	12	14	FERGUSON	BRAD	SAME	
27	208 5/8	CAMDEN	91	83 7/8	84 3/8	21 4/8	26 5/8	25 5/8	24 1/8	13	10	DUNCAN	DAVID	SAME	
28	208 3/8	PLATTE	91	73 0/8	74 2/8	18 4/8	48 3/8	25 0/8	27 2/8	14	8	HENSON	GREG	SAME	
29	208 2/8	GENTRY	90	76 2/8	71 1/8	20 5/8	45 5/8	25 7/8	24 7/8	9	12	SYBERT	ERIC	SAME	
30	207 7/8	ADAIR	94	82 3/8	83 1/8	20 6/8	23 7/8	28 3/8	28 6/8	7	8	HIGGINS	LARRY	SAME	
31	207 3/8	LINCOLN	55	83 5/8	76 5/8	18 5/8	44 0/8	28 7/8	29 1/8	10	10	ZUMWALT	MELVIN	SAME	
32	207 2/8	ANDREW	81	84 6/8	87 6/8	21 0/8	18 6/8	30 1/8	29 5/8	8	7	KELSO	FRANK	KELSO	MRS. FRANK

STATE RANK	SCORE	COUNTY	YEAR TAKEN	INCHES TYPICAL R	L	INSIDE SPREAD	INCHES ABNORMAL	LENGTH MAIN BEAM R	L	NUMBER POINTS R	L	HUNTER	FIRST NAME	OWNER	FIRST NAME
32	207 2/8	ADAIR	88	87 5/8	86 4/8	18 7/8	16 1/8	26 2/8	25 5/8	7	7	ELSEA	KEVIN	SAME	
34	206 1/8	CALDWELL	96	71 7/8	69 4/8	20 2/8	49 5/8	24 7/8	24 7/8	10	12	MIDDLETON	PAUL	SAME	
35	206 0/8	CLARK	83	78 2/8	79 1/8	17 5/8	33 4/8	23 2/8	23 3/8	9	13	COURTNEY	ALLEN L.	SAME	
36	205 7/8	ATCHISON	90	72 3/8	80 0/8	25 4/8	36 3/8	28 1/8	28 0/8	11	9	POPPA	LARRY	LOVEKAMP	TERRY L.
36	205 7/8	MACON	94	69 2/8	71 4/8	19 7/8	50 6/8	24 2/8	27 5/8	9	7	EASLEY	CLINT	LOVEKAMP	TERRY L.
38	205 1/8	ST. CLAIR	74	69 4/8	69 7/8	16 3/8	54 0/8	25 5/8	25 2/8	15	13	PIPER	CARROLL W.	SAME	
39	204 4/8	MONROE	96	82 3/8	81 3/8	20 4/8	31 4/8	28 6/8	29 0/8	10	7	BAUTISTA, M.D.	ROGELIO L.	SAME	
40	204 3/8	SALINE	60	88 5/8	78 1/8	22 4/8	28 3/8	28 2/8	27 3/8	9	9	POINTER	WILLIAM	SAME	
41	204 2/8	BOONE	85	84 0/8	87 3/8	22 2/8	15 6/8	26 2/8	26 4/8	5	8	BROWN	GENE	SAME	
42	204 1/8	PIKE	95	85 0/8	85 4/8	19 5/8	17 0/8	25 4/8	26 3/8	11	10	JEFFRIES	ROBERT	SAME	
43	203 6/8	ANDREW	89	74 3/8	80 5/8	17 5/8	23 7/8	24 7/8	25 1/8	10	16	HOWARD	MARTY	SAME	
44	203 5/8	CHARITON	53	68 7/8	70 3/8	15 5/8	56 0/8	26 6/8	28 0/8	18	13	SOWERS	VERNON	SAME	
44	203 5/8	CHARITON	95	67 2/8	77 3/8	15 2/8	56 1/8	23 6/8	24 7/8	10	10	STROUP	KEVIN RAYMOND	WALTON	ANN
46	203 2/8	ANDREW	95	86 5/8	85 6/8	22 2/8	24 2/8	26 7/8	26 7/8	13	7	SCHWEIZER	CRAIG	SAME	
47	203 1/8	LIVINGSTON	54	81 2/8	75 6/8	22 1/8	34 4/8	25 0/8	25 2/8	15	8	DAVIS	CLIFFORD	SAME	
48	202 6/8	DAVIESS	83	79 2/8	85 5/8	18 3/8	30 1/8	27 6/8	26 7/8	10	9	HEIDENBRAND	DENNIS	SAME	
48	202 6/8	MERCER	90	87 4/8	78 5/8	18 4/8	27 4/8	29 1/8	25 7/8	12	11	MOORE	MIKE	SAME	
50	202 0/8	NODAWAY	72	86 5/8	84 1/8	15 5/8	26 1/8	28 6/8	27 3/8	12	11	STEWART	RICHARD	SAME	
51	202 0/8	PLATTE	91	86 3/8	89 1/8	14 7/8	19 1/8	25 0/8	24 6/8	8	9	RICHARDSON	STEVEN	SAME	
51	202 0/8	MACON	94	66 0/8	70 5/8	17 4/8	54 0/8	20 4/8	22 4/8	12	15	ALLEN	LARRY	SAME	
51	202 0/8	CALLAWAY	95	84 7/8	85 3/8	18 5/8	17 7/8	26 4/8	26 1/8	8	10	MENG	MARC	SAME	
54	201 7/8	ADAIR	90	64 1/8	66 2/8	20 0/8	57 1/8	23 2/8	22 3/8	14	10	CAIN	RONALD	RINNE	KENNETH
55	201 5/8	HOWARD	83	75 4/8	77 4/8	21 6/8	29 7/8	25 2/8	26 6/8	10	10	O'BRIAN	GREG	SAME	
55	201 5/8	CLINTON	89	83 1/8	83 7/8	24 7/8	19 2/8	26 7/8	26 2/8	8	8	EADS	DAVID	SAME	
55	201 5/8	SCHUYLER	94	81 5/8	83 7/8	19 2/8	22 3/8	26 6/8	27 1/8	9	11	PAILEY	WAYNE	SAME	
58	201 4/8	WAYNE	92	75 7/8	72 4/8	14 0/8	45 4/8	22 4/8	21 2/8	13	13	HAYS	DAVID	SAME	
59	201 3/8	ATCHISON	88	79 3/8	74 1/8	17 6/8	36 1/8	24 7/8	23 6/8	10	9	THOMPSON	STEVE	BROWNING	RON
60	201 0/8	HOWARD	72	88 5/8	89 5/8	20 6/8	11 7/8	27 3/8	26 5/8	8	7	WYATT	ROBERT LEE	SAME	
60	201 0/8	JASPER	91	56 0/8	61 2/8	15 4/8	76 4/8	22 1/8	25 6/8	6	13	MORRIS	RICHARD	SAME	
62	200 7/8	PETTIS	95	75 2/8	77 2/8	24 0/8	30 5/8	26 4/8	25 2/8	11	10	KEMPKER	STEVE	SAME	
63	200 6/8	LINN	91	79 4/8	79 1/8	19 7/8	25 7/8	25 3/8	26 3/8	8	8	YOUNG	JASON	SAME	
64	200 4/8	CLINTON	91	77 1/8	76 0/8	19 2/8	32 2/8	23 1/8	23 2/8	11	9	NORTON	REA	SAME	

STATE RANK	SCORE	COUNTY	YEAR TAKEN	INCHES TYPICAL R	L	INSIDE SPREAD	INCHES ABNORMAL	LENGTH MAIN BEAM R	L	NUMBER POINTS R	L	HUNTER	FIRST NAME	OWNER	FIRST NAME
65	200 2/8	DOUGLAS	79	86 3/8	85 3/8	17 6/8	16 2/8	22 6/8	23 1/8	11	8	STITES	JOE	SAME	
66	200 1/8	HOLT	94	85 1/8	83 0/8	19 3/8	25 2/8	26 2/8	24 4/8	10	13	COPSEY	BRUCE	SAME	
67	200 0/8	LINCOLN	83	83 3/8	89 3/8	22 6/8	15 0/8	26 3/8	25 3/8	8	9	RODRIGUEZ	RALPH	SAME	
68	199 7/8	HICKORY	71	63 3/8	61 6/8	14 0/8	66 1/8	20 1/8	20 7/8	7	14	STOGSDILL	DARWIN	SAME	
69	199 6/8	PUTNAM	78	82 4/8	82 0/8	13 2/8	25 0/8	26 2/8	26 1/8	5	9	HORNADY	DAVE	SAME	
69	199 6/8	JACKSON	89	79 4/8	70 3/8	18 2/8	43 4/8	28 3/8	28 4/8	8	16	HOLLINGSWORTH	JACK	SAME	
71	199 5/8	BOONE	91	84 3/8	84 7/8	18 1/8	15 2/8	26 2/8	27 0/8	8	8	KRUEGER	STEVEN LEE	SAME	
72	199 4/8	ST. FRANCOIS	84	76 0/8	73 5/8	17 5/8	36 1/8	26 2/8	25 4/8	13	11	HULL	HENRY A.	SAME	
73	199 3/8	CLARK	73	80 3/8	79 0/8	21 6/8	24 7/8	28 0/8	26 4/8	10	8	ARNOLD	BOB	SAME	
74	199 0/8	CLAY	90	47 3/8	67 1/8	20 2/8	84 0/8	21 6/8	23 6/8	11	9	CALLAHAN	PATRICK M.	SAME	
75	198 2/8	CLARK	95	83 6/8	87 5/8	21 0/8	18 0/8	26 6/8	27 6/8	8	9	WARD	STEWART W.	SAME	
76	197 6/8	HOLT	86	77 1/8	90 2/8	16 6/8	26 6/8	26 1/8	27 3/8	12	10	WILSON	RON	SAME	
77	197 1/8	WORTH	82	76 3/8	75 7/8	18 7/8	32 0/8	28 2/8	26 6/8	9	11	KINDER	GARY	SAME	
77	197 1/8	JACKSON	84	78 0/8	80 7/8	17 3/8	27 0/8	26 1/8	26 3/8	8	7	MARTIN	JIM	SAME	
77	197 1/8	CALDWELL	90	72 0/8	75 5/8	17 3/8	46 0/8	22 6/8	24 4/8	8	6	NICKLES	JAMES	SAME	
77	197 1/8	CARROLL	90	84 0/8	85 4/8	19 2/8	13 1/8	25 6/8	26 2/8	6	7	OSER	DALE	SAME	
81	197 0/8	SALINE	86	81 2/8	81 7/8	21 5/8	17 7/8	30 3/8	28 2/8	7	8	BARTLETT	TOMMY	SAME	
82	196 7/8	PIKE	85	81 0/8	84 1/8	19 6/8	16 7/8	26 1/8	27 2/8	7	8	GROTE	HARRY	SAME	
83	196 5/8	NEWTON	93	77 6/8	83 5/8	12 5/8	28 4/8	22 1/8	22 4/8	8	10	PRITCHARD	WALTER P.	SAME	
84	196 3/8	MILLER	82	88 5/8	81 7/8	18 7/8	15 2/8	26 0/8	25 5/8	10	9	HEDDEN	RICK	SAME	
85	196 1/8	LACLEDE	72	66 2/8	68 0/8	18 3/8	52 0/8	23 5/8	22 4/8	10	9	WEST	JOHN	WEST	HARRY
85	196 1/8	SULLIVAN	95	87 0/8	83 6/8	16 5/8	14 2/8	26 3/8	25 3/8	7	8	WALKER	CARROLL	SAME	
87	195 5/8	STE. GENEIEVE	53	73 4/8	76 2/8	18 7/8	38 0/8	21 6/8	26 3/8	16	13	WEILER	MARTIN	SAME	
87	195 5/8	SCHUYLER	95	75 0/8	78 7/8	23 3/8	27 0/8	27 3/8	27 0/8	8	10	FARLEY	JOE	SAME	
89	195 3/8	CAMDEN	82	82 1/8	79 3/8	19 0/8	20 7/8	27 3/8	27 2/8	8	9	STEPHENS	CARLIS	DEATON	GLEN
89	195 3/8	PUTNAM	91	77 3/8	78 6/8	16 3/8	28 0/8	25 1/8	25 7/8	10	12	VALENTINE	JASON	SAME	
91	195 2/8	PLATTE	89	73 0/8	77 0/8	19 2/8	33 2/8	22 6/8	23 0/8	7	10	UTZ	JEFF	SAME	
91	195 2/8	WASHINGTON	91	81 2/8	86 0/8	16 3/8	17 5/8	25 2/8	24 7/8	12	8	RATH	ROBERT	SAME	
93	195 0/8	WAYNE	89	83 0/8	80 4/8	18 1/8	19 3/8	27 3/8	26 4/8	6	6	SICG	JOYCE	SAME	
94	194 7/8	WARREN	82	77 1/8	82 5/8	19 0/8	27 5/8	27 7/8	26 1/8	11	10	JONES	DENNIS	SAME	
95	194 6/8	COOPER	70	80 0/8	79 4/8	17 7/8	19 7/8	26 0/8	25 6/8	10	8	BURNETT	DONALD	SAME	
96	194 5/8	MERCER	83	77 0/8	84 1/8	19 2/8	24 1/8	26 7/8	28 2/8	8	11	GALETTI	DAN & JIM	SAME	

MISSOURI SHOW-ME BIG BUCKS CLUB RECORDS OF WHITETAIL DEER BY STATE, NON-TYP

STATE RANK	SCORE	COUNTY	YEAR TAKEN	INCHES TYPICAL R	INCHES TYPICAL L	INSIDE SPREAD	INCHES ABNORMAL	LENGTH MAIN BEAM R	LENGTH MAIN BEAM L	NUMBER POINTS R	NUMBER POINTS L	HUNTER	FIRST NAME	OWNER	FIRST NAME
97	194 4/8	CLARK	88	76 4/8	77 1/8	18 0/8	25 2/8	24 4/8	25 2/8	9	11	WHEATON	RALPH	SAME	
98	194 2/8	PIKE	80	84 4/8	77 6/8	23 5/8	19 7/8	27 1/8	26 0/8	9	6	KNOWLES	WILLIAM E.	SAME	
98	194 2/8	PHELPS	86	83 3/8	81 4/8	16 3/8	20 4/8	24 3/8	25 1/8	9	12	BRAIDLOW	DOUG	SAME	
98	194 2/8	HOWARD	87	80 5/8	81 1/8	19 4/8	22 2/8	23 3/8	22 5/8	8	8	RAYMORE	DAVID	SAME	
98	194 2/8	MERCER	89	77 4/8	76 1/8	24 1/8	19 1/8	28 7/8	28 7/8	5	6	SCHMIDT	DENNIS	SAME	
98	194 2/8	LINCOLN	96	74 6/8	70 0/8	18 2/8	39 0/8	22 0/8	21 5/8	7	9	THIEMET	DAVE	SAME	
103	194 1/8	LINCOLN	88	77 3/8	77 2/8	18 4/8	22 5/8	27 2/8	28 0/8	9	7	VAUGHAN	DOUG	SAME	
104	193 7/8	BOONE	92	78 0/8	75 7/8	24 1/8	21 4/8	25 2/8	24 0/8	12	9	QUEVREAUX	AL	SAME	
105	193 6/8	WARREN	71	79 4/8	78 4/8	21 6/8	20 0/8	28 5/8	27 0/8	6	9	TONIOLI, SR.	JERRY L.	SAME	
106	193 3/8	ANDREW	76	72 7/8	72 5/8	16 1/8	36 2/8	23 2/8	24 4/8	10	12	HERBERT	RICHARD	SAME	
107	193 1/8	HARRISON	75	82 0/8	83 6/8	18 1/8	15 6/8	28 6/8	28 4/8	9	8	MORELAND	STEVE	SAME	
108	193 0/8	CHARITON	71	86 2/8	81 6/8	19 6/8	15 0/8	28 5/8	26 1/8	9	6	COKERHAM	GARY	SAME	
108	193 0/8	HOWARD	82	0	0	0	0	0	0	0	0	FUEMMELER	MYRL	SAME	
108	193 0/8	SULLIVAN	84	77 6/8	83 5/8	17 5/8	28 3/8	25 6/8	27 0/8	8	9	HUGHES	GEORGE	SAME	
111	192 7/8	PULASKI	73	90 7/8	80 1/8	15 6/8	19 7/8	27 4/8	26 4/8	11	10	LAWSON	BILL	SAME	
111	192 7/8	ST. LOUIS	94	74 3/8	73 6/8	19 3/8	32 4/8	24 4/8	24 3/8	7	9	LUETHAUSER	SCOTT	SAME	
113	192 5/8	PUTNAM	95	77 5/8	81 4/8	20 7/8	19 0/8	27 5/8	27 5/8	9	8	MURCHISON	TIMOTHY N.	SAME	
114	192 4/8	HARRISON	85	81 3/8	78 1/8	18 5/8	19 5/8	25 4/8	25 0/8	6	8	SHAIN	ROD	SAME	
115	192 2/8	LINN	69	77 3/8	79 3/8	19 4/8	23 4/8	23 6/8	24 5/8	9	9	NICKERSON	MARK	SAME	
115	192 2/8	SHELBY	71	73 6/8	74 1/8	16 4/8	32 6/8	22 2/8	24 5/8	9	8	PARSONS	LINDELL	SAME	
117	192 1/8	MERCER	71	82 1/8	79 2/8	19 4/8	14 5/8	26 1/8	25 1/8	8	7	STOTTS	MELVIN E.	SAME	
118	191 7/8	BOONE	83	66 4/8	58 4/8	17 2/8	63 5/8	19 7/8	14 3/8	8	11	WIESCHAUS	PAUL	SAME	
118	191 7/8	CARTER	92	77 0/8	74 6/8	15 7/8	29 0/8	25 4/8	25 7/8	8	12	DENNIS	MICHAEL	SAME	
118	191 7/8	ST. LOUIS	95	78 3/8	76 7/8	18 6/8	22 7/8	26 6/8	26 1/8	8	7	DAUSTER	DAVID	SAME	
121	191 5/8	CHARITON	96	74 3/8	78 4/8	16 0/8	28 7/8	25 2/8	25 4/8	9	8	GLADBACH	TIM	SAME	
122	191 4/8	PUTNAM	89	79 2/8	75 0/8	23 7/8	17 5/8	24 3/8	22 5/8	6	7	COWAN	WADE	SAME	
123	191 3/8	MONTGOMERY	74	85 1/8	84 1/8	18 6/8	10 5/8	26 6/8	27 4/8	8	8	CARPENTER	PHILIP	SAME	
123	191 3/8	BOLLINGER	94	79 2/8	77 7/8	19 0/8	17 7/8	25 2/8	25 3/8	7	9	DEROUSSE	DAVE	SAME	
125	191 1/8	MARIES	83	74 7/8	79 4/8	16 0/8	29 5/8	22 7/8	23 4/8	8	13	ROLLINS	GARY KYLE	SAME	
125	191 1/8	ST. LOUIS	96	73 4/8	71 0/8	15 2/8	41 3/8	21 5/8	21 5/8	10	11	WERGES	GENE	SAME	
127	191 0/8	SALINE	88	76 4/8	78 3/8	19 7/8	19 5/8	26 4/8	26 2/8	7	9	STEDING	LARRY	SAME	
128	190 7/8	JACKSON	88	79 5/8	71 0/8	18 6/8	33 1/8	27 5/8	27 0/8	9	10	POTTS	DAVID	SAME	

MISSOURI SHOW-ME BIG BUCKS CLUB RECORDS OF WHITETAIL DEER BY STATE, NON-TYP

STATE RANK	SCORE	COUNTY	YEAR TAKEN	INCHES TYPICAL R	INCHES TYPICAL L	INSIDE SPREAD	INCHES ABNORMAL	LENGTH MAIN BEAM R	LENGTH MAIN BEAM L	NUMBER POINTS R	NUMBER POINTS L	HUNTER	FIRST NAME	OWNER	FIRST NAME
129	190 6/8	CAPE GIRARDEAU	89	77 3/8	77 2/8	23 4/8	21 4/8	27 7/8	28 1/8	11	6	SNELL	GARY	SAME	
129	190 6/8	OSAGE	92	80 0/8	82 2/8	21 0/8	12 6/8	27 2/8	26 3/8	7	7	POINTER	GREG	SAME	
131	190 5/8	MONROE	89	72 2/8	71 2/8	21 6/8	29 7/8	26 1/8	25 6/8	9	8	STRUNK	MIKE	SAME	
132	190 3/8	MORGAN	86	75 6/8	75 6/8	21 5/8	22 6/8	26 1/8	28 3/8	6	6	DOYLE	MARCUS D.	SAME	
133	190 2/8	CHARITON	83	78 5/8	83 4/8	19 0/8	16 2/8	25 6/8	25 2/8	8	9	WALTON	ANN	SAME	
134	190 0/8	COOPER	71	75 0/8	76 4/8	17 7/8	23 5/8	24 1/8	24 2/8	7	8	NIXON	H.A.	SAME	
134	190 0/8	GRUNDY	88	82 6/8	84 1/8	19 2/8	12 6/8	25 1/8	26 1/8	6	8	WHITAKER	JACY F.	SAME	
136	189 7/8	SCOTLAND	73	81 3/8	80 0/8	19 7/8	14 0/8	26 3/8	27 7/8	8	7	GUFFEY	DICK	SAME	
136	189 7/8	ST. CLAIR	76	78 4/8	76 0/8	18 0/8	24 7/8	25 6/8	25 3/8	8	6	CRAWFORD	BILLY G.	SAME	
138	189 5/8	HOLT	82	75 7/8	79 3/8	15 7/8	24 0/8	24 6/8	25 0/8	9	7	LONG	MIKE	SAME	
138	189 5/8	CLINTON	84	83 1/8	82 3/8	20 0/8	13 3/8	28 1/8	27 2/8	8	6	AITKENS	RONNIE	SAME	
140	189 4/8	MORGAN	96	82 1/8	74 6/8	19 5/8	20 7/8	27 2/8	26 5/8	10	10	JAMES	EDDIE	SAME	
141	189 3/8	CAMDEN	74	86 1/8	88 3/8	15 4/8	8 1/8	27 2/8	25 7/8	10	10	SULGROVE	A.D.	SAME	
141	189 3/8	HOLT	88	74 4/8	80 4/8	17 3/8	28 6/8	25 3/8	23 2/8	7	8	REHN	JOHN A.	SAME	
143	189 2/8	BUCHANAN	84	84 6/8	75 6/8	21 1/8	21 1/8	24 0/8	25 0/8	9	8	DELK	DEAN M.	SAME	
144	189 0/8	CRAWFORD	68	75 2/8	79 2/8	19 7/8	19 7/8	26 4/8	26 4/8	8	7	TAYLOR	HAROLD	HAVENS	MARK
144	189 0/8	PIKE	92	71 0/8	80 3/8	18 6/8	28 4/8	25 4/8	25 3/8	10	6	DRURY	TOMMY	SAME	
146	188 7/8	MERCER	85	78 6/8	82 1/8	18 0/8	19 1/8	23 0/8	27 4/8	10	6	NOLAND, JR.	JIM L.	SAME	
146	188 7/8	CLINTON	94	80 6/8	79 3/8	15 4/8	18 5/8	25 4/8	25 0/8	8	10	JONES	MARTIN	SAME	
148	188 6/8	ANDREW	59	77 6/8	81 7/8	20 2/8	20 2/8	25 0/8	27 4/8	8	8	CORDONNIER	DAVID	SAME	
148	188 6/8	JOHNSON	83	72 6/8	66 0/8	10 5/8	57 7/8	19 5/8	19 6/8	11	17	MILLER	CHARLES E.	SAME	
148	188 6/8	NODAWAY	85	78 6/8	80 6/8	20 0/8	15 4/8	27 5/8	27 6/8	6	7	AUFFERT	CHARLES	SAME	
148	188 6/8	ADAIR	91	73 1/8	72 5/8	19 1/8	27 7/8	23 5/8	22 6/8	8	10	REID	DAVID C.	SAME	
148	188 6/8	PETTIS	91	79 /8	84 4/8	18 0/8	17 4/8	23 2/8	25 7/8	8	7	TETER	MARK R.	SAME	
148	188 6/8	WARREN	95	81 1/8	72 5/8	15 1/8	30 3/8	23 6/8	24 6/8	8	11	BLAIR	JESSE	SAME	
154	188 5/8	COOPER	94	84 0/8	82 7/8	14 5/8	14 4/8	25 2/8	24 5/8	10	12	DEUSCHLE	STEVE	SAME	
155	188 1/8	MONROE	74	83 6/8	86 1/8	17 1/8	12 1/8	26 2/8	25 2/8	7	8	HOLLINGSWORTH	PAUL	SAME	
155	188 1/8	JACKSON	90	79 3/8	78 3/8	19 3/8	13 6/8	23 5/8	23 5/8	7	6	BUCHANAN	CHAD E.	SAME	
155	188 1/8	CLAY	92	81 3/8	77 4/8	19 7/8	19 4/8	26 6/8	27 2/8	6	8	COPELAND	DON	SAME	
158	188 0/8	WAYNE	72	77 3/8	78 4/8	21 5/8	18 5/8	28 5/8	27 6/8	9	11	KYRO	JAMES	SAME	
159	187 6/8	FRANKLIN	94	83 0/8	74 1/8	17 5/8	25 3/8	21 4/8	21 4/8	9	6	NUNN	BOBBY	SAME	
160	187 5/8	STE. GENEIEVE	64	74 5/8	76 0/8	23 3/8	43 6/8	26 2/8	24 3/8	9	13	VOLZ	KARL	SAME	

STATE RANK	SCORE	COUNTY	YEAR TAKEN	INCHES TYPICAL R	L	INSIDE SPREAD	INCHES ABNORMAL	LENGTH MAIN BEAM R	L	NUMBER POINTS R	L	HUNTER	FIRST NAME	OWNER	FIRST NAME
161	187 4/8	ST. CHARLES	66	74 3/8	80 6/8	19 6/8	19 4/8	25 4/8	26 4/8	7	6	DETJEN	JOHN	SAME	
162	187 3/8	PLATTE	85	64 2/8	66 3/8	16 7/8	43 4/8	22 4/8	24 2/8	12	10	ROWE	JOHN	SAME	
163	187 2/8	CALLAWAY	86	81 4/8	77 6/8	16 3/8	19 7/8	24 3/8	24 1/8	8	8	COX	BRUCE	SAME	
163	187 2/8	ADAIR	87	80 7/8	78 7/8	16 1/8	14 5/8	22 3/8	21 7/8	7	10	GIBBS	JOHN R.	SAME	
165	187 1/8	PIKE	67	80 0/8	78 0/8	20 6/8	14 7/8	25 0/8	24 6/8	7	8	WINTERBOWER	WILLIAM	SAME	
165	187 1/8	MONITEAU	84	78 4/8	79 6/8	17 7/8	18 6/8	25 2/8	25 6/8	9	10	KUEFFER	GARY	SAME	
165	187 1/8	ST. CHARLES	94	81 2/8	82 6/8	16 7/8	19 0/8	26 2/8	27 7/8	8	16	STRAUSS	MARK	SAME	
168	187 0/8	PUTNAM	87	74 7/8	77 0/8	23 6/8	14 0/8	27 2/8	28 1/8	6	9	RENNELLS	JOSH	SAME	
169	186 7/8	RAY	92	75 0/8	80 1/8	16 4/8	28 3/8	22 6/8	24 6/8	12	10	BROWN	BOB	SAME	
170	186 6/8	LINN	72	79 5/8	77 7/8	21 2/8	14 2/8	27 1/8	25 7/8	7	9	SCHUENEMAN	LESTER	SAME	
170	186 6/8	BOONE	86	71 1/8	82 5/8	16 4/8	20 4/8	27 1/8	25 7/8	9	9	PALMER	DALE	SAME	
172	186 5/8	MONROE	76	71 4/8	69 5/8	18 2/8	30 7/8	24 3/8	23 7/8	6	7	CHARLICK	DAVID	SAME	
172	186 5/8	NODAWAY	93	82 0/8	76 4/8	20 2/8	20 3/8	23 4/8	24 3/8	10	6	BOWLIN	DENNIS	SAME	
174	186 4/8	CHARITON	59	77 5/8	79 0/8	19 3/8	20 1/8	24 1/8	26 3/8	9	8	CHILDERS	HARLEY	SAME	
174	186 4/8	NODAWAY	85	73 3/8	72 0/8	22 5/8	23 4/8	26 1/8	26 4/8	7	7	RAUCH	VALERIE	SAME	
176	186 3/8	PHELPS	59	78 2/8	79 2/8	18 4/8	14 5/8	26 5/8	27 7/8	7	11	YOWELL	RAYMOND	SAME	
176	186 3/8	LINN	77	84 3/8	77 6/8	19 1/8	12 6/8	27 1/8	27 2/8	7	9	COOPER	JERRY	SAME	
176	186 3/8	REYNOLDS	96	78 6/8	78 0/8	23 7/8	11 4/8	26 0/8	25 1/8	8	6	LARAMORE	DANNY	SAME	
179	186 2/8	RAY	88	76 3/8	78 7/8	23 1/8	11 7/8	27 3/8	26 5/8	6	10	PIERCE	DAVID L.	SAME	
180	186 0/8	PIKE	90	76 5/8	77 3/8	16 7/8	17 5/8	23 3/8	23 4/8	7	7	BOSTON	BILLY	SAME	
181	185 7/8	MARION	74	76 0/8	79 6/8	22 6/8	13 3/8	24 2/8	25 0/8	6	9	STOUT	LARRY	SAME	
181	185 7/8	PUTNAM	88	59 6/8	69 2/8	17 6/8	49 7/8	22 5/8	25 6/8	10	10	SMITH	PAUL	SAME	
183	185 7/8	MORGAN	92	74 5/8	72 6/8	19 6/8	21 5/8	25 4/8	25 6/8	12	7	GANT	BRIAN	SAME	
184	185 6/8	LINN	89	67 6/8	78 4/8	16 4/8	36 4/8	23 2/8	23 0/8	10	6	QUIGLEY	DAVE	SAME	
185	185 5/8	SCOTLAND	84	77 1/8	75 6/8	20 2/8	17 0/8	25 3/8	25 0/8	7	9	SMITH	CHARLES L.	SAME	
186	185 4/8	KNOX	67	76 6/8	74 1/8	18 2/8	26 2/8	23 2/8	23 7/8	9	6	RHOADES	RAYMOND G.	SAME	
187	185 3/8	MACON	60	74 4/8	84 0/8	25 5/8	15 0/8	28 2/8	27 0/8	8	7	BRAGG	RONALD	SAME	
187	185 3/8	PUTNAM	90	78 7/8	73 2/8	22 0/8	17 5/8	24 2/8	24 5/8	6	7	MILBURN	CHRISTINA	SAME	
187	185 3/8	RANDOLPH	95	74 6/8	68 7/8	14 0/8	35 1/8	20 5/8	20 6/8	9	9	McCAWLEY	MIKE	SAME	
190	185 1/8	HOLT	83	70 7/8	75 0/8	20 4/8	26 3/8	22 7/8	22 3/8	11	12	HALEY	BECKY BREWER	SAME	
190	185 1/8	CRAWFORD	95	78 4/8	73 5/8	17 4/8	20 3/8	24 5/8	24 1/8	12	8	YOUNG	EUGENE P.	SAME	
192	185 0/8	CLARK	81	77 3/8	75 7/8	21 1/8	14 7/8	25 0/8	25 4/8	9	9	HARMON	TOM	SAME	

STATE RANK	SCORE	COUNTY	YEAR TAKEN	INCHES TYPICAL R	L	INSIDE SPREAD	INCHES ABNORMAL	LENGTH MAIN BEAM R	L	NUMBER POINTS R	L	HUNTER	FIRST NAME	OWNER	FIRST NAME
192	185 0/8	SALINE	83	72 1/8	78 1/8	24 5/8	17 3/8	26 5/8	26 5/8	6	8	WISSMAN, JR.	GLEN	SAME	
192	185 0/8	JOHNSON	95	78 6/8	69 1/8	16 6/8	30 0/8	25 4/8	24 5/8	10	10	COEN	ROCKY	SAME	
192	185 0/8	ST. FRANCOIS	95	73 3/8	80 1/8	18 6/8	20 6/8	26 4/8	26 3/8	8	11	JONES	BRUCE L.	SAME	
196	184 6/8	RANDOLPH	68	74 4/8	79 5/8	24 2/8	12 2/8	28 2/8	28 1/8	9	6	BELZER	R.L.	SAME	
197	184 5/8	SULLIVAN	89	75 5/8	74 7/8	17 6/8	18 7/8	23 5/8	24 1/8	8	8	GOOCH	MARTY	SAME	
197	184 5/8	CLARK	91	73 2/8	80 1/8	18 2/8	24 3/8	25 2/8	25 0/8	7	9	HOWARD	J. DAVID	SAME	
199	184 4/8	ANDREW	72	80 0/8	83 5/8	17 2/8	10 0/8	25 5/8	24 6/8	7	10	MARTIN	LOREN	SAME	
199	184 4/8	PULASKI	72	81 3/8	84 1/8	16 0/8	10 0/8	26 5/8	27 1/8	8	6	MELTON	JOHN W.	SAME	
199	184 4/8	CLARK	85	76 3/8	77 3/8	20 7/8	13 7/8	24 4/8	25 4/8	9	8	YATES	KEVIN	SAME	
199	184 4/8	MACON	95	74 2/8	73 7/8	19 1/8	23 1/8	24 5/8	25 4/8	8	9	LATCHFORD	BRUCE	SAME	
203	184 2/8	CRAWFORD	65	70 0/8	72 4/8	15 3/8	30 3/8	23 0/8	23 0/8	11	7	ROBINSON	JAMES R.	SAME	
204	184 1/8	ST. CHARLES	62	69 0/8	69 6/8	21 3/8	27 4/8	25 1/8	26 3/8	8	6	STELZER	LARRY D.	SAME	
204	184 1/8	LINCOLN	76	80 5/8	75 5/8	17 1/8	22 2/8	23 5/8	23 4/8	8	8	KEETEMAN	HAROLD	SAME	
206	184 0/8	PIKE	78	70 4/8	66 1/8	18 4/8	33 7/8	26 3/8	26 0/8	9	8	HAGEMEIER	GARY E.	SAME	
207	183 7/8	LIVINGSTON	78	81 1/8	75 1/8	24 7/8	12 2/8	28 6/8	28 1/8	5	9	LAMP	DONALD	SAME	
207	183 7/8	COOPER	86	82 3/8	86 1/8	15 4/8	16 1/8	26 0/8	22 4/8	8	7	THURMAN	TROY	SAME	
209	183 5/8	CHARITON	92	77 6/8	70 1/8	20 1/8	26 2/8	26 4/8	26 2/8	8	6	CUNNINGHAM	PATRICK	SAME	
209	183 5/8	ADAIR	95	71 4/8	77 4/8	19 0/8	24 7/8	24 4/8	24 3/8	10	10	GROSSNICKLE	JOHN B.	SAME	
211	183 4/8	ADAIR	61	82 5/8	75 4/8	17 0/8	17 0/8	26 1/8	26 2/8	7	8	SEVITS	WENDELL	SAME	
211	183 4/8	CRAWFORD	67	76 3/8	78 4/8	19 3/8	12 2/8	26 0/8	26 0/8	6	7	HARTKE	WARREN	SAME	
211	183 4/8	STE. GENEVIEVE	90	62 3/8	71 1/8	20 4/8	39 6/8	22 0/8	21 2/8	12	15	CARRON	JIM	SAME	
211	183 4/8	JACKSON	94	74 1/8	74 4/8	24 3/8	15 7/8	24 6/8	24 7/8	9	7	GILFOY	CARLTON	SAME	
215	183 3/8	DALLAS	62	79 5/8	72 3/8	20 6/8	19 1/8	24 1/8	23 0/8	9	7	HAMLET	D.W.	SAME	
216	183 2/8	KNOX	74	78 2/8	78 2/8	17 1/8	14 3/8	24 4/8	22 4/8	9	7	DAVIS	HASKEL	SAME	
216	183 2/8	SULLIVAN	90	70 6/8	70 0/8	14 2/8	36 4/8	22 7/8	22 4/8	14	10	COURTNEY	LONNIE	SAME	
218	183 1/8	AUDRAIN	86	73 0/8	69 5/8	17 1/8	33 6/8	23 4/8	24 4/8	10	8	McCUBBIN	DENNIS	SAME	
218	183 1/8	ANDREW	96	73 3/8	74 6/8	18 3/8	22 4/8	20 4/8	22 1/8	8	8	WAEGELE	RANDY	SAME	
220	182 5/8	OSAGE	95	77 5/8	74 7/8	18 4/8	14 7/8	23 7/8	23 6/8	8	8	TYREE	RONNIE LEE	SAME	
220	182 5/8	MARION	96	79 4/8	73 7/8	18 2/8	18 5/8	26 0/8	24 6/8	9	8	HILLS	TIM	SAME	
222	182 4/8	GRUNDY	87	66 4/8	66 3/8	14 4/8	39 0/8	19 3/8	20 4/8	10	11	COOLEY	MIKE	SAME	
222	182 4/8	MONROE	96	71 3/8	70 5/8	21 4/8	22 4/8	22 3/8	23 0/8	9	9	SAUNDERS	GEORGE L.	SAME	
224	182 3/8	CAMDEN	55	74 4/8	74 6/8	17 4/8	21 1/8	25 0/8	26 4/8	10	12	COURTNEY	BERT	COURTNEY	HERB

STATE RANK	SCORE	COUNTY	YEAR TAKEN	INCHES TYPICAL R	L	INSIDE SPREAD	INCHES ABNORMAL	LENGTH MAIN BEAM R	L	NUMBER POINTS R	L	HUNTER	FIRST NAME	OWNER	FIRST NAME
224	182 3/8	WARREN	74	72 2/8	78 3/8	18 1/8	27 0/8	23 1/8	24 1/8	9	8	FORBIS	GERALD F.	SAME	
224	182 3/8	SHELBY	96	78 4/8	76 3/8	19 1/8	12 4/8	26 1/8	27 1/8	8	7	CARR	RODNEY A.	SAME	
227	182 2/8	CALLAWAY	84	78 4/8	79 2/8	17 2/8	17 6/8	27 0/8	26 5/8	9	6	BROWN	ROGER	SAME	
228	182 1/8	SHELBY	87	82 7/8	79 7/8	21 1/8	12 2/8	26 6/8	24 3/8	7	8	OTTO	WILLARD	SAME	
229	181 7/8	PHELPS	91	79 7/8	75 6/8	18 6/8	12 7/8	25 4/8	24 5/8	6	8	MACORMIC	DOUG	SAME	
230	181 6/8	VERNON	91	73 6/8	81 2/8	20 4/8	15 6/8	24 4/8	26 4/8	6	8	YOUNT	TIM	SAME	
230	181 6/8	CALLAWAY	95	72 4/8	72 3/8	17 7/8	25 5/8	22 1/8	22 4/8	12	11	FOWLER	DONALD	SAME	
232	181 5/8	BENTON	66	78 1/8	80 6/8	18 3/8	12 6/8	25 4/8	25 3/8	9	10	WISE	CHARLES	SAME	
232	181 5/8	ST. FRANCOIS	89	71 5/8	71 4/8	17 6/8	23 7/8	25 3/8	26 5/8	12	7	ISGRIG	GENE	SAME	
232	181 5/8	ST. LOUIS	91	71 3/8	68 3/8	17 6/8	27 7/8	25 1/8	22 6/8	11	7	HETH	DAVID	SAME	
232	181 5/8	PUTNAM	92	71 1/8	72 4/8	20 2/8	26 3/8	25 3/8	23 0/8	7	9	MAHONEY	RANDY V.	SAME	
236	181 4/8	JACKSON	88	72 0/8	65 6/8	20 0/8	33 2/8	24 5/8	23 0/8	9	9	BARNES	BOB	SAME	
237	181 3/8	HICKORY	68	79 4/8	77 7/8	15 1/8	15 2/8	24 0/8	21 3/8	10	9	PLUMMER	CHARLES L.	SAME	
237	181 3/8	OSAGE	69	68 7/8	68 1/8	15 1/8	35 6/8	24 2/8	23 0/8	7	6	SESTAK	PAUL	SAME	
237	181 3/8	OZARK	96	75 3/8	77 1/8	18 7/8	14 0/8	23 6/8	25 0/8	8	9	WARREN	MARK	SAME	
240	181 2/8	LINN	70	69 0/8	72 0/8	19 4/8	26 4/8	22 4/8	23 6/8	8	13	BELZER	BILL	SAME	
240	181 2/8	PIKE	87	74 6/8	77 3/8	20 1/8	16 7/8	25 5/8	25 0/8	8	8	JOE'S JUG		SAME	
242	181 1/8	RANDOLPH	96	75 6/8	81 6/8	18 3/8	15 2/8	23 6/8	25 6/8	6	9	PALMATORY	DONNIE LEE	SAME	
243	180 6/8	SCHUYLER	60	77 5/8	72 5/8	20 3/8	17 5/8	26 4/8	26 6/8	6	10	BLUE	BASIL	SAME	
243	180 6/8	SCOTLAND	85	74 5/8	74 2/8	18 1/8	18 7/8	24 5/8	24 6/8	8	7	SIMPSON	STEVE	SAME	
243	180 6/8	CARTER	87	66 2/8	63 7/8	21 7/8	31 3/8	26 2/8	25 5/8	8	11	BOSTIC	IVAN	SAME	
243	180 6/8	LINCOLN	89	77 0/8	71 7/8	25 1/8	21 3/8	27 5/8	27 6/8	9	10	HATCHER	DON	SAME	
247	180 5/8	SALINE	95	80 2/8	75 6/8	20 1/8	13 2/8	23 2/8	25 0/8	8	5	HAYSLIP	JAMES W.	SAME	
247	180 5/8	DAVIESS	96	77 1/8	82 1/8	14 1/8	17 2/8	25 4/8	25 0/8	11	13	SHAUL	NORM	SAME	
249	180 4/8	BOONE	94	70 1/8	74 1/8	19 4/8	22 0/8	22 5/8	23 1/8	10	9	CALVERT, JR.	HOWARD	SAME	
250	180 3/8	JEFFERSON	92	76 0/8	79 2/8	17 0/8	13 5/8	26 1/8	25 7/8	10	9	RICHARDSON	DALE C.	SAME	
251	180 2/8	ANDREW	85	0	0	0	0	0	0	0	0	KAPP	BRENT	SAME	
252	180 1/8	LIVINGSTON	68	77 2/8	80 3/8	20 7/8	9 0/8	25 6/8	25 4/8	7	8	WOOD	FRANCIS P.	SAME	
252	180 1/8	HARRISON	81	71 2/8	70 2/8	16 2/8	26 5/8	22 5/8	21 1/8	9	12	IRVIN	MICHAEL	SAME	
254	180 0/8	RANDOLPH	77	78 7/8	71 2/8	17 2/8	20 2/8	25 3/8	25 2/8	9	7	HUDSON	RANDY	SAME	
254	180 0/8	ST. FRANCOIS	86	69 6/8	67 7/8	20 4/8	30 6/8	26 1/8	21 2/8	6	9	BROWN	PAUL W.	SAME	
256	179 7/8	OSAGE	78	80 0/8	72 7/8	18 4/8	16 3/8	27 1/8	27 0/8	7	7	BRANDT	DAVE	SAME	

STATE RANK	SCORE	COUNTY	YEAR TAKEN	INCHES TYPICAL R	INCHES TYPICAL L	INSIDE SPREAD	INCHES ABNORMAL	LENGTH MAIN BEAM R	LENGTH MAIN BEAM L	NUMBER POINTS R	NUMBER POINTS L	HUNTER	FIRST NAME	OWNER	FIRST NAME
256	179 7/8	STE. GENEVIEVE	81	80 7/8	78 4/8	20 1/8	10 6/8	24 2/8	24 2/8	8	8	DEMARCO	VINCENT	SAME	
256	179 7/8	SCOTLAND	89	66 4/8	76 5/8	17 6/8	29 7/8	24 6/8	24 6/8	8	6	MARTIN	DALE W.	SAME	
259	179 5/8	CALLAWAY	89	78 6/8	77 4/8	16 4/8	16 3/8	24 1/8	24 1/8	8	7	BUCKHOLZ	KENNY	SAME	
259	179 5/8	SCOTLAND	95	77 6/8	75 3/8	15 4/8	13 5/8	25 2/8	25 1/8	6	7	DOTSON	DAN	SAME	
261	179 3/8	GASCONADE	70	73 6/8	77 1/8	18 0/8	16 5/8	22 7/8	22 6/8	8	6	FARRIS	JOHN W.	SAME	
261	179 3/8	ST. CHARLES	82	73 2/8	63 5/8	20 2/8	31 7/8	23 7/8	23 7/8	12	10	SCHIPPER	RONALD H.	SAME	
263	179 2/8	TEXAS	59	73 1/8	78 5/8	17 2/8	17 0/8	24 6/8	26 3/8	7	8	AMBURN	BILL	SAME	
263	179 2/8	DENT	83	78 5/8	74 4/8	19 5/8	14 7/8	22 1/8	24 0/8	6	6	SIMPHER	MICHAEL	SAME	
263	179 2/8	JASPER	86	72 1/8	74 2/8	21 0/8	16 2/8	25 3/8	25 3/8	10	7	THORNTON	JACK	SAME	
263	179 2/8	SALINE	91	77 5/8	78 0/8	18 0/8	14 3/8	25 1/8	23 7/8	9	9	BLAKE	HAROLD	SAME	
267	179 1/8	PULASKI	76	75 2/8	70 3/8	14 6/8	24 7/8	23 5/8	23 4/8	8	9	GLAWSON	MICHAEL	SAME	
267	179 1/8	HOLT	81	72 5/8	74 6/8	21 3/8	12 6/8	23 2/8	24 0/8	7	6	ARCHER	DAVE	SAME	
267	179 1/8	LINCOLN	86	75 4/8	68 1/8	18 5/8	27 6/8	24 1/8	25 4/8	12	11	KERKER	EUGENE	SAME	
270	179 0/8	NODAWAY	66	75 7/8	66 6/8	22 4/8	25 6/8	28 0/8	26 1/8	9	9	PEVE	BOB	SAME	
270	179 0/8	MACON	74	72 2/8	72 3/8	14 7/8	14 7/8	25 2/8	26 6/8	5	6	DILLINGHAM	THEODORE	SAME	
270	179 0/8	RANDOLPE	94	73 1/8	71 6/8	19 6/8	19 2/8	22 0/8	22 2/8	10	9	HENDRIX	SHIRLEY	SAME	
273	178 7/8	KNOX	71	69 4/8	66 2/8	20 5/8	35 3/8	25 2/8	22 2/8	8	10	SCHRAGE	DAVID	SAME	
273	178 7/8	GRUNDY	94	72 5/8	68 7/8	17 4/8	24 1/8	24 4/8	24 6/8	7	7	SHERLEY	STANLEY	SAME	
275	178 5/8	CLARK	67	78 6/8	74 3/8	17 0/8	14 1/8	26 0/8	26 2/8	7	8	O'DAY	ROSS L.	SAME	
276	178 4/8	BOONE	83	76 1/8	71 0/8	20 3/8	17 1/8	26 5/8	26 5/8	7	9	LADDON	PHIL	SAME	
276	178 4/8	LINN	84	73 6/8	71 7/8	18 6/8	17 4/8	27 0/8	25 1/8	10	8	SCHUENEMAN	LESTER	SAME	
276	178 4/8	ADAIR	86	73 4/8	68 0/8	19 4/8	24 0/8	25 3/8	25 2/8	10	10	FARLEY	BILL	SAME	
276	178 4/8	HOLT	90	71 1/8	76 2/8	18 6/8	18 2/8	22 1/8	22 6/8	7	8	NANCE	LARRY R.	SAME	
276	178 4/8	ST. LOUIS	93	72 6/8	74 5/8	21 4/8	14 4/8	27 1/8	27 5/8	6	9	SMITH	ORLANDO A.	SAME	
281	178 3/8	SCOTLAND	64	70 4/8	71 5/8	19 0/8	21 4/8	21 2/8	22 4/8	9	8	FRANKLIN	PAUL R.	SAME	
281	178 3/8	OZARK	72	70 6/8	68 4/8	19 0/8	23 7/8	22 4/8	22 0/8	10	7	APPEL	GENE	SAME	
281	178 3/8	ST. LOUIS	81	71 3/8	83 1/8	17 7/8	25 4/8	22 6/8	28 0/8	9	9	WRIGHT	CECIL	SAME	
281	178 3/8	PETTIS	90	74 6/8	73 3/8	19 1/8	14 4/8	25 5/8	25 0/8	7	7	LUETJEN	ROBERT	SAME	
281	178 3/8	SALINE	92	76 7/8	74 6/8	17 2/8	14 5/8	25 6/8	24 4/8	9	8	O'BRYAN	ROBBIE	SAME	
286	178 2/8	STE. GENEVIEVE	73	68 2/8	68 3/8	17 0/8	27 2/8	23 2/8	23 2/8	9	9	SHELTON	GLENN	SAME	
286	178 2/8	CARROLL	96	71 2/8	72 5/8	20 4/8	16 4/8	26 0/8	26 1/8	8	7	GERMANN	MARK	SAME	
288	178 0/8	PHELPS	73	69 2/8	69 3/8	15 0/8	30 2/8	25 3/8	24 6/8	13	14	LEWIS	MICHAEL	SAME	

MISSOURI SHOW-ME BIG BUCKS CLUB RECORDS OF WHITETAIL DEER BY STATE, NON-TYP

STATE RANK	SCORE	COUNTY	YEAR TAKEN	INCHES TYPICAL R	L	INSIDE SPREAD	INCHES ABNORMAL	LENGTH MAIN BEAM R	L	NUMBER POINTS R	L	HUNTER	FIRST NAME	OWNER	FIRST NAME
288	178 0/8	HARRISON	81	74 0/8	74 0/8	18 5/8	13 1/8	24 4/8	24 6/8	5	5	PERKINS	DENNIS	SAME	
290	177 7/8	DALLAS	94	81 3/8	70 2/8	15 6/8	34 3/8	24 2/8	23 6/8	11	10	LEWIS	BOBBY A.	SAME	
291	177 6/8	LEWIS	94	74 0/8	75 2/8	16 6/8	15 4/8	22 4/8	21 4/8	6	7	MILLER	CLIFTON A.	SAME	
292	177 5/8	CRAWFORD	62	72 6/8	72 6/8	17 1/8	17 2/8	25 0/8	24 1/8	9	10	WEBB	RAYMOND	SAME	
292	177 5/8	PIKE	85	78 1/8	77 1/8	19 3/8	17 2/8	26 5/8	27 0/8	7	8	RUDD	FREDRICK	SAME	
294	177 4/8	COOPER	73	70 4/8	75 0/8	21 1/8	12 6/8	26 1/8	25 7/8	9	10	WALJE	WILLARD	SAME	
294	177 4/8	BENTON	79	70 5/8	70 2/8	17 1/8	17 1/8	24 3/8	26 0/8	7	6	DRENNON	CHIP	SAME	
294	177 4/8	PETTIS	94	71 6/8	70 0/8	21 2/8	20 2/8	25 6/8	26 2/8	7	10	SCHMUTZ	GEORGE	SAME	
297	177 3/8	BARTON	85	76 4/8	76 4/8	17 7/8	15 4/8	25 3/8	21 3/8	7	7	RANDALL	RODNEY	SAME	
297	177 3/8	HOLT	86	65 5/8	67 1/8	18 6/8	28 7/8	22 0/8	22 4/8	10	13	VOLTMER	DALE	SAME	
299	177 2/8	WARREN	80	77 2/8	74 5/8	16 5/8	8 6/8	23 0/8	21 0/8	6	7	HELLE	CHARLES E.	SAME	
299	177 2/8	DAVIESS	91	74 4/8	75 7/8	17 6/8	15 6/8	24 0/8	23 6/8	5	10	EADS	JOHN	SAME	
301	177 0/8	ANDREW	94	65 7/8	73 6/8	19 5/8	25 5/8	24 6/8	25 1/8	6	11	COLE	MIKE	SAME	
302	176 7/8	ANDREW	73	70 7/8	67 5/8	21 3/8	21 2/8	25 0/8	24 3/8	8	8	SMITH	LUCIAN	SAME	
303	176 6/8	KNOX	75	82 5/8	74 2/8	19 5/8	8 7/8	28 4/8	27 5/8	9	8	DENT	DALE	SAME	
303	176 6/8	ST. LOUIS	94	80 0/8	75 3/8	22 6/8	10 2/8	28 0/8	29 7/8	6	6	HELLWEG, III	NORBERT A.	SAME	
305	176 5/8	COOPER	82	68 0/8	67 0/8	18 2/8	27 5/8	27 0/8	26 6/8	10	7	TEMPLETON	JESSIE	SAME	
305	176 5/8	ST. LOUIS	89	74 2/8	73 7/8	18 6/8	14 1/8	25 4/8	24 4/8	10	7	GRELLNER	RICHARD A.	SAME	
307	176 4/8	HARRISON	83	68 1/8	66 0/8	18 3/8	29 1/8	22 2/8	22 0/8	7	9	HYRE	LARRY	SAME	
308	176 2/8	LINN	65	71 7/8	77 1/8	20 7/8	15 3/8	24 5/8	25 2/8	10	7	WALTZ	FLOYD	SAME	
308	176 2/8	IRON	93	75 3/8	75 4/8	15 6/8	12 0/8	23 2/8	23 7/8	7	7	WILSON, JR.	WILLIAM T.	SAME	
310	176 0/8	PUTNAM	81	69 6/8	68 1/8	22 0/8	22 6/8	24 6/8	23 0/8	7	5	DUNKIN	GREG D.	SAME	
310	176 0/8	MILLER	89	85 2/8	69 7/8	19 5/8	17 5/8	26 1/8	26 2/8	11	8	HAWK	TIM	SAME	
312	175 7/8	FRANKLIN	67	76 1/8	72 2/8	18 3/8	14 6/8	25 6/8	26 0/8	4	7	GLATZ	HILMAR	SAME	
312	175 7/8	MARIES	75	75 0/8	71 2/8	17 6/8	21 1/8	24 4/8	23 3/8	8	7	REDEL	LAWRENCE	SAME	
312	175 7/8	WAYNE	86	68 2/8	64 6/8	17 0/8	32 5/8	26 0/8	27 0/8	11	9	CHANDLER	STEVE L.	SAME	
315	175 6/8	SHELBY	67	72 5/8	72 3/8	22 1/8	11 1/8	25 3/8	24 4/8	7	6	FISER	BILL	SAME	
315	175 6/8	MACON	70	76 1/8	73 2/8	23 2/8	9 4/8	25 0/8	24 1/8	6	8	MORRIS	LARRY W.	SAME	
317	175 5/8	HOLT	91	77 4/8	76 1/8	19 2/8	13 3/8	26 4/8	26 7/8	8	7	GILLELAND	MAX	SAME	
317	175 5/8	CHARITON	96	80 2/8	75 1/8	15 2/8	12 1/8	25 3/8	24 2/8	7	6	WEIMER	MICHAEL	SAME	
319	175 4/8	WARREN	71	76 0/8	80 1/8	18 1/8	9 3/8	23 2/8	23 5/8	7	7	DOLL	RANSOM A.	DOLL	DANIEL F.
319	175 4/8	WARREN	94	76 3/8	80 0/8	17 2/8	10 0/8	27 5/8	27 7/8	7	9	HINCH	MARK	SAME	

STATE RANK	SCORE	COUNTY	YEAR TAKEN	INCHES TYPICAL R	INCHES TYPICAL L	INSIDE SPREAD	INCHES ABNORMAL	LENGTH MAIN BEAM R	LENGTH MAIN BEAM L	NUMBER POINTS R	NUMBER POINTS L	HUNTER	FIRST NAME	OWNER	FIRST NAME
321	175 3/8	TEXAS	69	72 7/8	66 3/8	17 6/8	24 7/8	21 6/8	21 4/8	10	8	BURCH	DON	SAME	
321	175 2/8	FRANKLIN	56	70 2/8	72 3/8	18 3/8	17 7/8	25 1/8	26 0/8	8	8	WAGNER	J.L.	SAME	
321	175 2/8	LIVINGSTON	89	74 2/8	71 4/8	17 0/8	16 2/8	22 1/8	22 2/8	7	7	HUSSEY	JAMES	SAME	
321	175 2/8	PIKE	92	74 0/8	73 3/8	19 4/8	13 7/8	23 5/8	24 3/8	6	7	KALLASH	KENNETH	SAME	
325	175 1/8	RANDOLPH	76	74 5/8	70 5/8	18 0/8	18 7/8	23 7/8	24 3/8	7	8	JOHNSON	GEORGE	SAME	
325	175 1/8	WAYNE	88	75 5/8	71 3/8	18 6/8	17 3/8	24 6/8	24 5/8	7	9	WHITTLEY, JR.	JESSE	SAME	
327	175 0/8	DADE	83	76 5/8	76 4/8	16 2/8	11 6/8	24 6/8	21 7/8	9	8	SLATTEN	DANNY	SAME	
327	175 0/8	BENTON	95	69 6/8	73 3/8	17 2/8	19 6/8	23 1/8	23 2/8	8	8	KOLL	BOB	SAME	
329	174 7/8	MERCER	85	67 2/8	55 4/8	15 7/8	48 0/8	23 0/8	17 0/8	10	6	HASHMAN	FRED	SAME	
329	174 7/8	MORGAN	93	70 4/8	69 7/8	18 4/8	19 7/8	21 5/8	21 7/8	7	9	UPTEGROVE	MICAH	SAME	
331	174 6/8	GRUNDY	83	66 0/8	67 7/8	14 5/8	33 5/8	22 6/8	21 5/8	11	8	TUTTLE	LARRY	SAME	
332	174 5/8	HARRISON	79	76 2/8	71 4/8	17 0/8	19 3/8	24 1/8	22 0/8	7	8	O'NEIL	TOM	SAME	
332	174 5/8	MERCER	96	68 5/8	65 5/8	16 6/8	27 7/8	24 0/8	23 1/8	9	8	HENLEY	TRACY	SAME	
334	174 4/8	HOWARD	83	77 6/8	71 3/8	21 5/8	15 5/8	24 7/8	25 6/8	8	6	KIRRANE	GARY	SAME	
335	174 3/8	HICKORY	69	71 3/8	78 6/8	22 7/8	17 0/8	23 0/8	25 1/8	7	11	CHAMBERS	DOUGLAS	SAME	
335	174 3/8	SHELBY	96	71 0/8	79 2/8	16 4/8	18 3/8	23 0/8	22 1/8	8	9	HENDRIX	ROGER	SAME	
337	174 2/8	PULASKI	72	74 2/8	72 2/8	15 2/8	19 0/8	22 5/8	23 2/8	9	14	DOYLE	ROY LEE	SAME	
337	174 2/8	GREENE	93	74 4/8	74 7/8	16 1/8	9 5/8	22 3/8	22 4/8	6	7	NOTHNAGEL	NORM	SAME	
337	174 2/8	RALLS	94	77 7/8	72 1/8	14 3/8	19 3/8	23 2/8	23 6/8	8	8	HARDY	STEVE	SAME	
337	174 2/8	AUDRAIN	96	79 2/8	74 5/8	15 2/8	10 2/8	25 7/8	25 5/8	6	9	DAY	JUSTIN	SAME	
341	174 0/8	KNOX	88	72 0/8	76 4/8	16 3/8	16 1/8	26 1/8	26 6/8	6	10	PETERS	STEVE	SAME	
341	174 0/8	DEKALB	89	72 4/8	70 4/8	16 7/8	21 1/8	25 3/8	26 1/8	6	5	SKOUBY	LESTER	SAME	
341	174 0/8	CASS	95	81 5/8	71 6/8	18 3/8	14 5/8	27 3/8	26 7/8	8	6	THOMAS	DAVID	SAME	
344	173 7/8	BENTON	70	73 0/8	85 5/8	16 5/8	12 0/8	23 6/8	23 4/8	6	8	COCKERELL	EDWARD	SAME	
344	173 7/8	ST. CHARLES	81	67 1/8	59 0/8	18 1/8	40 0/8	25 2/8	25 6/8	8	10	STREET	MELVIN	SAME	
346	173 6/8	COOPER	71	76 0/8	75 4/8	20 2/8	10 0/8	25 3/8	26 6/8	7	5	FRIEDRICH	RON	SAME	
346	173 6/8	CALLAWAY	88	79 7/8	73 3/8	15 6/8	13 6/8	24 6/8	24 6/8	10	10	SCHAEFER	RONALD ERIC	SAME	
348	173 5/8	ST. LOUIS	89	68 6/8	65 0/8	17 2/8	28 3/8	23 1/8	22 3/8	11	7	BRANSON	MICHAEL M.	SAME	
348	173 5/8	PUTNAM	96	78 2/8	68 3/8	17 6/8	20 1/8	25 4/8	22 1/8	6	9	REAM	JOE	SAME	
350	173 4/8	KNOX	72	65 3/8	64 7/8	20 2/8	29 0/8	23 1/8	22 2/8	10	8	SIMMONS	LARRY	SAME	
350	173 4/8	JOHNSON	72	71 4/8	73 5/8	17 2/8	17 0/8	27 5/8	28 1/8	7	6	WALTERS	VAUGEN	SAME	
350	173 4/8	GASCONADE	73	70 2/8	65 4/8	21 5/8	23 7/8	23 0/8	23 2/8	10	8	SCHNEIDER	ROBERT	SAME	

MISSOURI SHOW-ME BIG BUCKS CLUB RECORDS OF WHITETAIL DEER BY STATE, NON-TYP

STATE RANK	SCORE	COUNTY	YEAR TAKEN	INCHES TYPICAL R	L	INSIDE SPREAD	INCHES ABNORMAL	LENGTH MAIN BEAM R	L	NUMBER POINTS R	L	HUNTER	FIRST NAME	OWNER	FIRST NAME
350	173 4/8	ANDREW	93	42 6/8	51 7/8	17 6/8	74 2/8	19 1/8	21 4/8	12	13	SCHOTTEL	ROD	SAME	
354	173 3/8	MACON	85	72 6/8	71 1/8	18 0/8	17 3/8	24 5/8	24 7/8	10	5	PAGLIAI	DANIEL R.	SAME	
354	173 3/8	CALLAWAY	95	73 1/8	81 5/8	16 0/8	13 5/8	24 2/8	24 3/8	7	7	REANY	BILL	SAME	
354	173 3/8	STE. GENEIEVE	96	77 0/8	72 1/8	18 2/8	15 3/8	24 1/8	23 3/8	8	6	HURST	CHARLES E.	SAME	
357	173 2/8	CASS	84	72 7/8	73 5/8	19 2/8	12 2/8	25 7/8	25 5/8	10	8	STARK	ED	SAME	
357	173 2/8	BUCHANAN	89	71 3/8	76 /78	19 4/8	13 0/8	24 1/8	24 1/8	6	7	BILLINGTON	PAUL	SAME	
359	173 1/8	JASPER	91	66 7/8	68 4/8	18 0/8	24 5/8	24 1/8	23 5/8	9	9	GETTINGS	DOYLE	SAME	
359	173 1/8	ST. LOUIS	92	75 2/8	68 7/8	19 6/8	17 7/8	27 1/8	27 1/8	6	5	GEVERMUEHLE	RAY	SAME	
361	173 0/8	MERCER	67	70 7/8	71 1/8	17 0/8	16 4/8	24 7/8	25 4/8	7	6	CLAPHAM	CODA	SAME	
361	173 0/8	GENTRY	89	70 4/8	65 2/8	17 6/8	29 6/8	21 4/8	21 5/8	7	7	PIERICK	FRANK	SAME	
361	173 0/8	KNOX	92	70 7/8	70 2/8	18 0/8	18 0/8	23 6/8	24 0/8	7	7	DOSS	RANDY	SAME	
361	173 0/8	LINN	92	69 1/8	70 3/8	15 6/8	20 2/8	22 6/8	23 7/8	12	8	BERRY	DON	SAME	
365	172 7/8	SCOTLAND	88	74 5/8	74 3/8	17 6/8	14 1/8	22 0/8	22 7/8	10	6	HUGHES	BOB	SAME	
366	172 6/8	PUTNAM	92	71 5/8	71 5/8	19 2/8	13 6/8	24 0/8	24 4/8	5	5	STRINGER	ALLAN	SAME	
366	172 6/8	PUTNAM	94	71 1/8	76 1/8	18 7/8	12 3/8	25 5/8	5 3/8	9	9	BURNS	KRIS	SAME	
366	172 6/8	CLINTON	95	77 3/8	73 0/8	16 1/8	17 1/8	25 7/8	25 4/8	7	7	KECK	JIM	SAME	
369	172 5/8	CARROLL	76	68 4/8	68 2/8	21 5/8	20 6/8	22 3/8	22 6/8	9	8	BROOKE	WALTER	SAME	
369	172 5/8	SCOTLAND	78	71 3/8	74 0/8	18 4/8	13 5/8	21 6/8	21 6/8	8	5	BLAKE	CAROLYN	SAME	
371	172 4/8	HOWARD	90	62 4/8	67 4/8	15 5/8	36 1/8	23 4/8	23 1/8	10	7	COLVIN	ERIC	SAME	
371	172 4/8	CLARK	94	69 1/8	71 6/8	18 4/8	17 6/8	22 5/8	23 1/8	7	7	COPPLER	BRUCE H.	SAME	
373	172 3/8	CALLAWAY	75	71 7/8	72 6/8	17 0/8	16 1/8	21 7/8	21 0/8	7	12	SHANNON	MIKE	SAME	
373	172 3/8	ADAIR	91	76 1/8	72 3/8	20 0/8	10 7/8	26 7/8	25 2/8	8	7	STRIBLING	SONNY	SAME	
375	172 2/8	DAVIESS	74	72 6/8	73 0/8	18 1/8	13 5/8	22 1/8	22 5/8	7	7	YOST	KENNETH	SAME	
375	172 2/8	CLARK	87	73 3/8	70 1/8	20 1/8	15 5/8	24 1/8	24 2/8	8	6	YOUNG	RONALD L.	SAME	
375	172 2/8	CASS	92	68 4/8	73 2/8	25 2/9	14 4/8	25 0/8	25 2/8	9	8	WALTON	JERROL	SAME	
378	172 1/8	SALINE	86	65 5/8	63 1/8	17 0/8	29 1/8	23 3/8	63 3/8	8	7	BLUMHORST	ANTHONY	SAME	
378	172 1/8	WORTH	94	66 1/8	62 4/8	16 5/8	35 6/8	22 3/8	23 1/8	9	9	ATKISON	RICK	SAME	
378	172 1/8	LEWIS	95	69 1/8	70 4/8	20 7/8	15 2/8	23 7/8	24 3/8	6	6	MYERS	EARL J.	SAME	
381	171 7/8	OSAGE	71	74 1/8	76 2/8	19 6/8	9 7/8	26 0/8	26 3/8	8	7	WEBSTER	MURRAY	SAME	
381	171 7/8	HARRISON	74	84 4/8	71 3/8	15 0/8	17 5/8	25 0/8	25 1/8	8	8	WILCOXSON	DANA	SAME	
381	171 7/8	CARROLL	89	72 1/8	71 7/8	18 0/8	14 3/8	27 0/8	25 4/8	5	5	STARK	LEE	SAME	
381	171 7/8	SULLIVAN	94	72 6/8	73 1/8	16 3/8	11 4/8	23 4/8	23 7/8	5	6	STEPHENSON	JOSH	SAME	

MISSOURI SHOW-ME BIG BUCKS CLUB RECORDS OF WHITETAIL DEER BY STATE, NON-TYP

STATE RANK	SCORE	COUNTY	YEAR TAKEN	INCHES TYPICAL R	INCHES TYPICAL L	INSIDE SPREAD	INCHES ABNORMAL	LENGTH MAIN BEAM R	LENGTH MAIN BEAM L	NUMBER POINTS R	NUMBER POINTS L	HUNTER	FIRST NAME	OWNER	FIRST NAME
385	171 5/8	LACLEDE	83	66 7/8	69 1/8	17 7/8	20 0/8	24 0/8	24 3/8	7	8	HUNT	RON	SAME	
385	171 5/8	JACKSON	87	78 1/8	75 0//8	20 0/8	12 1/8	24 6/8	25 2/8	7	7	DICKEY, SR.	GLEN S.	SAME	
387	171 4/8	ANDREW	81	70 7/8	72 3/8	17 5/8	14 7/8	23 2/8	24 /8	7	7	TAYLOR	CAROLYN	SAME	
387	171 4/8	COLE	86	69 3/8	79 5/8	16 5/8	16 3/8	22 3/8	23 3/8	6	8	VARNADORE	ROBERT	SAME	
389	171 3/8	SCOTLAND	86	78 1/8	71 7/8	16 4/8	14 3/8	24 1/8	24 7/8	9	7	FOX	EDWIN	SAME	
389	171 3/8	HENRY	88	68 2/8	68 2/8	16 4/8	20 1/8	24 3/8	24 2/8	11	9	ALBIN	WOODY	SAME	
389	171 3/8	GENTRY	93	73 2/8	73 2/8	17 5/8	10 4/8	23 7/8	24 3/8	5	9	ROBERTS	KEATON	SAME	
392	171 1/8	SCOTLAND	82	70 6/8	73 5/8	18 0/8	14 1/8	24 6/8	24 7/8	7	8	WHITAKER	RICHARD D.	SAME	
393	171 0/8	LINCOLN	74	74 0/8	74 1/8	16 3/8	13 3/8	23 3/8	24 4/8	9	5	SCHLESINGER	RONALD	SAME	
393	171 0/8	MORGAN	81	76 2/8	70 0/8	16 5/8	15 7/8	24 3/8	21 7/8	8	8	BLAKE	THOMAS A.	SAME	
393	171 0/8	CLAY	83	78 4/8	86 1/8	17 0/8	25 4/8	21 6/8	27 0/8	7	6	NAPPI	VICTOR A.	SAME	
393	171 0/8	WORTH	83	69 5/8	57 1/8	18 1/8	39 5/8	21 0/8	21 0/8	9	9	McGHEE	DAVID	SAME	
397	170 7/8	HOLT	61	69 6/8	70 4/8	19 7/8	12 6/8	25 3/8	25 0/8	7	7	NASH	JAMES H.	SAME	
397	170 7/8	HENRY	70	73 2/8	70 0/8	21 3/8	10 0/8	26 4/8	25 3/8	5	6	EASTER	ROBERT LEE	SAME	
397	170 7/8	GENTRY	87	68 6/8	72 7/8	17 7/8	16 4/8	23 7/8	24 2/8	8	8	LUPFER	JOEY	SAME	
397	170 7/8	ST. CLAIR	92	68 7/8	73 1/8	18 1/8	16 0/8	25 2/8	26 1/8	5	9	PIEPMEIER	LISA	SAME	
397	170 7/8	CARROLL	93	65 4/8	72 2/8	15 4/8	26 5/8	20 0/8	20 0/8	8	10	HUTCHINSON	DENNIS	SAME	
397	170 7/8	SULLIVAN	95	68 4/8	70 5/8	19 2/8	17 3/8	24 7/8	26 3/8	6	10	VAN VELZER	DWAYNE	SAME	
403	170 6/8	NODAWAY	79	73 1/8	71 4/8	21 0/8	8 6/8	27 3/8	27 3/8	6	8	McBRIDE	DARRELL W.	SAME	
403	170 6/8	DEKALB	86	65 2/8	65 0/8	16 5/8	28 3/8	24 5/8	25 3/8	6	8	PENCE	BARB	SAME	
403	170 6/8	SULLIVAN	90	72 7/8	75 0/8	19 3/8	11 5/8	24 7/8	25 2/8	8	9	CASON	CHERI	SAME	
403	170 6/8	GRUNDY	90	73 4/8	73 /8	16 0/8	11 2/8	24 3/8	25 3/8	7	8	JONES	JEFF	SAME	
403	170 6/8	MONTGOMERY	94	70 3/8	73 4/8	16 5/8	23 3/8	23 6/8	23 6/8	11	8	BOKERMANN	JIM	SAME	
408	170 5/8	BUCHANAN	80	73 2/8	78 7/8	16 6/8	18 7/8	23 6/8	24 5/8	10	6	MUSSER	ROBERT	SAME	
408	170 5/8	POLK	85	71 0/8	74 2/8	17 6/8	17 3/8	25 5/8	26 4/8	6	8	AYRES	PERRY	SAME	
410	170 4/8	ADAIR	76	73 1/8	76 6/8	17 5/8	9 1/8	23 5/8	22 3/8	7	7	GIBSON	JOHN	SAME	
410	170 4/8	ATCHISON	86	72 0/8	69 6/8	18 0/8	19 1/8	26 3/8	26 7/8	8	9	SHAUL	NORM	SAME	
410	170 4/8	LEWIS	93	69 0/8	70 3/8	20 2/8	18 6/8	23 0/8	19 6/8	9	9	GUERDAN	LARRY	SAME	
413	170 3/8	HOLT	81	65 7/8	74 1/8	17 4/8	21 3/8	24 3/8	25 0/8	8	7	WRIGHT	ROBERT	SAME	
413	170 3/8	CALLAWAY	90	73 0/8	73 6/8	16 2/8	15 1/8	22 7/8	22 6/8	5	9	EDMUNDS	JAMES THOMAS	SAME	
413	170 3/8	CLARK	90	71 0/8	72 0/8	16 2/8	17 1/8	24 2/8	23 1/8	9	6	COOK	JIM	SAME	
413	170 3/8	LACLEDE	96	69 3/8	71 0/8	20 6/8	13 7/8	26 2/8	25 5/8	6	7	ALKIRE	RAYMOND	SAME	

STATE RANK	SCORE	COUNTY	YEAR TAKEN	INCHES TYPICAL R	INCHES TYPICAL L	INSIDE SPREAD	INCHES ABNORMAL	LENGTH MAIN BEAM R	LENGTH MAIN BEAM L	NUMBER POINTS R	NUMBER POINTS L	HUNTER	FIRST NAME	OWNER	FIRST NAME
417	170 2/8	CALLAWAY	88	66 3/8	69 2/8	17 6/8	22 2/8	24 7/8	25 5/8	11	9	MURPHY	LARRY	SAME	
418	170 1/8	ANDREW	72	71 7/8	71 3/8	22 1/8	10 2/8	24 7/8	24 4/8	7	9	PELLERSELS	DAVID	SAME	
417	170 1/8	HOLT	72	65 4/8	63 5/8	18 0/8	26 7/8	21 7/8	20 5/8	5	6	HOOD	JOHN	SAME	
417	170 1/8	OSAGE	73	68 6/8	84 0/8	14 7/8	18 0/8	23 6/8	24 2/8	7	14	KAUFFMAN	BOB	SAME	
417	170 1/8	CARROLL	92	71 6/8	70 1/8	18 1/8	15 0/8	26 1/8	27 0/8	5	9	BAGGS	TODD	SAME	
417	170 1/8	ADAIR	94	77 5/8	72 7/8	14 1/8	11 0/8	25 0/8	24 7/8	6	6	WAYBILL	JANET	SAME	
423	170 0/8	NODAWAY	70	68 2/8	69 4/8	15 5/8	21 7/8	21 5/8	21 7/8	10	9	BRUSHWOOD	HENRY	SAME	
423	170 0/8	RAY	73	67 0/8	74 4/8	19 7/8	18 5/8	26 3/8	25 7/8	6	7	WHITE	ALLEN	SAME	
423	170 0/8	SHELBY	74	78 0/8	73 2/8	16 0/8	11 4/8	24 4/8	25 7/8	10	6	McWILLIAMS	DAVID	SAME	
423	170 0/8	PIKE	77	75 5/8	74 2/8	14 3/8	9 7/8	22 6/8	21 7/8	8	6	INGRAM	BOB	SAME	
423	170 0/8	MERCER	85	71 7/8	79 2/7	15 5/8	19 7/8	25 7/8	26 1/8	6	7	CLEM	VELDON	SAME	
423	170 0/8	BENTON	89	66 4/8	73 3/8	17 0/8	21 4/8	20 5/8	20 2/8	10	7	McKINNEY	TROY	SAME	
429	169 6/8	TEXAS	72	71 1/8	67 1/8	19 6/8	17 2/8	25 2/8	24 6/8	8	9	MITCHELL	EVERETT	SAME	
429	169 6/8	DAVIESS	96	61 6/8	64 2/8	15 3/8	35 7/8	22 7/8	22 0/8	8	13	COLE	CHARLES R.	SAME	
431	169 4/8	DOUGLAS	71	75 1/8	74 5/8	16 0/8	8 2/8	21 4/8	23 2/8	9	5	ROY	RONNIE R.	SAME	
431	169 4/8	BENTON	94	69 4/8	76 3/8	16 5/8	14 5/8	23 0/8	22 7/8	10	7	MACKAY	ALAN D.	SAME	
433	169 3/8	TEXAS	80	70 4/8	73 0/8	23 2/8	11 3/8	25 0/8	24 0/8	6	8	BELEW	DON	SAME	
434	169 2/8	TEXAS	84	68 0/8	68 1/8	14 3/8	23 7/8	21 6/8	21 5/8	12	9	ADEY	FREDDIE	SAME	
434	169 2/8	MERCER	89	84 3/8	72 1/8	17 2/8	12 3/8	22 1/8	23 4/8	9	8	RIDENHOUR	KEITH	SAME	
434	169 2/8	WAYNE	93	75 6/8	72 5/8	17 2/8	10 0/8	25 2/8	25 4/8	11	5	DODD	KEVIN	SAME	
437	169 1/8	HARRISON	89	69 0/8	70 3/8	16 0/8	19 5/8	23 0/8	22 7/8	11	11	HARROLD	GLEN	SAME	
438	169 0/8	CARTER	59	68 7/8	69 0/8	17 5/8	19 1/8	24 0/8	24 4/8	9	9	DAWSON	GEORGE	DAWSON	GARY E.
438	169 0/8	TEXAS	70	64 3/8	68 4/8	17 2/8	28 6/8	22 3/8	21 4/8	8	5	NELSON	LARRY	SAME	
438	169 0/8	IRON	83	65 7/8	64 5/8	18 4/8	22 4/8	23 0/8	22 2/8	9	10	SUTTON	NORMAN	SAME	
438	169 0/8	BATES	84	64 3/8	81 5/8	21 3/8	20 3/8	25 0/8	25 0/8	8	9	DURST	MIKE	SAME	
442	168 7/8	STE. GENEVIEVE	57	80 3/8	59 0/8	16 4/8	50 3/8	16 3/8	21 4/8	9	17	HUCK, SR.	JOE	SAME	
422	168 7/8	ADAIR	88	63 5/8	68 1/8	20 2/8	24 1/8	26 7/8	29 1/8	10	8	ANDERSON	JAMES M.	SAME	
444	168 6/8	FRANKLIN	79	62 5/8	65 3/8	20 2/8	24 0/8	22 4/8	23 3/8	7	6	KOSSMANN	MIKE	SAME	
444	168 6/8	CRAWFORD	89	68 4/8	66 4/8	17 7/8	19 7/8	24 2/8	23 1/8	7	8	LEACH	JAMES C.	SAME	
446	168 5/8	GASCONADE	78	66 0/8	63 3/8	14 6/8	27 3/8	24 0/8	23 4/8	9	7	FILECCIA	JOE	SAME	
447	168 4/8	CRAWFORD	94	55 2/8	60 1/8	16 2/8	45 0/8	21 6/8	23 5/8	8	6	THORPE	BRENT C.	SAME	
448	168 2/8	WASHINGTON	94	76 4/8	71 2/8	17 7/8	9 3/8	25 6/8	25 0/8	7	10	PRATT, JR.	DEL A.	SAME	

MISSOURI SHOW-ME BIG BUCKS CLUB RECORDS OF WHITETAIL DEER BY STATE, NON-TYP

STATE RANK	SCORE	COUNTY	YEAR TAKEN	INCHES TYPICAL R	L	INSIDE SPREAD	INCHES ABNORMAL	LENGTH MAIN BEAM R	L	NUMBER POINTS R	L	HUNTER	FIRST NAME	OWNER	FIRST NAME
449	168 1/8	BENTON	85	66 2/8	69 6/8	13 4/8	25 7/8	20 0/8	21 5/8	12	13	HILTY	JOHN	SAME	
449	168 1/8	LINCOLN	96	72 6/8	75 7/8	15 5/8	16 2/8	23 5/8	23 0/8	9	9	REED	DENIS	SAME	
451	168 0/8	VERNON	86	70 6/8	66 2/8	18 0/8	18 4/8	24 6/8	24 4/8	5	7	ROBINSON	BILL	SAME	
451	168 0/8	STE. GENEIEVE	88	69 1/8	72 6/8	19 0/8	15 0/8	23 4/8	22 3/8	8	11	REECE	CHARLES E.	SAME	
451	168 0/8	BARTON	91	69 4/8	76 1/8	16 3/8	13 3/8	25 0/8	26 5/8	8	8	CARDER	GEORGE E.	SAME	
454	167 7/8	JOHNSON	79	66 6/8	68 3/8	16 2/8	25 3/8	18 6/8	22 1/8	10	6	BLAIR	PATRICK	SAME	
454	167 7/8	BATES	91	75 1/8	70 4/8	18 0/8	14 7/8	24 4/8	21 1/8	9	7	PIPES	MARK	SAME	
456	167 6/8	CASS	93	71 0/8	69 2/8	15 4/8	15 2/8	22 4/8	22 2/8	7	7	GRAVES	ED	SAME	
456	167 6/8	COOPER	95	71 5/8	71 6/8	18 7/8	9 3/8	25 0/8	26 4/8	6	6	ZUMSTEG	PAUL	SAME	
458	167 4/8	FRANKLIN	75	69 3/8	69 3/8	19 7/8	11 3/8	22 5/8	22 7/8	6	7	KERBY	JESSE	SAME	
459	167 3/8	CAPE GIRARDEAU	90	75 3/8	63 4/8	19 3/8	21 0/8	25 0/8	20 3/8	7	7	TALLEY	KENNY	SAME	
460	167 2/8	OSAGE	84	78 1/8	62 5/8	15 4/8	26 4/8	23 1/8	22 0/8	7	6	GENTGES	PHILIP	SAME	
460	167 2/8	RANDOLPH	89	67 0/8	69 2/8	19 2/8	20 2/8	23 6/8	25 6/8	8	9	SPRINGS	RON	SAME	
462	167 0/8	JEFFERSON	87	62 5/8	72 1/8	15 4/8	28 2/8	23 4/8	23 1/8	15	9	JOHNSON	BARNEY	SAME	
462	167 0/8	COOPER	91	63 5/8	62 1/8	18 4/8	27 2/8	23 7/8	22 4/8	5	7	HUTH	STEVE	SAME	
464	166 6/8	OSAGE	81	68 7/8	69 4/8	15 7/8	17 3/8	25 4/8	24 1/8	6	10	LAUX	JOHN	SAME	
464	166 4/8	GREENE	72	67 5/8	70 3/8	15 4/8	16 2/8	22 2/8	22 2/8	7	6	TRACY	CLAUDE	SAME	
464	166 4/8	VERNON	73	68 0/8	65 4/8	19 0/8	19 6/8	22 2/8	22 1/8	8	7	YURK	BILL	SAME	
464	166 4/8	MONTGOMERY	87	66 5/8	71 3/8	16 4/8	17 6/8	23 0/8	23 2/8	0	0	STRUBE	KENNY	SAME	
464	166 4/8	OREGON	94	70 3/8	73 7/8	16 4/8	12 6/8	23 7/8	23 7/8	7	8	CALDWELL	WAYNE	SAME	
469	166 1/8	PHELPS	82	72 4/8	74 1/8	17 4/8	14 3/8	25 6/8	23 1/8	7	10	THORPE	ERNEST	SAME	
469	166 1/8	FRANKLIN	91	71 2/8	66 7/8	14 2/8	26 5/8	21 7/8	22 0/8	11	9	CAREY	MIKE	SAME	
471	166 0/8	KNOX	86	71 7/8	70 3/8	18 0/8	10 2/8	25 1/8	23 5/8	6	8	WHITMIRE	KEVIN	SAME	
471	166 0/8	CLINTON	96	70 2/8	71 5/8	17 3/8	13 5/8	25 2/8	24 7/8	10	6	THOMAS	CHRIS	SAME	
473	165 6/8	SALINE	92	70 5/8	67 4/8	17 5/8	14 3/8	25 1/8	24 7/8	8	8	MORTON	PHILLIP	SAME	
474	165 5/8	HENRY	77	68 4/8	70 5/8	15 5/8	15 0/8	24 5/8	24 1/8	10	10	CHRONISTER	DAVID	SAME	
474	165 5/8	LINCOLN	91	84 2/8	70 0/8	18 7/8	11 0/8	27 0/8	24 7/8	5	7	COAN	JASON	SAME	
474	165 5/8	PUTNAM	95	68 0/8	63 7/8	19 7/8	19 0/8	25 1/8	24 0/8	7	8	GRAY	JEFF	SAME	
477	165 3/8	GREENE	90	76 5/8	68 7/8	18 7/8	12 4/8	23 6/8	21 6/8	8	6	HAYNES	JAMES L.	SAME	
477	165 3/8	PERRY	91	70 1/8	72 6/8	19 1/8	12 4/8	26 6/8	23 4/8	6	7	SCHOLL	DUANE	SAME	
477	165 3/8	HICKORY	91	73 6/8	71 6/8	15 4/8	11 5/8	22 3/8	24 4/8	7	5	ANDERSON	MARK	SAME	
480	165 1/8	CEDAR	74	54 3/8	58 7/8	17 1/8	39 2/8	20 1/8	20 2/8	10	8	ESSEX	NORMA	SAME	

STATE RANK	SCORE	COUNTY	YEAR TAKEN	INCHES TYPICAL R	L	INSIDE SPREAD	INCHES ABNORMAL	LENGTH MAIN BEAM R	L	NUMBER POINTS R	L	HUNTER	FIRST NAME	OWNER	FIRST NAME
481	165 0/8	PULASKI	83	65 3/8	44 1/8	12 6/8	70 0/8	16 2/8	18 0/8	13	13	RANSOM	CHARLES R.	SAME	
482	164 6/8	WAYNE	87	53 4/8	51 6/8	13 1/8	49 5/8	20 5/8	20 2/8	9	7	COOK	JAY	SAME	
483	164 5/8	TANEY	90	66 2/8	67 3/8	21 4/8	15 5/8	20 6/8	22 2/8	8	5	WALKER	LLOYD	SAME	
483	164 5/8	CHARITON	90	63 5/8	65 4/8	15 3/8	26 0/8	22 0/8	22 6/8	12	9	BILLUPS	RANDY	SAME	
485	164 4/8	GASCONADE	67	70 7/8	73 1/8	20 3/8	5 3/8	24 5/8	23 4/8	6	5	MEYER	LOUIS H.	SAME	
485	164 4/8	PHELPS	69	69 7/8	70 1/8	14 6/8	12 6/8	21 0/8	20 7/8	6	9	WATSON	REX	SAME	
485	164 4/8	STE. GENEIEVE	91	67 3/8	65 2/8	14 6/8	22 2/8	21 2/8	21 1/8	11	12	ETLING	KATHY	SAME	
488	164 2/8	LAFAYETTE	92	72 6/8	66 3/8	20 4/8	19 6/8	26 0/8	23 1/8	4	9	WRIGHT	MITCH	SAME	
488	164 2/8	LACLEDE	96	71 7/8	70 7/8	18 0/8	7 6/8	24 3/8	25 3/8	8	7	GOANS	JERRY	SAME	
490	164 1/8	COOPER	74	73 5/8	69 6/8	16 7/8	15 4/8	23 0/8	24 2/8	6	6	FRIEDRICH	TOMMY	SAME	
491	163 5/8	CRAWFORD	92	72 5/8	65 5/8	16 5/8	19 2/8	25 5/8	22 2/8	7	6	MATHEWS	BRIAN	SAME	
492	163 4/8	TEXAS	51	71 5/8	67 7/8	18 0/8	23 0/8	22 5/8	22 0/8	11	8	LANIER	WAYNE	SAME	
492	163 4/8	TEXAS	81	69 7/8	69 0/8	14 3/8	15 7/8	23 2/8	23 1/8	6	10	NOEL	BOBBY	SAME	
494	163 3/8	PETTIS	90	64 4/8	65 0/8	20 6/8	16 5/8	23 4/8	24 1/8	9	6	WALTERS	JIM	SAME	
495	163 2/8	GENTRY	73	71 1/8	68 4/8	14 7/8	13 3/8	24 0/8	23 6/8	10	9	HEATH	JOE	SAME	
496	163 0/8	OSAGE	66	76 1/8	67 0/8	15 6/8	17 4/8	22 5/8	24 2/8	10	7	BACON	SCOTT	SAME	
496	163 0/8	WASHINGTON	82	68 7/8	63 1/8	22 1/8	19 1/8	24 6/8	25 0/8	5	9	MERCER	RONNIE	SAME	
496	163 0/8	BENTON	84	69 6/8	64 5/8	20 1/8	13 7/8	25 4/8	25 0/8	7	6	DURRILL	RANDOLPH	SAME	
496	163 0/8	COOPER	87	69 4/8	75 7/8	19 0/8	7 2/8	22 7/8	23 2/8	5	9	REX	MIKE	SAME	
496	163 0/8	SALINE	91	69 6/8	63 7/8	13 3/8	22 1/8	22 5/8	22 0/8	6	10	RILEY, JR.	DONALD	SAME	
501	162 7/8	BARTON	91	68 2/8	68 2/8	19 7/8	12 2/8	26 2/8	27 7/8	6	5	YORK	ROBERT GLENN	SAME	
501	162 7/8	SALINE	95	69 1/8	65 4/8	19 4/8	12 5/8	23 0/8	23 0/8	6	6	HAMILTON	KURT K.	SAME	
503	162 6/8	HOWELL	91	61 5/8	61 5/8	15 7/8	34 0/8	20 5/8	20 7/8	9	11	MYRICK	JOHN R.	SAME	
504	162 5/8	CEDAR	71	73 5/8	71 7/8	17 0/8	10 1/8	20 4/8	20 2/8	8	9	DURHAM	LARRY	SAME	
505	162 4/8	RANDOLPH	92	72 0/8	68 4/8	16 0/8	10 0/8	23 5/8	23 0/8	8	7	AKINS	ROBERT P.	SAME	
506	162 3/8	DOUGLAS	74	65 2/8	70 3/8	14 3/8	18 4/8	20 5/8	20 3/8	8	8	CLAYTON	JOHN	SAME	
506	162 3/8	PHELPS	84	67 5/8	70 3/8	16 3/8	13 0/8	23 6/8	23 1/8	7	8	POUND	DAVID	SAME	
506	162 3/8	WASHINGTON	92	66 3/8	67 1/8	20 2/8	14 3/8	24 5/8	23 6/8	7	8	HIGGINS	STEVEN A.	SAME	
509	162 1/8	CAPE GIRARDEAU	88	63 0/8	61 2/8	21 3/8	22 6/8	22 0/8	21 4/8	7	7	FARROW	BRYAN	SAME	
509	162 1/8	TEXAS	92	72 3/8	70 3/8	21 0/8	5 3/8	25 6/8	25 5/8	8	6	PARKER	ROBERT D.	SAME	
509	162 1/8	FRANKLIN	92	68 1/8	62 5/8	17 6/8	20 7/8	26 4/8	25 0/8	7	6	FUNKHOUSER	GERRY	SAME	
512	162 0/8	HARRISON	95	64 7/8	68 0/8	16 0/8	19 0/8	22 1/8	24 2/8	7	5	BOWEN	BOBBY	SAME	

STATE RANK	SCORE	COUNTY	YEAR TAKEN	INCHES TYPICAL R	INCHES TYPICAL L	INSIDE SPREAD	INCHES ABNORMAL	LENGTH MAIN BEAM R	LENGTH MAIN BEAM L	NUMBER POINTS R	NUMBER POINTS L	HUNTER	FIRST NAME	OWNER	FIRST NAME
513	161 7/8	MORGAN	94	70 5/8	67 7/8	14 0/8	14 3/8	21 2/8	21 5/8	7	5	HILLDON	JAMES	SAME	
514	161 6/8	CALLAWAY	96	68 1/8	71 4/8	17 7/8	9 5/8	22 0/8	21 7/8	7	9	HOOK	BRIAN K.	SAME	
515	161 5/8	HENRY	70	0	0	0	0	0	0	0	0	KERNS	BOBBIE	SAME	
516	161 4/8	MADISON	86	68 2/8	69 3/8	17 6/8	9 0/8	25 1/8	25 0/8	7	7	STEPHENS	ERNEST J.	SAME	
516	161 4/8	ST. LOUIS	96	68 4/8	72 4/8	15 0/8	12 6/8	23 0/8	22 6/8	8	7	LEUTHAUSER	SCOTT	SAME	
518	161 3/8	OSAGE	73	62 5/8	66 6/8	17 6/8	18 5/8	24 0/8	25 7/8	9	5	WILSON	BILL	SAME	
519	161 2/8	WASHINGTON	65	70 6/8	61 0/8	18 4/8	28 0/8	25 2/8	22 2/8	8	12	NELSON	JAMES B.	SAME	
519	161 2/8	PETTIS	88	76 6/8	81 1/8	20 4/8	8 4/8	27 3/8	25 3/8	7	7	THIERFELDER	CHRIS	SAME	
521	161 0/8	PUTNAM	83	68 4/8	70 0/8	19 1/8	10 1/8	24 3/8	24 7/8	5	7	REAM, JR.	DALE H.	SAME	
522	160 7/8	BARTON	90	63 1/8	64 6/8	18 2/8	20 3/8	23 2/8	25 4/8	8	7	TODD	DONALD	SAME	
522	160 7/8	MILLER	96	69 2/8	70 1/8	18 0/8	9 3/8	22 0/8	23 2/8	8	9	WHITNEY	JON	SAME	
524	160 6/8	PULASKI	72	61 6/8	63 2/8	15 1/8	22 5/8	21 2/8	21 6/8	13	11	YORK	DARREL J.	SAME	
524	160 6/8	MONROE	96	77 3/8	68 5/8	16 3/8	14 7/8	23 7/8	22 4/8	8	6	MUDD	JAMIE	SAME	
526	160 5/8	BENTON	96	58 3/8	52 2/8	14 7/8	45 0/8	16 4/8	18 1/8	11	13	IRWIN	JACOB	SAME	
527	160 4/8	GASCONADE	52	59 1/8	69 0/8	18 4/8	22 7/8	23 2/8	24 4/8	6	7	BRANDT	WESLEY E.	SAME	
527	160 4/8	CASS	84	66 5/8	67 3/8	18 1/8	15 5/8	24 1/8	23 6/8	8	7	JOHNSON	STEVE	SAME	
527	160 4/8	REYNOLDS	95	67 0/8	63 4/8	23 4/8	11 2/8	24 6/8	24 5/8	8	5	MARTIN	JOHN W.	SAME	
530	160 3/8	JACKSON	91	76 6/8	65 2/8	16 7/8	16 2/8	22 0/8	23 5/8	9	7	HOOD	WENDELL E.	SAME	
530	160 3/8	FRANKLIN	91	70 4/8	64 1/8	15 2/8	20 7/8	22 2/8	21 1/8	7	6	MINKS	DAN	SAME	
530	160 3/8	CHRISTIAN	92	58 0/8	57 7/8	13 6/8	34 3/8	20 7/8	20 6/8	6	8	PLANK	TERRY	SAME	
533	160 2/8	PHELPS	94	61 7/8	69 3/8	16 7/8	20 7/8	22 2/8	23 5/8	10	7	WASSILAK	TOM	SAME	
534	160 1/8	STONE	76	66 5/8	74 5/8	21 2/8	7 7/8	20 2/8	23 4/8	7	6	WILLIAMS	ELSIE	SAME	
534	160 1/8	HOWELL	89	65 6/8	68 3/8	20 3/8	9 2/8	23 6/8	24 4/8	8	6	HARLAN	JAMES	SAME	
536	160 0/8	HENRY	74	84 7/8	65 0/8	19 6/8	16 0/8	28 4/8	22 2/8	8	8	WISKUR	HENRY	SAME	
537	159 2/8	HOWARD	95	61 3/8	63 3/8	17 6/8	20 4/8	24 4/8	24 3/8	7	7	BELSTLE	GARY	SAME	
538	159 1/8	REYNOLDS	96	52 1/8	69 1/8	21 1/8	33 6/8	21 2/8	23 3/8	10	7	BARTON	QUINTON	SAME	
539	158 7/8	WARREN	96	70 0/8	68 1/8	15 4/8	11 5/8	23 0/8	22 4/8	7	6	MARSCHEL	JASON	SAME	
540	157 3/8	ATCHISON	94	71 1/8	65 0/8	15 6/8	12 7/8	21 6/8	22 0/8	9	7	HEANY	RONNIE	SAME	
541	156 6/8	HARRISON	96	66 4/8	65 1/8	14 2/8	16 4/8	21 2/8	21 6/8	7	8	HARTSCHEN	TRACY	SAME	

Walsworth Publishing Company
306 North Kansas Avenue / Marceline, Missouri 64658 USA